Bright Pages

D1474412

Yale Book Award

LUX ET VERITAS

PRESENTED BY

Yale Club of Boston

TO

Jake Montoya

*For Outstanding Personal Character
and Intellectual Promise*

June 11 2012

Date

ASSOCIATION OF YALE ALUMNI

Bright Pages

Yale Writers
1701–2001

edited and

with an

introduction by

J. D. McClatchy

Yale
University
Press
New Haven
& London

Published with assistance from the
Mary Cady Tew Memorial Fund.

Designed by Nancy Ovedovitz and set
in Adobe Garamond type by Keystone
Typesetting, Inc. Printed in the United
States of America by Edwards Brothers,
Inc.

ISBN 0-300-08944-9 (cloth: alk. paper)
ISBN 0-300-08945-7 (pbk.: alk. paper)

Library of Congress Card Number:
00-111040

A catalogue record for this book is
available from the British Library.

The paper in this book meets the
guidelines for permanence and
durability of the Committee on
Production Guidelines for Book
Longevity of the Council on Library
Resources.

10 9 8 7 6 5 4 3 2 1

Contents

t he familiar dictum of Horace—that poets are born, not made—may be true, but any writer's true cradle is a school. No one would think to write without first having read, without having been intrigued enough to imitate. At a mother's knee, on a father's lap, before the stage or pulpit—the fledgling may first be excited by all manner of performance, but books themselves finally inspire and instruct. It is usually when adolescents begin to explore the chaos of their feelings that they discover a mirror in the fantasies and intrigues of literature. By the time they are at college, though, they have developed as well a sense of irony and paradox, an altogether more sophisticated sense of possibilities. If they would be writers, there is still the long study of craft ahead. But these are years when ideas collide, when historical perspectives are brought to bear on a life, when science reveals hidden forces, when lasting passions are first fired; it is the time when the library becomes the landscape, and eloquent teachers the truest guides. This book gathers the work of sixty-two writers whose dedication to their calling was formed or nurtured at Yale—or rather, *by* Yale, whose unique intellectual resources and brilliant faculty have, down the years, helped give shape to a remarkable part of our nation's literary heritage.

That Yale turned out writers at all during its first two centuries still seems something of a mystery. After all, Yale College had begun as a stern Puritan refuge from the perceived heresies—things like Congregationalism and novel-reading—already brewing at a little college in the Massachusetts Bay Colony and elsewhere in the wilderness that was then America. The *lux et veritas* Yale wanted was God's own, and it set about training young men in the rigors of orthodoxy and the strictures of correct biblical interpretation. Not until 1899 did Yale have a president who was not an ordained minister (and not until 1925 was compulsory chapel ended). For well beyond its first century, Yale insisted that its students speak Latin, even in private. Nothing so frivolous as belles-lettres was taught; the early course of study included Latin, Greek, and Hebrew, along with logic, metaphysics, mathematics, physics, rhetoric, and religion. English grammar and literature were finally added to the curriculum in the late eighteenth century; the library's holdings were expanded and literary societies were founded—first the Crotonia, then the Linonia, followed by Brothers in Unity. Plays were even performed. (This no doubt accounts for the fact that young Nathan Hale's famous last words, "I only regret that I have but one life to lose for my country," are an echo of Joseph Addison's popular play *Cato,* which Hale read at the Linonia. Cato's words are: "What pity is it that we can die but once to serve our country.") Still, dancing teachers were driven out of New Haven. And when Timothy Dwight, himself an enlightened teacher and an admired poet, became president of Yale in 1795, he inaugurated an annual public debate among the student body. One favorite subject was "Are novels beneficial?" President Dwight himself would give the closing argument, and always in the negative. In spite of such attitudes, a writer of such apocalyptic power as Jonathan Edwards, a poet of such grand ambition as Joel Barlow, a novelist of such inventive scope as James Fenimore Cooper all emerged from Yale during this period.

In time, the great flowering of learning and achievement that surrounded the years of the War of Independence faded. Professors were aloof and tutors were drill masters; grammar and rhetoric were a frog march. Finally, French and German were grudgingly admitted to the curriculum, but when the study of Anglo-Saxon was allowed in 1839, Yale's president Jeremiah Day remarked "that it might soon be necessary to appoint an instructor in *whittling.*" The college library in these days was seldom open to students, and in any case contained little literature beyond the esteemed classics. Still, the *Yale Literary Magazine*—since termed "the most successful periodical in American college literature"—appeared in 1836, and the literary societies continued as a beacon of pleasure and as an encouragement to students with literary pretensions. But by the mid-nineteenth century the societies, too, began to fade. The faculty feared they could not control them, and students who wished to read poetry together were deemed suspicious. Eventually, Yale's extreme educational conservatism was replaced by a palpable anti-intellectualism—except in the sciences and divinity—that in the twilight of the nineteenth century made the term "Yale man" synonymous with the sort of bullying scamp who grew up to be a robber baron—or preacher or university president or lawyer or statesman.

In 1870, Thomas Lounsbury was named Yale's first professor of English—a term that until then referred only to rhetoric, not literature. Lounsbury soon had his students reading Chaucer, Shakespeare, Milton, and Pope, and in the back of his mind must have been the memory that when he himself was an undergraduate at Yale he had never studied or even heard the names of the major English or American authors. But it was not until the arrival of a few younger, vigorous teachers—William Lyon Phelps, Henry Seidel Canby, Wilbur Cross, and Chauncey Brewster Tinker—decades later that the situation changed dramatically. Phelps, the most famous and dynamic of them all, remembered that when he started teaching at Yale in the 1890s there seemed to be "a blight, a curse on the teaching. . . . In the traditional teaching at Yale, formality was the rule. Nearly all the members of the Faculty wore dark clothes, frock coats, high collars; in the class room their manners had an icy formality; humor was usually absent, except occasional irony at the expense of a dull student." Phelps's own easy, unbuttoned manner made him at once a popular lecturer—and a target of scorn to his peers. He had to struggle to be made a full professor. But once in place, his energies bore fruit. In 1899, he boldly offered a course in the American novel, and Yale was never the same.

In the closing years of the eighteenth century, the Connecticut Wits wrote in a period of great tension between the forces of progress and regression that prevailed after the Revolution. They wrote with wit and dread, with satire and rapture, of what they foresaw. Timothy Dwight, John Trumbull, Joel Barlow, and the others had been Yale undergraduates and tutors, a part of the intellectual flowering that accompanied the rise of the spirit of independence in this country. First in New Haven, as later in Hartford, they envisioned the genial, literate life in the peaceful Connecticut Valley as an ideal, threatened by the crass new forces of modern democracy. It was their Walden. And it was the last time that Yale was, even by extension, a center for the kind of literary culture that debated ideas of national destiny. Unlike Harvard, with its concentric literary circles in Cambridge, Boston, and Concord, Yale never had much of a self-conscious community of authors and audiences—or not until the charismatic William Lyon Phelps galvanized things. Not only did he and Tinker and Canby vitalize the literary curriculum, they mixed with students and encouraged their stories and poems and plays. They invited living authors to the campus to read their work. In 1908, Yale University Press was founded, and eleven years later it inaugurated the Yale Series of Younger Poets. In 1911, Wilbur Cross translated the stodgy *Yale Review* into a journal filled with the best writers and thinkers here and abroad. In that same year, the Elizabethan Club was formed, a haven for literary discussion and plans. The Yale Dramat gained new distinction under the direction of Monty Woolley (Class of 1911), and then in 1924 a drama department with its own building and faculty was founded and George Pierce Baker was lured from Harvard to teach the famous English 47 "Workshop." The *Courant* and the *Record* were homes for student writers. Undergraduate composers like Douglas Moore and Quincy Porter were around in these days—to say nothing of Cole Porter—and painters like Reginald Marsh, but above all there was a new literary seriousness in the air. Where earlier there had been a sharp divide between Harvard's Athens and Yale's Sparta, between the parlor aesthetes and the knockabout athletes, the literary renaissance at Yale was part of a broader awakening that made scholarship more earnest and the intellectual respectable. By 1910, an article in the *New York Times* could even refer to "a Yale school of belles-lettres." The likes of Sinclair Lewis, Thornton Wilder, Stephen Vincent Benét, and Archibald MacLeish were contributing their early work to the *Yale Lit.* Instead of turning instinctively to the law, Yale graduates like John Farrar and Henry Luce (who also contributed poems to the *Yale Lit*) were running magazine empires and publishing houses.

In 1915, Phelps lamented that Yale had for so long neglected the creative arts, but he took heart in his conviction that "Yale's greatness as the mother of authors lies in the future." By 1922, Heywood Broun was complaining that while Harvard at last had a successful football team, "literature thrives at Yale and, more than that, is fashionable. Our magazines are filled with poems from New Haven and essays. Within a year we have seen with our own eyes a Yale football captain listening to a reading of lyric poetry."

From that day to this, the arts have flourished at Yale. Its composers, painters, architects, directors, actors, set and lighting designers, sculptors, musicians, graphic artists, and printers have dominated and enriched their fields. Its writers, too, over the course of the past half century, have shown an unparalleled richness and diversity. The genial wit of Brendan Gill and Calvin Trillin, the narrative command of David McCullough and Robert K. Massie, the haunted austerities of Mark Strand and Rosanna Warren, the fictive ingenuity of Peter Matthiessen and Claire Messud and Christopher Tilghman, the theatrical panache of Wendy Wasserstein and John Guare. . . . Each star shines; constellated, they are a sky filled with fables.

Bright Pages is divided into three sections. The last surveys the lofty distance. Jonathan Edwards's sermons are, or used to be, well known, and the power of their ominous shudders can still be felt. It cannot surprise that men wept and women miscarried while listening to him preach. From James Fenimore Cooper to Clarence Day, from Philip Barry to Thornton Wilder, I have drawn on material that is meant to recall the wider achievements of these popular writers. I have also tried to retrieve less familiar material. Noah Webster on the future of English as the language of Americans or Cole Porter's undergraduate lyrics—these are byways that deserve a leisurely stroll. This anthology's middle section is the longest, and includes writers who have been working since the end of the Second World War. History will make its own slow judgments, as it has of writers from the earlier centuries, but the plenitude here will give any critic pause and any reader pleasure. I have chosen work that casts a strong light on an author, the better to throw his or her work into strong profile. Juxtapositions have been created by chronology, but the effect is dramatic. This book opens with a section devoted to the four teachers of writing at Yale who have had the most influence during the past few decades. I have done so not only to highlight their own work but to emphasize just how a young writer learns, how traditions are passed on. It must be said, however, that Yale, unlike most colleges these days, has never institutionalized creative writing. The College Seminar system has brought distinguished visitors to the campus as guest lecturers every year. The famous "Daily Themes" class is always thronged with students. But there has never been a graduate program in writing, and undergraduates are still encouraged to consider the library their best classroom. The young writer learns most from Herman Melville and Franz Kafka, John Milton and Emily Dickinson. But the encounter of master and apprentice is always decisive, and can stamp a young writer for life. No beginners first coached and corrected by John Hersey or Robert Penn Warren, by John Hollander or Robert Stone, or by such visitors as Richard Howard and Peter Matthiessen and Maureen Howard, have ever forgotten the lessons learned during their struggles with silence under the watchful eyes of the wise instructor. As in the past, these teachers have had the most direct contact with students; they have inspired their ambitions and helped shape their sense of themselves as writers. This is where everything in *Bright Pages* began—a pile of books, a compelling example, the spur of admiration, a blank page.

Any collection that attempts to represent the full range of Yale writers over three centuries, and to sample the depth and variety of their work, should properly run to several volumes. Budgetary constraints, however, forbid the generous overview. For all the dazzle of the work included in this anthology, I am not blinded to the sorry fact that so much else is missing. Among those in an earlier age, the great chemist Benjamin Silliman wrote a fascinating account of his travels in early nineteenth-century Europe. Not only have scores of talented individual writers been stranded in the wings, but whole categories of important writers have been ignored. There are, for instance, scholars whose work transcended the academy, from William Lyon Phelps himself, who became a well-known public figure, to Robert Maynard Hutchins, who was such an influential educator, to F. O. Matthiessen, who more or less started American Studies, on to more recent figures like William Sloan Coffin, Jr., or Henry Louis Gates, Jr. Gone, too, are those statesmen who wrote their own words, from William Howard Taft to Dean Acheson and McGeorge Bundy. Nonfiction takes a heavy blow; I have had to omit countless popular historians, essayists, and journalists whose work has stirred and enlightened their readers. I should note, too, that the most widely read and influential author in the second half of the twentieth century, and a sprightly stylist at that, was also a Yale graduate—Dr. Benjamin Spock. In the end, I wince to admit, it was not possible to include notable contemporary writers—many of them winners of prestigious awards for their work—like Richard Rhodes, Garry Wills, Henry S. F. Cooper, C. D. B. Bryan, Lewis Lapham, and Mark Singer. Then there are playwrights like Frank Gilroy, Tad Mosel, Christopher Durang, Albert Innaurato, Thomas Babe, David Henry Hwang, Paul Rudnick, and David Ives; young novelists like Mark Salzman, Allen Kurzweil, Jane Mendelsohn, Sylvia Brownrigg, Tom Perrotta, and Jonathan Levi; poets like Harvey Shapiro, Sydney Lea, Robert B. Shaw, Peter Sacks, Jonathan Aaron, Rika Lesser, John Burt, and Tony Sanders. . . . Their achievements, of course, are not being judged because I couldn't find a seat for them on this over-booked express train.

When in 1901 Theodore Roosevelt (along with Mark Twain) was given an honorary degree by Yale, the Public Orator at the ceremony proclaimed that the president "is a Harvard man by nature; but in his democratic spirit, his breadth of national feeling, and his earnest pursuit of what is true and right, he possesses those qualities which represent the distinctive ideals of Yale." Where we might today smile at the chauvinistic comparison, I wonder instead if there isn't here a clue to follow when trying to trace the characteristics of A Yale Writer. After all, it is a note sounded over and over. In 1915, Arthur Twining Hadley, Yale's thirteenth president, outlined the five aims of a Yale education. The first is that it must contribute to "the intellectual training of the student," and as his example he noted that "we do not count the ability to play an instrument . . . unless it is accompanied by a knowledge of musical theory and musical composition." His fifth and summarizing point was this: "It must make him a profounder thinker and a better citizen. A public motive rather than a private one must constitute the dominant note in its appeal." The link between artistic knowledge and moral understanding has, during three centuries now, been at the heart of a Yale education. There are those for whom the world means only itself and others for whom the inner soul and destinies of humanity are their subject. It is not by accident that this book opens with John Hersey's *Hiroshima*.

There are writers whose appetites are for extremities and those for whom the middle ground is mined. Socrates says that a man is not to be considered a master of harmony simply because he knows how to produce the highest possible note and the lowest possible on his strings. If Yale has taught its writers anything, it is where to find the world's true harmonies: in the bitter prosperities and redemptive sadnesses of our lives. More than many other groups of writers, I think, Yalies have cultivated an instinct to probe the moral dimension of experience, to turn emotions in the light of thought, to site the private self within a complex of public allegiances and pressures. They are drawn to outsize events, whether in history or in the self. Yale's motto—*lux et veritas,* light and truth—has become their own. In the bright pages that follow, you can watch an extraordinary group of men and women as they use language to illuminate the truths they have discovered.

I **Four Teachers**

orn in Tientsin, China, where his mother was a missionary and his father the secretary of the YMCA, John Hersey (1914–1993) graduated from Yale in 1936. The next summer he worked as Sinclair Lewis's private secretary but was soon after a correspondent for *Time,* covering first China and Japan and later the war in the South Pacific, the Sicilian campaign, and Moscow. From 1945 until his death, he was a writer for the *New Yorker.* He returned to Yale in 1965 as master of Pierson College, and after his term he stayed on to teach writing, from 1971 until 1984. To many, he was the embodiment of the moral clarity and integrity that has guided Yale's educational mission down the years. Hersey understood that a proper understanding of history demands both lucidity and compassion. His first book, *Men on Bataan,* appeared in 1942. He published thirteen more books of nonfiction, two collections of stories, and fourteen novels, among them his Pulitzer Prize–winning *A Bell for Adano* (1944), *The Wall* (1950), *The War Lover* (1959), *The Child Buyer* (1960), and *The Call* (1985). Perhaps his best-known work is *Hiroshima* (1946), originally published in an entire single issue of the *New Yorker* and recently voted by reporters and scholars at the New York University School of Journalism as the single best work of twentieth-century American journalism. In 1949, he wrote: "Fiction is a clarifying agent. It makes truth plausible." That was the goal of all his work.

At exactly fifteen minutes past eight in the morning, on August 6, 1945, Japanese time, at the moment when the atomic bomb flashed above Hiroshima, Miss Toshiko Sasaki, a clerk in the personnel department of the East Asia Tin Works, had just sat down at her place in the plant office and was turning her head to speak to the girl at the next desk. At that same moment, Dr. Masakazu Fujii was settling down crosslegged to read the Osaka *Asahi* on the porch of his private hospital, overhanging one of the seven deltaic rivers which divide Hiroshima; Mrs. Hatsuyo Nakamura, a tailor's widow, stood by the window of her kitchen, watching a neighbor tearing down his house because it lay in the path of an air-raid-defense fire lane; Father Wilhelm Kleinsorge, a German priest of the Society of Jesus, reclined in his underwear on a cot on the top floor of his order's three-story mission house, reading a Jesuit magazine, *Stimmen der Zeit;* Dr. Terufumi Sasaki, a young member of the surgical staff of the city's large, modern Red Cross Hospital, walked along one of the hospital corridors with a blood specimen for a Wassermann test in his hand; and the Reverend Mr. Kiyoshi Tanimoto, pastor of the Hiroshima Methodist Church, paused at the door of a rich man's house in Koi, the city's western suburb, and prepared to unload a handcart full of things he had evacuated from town in fear of the massive B-29 raid which everyone expected Hiroshima to suffer. A hundred thousand people were killed by the atomic bomb, and these six were among the survivors. They still wonder why they lived when so many others died. Each of them counts many small items of chance or volition—a step taken in time, a decision to go indoors, catching one streetcar instead of the next—that spared him. And now each knows that in the act of survival he lived a dozen lives and saw more death than he ever thought he would see. At the time, none of them knew anything.

The Reverend Mr. Tanimoto got up at five o'clock that morning. He was alone in the parsonage, because for some time his wife had been commuting with their year-old baby to spend nights with a friend in Ushida, a suburb to the north. Of all the important cities of Japan, only two, Kyoto and Hiroshima, had not been visited in strength by *B-san,* or Mr. B, as the Japanese, with a mixture of respect and unhappy familiarity, called the B-29; and Mr. Tanimoto, like all his neighbors and friends, was almost sick with anxiety. He had heard uncomfortably detailed accounts of mass raids on Kure, Iwakuni, Tokuyama, and other nearby towns; he was sure Hiroshima's turn would come soon. He had slept badly the night before, because there had been several air-raid warnings. Hiroshima had been getting such warnings almost every night for weeks, for at that time the B-29s were using Lake Biwa, northeast of Hiroshima, as a rendezvous point, and no matter what city the Americans planned to hit, the Superfortresses streamed in over the coast near Hiroshima. The frequency of the warnings and the continued abstinence of Mr. B with respect to Hiroshima had made its citizens jittery; a rumor was going around that the Americans were saving something special for the city.

Mr. Tanimoto was a small man, quick to talk, laugh, and cry. He wore his black hair parted in the middle and rather long; the prominence of the frontal bones just above his eyebrows and the smallness of his mustache, mouth, and chin gave him a strange, old-young look, boyish and yet wise, weak and yet fiery. He moved nervously and fast, but with a restraint which suggested that he was a cautious, thoughtful man. He showed, indeed, just those qualities in the uneasy days before the bomb fell. Besides having his wife spend the nights in Ushida, Mr. Tanimoto had been carrying all the portable things from the church, in the close-packed residential district called Nagaragawa, to a house that belonged to a rayon manufacturer in Koi, two miles from the center of town. The rayon man, a Mr. Matsui, had opened his then unoccupied estate to a large number of his friends and acquaintances, so that they might evacuate whatever they wished to a safe distance from the probable target area. Mr. Tanimoto had had no difficulty in moving chairs, hymnals, Bibles, altar gear, and church records by pushcart himself, but the organ console and an upright piano required some aid. A friend of his named Matsuo had, the day before, helped him get the piano out to Koi; in return, he had promised this day to assist Mr. Matsuo in hauling out a daughter's belongings. That is why he had risen so early.

Mr. Tanimoto cooked his own breakfast. He felt awfully tired. The effort of moving the piano the day before, a sleepless night, weeks of worry and unbalanced diet, the cares of his parish—all combined to make him feel hardly adequate to the new day's work. There was another thing, too: Mr. Tanimoto had studied theology at Emory College, in Atlanta, Georgia; he had graduated in 1940; he spoke excellent English; he dressed in American clothes; he had corresponded with many American friends right up to the time the war began; and among a people obsessed with a fear of being spied upon—perhaps almost obsessed himself—he found himself growing increasingly uneasy. The police had questioned him several times, and just a few days before, he had heard that an influential acquaintance, a Mr. Tanaka, a retired officer of the Toyo Kisen Kaisha steamship line, an anti-Christian, a man famous in Hiroshima for his showy philanthropies and notorious for his personal tyrannies, had been telling people that Tanimoto should not be trusted. In compensation, to show himself publicly a good Japanese, Mr. Tanimoto had taken on the chairmanship of his local *tonarigumi,* or Neighborhood Association, and to his other duties and concerns this position had added the business of organizing air-raid defense for about twenty families.

Before six o'clock that morning, Mr. Tanimoto started for Mr. Matsuo's house.

There he found that their burden was to be a *tansu,* a large Japanese cabinet, full
of clothing and household goods. The two men set out. The morning was perfectly clear and so warm that the day promised to be uncomfortable. A few minutes after they started, the air-raid siren went off—a minute-long blast that
warned of approaching planes but indicated to the people of Hiroshima only a
slight degree of danger, since it sounded every morning at this time, when an
American weather plane came over. The two men pulled and pushed the handcart through the city streets. Hiroshima was a fan-shaped city, lying mostly on
the six islands formed by the seven estuarial rivers that branch out from the Ota
River; its main commercial and residential districts, covering about four square
miles in the center of the city, contained three-quarters of its population, which
had been reduced by several evacuation programs from a wartime peak of
380,000 to about 245,000. Factories and other residential districts, or suburbs, lay
compactly around the edges of the city. To the south were the docks, an airport,
and the island-studded Inland Sea. A rim of mountains runs around the other
three sides of the delta. Mr. Tanimoto and Mr. Matsuo took their way through
the shopping center, already full of people, and across two of the rivers to the
sloping streets of Koi, and up them to the outskirts and foothills. As they started
up a valley away from the tight-ranked houses, the all-clear sounded. (The Japanese radar operators, detecting only three planes, supposed that they comprised a
reconnaissance.) Pushing the handcart up to the rayon man's house was tiring,
and the men, after they had maneuvered their load into the driveway and to the
front steps, paused to rest awhile. They stood with a wing of the house between
them and the city. Like most homes in this part of Japan, the house consisted of a
wooden frame and wooden walls supporting a heavy tile roof. Its front hall,
packed with rolls of bedding and clothing, looked like a cool cave full of fat
cushions. Opposite the house, to the right of the front door, there was a large,
finicky rock garden. There was no sound of planes. The morning was still; the
place was cool and pleasant.

Then a tremendous flash of light cut across the sky. Mr. Tanimoto has a distinct recollection that it travelled from east to west, from the city toward the hills.
It seemed a sheet of sun. Both he and Mr. Matsuo reacted in terror—and both
had time to react (for they were 3,500 yards, or two miles, from the center of the
explosion). Mr. Matsuo dashed up the front steps into the house and dived
among the bedrolls and buried himself there. Mr. Tanimoto took four or five
steps and threw himself between two big rocks in the garden. He bellied up very
hard against one of them. As his face was against the stone, he did not see what
happened. He felt a sudden pressure, and then splinters and pieces of board and
fragments of tile fell on him. He heard no roar. (Almost no one in Hiroshima recalls hearing any noise of the bomb. But a fisherman in his sampan on the Inland
Sea near Tsuzu, the man with whom Mr. Tanimoto's mother-in-law and sister-in-

law were living, saw the flash and heard a tremendous explosion; he was nearly twenty miles from Hiroshima, but the thunder was greater than when the B-29s hit Iwakuni, only five miles away.)

When he dared, Mr. Tanimoto raised his head and saw that the rayon man's house had collapsed. He thought a bomb had fallen directly on it. Such clouds of dust had risen that there was a sort of twilight around. In panic, not thinking for the moment of Mr. Matsuo under the ruins, he dashed out into the street. He noticed as he ran that the concrete wall of the estate had fallen over—toward the house rather than away from it. In the street, the first thing he saw was a squad of soldiers who had been burrowing into the hillside opposite, making one of the thousands of dugouts in which the Japanese apparently intended to resist invasion, hill by hill, life for life; the soldiers were coming out of the hole, where they should have been safe, and blood was running from their heads, chests, and backs. They were silent and dazed.

Under what seemed to be a local dust cloud, the day grew darker and darker.

At nearly midnight, the night before the bomb was dropped, an announcer on the city's radio station said that about two hundred B-29s were approaching southern Honshu and advised the population of Hiroshima to evacuate to their designated "safe areas." Mrs. Hatsuyo Nakamura, the tailor's widow, who lived in the section called Nobori-cho and who had long had a habit of doing as she was told, got her three children—a ten-year-old boy, Toshio, an eight-year-old girl, Yaeko, and a five-year-old girl, Myeko—out of bed and dressed them and walked with them to the military area known as the East Parade Ground, on the northeast edge of the city. There she unrolled some mats and the children lay down on them. They slept until about two, when they were awakened by the roar of the planes going over Hiroshima.

As soon as the planes had passed, Mrs. Nakamura started back with her children. They reached home a little after two-thirty and she immediately turned on the radio, which, to her distress, was just then broadcasting a fresh warning. When she looked at the children and saw how tired they were, and when she thought of the number of trips they had made in past weeks, all to no purpose, to the East Parade Ground, she decided that in spite of the instructions on the radio, she simply could not face starting out all over again. She put the children in their bedrolls on the floor, lay down herself at three o'clock, and fell asleep at once, so soundly that when planes passed over later, she did not waken to their sound.

The siren jarred her awake at about seven. She arose, dressed quickly, and hurried to the house of Mr. Nakamoto, the head of her Neighborhood Association, and asked him what she should do. He said that she should remain at home unless an urgent warning—a series of intermittent blasts of the siren—was sounded.

She returned home, lit the stove in the kitchen, set some rice to cook, and sat down to read that morning's Hiroshima *Chugoku*. To her relief, the all-clear sounded at eight o'clock. She heard the children stirring, so she went and gave each of them a handful of peanuts and told them to stay on their bedrolls, because they were tired from the night's walk. She had hoped that they would go back to sleep, but the man in the house directly to the south began to make a terrible hullabaloo of hammering, wedging, ripping, and splitting. The prefectural government, convinced, as everyone in Hiroshima was, that the city would be attacked soon, had begun to press with threats and warnings for the completion of wide fire lanes, which, it was hoped, might act in conjunction with the rivers to localize any fires started by an incendiary raid; and the neighbor was reluctantly sacrificing his home to the city's safety. Just the day before, the prefecture had ordered all able-bodied girls from the secondary schools to spend a few days helping to clear these lanes, and they started work soon after the all-clear sounded.

Mrs. Nakamura went back to the kitchen, looked at the rice, and began watching the man next door. At first, she was annoyed with him for making so much noise, but then she was moved almost to tears by pity. Her emotion was specifically directed toward her neighbor, tearing down his home, board by board, at a time when there was so much unavoidable destruction, but undoubtedly she also felt a generalized, community pity, to say nothing of self-pity. She had not had an easy time. Her husband, Isawa, had gone into the Army just after Myeko was born, and she had heard nothing from or of him for a long time, until, on March 5, 1942, she received a seven-word telegram: "Isawa died an honorable death at Singapore." She learned later that he had died on February 15th, the day Singapore fell, and that he had been a corporal. Isawa had been a not particularly prosperous tailor, and his only capital was a Sankoku sewing machine. After his death, when his allotments stopped coming, Mrs. Nakamura got out the machine and began to take in piecework herself, and since then had supported the children, but poorly, by sewing.

As Mrs. Nakamura stood watching her neighbor, everything flashed whiter than any white she had ever seen. She did not notice what happened to the man next door; the reflex of a mother set her in motion toward her children. She had taken a single step (the house was 1,350 yards, or three-quarters of a mile, from the center of the explosion) when something picked her up and she seemed to fly into the next room over the raised sleeping platform, pursued by parts of her house.

Timbers fell around her as she landed, and a shower of tiles pommelled her: everything became dark, for she was buried. The debris did not cover her deeply. She rose up and freed herself. She heard a child cry, "Mother, help me!," and saw her youngest—Myeko, the five-year-old—buried up to her breast and unable to move. As Mrs. Nakamura started frantically to claw her way toward the baby, she could see or hear nothing of her other children.

In the days right before the bombing, Dr. Masakazu Fujii, being prosperous, hedonistic, and at the time not too busy, had been allowing himself the luxury of sleeping until nine or nine-thirty, but fortunately he had to get up early the morning the bomb was dropped to see a house guest off on a train. He rose at six, and half an hour later walked with his friend to the station, not far away, across two of the rivers. He was back home by seven, just as the siren sounded its sustained warning. He ate breakfast and then, because the morning was already hot, undressed down to his underwear and went out on the porch to read the paper. This porch—in fact, the whole building—was curiously constructed. Dr. Fujii was the proprietor of a peculiarly Japanese institution: a private, single-doctor hospital. This building, perched beside and over the water of the Kyo River, and next to the bridge of the same name, contained thirty rooms for thirty patients and their kinfolk—for, according to Japanese custom, when a person falls sick and goes to a hospital, one or more members of his family go and live there with him, to cook for him, bathe, massage, and read to him, and to offer incessant familial sympathy, without which a Japanese patient would be miserable indeed. Dr. Fujii had no beds—only straw mats—for his patients. He did, however, have all sorts of modern equipment: an X-ray machine, diathermy apparatus, and a fine tiled laboratory. The structure rested two-thirds on the land, one-third on piles over the tidal waters of the Kyo. This overhang, the part of the building where Dr. Fujii lived, was queer-looking, but it was cool in summer and from the porch, which faced away from the center of the city, the prospect of the river, with pleasure boats drifting up and down it, was always refreshing. Dr. Fujii had occasionally had anxious moments when the Ota and its mouth branches rose to flood, but the piling was apparently firm enough and the house had always held.

Dr. Fujii had been relatively idle for about a month because in July, as the number of untouched cities in Japan dwindled and as Hiroshima seemed more and more inevitably a target, he began turning patients away, on the ground that in case of a fire raid he would not be able to evacuate them. Now he had only two patients left—a woman from Yano, injured in the shoulder, and a young man of twenty-five recovering from burns he had suffered when the steel factory near Hiroshima in which he worked had been hit. Dr. Fujii had six nurses to tend his patients. His wife and children were safe; his wife and one son were living outside Osaka, and another son and two daughters were in the country on Kyushu. A niece was living with him, and a maid and a manservant. He had little to do and did not mind, for he had saved some money. At fifty, he was healthy, convivial, and calm, and he was pleased to pass the evenings drinking whiskey with friends, always sensibly and for the sake of conversation. Before the war, he had affected brands imported from Scotland and America; now he was perfectly satisfied with the best Japanese brand, Suntory.

Dr. Fujii sat down cross-legged in his underwear on the spotless matting of the porch, put on his glasses, and started reading the Osaka *Asahi*. He liked to read the Osaka news because his wife was there. He saw the flash. To him—faced away from the center and looking at his paper—it seemed a brilliant yellow. Startled, he began to rise to his feet. In that moment (he was 1,550 yards from the center), the hospital leaned behind his rising and, with a terrible ripping noise, toppled into the river. The Doctor, still in the act of getting to his feet, was thrown forward and around and over; he was buffeted and gripped; he lost track of everything, because things were so speeded up; he felt the water.

Dr. Fujii hardly had time to think that he was dying before he realized that he was alive, squeezed tightly by two long timbers in a V across his chest, like a morsel suspended between two huge chopsticks—held upright, so that he could not move, with his head miraculously above water and his torso and legs in it. The remains of his hospital were all around him in a mad assortment of splintered lumber and materials for the relief of pain. His left shoulder hurt terribly. His glasses were gone.

Father Wilhelm Kleinsorge, of the Society of Jesus, was, on the morning of the explosion, in rather frail condition. The Japanese wartime diet had not sustained him, and he felt the strain of being a foreigner in an increasingly xenophobic Japan; even a German, since the defeat of the Fatherland, was unpopular. Father Kleinsorge had, at thirty-eight, the look of a boy growing too fast—thin in the face, with a prominent Adam's apple, a hollow chest, dangling hands, big feet. He walked clumsily, leaning forward a little. He was tired all the time. To make matters worse, he had suffered for two days, along with Father Cieslik, a fellow-priest, from a rather painful and urgent diarrhea, which they blamed on the beans and black ration bread they were obliged to eat. Two other priests then living in the mission compound, which was in the Nobori-cho section—Father Superior LaSalle and Father Schiffer—had happily escaped this affliction.

Father Kleinsorge woke up about six the morning the bomb was dropped, and half an hour later—he was a bit tardy because of his sickness—he began to read Mass in the mission chapel, a small Japanese-style wooden building which was without pews, since its worshippers knelt on the usual Japanese matted floor, facing an altar graced with splendid silks, brass, silver, and heavy embroideries. This morning, a Monday, the only worshippers were Mr. Takemoto, a theological student living in the mission house; Mr. Fukai, the secretary of the diocese; Mrs. Murata, the mission's devoutly Christian housekeeper; and his fellow-priests. After Mass, while Father Kleinsorge was reading the Prayers of Thanksgiving, the siren sounded. He stopped the service and the missionaries retired across the compound to the bigger building. There, in his room on the ground floor, to the right of the front door, Father Kleinsorge changed into a military uniform which he had acquired when he was teaching at the Rokko Middle School in Kobe and which he wore during air-raid alerts.

After an alarm, Father Kleinsorge always went out and scanned the sky, and in this instance, when he stepped outside, he was glad to see only the single weather plane that flew over Hiroshima each day about this time. Satisfied that nothing would happen, he went in and breakfasted with the other Fathers on substitute coffee and ration bread, which, under the circumstances, was especially repugnant to him. The Fathers sat and talked awhile, until, at eight, they heard the all-clear. They went then to various parts of the building. Father Schiffer retired to his room to do some writing. Father Cieslik sat in his room in a straight chair with a pillow over his stomach to ease his pain, and read. Father Superior LaSalle stood at the window of his room, thinking. Father Kleinsorge went up to a room on the third floor, took off all his clothes except his underwear, and stretched out on his right side on a cot and began reading his *Stimmen der Zeit*.

After the terrible flash—which, Father Kleinsorge later realized, reminded him of something he had read as a boy about a large meteor colliding with the earth—he had time (since he was 1,400 yards from the center) for one thought: A bomb has fallen directly on us. Then, for a few seconds or minutes, he went out of his mind.

Father Kleinsorge never knew how he got out of the house. The next things he was conscious of were that he was wandering around in the mission's vegetable garden in his underwear, bleeding slightly from small cuts along his left flank; that all the buildings round about had fallen down except the Jesuits' mission house, which had long before been braced and double-braced by a priest named Gropper, who was terrified of earthquakes; that the day had turned dark; and that Murata-*san,* the housekeeper, was nearby, crying over and over, "*Shu Jesusu, awaremi tamai!* Our Lord Jesus, have pity on us!"

On the train on the way into Hiroshima from the country, where he lived with his mother, Dr. Terufumi Sasaki, the Red Cross Hospital surgeon, thought over an unpleasant nightmare he had had the night before. His mother's home was in Mukaihara, thirty miles from the city, and it took him two hours by train and tram to reach the hospital. He had slept uneasily all night and had awakened an hour earlier than usual, and, feeling sluggish and slightly feverish, had debated whether to go to the hospital at all; his sense of duty finally forced him to go, and he had started out on an earlier train than he took most mornings. The dream had particularly frightened him because it was so closely associated, on the surface at least, with a disturbing actuality. He was only twenty-five years old and had just completed his training at the Eastern Medical University, in Tsingtao, China. He was something of an idealist and was much distressed by the inadequacy of medical facilities in the country town where his mother lived. Quite on his own, and without a permit, he had begun visiting a few sick people out there in the evenings, after his eight hours at the hospital and four hours' commuting. He had recently learned that the penalty for practicing without a permit was severe; a fellow-doctor whom he had asked about it had given him a serious scolding. Nevertheless, he had continued to practice. In his dream, he had been at the bedside of a country patient when the police and the doctor he had consulted burst into the room, seized him, dragged him outside, and beat him up cruelly. On the train, he just about decided to give up the work in Mukaihara, since he felt it would be impossible to get a permit, because the authorities would hold that it would conflict with his duties at the Red Cross Hospital.

At the terminus, he caught a streetcar at once. (He later calculated that if he had taken his customary train that morning, and if he had had to wait a few minutes for the streetcar, as often happened, he would have been close to the center at the time of the explosion and would surely have perished.) He arrived at the hospital at seven-forty and reported to the chief surgeon. A few minutes later, he went to a room on the first floor and drew blood from the arm of a man in order to perform a Wassermann test. The laboratory containing the incubators for the test was on the third floor. With the blood specimen in his left hand, walking in a kind of distraction he had felt all morning, probably because of the dream and his restless night, he started along the main corridor on his way toward the stairs. He was one step beyond an open window when the light of the bomb was reflected, like a gigantic photographic flash, in the corridor. He ducked down on one knee and said to himself, as only a Japanese would, "Sasaki, *gambare!* Be brave!" Just then (the building was 1,650 yards from the center), the blast ripped through the hospital. The glasses he was wearing flew off his face; the bottle of blood crashed against one wall; his Japanese slippers zipped out from under his feet—but otherwise, thanks to where he stood, he was untouched.

Dr. Sasaki shouted the name of the chief surgeon and rushed around to the man's office and found him terribly cut by glass. The hospital was in horrible confusion: heavy partitions and ceilings had fallen on patients, beds had overturned, windows had blown in and cut people, blood was spattered on the walls and floors, instruments were everywhere, many of the patients were running about screaming, many more lay dead. (A colleague working in the laboratory to which Dr. Sasaki had been walking was dead; Dr. Sasaki's patient, whom he had just left and who a few moments before had been dreadfully afraid of syphilis, was also dead.) Dr. Sasaki found himself the only doctor in the hospital who was unhurt.

Dr. Sasaki, who believed that the enemy had hit only the building he was in, got bandages and began to bind the wounds of those inside the hospital; while outside, all over Hiroshima, maimed and dying citizens turned their unsteady steps toward the Red Cross Hospital to begin an invasion that was to make Dr. Sasaki forget his private nightmare for a long, long time.

Miss Toshiko Sasaki, the East Asia Tin Works clerk, who was not related to Dr. Sasaki, got up at three o'clock in the morning on the day the bomb fell. There was extra housework to do. Her eleven-month-old brother, Akio, had come down the day before with a serious stomach upset; her mother had taken him to the Tamura Pediatric Hospital and was staying there with him. Miss Sasaki, who was about twenty, had to cook breakfast for her father, a brother, a sister, and herself, and—since the hospital, because of the war, was unable to provide food—to prepare a whole day's meals for her mother and the baby, in time for her father, who worked in a factory making rubber earplugs for artillery crews, to take the food by on his way to the plant. When she had finished and had cleaned and put away the cooking things, it was nearly seven. The family lived in Koi, and she had a forty-five minute trip to the tin works, in the section of town called Kannonmachi. She was in charge of the personnel records in the factory. She left Koi at seven, and as soon as she reached the plant, she went with some of the other girls from the personnel department to the factory auditorium. A prominent local Navy man, a former employee, had committed suicide the day before by throwing himself under a train—a death considered honorable enough to warrant a memorial service, which was to be held at the tin works at ten o'clock that morning. In the large hall, Miss Sasaki and the others made suitable preparations for the meeting. This work took about twenty minutes.

Miss Sasaki went back to her office and sat down at her desk. She was quite far from the windows, which were off to her left, and behind her were a couple of tall bookcases containing all the books of the factory library, which the personnel department had organized. She settled herself at her desk, put some things in a drawer, and shifted papers. She thought that before she began to make entries in her lists of new employees, discharges, and departures for the Army, she would chat for a moment with the girl at her right. Just as she turned her head away from the windows, the room was filled with a blinding light. She was paralyzed by fear, fixed still in her chair for a long moment (the plant was 1,600 yards from the center).

Everything fell, and Miss Sasaki lost consciousness. The ceiling dropped suddenly and the wooden floor above collapsed in splinters and the people up there came down and the roof above them gave way; but principally and first of all, the bookcases right behind her swooped forward and the contents threw her down, with her left leg horribly twisted and breaking underneath her. There, in the tin factory, in the first moment of the atomic age, a human being was crushed by books.

robert Penn Warren (1905–1989) first came to Yale in 1927, intent on pursuing his doctoral studies. He had already graduated from Vanderbilt University and studied at Berkeley, but was restive in New Haven. "What I really wanted," he wrote to a friend in 1928, "was to get in an environment where men were actually doing creative writing, but Yale is not the place for that, I learned too late." Instead, he went to Oxford as a Rhodes Scholar, where he took his B.Litt. He then taught at Vanderbilt, Louisiana State, and the University of Minnesota, where he forged famous critical alliances with Cleanth Brooks and Allen Tate. As an influential prose writer and critic, his early books were *John Brown: The Making of a Martyr* (1929), *I'll Take My Stand* (1930), and, with Cleanth Brooks, *Understanding Poetry* (1930). His career as a poet began with *XXXVI Poems* (1935) and *Eleven Poems on the Same Theme* (1942). *Promises: Poems, 1954–1956* (1957) won both the Pulitzer Prize and the National Book Award. His greatest work came later, beginning with *Incarnations* (1968). He won the Pulitzer again for his 1979 collection, *Now and Then: Poems, 1976–1978*. The style of his early poems, knottily or delicately metaphysical, later gave way to a vigorous narrative drive, to moralized anecdotes and memories written up in ways that are craggy and powerful. Regarded as one of the best poets of his strong generation, Warren was equally at home in the novel. His best-known novel is *All the King's Men*, published in 1946 and awarded the Pulitzer. Among his other novels are *Night Rider* (1938), *At Heaven's Gate* (1943), *World Enough and Time* (1950), *Flood* (1964), and *A Place to Come To* (1977). In 1950 he returned to Yale as a visiting professor, and the next year he accepted an appointment as professor of playwriting in the Yale School of Drama. Beginning in 1962, and for the next eleven years, as a member of Yale's English Department he taught writing one semester a year. When in 1986 he was named the nation's first official Poet Laureate, he had long since been the dean of American letters. The breadth of his achievements and sympathies is nearly unrivaled, and his influence on generations of students has been profound.

MASTS AT DAWN

Past second cock-crow yacht masts in the harbor go slowly white.

No light in the east yet, but the stars show a certain fatigue.
They withdraw into a new distance, have discovered our unworthiness. It is long
    since

The owl, in the dark eucalyptus, dire and melodious, last called, and
Long since the moon sank and the English
Finished fornicating in their ketches. In the evening there was a strong swell.

Red died the sun, but at dark wind rose easterly, white sea nagged the black
    harbor headland.

When there is a strong swell, you may, if you surrender to it, experience
A sense, in the act, of mystic unity with that rhythm. Your peace is the sea's will.

But now no motion, the bay-face is glossy in darkness, like

An old window pane flat on black ground by the wall, near the ash heap. It neither
Receives nor gives light. Now is the hour when the sea

Sinks into meditation. It doubts its own mission. The drowned cat
That on the evening swell had kept nudging the piles of the pier and had seemed

To want to climb out and lick itself dry, now floats free. On that surface a slight
    convexity only, it is like
An eyelid, in darkness, closed. You must learn to accept the kiss of fate, for

The masts go white slow, as light, like dew, from darkness
Condensed on them, on oiled wood, on metal. Dew whitens in darkness.

I lie in my bed and think how, in darkness, the masts go white.

The sound of the engine of the first fishing dory dies seaward. Soon
In the inland glen wakes the dawn-dove. We must try

To love so well the world that we may believe, in the end, in God.

BIRTH OF LOVE

Season late, day late, sun just down, and the sky
Cold gunmetal but with a wash of live rose, and she,
From water the color of sky except where
Her motion has fractured it to shivering splinters of silver,
Rises. Stands on the raw grass. Against
The new-curdling night of spruces, nakedness
Glimmers and, at bosom and flank, drips
With fluent silver. The man,

Some ten strokes out, but now hanging
Motionless in the gunmetal water, feet
Cold with the coldness of depth, all
History dissolving from him, is
Nothing but an eye. Is an eye only. Sees

The body that is marked by his use, and Time's,
Rise, and in the abrupt and unsustaining element of air,
Sway, lean, grapple the pond-bank. Sees
How, with that posture of female awkwardness that is,
And is the stab of, suddenly perceived grace, breasts bulge down in
The pure curve of their weight and buttocks
Moon up and, in that swelling unity,
Are silver, and glimmer. Then,

The body is erect, she is herself, whatever
Self she may be, and with an end of the towel grasped in each hand,
Slowly draws it back and forth across back and buttocks, but
With face lifted toward the high sky, where
The over-wash of rose color now fails. Fails, though no star
Yet throbs there. The towel, forgotten,
Does not move now. The gaze
Remains fixed on the sky. The body,

Profiled against the darkness of spruces, seems
To draw to itself, and condense in its whiteness, what light
In the sky yet lingers or, from
The metallic and abstract severity of water, lifts. The body,
With the towel now trailing loose from one hand, is
A white stalk from which the face flowers gravely toward the high sky.
This moment is non-sequential and absolute, and admits

Of no definition, for it
Subsumes all other, and sequential, moments, by which
Definition might be possible. The woman,

Face yet raised, wraps,
With a motion as though standing in sleep,
The towel about her body, under the breasts, and,
Holding it there, hieratic as lost Egypt and erect,
Moves up the path that, stair-steep, winds
Into the clamber and tangle of growth. Beyond
The lattice of dusk-dripping leaves, whiteness
Dimly glimmers, goes. Glimmers and is gone, and the man,

Suspended in his darkling medium, stares
Upward where, though not visible, he knows
She moves, and in his heart he cries out that, if only
He had such strength, he would put his hand forth
And maintain it over her to guard, in all
Her out-goings and in-comings, from whatever
Inclemency of sky or slur of the world's weather
Might ever be. In his heart
He cries out. Above

Height of the spruce-night and heave of the far mountain, he sees
The first star pulse into being. It gleams there.

I do not know what promise it makes to him.

RATTLESNAKE COUNTRY

for James Dickey

I
Arid that country and high, anger of sun on the mountains, but
One little patch of cool lawn:

                    Trucks
Had brought in rich loam. Stonework
Held it in place like a shelf, at one side backed
By the length of the house porch, at one end
By rock-fall. Above that, the mesquite, wolf-waiting. Its turn

Will, again, come.

Meanwhile, wicker chairs, all day,
Follow the shimmering shade of the lone cottonwood, the way that
Time, sadly seeking to know its own nature, follows
The shadow on a sun-dial. All day,
The sprinkler ejects its misty rainbow.

All day,
The sky shivers white with heat, the lake,
For its fifteen miles of distance, stretches
Tight under the white sky. It is stretched
Tight as a mystic drumhead. It glitters like neurosis.
You think it may scream, but nothing
Happens. Except that, bit by bit, the mountains
Get heavier all afternoon.

One day,
When some secret, high drift of air comes eastward over the lake,
Ash, gray, sifts minutely down on
Our lunch-time ice cream. Which is vanilla, and white.

There is a forest fire on Mount Ti-Po-Ki, which
Is at the western end of the lake.

2
If, after lunch, at God's hottest hour,
You make love, flesh, in that sweat-drench,
Slides on flesh slicker than grease. To grip
Is difficult.

At drink-time,
The sun, over Ti-Po-Ki, sets
Lopsided, and redder than blood or bruised cinnabar, because of
The smoke there. Later,
If there is no moon, you can see the red eyes of fire
Wink at you from
The black mass that is the mountain.

At night, in the dark room, not able to sleep, you
May think of the red eyes of fire that
Are winking from blackness. You may,
As I once did, rise up and go from the house. But,
When I got out, the moon had emerged from cloud, and I

Entered the lake. Swam miles out,
Toward moonset. Motionless,
Awash, metaphysically undone in that silvered and
Unbreathing medium, and beyond
Prayer or desire, saw
The moon, slow, swag down, like an old woman's belly.

Going back to the house, I gave the now-dark lawn a wide berth.

At night the rattlers come out from the rock-fall.
They lie on the damp grass for coolness.

3
I-yee!—
        and the wranglers, they cry on the mountain, and waking
At dawn-streak, I hear it.

                High on the mountain
I hear it, for snow-water there, snow long gone, yet seeps down
To green the raw edges and enclaves of forest
With a thin pasturage. The wranglers
Are driving our horses down, long before daylight, plunging
Through gloom of the pines, and in their joy
Cry out:

        I-yee!

            We ride this morning, and,
Now fumbling in shadow for *levis,* pulling my boots on, I hear
That thin cry of joy from the mountain, and what once I have,
Literally, seen, I now in my mind see, as I
Will, years later, in my mind, see it—the horsemen
Plunge through the pine-gloom, leaping
The deadfall—*I-yee!*—
Leaping the boulder—*I-yee!*—and their faces
Flee flickering white through the shadow—*I-yee!*—
And before them,
Down the trail and in dimness, the riderless horses,
Like quicksilver spilled in dark glimmer and roil, go
Pouring downward.

            The wranglers cry out.

                And nearer.

                                                    But,
Before I go for my quick coffee-scald and to the corral,
I hear, much nearer, not far from my open window, a croupy
Gargle of laughter.

              It is Laughing Boy.

4
Laughing Boy is the name that my host—and friend—gives his yard-hand.
Laughing Boy is Indian, or half, and has a hare-lip.
Sometimes, before words come, he utters a sound like croupy laughter.
When he utters that sound his face twists. Hence the name.

Laughing Boy wakes up at dawn, for somebody
Has to make sure the rattlers are gone before
The nurse brings my host's twin baby daughters out to the lawn.
Laughing Boy, who does not like rattlers, keeps a tin can
Of gasoline covered with a saucer on an outer ledge of the porch.
Big kitchen matches are in the saucer. This
At the porch-end toward the rock-fall.

The idea is: Sneak soft-foot round the porch-end,
There between rattlers and rock-fall, and as one whips past,
Douse him. This with the left hand, and
At the same instant, with the nail of the right thumb,
Snap a match alight.

              The flame,
If timing is good, should, just as he makes his rock-hole,
Hit him.

The flame makes a sudden, soft, gaspy sound at
The hole-mouth, then dances there. The flame
Is spectral in sunlight, but flickers blue at its raw edge.

Laughing Boy has beautiful coordination, and sometimes
He gets a rattler. You are sure if
The soft, gasping sound and pale flame come before
The stub-buttoned tail has disappeared.

                    Whenever
Laughing Boy really gets a rattler, he makes that sound like
Croupy laughter. His face twists.

Once I get one myself. I see, actually, the stub-buttoned tail
Whip through pale flame down into earth-darkness.

"The son-of-a-bitch," I am yelling, "did you see me, I got him!"
I have gotten that stub-tailed son-of-a-bitch.

I look up at the sky. Already, that early, the sky shivers with whiteness.

5
What was *is* is now *was*. But
Is *was* but a word for wisdom, its price? Some from
That long-lost summer are dead now, two of the girls then young,
Now after their pain and delusions, worthy endeavors and lies, are,
Long since, dead.

        The third
Committed her first adultery the next year, her first lover
A creature odd for her choosing, he who
Liked poetry and had no ambition, and
She cried out in his arms, a new experience for her. But
There were the twins, and she had, of course,
Grown accustomed to money.

        Her second,
A man of high social position, who kept a score-card. With her,
Not from passion this time, just snobbery. After that,
From boredom. Forgot, finally,
The whole business, took up horse-breeding, which
Filled her time and even, I heard, made unneeded money, and in
The old news photo I see her putting her mount to the jump.
Her yet beautiful figure is poised forward, bent elbows
Neat to her tight waist, face
Thrust into the cleansing wind of her passage, the face
Yet smooth as a girl's, no doubt from the scalpel
Of the plastic surgeon as well as
From her essential incapacity
For experience.

        The husband, my friend,
Would, by this time, be totally cynical. The children
Have been a disappointment. He would have heavy jowls.
Perhaps he is, by this time, dead.

As for Laughing Boy, he wound up in the pen. Twenty years.
This for murder. Indians
Just ought to leave whiskey to the white folks.

I can't remember the names of the others who came there,
The casual weekend-ers. But remember

What I remember, but do not
Know what it all means, unless the meaning inheres in
The compulsion to try to convert what now is *was*
Back into what was *is*.

    I remember
The need to enter the night-lake and swim out toward
The distant moonset. Remember
The blue-tattered flick of white flame at the rock-hole
In the instant before I lifted up
My eyes to the high sky that shivered in its hot whiteness.

And sometimes—usually at dawn—I remember the cry on the mountain.

All I can do is to offer my testimony.

EVENING HAWK

From plane of light to plane, wings dipping through
Geometries and orchids that the sunset builds,
Out of the peak's black angularity of shadow, riding
The last tumultuous avalanche of
Light above pines and the guttural gorge,
The hawk comes.

    His wing
Scythes down another day, his motion
Is that of the honed steel-edge, we hear
The crashless fall of stalks of Time.

The head of each stalk is heavy with the gold of our error.

Look! Look! he is climbing the last light
Who knows neither Time nor error, and under
Whose eye, unforgiving, the world, unforgiven, swings
Into shadow.

Long now,
The last thrush is still, the last bat
Now cruises in his sharp hieroglyphics. His wisdom
Is ancient, too, and immense. The star
Is steady, like Plato, over the mountain.

If there were no wind we might, we think, hear
The earth grind on its axis, or history
Drip in darkness like a leaking pipe in the cellar.

John Hollander

orn in New York City in 1929, John Hollander first visited Yale in 1957 to confer with Yale University Press about his debut collection of poems, *A Crackling of Thorns,* which was to be published the next year, having been chosen by W. H. Auden for the Yale Series of Younger Poets. He then taught at Yale from 1959 until 1966 and was one of the founding fellows of Ezra Stiles College. After a decade at Hunter College, in 1977 Hollander returned to Yale, where he is now Sterling Professor of English. During the past quarter-century, he has invigorated Yale's offerings in creative writing by refashioning the famous Daily Themes course and by teaching a seminar on writing verse out of which many of today's prominent younger poets have emerged. His scholarly life has resulted in many important volumes, including *The Untuning of the Sky* (1961), *Vision and Resonance* (1975), *The Figure of Echo* (1981), *The Gazer's Spirit* (1995), and *The Work of Poetry* (1997). He has edited dozens of other books and has collaborated on important operatic and lyric works with such composers as Milton Babbitt, George Perle, Alexander Goehr, and Hugo Weisgall. Having added a philosopher's rigor and a fabulist's ingenuity to the wit and erudition that already marked his early poetry, Hollander's later poems, often parables with a dark moral force, have only grown in power and depth. He has published seventeen collections of poetry, among them *Movie-Going* (1962), *The Night Mirror* (1971), *Reflections on Espionage* (1976), *Powers of Thirteen* (1983), for which he was awarded the Bollingen Prize, *Selected Poetry* (1993), and *Figurehead* (1999). "In my first semester at Yale," he recalls, "I taught a freshman composition course and after class would usually walk over to what was then George and Harry's restaurant on Temple Street. One morning—in October, I think it was—it occurred to me that I owed a promised letter to a friend (the late Mackie Jarrell) in which I would undertake to explain why, with similar literary tastes, we seemed to disagree so strongly about movies. I couldn't seem to get the tone of the letter right, hearing what I had started to write as too didactic for a letter. Then I decided to *be* didactic, in the high, imperative mode of Horace's *Ars Poetica,* and propound a list of instructions. The beginning of the first line ("Drive-ins are out, to start with") was one of those phrases given to poets by the idioms of their language, to which they could hardly lay personal claim. But the list went on, cast in loose accentual hexameters, for several pages. These were written over two days at the same table, and were published as 'Movie-Going,' the title poem of my second volume. Lurking in the dark wood of George and Harry's booths are shadows, of times I had written there and of other people—I think of my then great senior colleague and informal mentor, W. K. Wimsatt—who used to work regularly there as well."

ADAM'S TASK

And Adam gave names to all cattle, and
to the fowl of the air, and to every
beast of the field . . . Gen. 2:20

Thou, paw-paw-paw; thou, glurd; thou, spotted
   Glurd; thou, whitestap, lurching through
The high-grown brush; thou, pliant-footed,
   Implex; thou, awagabu.

Every burrower, each flier
   Came for the name he had to give:
Gay, first work, ever to be prior,
   Not yet sunk to primitive.

Thou, verdle; thou, McFleery's pomma;
   Thou; thou; thou—three types of grawl;
Thou, flisket; thou, kabasch; thou, comma-
   Eared mashawk; thou, all; thou, all.

Were, in a fire of becoming,
   Laboring to be burned away,
Then work, half-measuring, half-humming,
   Would be as serious as play.

Thou, pambler; thou, rivarn; thou, greater
   Wherret, and thou, lesser one;
Thou, sproal; thou, zant; thou, lily-eater.
   Naming's over. Day is done.

THE MAD POTTER

Now at the turn of the year this coil of clay
Bites its own tail: a New Year starts to choke
On the old one's ragged end. I bite my tongue
As the end of me—of my rope of stuff and nonsense
(The nonsense held, it was the stuff that broke),
Of bones and light, of levity and crime,
Of reddish clay and hope—still bides its time.

Each of my pots is quite unusable,
Even for contemplating as an object
Of gross unuse. In its own mode of being
Useless, though, each of them remains unique,
Subject to nothing, and themselves unseeing,
Stronger by virtue of what makes them weak.

I pound at all my clay. I pound the air.
This senseless lump, slapped into something like
Something, sits bound around by my despair.
For even as the great Creator's free
Hand shapes the forms of life, so—what? This pot,
Unhollowed solid, too full of itself,
Runneth over with incapacity.
I put it with the others on the shelf.

These tiny cups will each provide one sip
Of what's inside them, aphoristic prose
Unwilling, like full arguments, to make
Its points, then join them in extended lines
Like long draughts from the bowl of a deep lake.
The honey of knowledge, like my milky slip,
Firms slowly up against what merely flows.

Some of my older pieces bore inscriptions
That told a story only when you'd learned
How not to read them: LIVE reverted to EVIL,
EROS kept running backwards into SORE.
Their words, all fired up for truth, got burned.
I'll not write on weak vessels any more.

My juvenilia? I gave them names
In those days: Hans was all handles and no spout;
Bernie believed the whole world turned about
Himself alone; Sadie was close to James
(But Herman touched her bottom when he could);
Paul fell to pieces; Peter wore away
To nothing; Len was never any good;
Alf was a flat, random pancake, May
An opened blossom; Bud was an ash-tray.
Even their names break off, though: Whatsisface,

That death-mask of Desire, and—you know!—
The smaller version of that (Oh, what was it?—
You know . . .) All of my pots now have to go
By number only. Which is no disgrace.

Begin with being—in an anagram
Of unending—conclude in some dark den;
This is no matter. What I've been, I am:
What I will be is what I make of all
This clay, this moment. Now begin again . . .
Poured out of emptiness, drop by slow drop,
I start up at the quarreling sounds of water.
Pots cry out silently at me to stop.

What are we like? A barrelfull of this
Oozy wet substance, shadow-crammed, whose smudges
Of darkness lurk within but rise to kiss
The fingers that disturb the gentle edges
Of their bland world of shapelessness and bliss.

The half-formed cup cries out in agony,
The lump of clay suffers a silent pain.
I heard the cup, though, full of feeling, say
"O clay be true, O clay keep constant to
Your need to take, again and once again,
This pounding from your mad creator who
Only stops hurting when he's hurting you."

What will I then have left behind me? Over
The years I have originated some
Glazes that wear away at what they cover
And weep for what they never can become.
My Deadware, widely imitated; blue
Skyware of an amazing lightness; tired
Hopeware that I abandoned for my own
Good reasons; Hereware; Thereware; ware that grew
Weary of everything that earth desired;
Hellware that dances while it's being fired,
Noware that vanishes while being thrown.

Appearing to be silly, wisdom survives
Like tribes of superseded gods who go
Hiding in caves of triviality

From which they laughingly control our lives.
So with my useless pots: safe from the blow
Of carelessness, or outrage at their flaws,
They brave time's lion and his smashing paws.
—All of which tempts intelligence to call
Pure uselessness one more commodity.
The Good-for-Nothing once became our Hero,
But images of him, laid-back, carelessly
Laughing, were upright statues after all.
From straight above, each cup adds up to zero.

Clay to clay: Soon I shall indeed become
Dumb as these solid cups of hardened mud
(Dull *terra cruda* colored like our blood);
Meanwhile the slap and thump of palm and thumb
On wet mis-shapenness begins to hum
With meaning that was silent for so long.
The words of my wheel's turning come to ring
Truer than Truth itself does, my great *Ding
Dong-an-sich* that echoes everything
(Against it even lovely bells ring wrong):
Its whole voice gathers up the purest parts
Of all our speech, the vowels of the earth,
The aspirations of our hopeful hearts
Or the prophetic sibillance of song.

AN OLD-FASHIONED SONG

(*Nous n'irons plus au bois*)

No more walks in the wood:
The trees have all been cut
Down, and where once they stood
Not even a wagon rut
Appears along the path
Low brush is taking over.

No more walks in the wood;
This is the aftermath
Of afternoons in the clover

Fields where we once made love
Then wandered home together
Where the trees arched above,
Where we made our own weather
When branches were the sky.
Now they are gone for good,
And you, for ill, and I
Am only a passer-by.

We and the trees and the way
Back from the fields of play
Lasted as long as we could.
No more walks in the wood.

X'S SYNDROME

Phi Beta Kappa poem, Yale University, 1996

Quinsy, archaically dogging the throat, the whiffles
(Where did they go?), the glanders poor horses get,
The pip (a disease of chickens), the purely invented
Candlemaker's glottis (by Peter Shaffer
In nineteen fifty-one): these prebiomedical
Names for blights that afflict us afflict us themselves
With a charm and a horror (those unknowns! lying behind
The folksy masks of such names in an aetiological
Void . . .) And even if now, with a greater degree
Of sophistication, still named after a place
The illness appeared to haunt—Tapanuli fever,
The Black Formosa corruption, Madura foot—
And perhaps the citizens of wherever it was
Bleating objections (as if Lyme, say, didn't want
To have its name stigmatized with a spreading disease
That possibly anyway came from deer on Naushon).

But nature disposes and medical science proposes
Other arrangements of naming: a disease like a rare
Flower is given a crypto-Linnaean name
By its responsible discoverer, as with
A wild surmise he gazes on the specific

Symptom that might be ascribed to Y's disease
Or W's, but given the facts of the case,
Had to be acknowledged as something new.

And so "X's syndrome"—the name of a manifestation,
A race of observable elements of illness
Running together (as if for their health? as if
For the sport of it?); not to be named for even
Some singular victim of its incursions or torments
But for the physician who first distinguished it.

And who was X after all? what story could truth
Tell us of him as a person? What of his childhood?
What beach did he play upon in summer twilight
As the golden sand reddened, grew cold, and the tide receded
Into the menacing dark? Or what fair field
Empty of folk, far from larger bodies of water
Did he gaze across, under a leaden sky?
X: was it always his name? was it shortened from something
Polysyllabic? And what was the name of the journal
He published his great result in? No matter. I quote from The
Paper that brought an entity into the world
By naming it, having established the right to do so:
The patient first presented with longer and longer
Periods of silence, matching the silent prognosis
He was presented with; on alternate days
The fever peaked at dawn or evening twilight . . .
A cessation of speech? a silencing, (a muteation?
—Ha, ha!) that may abate if death does not,
Come first with that other silence of the grave . . .

X's Syndrome. Not ours. The illness is ours:
The disease with its causes and slowly evolving rituals
Of treatment will always have been Dr. X's construction.

But now that I know what it's called, we should be well
On our way to recovery, coming around again,
From what it is we're said to suffer from.

b orn in New York City in 1937, Robert Stone joined the navy as a young man and only later went to school, at New York University and Stanford. He has worked as a caption writer for the *New York Daily News,* as an actor in New Orleans, as a copywriter on Madison Avenue, as a prankster with Ken Kesey, and as a freelance writer in London, Hollywood, and Saigon. As a novelist, he has wrenchingly explored the underbelly of American society, its brutality and glamour, with an almost reckless precision and force. He has written a collection of short stories, *Bear and His Daughter* (1997), and six novels: *A Hall of Mirrors* (1967), *Dog Soldiers* (1974), *A Flag for Sunrise* (1981), *Children of Light* (1986), *Outerbridge Reach* (1989), and *Damascus Gate* (1998). Two of his novels were made into major motion pictures, and his writing has won the Faulkner Award, the National Book Award, and the *Los Angeles Times* Book Prize. Since 1994, he has been the Rosencrantz Writer in Residence at Yale. "Where other than at Yale," he writes, "would I find myself discussing Ecclesiastes, T. S. Eliot, and Nathanael West with a student from Malaysia who reads Chinese, Malaysian, English, German, and Japanese, and writes poetry in all of them? Where else would I be likely to examine prose tropes with the undergraduate author and illustrator of the best available American book on fly-fishing? Or with a freshman contributor to *The Best American Poetry 1996?* Teaching at Yale is often a special pleasure, a source of exhilaration and even inspiration."

Mary Urquhart had just finished story hour at the library when the muted phone rang at the circulation desk. She had been reading the children *Prince Caspian.*

Camille Innaurato was on the line and as usual she was beside herself.

"Mary, Mary, so listen . . ." Camille began. It sounded almost prayerful. Then Camille began to hyperventilate.

"Oh, Camille," Mrs. Urquhart said. "Try to be calm. Are you all right, dear? Do you have your inhaler?"

"I have more!" Camille croaked fiercely at last. The force of the words in her constricted throat made her sound, Mary Urquhart thought, like her counterpart in *Traviata.*

"More?" Although Mary knew at once what Camille meant, she needed the extra moment of freedom.

"More babies!" Camille shouted. She spoke so loudly that even with the receiver as close to her ear as she could bear, Mary Urquhart thought that everyone around the circulation desk must be able to hear her voice on the phone, its unsound passion.

"My brother, he found them!" cried Camille. "And he took them here. So I got them now."

"I see," said Mary Urquhart.

Outside, Mrs. Carter, the African-American head librarian, was supervising the reuniting of the story-hour children with their mothers. The children were, without exception, black and Hispanic. The mothers of the black children were mostly West Indian domestics; they were the most scrupulous of the story-hour mothers and they loved their children to have English stories, British stories.

"Mary . . ." Camille gasped over the phone. "Mary?"

Outside the library windows, in the darkening winter afternoon, the children looked lively and happy and well behaved and Mary was proud of them. The mothers were smiling, and Mrs. Carter too.

"Easy does it," said Mary Urquhart to her friend Camille. For years after Mary had stopped drinking, she had driven around with a bumper sticker to that effect. Embarrassing to consider now.

"You'll come, Mary? You could come today? Soon? And we could do it?"

The previous year Mrs. Urquhart had bought little books of C. S. Lewis tales with her own money for the children to take home. That way at least some might learn to read them. She liked to meet the mothers herself and talk with them. Looking on wistfully, she wished herself out on the sidewalk too, if only to say hello and remind herself of everyone's name. But Mrs. Carter was the chief librarian and preempted the privilege of overseeing the dismissal of story hour.

"Yes, dear," Mary said to Camille. "I'll come as soon as we close."

They closed within the hour because the New Jersey city in which Mary worked had scant funds to spare for libraries. It was largely a city of racial minorities, in the late stages of passing from the control of a corrupt white political machine to that of a corrupt black one. Its schools were warrens of pathology and patronage. Its police, still mainly white, were frequently criminals.

Mary Urquhart looked carefully about her as she went out the door into the library parking lot for the walk to her old station wagon. It was nearly night, though a faint stain of the day persisted. At the western horizon, across the river and over the stacks and gables of the former mills, hung a brilliant patch of clear night sky where Venus blazed. Some of the newer street lights around the library's block were broken, their fixtures torn away by junkies for sale to scrap dealers. There were patchy reefs and banks of soiled frozen snow on the ground. Not much had fallen for a week, but the weather was bitter and the north-facing curbs and margins were still partly covered.

"Thou fair-haired angel of the evening," Mary recited silently to the first star. She could not keep the line from her mind.

Temple Street, the road Mary drove toward the strip that led her home, was one of crumbling wooden houses. In some of them, bare lights glowed behind gypsy-colored bedspreads tacked over the taped windows. About every fifth house was derelict and inside some of these candlelight was already flickering. They were crack houses. Mary had worked as an enumerator in the neighborhood during the last census and, for all its transience, she knew it fairly well. Many of the houses were in worse condition inside than out. The official census description for all of them was "Dilapidated." A few of her story children lived on the street.

The odd corner had a bodega in a cinderblock building with a faint neon beer sign in its window. The cold had driven the brown-bagging drinkers away from the little strip mall that housed Mashona's Beauty Shoppe, a cheap lamp store and a takeout ribs joint called Floyd's, which kept erratic hours. All the shops closed at dusk and God knew, she thought, where the alcoholics had gone. Maybe out of the bitter wind into the crack houses. Mary knew a lot of the older alcoholics who hung out there by sight and sometimes, in daytime, she stopped for Floyd's ribs, which were not at all bad. Floyd, who always had a smile for her, kept a sign over his register that read CHRIST IS THE ANSWER.

She had an ongoing dialogue with a few of the men. Those who would speak to a middle-aged white woman like herself called her "Mary" and sometimes, in the case of the beat old-timers from down home, "Miss Mary." She had begun by addressing them all as "sir," but she had soon perceived that this offended them as patronizing and was not appropriate to street banter. So, if she did not know them by name, she addressed them as "guy," which amused them. It was how her upper-class Southern husband had addressed his social equals. He had used it long before one heard it commonly; he had been dead for thirteen years.

"I know your story, guy," she would say to a brown-bagging acquaintance as she carried her paper container of ribs to the car. "I'm a juicehead. I'm a boozer."

"But you gotta enjoy your life, Mary," an old man had said to her once. "You ain't got but one, chere?"

And that had stopped her cold.

"But that's it," she had told the man. "You're so right."

He had shaken his head, telling her really, well, she'd never understand. Her life and his? But she'd persisted.

"That's why I don't have my bottle today as you do. Because there was a time, guy. Yes, you best believe it."

Then he'd heard her vestigial Southernness and cocked his head and said, in a distinctly sarcastic but not altogether unfriendly way, "Do it right, Mary. You say so."

"God bless, guy."

"Be right, Mary."

Poor fellow, she'd thought. Who was he? Who might he have become? She wished him grace.

A short distance before Temple Street doglegged into the strip of Route 4, it passed the dangerous side of a city park in which there was a large lake. The cold weather had frozen the lake to a depth that Mary knew must be many feet. After the cold weeks they'd had, it must be safe for skating. In some towns there would be lights by the lakeside and skating children; not in this one. And for that she could only be grateful, because she did not think she could bear the sight of children skating or lights on the icy surface of a frozen lake. Even after the thirteen years.

Along its last quarter mile, Temple Street acquired an aluminum guardrail and some halogen overhead lights, though on these, too, the metal was torn up, unscrewed, pried loose by the locust-junkies.

At the light that marked the intersection with Route 4 stood a large gas station. It was one of a number owned by an immigrant from India. Once the immigrant himself had worked in it, then he'd bought it, then bought others and real estate to go with them. Now he employed other Indian immigrants who worked long shifts, day and night. In the previous twelve months, according to the county newspaper, no fewer than four of the immigrants had been shot dead in holdups and another four wounded.

Mary waited at the light, and it was really easier to think about the poor slaughtered Gujaratis than about the frozen lake. She prayed for them, in her way, eyes focused on the turn signal. It did not suit her to utter repetitions.

Rather the words came to her on all the music she had heard, so many settings, that prayer sung over and over since the beginning of music itself.

Agnus Dei, qui tollis peccata mundi,
Miserere nobis.

Then there was Route 4, the American Strip. And this was New Jersey, where she had ended up, its original home and place of incubation, whence it had been nourished to creep out and girdle the world. It had come in time to her own stately corner of North Carolina, looking absolutely the same.

Since her widowhood and recovery, Mary Urquhart had lived in a modest house in what had once been a suburb of this New Jersey city, only a few blocks beyond its formal border. At the suburban end of her street was a hill from which the towers of Manhattan were visible on the clearer mornings. All day and most of the night, planes on a southward descent for Newark passed overhead and, even after so many years, often woke her.

But Mary was not, that afternoon, on her way home. A mile short of the city line, she pulled off Route 4 onto Imperial Avenue. The avenue led to a neighbor-hood called Auburn Hill, which had become an Italian enclave in the Spanish-speaking section of the ghetto. Auburn Hill could be relied upon for neat lawns and safe streets, their security reinforced by grim anecdotes of muggers' and housebreakers' summary punishments. Young outlaws nailed to tar rooftops with screwdrivers. Or thrown from an overpass onto the Jersey Central tracks fifty feet below. At Christmastime, the neighborhood sparkled with cheery lights. Mary had come to know it well and, comprehending both the bitter and the sweet of Auburn Hill, was fond of it.

Camille Innaurato's was like the other houses in that end of town. It was a brick, three-bedroom single-story with aluminum siding and a narrow awning of the same. It had a small lawn in front, surrounded by a metal fence, and a garden in the back where Camille grew tomatoes and peppers in season.

When Mary pulled into the driveway, she saw Camille's pale, anxious face at the picture window. Camille was mouthing words, clasping her hands. In a mo-ment she opened the door to the winter wind, as Mary emerged from her car and locked it.

"Oh, Mary. I'm thanking God Almighty you could come. Yeah, I'm thanking him."

Camille was one of those women who had grown older in unquestioning service to her aged parents. She had helped raise her younger brother. Later she had shared with her father the care of her sick mother. Then, when he died, she had assumed it all—her mother, the house, everything. Camille worked in a garment-sewing shop that had set itself up on two floors of a former silk mill; she oversaw the Chinese and Salvadoran women employed there.

Her younger brother, August, was technically a policeman, though not an actively corrupt one. In fact, he had no particular constabulary duties. The family had had enough political connections to secure him a clerical job with the department. He was a timid, excitable man, married, with grown children, who lived with his domineering wife in an outer suburb. But as a police insider he knew the secrets of the city.

The Innauratos, brother and sister, had inherited nothing from their parents except the house Camille occupied and their sick mother's tireless piety.

Mary Urquhart stepped inside and took Camille by the shoulders and looked at her.

"Now, Camille, dear, are you all right? Can you breathe?"

She inspected Camille and, satisfied with her friend's condition, checked out the house. The living room was neat enough, although the television set was off, a sure sign of Camille's preoccupation.

"I gotta show you, Mary. Oh I gotta show you. Yeah I gotta." She sounded as though she were weeping, but the beautiful dark eyes she fixed on Mary were dry. Eyes out of Alexandrian portraiture, Mary thought, sparkling and shimmering with their infernal vision. For a moment it seemed she had returned from some transport. She gathered Mary to her large, soft, barren breast. "You wanna coffee, Mary honey? You wanna *biscote?* A little of wine?"

In her excitement, Camille always offered the wine when there were babies, forgetting Mary could not drink it.

"I'll get you a glass of wine," Mary suggested. "And I'll get myself coffee."

Camille looked after Mary anxiously as she swept past her toward the kitchen.

"Sit down, dear," Mary called to her. "Sit down and I'll bring it out."

Slowly, Camille seated herself on the edge of the sofa and stared at the blank television screen.

In the immaculate kitchen, Mary found an open bottle of sangiovese, unsoured, drinkable. She poured out a glass, then served herself a demitasse of fresh-made espresso from Camille's machine. In the cheerless, spotless living room, they drank side by side on the faded floral sofa, among the lace and the pictures of Camille's family and the portrait photograph of the Pope.

"I used to love sangiovese," Mary said, watching her friend sip. "The wine of the Romagna. Bologna. Urbino."

"It's good," Camille said.

"My husband and I and the children once stayed in a villa outside Urbino. It rained. Yes, every day, but the mountains were grand. And the hill towns down in Umbria. We had great fun."

"You saw the Holy Father?"

Mary laughed. "We were all good Protestants then."

Camille looked at her in wonder, though she had heard the story of Mary's upbringing many times. Then her face clouded.

"You gotta see the babies, Mary."

"Yes," Mary sighed. "But do finish your wine."

When the wine was done they both went back to look at the fetuses. There were four. Camille had laid them on a tarpaulin, under a churchy purple curtain on the floor of an enclosed, unheated back porch, where it was nearly as cold as the night outside. On top of the curtain she had rested one of her wall crucifixes.

Mary lifted the curtain and looked at the little dead things on the floor. They had lobster-claw, unseparated fingers, and one had a face. Its face looked like a Florida manatee's, Mary thought. It was the only living resemblance she could bring to bear—a manatee, bovine, slope-browed. One was still enveloped in some kind of fibrous membrane that suggested bat wings.

"So sweet," Camille sobbed. "So sad. Who could do such a thing? A murderer!" She bit her thumb. "A murderer, the degenerate fuck, his eyes should be plucked out!" She made the sign of the cross, to ask forgiveness for her outburst.

"Little lamb, who made thee?" Mary Urquhart asked wearily. The things were so disgusting. "Well, to work then."

Camille's brother August had discovered that the scavenger company that handled the county's medical waste also serviced its abortion clinics, which had no incinerators of their own. The fetuses were stored for disposal along with everything else. August had fixed it with the scavengers to report specimens and set them aside. He would pass on the discovery to Camille. Then Camille and a friend—most often Mary—would get to work.

Mary knew a priest named Father Hooke, the pastor of a parish in a wealthy community in the Ramapos. They had known each other for years. Hooke had been, in a somewhat superficial way, Mary's spiritual counselor. He was much more cultivated than most priests and could be wickedly witty, too. Their conversations about contemporary absurdities, Scripture and the vagaries of the Canon, history and literature had helped her through the last stage of her regained abstinence. She knew of Julian of Norwich through his instruction. He had received her into the Catholic Church and she had been a friend to him. Lately, though, there had been tension between them. She used Camille's telephone to alert him.

"Frank," she said to the priest, "we have some children."

He gave her silence in return.

"Hello, Frank," she said again. "Did you hear me, Father? I said we have some children."

"Yes," said Hooke, in what Mary was coming to think of as his affected tone, "I certainly heard you the first time. Tonight is . . . difficult."

"Yes, it surely is," Mary said. "Difficult and then some. When will you expect us?"

"I've been meaning," Hooke said, "to talk about this before now."

He had quoted Dame Julian to her. "All shall be well, and all shall be well, and all manner of thing shall be well." Those were lines he liked.

"Have you?" she inquired politely. "I see. We can talk after the interment."

"You know, Mary," Father Hooke said with a nervous laugh, "the bishop, that pillar of intellect, our spiritual prince, has been hearing things that trouble him."

Mary Urquhart blushed to hear the priest's lie.

"The bishop," she told him, "is not a problem in any way. You are."

"Me?" He laughed then, genuinely and bitterly. "I'm a problem? Oh, sorry. There are also a few laws . . ."

"What time, Father? Camille works for a living. So do I."

"The thing is," Father Hooke said, "you ought not to come tonight."

"Oh, Frank," Mary said. "Really, really. Don't be a little boy on me. Take up your cross, guy."

"I suppose," Hooke said, "I can't persuade you to pass on this one?"

"Shame on you, Frank Hooke," she said.

The drive to the clean outer suburbs led through subdivisions and parklands, then to thick woods among which colonial houses stood, comfortably lighted against the winter night. Finally there were a few farms, or estates laid out to resemble working farms. The woods were full of frozen lakes and ponds.

The Buick wagon Mary drove was almost fifteen years old, the same one she had owned in the suburbs of Boston as a youngish mother, driving all the motherly routes, taking Charles Junior to soccer practice and Payton to girls' softball and little Emily to play school.

The fetuses were secured with blind cord in the back of the station wagon, between the tarp and the curtain in which Camille had wrapped them. It was a cargo that did not shift or rattle and they had not tried to put a crucifix on top. More and more, the dark countryside they rode through resembled the town where she had lived with Charles and her children.

"Could you say the poem?" Camille asked. When they went to an interment Camille liked to hear Mary recite poetry for her as they drove. Mary preferred poetry to memorized prayer, and the verse was always new to Camille. It made her cry, and crying herself out on the way to an interment, Mary had observed, best prepared Camille for the work at hand.

"But which poem, Camille?"

Sometimes Mary recited Crashaw's "To the Infant Martyrs," or from his hymn to Saint Teresa. Sometimes she recited Vaughan or Blake.

"The one with the star," Camille said. "The one with the lake."

"Oh," Mary said cheerfully. "Funny, I was thinking about it earlier."

Once, she could not imagine how, Mary had recited Blake's "To the Evening

Star" for Camille. It carried such a weight of pain for her that she dreaded its every line and trembled when it came to her unsummoned:

Thou fair-hair'd angel of the evening,
Now, whilst the sun rests on the mountains, light
Thy bright torch of love; thy radiant crown
Put on, and smile upon our evening bed!

It had almost killed her to recite it the first time, because that had been her and Charles's secret poem, their prayer for the protection that was not forthcoming. The taste of it in her mouth was of rage unto madness and the lash of grief and above all of whiskey to drown it all, whiskey to die in and be with them. That night, driving, with the dark dead creatures at their back, she offered up the suffering in it.

Camille wept at the sound of the words. Mary found herself unable to go on for a moment.

"There's more," Camille said.

"Yes," said Mary. She drew upon her role as story lady.

Let thy west wind sleep on
The lake; speak silence with thy glimmering eyes,
And wash the dusk with silver. Soon, full soon,
Dost thou withdraw; then the wolf rages wide,
And the lion glares thro' the dun forest:
The fleeces of our flocks are cover'd with
Thy sacred dew: protect them with thine influence.

Camille sobbed. "Oh, Mary," she said. "Yours weren't protected."

"Well, stars . . ." Mary Urquhart said, still cheerfully. "Thin influence. Thin ice."

The parlor lights were lighted in the rectory of Our Lady of Fatima when they pulled off the genteel main street of the foothill town and into the church parking lot. Mary parked the station wagon close to the rectory door, and the two women got out and rang Father Hooke's bell.

Hooke came to the door in a navy cardigan, navy-blue shirt and chinos. Camille murmured and fairly curtsied in deference. Mary looked the priest up and down. His casual getup seemed like recalcitrance, an unreadiness to officiate. Had he been working himself up to deny them?

"Hello, Frank," said Mary. "Sorry to come so late."

Hooke was alone in the rectory. There was no assistant and he did his own housekeeping, resident rectory biddies being a thing of the past.

"Can I give you coffee?" Father Hooke asked.

"I've had mine," Mary said.

He had a slack, uneasy smile. "Mary," the priest said. "And Miss . . . won't you sit down?"

He had forgotten Camille's name. He was a snob, she thought, a suburban snob. The ethnic, Mariolatrous name of his parish, Our Lady of Fatima, embarrassed him.

"Father," she said, "why don't we just do it?"

He stared at her helplessly. Ashamed for him, she avoided his eye.

"I think," he said, dry-throated, "we should consider from now on."

"Isn't it strange?" she asked Camille. "I had an odd feeling we might have a problem here tonight." She turned on Hooke. "What do you mean? Consider what?"

"All right, all right," he said. A surrender in the pursuit of least resistance. "Where is it?"

"They," Mary said.

"The babies," said Camille. "The poor babies are in Mary's car outside."

But he hung back. "Oh, Mary," said Father Hooke. He seemed childishly afraid.

She burned with rage. Was there such a thing as an adult Catholic? And the race of priests, she thought, these self-indulgent, boneless men.

"Oh, dear," she said. "What can be the matter now? Afraid of how they're going to look?"

"Increasingly . . ." Father Hooke said, "I feel we're doing something wrong."

"Really?" Mary asked. "Is that a fact?" They stood on the edge of the nice red Bolivian rectory carpet, in the posture of setting out for the station wagon. Yet not setting out. There was Haitian art on the wall. No lace curtains here. "What a shame," she said, "we haven't time for an evening of theological discourse."

"We may have to make time," Father Hooke said. "Sit down, girls."

Camille looked to Mary for reassurance and sat with absurd decorousness on the edge of a bare-boned Spanish chair. Mary stood where she was. The priest glanced at her in dread. Having given them an order, he seemed afraid to take a seat himself.

"It isn't just the interments," he told Mary. He ignored Camille. "It's the whole thing. Our whole position." He shuddered and began to pace up and down on the rug, his hands working nervously.

"Our position," Mary repeated tonelessly. "Do you mean *your* position? Are you referring to the Church's teaching?"

"Yes," he said. He looked around as though for help, but as was the case so often with such things, it was not available. "I mean I think we may be wrong."

She let the words reverberate in the rectory's quiet. Then she asked, "Prodded by conscience, are you, Father?"

"I think we're wrong on this," he said with sudden force. "I think women have a right. I do. Sometimes I'm ashamed to wear my collar."

She laughed her pleasant, cultivated laughter. "Ashamed to wear your collar? Poor Frank. Afraid people will think badly of you?"

He summoned anger. "Kindly spare me the ad hominem," he said.

"But Frank," she said, it seemed lightly, "there is only ad hominem."

"I'm afraid I'm not theologian enough," he said, "to follow you there."

"Oh," said Mary, "I'm sorry, Father. What I mean in my crude way is that what is expected of you is expected personally. Expected directly. Of *you,* Frank."

He sulked. A childish resentful silence. Then he said, "I can't believe God wants us to persecute these young women the way you people do. I mean you particularly, Mary, with your so-called counseling."

He meant the lectures she gave the unwed mothers who were referred to her by pamphlet. Mary had attended anti-war and anti-apartheid demonstrations with pride. The abortion clinic demonstrations she undertook as an offered humiliation, standing among the transparent cranks and crazies as a penance and a curb to pride. But surprisingly, when she was done with them in private, over coffee and cake, many pregnant women brought their pregnancies to term.

She watched Father Hooke. He was without gravitas, she thought. The hands, the ineffectual sputter.

"For God's sake," he went on, "look at the neighborhood where you work! Do you really think the world requires a few million more black, alienated, unwanted children?"

She leaned against one of his antique chests and folded her arms. She was tall and elegant, as much an athlete and a beauty at fifty as she had ever been. Camille sat open-mouthed.

"How contemptible and dishonest of you to pretend an attack of conscience," she told Hooke quietly. "It's respectability you're after. And to talk about what God wants?" She seemed to be politely repressing a fit of genuine mirth. "When you're afraid to go out and look at his living image? Those things in the car, Frank, that poor little you are afraid to see. That's man, guy, those little forked purple beauties. That's God's image, don't you know that? That's what you're scared of."

He took his glasses off and blinked helplessly.

"Your grief . . ." he began. A weakling, she thought, trying for the upper hand. Trying to appear concerned. In a moment he had lost his nerve. "It's made you cruel . . . Maybe not *cruel,* but . . ."

Mary Urquhart pushed herself upright. "Ah," she said with a flutter of gracious laughter, "the well-worn subject of my grief. Maybe I'm drunk again tonight, eh Father? Who knows?"

Thirteen years before on the lake outside Boston, on the second evening before Christmas, her husband had taken the children skating. First young Charley had wanted to go and Charles had demurred; he'd had a few drinks. Then he had agreed in his shaggy, teasing, slow-spoken way—he was rangy, wry, a Carolina Scot like Mary. It was almost Christmas and the kids were excited and how long would it stay cold enough to skate? Then Payton had demanded to go, and then finally little Emily, because Charles had taught them to snap the whip on ice the day before. And the lake, surrounded by woods, was well lighted and children always skated into the night although there was one end, as it turned out, where the light failed, a lonely bay bordered with dark blue German pine where even then maybe some junkie had come out from Roxbury or Southie or Lowell or God knew where and destroyed the light for the metal around it. And Emily still had her cold and should not have gone.

But they went and Mary waited late, and sometimes, listening to music, having a Wild Turkey, she thought she heard voices sounding strange. She could remember them perfectly now, and the point where she began to doubt, so faintly, that the cries were in fun.

The police said he had clung to the ice for hours, keeping himself alive and the children clinging to him, and many people had heard the calling out but taken it lightly.

She was there when the thing they had been was raised, a blue cluster wrapped in happy seasonal colors, woolly reindeer hats and scarves and mittens, all grasping and limbs intertwined, and it looked, she thought, like a rat king, the tangle of rats trapped together in their own naked tails and flushed from an abandoned hull to float drowned, a raft of solid rat on the swells of the lower Cape Fear River. The dead snarls on their faces, the wild eyes, a paradigm she had seen once as a child she saw again in the model of her family. And near Walden Pond, no less, the west wind slept on the lake, eyes glimmered in the silver dusk, a dusk at morning. She had lost all her pretty ones.

"Because," she said to Father Hooke, "it would appear to me that you are a man—and I know men, I was married to a man—who is a little boy, a little boy-man. A tiny boy-man, afraid to touch the cross or look in God's direction."

He stared at her and swallowed. She smiled as though to reassure him.

"What you should do, Father, is this. Take off the vestments you're afraid to wear. Your mama's dead for whom you became a priest. Become the nice little happy homosexual nonentity you are."

"You are a cruel bitch," Hooke said, pale-faced. "You're a sick and crazy woman."

Camille in her chair began to gasp. Mary bent to attend her.

"Camille? Do you have your inhaler?"

Camille had it. Mary helped her adjust it and waited until her friend's breathing was under control. When she stood up, she saw that Father Hooke was in a bad way.

"You dare," Mary said to him, "you wretched tiny man, to speak of black un-wanted children? Why, there is not a suffering black child—God bless them all—not a black child in this unhappy foolish country that I would not exalt and nourish on your goddamn watery blood. I would not risk the security of the most doomed, lost, deformed black child for your very life, you worthless pussy!"

Father Hooke had become truly upset. My Lord, she thought, now I've done it. Now I'll see the creature cry. She looked away.

"You were my only friend," Father Hooke told her when he managed to speak again. "Did you know that?"

She sighed. "I'm sorry, Father. I suppose I have my ignorant cracker side and God help me I am sick and I am crazy and cruel. Please accept my sincerest apologies. Pray for me."

Hooke would not be consoled. Kind-hearted Camille, holding her inhaler, took a step toward him as though she might help him somehow go on breathing.

"Get out," he said to them. "Get out before I call the police."

"You have to try to forgive me, Charles." Had she called him Charles? How very strange. Poor old Charles would turn in his grave. "Frank, I mean. You have to try and forgive me, Frank. Ask God to forgive me. I'll ask God to forgive you. We all need it, don't we, Father."

"The police!" he cried, his voice rising. "Because those things, those goddamn things in your car! Don't you understand? People accuse us of violence!" he shouted. "And you are violence!" Then he more or less dissolved.

She went and put a hand on his shoulder as Camille watched in amazement.

"God forgive us, Frank." But he leaned on the back of his leather easy chair and turned from her, weeping. "Oh Frank, you lamb," she said, "what did your poor mama tell you? Did she say that a world with God was easier than one without him?"

She gave Father Hooke a last friendly pat and turned to Camille. "Because that would be mistaken, wouldn't it, Camille?"

"Oh, you're right," Camille hastened to say. The tearful priest had moved her too. But still she was dry-eyed, staring, Alexandrian. "You're so right, Mary."

When they were on the road again it was plain Camille Innaurato was exhausted.

"So, Mary," she asked. "So where're we going now, honey?"

"Well," Mary said, "as it happens, I have another fella up my sleeve." She laughed. "Yes, another of these worthies Holy Mother Church provides for our direction. Another selfless man of the cloth."

"I'll miss Mass tomorrow."

"This is Mass," Mary said.

"Right. OK."

This is Mass, she thought, this is the sacrifice nor are we out of it. She reached over and gave Camille a friendly touch.

"You don't work tomorrow, do you, love?"

"Naw, I don't," Camille said. "I don't, but . . ."

"I can take you home. I can get this done myself."

"No," said Camille, a little cranky with fatigue. "No way."

"Well, we'll get these children blessed, dear."

The man Mary had up her sleeve was a priest from Central Europe called Monsignor Danilo. It was after ten when Mary telephoned him from a service station, but he hurriedly agreed to do what she required. He was smooth and obsequious and seemed always ready to accommodate her.

His parish, St. Macarius, was in an old port town on Newark Bay, and to get there they had to retrace their drive through the country and then travel south past several exits of the Garden State.

It took them nearly an hour, even with the sparse traffic. The church and its rectory were in a waterfront neighborhood of refineries and wooden tenements little better than the ones around Temple Street. The monsignor had arranged to meet them in the church.

The interior was an Irish-Jansenist nightmare of tarnished marble, white-steepled tabernacles and cream columns. Under a different patron, it had served the Irish dockers of a hundred years before. Its dimensions were too mean and narrow to support the mass of decoration, and Father Danilo's bunch had piled the space with their icons, vaguely Byzantine Slavic saints and Desert Fathers and celebrity saints in their Slavic aspect.

Candles were flickering as the two women entered. The place smelled of wax, stale wine and the incense of past ceremony. Mary carried the babies under their purple cloth.

Monsignor Danilo waited before the altar, at the end of the main aisle. He wore his empurpled cassock with surplice and a silk stole. His spectacles reflected the candlelight.

Beside him stood a tall, very thin, expressionless young man in cassock and surplice. The young man, in need of a shave, held a paten on which cruets of holy water and chrism and a slice of lemon had been set.

Monsignor Danilo smiled his lupine smile, and when Mary had set the babies down before the altar, he took her hand in his. In the past he had sometimes kissed it; tonight he pressed it to his breast. The intrusion of his flabby body on her senses filled Mary with loathing. He paid no attention to Camille Innaurato and he did not introduce the server.

"Ah," he said, bending to lift the curtain under which the creatures lay, "the little children, no?"

She watched him regard the things with cool compassion, as though he were moved by their beauty, their vestigial humanity, the likeness of their Creator. But perhaps, she thought, he had seen ghastly sights before and smiled on them. Innocent as he might be, she thought, he was the reeking model of every Jew-baiting, clerical fascist murderer who ever took orders east of the Danube. His merry countenance was crass hypocrisy. His hands were huge, thick-knuckled, the hands of a brute, as his face was the face of a smiling Cain.

"So beautiful," he said. Then he said something in his native language to the slovenly young man, who looked at Mary with a smirk and shrugged and smiled in a vulgar manner. She did not let her gaze linger.

Afterward, she would have to hear about Danilo's mother and her trip to behold the apparition of the Virgin in some Bessarabian or Balkan hamlet and the singular misfortunes, historically unique, of Danilo's native land. And she would have to give him at least seventy-five dollars or there would be squeals and a disappointed face. And now something extra for the young man, no doubt an illegal alien, jumped-ship and saving his pennies.

Camille Innaurato breathed through her inhaler. Father Danilo took a cruet from the paten and with his thick fingers sprinkled a blessing on the lifeless things. Then they all faced the altar and the Eastern crucifix that hung suspended there. They prayed together in the Latin each knew:

Agnus Dei, qui tollis peccata mundi,
Miserere nobis.

Finally, she was alone with the ancient Thing before whose will she still stood amazed, whose shadow and line and light they all were: the bad priest and the questionable young man and Camille Innaurato, she herself and the unleavened flesh fouling the floor. Adoring, defiant, in the crack-house flicker of that hideous, consecrated half-darkness, she offered It Its due, by old command.

Lamb of God, who takest away the sins of the world,
Have mercy on us.

II **After the War**

b orn in Hartford, Connecticut, Brendan Gill (1914–1997) had already published a book, *Death in April and Other Poems,* before he graduated from Yale in 1936. It was followed by so many others, and in so many different genres—novels, biographies, architectural studies, portraiture, and memoirs—that he truly earned his title of man of letters. Immediately after graduation, he joined the staff of the *New Yorker,* where he remained until his death; he was the magazine's film critic from 1961 until 1967, and for the next two decades was its drama critic before again switching hats to become its columnist on architecture. He worked to preserve and celebrate New York City's grandest buildings, both by serving on the board of the Landmark Conservancy and the Whitney Museum of American Art and by writing books about the Customs House, Saint Patrick's Cathedral, and the Flatiron Building. He wrote biographies of Cole Porter, Tallulah Bankhead, Frank Lloyd Wright, and Charles Lindbergh, as well as *Late Bloomers* (1996), a gathering of character portraits. His novels include *The Trouble of One House,* which won the National Book Award in 1951, and *The Day the Money Stopped* (1957), which Maxwell Anderson adapted into a play. *Ways of Loving: Two Novellas and Eighteen Short Stories* appeared in 1974. And Gill's *Here at "The New Yorker,"* published to coincide with the magazine's fiftieth anniversary, is a classic. He once told an interviewer: "Fiction is my chief interest, followed by architectural history, followed by literary and dramatic criticism. If these fields were to be closed to me, I would write copy for a birdseed catalogue. In any event, I would write."

Happy writers have histories shorter even than happy families. The whole of my professional career can be summed up by saying that I started out at the place where I wanted most to be— *The New Yorker* magazine—and with much pleasure and very little labor have remained here ever since. Sometimes, and with reason, I boast of never having done an honest day's work in my life. An honest day's play—oh, that I have accomplished on a thousand occasions, or ten thousand, but work implies a measure of drudgery and fatigue, and these are states as yet unknown to me. With *The New Yorker* serving as my passport and letter of credit, how easy I have found it for almost forty years to rush pell-mell through the world, playing the clown when the spirit of darkness has moved me and colliding with good times at every turn!

Such a confession will no doubt make unwelcome reading to my colleagues, for the fashion among them is to hold that writing is a prolonged and disenchanting misery. A friend of mine, Patrick Kavanagh, who was the premier poet in Ireland after Yeats, said of the peasantry from which he sprang that they live in the dark cave of the unconscious and they scream when they see the light. They *scream* when they see the light. Now, most *New Yorker* writers share this attribute with Irish peasants. They tend to be lonely, molelike creatures, who work in their own portable if not peasant darkness and who seldom utter a sound above a groan. It happens that I am not like that. On the contrary, I am among those who enjoy the light and even, to a certain extent, the limelight—a predilection that has its hazards. Once I was showing off at a cocktail party, and I mentioned some very arcane fact that we had dug up for "Talk of the Town," like that Saint Ambrose was the first person in history reputed to have been able to read without moving his lips. Somebody asked me how I knew that, and I replied grandly, "I know everything." And a pretty girl was there, an Italian model, and she looked up at me with great melting dark eyes and said softly, "Tell me about the Battle of Mukden." I burst out in dismay, "Mukden, Mukden, the Battle of Mukden—!" For, sure enough, I knew nothing whatever about that very important event.

Nevertheless, I am always so ready to take a favorable view of my powers that even when I am caught out and made a fool of, I manage to twist this circumstance about until it becomes a proof of how exceptional I am. The ingenuities we practice in order to appear admirable to ourselves would suffice to invent the telephone twice over on a rainy summer morning.

Writer-moles avoid another hazard of the limelight: the public occasion that fails. In my youth, having gained a little fame by some short stories in *The New Yorker,* I was invited to give a talk about the magazine at Indiana University, and it turned out to be a nightmare, because the audience was academic. I didn't know then what I know now—that college professors like a talk to last at least an hour, with everything being said at least three times. The third time they hear a thing, they feel that famous shock of recognition, and a pleased smile begins to play over their faces. Well, in my ignorance on that occasion, I simply got up and talked, and having told them everything I knew about my assigned topic, I found I had consumed only ten minutes. I then went nattering on, in greater and greater panic, about metalinguistics, pendentive arches, and the decline of materialism in third-century Greece. Oh, God! That took but ten minutes more. All I could think of to do was sit down, and I did. Silence. No applause. The audience stared at me and I stared back. Little by little, I perceived that they thought I was having a heart attack, or a massive cerebral hemorrhage, or some such tiresome little thing as that; as soon as it was over, they expected me to get to my feet and go on. No doubt many of *them* had had heart attacks or massive cerebral hemorrhages in the course of those sixty-minute talks of theirs and had gone on speaking without the slightest trace of discomfort. Anyhow, I finally got to my feet, bowed, or, rather, lowered my head in a protective fashion, and slunk offstage.

In the offices of *The New Yorker* is a long corridor off which Joseph Mitchell, Philip Hamburger, and a couple of dozen other writers and editors have their bleak little ill-painted cells. The silence in that corridor is so profound and continuous that Hamburger long ago christened it Sleepy Hollow. At this moment, I am breaking the silence of Sleepy Hollow with the thud and clatter of an ancient sea-green Olivetti 82. Fortunately, my neighbors on either side are away on holiday; their daily naps will not be interrupted by my zeal. I foresee that writing about the magazine will be a lighter task than talking about it proved to be in Indiana. My intention is to follow the principle upon which the "Talk of the Town" department of the magazine is based: I will try to cram these paragraphs full of facts and give them a weight and shape no greater than that of a cloud of blue butterflies.

Not that this is how the principle of "Talk" would have been enunciated by Harold Wallace Ross, the founder and first editor of the magazine. Butterflies, and especially metaphorical butterflies, were the kind of thing that made Ross nervous. He was a self-taught man, and his teaching had been spectacularly hit-or-miss. He was rumored to have read only one book all the way through—a stout volume on sociology by Herbert Spencer. The truth was that he had read other books, but not many. He had the uneducated man's suspicion of the fickleness of words; he wanted them to have a limited, immutable meaning, but the sons of bitches kept hopping about from one sentence to the next. Ross was a foul-tongued man and he used curse-words to curse words. Nor were the goddam dictionaries the allies he thought they ought to be; they nearly always betrayed him by granting a word several definitions, some of which were maddeningly at odds with others. That was why Ross fell back with such relish upon Fowler's *Modern English Usage*—the work of a petty tyrant, who imposed idiosyncrasies by fiat. Ross was awed by Fowler; he would have liked to hold the whip hand over words and syntax as Fowler did. If words in themselves were not to be trusted, figures of speech were suspicious in the extreme. Metaphors and similes were Ross's adversaries; my blue butterflies would have been wiped out by a single sweep of his big nicotine-stained hand, a single agitated "Jesus!"

Ross's way of stating the principle of "Talk" was simple and direct. "If you can't be funny," he would growl, "be interesting." Like so many Ross formulations, this is something easier said than done.

By now I am half-convinced that I came to work for *The New Yorker* as a child. I make up stories to the effect that I was too small to reach above the lowest row of typewriter keys and therefore had to write pieces that consisted largely of words containing the letters z, x, c, v, b, n, and m. In truth, I sold my first short story to the magazine in 1936, when the magazine was eleven and I was approaching my twenty-second birthday. I was well able to strike all those shapely, necessary vowels in the upper row of keys, and I did so with eagerness. I had graduated from Yale in June of that year and had got married the next day. My wife and I spent the summer honeymooning in Europe, from time to time accompanied, not altogether to our convenience, by some seventy members of the Yale Glee Club. I felt thoroughly grown-up at twenty-one—more grown-up, indeed, than I have ever succeeded in feeling since. The confidence of ignorant youth seeps slowly, slowly away and to our astonishment no confidence of sapient age comes surging in to take its place.

When I started at *The New Yorker,* I felt an unshakable confidence in my talent and intelligence. I revelled in them openly, like a dolphin diving skyward out of the sea. After almost forty years, my assurance is less than it was; the revellings, such as they are, take place in becoming seclusion. This steady progress downward in the amount of one's confidence is a commonplace at the magazine—one might almost call it a tradition. Again and again, some writer who has made a name for himself in the world will begin to write for us and will discover as if for the first time how difficult writing is. The machinery of benign skepticism that surrounds and besets him in the form of editors, copy editors, and checkers, to say nothing of fellow-writers, digs a yawning pit an inch or so beyond his desk. He hears it repeated as gospel that there are not three people in all America who can set down a simple declarative sentence correctly; what are the odds against his being one of this tiny elect?

In some cases, the pressure of all those doubting eyes upon his copy is more than the writer can bear. When the galleys of a piece are placed in front of him, covered with scores, perhaps hundreds, of pencilled hen-tracks of inquiry, suggestion, and correction, he may sense not the glory of creation but the threat of being stung to death by an army of gnats. Upon which he may think of nothing better to do than lower his head onto his blotter and burst into tears. Thanks to the hen-tracks and their consequences, the piece will be much improved, but the author of it will be pitched into a state of graver self-doubt than ever. Poor devil, he will type out his name on a sheet of paper and stare at it long and long, with dumb uncertainty. It looks—oh, Christ!—his name looks as if it could stand some working on.

As I was writing the above, Gardner Botsford, the editor who, among other duties, handles copy for "Theatre," came into my office with the galleys of my latest play review in his hand. Wearing an expression of solemnity, he said, "I am obliged to inform you that Miss Gould has found a buried dangling modifier in one of your sentences." Miss Gould is our head copy editor and unquestionably knows as much about English grammar as anyone alive. Gerunds, predicate nominatives, and passive periphrastic conjugations are mother's milk to her, as they are not to me. Nevertheless, I boldly challenged her allegation. My prose was surely correct in every way. Botsford placed the galleys before me and indicated the offending sentence, which ran, "I am told that in her ninth decade this beautiful woman's only complaint in respect to her role is that she doesn't have enough work to do."

I glared blankly at the galleys. Humiliating enough to have buried a dangling modifier unawares; still more humiliating not to be able to disinter it. Botsford came to my rescue. "Miss Gould points out that as the sentence is written, the meaning is that the complaint is in its ninth decade and has, moreover, suddenly and unaccountably assumed the female gender." I said that in my opinion the sentence could only be made worse by being corrected—it was plain that "The only complaint of this beautiful woman in her ninth decade . . ." would hang on the page as heavy as a sash-weight. "Quite so," said Botsford. "There are times when to be right is wrong, and this is one of them. The sentence stands."

alter Lord was born in Baltimore in 1917. After graduating from Princeton, he served in the Office of Strategic Services during World War II and was head of the OSS Secretariat in London in 1945. After the war, he entered Yale Law School and graduated with an LL.B. in 1946. His writing career began in 1954 with the publication of *The Freemantle Diary,* and he has gone on to write many other books of popular history, including *Day of Infamy* (1957), *The Good Years* (1960), *A Time to Stand* (1961), *Peary to the Pole* (1963), *The Past That Would Not Die* (1965), *Incredible Victory* (1967), *The Dawn's Early Light* (1972), *Lonely Vigil* (1977), *The Miracle of Dunkirk* (1982), and *The Night Lives On* (1986). He was given the Francis Parkman Prize for Special Achievement by the Society of American Historians in 1994. His most famous book is *A Night to Remember,* published in 1955 and made into a memorable film. Lord's account of the sinking of the *Titanic,* which has held at least a couple of generations spellbound, has never been surpassed.

With the boats all gone, a curious calm came over the *Titanic*. The excitement and confusion were over, and the hundreds left behind stood quietly on the upper decks. They seemed to cluster inboard, trying to keep as far away from the rail as possible.

Jack Thayer stayed with Milton Long on the starboard side of the boat deck. They studied an empty davit, using it as a yardstick against the sky to gauge how fast she was sinking. They watched the hopeless efforts to clear two collapsibles lashed to the roof of the officers' quarters. They exchanged messages for each other's families. Sometimes they were just silent.

Thayer thought of all the good times he had had and of all the future pleasures he would never enjoy. He thought of his father and his mother, of his sisters and brother. He felt far away, as though he were looking on from some distant place. He felt very, very sorry for himself.

Colonel Gracie, standing a little way off, felt curiously breathless. Later he rather stuffily explained it was the feeling when "*vox faucibus haesit,* as frequently happened to the old Trojan hero of our schooldays." At the time he merely said to himself, "Good-bye to all at home."

In the wireless shack there was no time for either self-pity or *vox faucibus haesit.* Phillips was still working the set, but the power was very low. Bride stood by, watching people rummage the officers' quarters and the gym, looking for extra lifebelts.

It was 2:05 when Captain Smith entered the shack for the last time: "Men, you have done your full duty. You can do no more. Abandon your cabin. Now it's every man for himself."

Phillips looked up for a second, then bent over the set once more. Captain Smith tried again, "You look out for yourselves. I release you." A pause, then he added softly, "That's the way of it at this kind of time . . ."

Phillips went on working. Bride began to gather up their papers. Captain Smith returned to the boat deck, walked about speaking informally to men here and there. To fireman James McGann, "Well, boys, it's every man for himself." Again, to oiler Alfred White, "Well, boys, I guess it's every man for himself." To steward Edward Brown, "Well, boys, do your best for the women and children, and look out for yourselves." To the men on the roof of the officers' quarters, "You've done your duty, boys. Now, every man for himself." Then he walked back on the bridge.

Some of the men took the Captain at his word and jumped overboard. Night baker Walter Belford leaped as far out as he could, cannon-balled into the water in a sitting position. He still shudders and sucks his breath sharply when he thinks of the stabbing cold. Greaser Fred Scott, just up from boiler room 4, tried to slide down an empty fall, missed, and took a belly-flopper into the sea. He was picked up by boat 4, still standing by the ship but trying to row clear of the barrels and deck chairs that were now hurtling down. Steward Cunningham made a hefty leap and also managed to reach No. 4.

But most of the crew stuck to the ship. On top of the officers' quarters, Lightoller noticed trimmer Hemming at work on one of the tangled collapsibles . . . yet Hemming should have gone long ago as part of the crew in No. 6.

"Why haven't you gone, Hemming?"

"Oh, plenty of time yet, sir."

Not far away two young stewards idly watched Lightoller, Hemming, and the others at work. In the fading light of the boat deck, their starched white jackets stood out as they leaned against the rail, debating how long the ship could last. Scattered around the boat deck, some fifteen first-class bellboys were equally at ease—they seemed pleased that nobody cared any longer whether they smoked. Nearby, gymnasium instructor T. W. McCawley, a spry little man in white flannels, explained why he wouldn't wear a life jacket—it kept you afloat but it slowed you down; he felt he could swim clear more quickly without it.

By the forward entrance to the grand staircase, between the first and second funnel, the band—now wearing life jackets on top of their overcoats—scraped lustily away at ragtime.

The passengers were just as calm, although they too had their jumpers. Frederick Hoyt saw his wife into collapsible D, leaped and swam to where he thought the boat might pass. He guessed well. In a few minutes boat D splashed by and hauled him in. For the rest of the night he sat soaked to the skin, rowing hard to keep from freezing.

But for the most part the passengers merely stood waiting or quietly paced the boat deck. New York and Philadelphia society continued to stick together— John B. Thayer, George and Harry Widener, Duane Williams formed a little knot . . . lesser luminaries like Clinch Smith and Colonel Gracie hovering nearby. Astor remained pretty much alone, and the Strauses sat down on deck chairs.

Jack Thayer and Milton Long debated whether to jump. The davit they were using as a gauge showed the *Titanic* was going much faster now. Thayer wanted to jump out, catch an empty lifeboat fall, slide down and swim out to the boats he could dimly see 500 or 600 yards away. He was a good swimmer. Long, not nearly as good, argued against it and persuaded Thayer not to try.

Further forward, Colonel Gracie lent his penknife to the men struggling with the collapsibles lashed to the officers' quarters. They were having a hard time, and Gracie wondered why.

Some of the third-class passengers had now worked their way up to the boat deck, and others were drifting towards the gradually rising stern. The after poop deck, normally third-class space anyhow, was suddenly becoming attractive to all kinds of people.

Olaus Abelseth was one of those who reached the boat deck. Most of the evening he had been all the way aft with his cousin, his brother-in-law, and the two Norwegian girls. With other steerage men and women, they aimlessly waited for someone to tell them what to do.

Around 1:30 an officer opened the gate to first class and ordered the women to the boat deck. At 2:00 the men were allowed up too. Many now preferred to stay where they were—this would clearly be the last point above water. But Abelseth, his cousin and brother-in-law went up on the chance there was still a boat left. The last one was pulling away.

So they just stood there, as worried about being in first class as by the circumstances that brought them there. Abelseth watched the crew trying to free the collapsibles. Once an officer, searching for extra hands, called, "Are there any sailors here?"

Abelseth had spent sixteen of his twenty-seven years on the sea and felt he should speak up. But his cousin and brother-in-law pleaded, "No, let us just stay here together."

So they did. They felt rather awkward and said very little. It was even more awkward when Mr. and Mrs. Straus drew near. "Please," the old gentleman was saying, "get into a lifeboat and be saved."

"No, let me stay with you," she replied. Abelseth turned and looked the other way.

Within the ship the heavy silence of the deserted rooms had a drama of its own. The crystal chandeliers of the *à la carte* restaurant hung at a crazy angle, but they still burned brightly, lighting the fawn panels of French walnut and the rose-coloured carpet. A few of the little table lights with their pink silk shades had fallen over, and someone was rummaging in the pantry, perhaps for something to fortify himself.

The Louis Quinze lounge with its big fireplace was silent and empty. The Palm Court was equally deserted—one passer-by found it hard to believe that just four hours ago it was filled with exquisitely dressed ladies and gentlemen, sipping after-dinner coffee, listening to chamber music by the same men who now played gay songs on the boat deck above.

The smoking-room was not completely empty. When a steward looked in at 2:10, he was surprised to see Thomas Andrews standing all alone in the room. Andrews' lifebelt lay carelessly across the green cloth top of a card table. His arms were folded over his chest; his look was stunned; all his drive and energy were gone. A moment of awed silence, and the steward timidly broke in: "Aren't you going to have a try for it, Mr. Andrews?"

There was no answer, not even a trace that he heard. The builder of the *Titanic* merely stared aft.

Outside on the decks, the crowd still waited; the band still played. A few prayed with the Reverend Thomas R. Byles, a second-class passenger. Others seemed lost in thought.

There was much to think about. For Captain Smith there were the four ice messages he received during the day—a fifth, which he may not have seen, told exactly where to expect the berg. And there was the thermometer that fell from forty-three degrees at seven o'clock to thirty-two degrees at ten o'clock. And the temperature of the sea, which dropped to thirty-one degrees at 10:30 p.m.

Wireless operator Jack Phillips could ponder over the sixth ice warning—when the *Californian* broke in at 11:00 p.m. and Phillips told her to shut up. That one never even reached the bridge.

George Q. Clifford of Boston had the rueful satisfaction of remembering that he took out 50,000 dollars' extra life insurance just before the trip.

For Isidor Straus there was the irony of his will. A special paragraph urged Mrs. Straus to "be a little selfish; don't always think only of others." Through the years she had been so self-sacrificing that he especially wanted her to enjoy life after he was gone. Now the very qualities he admired so much meant he could never have his wish.

Little things too could return to haunt a person at a time like this. Edith Evans remembered a fortune-teller who once told her to "beware of the water." William T. Stead was nagged by a dream about somebody throwing cats out of a top-storey window. Charles Hays had prophesied just a few hours earlier that the time would soon come for "the greatest and most appalling of all disasters at sea."

Two men perhaps wondered why they were there at all. Archie Butt didn't want to go abroad, but he needed a rest; and Frank Millet badgered President Taft into sending Butt with a message to the Pope—official business but spring in Rome, too. Chief Officer Wilde didn't plan to be on board either. He was regularly on the *Olympic,* but the White Star Line transferred him at the last minute for this one voyage. They thought his experience would be useful in breaking in the new ship. Wilde had considered it a lucky break.

In the wireless shack Phillips struggled to keep the set going. At 2:10 he sounded two V's—heard faintly by the *Virginian*—as he tried to adjust the spark for better results. Bride made a last inspection tour. He returned to find a fainting lady had been carried into the shack. Bride got her a chair and a glass of water, and she sat gasping while her husband fanned her. She came to, and the man took her away.

Bride went behind the curtain where he and Phillips slept. He gathered up all the loose money, took a last look at his rumpled bunk, pushed through the curtain again. Phillips still sat hunched over the set, completely absorbed. But a stoker was now in the room, gently unfastening Phillips' lifejacket.

Bride leaped at the stoker, Phillips jumped up, and the three men wrestled around the shack. Finally Bride wrapped his arms about the stoker's waist, and Phillips swung again and again until the man slumped unconscious in Bride's arms.

A minute later they heard the sea gurgling up the A deck companionway and washing over the bridge. Phillips cried, "Come on, let's clear out!" Bride dropped the stoker, and the two men ran out on to the boat deck. The stoker lay still where he fell.

Phillips disappeared aft. Bride walked forward and joined the men on the roof of the officers' quarters who were trying to free collapsibles A and B. It was a ridiculous place to stow boats—especially when there were only twenty for 2,207 people. With the deck slanting like this, it had been hard enough launching C and D, the two collapsibles stowed right beside the forward davits. It was impossible to do much with A and B.

But the crew weren't discouraged. If the boats couldn't be launched, they could perhaps be floated off. So they toiled on—Lightoller, Murdoch, trimmer Hemming, steward Brown, greaser Hurst, a dozen others.

On the port side Hemming struggled with the block and tackle for boat B. If he could only iron out a kink in the fall, he was sure it could still be launched. He finally got the lines working, passed the block up to Sixth Officer Moody on the roof, but Moody shouted back, "We don't want the block; we'll leave the boat on the deck."

Hemming saw no chance of clearing boat B this way; so he jumped and swam for it. Meanwhile the boat was pushed to the edge of the roof and slid down on some oars to the deck. It landed upside down.

On the starboard side they were having just as much trouble with boat A. Somebody propped planks against the wall of the officers' quarters, and they eased the boat down bow first. But they were still a long way from home, for the *Titanic* was now listing heavily to port, and they couldn't push the boat "uphill" to the edge of the deck.

The men were tugging at both collapsibles when the bridge dipped under at 2:15 and the sea rolled aft along the boat deck. Colonel Gracie and Clinch Smith turned and headed for the stern. A few steps, and they were blocked by a sudden crowd of men and women pouring up from below. They all seemed to be steerage passengers.

At this moment bandmaster Hartley tapped his violin. The ragtime ended, and the strains of the Episcopal hymn "Autumn" flowed across the deck and drifted in the still night far out over the water.

In the boats women listened with wonder. From a distance there was an agonizing stateliness about the moment. Close-up, it was different. Men could hear the music, but they paid little attention. Too much was happening.

"Oh, save me! Save me!" cried a woman to Peter Daly, Lima representative of the London firm Haes and Sons, as he watched the water roll on to the deck where he stood.

"Good lady," he answered, "save yourself. Only God can save you now."

But she begged him to help her make the jump, and on second thoughts he realized he couldn't shed the problem so easily. Quickly he took her by the arm and helped her overboard. As he jumped himself, a big wave came sweeping along the boat deck, washing him clear of the ship.

The sea foamed and swirled around steward Brown's feet as he sweated to get boat A to the edge of the deck. Then he realized he needn't try any longer—the boat was floating off. He jumped in . . . cut the stern lines . . . yelled for someone to free the bow . . . and in the next instant was washed out by the same wave that swept off Peter Daly.

Down, down dipped the *Titanic*'s bow, and her stern swung slowly up. She seemed to be moving forward too. It was this motion which generated the wave that hit Daly, Brown, and dozens of others as it rolled aft.

Lightoller watched the wave from the roof of the officers' quarters. He saw the crowds retreating up the deck ahead of it. He saw the nimbler ones keep clear, the slower ones overtaken and engulfed. He knew that this kind of retreat just prolonged the agony. He turned and, facing the bow, dived in. As he reached the surface, he saw just ahead of him the crow's-nest, now level with the water. Blind instinct seized him, and for a moment he swam towards it as a place of safety.

Then he snapped to and tried to swim clear of the ship. But the sea was pouring down the ventilators just in front of the forward funnel, and he was sucked back and held against the wire grating of an air shaft. He prayed it would hold. And he wondered how long he could last, pinned this way to the grating.

He never learned the answer. A blast of hot air from somewhere deep below came rushing up the ventilator and blew him to the surface. Gasping and spluttering, he finally paddled clear.

Harold Bride kept his head too. As the wave swept by, he grabbed an oarlock of collapsible B, which was still lying upside down on the boat deck near the first funnel. The boat, Bride and a dozen others were washed off together. The collapsible was still upside down, and Bride found himself struggling underneath it.

Colonel Gracie was not as sea-wise. He stayed in the crowd and jumped with the wave—it was almost like Newport. Rising on the crest, he caught the bottom rung of the iron railing on the roof of the officers' quarters. He hauled himself up and lay on his stomach right at the base of the second funnel.

Before he could rise, the roof too had dipped under. Gracie found himself spinning round and round in a whirlpool of water. He tried to cling to the railing, then realized this was pulling him down deeper. With a mighty kick he pushed himself free and swam clear of the ship, far below the surface.

Chef John Collins couldn't do much of anything about the wave. He had a baby in his arms. For five minutes he and a deck steward had been trying to help a steerage woman with two children. First they heard there was a boat on the port side. They ran there and heard it was on the starboard side. When they got there, somebody said their best chance was to head for the stern. Bewildered, they were standing undecided—Collins holding one of the babies—when they were all swept overboard by the wave. He never saw the others again, and the child was washed out of his arms.

h arvey Shapiro was born in Chicago in 1924. He entered Yale with the class of 1945 but graduated two years later, having interrupted his studies to serve as a B-17 gunner in the war—for which he received the Distinguished Flying Cross and the Air Medal with three oak-leaf clusters. While at Yale he helped edit the *Yale Poetry Review,* whose pages included work by Wallace Stevens and Ezra Pound. Shapiro has since published eleven books of poems. For much of his career he has worked at the *New York Times,* first at its magazine, then as editor of its book review from 1975 until 1983. He is now a contributing editor at the *Times Magazine.* "When I returned to Yale in September 1945 after the war," Shapiro recalls, "I knew I wanted to write poetry but there were no courses for doing that, so I took an advanced expository writing course with the poet Theodore Weiss. He was the editor of the *Quarterly Review of Literature,* one of the first journals I published in. He was a brilliant teacher, and became a friend for life. I studied French with Wallace Fowlie, who pointed me towards the Gotham Book Mart in New York and told me to read. And I had the good fortune to take a course in the epic and a graduate seminar in criticism with W. K. Wimsatt. The basic message of the Yale English Department in those days was that to know a few lines of Shakespeare and possibly Chaucer was the attribute of a gentleman. Wimsatt taught me that literature has nothing to do with being a gentleman, that matters of life and death are being fought out on the page."

from BATTLE REPORT

I

The Adriatic was no sailor's sea.
We raced above that water for our lives
Hoping the green curve of Italy
Would take us in. Rank, meaningless fire

That had no other object but our life
Raged in the stunned engine. I acquired
From the scene that flickered like a silent film
New perspective on the days of man.

Now the aviators, primed for flight,
Gave to the blue expanse can after can
Of calibers, armored clothes, all
The rich paraphernalia of our war.

Death in a hungry instant took us in.
He touched me where my lifeblood danced
And said, the cold water is an ample grin
For all your twenty years.

Monotone and flawless, the blue sky
Shows to my watching face this afternoon
The chilled signal of our victory.
Again the lost plane drums home.

NATIONAL COLD STORAGE COMPANY

The National Cold Storage Company contains
More things than you can dream of.
Hard by the Brooklyn Bridge it stands
In a litter of freight cars,
Tugs to one side; the other, the traffic
Of the Long Island Expressway.
I myself have dropped into it in seven years
Midnight tossings, plans for escape, the shakes.
Add this to the national total—
Grant's tomb, the Civil War, Arlington,
The young President dead.
Above the warehouse and beneath the stars
The poets creep on the harp of the Bridge.
But see,
They fall into the National Cold Storage Company
One by one. The wind off the river is too cold,
Or the times too rough, or the Bridge
Is not a harp at all. Or maybe
A monstrous birth inside the warehouse
Must be fed by everything—ships, poems,
Stars, all the years of our lives.

[on the death of John Fitzgerald Kennedy]

RIDING WESTWARD

It's holiday night
And crazy Jews are on the road,
Finished with fasting and high on prayer.
On either side of the Long Island Expressway
The lights go spinning
Like the twin ends of my tallis.
I hope I can make it to Utopia Parkway
Where my father lies at the end of his road.
And then home to Brooklyn.
Jews, departure from the law
Is equivalent to death.
Shades, we greet each other.
Darkly, on the Long Island Expressway,
Where I say my own prayers for the dead,
Crowded in Queens, remembered in Queens,
As far away as Brooklyn. Cemeteries
Break against the City like seas,
A white froth of tombstones
Or like schools of herring, still desperate
To escape the angel of death.
Entering the City, you have to say
Memorial prayers as he slides overhead
Looking something like my father approaching
The Ark as the gates close on the Day of Atonement
Here in the car and in Queens and in Brooklyn.

t he novelist John Knowles was born in Fairmont, West Virginia, in 1926 and graduated from Yale College in 1949. He worked as a newspaper reporter and magazine editor, but he is best known for his 1959 novel *A Separate Peace,* which along with *The Catcher in the Rye* has achieved cult status and become a rite of passage. Among his other novels are *Morning in Antibes* (1962), *Phineas* (1968), *Spreading Fires* (1974), *A Vein of Riches* (1978), *A Stolen Past* (1983), and *The Private Life of Axie Reed* (1986). With a delicate sensibility and a sense of the absurd that predicted the more antic work of Kurt Vonnegut, Knowles set *A Separate Peace* at the fictional Devon School in 1942, its preppies soon to be torn from their private world of privileges and longings and sent to war. The narrator, Gene Forrester, sets in motion a train of accidents that result in the death of his roommate and best friend, Phineas. By the end of the novel—the final chapter is printed here—the war effort has taken over the campus, and young Gene is graduated into the world.

The quadrangle surrounding the Far Common was never considered absolutely essential to the Devon School. The essence was elsewhere, in the older, uglier, more comfortable halls enclosing the Center Common. There the School's history had unrolled, the fabled riot scenes and Presidential visits and Civil War musterings, if not in these buildings then in their predecessors on the same site. The upperclassmen and the faculty met there, the budget was compiled there, and there students were expelled. When you said "Devon" to an alumnus ten years after graduation he visualized the Center Common.

The Far Common was different, a gift of the rich lady benefactress. It was Georgian like the rest of the school, and it combined scholasticism with grace in the way which made Devon architecturally interesting. But the bricks had been laid a little too skillfully, and the woodwork was not as brittle and chipped as it should have been. It was not the essence of Devon, and so it was donated, without too serious a wrench, to the war.

The Far Common could be seen from the window of my room, and early in June I stood at the window and watched the war moving in to occupy it. The advance guard which came down the street from the railroad station consisted of a number of Jeeps, being driven with a certain restraint, their gyration-prone wheels inactive on these old ways which offered nothing bumpier than a few cobblestones. I thought the Jeeps looked noticeably uncomfortable from all the power they were not being allowed to use. There is no stage you comprehend better than the one you have just left, and as I watched the Jeeps almost asserting a wish to bounce up the side of Mount Washington at eighty miles an hour instead of rolling along this dull street, they reminded me, in a comical and a poignant way, of adolescents.

Following them there were some heavy trucks painted olive drab, and behind them came the troops. They were not very bellicose-looking; their columns were straggling, their suntan uniforms had gotten rumpled in the train, and they were singing *Roll Out the Barrel.*

"What's that?" Brinker said from behind me, pointing across my shoulder at some open trucks bringing up the rear. "What's in those trucks?"

"They look like sewing machines."

"They *are* sewing machines!"

"I guess a Parachute Riggers' school has to have sewing machines."

"If only Leper had enlisted in the Army Air Force and been assigned to Parachute Riggers' school . . ."

"I don't think it would have made any difference," I said. "Let's not talk about Leper."

"Leper'll be all right. There's nothing like a discharge. Two years after the war's over people will think a Section Eight means a berth on a Pullman car."

"Right. Now do you mind? Why talk about something you can't do anything about?"

"Right."

I had to be right in never talking about what you could not change, and I had to make many people agree that I was right. None of them ever accused me of being responsible for what had happened to Phineas, either because they could not believe it or else because they could not understand it. I would have talked about that, but they would not, and I would not talk about Phineas in any other way.

The Jeeps, troops, and sewing machines were now drawn up next to the Far Common quadrangle. There was some kind of consultation or ceremony under way on the steps of one of the buildings, Veazy Hall. The Headmaster and a few of the senior members of the faculty stood in a group before the door, and a number of Army Air Force officers stood in another group within easy speaking distance of them. Then the Headmaster advanced several steps and enlarged his gestures; he was apparently addressing the troops. Then an officer took his place and spoke longer and louder; we could hear his voice fairly well but not make out the words.

Around them spread a beautiful New England day. Peace lay on Devon like a blessing, the summer's peace, the reprieve, New Hampshire's response to all the cogitation and deadness of winter. There could be no urgency in work during such summers; any parachutes rigged would be no more effective than napkins.

Or perhaps that was only true for me and a few others, our gypsy band of the summer before. Or was it rarer even than that; had Chet and Bobby sensed it then, for instance? Had Leper, despite his trays of snails? I could be certain of only two people, Phineas and myself. So now it might be true only for me.

The company fell out and began scattering through the Far Common. Dormitory windows began to fly open and olive drab blankets were hung over the sills by the dozens to air. The sewing machines were carried with considerable exertion into Veazy Hall.

"Dad's here," said Brinker. "I told him to take his cigar down to the Butt Room. He wants to meet you."

We went downstairs and found Mr. Hadley sitting in one of the lumpy chairs, trying not to look offended by the surroundings. But he stood up and shook my hand with genuine cordiality when we came in. He was a distinguished-looking man, taller than Brinker so that his portliness was not very noticeable. His hair was white, thick, and healthy-looking and his face was healthily pink.

"You boys look fine, fine," he said in his full and cordial voice, "better I would say than those dough-boys—G.I.'s—I saw marching in. And how about their artillery! Sewing machines!"

Brinker slid his fingers into the back pockets of his slacks. "This war's so technical they've got to use all kinds of machines, even sewing machines, don't you think so, Gene?"

"Well," Mr. Hadley went on emphatically, "I can't imagine any man in my time settling for duty on a sewing machine. I can't picture that at all." Then his temper switched tracks and he smiled cordially again. "But then times change, and wars change. But men don't change, do they? You boys are the image of me and my gang in the old days. It does me good to see you. What are you enlisting in, son," he said, meaning me, "the Marines, the Paratroops? There are doggone many exciting things to enlist in these days. There's that bunch they call the Frogmen, underwater demolition stuff. I'd give something to be a kid again with all that to choose from."

"I was going to wait and be drafted," I replied, trying to be polite and answer his question honestly, "but if I did that they might put me straight in the infantry, and that's not only the dirtiest but also the most dangerous branch of all, the worst branch of all. So I've joined the Navy and they're sending me to Pensacola. I'll probably have a lot of training, and I'll never see a foxhole. I hope."

"Foxhole" was still a fairly new term and I wasn't sure Mr. Hadley knew what it meant. But I saw that he didn't care for the sound of what I said. "And then Brinker," I added, "is all set for the Coast Guard, which is good too." Mr. Hadley's scowl deepened, although his experienced face partially masked it.

"You know, Dad," Brinker broke in, "the Coast Guard does some very rough stuff, putting the men on the beaches, all that dangerous amphibious stuff."

His father nodded slightly, looking at the floor, and then said, "You have to do what you think is the right thing, but just make sure it's the right thing in the long run, and not just for the moment. Your war memories will be with you forever, you'll be asked about them thousands of times after the war is over. People will get their respect for you from that—*partly* from that, don't get me wrong—but if you can say that you were up front where there was some real shooting going on, then that will mean a whole lot to you in years to come. I know you boys want to see plenty of action, but don't go around talking too much about being comfortable, and which branch of the service has too much dirt and stuff like that. Now I know you—I feel I know you, Gene, as well as I know Brink here—but other people might misunderstand you. You want to serve, that's all. It's your greatest moment, greatest privilege, to serve your country. We're all proud of you, and we're all—old guys like me—we're all darn jealous of you too."

I could see that Brinker was more embarrassed by this than I was, but I felt it was his responsibility to answer it. "Well, Dad," he mumbled, "we'll do what we have to."

"That's not a very good answer, Brink," he said in a tone struggling to remain reasonable.

"After all that's all we can do."

"You can do more! A lot more. If you want a military record you can be proud of, you'll do a heck of a lot more than just what you have to. Believe me."

Brinker sighed under his breath, his father stiffened, paused, then relaxed with an effort. "Your mother's out in the car. I'd better get back to her. You boys clean up—ah, those shoes," he added reluctantly, in spite of himself, having to, "those shoes, Brink, a little polish?—and we'll see you at the Inn at six."

"Okay, Dad."

His father left, trailing the faint, unfamiliar, prosperous aroma of his cigar.

"Dad keeps making that speech about serving the country," Brinker said apologetically, "I wish to hell he wouldn't."

"That's all right." I knew that part of friendship consisted in accepting a friend's shortcomings, which sometimes included his parents.

"I'm enlisting," he went on, "I'm going to 'serve' as he puts it, I may even get killed. But I'll be damned if I'll have that Nathan Hale attitude of his about it. It's all that World War I malarkey that gets me. They're all children about that war, did you ever notice?" He flopped comfortably into the chair which had been disconcerting his father. "It gives me a pain, personally. I'm not any kind of hero, and neither are you. And neither is the old man, and he never was, and I don't care what he says he almost did at Château-Thierry."

"He's just trying to keep up with the times. He probably feels left out, being too old this time."

"Left out!" Brinker's eyes lighted up. "Left out! He and his crowd are responsible for it! And *we're* going to fight it!"

I had heard this generation-complaint from Brinker before, so often that I finally identified this as the source of his disillusionment during the winter, this generalized, faintly self-pitying resentment against millions of people he did not know. He did know his father, however, and so they were not getting along well now. In a way this was Finny's view, except that naturally he saw it comically, as a huge and intensely practical joke, played by fat and foolish old men bungling away behind the scenes.

I could never agree with either of them. It would have been comfortable, but I could not believe it. Because it seemed clear that wars were not made by generations and their special stupidities, but that wars were made instead by something ignorant in the human heart.

Brinker went upstairs to continue his packing, and I walked over to the gym to clean out my locker. As I crossed the Far Common I saw that it was rapidly becoming unrecognizable, with huge green barrels placed at many strategic points, the ground punctuated by white markers identifying offices and areas, and also certain less tangible things: a kind of snap in the atmosphere, a professional optimism, a conscious maintenance of high morale. I myself had often been happy at Devon, but such times it seemed to me that afternoon were over now. Happiness had disappeared along with rubber, silk, and many other staples, to be replaced by the wartime synthetic, high morale, for the Duration.

At the gym a platoon was undressing in the locker room. The best that could be said for them physically was that they looked wiry in their startling sets of underwear, which were the color of moss.

I never talked about Phineas and neither did anyone else; he was, however, present in every moment of every day since Dr. Stanpole had told me. Finny had a vitality which could not be quenched so suddenly, even by the marrow of his bone. That was why I couldn't say anything or listen to anything about him, because he endured so forcefully that what I had to say would have seemed crazy to anyone else—I could not use the past tense, for instance—and what they had to say would be incomprehensible to me. During the time I was with him, Phineas created an atmosphere in which I continued now to live, a way of sizing up the world with erratic and entirely personal reservations, letting its rocklike facts sift through and be accepted only a little at a time, only as much as he could assimilate without a sense of chaos and loss.

No one else I have ever met could do this. All others at some point found something in themselves pitted violently against something in the world around them. With those of my year this point often came when they grasped the fact of the war. When they began to feel that there was this overwhelmingly hostile thing in the world with them, then the simplicity and unity of their characters broke and they were not the same again.

Phineas alone had escaped this. He possessed an extra vigor, a heightened confidence in himself, a serene capacity for affection which saved him. Nothing as he was growing up at home, nothing at Devon, nothing even about the war had broken his harmonious and natural unity. So at last I had.

The parachute riggers sprinted out of the hallway toward the playing fields. From my locker I collected my sneakers, jock strap, and gym pants and then turned away, leaving the door ajar for the first time, forlornly open and abandoned, the locker unlocked. This was more final than the moment when the Headmaster handed me my diploma. My schooling was over now.

I walked down the aisle past the rows of lockers, and instead of turning left toward the exit leading back to my dormitory, I turned right and followed the Army Air Force out onto the playing fields of Devon. A high wooden platform had been erected there and on it stood a barking instructor, giving the rows of men below him calisthenics by the numbers.

This kind of regimentation would fasten itself on me in a few weeks. I no longer had any qualms about that, although I couldn't help being glad that it would not be at Devon, at anywhere like Devon, that I would have that. I had no qualms at all; in fact I could feel now the gathering, glowing sense of sureness in the face of it. I was ready for the war, now that I no longer had any hatred to contribute to it. My fury was gone, I felt it gone, dried up at the source, withered and lifeless. Phineas had absorbed it and taken it with him, and I was rid of it forever.

The P.T. instructor's voice, like a frog's croak amplified a hundred times, blared out the Army's numerals, "Hut! Hew! Hee! Hore!" behind me as I started back toward the dormitory, and my feet of course could not help but begin to fall involuntarily into step with that coarse, compelling voice, which carried to me like an air-raid siren across the fields and commons.

They fell into step then, as they fell into step a few weeks later under the influence of an even louder voice and a stronger sun. Down there I fell into step as well as my nature, Phineas-filled, would allow.

I never killed anybody and I never developed an intense level of hatred for the enemy. Because my war ended before I ever put on a uniform; I was on active duty all my time at school; I killed my enemy there.

Only Phineas never was afraid, only Phineas never hated anyone. Other people experienced this fearful shock somewhere, this sighting of the enemy, and so began an obsessive labor of defense, began to parry the menace they saw facing them by developing a particular frame of mind, "You see," their behavior toward everything and everyone proclaimed, "I am a humble ant, I am nothing, I am not worthy of this menace," or else, like Mr. Ludsbury, "How dare this threaten me, I am much too good for this sort of handling, I shall rise above this," or else, like Quackenbush, strike out at it always and everywhere, or else, like Brinker, develop a careless general resentment against it, or else, like Leper, emerge from a protective cloud of vagueness only to meet it, the horror, face to face, just as he had always feared, and so give up the struggle absolutely.

All of them, except Phineas, constructed at infinite cost to themselves these Maginot Lines against this enemy they thought they saw across the frontier, this enemy who never attacked that way—if he ever attacked at all; if he was indeed the enemy.

robert K. Massie was born in 1929 in Lexington, Kentucky, and after graduating from Yale went on to Oxford as a Rhodes Scholar. He served in the navy during the Korean War and later launched himself on a career as a journalist at *Newsweek,* where he was a book reviewer, a foreign news writer, the United Nations bureau chief, and an associate editor. His first book, *Nicholas and Alexandra,* appeared in 1967; it was an international best-seller and was made into a film. His other books include *Journey* (1975), *Dreadnought: Britain, Germany, and the Coming of the Great War* (1991), and *The Romanovs: The Final Chapter* (1995). At Yale, he says, "I enrolled in a new interdepartmental major, American Studies. My thesis was a comparison of the contrasting values represented by the two great American autobiographers, Benjamin Franklin and Henry Adams. In retrospect, it seems a solitary undergraduate Charge of the Light Brigade: bold, gallant, and probably headed up the wrong valley. My adviser, the mysterious, charismatic Norman Holmes Pearson, patted my back and said he admired my courage." Massie also remembers that, as a boy living in the American South, and following the dramatic course of World War II in the papers, he learned "three elements which I have come to believe are vital to involving a reader in a narration of history." They are relevance, suspense, and immediacy. Those are certainly qualities of Massie's own 1980 biography, *Peter the Great,* which was awarded the Pulitzer Prize. At the start of the book is a portrait of Moscow at the time of Peter's birth in 1689, when Russia was ruled by Peter's father, the tsar Alexis.

Around Moscow, the country rolls gently up from the rivers winding in silvery loops across the pleasant landscape. Small lakes and patches of woods are sprinkled among the meadowlands. Here and there, a village appears, topped by the onion dome of its church. People are walking through the fields on dirt paths lined with weeds. Along the riverbanks, they are fishing, swimming and lying in the sun. It is a familiar Russian scene, rooted in centuries.

In the third quarter of the seventeenth century, the traveler coming from Western Europe passed through this countryside to arrive at a vantage point known as the Sparrow Hills. Looking down on Moscow from this high ridge, he saw at his feet "the most rich and beautiful city in the world." Hundreds of golden domes topped by a forest of golden crosses rose above the treetops; if the traveler was present at a moment when the sun touched all this gold, the blaze of light forced his eyes to close. The white-walled churches beneath these domes were scattered through a city as large as London. At the center, on a modest hill, stood the citadel of the Kremlin, the glory of Moscow, with its three magnificent cathedrals, its mighty bell tower, its gorgeous palaces, chapels and hundreds of houses. Enclosed by great white walls, it was a city in itself.

In summer, immersed in greenery, the city seemed like an enormous garden. Many of the larger mansions were surrounded by orchards and parks, while swaths of open space left as firebreaks burst out with grasses, bushes and trees. Overflowing its own walls, the city expanded into numerous flourishing suburbs, each with its own orchards, gardens and copses of trees. Beyond, in a wide circle around the city, the manors and estates of great nobles and the white walls and gilded cupolas of monasteries were scattered among meadows and tilled fields to stretch the landscape out to the horizon.

Entering Moscow through its walls of earth and brick, the traveler plunged immediately into the bustling life of a busy commercial city. The streets were crowded with jostling humanity. Tradespeople, artisans, idlers and ragged holy men walked beside laborers, peasants, black-robed priests and soldiers in bright-colored caftans and yellow boots. Carts and wagons struggled to make headway through this river of people, but the crowds parted for a fat-bellied, bearded boyar, or nobleman, on horseback, his head covered with a fine fur cap and his girth with a rich fur-lined coat of velvet or stiff brocade. At street corners, musicians, jugglers, acrobats and animal handlers with bears and dogs performed their tricks. Outside every church, beggars clustered and wailed for alms. In front of taverns, travelers were sometimes astonished to see naked men who had sold every stitch of clothing for a drink; on feast days, other men, naked and clothed alike, lay in rows in the mud, drunk.

The densest crowds gathered in the commercial districts centered on Red

Square. The Red Square of the seventeenth century was very different from the silent, cobbled desert we know today beneath the fantastic, clustered steeples and cupolas of St. Basil's Cathedral and the high Kremlin walls. Then it was a brawling, open-air marketplace, with logs laid down to cover the mud, with lines of log houses and small chapels built against the Kremlin wall where Lenin's tomb now stands, and with rows and rows of shops and stalls, some wood, some covered by tent-like canvas, crammed into every corner of the vast arena. Three hundred years ago, Red Square teemed, swirled and reverberated with life. Merchants standing in front of stalls shouted to customers to step up and inspect their wares. They offered velvet and brocade, Persian and Armenian silk, bronze, brass and copper goods, iron wares, tooled leather, pottery, innumerable objects made of wood, and rows of melons, apples, pears, cherries, plums, carrots, cucumbers, onions, garlic and asparagus as thick as a thumb, laid out in trays and baskets. Peddlers and pushcart men forced their way through the crowds with a combination of threats and pleas. Vendors sold pirozhki (small meat pies) from trays suspended by cords from their shoulders. Tailors and street jewelers, oblivious to all around them, worked at their trades. Barbers clipped hair, which fell to the ground unswept, adding a new layer to a matted carpet decades in the forming. Flea markets offered old clothes, rags, used furniture and junk. Down the hill, nearer the Moscow River, animals were sold, and live fish from tanks. On the riverbank itself, near the new stone bridge, rows of women bent over the water washing clothes. One seventeenth-century German traveler noted that some of the women selling goods in the square might also sell "another commodity."

At noon, all activity came to a halt. The markets would close and the streets empty as people ate dinner, the largest meal of the day. Afterward, everyone napped and shopkeepers and vendors stretched out to sleep in front of their stalls.

With the coming of dusk, swallows began to soar over the Kremlin battlements and the city locked itself up for the night. Shops closed behind heavy shutters, watchmen looked down from the rooftops and bad-tempered dogs paced at the end of long chains. Few honest citizens ventured into the dark streets, which became the habitat of thieves and armed beggars bent on extracting by force in the dark what they had failed to get by pleading during the daylight hours. "These villains," wrote an Austrian visitor, "place themselves at the corners of streets and throw swinging cudgels at the heads of those that pass by, in which practice they are so expert that these mortal blows seldom miss." Several murders a night were common in Moscow, and although the motive for these crimes was seldom more than simple theft, so vicious were the thieves that no one dared respond to cries for help. Often, terrorized citizens were afraid even to look out their own doors or windows to see what was happening. In the morning, the police routinely carried the bodies found lying in the streets to a central field where relatives could come to check for missing persons; eventually, all unidentified corpses were tumbled into a common grave.

Moscow in the 1670's was a city of wood. The houses, mansions and hovels alike, were built of logs, but their unique architecture and the superb carved and painted decoration of their windows, porches and gables gave them a strange beauty unknown to the stolid masonry of European cities. Even the streets were made of wood. Lined with rough timbers and wooden planks, thick with dust in summer or sinking into the mud during spring thaws and September rains, the wood-paved streets of Moscow attempted to provide footing for passage. Often, they failed. "The autumnal rains made the streets impassable for wagons and horses," complained an Orthodox churchman visiting from the Holy Land. "We could not go out of the house to market, the mud and clay being deep enough to sink in overhead. The price of food rose very high, as none could be brought in from the country. All the people, and most of all ourselves, prayed to God that He would cause the earth to freeze."

Not unnaturally in a city built of wood, fire was the scourge of Moscow. In winter when primitive stoves were blazing in every house, and in summer when the heat made wood tinder-dry, a spark could create a holocaust. Caught by the wind, flames leaped from one roof to the next, reducing entire streets to ashes. In 1571, 1611, 1626 and 1671, great fires destroyed whole quarters of Moscow, leaving vast empty spaces in the middle of the city. These disasters were exceptional, but to Muscovites the sight of a burning house with firemen struggling to localize the fire by hastily tearing down other buildings in its path was a part of daily life.

As Moscow was built of logs, Muscovites always kept spares on hand for repairs or new construction. Logs by the thousand were piled up between houses or sometimes hidden behind them or surrounded by fences as protection from thieves. In one section, a large wood market kept thousands of prefabricated log houses of various sizes ready for sale; a buyer had only to specify the size and number of rooms desired. Almost overnight, the timbers, all clearly numbered and marked, would be carried to his site, assembled, the logs chinked with moss, a roof of thin planks laid on top and the new owner could move in. The largest logs, however, were saved and sold for a different purpose. Cut into six-foot sections, hollowed out with an axe and covered with lids, they became the coffins in which Russians were buried.

Rising from a hill 125 feet above the Moscow River, the towers, cupolas and battlements of the Kremlin dominated the city. In Russian, the word "kreml" means "fortress," and the Moscow Kremlin was a mighty citadel. Two rivers and a deep moat rippled beneath its powerful walls. These walls, twelve to sixteen feet thick and rising sixty-five feet above the water, formed a triangle around the crest of the hill, with a perimeter of a mile and a half and a protected enclosure of sixty-nine acres. Twenty massive towers studded the wall at intervals, each a self-contained fortress, each designed to be impregnable. The Kremlin was not impregnable; archers and pikemen and later musketeers and artillerymen could be made to surrender to hunger if not to assault, but the most recent siege, early in the seventeenth century, had lasted two years. Ironically, the besiegers were Russian and the defenders Poles, supporters of a Polish claimant, the False Dmitry, who temporarily occupied the throne. When the Kremlin finally fell, the Russians executed Dmitry, burned his body, primed a cannon on the Kremlin wall and fired his ashes back toward Poland.

In normal times, the Kremlin had two masters, one temporal, the other spiritual: the tsar and the patriarch. Each lived within the fortress and governed his respective realm from there. Crowding around the Kremlin squares were government offices, lawcourts, barracks, bakeries, laundries and stables; nearby stood other palaces and offices and more than forty churches and chapels of the patriarchate of the Russian Orthodox Church. At the center of the Kremlin, on the crest of the hill around the edges of a wide square, stood four magnificent buildings—three superb cathedrals and a majestic, soaring bell tower—which, then and now, may be considered the physical heart of Russia. Two of these cathedrals, along with the Kremlin wall and many of its towers, had been designed by Italian architects.

The largest and most historic of these cathedrals was the Assumption Cathedral (Uspensky Sobor), in which every Russian tsar or empress from the fifteenth century to the twentieth was crowned. It had been built in 1479 by Ridolfo Fioravanti of Bologna but reflected many essential Russian features of church design. Before beginning its construction, Fioravanti had visited the old Russian cities of Vladimir, Yaroslavl, Rostov and Novgorod to study their beautiful cathedrals, and then produced a Russian church with far more space inside than any Russian had ever seen. Four huge circular columns supported the onion-shaped central dome and its four smaller satellite domes without the complicated webbing of walls and buttressing previously thought necessary. This gave an airiness to the ceiling and a spaciousness to the nave entirely unique in Russia, where the power as well as the beauty of the Gothic arch were unknown.

Across the square from the Assumption Cathedral stood the Cathedral of the Archangel Michael, where the tsars were entombed. Built by Alvesio Novy of Milan, it was considerably more Italianate than either of its two sisters. Inside, amidst its several chapels, the deceased rulers were clustered in groups. In the middle of one small room, three carved stone coffins held Ivan the Terrible and his two sons. Other tsars lay in rows along the walls, their coffins of brass and stone covered with embroidered velvet cloths with inscriptions sewn in pearls around the hems. Tsar Alexis, father of Peter the Great, and two of his sons, Fedor and Ivan VI, also both tsars, would lie in this small room, but they would be the last. Alexis' third son, Peter, would build a new cathedral in a new city on the Baltic where he and all the Romanovs who followed would be entombed.*

The smallest of the three cathedrals, the Cathedral of the Annunciation, had nine towers and three porches, and was the only one designed by Russian architects. Its builders came from Pskov, which was famous for its carved stone churches. Used extensively as a private chapel by the tsars and their families, its iconostasis was set with icons by the two most famous painters of this form of religious art in Russia, Theophanes the Greek, who came from Byzantium, and his Russian pupil Andrei Rublev.

On the eastern side of the square, towering above the three cathedrals, stood the whitewashed brick bell towers of Ivan the Great, the Bono Tower and the Tower of the Patriarch Philaret, now joined into a single structure. Beneath its highest cupola, 270 feet in the air, rows of bells hung in laddered niches. Cast in silver, copper, bronze and iron, in many sizes and timbres (the largest weighed thirty-one tons), they rang with a hundred messages: summoning Muscovites to early mass or vespers, reminding them of fasts and festivals, tolling the sadness of death, chiming the happiness of marriage, jangling warnings of fire or booming the celebration of victory. At times, they rang all night, driving foreigners to consternation. But Russians loved their bells. On holidays, the common people crowded to the belfries to take turns pulling the ropes. The first bells usually sounded from the Kremlin, then the sound was taken up by all the bells of Moscow's "forty times forty" churches. Before long, waves of sound passed over the city and "the earth shook with their vibrations like thunder" according to one awed visitor.

From building cathedrals, the Italian architects turned to building palaces. In 1487, Ivan the Great commissioned the first stone palace of the Kremlin, the Palace of Facets (Granovitaya Palata), so named because its gray stone exterior walls were cut prismatically to resemble the surface of facet-cut jewels. Its most notable architectural feature was a throne room seventy-seven feet on each side, whose roof was supported by a single, massively arched column in the middle. When foreign ambassadors were being received, and on other state occasions, a small curtained window near the ceiling permitted the cloistered women of the tsar's family to peek down and watch.

The Palace of Facets was primarily an official state building, and thus, in 1499, Ivan the Great ordered another palace of brick and stone in which to live. This five-story building, called the Terem Palace, contained a honeycomb of low-ceilinged, vaulted apartments for himself and the many women—wives, widows, sisters, daughters—of the royal family. The building was badly damaged by fire

*Except Peter II, whose body is in the Kremlin, and Nicholas II, the last tsar, whose body was destroyed in a pit outside Ekaterinburg in the Urals.

several times during the sixteenth and early seventeenth centuries, but both of
the first Romanov tsars, Michael and his son Alexis, lavished great efforts to restore the building. In Alexis' time, the doors, windows, parapets and cornices
were made of white stone carved into foliage and figures of birds and animals,
then painted bright colors. Alexis devoted special effort to refurbishing the fourth
floor as a dwelling for himself. The five principal rooms—anteroom, throne room
(known as the Golden Hall), study, bedroom and private chapel—were fitted
with wooden walls and floors to prevent the dampness caused by moisture con-
densing on brick and stone, and the walls were covered with hangings of embroidered silk, woolen tapestries or tooled leather, depicting scenes from the Old and
New Testaments. The arches and ceilings were intersected by curving arabesques
and Eastern versions of plants and fairy-tale birds, all done in brilliant colors with
lavish inlays of silver and gold. The furnishing of the tsar's apartment was partly
traditional and partly modern. The old, carved oaken benches and chests and
polished wooden tables were there, but so also were upholstered armchairs, elaborate gilded and ebony tables, clocks, mirrors, portraits and bookcases filled with
books of theology and history. One window of the tsar's study was known as the
Petitioner's Window. Outside was a small box which could be lowered to the
ground, stuffed with petitions and complaints, then raised to be read by the sovereign. The tsar's bedroom was upholstered with Venetian velvet and contained
an intricately carved four-poster oak bed, curtained and canopied with brocade
and silk and heaped with furs, eiderdown and cushions to ward off the icy currents of winter air that blasted against the windows and eddied under the doors.
All these rooms were simultaneously heated and decorated by huge stoves of
glazed, colored tiles whose radiant warmth also kept Russia's rulers warm.

The major drawback to these splendid chambers was their lack of light. Little
sunlight could filter through the narrow windows with their double sheets of
mica separated by strips of lead. Not only at night and on the short, gray days of
winter, but even in summertime, most of the illumination in the Terem Palace
came from the light of flickering candles in the alcoves and along the walls.

In the third quarter of the seventeenth century, the royal chambers were occupied
by the second tsar of the Romanov dynasty, "the Great Lord, Tsar and Grand
Duke, Alexis Mikhailovich, of all Great and Little and White Russia, Autocrat."
Remote and inaccessible to his subjects, this august figure was enclosed in an aura
of semi-divinity. An embassy of Englishmen, come in 1664 to thank the Tsar for
his constant support of their once-exiled monarch, Charles II, was deeply impressed by the sight of Tsar Alexis seated on his throne:

The Tsar like a sparkling sun darted forth most sumptuous rays, being most magnifi-
cently placed upon his throne, with his scepter in his hand and having his crown on his

head. His throne was of massy silver gilt, wrought curiously on top with several works and pyramids; and being seven or eight steps higher than the floor, it rendered the person of the Prince transcendently majestic. His crown (which he wore upon a cap lined with black sables) was covered quite over with precious stones, terminating toward the top in the form of a pyramid with a golden cross at the spire. The scepter glittered also all over with jewels, his vest was set with the like from the top to the bottom and his collar was answerable to the same.

From infancy, Russians had been taught to regard their ruler as an almost god-like creature. Their proverbs embodied this view: "Only God and the tsar know," "One sun shines in heaven and the Russian tsar on earth," "Through God and the tsar, Russia is strong," "It is very high up to God; it is a very long way to the tsar."

Another proverb, "The sovereign is the father, the earth the mother," related the Russian's feeling for the tsar to his feeling for the land. The land, the earth, the motherland, "rodina," was feminine. Not the pure maiden, the virgin girl, but the eternal, mature woman, the fertile mother. All Russians were her children. In a sense, long before communism, the Russian land was communal. It belonged to the tsar as father, but also to the people, his family. Its disposal belonged to the tsar—he could give away vast tracts to favored noblemen—yet it still remained the joint property of the national family. When it was threatened, all were willing to die for it.

The tsar, in this familial scheme, was the father, "Batushka," of the people. His autocratic rule was patriarchal. He addressed his subjects as his children and had the same unlimited power over them that a father has over his children. The Russian people could not imagine any limitation of the power of the tsar, "for how can a father's authority be limited except by God?" When he commanded, they obeyed for the same reason that when a father commands, the child must obey, without question. At times, obeisance before the tsar took on a slavish, Byzantine quality. Russian noblemen, when greeting or receiving favors from the tsar, prostrated themselves in front of him, touching the ground with their foreheads. When addressing his royal master, Artemon Matveev, who was Tsar Alexis' leading minister and close friend, declared, "We humbly beseech you, we your slave Artemushka Matveev, with the lowly worm, my son Adrushka, before the high throne of Your Royal Majesty, bowing our faces to the earth. . . ." In addressing the tsar, his whole lengthy official title had to be used. In so doing, the accidental omission of a single word could be considered an act of personal disrespect almost equivalent to treason. The tsar's own conversation was sacrosanct: " 'Tis death for anyone to reveal what is spoken in the tsar's palace," declared an English resident.

In fact, the demi-god who bore these titles, who wore a crown braided with "tufts of diamonds as big as peas, resembling bunches of glittering grapes" and the imperial mantle embroidered with emeralds, pearls and gold, was a relatively unassuming mortal. Tsar Alexis was recognized in his own time as "tishaishy tsar," the quietest, gentlest and most pious of all the tsars, and when he succeeded his father on the throne in 1645 at the age of sixteen, he was already known as "the Young Monk." In manhood, he grew taller than most Russians, about six feet, well built, inclined to fat. His roundish face was framed by light-brown hair, a mustache and a flowing brown beard. His eyes also were brown, their tone ranging from hardness in anger to warmth in affection and religious humility. "His Imperial Majesty is a goodly person, about two months older than King Charles II," reported his English physician, Dr. Samuel Collins, adding that his patron was "severe in his chastisements but very careful of his subjects' love. Being urged by a stranger to make it [punishable by] death for any man to desert his colors, he answered, 'It was a hard case to do that, for God has not given courage to all men alike.' "

Although he was tsar, Alexis' life inside the Kremlin was more like that of a monk. At four a.m., the Tsar threw aside his sable coverlet and stepped from his bed clad in shirt and drawers. He dressed and went immediately to the chapel next to his bedroom for twenty minutes of prayers and readings from devotional books. When he had kissed the icons and been sprinkled with holy water, he emerged and sent a chamberlain to bid the Tsaritsa good morning and ask after her health. A few minutes later, he went to her chamber to escort her to another chapel, where together they heard morning prayers and early mass.

Meanwhile, boyars, government officials and secretaries had gathered in a public anteroom awaiting the arrival of the Tsar from his private chambers. As soon as they saw "the bright eyes of the Tsar," they began to bow to the ground, some as many as thirty times, in gratitude for favors granted. For a while, Alexis listened to reports and petitions; then, at about nine a.m., the entire group went to hear a two-hour mass. During the service, however, the Tsar continued to converse quietly with his boyars, conducting public business and issuing instructions. Alexis never missed any divine service. "If he be well, he goes to it," said Dr. Collins. "If sick, it comes to him in his chamber. On fast days he frequents midnight prayers, standing four, five, or six hours together, prostrating himself on the ground, sometimes a thousand times, and on great festivals, fifteen hundred."

Following morning mass, the Tsar returned to administrative work with his boyars and secretaries until time for dinner at noon. He ate alone at a high table surrounded by boyars who dined at lower tables along the walls of the room. He was served only by special boyars, who tasted his food and sipped his wine before offering the cup. Meals were gargantuan; on festival days, as many as seventy dishes might be served at the Tsar's table. Zakuski, or hors d'oeuvres, included raw vegetables, especially cucumbers, salted fish, bacon and innumerable pirozhki, sometimes stuffed with egg, fish, rice or cabbage and herbs instead of meat. Then came soups and roasts of beef, mutton and pork, seasoned with onion, garlic, saffron and pepper. There were dishes of game and fish such as salmon, sturgeon and sterlet. Dessert was cakes, cheeses, preserves, fruits. Russians drank mostly vodka, beer or a milder drink called kvas, made of fermented black bread, variously flavored with raspberry, cherry or other fruits.

But Alexis rarely touched any of the succulent dishes that were presented to him. Instead, he sent them as presents to various boyars to show special favor. His own palate was monastically simple. He ate only plain rye bread and drank light wine or beer, perhaps with a few drops of cinnamon added; cinnamon, Dr. Collins reported, was the "aroma imperiale." During periods of religious fasting, said Dr. Collins, the Tsar "eats but three meals a week; for the rest, he takes a piece of brown bread and salt, a pickled mushroom or cucumber and drinks a cup of small beer. He eats fish but twice in Lent and observes it seven weeks altogether. . . . In fine, no monk is more observant of canonical hours than he is of fasts. We may reckon he fasts almost eight months in twelve."

Following dinner, the Tsar slept for three hours until time to return to church for vespers, again with his boyars, again to consult on affairs of state during the religious service. Supper and the end of the day were spent either with his family or with intimate friends playing backgammon or chess. Alexis' special pleasure during these hours was to listen to people read or tell stories. He liked hearing passages from books of church history, or the lives of saints, or the presentation of religious dogma, but he also liked to hear the reports of Russian ambassadors traveling abroad, extracts from foreign newspapers or simple tales told by pilgrims and wanderers who had been brought to the palace to entertain the monarch. In warmer weather, Alexis left the Kremlin to visit his country mansions outside Moscow. One of these at Preobrazhenskoe on the Yauza River was the center of Alexis' favorite sport, falconry. Over the years, the enthusiastic huntsman built up an immense establishment of 200 falconers, 3,000 falcons and 100,000 pigeons.

Most of the time, however, Alexis prayed and worked. He never questioned his own divinely granted right to rule; in his mind, he and all monarchs were chosen by God and responsible only to God.* Beneath the tsar stood the nobility, divided into almost a dozen ranks. The greatest noblemen held the highest rank, that of boyar, and were members of the old princely families who held hereditary landed estates. Below were the lesser aristocracy and gentry who had been given estates in return for service. There was a small middle class of merchants, artisans

*When the English Parliamentarians cut off the head of King Charles I, in 1649, Tsar Alexis was so shocked and personally outraged that he expelled all English merchants from the interior of Russia, a move which gave great advantage to Dutch and German merchants. While King Charles II remained in exile, Alexis sent him money and his tenderest wishes for "the disconsolate widow of that glorious martyr, King Charles I."

and other townspeople and then—the huge base of the pyramid—the peasants and serfs who made up the overwhelming mass of Russian society; their conditions of life and methods of farming were roughly similar to those of those serfs of medieval Europe. Most Muscovites used the title "boyar" to include all noblemen and high officials. Meanwhile, the actual daily work of administering the tsar's government was in the hands of between thirty and forty departments known as Prikazy. Generally speaking, they were inefficient, wasteful, overlapping, difficult to control and corrupt—in brief, a bureaucracy which nobody had designed and over which no one had any real control.

From his dimly lit, incense-scented Kremlin rooms and chapels, Tsar Alexis ruled the largest nation on earth. Vast plains, endless tracts of dark forest and boundless expanses of desert and tundra stretched from Poland to the Pacific. Nowhere in this immensity of space was the wide horizon broken by more than shallow mountains and rolling hills. The only natural barriers to movement on the broad plain were the rivers, and from the earliest times these had been converted into a network of watery highways. In the region around Moscow, four great rivers had their tributary headwaters: the Dnieper, the Don and the mighty Volga flowed south to the Black and the Caspian seas; the Dvina flowed north to the Baltic and the frozen Arctic.

Scattered over this immense landscape was a thin sprinkling of human beings. At the time of Peter's birth—near the end of Tsar Alexis' reign—the population of Russia was roughly eight million people. This was about the same as that of Russia's western neighbor, Poland, although the Russians were dispersed over a far greater area. It was much larger than the population of Sweden (less than two million) or England (slightly more than five million), but less than half that of the most populous and powerful state in Europe, the France of Louis XIV (nineteen million). A fraction of the Russian population lived in the old Russian towns—Nizhni-Novgorod, Moscow, Novgorod, Pskov, Vologda, Archangel, Yaroslavl, Rostov, Vladimir, Suzdal, Tver, Tula—and in the more recently acquired Kiev, Smolensk, Kazan and Astrachan. Most of the people lived on the land, where they wrenched a living from the earth, the forest and the waters.

Enormous though Alexis' tsardom was, Russia's boundaries were fragile and under pressure. In the east, under Ivan the Terrible and his successors, Muscovy had conquered the middle Volga and the khanate of Kazan, extending the Russian empire to Astrachan and the Caspian Sea. The Urals had been crossed and the immense, largely empty spaces of Siberia added to the tsar's domain. Russian pioneers had penetrated to the northern Pacific and established a few bleak settlements there, although a clash with the aggressive Manchu Dynasty of China had forced a withdrawal of Russian outposts along the Amur River.

To the west and the south, Russia was ringed by enemies who struggled to keep the giant landlocked and isolated. Sweden, then reigning as Mistress of the Baltic, stood guard across this seaborne road to the West. Westward lay Catholic Poland, the ancient enemy of Orthodox Russia. Only recently, Tsar Alexis had reconquered Smolensk from Poland, although that Russian fortress town lay a mere 150 miles from Moscow. Late in his reign, Alexis had won back from Poland the shining prize of Kiev, mother of all Russian cities and the birthplace of Russian Christianity. Kiev and the fertile regions both east and west of the Dnieper were the lands of the Cossacks. These were Orthodox people, originally vagabonds, freebooters and runaways who had fled the onerous conditions of life in old Muscovy to form bands of irregular cavalry and then to become pioneers, colonizing farms, villages and towns throughout the upper Ukraine. Gradually, this line of Cossack settlements was spreading southward, but the limits still were 300 or 400 miles above the shores of the Black Sea.

The ground in between, the famous black-earth steppe of the lower Ukraine, was empty. Here, tall grasses grew so high that sometimes only the head and shoulders of a man on horseback could be seen moving along above the grass. In Alexis' day, this steppe was the hunting and grazing ground of the Crimean Tatars, Islamic descendants of the old Mongol conquerors and vassals of the Ottoman sultan, who lived in villages along the slopes and among the crags of the mountainous Crimean peninsula. Every spring and summer, they brought their cattle and horses down to feed on the steppe grasslands. Often enough, they strapped on their bows, arrows and scimitars and rode north to raid and plunder among the Russian and Ukrainian villages, sometimes storming the wooden stockade of a town and leading the entire population off into slavery. These massive raids, bringing thousands of Russian slaves annually into the Ottoman slave markets, were a source of embarrassment and anguish to the tsars in the Kremlin. But there was nothing so far that anyone could do. Indeed, twice, in 1382 and 1571, the Tatars had sacked and burned Moscow itself.

Beyond the massive white Kremlin battlements, beyond the gilt and blue onion domes and the wooden buildings of Moscow lay the fields and the forest, the true and eternal Russia. For centuries, everything had come from the forest, the deep, rich, virgin forest which stretched as far as an ocean. Amidst its birches and firs, its bushes with berries, its mosses and soft ferns, the Russian found most of what he needed for life. From the forest came logs for his house and firewood for warmth, moss to chink his walls, bark for his shoes, fur for his clothing, wax for his candles, and meat, sweet honey, wild berries and mushrooms for his dinner. Through most of the year, the forest groves rang with the sound of axes. On lazy summer days, men, women and children searched beneath the dark trunks for mushrooms, or brushed through the high grasses and flowers to pick wild raspberries and red and black currants.

Russians are a communal people. They did not live alone deep in the forest, contesting the primeval weald with wolf and bear. Rather they chose to cluster in tiny villages built in forest clearings, or on the edges of lakes or the banks of slow-moving rivers. Russia was an empire of such villages: lost at the end of a dusty road, surrounded by pasture and meadowland, a collection of simple log houses centered on a church whose onion dome gathered up the prayers of the villagers and passed them along to heaven. Most of the houses had only a single room without a chimney; smoke from the fire burning inside the stove found its way outdoors as best it could, through cracks in the logs. Usually, as a result, everything and everyone inside was black with soot. For this reason, too, public baths were a common institution in Russia. Even the smallest village had its steaming bathhouse where men and women together could scrub themselves clean and then go outside, even in winter, to permit the wind to cool and dry their heated, naked bodies.

When the Russian peasant dressed, first combing his beard and hair, he put on a shirt of rough cloth which hung over his waist and was tied with a string. His trousers were loose and were stuffed into boots if he owned them, or, more often, into cloth leggings tied with heavy threads. "Their hair is cropt to their ears and their heads covered winter and summer with a fur cap," wrote a Western visitor. "Their beards remain yet untouched. . . . Their shoes are tied together with bast. About their neck they wear from the time of their baptism a cross, and next to it their purse, though they commonly keep the small money, if it be not much, a good while in their mouth, for as soon as they receive any, either as a present, or as their due, they put it into their mouths and keep it under their tongue."

Few people in the world live in such harmony with nature as the Russians. They live in the North, where winter comes early. In September, the light is fading by four in the afternoon and an icy rain begins. Frost comes quickly, and the first snow falls in October. Before long, everything vanishes beneath a blanket of whiteness: earth, rivers, roads, fields, trees and houses. Nature takes on not only a majesty but a frightening omnipotence. The landscape becomes a broad white sea with mounds and hollows rising and falling. On days when the sky is gray, it is hard, even straining the eye, to see where earth merges with air. On brilliant days, when the sky is a gorgeous azure, the sunlight is blinding, as if millions of diamonds were scattered on the snow, refracting light.

After 160 days of winter, spring lasts only for several weeks. First the ice cracks and breaks on rivers and lakes, and the murmuring waters, the dancing waves return. On land, the thaw brings mud, an endless, vast sea of mud through which man and beast must struggle. But every day the dirty snow recedes, and soon the first sprouts of green grass appear. Forest and meadows turn green and come to life. Animals, larks and swallows reappear. In Russia, the return of spring is greeted with a joy inconceivable in more temperate lands. As the warming rays of the sun touch meadow grass and the backs and faces of peasants, as the days rapidly grow longer and the earth everywhere is coming to life, the glad feeling of revival, of deliverance, urges people to sing and celebrate. The 1st of May is an ancient holiday of rebirth and fertility when people dance and wander in the woods. And while youth revels, the older people thank God that they have lived to see this glory again.

Spring races quickly into summer. There is great heat and choking dust, but there is also the loveliness of an immense sky, the calm of the great land rolling gently to the horizon. There is the freshness of early morning, the coolness of shade in groves of birches or along the rivers, the mild air and warm wind of night. In June, the sun dips beneath the horizon for only a few hours and the red of sunset is followed quickly by the delicate rose-and-blue blush of dawn.

Russia is a stern land with a harsh climate, but few travelers can forget its deep appeal, and no Russian ever finds peace in his soul anywhere else on earth.

born in New York City in 1927, Peter Matthiessen published his first short story, written in his Daily Themes class, in the *Atlantic Monthly* in 1951, the year after he graduated from Yale. Since then he has published and traveled widely. His first novel, *Race Rock,* appeared in 1954 and was followed by *Partisans* (1955), *Raditzer* (1961), *At Play in the Fields of the Lord* (1965), *Far Tortuga* (1975), *Killing Mister Watson* (1990), *Lost Man's River* (1997), and *Bone in Bone* (1999). Among his many nonfiction books—he is the preeminent naturalist writer of our time—are *The Snow Leopard* (1978), which won a National Book Award, *In the Spirit of Crazy Horse* (1983), and *African Silences* (1991). "At New Haven," he writes, "I was an English major (with a strong side interest in zoology and ornithology courses at the Peabody Museum) and I co-wrote a hunting-fishing column for the *Yale Daily News.* Alas, in terms of higher education, I was a near ne'er-do-well, and never made the most of my Yale years, being more concerned with the excellent dry martinis at the Fence Club and my beautiful girlfriend at Smith College, whom I had met in Paris on our Junior Year Abroad. Fortunately, the final exam question concerned Faulkner, and I actually knocked out a good paper, or at least one sufficiently superior to my earlier endeavors that my exasperated professor, Norman Holmes Pearson, summoned me to the Grad School and chewed me out—'Where the hell have you been for the past three years? You could have won the English Prize!'—or words to that effect. I liked Pearson because he was a maverick and because he'd been a friend of my kinsman, the Harvard professor F. O. Matthiessen, who had jumped out of a hotel window the previous year (1949), leaving his Skull and Bones ring on the windowsill."

I

He comes by train out of the wilderness of cities, he has come from abroad this very day. At mid-life he has returned to a hometown where he knows no one.

The train tugs softly, slides away, no iron jolt and bang as in his childhood, no buck and yank of couplings, only a gathering clickety-click away along the glinting track, away along the river woods, the dull shine of the water, north and away toward the great bend in the Hudson.

Looking north, he thinks, The river has lost color. The track is empty, the soft late summer sunshine fills the bend, the day is isolate.

He is the one passenger left on the platform, exposed to the bare windows of Arcadia. He might be the one survivor of a cataclysm, emerging into the flat sun of the river street at the foot of this steep decrepit town fetched up against the railroad tracks on the east slope of the Hudson River Valley. What he hasn't remembered in the years he has been gone is the hard bad colors of its houses, the dirtied brick and fire bruises of the abandoned factory, the unbeloved dogs, the emptiness.

On this railroad street, a solitary figure with a suitcase might attract attention. To show that his business is forthright, he crosses the old cobbles quickly to the salesmen's hotel at the bottom of the downhill slide of human habitation. The dependent saloon has a boarded-up side door marked "Ladies Entrance," and the lobby reminds him, not agreeably, of looted colonial hotels in the new Africa that he supposes he will never see again.

The stranger's soft voice and quiet suit, his discreet manner, excite the suspicion of the clerk, who puts down a mop to shuffle behind the desk and slap out a registration form. This dog-eared old man spies on the name as it is being written. "We got a park here by that name," he says.

The man shakes his head as if shaking off the question. Asked where he's from, he says he has lived abroad. The foreign service. Africa.

"Africa," the clerk says, licking a forefinger and flicking the sports pages of a New York daily. "You'll feel right at home, then." He reads a while as if anticipating protest. "Goddam Afros overflowing right out of the city. Come up this way from Yonkers, come up at night along the river."

Nodding at his own words, the clerk looks up. "You have a wife?"

"I saw them," the stranger says. At Spuyten Duyvil, where the tracks emerged from the East River and turned north up the Hudson, black men had watched his train from the track sidings. The stranger's fingertips lie flat upon the counter as if he meant to spring into the air. "They were fishing," he says.

He is a well-made man of early middle age and good appearance, controlled and quiet in his movements. Dry blond hair is combed across a sun-scarred bald spot.

"Fishing," the clerk says, shaking his head. "I guess you learned to like 'em over there."

The man says nothing. He has shallow and excited eyes. He awaits his key.

Irritable and jittery under that gaze, the clerk picks out a key with yellowed fingers. "How many nights?"

The man shrugs. Who knows? Asked if he wishes to see the room, he shrugs again. He will see it soon enough. When he produces a thick roll of bills to pay the cash deposit in advance, the old man inspects the bills, lip curled, checking the stranger's face at the same time. Still holding the cash as if in evidence, he leans over the desk to glare at the large old-fashioned leather suitcase.

The stranger says, "I'll take it up. It's heavy."

"I'll bet," says the clerk, shaking his head over the weight he had almost been asked to hump up the steep stair. He snaps open the next page of his paper. "Bathroom down the hall."

On the floor above, the man listens a moment, wondering briefly why he sets people on edge even before trouble occurs. Their eyes reflect the distemper he is feeling.

He opens, closes, bolts the transomed door.

The room is penitential, it is high-ceilinged and skinny, with defunct fire pipes, no pictures, a cold-water sink, a scrawny radiator, a ruined mirror on the wall. The water-marked walls are the color of blue milk. The bedside table is so small that there is no room for a lamp. The Gideon Bible sits in the chipped washbasin. A rococo ceiling fixture overhead, a heavy dark armoire, an iron bed with a stained spread of slick green nylon.

The pieces stand in stiff relation, like spare mourners at a funeral whom no one is concerned to introduce.

His reflected face in the pocked mirror is unforgiving.

The room has no telephone, and there will be no visitors. He has no contacts in this place, which is as it should be. Checking carefully for surveillance devices, he realizes the precaution is absurd, desists, feels incomplete, finishes anyway.

Big lonesome autumn flies buzz on the windowsill. The high bare window overlooks the street, the empty railroad station, the river with its sour burden of industrial filth carried down from bleak ruined upstate valleys. Across the river the dark cliffs of the Palisades wall off the sky.

His mother had not felt well enough to see him off, nor had his father driven him down to the station. The Assistant Secretary for African Affairs had wished to walk his English setter, and had walked his son while he was at it.

We want you to gain the Prime Minister's confidence. He may trust you simply because you are my son.

Unfortunately the more . . . boyish? . . . elements in our government want another sort of prime minister entirely. They are sure to find some brutal flunky who, for a price, will protect Western interests.

The Assistant Secretary had not waited for the train.

Make the most of this opportunity, young man.

By which he meant, *You have this chance to redeem yourself, thanks to my influence.*

The gardener had brought the leather suitcase. From the empty platform they watched his father stride away. At the north end of the street, the tall straight figure passed through the iron gate into the park.

The gardener cried, *So it's off to Africa ye are! And what will ye be findin there, I'm askin?*

Turning from the window, he removes his jacket, drapes it on a chair; he does not remove the shoulder holster, which is empty. He contemplates the Assistant Secretary's ancient suitcase as if the solution to his life were bundled up in it.

He unpacks his clothes, takes out a slim chain, locks and binds the suitcase, chains it to the radiator.

On the bed edge he sits upright for a long time as if expecting something. He has trained himself to wait immobile hour after hour, like a sniper, like a roadside African, like a poised hawk, ready for its chance, thinking of nothing.

A dying fly comes to his face. It wanders. Its touch is weak and damp. He does not brush it away.

By the river at the north end of town is a public park established by his grandfather, at one time a part of the old Harkness estate. His father's great-uncle, in the nineteenth century, had bought a large tract of valleyside and constructed a great ark of a house with an uplifting view of the magnificent Palisades across the river, and his descendants had built lesser houses in the park, in one of which, as an only child, he had spent the first years of his life.

Not wishing to hurry, he does not go there on the first day, contenting himself with climbing the uphill street and buying a new address book. He must make sure that each day has its errand, that there is a point to every day, day after day.

Soon he visits the real-estate agent's office. The agent, a big man with silver hair slicked hard and puffy dimpled chin, concludes that the old Harkness property will have just the "estate" that Mr. . . .? might be looking for.

"Call me Ed," the agent says, sticking out his hand. The client shakes it after a brief pause but does not offer his name.

All but the river park presented to the village was sold off for development, the agent explains, when the last Harkness moved away some years before. But the

big trees and the big stone houses—the "manor houses," the agent calls them—
are still there, lending "class" to the growing neighborhood.

Mother says you are obliged to sell the house. I'd like to buy it.
Absolutely not!

The narrow road between high ivied walls was formerly the service driveway, and
the property the realtor has in mind is the gardener's brick cottage, which shares
the river prospect with "the big house" on the other side of an old stand of oak
and hickory.

As a child he fled his grandmother's cambric tea to take refuge in this cottage
full of cooking smells. His nurse was married to the gardener, and he knows at
once that he will buy the cottage even if the price is quite unreasonable. So gleeful is he in this harmony of fate that his fingers work in his coat pockets.

He has no wish to see the rooms until all intervening life has been cleaned out
of them. Before the agent can locate the keys, he says, "I'll take it."

When the agent protests—"You don't want to look inside?"—he counts off five
thousand dollars as a deposit and walks back to the car, slipping into the passenger seat, shutting the door.

Not daring to count or pocket so much cash, the agent touches the magic
bricks in disbelief. He pats the house as he might pat a horse and stands back
proudly. "Nosir, they don't make 'em like this, not anymore."

The one thing missing here is burglar lights, the agent says—a popular precaution these days, he assures his client, climbing back into the car. Like the man at
the hotel, he evokes the human swarm emerging from the slums and coming up
along the river woods at night. "Engage in criminal activity," he emphasizes
when the other man, by his silence, seems to question this.

"Ready to go?" the client says, looking out the window.

On the way home he inquires about New York State law in regard to shooting
burglars, and the agent laughs. "Depends on his color," he says, and nudges his
client, and wishes he had not. "Don't get me wrong," he says.

Back at the office the agent obtains the buyer's name to prepare the contract.
"You've come to the right place, all right! Any relation, Mr. Harkness?"

The man from Africa ignores the question. He will reveal that he belongs here
in his own good time. First he wants everything to be in place, the little house, its
furnishings, his history. The place will be redone in the style of the big house
across the hedge, with English wallpapers, old walnut furniture, big thick towels
and linen sheets, crystal and porcelain, such as his parents might have left him,
setting off the few good pieces he had put in storage after their deaths. The inside

walls will be painted ivory, as the house was, and the atmosphere will be sunny and cheerful, with an aura of fresh mornings in the spring.

Once the cottage is ready, his new life will commence, and the names of new friends will flower in his address book.

To his childhood house he wishes to return alone, on foot. Since he means to break in, he makes sure that he leaves the hotel unobserved, that he is not followed. Not that there is anyone to follow him, it is simply a good habit, sound procedure.

He enters the park by the iron gate beyond the railroad station, climbing transversely across a field, then skirting an old boxwood border so as not to be seen by the unknown people who have taken over his uncle's house. He trusts the feel of things and not his sight, for nothing about this shrunken house looks quite familiar. It was always a formal, remote house, steep-roofed and angular, but now it has the dark of rottenness, of waterlogged wood.

He hurries on, descending past the stables (no longer appended to his uncle's house or frequented by horses, to judge from the trim suburban cars parked at the front). In the old pines stands a grotesque disc of the sort recommended to him by his would-be friend the agent, drawing a phantasmagoria of color from the heavens.

He is seeking a childhood path down through the wood, across the brook, and uphill through the meadow.

From the trees come whacks and pounding, human cries.

A paddle-tennis court has spoiled the brook, which is now no more than an old shadow line of rocks and broken brush. Wary of his abrupt appearance, his unplayful air—or perhaps of a stranger not in country togs, wearing unsuitable shoes for a country weekend—the players challenge him. Can they be of help?

He says he is looking for the Harkness house.

"Who?" one man says.

Calling the name—*Harkness!*—through the trees, hearing his own name in his own voice, makes him feel vulnerable as well as foolish, and his voice is thickened by a flash of anger. He thinks, I have lost my life while soft and sheltered men like these dance at their tennis.

He manages a sort of smile, which fails to reassure them. They look at each other, they look back at him. They do not resume playing.

"Harkness," one man says finally, cocking his head. "That was long ago. My grandfather knew your father. Something like that."

Dammit, he thinks. Who said that was my name!

Now the players bat the ball, rally a little. He knows they watch him as he skirts the court and leaves the trees and climbs the lawn toward the stone house set against the hillside at the ridge top.

His father's house has a flagstone terrace with a broad prospect of the Hudson. It is a good-sized stone house, with large cellar rooms, a downstairs, upstairs, and a third story with servants' rooms and attic. Yet even more than his uncle's place it seems diminished since his childhood. Only the great red oak at this south end of the house seems the right size, which confuses him until he realizes that in the decades he has been away it has grown larger.

In a snapshot of himself beneath this tree, in baggy shorts, he brandishes a green garden stake shoved through the hole of a small flower pot, used as a hand guard. He is challenging to a duel the Great Dane, Inga.

The oak stands outside the old "sun room," with its player piano and long boxes of keyed scrolls, and a bare parquet floor for children's games and tea dancing. The world has changed since a private house had a room designed for sun and dancing.

The weather-greened cannon are gone from the front circle. Once this staid house stood alone, but now low dwellings can be seen, crowding forward like voyeurs through what is left of the thin woods farther uphill.

Completing the circuit of the house, he arrives at the formal garden—"the autumn garden," his mother called it, with its brick wall and flowered gate, its view down across the lawn to the woods and river. The garden is neglected, gone to weeds. Though most are fallen, his mother's little faded signs that identified the herb species still peep from a coarse growth of goldenrod, late summer asters.

In other days, running away, he had hidden past the dusk in the autumn garden, peering out at the oncoming dark, waiting for a voice to call him into the warm house. They knew his ways, and no one ever called. Choked with self-pity, a dull yearning in his chest, he would sneak up the back stairs without his supper.

The boiler room has an outside entrance under the broad terrace, on the downhill side. He draws on gloves to remove a pane, lever the lock. He crosses the spider-shrouded light to the cellar stair and enters the cold house from below, turning the latch at the top of the stair, edging the door open to listen. He steps into the hall. The house feels hollow, and white sheets hide the unsold furniture. In the kitchen he surprises an old cockroach, which scuttles beneath the pipes under the sink.

The silence follows him around the rooms. On his last visit before his father sold the house, faint grease spots still shone through the new paint on the ceiling of his former bedroom. Sometimes, sent up to his room for supper, he had used a banged spoon as a catapult to stick the ceiling with rolled butter pats and peanut-butter balls.

From his parents' bedroom, from the naked windows, he gazes down over the lawn, standing back a little to make sure he is unseen. The court is empty. He is still annoyed that the paddle-tennis players have his name. Possibly they are calling the police. To be arrested would reflect badly on his judgment, just when he has asked if there might be an assignment for him someplace else.

Hearing a car, he slips downstairs and out through the cellar doors.

"Looking for somebody?"

The caretaker stands in the service driveway by the corner of the house. He wears a muscle-tight black T-shirt and big sideburns. He is wary, set for trouble, for he comes no closer.

Had this man seen him leave the house?

He holds the man's eye, keeping both hands in his coat pockets, standing motionless, dead silent, until uneasiness seeps into the man's face.

"I got a call. The party said there was somebody lookin' for someone."

"Can't help you, I'm afraid." Casually he shrugs and keeps on going, down across the lawn toward the brook.

"Never seen them signs?" the man calls after him, when the stranger is a safe distance away. "What do you want around here, mister?"

2

With some idea of returning to the hotel by walking south beside the tracks, he makes his way down along the brook, his street shoes slipping on the aqueous green and sunshined leaves.

Whenever, in Africa, he thought of home, what he recalled most clearly was this brook below the house and a sandy eddy where the idle flow was slowed by his rock dam. Below this pool, the brook descended through dark river woods to a culvert that ran beneath the tracks into the Hudson. Lit by a swift sun that passed over the trees, the water crossed the golden sand—the long green hair of algae twined on bobbing stems, the clean frogs and quick fishes and striped ribbon snakes—the flow so clear that the diadem of a water skater's shadow would be etched on the sunny sand glinting below. One morning a snake seized a small frog—still a tadpole, really, a queer thing with new-sprouted legs and a thick tail—and swallowed it with awful gulps of its unhinged jaws. Another day, another year, perhaps, peering into the turmoil in a puff of sunlit sand of the stream bottom, he saw a minnow in the mouth and claws of a mud-colored dragon. The dragonfly nymph loomed in his dreams for years thereafter, and he hated the light-filled creature it became, the crazy sizzle of the dragonfly's glass wings, the unnatural hardness of this thing when it struck the skin.

For hours he would hunch upon a rock, knees to his ears, staring at the passages and deaths. Sometimes he thought he would like to study animals. How remote this dark brook was from the Smiling Pool in his Peter Rabbit book up in the nursery, a meadow pool all set about with daffodils and roses, birds, fat bumblebees, where mirthful frogs, fun-loving fish, and philosophical turtles fulfilled their life on earth without a care.

Even then he knew that Peter Rabbit was a mock-up of the world, meant to fool children.

Nearing the railroad, the old brook trickles free from the detritus, but the flow is a mere seepage, draining into a black pool filled with oil drums. An ancient car, glass-shattered, rust-colored, squats low in the thick Indian summer undergrowth where once—or so his father said—an Algonkin band had lived in a log village.

In the sun and silence of the river, he sits on the warm trunk of a fallen willow, pulling mean burrs from his city trousers. From here he can see across the tracks to the water and the Palisades beyond. Perhaps, he thinks, those sugar-maple yellows and hot hickory reds along the cliffs welcomed Henry Hudson, exploring upriver with the tide four centuries before, in the days when this gray flood—at that time blue—swirled with silver fishes.

Hudson's ship—or so his father always claimed—had an elephant chained on the foredeck, an imposing present for the anticipated Lord of the Indies. Turned back at last by the narrowing river from his quest for the Northwest Passage, fed up with the task of gathering two hundred pounds of daily fodder for an animal that daily burdened the small foredeck with fifteen to twenty mighty shits—his father's word, in its stiff effort at camaraderie, had astonished and delighted him—Henry the Navigator had ordered the elephant set free in the environs of present-day Poughkeepsie. Strewing its immense sign through the woods, blaring its longing for baobab trees to the rigid pines, the great beast surely took its place in Algonkin legend.

Misreading his son's eager smile, his father checked himself, sighed crossly, and stood up. *A vigorous Anglo-Saxon term, not necessarily a dirty word to be leered and giggled at. You should have outgrown all that by now.* He left the room before the boy found words to undo such awful damage.

Beyond the misted trees, upriver, lies Tarrytown—Had someone tarried there? his mother asked his father, purling demurely. Why his father smiled at this he did not know. From Tarrytown one might see across the water to the cliffs where Rip Van Winkle had slept for twenty years. As a child he imagined a deep warm cleft full of autumn light, sheltered from the northeast storms and northwest winds. He peers across the mile of water, as if that shelter high up in clean mountains were still there.

In the Indian summer mist the river prospect looks much as he remembered it—indeed, much as it had been portrayed by the Hudson River School of painters so admired by his maternal grandmother. *Atrocious painters, all of them,* his father said. The small landscape of this stretch of river—was that in the crate of family things he had in storage? How much he has lost track of, in those years away.

He places a penny on the railroad track.

He longs to reassemble things—well, not "things" so much as continuity, that was his mother's word. Her mother had been raised on the west banks of the Hudson, and she could recall, from her own childhood, her great-aunt relating how *her* grandmother had seen Alexander Hamilton sculling downriver one fine morning just below their house—"Good day, Mr. Hamilton!"—and how Mr. Hamilton had never returned, having lost his life that day to Mr. Burr in a duel at Weehawken.

His father loved this story, too, the more so because that reach of river cliff had changed so little in the centuries between. For both of them, the memory of Mr. Hamilton had an autumnal melancholy that reached far back across the nation's history, to the Founding Fathers.

It seemed he had not responded to it properly.

I suppose you find it merely quaint, his mother said.

At one time he attended Sunday school here in Arcadia, and he thinks he will rejoin the Episcopal Church. On sunny Sundays in white shirt and sober suit he will find himself sustained and calmed by stained-glass windows and Bach organ preludes. Afterward he will return to the garden cottage with its antique furniture, blue flowers in white rooms, fine editions, rare music, and a stately dog thumping its tail on a warm rug. He envisions an esoteric text, a string quartet, a glass of sherry on a sunlit walnut table in the winter—his parents' tastes, he realizes, acquired tastes he is determined to acquire.

In this civilized setting, smoking a pipe, he will answer questions from young women about Africa, and the nature of Africans, and how to deal judiciously with these Afro-Americans, so-called. Those who imagine that Africans are inferior do not know Africans, he'll say. Africans have their own sort of intelligence, they are simply not interested in the same things we are. Once their nature is understood, he'll say, Africans are Africans, wherever you find them, never mind what these bleeding-hearts may tell you.

A train comes from the north, clicketing by, no longer dull coal black, as in his childhood, but a tube of blue-and-silver cars, no light between. In his childhood he could make out faces, but with increased speed the human beings are pale blurs behind the glass, and nobody waves to the man on the dead tree by the railroad tracks.

The wind and buffet of the train, the sting of grit, intensify his sense of isolation. To his wave, the train responds with a shrill whistle that is only a signal to the station at Arcadia, a half mile south.

He gets up, stretching, hunts the penny. It glints at him among the cinders. Honest Abe, tarnished by commerce, has been wiped right off the copper, replaced by a fiery smooth shine.

Looking north and south, he picks his way across the tracks. The third rail—if such it is—is a sheathed cable between pairs of rails marked "Danger Zone 700 Volts." Has the voltage increased since his childhood? *If you so much as point at that third rail,* explained his mother, who worried about his solitary expeditions to the river, *you'll be electrocuted, like one of those ghastly criminals up at Sing-Sing!* He hesitates before he crosses, stepping over this rail higher than necessary.

The tracks nearest the river are abandoned, a waste of rusted rails and splintered oaken ties and hard dry weeds. Once across, he can see north to the broad bend where a shoulder of the Palisades juts out from the far shore into the Tappan Zee. A thick new bridge has been thrust across the water, cutting off the far blue northern mountains. In his childhood, a white steamer of the Hudson River Day Line might loom around that bend at any moment, or a barge of bright tomato-red being towed by a pea-green tug, both fresh as toys. His father would evoke the passage of Robert Fulton's steamship *Claremont,* and the river trade on this slow concourse, flowing south out of the far blue mountains.

In his own lifetime—is this really true?—the river has changed from blue to a dead gray-brown, so thickened with inorganic silt that a boy would not see his own feet in the shallows. The agent, not a local man but full of local lore, asserts that the Atlantic salmon have vanished from the Hudson, and that the striped bass and shad are so contaminated by the poisons dumped into these waters by the corporations that people are prohibited from eating them. Only the blacks, says he, come out to fish for them, prowling the no-man's-land of tracks and cinders.

A grit beach between concrete slabs of an old embankment is scattered with worn tires. He wonders, as his father had, at the sheer number of these tires, brought by forces unknown so very far from the roads and highways and dumped in low woods and spoiled sullen waters all across America, as if, in the ruined wake of the course of empire, the tires had spun away in millions down the highways and rolled off the bridges into the rivers and down into deep swamps of their own accord.

But the horizon is oblivious, the clouds are white, the world rolls on. Under the cliffs, the bend is yellow in the glow of maples, and the faraway water, reflecting the autumn sky, is gold and blue. Soiled though they are, the shining woods and glinting water and the bright steel tracks, the high golden cliffs across the river, seem far more welcoming than the valley slope above, with its tight driveways, smelly cars, vigilant houses.

For a long time, by the riverside, he sits on a drift log worn smooth by the flood, withdrawn into the dream of Henry Hudson's clear blue river, of that old

America off to the north toward the primeval mountains, off to the west under the shining sky.

3

The real-estate agent has persuaded him to come to dinner, to celebrate his move into the cottage, and a van has delivered a large crate containing what is left of the family things. On a journey home after his father's death, he had got rid of everything else, glad to have Arcadia behind him. But when his years in Africa were ended, and he was faced with a return to the United States, where he knew no one, this crate, in his imagination, had overflowed with almost everything from childhood. However, all he finds are a few small antiques that could not be sold quickly yet had seemed too valuable to abandon. There are also a few unaccountable small scraps—a baby-blue bathroom rug with faded bears, the Peter Rabbit book, the photograph of his duel with the Great Dane Inga.

His grandmother's riverscape is jammed in carelessly, its gold frame chipped. Wrapped around his father's Hardy reels and .410 Purdy shotgun is the Assistant Secretary's worn-out hunting jacket, the silver brandy flask still in the pocket, the hard brown canvas and scuffed corduroy irrevocably stained with gun oil, bird blood, and the drool of setter dogs.

The riverscape is hung over the mantel, with the Purdy on oak dowel pins beneath. He likes the feel of the quick gun, with its walnut stock and blue-black finish, its fine chasing. He will keep it loaded, as a precaution against looters and marauders. Agent Ed has advised him to emulate the plump homes of his neighbors, which are walleyed with burglar lights, atremble with alarms.

However, he hates all that night glare, he feels less protected than exposed. As soon as his pistol permit is restored—he concocts this plan over his evening whiskeys—he'll use a silencer to extinguish every burglar light in the whole neighborhood.

Why scare off marauders, he asks Mrs. Ed at supper, when the death of one burglar at the hands of a private citizen would do more to prevent crime than all the floodlights in Westchester County? He has said this for fun, to alarm this upstate couple. Poor Ed loves this dangerous talk, having no idea that his guest means it, and as for the hostess, the woman is agog, her eyes loom huge and round behind her spectacles.

"You're such a . . . well, a *disturbing* man!" she says.

"Disturbed *me* from the very first day I met him!" Ed cries jovially to soften his wife's inadvertent candor. "I suppose you're waiting for a new foreign service job?"

"There won't be one," he says abruptly, as if admitting this to himself for the first time.

He drinks the whiskey he has carried to the table. That these folks want a Harkness for a friend is all too plain. He picks up the wine, sips it, blinks, pulls his head back from it, sets his glass down again. "A bit sweet," he explains, when her stare questions him.

Ed jars the table and his face goes red with a resentment that he has avoided showing until now. "Well, shit," he says. "You're a damn snob," he says.

"Oh my." The woman does not take her round eyes off their guest.

Ed scrapes his chair back and goes to the front door and opens it. "We just thought you might be kind of lonely," Mrs. Ed mourns.

"Probably likes it that way," the agent says.

Things are awry again. Afraid of something, he takes a large swallow of wine and nods approvingly. "Not bad at all," he says, with a poor smile.

"It's not just the wine," the agent warns his wife. The woman has crossed her bare arms on her chest in the cold draft that wanders through the opened door.

"I was hoping you'd call me Henry," he says, drinking more wine. "Very nice," he says. She turns her face away, as if unable to look upon his desperation. "Forgive me," he says.

"Nosir," the voice says from the door. "Nosir, I don't think we will."

4

Not wanting his new house to be finished, leaving things undone, he takes long walks along suburban roads and drives. People stare to let him know they have their eye on him. Bad dogs run out. Even so, the walks are dull and pointless. More and more often he returns to the low river woods, the endless iron stretch of tracks, the silent river, flickered over by migrating swallows.

One day in October, he crosses the tracks and sits on a dock piling with twisted bolts, wrenched free by some upriver devastation. The piling's faint creosote smell brings back some childhood boat excursion, upriver through the locks of Lake Champlain.

The breeze is out of the northwest, and has an edge to it. With a fire-blackened scrap of siding, he scrapes out a shelter under the old pilings, partly hidden from the woods by the pale sumac saplings that struggle upward from the cinders.

In the early autumn afternoon, out of the wind, he is warmed by the westering sun across the river. If the beach litter were piled in front of him, he thinks, he would be unseen even from the water. Not that there is anyone to see him, it is just the sheltered feeling it would give him. The freighters headed up to Albany, the tugs and barges, an occasional fat white motor cruiser with its nylon Old Glory flying from the stern, pass too far offshore to be aware of a hat-shadowed face in a pile of flotsam.

He hunches down a little, squinting out between his knees.

He is safe and secret, sheltered from the world, just as he had been long ago in his tree houses and attic hideouts, in the spruce hollow in the corner behind the lode of packages under the Christmas tree, in warm nests in the high summer grass, peeping out at the Algonkin Indians. *Delawares,* his father said. *Algonkin is the language family.* In the daytime, at least, no one comes along the tracks. He has the river kingdom to himself. As to whether he is content, he does not know.

He has packed dry sherry in his father's silver flask, a sandwich, a hard apple, and also a new bleeding-heart account of modern politics in the former Belgian Congo. His name receives harsh passing mention. He thinks, To hell with it. I did what was asked of me. I did my duty. Having the courage to dirty one's hands, without glory and at great risk of ingratitude, may become one's higher duty to one's country, wasn't that true?

The trouble was, he had not liked Lumumba. He had wondered if the Prime Minister might be unstable. Lumumba's hostility toward Europeans flared and shuddered like a fire in the wind but never died. He ate distractedly in small brief fits, growing thinner and thinner. He was moody, loud, self-contradictory, he smoked too much hemp, he drank a lot, he took one woman after another despite his devotion to his wife, he could not stop talking or stand still.

Wild ducks pass by within gun range, flaring away from his little cove with hard quacks of alarm. He swings his arms as if holding a gun, and they crumple and fall in a downward arc as he follows through. Watching them fly onward, he feels an exhilaration tinged with loss that wild fowl still tried to migrate south along this shore of poisoned mud and rust and cinders. On a northeast wind, in rain, his hiding place would serve well as a duck blind, for in order to land into the wind the birds would hook around over the open water and come straight in to the gun.

More ducks appear farther upriver where the black stumps of an old dock jut from the surface. The long rust heads and silver-white bodies are magically unsullied in the somber water. There are five.

Needing something to look forward to, he decides upon a sacramental hunt. A hunter's stiff whiskey by the fire, the wild-duck supper with wild rice, the red Bordeaux from his mother's old colonial crystal decanter—thus will he consecrate the return of the Harkness family to Arcadia. Since it will happen only once, he can't be bothered with decoys, waders, far less a retriever. The river is too swift and deep to wade in, and in the unlikely event that a duck falls, the current is bound to carry it ashore.

To acquire a license to kill ducks he goes to Yonkers, not wishing to excite local curiosity. It seems absurd to bother about a license for one bird, when to shoot on the railroad right-of-way will be illegal in the first place. He applies for the permit for the same reason that he would feel obliged to retrieve and eat any bird he shot, rather than waste it. His father had been strict about licenses, bag limits, and using what one killed, even in the days when ducks were plentiful. To offend this code would violate the hunt ceremony in some way, make the supper pointless.

He has no proof of U.S. residence in the previous year—in the previous two decades, if it comes to that. He does not say this, lest his very citizenship be challenged by the hostile young black woman, who says he will have to identify himself, submit proof of residence, proof of citizenship. But he has no driver's license or certificate of birth, and can't tell her that his passport has been confiscated.

"Next!"

As for the huge hunting license, it looks nothing like the duck-stamp badge his father had worn upon his fishing hat. The new license is worn on the back, to facilitate identification by the game warden. Though he knows it is foolish, he feels he is being tricked into the open. One might as well wear a bull's-eye on one's back.

"Next!"

Are the authorities suggesting, he inquires, that the duck hunter is stupid as well as lawless, that he will shoot over his limit and make off with his booty, yet neglect to remove this grotesque placard from his back?

"We ain't suggesting nothing. That's the law." She waves him aside. "Next!"

He is surprised that the man behind him in the line is black.

"Move along please! Next!"

His stalling has permitted him to fold a twenty-dollar bill into his application form and ease it back across the counter, at the same time requesting her to be more careful how she talks to him. Raising her eyebrows at his tone, then at the money, she heaves around as if to summon her superior, giving him a chance to withdraw the bill. He does so quickly, winking at the black man, asking this female if he really requires proof that he is an American—doesn't he look like one?

With the back of her hand, she brushes away his application form, which flutters to the floor.

"I could bust you, mister. You just watch your step."

She is already processing the next application.

"*Everybody* looks American," she is saying. "*I* look American. And you know what, mister?" She looks up at him. "I *am* American. More than you." She points at the incomplete form in his hand. "I haven't lived in Africa for half my life."

Please do not confuse your activities in Africa with the foreign service, far less true service to your country, less still an honorable career that would make you a credit to this family.

When he raised his eyes, his mother averted hers. He flipped his father's note back at her, in a kind of spasm. The letter struck her at the collarbone and fell into her lap. She looked down at it for a long moment, then picked it up between two fingers and set it on the table. Her eyes glistened.

You've changed so, Henry, dear. When you went off to war, you grew so hard. It wasn't your fault, of course. Seeing all those dreadful things—it's enough to confuse anyone, *I'm sure!*

Before he could protest, she had slipped away from him.

You were such a lonely boy. How I wish you'd found somebody. Or become a naturalist! she added brightly. *Animals are so much easier, aren't they?*

Inappropriately, she tried to smile, as if to soothe him.

We shall always love you, dear.

His rivals killed him! he insisted. *Mother?* He had wanted to seize her, to shake from her frail body some pledge of loyalty. *Patrice was the Soviets' little macaque!*

She opened her eyes wide in mock astonishment—Patrice?

And your little Mr. Mobutu, dear? The dictator? Whose macaque is he?

He decides he will need decoys after all. His father's hand-carved balsa ducks, close-etched with wild colors, had been rigged with cedar keels and fine-smelling tarred cod line and square lead anchors on which the line was wrapped, leaving just enough room in the open center so that line and weight fitted neatly over bill and head. But sturdy wood decoys are no longer available, or not, at least, in these seedy river towns.

What are offered instead are swollen plastic mallards, drake mallards only, with heads the dead green of zinc alloy and the rest a bad industrial brown fit to attract those mongrel ducks that inhabited the dirty waters of the city parks and the pilings of old river docks in Yonkers. By means of gaudy plastic twine that would cut the hands in winter weather each duck is rigged to a scrap of pig iron, sure to drag in any sort of wind.

He cannot bring himself to acquire more than three (*Always set an odd number,* his father had said, *in case of a lone bird*), since he would not harbor such horrors in his house, and does not intend to hunt ever again. So irritated is he by wasting money on such rubbish that he feels justified in commandeering a rain parka in its slim packet and also a handful of shotgun shells.

At the cottage he finds a burlap sack for carrying and concealing the decoys, the dismantled gun, the shells, and a thermos of coffee in its leather case. That evening, he rigs a treble-hooked surf-casting lure on a length of line—a makeshift retrieval gear of his own devising.

Within a few days comes a forecast of northeast wind, with rain. Since his days are his own—the one activity left to him, now that the house is finished, is phoning for groceries, which are delivered daily—he will go hunting with the first change in the weather.

Bearing his sack over his shoulder like a burglar, he makes his way down toward the river. In the darkness, each house is fortified by its hard pool of light, and he half expects that his flashlight, spotted at the wood edge by some nosy oldster out of bed to pee, will bring police from all directions, filling the suburban night with whirling red, white, and blue beacons—the Nigger Hunters, as the hotel clerk referred to them, conveying contempt for cops and blacks alike.

In the woods he descends wet shadow paths, his sack catching and twisting in the thorns. At the track edge he peers north and south through a grim mist that hides him entirely from the world, then crosses the railroad to the river.

He lobs the decoys out upon the current, and the wind skids them quickly to the end of their strings, which swing too far inshore. In daybreak light, in choppy water, they in no way resemble three lorn ducks yearning for the companionship of a fourth.

He yanks his blind together, scrunching low as a train sweeps past toward the city. He feels clumsy, out of place, not nearly so well hidden as he had imagined. The upstate passengers, half-dozing in the fetid yellow light, cannot have seen him, though they stare straight at him through the grit-streaked windows. He breaks the light gun, loads two shells, and snaps it to, then sips his cup of coffee, peering outward.

As forecast, the wind is out of the northeast. Pale gulls sail past. But there is no rain, and the mist lifts, and the sun rises from the woods behind, filling the cliff faces across the river with a red-gold light.

The eerie windshine of the first day of a northeaster exposes the decoys for the poor things they are; the unnatural brightness of their anchor lines would flare a wild bird from five gunshots away. His folly is jeered at by clarion jays that cross back and forth among the yellow maples at the wood edge.

BANG

He has whirled and with a quick snap shot extinguished one of the jays, which flutters downward in the river woods like a blue leaf. He sinks back, strangely out of breath. And he is about to break his gun, retreat, slink home—he wants to drink—when there comes a small whispery sound, a small watery rush.

A black duck has landed just beyond the decoys. Struggling to make sense of its silent company, it quacks softly, turning back and forth. It rides the gray wavelets, wheat-colored head held high in wariness.

He has one shell left and no time to reload.

The gentle head switches back and forth, one eye seeking, then the other. In the imminence of the morning sun, in the wild light, the bird's tension holds the earth together.

The duck springs from the surface with a downward buffet of the wings. In one jump it is ten feet in the air, drops of water falling, silver-lined wings stretched to the wind that will whirl it out of range.

BANG

The dark wings close. The crumpled thing falls humbly to the surface, scarcely a splash, as the echo caroms from the cliffs across the river.

In the ringing silence, the river morning is resplendent. Time resumes, and the earth breathes again.

The duck floats upside down, head underwater, red legs on the bronze-black feathers twitching.

Not a difficult shot, his father would have said. *The trigger is squeezed when the bird levels off at the top of the jump, for just at that moment it seems almost motionless, held taut by wires—not a difficult shot.*

How often in his boyhood he had missed it, turning away so as not to see his father's mouth set at the corners. Then one day he outshot his father, finishing up with a neat double, trying not to grin.

With that second barrel he had overshot his limit. He had known this but could not resist, his father's good opinion had seemed more important. The Assistant Secretary's nod acknowledged the fine shot, but his voice said, *You've always been good at things, Henry. No need to be greedy.* It was no use blustering that he had followed through the double as his father had taught him. His father had no patience with excuses.

Often his mother felt obliged to say, *Your father's standards are so high, you see.* When he tried to ask just what she meant, she cut him off.

She smiled. *Sometimes what I think you lack is a sense of humor.*

He whirls his retrieval rig around his head and lets it go, looping the casting plug out beyond the duck, then tugging it back across the line of drift. On the third try it catches in the tail feathers and turns the bird around before pulling free. The next two tries are rushed, the last falls short.

The current has taken the diminished thing, it is moving more rapidly now, tending offshore.

Alone on the riverbank, peering about him, he takes a deep breath and regrets it, for the breath displaces his exhilaration, drawing into his lungs intuitions of final loneliness and waste and loss. That this black duck of the coasts and rivers should be reduced to a rotting tatter in the tidal flotsam, to be pulled at by the gulls, to be gnawed by rats, is not bearable, he cannot bear it, he veers from this bitter end of things with a grunt of pain. Or is it, he wonders, the waste that he cannot bear? Something else scares him: he dreads going home alone and empty-handed, to the life still to be lived in the finished cottage. If the hunt supper does not take place, nothing will follow.

Sooner or later, the black duck must enter an eddy and be brought ashore. Hiding the shells and thermos under the driftwood, abandoning the decoys to the river, he hurries down the tracks toward the city, gun across his shoulder.

The bird does not drift nearer, neither does it move out farther. Wind and current hold it in equilibrium, a dull dark thing like charred deadwood in the tidal water. Far ahead, the cliffs of both shores come together at the George Washington Bridge, and beyond the high arch, the sinking skyline of the river cities.

The world is littered with these puppet dictators of ours, protecting our rich business-men and their filthy ruination of poor countries, making obscene fortunes off the misery of the most miserable people on this earth!

The old man shifted his bones for a better look at his impassive son, as if he had forgotten who he was. He considered him carefully in a long mean silence. *Who do you really work for these days, Henry? What is it that you do, exactly?*

I am the government liaison with the western corporations.

And it's your idea, I'm told, that these corporations pay these governments for the right to dump their toxic wastes in Africa.

When his son was silent, the old man nodded. *I gather they pay you well for what you do.*

Mother says you are obliged to sell the house. I'd like to buy it.

Absolutely not! I'd sooner sell it to Mobutu!

Didn't you warn me once against idealism? The Cold War is not going to be won by the polite and passive intrigues of your day—

Stop that at once! Don't talk as if you had standards of your own—you don't! You're some damn kind of moral dead man! You don't know who the hell you are, and I don't either! You probably should have been an undertaker!

The old man rummaged his newspaper. When his son sat down by him, he drew his dressing gown closer. Stricken, he said, *Forgive me. Perhaps you cannot help what you have become. I asked too much of you, your mother says, I was too harsh.* He paused for a deep breath, then spoke shyly. *I'm sorry, Henry. Please don't come again.*

The mist has lifted, the sun rises.

Trudging south, he is overtaken by the heat, the early trains. In his rain parka with the stiff canvas beneath, lugging the gun, his body suffocates. It is his entire body, his whole being, that is growing angry. The trains roar past, they assail him with bad winds, faces stare stupidly. He waves them off, his curses lost in the trains' racketing. His jaw set in an iron rage, he concentrates on each railroad tie, tie after tie.

The dead bird is fifty yards offshore, bound for the sea. In the distance, the silver bridge glints in the mist. Nearer are the cliffs at Spuyten Duyvil, where the tracks turn eastward, following the East River. Once the bird had passed that channel mouth, he could only watch as it drifted down the west shore of Manhattan.

He trots a little. He can already see the rail yard and trestle where the tracks bend away under the cliffs.

5

There they are.

Perched on concrete slabs along the bank, thin dark-skinned figures turn dark heads to see this white man coming with a gun. Though the day is warm, they are wearing purple sweatshirts with sharp, pointed hoods drawn tight, as in some archaic sect in Abyssinia.

They pretend to ignore him, he ignores them, too. "Hey," one says, more or less in greeting. Rock music goes loud then soft again as he moves past paper bags, curled orange peels.

In painted silver, the purple sweatshirts read:

LUMUMBA LIVES

On a drift log lies a silver fish, twenty pounds or more, with lateral black stripes from gills to tail. In the autumn light, the silver scales glint with tints of brass. Should he tell these Africans that this shining New World fish carries cancer-causing poison in its gut?

Beyond the Africans, on the outside of the tracks between rails and river, is a small brick relay station. The wrecked windows are boarded up with plywood, and each plywood panel is marked with a single word scrawled in harsh black:

NAM COKE RUSH

Crouched behind the station, he hides the gun under a board, slips his wallet into a crevice, then his shoulder holster. He fits a shard of brick.

The plaint of a train, from far upriver. The Africans teeter on their slabs, craning to see where he has gone. The sun disappears behind swift clouds.

He strips to his shorts and picks his way across dirtied weeds and rocks, down to the water edge.

Where an eddy has brought brown scud onto the shore lie tarred scrap wood and burnt insulation, women's devices in pink plastic, rusted syringes, a broken chair, a large filth-matted fake-fur toy, a beheaded cat, a spent condom, a half grapefruit.

Ah shit, he says aloud, as if the sound of his own voice might be of comfort. He forces his legs into the flood, flinching in anticipation of glass shards, metal, rusty nails through splintered wood.

The hooded figures shout, waving their arms. They yell again, come running down the bank.

His chest is hollowed out, his lungs yawn mortally. He hurls himself outward, gasping as the hard cold strikes his temples, as a soft underwater shape nudges his thigh. In his thrash, he gasps up a half mouthful of the bitter water, losing his breath as he coughs it out, fighting the panic.

Rippling along his ear, the autumn water whispers of cold deeps, green-turning boulders. The river is tugging at his arms, heavy as mercury, entreating him to let go, to sink away. Through the earth's ringing he can hear his arms splash, as the surface ear hears the far whistle of a train, as yells diminish.

Cold iron fills his chest, and desolation. It is over now—this apprehension of the end comes to him simply, as if body and soul were giving up together. The earth is taking him, he is far out on the edge, in the turning current.

The duck floats belly up, head underwater, droplets of Adirondack water pearled on the night blue of its speculum, drifting downriver from the sunny bend, from the blue mountains.

His cold hand is dull as wood on the stiffened duck.

The cold constricts him and his throw is clumsy. The effort of the throw takes too much strength. The duck slides away downstream. He swallows more water, coughs and spits, and overtakes it, rolling over on his back to get a breath.

A rock nudges him. He sees bare trees whirl on the sky. The point-head purple hoods loom up, dark faces break.

"Yo, man! Lookin good, man! You all right?"

From the shallows, he slings the duck onto the litter. He crawls onto the rocks, knocks away a hand.

"Easy, man! We trying to help!"

"Yay man? What's happenin? How come you jumpin in the river?"

"October, man! *Bad* river, man!"

"Never catch no *nigger* swimmin! Not out there!"

"*No,* man! Niggers *sink!* Any fool know *dat!*"

They yell with laughter.

"Goodbye cruel world, look like to me!"

"Cruel world!" another hoots, delighted. "That's about it!"

His wet underwear is transparent. He feels exposed, caught in the open. Rage grasps him, but he has no strength. He fights for breath.

"Hey man? You hearin me? Next time you need duck meat bad as that, you let me know. Go walkin in the park, toss me some crumbs, noose all you want! Two bucks apiece! Yeah man! Gone give you my card!"

They laugh some more. "Gone give the man his *card,* that nigger say!"

"Like to eat fish? We gone fry fish!"

He gazes from one black man to another, trying to bring the turmoil in his head under control. Four are middle-aged, in old suit trousers and broken street shoes. The fifth might be a son, and wears new running sneakers.

LUMUMBA LIVES

They smile at him. He knows these Africans, he knows how well they feign subservience and admiration, laughing at someone when they have him at their mercy. He gets slowly to his feet.

"Who's Lumumba?" he inquires, playing for time.

"Who Lumumba *is?*"

This man looks down, he spreads his lettering with all eight fingers, then looks up at the younger man, who must be twenty.

"My boy Junius our Lumumba man. Who Lumumba, Junius?"

"*Frag!*"

"Who Lumumba, Frag?"

The white man coughs. Wasn't that the problem? That he had not liked Lumumba? Wasn't that it?

Ashamed of his elders, Frag rolls his eyes. Frag is feverish and skinny, wild-eyed, angry. "Have Lumumba on your fuckin shirt, don't know who he *is?*" He glares at the white man.

"Who he *was,* Lumumba Man. He's dead."

Frag shrieks, "You makin fun? You makin fun with me?"

The white man does a stiff shuffle, almost falling. "Wholumumba, wholumumba, wholumumba, WHO!" He is foot-numb, goosefleshed, shuddering with cold. Nothing seems real to him.

The faces in the purple hoods look mystified. He thinks, Come on, get it over with.

He starts out along the rail bed for the relay station, on the dead city stones and broken glass and metal litter.

At a sharp whistle he turns. Frag pitches the duck underhand, too hard, straight at his gut. He lets it fall.

"Shot it and swam for it, almost got drownded," one man says. "So why you *leavin* it? Ain't got no license?"

He points toward their fishing poles, upriver. They have no license, either. And possession of striped bass, he says, is against the law.

They exchange looks of comic disbelief. One raises both hands. "Whoo!" he says.

"Ol' fish washed up out of the river!"

"Yessir, that fish *all* washed up!"

They hoot, delighted, then frown and mutter when he will not laugh with them.

"Hey, we ain't gone *possess* that fish!"

"No, man! We gone *eat* him! You *invited!*"

When he tells them that their fish is poisoned, they stare back in mock outrage.

"Shit, man! Ain't niggers poisoned it!"

He goes on, knowing they will follow. They are after his wallet, and the gun.

"Where's that gun at, Whitey?"

There it is. They have come up fast, they are right behind him.

"None of your business, Blacky," he says, and keeps on going. He feels giddy.

"Blacky" is repeated, bandied about. He hears a whoop, a cry of warning, and he turns again.

An older man with silver grizzle at the temples, dark wet eyes, has his hand on Frag's arm. In Frag's hand is a large rock. The others jabber.

"What's happenin, man? What's up wit' you?"

"Come downriver see if we can help, and you just don't do right."

He resumes walking, paying no attention to the rock. Hauteur, he thinks, will always impress Africans. All the same, he feels confused, and tries to focus. On impulse he admits over his shoulder that he hid the gun, since they know this anyway.

"Scared we steal it, right?" Frag's voice is a near-screech. "Seen niggers hangin around, right?" Frag bounces his big rock off a rail.

He wants to shout "Right!" but restrains himself.

An older voice says, "Easy, Junius, don't excite yourself."

"*Frag!*"

"Easy, Frag, don't excite yourself. You okay, Frag?"

At the relay station, his clothes are undisturbed. He sees the corner of his wallet in the crevice.

NAM COKE RUSH

He pulls the pants on over his wet underwear, realizes that he does this out of modesty, stops himself, strips. They whoop and whistle. When he reaches for his pants a second time, Frag snaps them from his hand.

"Don't like niggers, right? Scared of 'em, right? We smell it! Oh, we *hate* that honky smell, man!"

His foot is right beside the board, he slides his toe beneath it.

"Mister? Frag excites hisself, okay?"

"Truth!" Frag yells. "Fuckin truth, man! We can take it! Don't like niggers, right?"

"Right," he says, because the timing is so satisfying. He doesn't care whether or not it's true. Five blacks, one white—a clear case of self-defense. He flips the board, stoops quick, brings up the gun.

"Let's have those pants," he says. "I'm tired of this."

The black men back away, form a loose circle neither out of range nor close enough to threaten him. Breathing raggedly, beside himself, Frag stays where he is, as if transfixed by the twin black holes of the gun muzzle.

"Don' point that mothafucka, man!" he gasps at last.

"Toss the man his damn pants, Junius! Go ahead, now!"

"Man might do it, Junius! See them eyes?"

"Fuck!" Frag yells, beside himself. "Li'l popgun!"

The father's soft voice is a plea. "Easy, mister, please, what's up wit' you? That boy can't help hisself."

He sees their fear of what they take to be his naked craziness.

At the train whistle, the black men look relieved. Frag jabs his finger, furious and scared. He keeps staring at the gun, he will not back off.

"Toss the man them pants now, Junius."

The train is coming down the track toward the city, loud as a riveting machine, as a machine gun.

"Train comin, man."

But he makes no move to hide himself. He steps farther out onto the tracks. What the engineer must see is a naked white man surrounded and beset by a gang of blacks.

The train blows three shrill whistles, lurches, and begins to slow.

"Junius? Trouble, boy! You got enough!"

"Shit!" the boy snarls. "Ain't us done nothin!"

He slings the pants. The older man grabs him from behind, spins him away. The boy curses in a vicious stream, angling out across the tracks toward the woods on the river slope behind the train, ready to run if anyone on the train starts to descend. He yells, "You ain't done with Frag yet, shithead! Honky mothafuck!"

The train eases to a stop. A hiss of steam. High cirrus clouds come out over the trees, over the river.

"Put them pants on, mister! Folks is *lookin* at you!"

"Back up," he says, lifting the gun. And right now, remembering that both shells in the gun have been expended, he feels a sharp tingle at the temples.

A voice from the train calls, "You all right?" He waves his hand, then lays the gun down and begins to dress.

Sullen and sad, the black men shake their heads. They mutter, but they do not speak, they will not meet the stares from the train windows. They watch him dress, watch him take his wallet from the crevice in the wall. When he straps on the empty shoulder holster, they groan and retreat farther.

The train departs. He starts away, walking upriver.

He wonders now if they meant him any harm, but he takes no chances. Every little while he turns to be sure he is not followed.

The figures stand in silhouette. Three wave and point as the fourth raises the wild duck, bill pointed against the city. They seem to entreat him, but it is too late. What are they calling?

The hurled duck arches on the sky, falls fast, and bounces, coming to rest in the junk along the river.

When he goes back for it, they scatter, abandoning their fish. He puts the gun down, raises both his arms. "Wait a minute!" he calls. "Listen!"

"Get outta here!" they holler back. "Jus' you get *outta* here!"

At his blind he retrieves his equipment, leaving the three decoys to the river. With his burlap sack, he starts across the tracks toward the woods. Near the mouth of the old brook, he spins, recoiling from a clip of wind right past his ear.

A purple hood sinks back behind the auto body in the swamp. He circles the auto, crouching and running, but the rock-thrower has vanished, and the woods are silent.

He hunts quickly through the woods, chasing scared footfalls, then retreats half backward, swinging the gun. Moving slowly so that Frag can tail him without difficulty, he climbs the steep lawn below his father's house. Someone is shouting.

Inside, the cottage seems to enclose him. He listens to the clock tick. The house creaks. He pours himself a whiskey.

No one answers at the real-estate office. To the answering machine he whispers, "This is Henry Harkness. I have a wild duck here, and some wild rice and good wine. I was hoping you and . . ." He doesn't want to say "your wife," but he cannot recall the round-eyed woman's name. He puts the phone down. Somewhere his life took a turn without his knowledge.

The duck drips blood and water from its bill onto the white enamel of the kitchen table.

He slips out the back door and through the trees to the autumn garden. From here he can spot the purple hood coming up along the woods. The running, the game of it, the ambush are exhilarating, but the excitement dies quickly with the whiskey flush and does not return.

He settles down to wait behind the wall.

The light has gone wrong in some way. The sky is darkening in the noon sun, the dusk is waiting in the trees, and nowhere is there any shelter.

The African will come, perhaps at dark. Even now that face is peering from the trees. Neighbors will come to pay respects once it is over.

A police car comes and goes, lights flashing slowly, humping around the drive on its fat tires. The caretaker rides in the front seat.

No one comes up from the woods, the glinting river. Still he waits there in the autumn garden, cooling his forehead on the night-blue metal, in the haunted sunlight, in the dread of home.

William F. Buckley, Jr.

born in New York City in 1925, William F. Buckley, Jr., graduated from Yale College in 1950, promptly got married, taught Spanish at Yale, and set about writing the polemical book, *God and Man at Yale* (1951), that made an early name for him. As an undergraduate he had been chairman of the *Yale Daily News,* and he recalls receiving "a letter from Professor Norman Holmes Pearson protesting my editorials and instructing us to cancel his subscription. When, ten years later, a letter from a subscriber to *National Review* wrote to say the same thing, I published the letter with the editorial note, 'Cancel your own goddam subscription.'" Buckley founded the *National Review* in 1955, began writing a syndicated column in 1962, and started his television program, *Firing Line,* in 1966. In each of these venues he held forth as an eloquent contrarian. Among his books are *Up from Liberalism* (1959), *United Nations Journal* (1974), and *Right Reason* (1985). He is also a prolific novelist, from *Saving the Queen* (1976) to *High Jinks* (1997) and *The Redhunter* (1999). The recipient of many honors and awards, he must be most proud of the Presidential Medal of Freedom, bestowed on him in 1991.

THE HARPSICHORD

(Published in the New York *Time Magazine,* January 2, 1983, under the title "Queen of All Instruments")

January 2, 1983

At *National Review,* we give (of course) a Christmas party. For ten years or so, up until a year ago, the guest performer was Fernando Valenti, once designated (in *Time* magazine) as "the most exciting" recitalist alive, performing on the harpsichord. Then the cancer hit (from which, happily, he is in remission) and, of course, he was making no commitments for the indefinite future. I thought of asking Judith Norell, not only a brilliant musician but also a courageous one, as witness that for a couple of years she consented to be my teacher. But I thought that to present another harpsichordist would skirt insouciance—too much like the King is dead, long live the King. Better something completely different. Michael Sweeley, the president of the Caramoor music center near Katonah, New York, suggested Richard Vogt, Caramoor's choral director, who arrived on a snowy Friday in December at our place in Manhattan with an incredible thirteen performers—singers, a cellist, a harpsichord accompanist and a clarinetist.

Later that night, I measured the reactions of an audience of about eighty—staff and friends of the magazine. The reaction to Valenti had always been more than merely courteous. He weaves his wonders so engagingly that even those who had never before heard the instrument knew that a magic of sorts was being brewed. But one simply has to acknowledge that there are more popular forms of music, and those carried the day when the happy and talented choristers sang and played, everything from old English madrigals to "O Little Town of Bethlehem." The harpsichord is not, in my opinion, a difficult instrument to listen to, in the sense that one might say of a bagpipe that an evening with it would prove long. But the pow is not instantly there in a harpsichord. It requires habituation. I suppose it is only safe to say it because the experiment is unlikely, but I warrant that if those children in *The Blue Lagoon* had had a wind-up gramophone that survived the shipwreck, along with a record collection one-half harpsichord music, one-half rock and roll, they'd have learned to prefer the former to the latter well before they learned to mate. But it isn't an instrument made for singing along with Mitch, and it makes sense to acknowledge this going in.

And so we concede that the harpsichord, although there is no question about the renaissance of early music of which it is an integral part, continues to be a relatively neglected instrument, in need of a little affirmative action. God knows it was once worse.

In the winter of 1816, the cold in Paris got most awfully severe and heating materials scarce. The governors of the Paris Conservatory met their own crisis with Gallic wit: by burning, one after another, their abundant supply of harpsichords.

What do you do with a bulky object that has become, quite simply, useless? Why, dispose of it. If in the course of doing so you can tease out of it some highly desirable British thermal units—then why not dispose of it into the fireplaces, rather than the dustbin?

The act of 1816 is as horrifying as it would be if the Goya collection in the Prado Museum were burned on the grounds that Goya was no longer in style. Worse, in a way—because you cannot any longer "destroy" Goya, whose works are definitely reproduced, even to the point where experts are occasionally needed to authenticate an original. With the burning of so many Stradivarius-class French harpsichords, a treasury was depreciated which proved unreplenishable.

Consider. There resides, in the Yale Collection, a Taskin. There are those who hold that this harpsichord's sound does not elsewhere, in its singular beauty, exist (so much, by the way, for the position that sounding boards necessarily deteriorate with age). Pascal Taskin the Elder was a harpsichord maker who made wonderful instruments in the French school (the others were Italian, Flemish, German, English) during the third of the three centuries preceding the unconditional victory of the piano. Call that year 1800. The instrument for which Couperin and Rameau, Soler and Scarlatti, Bach and Handel had written was, for a very dark age, held to be forever anachronized. The Western world was entering exuberantly the age of romance. Schubert was already there, and even Chopin would soon be born; Keats and Byron were stirring, Turner and Goya exhibiting, and the artist's vision was of a pretty girl, just like a melody; even though the girl could be sad and, in opera, was often expected to commit suicide. The relative austerity of the (relatively astringent) harpsichord was something people were entirely disposed to discard, in favor of the mellifluous, sound-variable piano.

But it is not really safe to say that the piano was, so to speak, the evolutionary next step in the development of the harpsichord, as one might say that the DC-4 was the outgrowth of the DC-3. It is the beginning of knowledge of the harpsichord to know that it is a different instrument from the piano. A corollary is that the end of the harpsichord might well have been dictated, along around 1800, not so much by the realization of the piano, as by the desuetude of Baroque music. The early sonatas of Beethoven were written for the harpsichord. His later sonatas could not even be played on a harpsichord (Beethoven was now absolutely depending, for the communication of his art, on a pedal that sustained notes that had already been struck, by fingers now otherwise occupied; and on volume differentials from *pianissimo—pp—*to *fortissimo—ff*). It is more accurate to think in terms, not of a better mousetrap's having replaced its predecessor, but of the awakening of exclusivist artistic appetites appeased only at the expense of totally ignoring what had gone before. There had come a period during which the public *would not listen* to Baroque music, even as, a century and a half later, there came a period during which the public, however briefly, *would not view,* enthusiastically, classical art. In any event the harpsichord, for all intents and purposes, disappeared.

One of several reasons for the unchallengeable supremacy of the modern piano is, of course, its unmatchable versatility. Its tone, however lovely and however interesting, is relatively "white": a clear, neutral voice which can sing any melody without imposing its own personality on its song. A "white" sound might be thought of as a sound unencumbered by extrinsically imposed character. The closer to midpoint between where any string is held down at both ends you pluck or strike it, the "whiter" the sound—i.e., the less affected by the nature of the instrument. Moreover, the highly developed mechanical action of the best grand pianos enables the performer to do almost anything he wishes with this basic, adaptable sound.

Skilled piano builders have even been able to minimize the effect of the piano's only significant limitation (shared with the harpsichord, and with all other keyboard instruments save the organ and certain electronic jazz-rock gizmos): its inability to sustain tones indefinitely at a given volume level (you can toot a horn at a constant level of sound, but a piano key, however hard you hit it, hammers a string whose resonance begins immediately to diminish). The result of all these characteristics is that the modern piano is the willing servant of its master, who may mold an interpretation as he wishes, limited only by his personal musical sensibility and technical skills.

But as Courtenay Caublé, the learned contemporary teacher, harpsichord authority and technician, comments, a fine harpsichord performance is the product of a sort of "musical contract between equal partners." In contrast to the piano, the harpsichord has a distinctive, highly complex tonal personality which substantially limits a performer's interpretation. Moreover, the means by which the sounds are produced imposes severe restrictions on how the performer can express musical textures and lines. And only certain kinds of music lend themselves at all to harpsichord performance.

To the piano-oriented performer, these limitations are fatal. But to the rare performer willing to accept his instrument as a willful rather than a willing partner, the results can be uniquely, stunningly gratifying. A classical attitude about artistic production—illustrated so well, for instance, in many of Igor Stravinsky's neoclassical works, as Caublé points out—is that a work of art gains increasing vigor and beauty as the artist focuses his energies by imposing on himself more and more demanding limitations. Some harpsichord music—for instance, compositions of Rameau and Couperin—is so idiomatic that it is unsuccessful when played on any other instrument, even the versatile piano. Other Baroque compositions—Bach's keyboard works, for instance—though they can be successfully reinterpreted by a modern pianist without doing violence to their inherent musicality, take on, under the fingers of a skilled harpsichordist, a shape and meaning uniquely theirs. Without the use of a sustaining pedal, for instance, and, thus, without dramatic increases or diminutions in volume, the music requires, once again, a *different* shaping. Bach's "Chromatic Fantasy and Fugue" can be played on the clavichord, harpsichord, piano and organ, and is exquisite on all four: But the sound and the shape, and the nature of the excitement, are different in each case. A modern listener can choose which rendering—the piano's or the harpsichord's—is more congenial to his taste. But it remains a fact that, to many listeners, the experience of Caublé's "tripartite marriage of composer, instrument and performer," done by the harpsichord, is not just revelation, but a quite ineffable joy.

During the last years of the century, a music craftsman named Arnold Dolmetsch began to fuss about, repairing old instruments, building new ones, and writing about the lost music of the preceding century. But Dolmetsch came, struggled, and went; and still the harpsichord was rare. But restoration was in the wings, and John Challis, Wanda Landowska and Frank Hubbard were about to happen.

In the fall of 1950, I was freshly graduated from Yale University and living in New Haven. I learned that Ralph Kirkpatrick, who was attached in some vague way to the Yale School of Music, would commemorate the two hundredth anniversary of the death of Johann Sebastian Bach by giving three concerts on successive Tuesdays. He would play the entire "Clavierübung," which includes the Six Partitas, the "Goldberg Variations," the "Chromatic Fantasy and Fugue," and four duets.

I had played the piano rather seriously as a boy and young teenager, but always my love and awe of the instrument purchased more of my enthusiasm than of my time: which is merciful, because those without serious talent in art are miserably misled if deluded into believing they can become serious artists, practicing hours on end to no significant effect. I puttered. I had an upright piano at Yale (cost, $100), and my attraction to the music of Bach led me to curiosity about the sound and the technique of Baroque instruments.

So I attended these concerts and heard a harpsichord performance in an auditorium for the first time. During the spring of that year, my father had made me a graduation gift. John Challis received a check for $1,000, and I received a beautiful little clavichord, the drawing-room contemporary of the harpsichord, back in its golden years. What surprised me was a telephone call, the day after the instrument arrived, from Ralph Kirkpatrick—asking whether he might come to my rooms to try out my clavichord. John Challis had written to say that he had experimented with the instrument's bridge, which lies across the sounding board, dictating the pitch of the strings, and Challis wanted Kirkpatrick's reaction to its effectiveness.

In those days (and even today, though to a lesser extent), harpsichord makers and performers made up a tight little fraternity, comparable to the computer engineers and builders of twenty and fifteen years ago in California and Boston, though less competitive. The financial stakes, in harpsichord building, are not very high (the artistic stakes are infinite). Someday someone should write "The Soul of the New Machine" around the restoration of the harpsichord—an achievement of the twentieth century.

I remember both the excitement of meeting the illustrious Kirkpatrick, then in his thirties, and the protracted anxiety after he sat down to play. He held a cigarette holder with lit cigarette between his lips. It must have been sadism. Surely it was with malice aforethought that he permitted the ash on his burning cigarette to grow to advanced defumescence, reaching the point where you become furiously certain that the long, dirty ashes would fall into the clavichord's womb, all over your delicate little wooden keys and brass tangents. But then—suddenly—the fingers of one of his hands, theretofore wholly engaged in the nimble articulation of complicated fugues, runs and trills, were unaccountably free. With them he would nonchalantly transport the cigarette holder from his lips to the ashtray at the side of the instrument, tap it, detaching the ash, and return to the keyboard to accompany his other hand, which had never stopped playing.

It was, under the circumstances, with special excitement that I went with my wife to Sprague Hill, filled for the occasion with 500 students, faculty and townfolk. We sat for the beginning of the five hours of the Kirkpatrick-Bach we would hear in the course of the fortnight. The experience was dazzling on several counts. There was the music: unusual, to the inexperienced ear; stringy, controlled, subtle, seductive; engaging, finally. The music, rococo; at times somnolently quiet, lyrical; then gay, turbulent. Finally, overpowering.

And virtuosity. It would be five hours of music profoundly intricate; music that, for the most part, cannot be hummed—because you cannot hum two, let alone three or four melodies at the same time. And so much of the music of the Baroque period is contrapuntal—vertical music, they call it; because, on the page, you see it as a column of melodies, so different from the single-line melody with accompanying chords. The awe would mount.

On the evening after the second concert, Kirkpatrick played the "Goldberg Variations." They are, arguably, the most difficult single keyboard work ever written. I attended a reception for the artist and found myself in conversation, once again, with the gentleman who, a few months earlier, had tried out my Challis. "When," I asked reverently, "did you commit yourself to giving these three concerts?"

"Oh," said Kirkpatrick matter-of-factly (he does not smile easily), "it was last spring, in Italy."

"When," I persevered, "did you *practice* the 'Goldberg'?"

"Oh," said Kirkpatrick, visibly struggling to remember a detail so inconsequential, "it was on a bus. From Perugia to Rome."

Since I think with the speed of light, I reasoned that Kirkpatrick had spent the entire summer riding buses every day from home to Perugia—you know, the kind of thing genius-eccentrics do, when they run out of conventionality—with one of those keyboard simulators on his lap, practicing away for the 300, 400 hours it would take to master the "Goldberg." I asked if he had used such a keyboard? He looked at me, perplexed. "Oh, no," he said. "I *rethought* the 'Goldberg' on that ride."

"Wait a minute," I said sternly, bringing the conversation to attention: "I . . . am . . . asking . . . you: When last did you actually *play* the 'Goldberg'?"

"Oh," he said, ruminatively, "I think it was when I was still at Harvard. I was twenty-one, I think." I wandered away, and have wandered ever since away from such fonts of immortality, awestruck. Although I assume there are complementary talents in the piano world, the impact of that epiphany stayed with me, and I thought for the first time about the infinite complexity of a mind that could recall so formidable a composition as the "Goldberg." I knew then and there that no human achievement I was likely to encounter would ever dwarf, in my estimation, this one. And the harpsichord was his chosen instrument. Kirkpatrick had begun on the piano and switched to the harpsichord as a student at Harvard. That he should have done so was terribly important to me.

During that year and the year or two after, the musical world suddenly found itself in the lap of Wanda Landowska. Although in her seventies, Madame Landowska had just released "The Well-Tempered Clavier." It was rapturously received, which did not surprise her, as I learned in the summer of 1950 when I visited her home in Lakeville, Conn., only five miles from my own home. The first words of the 4-foot-8-inch tiger were: "You ahrr familiar weeth my 'Vell-Temperred' recordings?" I told her I was. She closed her eyes: "Magnificent, no?" I agreed that they were.

It is hard to overestimate the influence of Landowska. For a while, she was virtually alone as a harpsichord performer. Her musicality combined with a sense of theater, concerning which, in the chaste afteryears of the harpsichord explosion of the 1950s and 1960s, there has been some reservation. You see, in the harpsichord you have more than one register, as they are called. The concert instrument normally has two keyboards. The lower of these plucks a set of strings at a given point along their length, producing the "lower-eight-foot" sound. This is the basic harpsichord sound. But if you depress a note on the upper keyboard you will hear a slightly different sound, because a different string is being twanged by the plucker (which is called a plectrum). The plectrum is here positioned under a different point of that other string, evoking the same pitch, but of a different quality—more nasal, stringier, muter, whatever. By depressing a "coupler" you can, by striking only the lower-keyboard eight-footer, simultaneously depress the same note in the upper keyboard. It goes without saying that the two timbres should complement each other, in agreeable harmony.

But you have just begun. The lower eight can also be struck, but this time using the buff stop, whereupon the sound is damped, giving off a pizzicato sound. This is an either-or situation, but if you wish, you can depress a pure note on the upper keyboard, using the regular eight-foot, while on the lower keyboard you can depress it in the so-called buff mode. A third alternative is to shift to the *peau de buffle* (buffalo hide) which gives you a dreamy-soft version of the regular eight. A third set of strings is pitched an octave higher than the eight-footers, and called the four-foot. Much of the time the performer will simultaneously engage the eight-foot and the four-foot, producing a more solid sound.

Now: Wanda Landowska (and indeed a lot of her immediate successors, most prominently Kirkpatrick and Valenti) regularly used yet another set of strings, those pitched one octave below the eight-foot. Now strike a chord and it will sound almost like an organ roll: the equivalent of three pianists playing with perfect coordination on three octaves. The sound produced by Landowska was wonderfully varied, with substantial reliance on the 16-foot, using every conceivable combination of register. By the late 1960s the use of a 16-foot register had become musically unfashionable. Why? For historical, practical and esthetic reasons. Only a few harpsichords, late in their epoch, had 16-foot registers. To supply the 16-foot, it is required that the instrument be stretched out in length considerably, and that heavy strings be used. The temptation to add the extra effect of the 16-foot tends to overcome many performers' taste, and then the sound of the 16-footer can affect adversely that of the other strings, except where a perfect balance is provided by numinous craftsmen—rare.

The disapproval of the 16-foot register, I barge in to say, is only in part justified. I walked once into the Unitarian Church in Westport, Connecticut, to hear Fernando Valenti record the sonatas of Soler, and he was using the famous Challis on which he had recorded more than fifty long-playing records. It is true that sometimes the sound was that of an organ. It is not true that the sound of a harpsichord working was indistinct. The sound was, well, perfect. I'd have shot anyone who threatened to take away Fernando's 16-footer.

The sound of an individual note of the harpsichord does not, if you are measuring decibels, increase measurably by pounding on it. Dynamic effects are therefore the consequence of balance: of rhythm and timing, of delicate releases, of notes properly held. The pleasure taken from hearing someone with these requisite skills performing on a fine instrument is the pleasure of petit point.

A friend was present at the Frick Collection at what proved to be the last public performance of Landowska. She was playing an obscure sonata by Fisher (J. A., 1744–1806) which my friend happened to have been studying. So that he knew it when what was being played suddenly ceased to be Fisher, becoming Landowska, improvising. My friend was concerned. What was she up to? Memory lapse? But, the work being largely unknown, the audience did not react, and in due course she was back, playing what Fisher wrote.

Next on the program was the famous "Chromatic Fantasy and Fugue." As was her habit, Landowska bowed her head slightly before beginning, bringing her hands—extended—to her lips, as if in prayer. Then the right hand was raised dramatically, as if to strike a hammer blow. Suddenly she stopped, wheeling thoughtfully about to address her audience in her heavily accented, high-pitched voice:

"Ladies and gentlemen, lahst night I had a visitor. It was Poppa Bach. We spoke, of corrse, in Cherrman. He said to me, 'Vanda, haff you ever trried *my* fingerring on the "Chromatic Fantasy"?' 'No,' I said to him, and he said the next time I *must trry*. So tonight, I will use a different fingerring and maybe the result will not be the same azz my *incomparable* recorrding."

Wheel back to the instrument. Hands pressed together, raised to the lips. Right hand up.

And then the "Fantasy." Landowska, having experienced the difficulty with Fisher, evidently did not know whether her memory, suddenly insecure, would sustain her through the "Fantasy" which, unlike the Fisher, is as familiar to Baroque-minded audiences as "Twinkle, Twinkle Little Star," precluding surreptitious improvisation.

No dramatist, given a full year's notice, could have written lines more disarming than those she extemporized. And, of course, no one, in her presence, would profess skepticism about her personal familiarity with Poppa Bach.

By the time she died (1959), musical America was thoroughly exposed to the harpsichord. Frank Hubbard, apprentice to Challis, apprentice to Dolmetsch, put down stakes in Boston. There, with William Dowd, he made instruments. In due course they separated, Hubbard more interested in history and theory, Dowd in making wonderful instruments. And soon there was Eric Herz. And before long Boston became known as the Antwerp of the harpsichord world, Antwerp being where Ruckers, the Flemish master, had captured the attention of the discriminating world of harpsichord listeners. Now there were 100 harpsichord makers, including the mass-production types, mostly out of Germany. W. J.

Zuckermann wrote a literate and splendidly illustrated book, *The Modern Harpsichord,* in 1969. "Hardly a day passes in New York," he commented, "in which a recording studio is not using a harpsichord. One musical instrument rental service alone possesses a fleet of 18 harpsichords which it was my lot for many years to tune and service daily. These instruments are used in Muzak for banks and supermarkets, incidental music for Shakespeare dramas, advertising jingles for television, background music for documentary films, Christmas music, children's music, cha-chas, rock-and- roll. . . . How long this fad (if that is what it is) will last, no one can say, but it still seems to be gathering force."

The answer to that question is that the fad did not last. It is over. But harpsichord devotees, if relatively few in number, can only be said to be beleaguered as, say, Israel is beleaguered. The harpsichord family is confident, proud, serene, and maybe just a little patronizing, like the folks who knew Acapulco before it was famous, or read *Lolita* when the Olympia Press brought it out. Their numbers, measured up against Mr. Zuckermann's graph, are static. This happened in part because the theatricality of the galvanizers of the 1950s became excommunicably unfashionable; in part, because the craze for build-it-yourself harpsichord kits proliferated instruments which, because they were so often inferior, were not up to communicating the singular beauty of the well-crafted machine of the masters. In part, also, because a harpsichord simply will not sound out in the big, standard auditoriums to which people go to hear music performed. O.K. So the true believers listen to the harpsichord through records. This is, for the obvious reason, disappointing to the performing artists, who are hard put to gather together audiences of sufficient size to earn a living by playing. Judith Norell, among the most gifted and versatile artists alive (she has even played Gershwin on the harpsichord), gets critical, not popular, acclaim—but the other day I reached her in Topeka, Kansas, where she was playing chamber music. The legendary Fernando Valenti played 100 Scarlatti sonatas on five consecutive evenings at Carnegie Recital Hall, but never to an audience of more than 100. Bleak stuff.

But it does not matter to *us,* because records are available (and some also own the instrument), so that when the spirit sags and (as Melville put it) we are drawn to the tail end of funeral processions, with only minor exertion over the turntable we can hear the "Goldberg," or Rameau, or the ineffable Scarlatti, and rejoice in communion with the eighteenth century, whose dominant figures, sometimes limited to a mere four octaves, created (some of us maintain) the greatest musical literature extant. Much of music, in all ages, is divine. But *Aïda,* with 100 musicians, 200 choristers, a stage designed by Zeffirelli costing a million dollars, and three elephants, does not bring more joy than the diffident, gifted Gerald Ranck does, seated alone by that little wooden instrument, using only ten fingers and giving us, at St. George's Episcopal Church in Manhattan, a prelude and a fugue written more than 200 years ago. For the harpsichord.

David McCullough

hen David McCullough was awarded an honorary degree by Yale, the citation read, "As an historian, he paints with words, giving us pictures of the American people that live, breathe, and above all, confront the fundamental issues of courage, achievement, and moral character." His early books are *The Johnstown Flood* (1968) and *The Great Bridge* (1972), his account of the building of the Brooklyn Bridge. For his book about Theodore Roosevelt's early years, *Mornings on Horseback* (1981), he received the National Book Award for biography. *Brave Companions* (1992) is a collection of profiles of exceptional men and women whose lives left a mark on the history of their time. *Truman,* his biography of the president, was published in the same year and awarded the Pulitzer Prize. An earlier book had won for McCullough his first National Book Award. It was *The Path Between the Seas* (1977), which recounts the epic struggle to build the Panama Canal. His portrait there of the French diplomat and canal promoter Ferdinand, vicomte de Lesseps, is especially vivid. Born in Pittsburgh in 1933, McCullough graduated from Yale in 1955. He writes: "As has been said, one of the greatest of the manifold benefits of a Yale education for an aspiring writer is the chance to meet in real life writers of genuine consequence; and certainly that was my experience as an undergraduate in the 1950s, when people like John O'Hara, Brendan Gill, John Hersey, and Thornton Wilder were on the campus, as visitors, or, in Thornton Wilder's case, as a college fellow. Yet for all this I have to say that it was Vincent Scully whose influence counted most of all for me, and I'm sure for many others. 'Make me see,' was Dickens's famous admonition to writers, and with his vivid lectures on the history of art and architecture, Professor Scully threw open the window as did no one else and taught us, inspired us to see as we never had before."

> *How dull it is to pause, to make an end,*
> *To rust unburnish'd not to shine in use!*
> —ALFRED, LORD TENNYSON, *Ulysses*

I

Independence, his vital source of strength, he often remarked, had come late in life to Vicomte Ferdinand de Lesseps. The charm, the pervasive, indomitable, world-famous de Lesseps charm that had carried him so very far, had been there right along, born in him, a family streak, it was said, like the zest for adventure and the good looks. From the very start of his career at Lisbon he had made a strong impression. Older observers likened him to his father and to his celebrated uncle, Barthélemy de Lesseps. Friends of both sexes were gathered effortlessly. "Ferdinand encounters friends everywhere," his first wife had written from the post at Málaga. "He is loved with true affection. . . . It is wonderful to have a husband so liked by everyone." And a little later on: "Ferdinand is so good, so amiable, he spreads life and gaiety everywhere."

He was gifted, passionate; he loved books, music, horses, his work, his children, his graceful, witty first wife, his stunning second wife, and occasionally, if we are to believe one admiring French biographer, the wives of others. But independence had not come until he was past forty, thrust upon him unexpectedly by forces not of his own making.

In the summer of 1870, when he stood on the flower-banked platform within the great Crystal Palace, beaming as the boys from the Lambeth Industrial Schools waved their "Egyptian Salute," Ferdinand de Lesseps was sixty-four years old, very nearly as old as the century. He had been born on November 19, 1805, the year of Austerlitz, in a beige-colored stone house with white shutters that still stands in the town of Versailles. Less than fifty yards from the house, through an iron gate at the end of the Rue de la Paroisse, were the gardens of the Versailles Palace, the great Neptune Basin with its spectacular fountains, and just beyond that, within a mile or so, the Grand Canal of Versailles, which once, in the time of Louis XIV, had been alive with brightly painted gondolas and had been the setting for mock naval battles staged by actual ships of the line.

His family was long distinguished in the French diplomatic service. The men were esteemed as "lovers of progress and movement"; they were cultivated, athletic, fond of extravagant living, and immensely attractive to women. A great-uncle, Dominique de Lesseps, had been ennobled for his services to the state a hundred years before Ferdinand's birth. Grandfather Martin de Lesseps had been

French consul general to the court of Catherine the Great, and Ferdinand's father, Comte Mathieu de Lesseps, had been an accomplished Napoleonic diplomat, a friend of Talleyrand's. In Egypt, at the time of the British occupation, or shortly before Ferdinand was born, the vivacious Mathieu de Lesseps had worked miracles for Franco-Egyptian relations, and in 1818, when young Ferdinand was entering the Lycée Napoleon, Mathieu had been posted to the United States. Some sixty years later, at the unveiling of the Statue of Liberty in New York, Ferdinand would tell how his father had negotiated the first commercial treaty between France and the United States.

Barthélemy de Lesseps, the famous uncle, had been able to speak three languages by the time he was ten. While still in his twenties, he had sailed on the final expedition of the navigator La Pérouse, around Cape Horn to California and, at length, to Petropavlovsk, in Kamchatka. From there, in 1787, on orders from La Pérouse, all alone and with winter approaching, he had set out to find his way home to France. A year later, dressed as a Kamchatkan, he was presented to Louis XVI at Versailles, having traveled the entire distance across Siberia to St. Petersburg, mostly by dog sled, then on to Paris. He was a national hero overnight and in his subsequent diplomatic career—first under the Monarchy, then under the Empire, finally under the Restoration—he distinguished himself repeatedly, surviving three years of imprisonment in Turkey and the retreat of the *Grande Armée* from Moscow. So throughout his boyhood Ferdinand had been nourished on tales of valiant endurance, of heroic quests and heroic triumphs at the far ends of the world.

His mother was Catherine de Grivignée, whose French father had settled in Spain, prospered in the wine business, and married a Spanish girl of good family. His mother had lived her entire life in Spain until her marriage; Spanish was her first language and she was very Spanish in temperament, as Ferdinand would recall. He had grown up speaking Spanish as well as he did French, all of which would be offered later in explanation for the special allure of Panama, "a country made to seduce him."

There was never an overabundance of money in the family, appearances to the contrary. His mother's jewels had been pawned privately at least once to meet family expenses and his father had died all but bankrupt. Nor did Ferdinand attain great wealth. Like his father, he married well; like his father, he always lived in grand style. But the reputed de Lesseps fortune was a fiction.

Whether as a youth he ever envisioned a life other than the diplomatic service is impossible to say. But at age nineteen, having studied a little law, he was appointed *élève-consul* to his uncle, then the French ambassador to Lisbon. He served in Tunis afterward, with his father, until 1832, the year of his father's death; then came a Biblical seven years in Egypt, where being the son of Mathieu de

Lesseps was a decided advantage. Later came Rotterdam, Málaga, and Barcelona. In 1848, at age forty-three, he was made minister to Madrid.

It was work he naturally enjoyed and he did it well. He was efficient; he was gallant. He sat a horse beautifully. He was a crack shot and a great favorite among sportsmen. ("These healthful occupations," wrote one high-Victorian biographer, "contributed largely to the promotion of that robust health and that iron constitution, thanks to which he was able to bear, without even feeling them, the innumerable fatigues, labors, and voyages in all parts of the world.")

Though of less than average height, he was handsomely formed. He had a fine head of thick black hair, a good chin, a flashing smile that people would remember. The eyes were dark and active. The mustache had still to make its appearance.

His wife, the former Agathe Delamalle, bore him five sons, only two of whom would live to maturity, and she appears to have been another important asset to his career. A French officer described her as "this young woman with the clear gaze, witty, decided . . ." "Diamonds glittered everywhere," reads another account from the time, a description of a ball she gave at Barcelona. "Madame de Lesseps received the guests with perfect grace. Her toilette was ravishing, and she wore it with that marvelous air of which only *Parisiennes* have the secret. Let us add that the affection which everyone bears her did not a little to increase the charm of this magnificent soirée, which lasted until dawn."

His interest in canal building began supposedly in Egypt in the early 1830's with the arrival of the Saint-Simonians, about twenty Frenchmen, many of them civil engineers, who were led by an improbable figure named Prosper Enfantin. They had come, they announced, to dig a Suez canal, a work of profound religious meaning.

Their messiah was the late Claude Henri de Rouvroy, the Comte de Saint-Simon, who had fought under Lafayette at Yorktown, then, back in France, founded his own radical philosophy aimed toward a new global order. It was he who wrote, "From each according to his ability, to each according to his work." Private property and nationalism were to be things of the past. The leadership of mankind was to be entrusted to an elite class of artists, scientists, and industrialists. Mainly the good society was to be attained through ennobling, regenerative work. The world was to be saved—from poverty, from war—through immense public improvements, networks of highways, railroads, and two great ship canals through the Isthmus of Suez and the Isthmus of Panama.

Prosper Enfantin had taken up the banner after the death of the Master, calling himself *Le Père,* "one half of the Couple of Revelation." The other half, he said, was a divine female who had still to make herself recognized. A "church" was established on the Rue Monsigny in Paris; lavish receptions were staged to welcome the female messiah, candidates for the honor being received in Father

Enfantin's ornate bedchamber. Further, at a private estate near Paris, he founded an all-male colony for the faithful, where the prescribed habit, an outfit designed by the artist Raymond Bonheur, was a long, flowing tunic, blue-violet in color, tight-fitting white trousers, scarlet vest, and an enormous sash of richly embroidered silk. Enfantin, a big, bearded man, had the words *"Le Père"* embroidered across the front of his blouse. When he was taken to court for his advocacy of free love, he appeared in Hessian boots and a velvet cloak trimmed with ermine. Asked to defend his behavior, he stood motionless and silent, then explained that he wished the court to have a quiet moment to reflect on his beauty.

But for all this he had a decisive intelligence. He had been an excellent student at the École Polytechnique, the ultimate in French scientific training. He was a financier of importance and converts to the creed included eminent financiers, respected business people, journalists, many of the ablest civil engineers in France.

Enfantin had judged Suez to be an easier undertaking than Panama. He was further inspired by a premonition that his female counterpart waited for him somewhere in the ancient cradle of civilization. So after serving a brief prison term, he had sailed for Egypt, and it was de Lesseps who persuaded the ruling viceroy of Egypt, Mohammed Ali, not to throw him out of the country. De Lesseps may also have provided Enfantin with financial assistance. At any rate, Enfantin and his engineers went into the Suez desert.

After four years, more than half of them had died of cholera and little of practical value had been accomplished. Nonetheless, the prospect of a Suez canal was being talked about in Europe with seriousness at last, as a result of Enfantin's proselytizing, and young de Lesseps, if not exactly a complete convert to Saint-Simonianism, had been uplifted by ideas that were to last a lifetime. "Do not forget that to accomplish great things you must have enthusiasm," Enfantin had said, repeating the deathbed exhortation of the Master.

There was, however, to be no immediate deviation from the progress of a model career, and by any reasonable standard of evaluation, nobody could possibly have prophesied the future the young diplomat had in store. What heights he personally aspired to can only be guessed at. Probably they were of the predictable kind.

Viewed in retrospect, de Lesseps' life stands out as one of the most extraordinary of the nineteenth century, even without the Panama venture. That he of all men of his time should have been the one to make "the miracle" happen at Suez is in itself miraculous. Suddenly there he was. Known after 1869 as "The Great Engineer," he was no such thing. He had no technical background, no experience in finance. His skills as an administrator were modest. Routine of any kind bored him quickly.

The great turning point, the traumatic personal watershed from which so much history was to flow, came in 1849. That it happened that particular year, the year of the gold rush, when Panama emerged from the shadows once again, seems a play of fate that not even a novelist of his day might have risked.

A French expeditionary force sent to subdue Mazzini's newborn Roman republic and restore papal rule had been unexpectedly thrown back at Rome by Garibaldi. De Lesseps, then in Paris, was told he was to leave at once to resolve the crisis. "Guided by circumstances," he was to please all parties and achieve a peaceful accommodation. With all eyes on him he had shown the incredible stamina and single-mindedness he could summon—and especially if all eyes were on him. Convinced that he could succeed, he very nearly had, and apparently quite blind to the fact that he was being used by his own government merely as a means to gain time. A temporary cease-fire was agreed to. But then French reinforcements arrived; Louis Napoleon, the new "Prince-President" of France, gave the order and the French army attacked.

Summarily recalled, de Lesseps was publicly reprimanded before the Assembly for exceeding his instructions. When Rome fell to the French army, he was left with no choice but to resign. The gossip was that the strain of the mission had been too much, that he had temporarily departed from his senses.

So at age forty-three he was without the career his background and natural gifts had so ideally suited him for, and to which he had given himself so wholeheartedly. The future was a blank page. He was in debt. Public disgrace was something he had never experienced. Yet outwardly he remained the man he had always been, jaunty, confident, up at dawn, busy all day. With his wife and three young sons he moved into a flat on the Rue Richepanse and for the next five years divided his time between Paris and a country estate in central France, an ancient, towered château in the province of Berri that had once belonged to Agnès Sorel, mistress of Charles VII. Known as La Chesnaye, it had been purchased at de Lesseps' urging by his mother-in-law, Madame Delamalle, who had recently come into a sizable inheritance. The estate was located near the little village of Vatan on an open plain, mostly wheat country and extremely good land, with a great belt of forest a few miles to the south. His ambition was to create a model farm and he plunged into the role of country gentleman.

To occupy his mind he returned to the old interest in an Egyptian canal, reading everything he could lay his hands on. He was in touch again with Prosper Enfantin, for whom the Egyptian dream still burned. Enfantin generously supplied studies and papers from his files in the belief that he and de Lesseps could join forces. De Lesseps, however, had no such intention. His destiny henceforth, he had decided, would be in his own hands. Once, years before in Egypt, Mohammed Ali had advised, "My dear Lesseps . . . when you have something important to do, if there are two of you, you have one too many."

France, meantime, had been wrenched by still another bloody political turn. The improbable Prince-President sprang a coup d'état, made himself dictator, and proclaimed the birth of the Second Empire. As Emperor Napoleon III, he would take France into a new age of progress, he said. "We have immense territories to cultivate, roads to open, harbors to deepen, canals to dig, rivers to make navigable, railroads to complete." The Saint-Simonians were among his strongest supporters.

He established a brilliant court at the Tuileries, and on a bright winter morning at Notre Dame, he married the spectacular Eugénie de Montijo, who was half Spanish, half Scottish, something of an adventuress, and a distant cousin of Ferdinand de Lesseps'. (His mother and her grandmother were sisters.) Young enough to be the daughter of her cousin Fernando, as she called him in Spanish, she had always looked to him for advice. Especially in her new responsibilities would she welcome his views, she wrote the week before the wedding.

A few months afterward, in the spring of 1853, Agathe Delamalle de Lesseps died of scarlet fever and a son, his father's namesake, died of the same cause. De Lesseps took refuge at La Chesnaye, pouring himself into routine projects and his canal studies. Life, he wrote to his oldest son, Charles, demanded courage, resignation, and trust in Providence. Charles, a bright, attentive boy of twelve, a student in Paris, had become a particular source of pride.

Then quite out of the blue came the news that Egypt's ruling viceroy had been murdered by two slaves. De Lesseps was on a scaffold working with some stonemasons on the old house when the postman appeared in the courtyard with the Paris mail. "The workmen passed my letters and papers from hand to hand. Imagine my astonishment when I read of the death of Abbas-Pasha . . . I hurried down, and at once wrote to the new Viceroy to congratulate him. . . ." The new viceroy was Mohammed Said, whom de Lesseps had befriended years before when Mohammed Said was a fat, unattractive, and friendless little boy.

Mohammed Said, for whom de Lesseps was to name Port Said, had since become a walleyed mountain of a man, a great eater and drinker and jovial teller of "French stories," a ruler who liked to have his pashas wade through gunpowder carrying lighted candles to test their nerve. More important, he was known for his generous impulses and so de Lesseps wasted no time in getting to Egypt. By way of welcome, Said arranged to go on maneuvers in the Western Desert with an army of ten thousand men. They were joined by Bedouin tribesmen and a military band. It was the sort of show de Lesseps adored. He traveled in style—his own private tent, mahogany furniture, quilted silk bedding, ice for his drinking water.

In the pages of his journal one senses a sudden exhilaration, a tremendous feeling of release and adventure.

He joined Said at his desert command post outside Alexandria on November 13,

1854. Both were in top spirits. Said expressed a singular desire to commence his re-
gime with some great enterprise. Did Ferdinand have any ideas? But de Lesseps
said nothing of the canal; he was waiting for a sign, as he explained later.

At night he searched the desert sky. Before dawn he was up and out of doors and
the day was spent galloping miles over the desert on a magnificent Arabian steed.
But the following morning, he knew the moment had come. He was standing at
the opening to his tent, wrapped in a red dressing gown, looking and feeling for all
the world like an Arab sheik. The description that follows is from his journal:

The sun's rays were already lighting up the eastern horizon; in the west it was still dark
and cloudy. Suddenly I saw a vivid-colored rainbow stretching across the sky from east to
west. I must admit that I felt my heart beat violently, for . . . this token of a covenant . . .
seemed to presage that the moment had come for the consummation of the Union between East and West. . . .

Before breakfast, but with everyone watching, he mounted his horse and went
sailing over a high wall, a bit of imprudence, he calls it in the journal, but one
"which afterward caused the Viceroy's entourage to give the necessary approval to
my scheme. The generals with whom I shared breakfast congratulated me and remarked that my boldness had greatly increased their opinion of me."

And thus was launched the great Suez Canal. He broached the subject to Said
at the close of day. Said asked a few questions, then declared the matter settled.
His staff was summoned to hear the news.

Nothing had been said about cost. That de Lesseps had no experience faintly
related to such an undertaking, that he represented no powerful organization, no
combination of interests, that he had neither rank nor office nor any entrée to financial sources, seems not to have concerned either of them.

For the next fifteen years he was everywhere at once—Egypt, London, Con-
stantinople, Paris—coaxing, flattering, convincing monarchs and newspaper editors, issuing endless reports, driving the work forward in the desert, watching
over every detail, frequently overruling his technical advisers, defying the European bankers, and facing the scorn of the English prime minister, Palmerston,
who called him a swindler and a fool and who saw the canal as nothing more
than a cheap French grab for power in the Mediterranean.

The engineer Stephenson, builder of the Britannia Bridge, member of Parlia-
ment, rose from a bench in Commons to pronounce the scheme preposterous.
De Lesseps, whose English was terrible and whose experience as a builder had
begun and ended with the restoration work at La Chesnaye, hung a French flag
from his hotel window on Piccadilly, and went traveling across England giving
more than eighty speeches in a month. "They never achieve anything who do not
believe in success," he loved to say.

When the Rothschilds wanted 5 percent for handling the initial stock subscription, he said he would hire an office and raise the money himself. "You will not succeed," said Baron de Rothschild, an old friend. "We shall see," De Lesseps had answered.

Approximately half the money had come from France (from twenty-five thousand small investors), the rest from Mohammed Said. When Said died, in 1863, his replacement, Khedive Ismail, was even more beneficent, so much so that by 1869 he had nearly put Egypt into bankruptcy. In the final stages it had been the colossal steam dredges designed by French engineers that made the difference. Nor can the repeated influence of the empress, her faith in her brilliant cousin, be discounted. Yet de Lesseps remained the driving spirit, and in truth he was something new under the sun; he had no historical counterpart. What he was—what he became—was the *entrepreneur extraordinaire,* with all the requisite traits for the role: nerve, persistence, dynamic energy, a talent for propaganda, a capacity for deception, imagination. He was a bit of an actor and as shrewd and silky a diplomat as anyone of his time.

He had no interest in making money, as he professed. "I am going to accomplish something without expediency, without personal gain," he once wrote in his quick, sure, upward-sloping hand. "That, thank God, is what has up to now kept my sight clear and my course away from the rocks." At any time he could have sold his precious concession and realized a fortune, but this he never did; his driving ambition throughout was to build the canal, *"pour le bien de l'humanité."*

"He persevered, you see," a grandson would recall. "He was a very stubborn man." Jules Verne called it "the genius of will." But de Lesseps spoke of patience. "I wait with patience," he wrote to a correspondent in the final year of the work, "patience which I assure you requires more force of character than does action."

On the morning of the Grand Opening, November 17, 1869, tens of thousands of people lining both banks of the canal saw him ride by. Radiant with health, his hair turned nearly white by now, he stood beside the empress on the deck of the imperial yacht, *Aigle.* She was wearing a big straw hat and waving a white handkerchief.

Khedive Ismail had spared no expense on the inaugural ceremonies. Six thousand invitations were sent, offering to pay all travel and hotel expenses. A Cairo opera house had been built for the occasion and Verdi had been commissioned to write a spectacular new work, *Aïda.** Five hundred cooks and a thousand waiters were imported from Europe. At Lake Timsah, halfway down the canal, a whole town, Ismailia, had been created, trees planted, hotels put up, a palace built.

Behind *Aigle* steamed an Austrian frigate carrying Emperor Franz Josef, who was turned out in scarlet trousers, white tunic, and a cocked hat with a green

*The opera was not ready in time, so the performance was put off until 1871.

feather. There were two Austrian corvettes, five British ironclads, a Russian sloop of war, several French steamers—fifty ships in all. "There was a real Egyptian sky," Eugénie would remember, "a light of enchantment, a dreamlike resplendence. . . ."

For the next eight months, until the outbreak of the Franco-Prussian War, he was Europe's reigning hero. The empress presented the Grand Cross of the Legion of Honor. The emperor hailed his perseverance and genius. He was cause for dozens of banquets in Paris. His name was constantly in the papers, his face in the illustrated magazines. And the fact that he had also become a bridegroom added immeasurably to his hold on the public imagination.

A small, private ceremony had been performed at Ismailia a few days after the opening of the canal. The bride was a stunning French girl of twenty, with large, dark eyes and great spirit, Louise Hélène Autard de Bragard, the daughter of an old and wealthy friend of de Lesseps' and of a magnificent mother who, in her own youth, had been the inspiration for a sonnet by Baudelaire. She had been raised on the island of Mauritius, in the Indian Ocean, where her family, Huguenots, owned large plantations. According to the traditional story, it was love at first sight when she and de Lesseps met at one of Eugénie's "Mondays." By this second marriage he was to produce no fewer than twelve children—six sons, six daughters—which in some circles was considered a more notable accomplishment than the canal.

Palmerston was in his grave. In London, a few days after the great Crystal Palace reception, Prime Minister Gladstone informed the hero of Suez that Her Majesty had bestowed upon him the Grand Cross of the Star of India.

Few men had ever been so vindicated or extolled while they lived.

II

The first skirmish of the war, "*La Débâcle*" that overcame France with such appalling fury in 1870, was fought on August 4, the day Ferdinand de Lesseps returned from London, and the outcome, despite French heroism, was plain almost immediately. Napoleon III was suddenly aged and so ill he could barely sit a horse; yet he insisted on commanding an army in the field. An American observer, General Sheridan, wrote of the "marvelous mind" of Moltke and called the German infantry "as fine as I ever saw." The steel guns from the Krupp Works had twice the range of the French bronze pieces.

Within two weeks the main French army was penned in at Metz. On September 2, at Sedan, Napoleon III and 100,000 of his troops surrendered. It was the most stunning, humiliating defeat in French history. The Second Empire collapsed instantly. Sunday, September 4, Léon Gambetta climbed out onto a window sill at the Hôtel de Ville to proclaim to a Paris mob the birth of the Third French Republic. The empress, with the help of Ferdinand de Lesseps, escaped from the Tuileries and rushed to the home of her American dentist, a Dr. Evans, who got her to the Normandy coast and arranged for a yacht that carried her to asylum in England.

The war ended with the capitulation of Paris in January, after a siege of four months, during which the beleaguered citizens ate pet cats and elephants from the Paris zoo. The French dead were three times the German casualties, and by the peace terms France lost the rich, industrial provinces of Alsace and Lorraine. Further, Bismarck demanded an indemnity of 5,000,000,000 francs—$1,000,000,000—enough, he thought, to keep France crippled and subservient for another generation. And as a final humiliation, the despised German troops with their spiked helmets were to be permitted to parade down the Champs Élysées.

Then, with the return of spring, the tragedy was compounded. While a German army of occupation stood idly by, a vicious civil war raged; the savage days of the Commune became a bloodier time even than the infamous Terror.

Yet the Third Republic survived and the sudden resurgence of France after the war was as astonishing as her defeat. It was as if Sedan had released a vital inner resource. Everywhere people doubled their efforts, fired by a spirit of *revanche*. It was to be a revenge won on battlefields of "peace and progress"—for the while, anyway. In Paris the rubble was carted off and the new government carried on with the grandiose construction programs of Napoleon III and Baron Haussmann. Coal and iron production increased even without Alsace and Lorraine. Money was plentiful, furthermore, for capitalizing new enterprises, for foreign investments. Amazingly, the German indemnity was paid off in full by 1873, two years ahead of schedule. The days of *grandeur* were not past; France would be herself again.

For his own part Ferdinand de Lesseps was no more interested in retirement than he had been twenty years earlier. Inspirited by his new marriage and constant public attention, he was openly casting about for new worlds to conquer. He had been untarnished by the war; he was among the few. People spoke of him as the living embodiment of French vitality and the century's "splendid optimism." "We have had a lot of other men who have done things perhaps more remarkable and who have been less popular," a grandson would remember, "but that's the way he was." Once, on Bastille Day, when he was on his way to the station to take the train to his country place, a cheering crowd stopped his carriage, unhitched the horses, and pulled the carriage the rest of the way to the station. Gambetta called him *Le Grand Français*—The Great Frenchman, The Great Patriot—and the name was picked up by everyone.

He kept in excellent physical condition. He exercised regularly—fencing, riding—and with the zest of a man half his age. He looked at least ten to fifteen years younger than he was. An admiring American of the day described him as "a small man, French in detail, with . . . what is called a magnetic presence." A reporter for the New York *Herald* provided this description:

He bears his years with ease and grace, showing no sign of age in his movements, which are quick and frequent, though never jerky. . . . His hair is almost white. His eyes are black, large, restless, and fringed by heavy lashes over which are shaggy eyebrows. His face is tanned . . . and ruddy with the evidence of perfect health. A mustache is the only one hirsute adornment on his face. It is small, iron-gray, bristling and has an aggressive look. In stature he is a little below medium height. His bearing is erect, his manner suave, courteous and polished.

Come winter he was usually off to Egypt with his wife and children, and wherever they went she attracted still more attention for him. "Her form is the admiration of every dressmaker in the French capital," reported the Paris correspondent of the Chicago *News,* "and a tight fitting dress sets off her elegant figure to the greatest advantage." They were seen riding in the Bois, at balls at the Élysée, where the stately Marshal MacMahon, president of the Republic, and his lady led "the decorous waltz" past flower-wreathed panels that still bore the imperial initials of "N" and "E."

They entertained often and grandly at a new apartment on the Rue Saint Florentin, a home with "every elegance"—Persian rugs, walls of family photographs and paintings in heavy gilt frames, a pair of tremendous elephant tusks in one antechamber, in another a display of his decorations. Presently, with her money, a larger, more impressive residence was purchased, a five-story private mansion, or *hôtel particulier,* on the chic new Avenue Montaigne, where, as at La Chesnaye, the custom was never-ending hospitality. There were always ten to twelve people at dinner, always some old Suez comrade or distant kinsman or other stopping over for the night and staying a week or six months.

As chairman and president of the Suez Canal Company, he remained for thousands of shareholders the charmed guardian of their fortunes, which kept gaining steadily as the value of the stock grew ever greater. He thrived on the public role expected of him, rising to all occasions—banquets, newspaper interviews—with exuberant renditions of his adventures in the desert, or, increasingly, with talk of some vast new scheme in the wind. He talked of building a railroad to join Paris with Moscow, Peking, and Bombay. He had an astonishing plan to create an inland sea in the Sahara by breaking through a low-lying ridge on Tunisia's Gulf of Gabès and flooding a depression the size of Spain.

Interestingly, when a special commission of engineers was appointed to appraise this particular scheme, his absolute faith in it was not enough. Among the members was Sadi Carnot, a future president of France, who would recall de Lesseps' performance years later. "We had no difficulty in showing him that the whole thing was a pure chimera. He seemed very much astonished, and we saw that we had not convinced him. Take it from me that as a certainty he would have spent millions upon millions to create his sea, and that with the best faith in the world."

It was said that he could command money as no one else alive, and encouragement came from every quarter. Victor Hugo urged that he "astonish the world by the great deeds that can be won without a war!"

A forum for de Lesseps' interests, now a favorite gathering place for those most intrigued by his future plans, was the Société de Géographie de Paris, where Humboldt had once been a reigning light. Geography, since the war, had become something of a national cause. Among men of position it had also become extremely fashionable. It was said that ignorance of the world beyond her borders had put France in an inferior position commercially, that it had contributed to her disgraceful performance in the late war. Geographical societies sprouted in the provinces. Geography was made mandatory in the schools. Membership in the Paris society increased four times, and Vice Admiral Clement Baron de La Roncière-Le Noury, president of the society, wrote of "this ardor for geography" as one of the characteristics of the epoch. When the first serialized chapters of *Around the World in Eighty Days* appeared in *Le Temps* in 1872, Paris correspondents for foreign papers cabled their contents to home offices as though filing major news stories. Nothing else had ever made the geographical arrangement of the planet quite so clear or so interesting in human terms. An extravagant stage production of the novel opened in Paris, complete with live snakes and elephants, and between acts audiences jammed the theater lobby to watch an attendant mark Phileas Fogg's progress on a huge world map.

Jules Verne, strictly an armchair adventurer, worked in a tower study in his home at Amiens, but came often to Paris to attend meetings of the Société de Géographie and to do his research in its library. When he was made Chevalier of the Legion of Honor, it was on the nomination of Ferdinand de Lesseps, and the sight of two such men at Société functions, talking, shaking hands with admirers, was in itself a measure of the organization's standing.

It was at an international congress held under the auspices of the Société the summer of 1875 that de Lesseps made his first public declaration of interest in an interoceanic canal. The meetings opened at the Louvre, in conjunction with a huge geographical exhibition, the first of its kind, that took Paris by storm. Crowds ranged from ten to twelve thousand people a day.

Two issues must be resolved, he said. First was the best route; second was the type of canal to be built, whether at sea level (*à niveau* was the French expression) or whether a canal with locks. Several French explorers who had been to Darien spoke on their experiences and presented proposals. Joseph E. Nourse, of the United States Naval Observatory, reported on the recent American expeditions to

Nicaragua and Panama. But de Lesseps was the center of attention, and when he declared that the canal through the American Isthmus must be *à niveau* and *sans écluses* (without locks), it seemed that side of the problem had been settled.

Events began to gather momentum. Aided by the Rothschilds, England suddenly acquired financial control of the Suez Canal, and de Lesseps, while still head of the company, with offices in Paris, found his influence substantially undercut. The beloved enterprise, the pride of France, had become the lifeline of the *British* Empire.

Then before winter was out came the decision of President Grant's Interoceanic Canal Commission. Having weighed the results of its surveys in Central America, the commission had decided in favor of Nicaragua. The decision was unanimous. Panama received little more than passing mention.

Within weeks it was announced that the Société de Géographie would sponsor a great international congress for the purpose of evaluating the scientific considerations at stake in building a Central American canal. The American efforts had been insufficient, it was stated.

III

Whether Ferdinand de Lesseps was merely an adornment for the Türr Syndicate or a willing confederate or its guiding spirit were to become questions of much debate. In some accounts he would be portrayed as the victim of forces beyond his control. "Inevitably the whirlpool began to draw Ferdinand nearer and nearer its vortex," reads one interpretation of events surrounding the origins of the Panama venture, and he is pictured struggling valiantly against the current. To a great many contemporary American observers he would appear more the innocent dupe of furtive schemers—"insidious influences," as one of the New York papers said—who were placing the old hero out in front of the French people like a goat before sheep.

Had things turned out differently, however, it is unlikely that the galvanizing leadership of the effort would ever have been attributed to anybody other than Ferdinand de Lesseps, which, from the available evidence, not to mention the man's very nature, appears to have been the truth of the matter. As he himself once remarked to an American reporter, "Either I am the head or I refuse to act at all."

The newly formed Türr Syndicate was quite small but made up of such "well-selected" figures as to command immediate attention and confidence. Its better-known stockholders included Senator Émile Littré, author of the great French dictionary, and Octave Feuillet, the novelist. (Littré declared that the five thousand francs he put in represented the first financial investment of his life.) There were General Claude Davout, Charles Cousin, of the Chemin de Fer du Nord, the Saint-Simonian financier Isaac Periere, and Jules Bourdon, who was curator of the Opéra. Dr. Henri Bionne, an official of the Société de Géographie, was an authority on international finance, a former lieutenant commander in the French Navy, who had degrees in both medicine and law. Dr. Cornelius Herz, a newcomer to Paris and an American, was a physician and entrepreneur who claimed a personal friendship with Thomas Edison.

The syndicate's formal title was the Société Civile Internationale du Canal Interocéanique de Darien. It had a capital of 300,000 francs represented by some sixty shares and de Lesseps was neither a shareholder nor an officer. The leadership and the bulk of the stock were in the hands of three directors. The most conspicuous of these was General Istvan Türr, a Hungarian who had covered himself with glory in Sicily as Garibaldi's second in command and who for a time had been employed by King Victor Emmanuel II for diplomatic missions. With his long, elegant figure, his long, handsome face and spectacular Victor Emmanuel mustache—it must have been the largest mustache in all Paris in the 1870's— Istvan Türr had become something of a celebrity, the sort of personage people pointed out on the boulevards. His social connections included *Le Grande Français.*

The second man was the financier Baron Jacques de Reinach, a short, stout, affable man about town, known for his political pull and his voracious interest in young women. Like Türr, he was foreign-born, but a German and a Jew, as would be made much of later. He had founded the Paris banking firm of Kohn, de Reinach et Compagnie and had become rich speculating in French railroads and selling military supplies to the French government. His dealings had been subject to some question, although as yet nothing serious had come of it.

Most important of the three was Lieutenant Wyse, Lieutenant Lucien Napoleon-Bonaparte Wyse, who was the illegitimate son of the first Napoleon's niece Princess Laetitia. Temporarily on leave from the French Navy, Wyse was twenty-nine years old. He did not look much like a Bonaparte. Tall and slender, he had an open, friendly face with a high forehead, blue eyes, and full beard. His mother, a sensational woman who had been known in every capital in Europe, was the daughter of Napoleon's wayward brother Lucien Bonaparte, Prince of Canino. Her early marriage to Sir Thomas Wyse, an Irish diplomat, had failed, but was never dissolved legally, and by the time Lieutenant Wyse was born, nineteen years had passed since she and her husband had even seen each other. Two illegitimate daughters had also resulted, magnificent-looking women, very much like their mother, one of whom married Istvan Türr (which made Türr and Wyse brothers-in-law). The other, known as Madame Rattazzi, was a literary figure of sorts and one of the most dazzling and publicized figures of the day. The father of the sisters was an English Army officer who had pulled Princess Laetitia from a pond in St. James's Park after she had attempted a public and rather ridiculous suicide at the time her marriage was breaking up. But the identity of the young lieutenant's father was never divulged, though naturally there was speculation on the subject and especially when the Panama venture commenced. The money he put into the syndicate had come from his wife, a wealthy Englishwoman.

It was Wyse who went to see de Lesseps and in the early stages de Lesseps appears to have found him a young man much after his own heart. Wyse would also be the sole member of the syndicate to subject himself to any physical danger or hardship.*

The initial plan announced by the Société de Géographie was for a series of definitive explorations and surveys, a binational, wholly nonpartisan effort, with the world's leading scientific societies participating. But all such talk ceased the moment the Türr Syndicate made itself available, offering to handle everything. Permission to conduct explorations within Colombian territory was secured by sending an intermediary to Bogotá, and six months later, in early November 1876, an expedition of seventeen men sailed on the steamer *Lafayette,* flagship of the French West Indies line. Lieutenant Wyse was in command, assisted by another French naval officer, Lieutenant Armand Réclus, and their orders were to find and survey a canal route, but to confine their activities to Darien, east of the railroad, since the Colombian government had forbidden any intrusion along the railroad's right of way. In other words they were to look only in that area wherein the syndicate had a legal right to carry on its business, which was scarcely the broad-range perspective embodied in the Société's original proposal.

The party was gone six months, two of which were spent at sea. Everyone suffered from malaria, two men died in the jungle, a third died during the voyage home. Wyse returned thin and drawn and covered with tiny scars from insect bites. He was thoroughly discouraged and made little effort to hide it. Though they had managed to cross the divide, the terrain, the punishing heat, the rains, had defeated them. The best he could recommend—and purely by guesswork—was a Darien canal with a tunnel as much as nine miles in length.

De Lesseps was wholly dissatisfied. How instrumental he had been in planning the expedition, if at all, is not apparent. His role was supposedly that of an arbiter only. He was the head of the Société's Committee of Initiative.

At any rate, having heard the young officer's report, he declared it as good as worthless. He would agree only to a canal at sea level—no locks, no tunnels. Furthermore, he now knew where to build the canal. As he would remark later to a

*In examining the relationship that developed between Wyse and de Lesseps, their kinship of purpose, the shared sense of adventure, the almost father-son spirit, the question inevitably arises: Might de Lesseps have been the unknown father? There is, however, nothing in the available record to suggest this was so. About all we can safely assume is that for a young man of such background, with his paternity in doubt and his aspirations so high, de Lesseps must have been an appealing figure and one to which he might very naturally wish to attach himself.

New York newspaperman, "I told Messrs. Wyse and Réclus when they made their report that there could be no other route than that of the railroad. 'If you come back with a favorable report on a sea-level canal on that route I shall favor it.'"

So Wyse and Réclus sailed again, accompanied by many of the same men who had been on the first expedition. And this time things went differently. Considering how much was to hang on their efforts, how much would be risked on the so-called Wyse Survey at Panama, it is interesting to see just how their time was occupied.

Landing at Colón and crossing to Panama City, Wyse assembled the necessary provisions and sailed for the Pacific shores of San Blas, where his efforts appear to have been half-hearted. Indeed, it is puzzling why he bothered at all, knowing de Lesseps' attitude. In three weeks, certain that no canal could be built at San Blas without a tunnel, Wyse ordered everybody back to Panama City.

Lieutenant Réclus was told to explore the Panama route, keeping to the line of the railroad, and since this was in violation of the agreement secured earlier, Wyse decided to go himself to Bogotá. Time suddenly was of the essence. On the first of April the president of Colombia, Aquileo Parra, would be retiring from office and President Parra was known to favor the Wyse-Türr enterprise.

Lieutenant Réclus, meantime, began an informal reconnaissance of the Pacific slope a few miles east of the railroad, assisted by a young Panamanian engineer, Pedro Sosa. It was, as Réclus himself noted in his diary, "not an exploration in the true sense of the word." It was more of a walk, a ride on the railroad even. Sosa became ill within a week. Then Réclus too was stricken with an excruciating earache, and so he called the whole thing off. On April 20, they were back in Panama City and ten days later, with no word from Wyse, Réclus sailed for France.

And that was the sum total of the Wyse Survey. The exploration of the Panama route that was "not an exploration" had occupied all of two weeks, four days. Wyse had played no part in it and in fact no survey had resulted.

By contrast, the American expedition of three years before had remained two and a half months in Panama and virtually all that time had been spent in the field. The Americans, more than a hundred in number, had run a line of levels from ocean to ocean, explored the Chagres watershed, and prepared maps, charts, and statistical tables. And the Government Printing Office in Washington had made most of these findings, except for the maps and plans, available in a document of several hundred pages, a document Wyse would be perfectly happy to rely upon. Such borrowing would pose no conflict presumably, since the material had been published in the spirit of open exchange of scientific information and the Americans had already rejected the Panama route.

It was well afterward, when he was safely back in Paris, that Wyse wrote of his mission to Bogotá, then one of the most inaccessible cities on the face of the earth. From Panama City to Bogotá was normally a journey of three, even four weeks, though the distance on a straight line was only about five hundred miles. Moreover, it was a vastly different world from Panama that one found on arrival—a gray stone city set on a tableland at 8,600 feet and hemmed in by two of the three tremendous ranges of the Andes that divide Colombia like giant fingers; a mild damp climate that seldom varies, skies often clouded; a solemn, impoverished populace clothed in black; a proud ruling class of bankers, scholars, poets, who spoke the most perfect Castilian to be heard in Latin America.

Because the Darien wilderness stood between Panama and the rest of Colombia, Panama was as removed as if it were an island, and Colombia could be reached only by sea, either by the Caribbean or the Pacific. One sailed first either to Barranquilla or to Buenaventura. The journey from Barranquilla to Bogotá involved a four-hundred-mile trip by river steamer up the Magdalena to a point called Honda, then another hundred miles over the mountains by horse or wagon. There were no railroads.

The other way, by Buenaventura, the route Wyse took, was shorter but considerably more arduous, covering nearly four hundred miles. Wyse went by horseback, traveling with one companion, a French lawyer, Louis Verbrugghe, the two of them in serapes and big Panama hats. The general direction, as Wyse wrote, was "*perpendiculaire.*"

They reached Bogotá in just eleven days, during which they sometimes spent twenty-four hours in the saddle. They arrived unshaven, their clothes torn and filthy. Wyse was missing one spur and had broken the other so that it clanked disconcertingly as they walked along the streets. Hotels turned them away because of their appearance, as Wyse would tell the story. But the following morning, March 13, bathed, shaved, looking most presentable, Wyse met with Eustorgio Salgar, Secretary of Foreign Relations. On March 14 he saw President Parra, who was especially "well disposed" toward his proposition.

The newspapers in Bogotá, all closely tied to the party in power, the Liberals, took little notice of Wyse's presence in the capital. That the visit was one of the utmost importance to the future of Colombia, that Wyse was there in fact to settle the basic contract to build a Panama canal, a contract that could mean a world of difference to Colombia for centuries to come, or more immediately help solve the country's dire financial troubles, was in no way suggested. Possibly someone somewhere along the line had decided that a better bargain might be driven with the young man by playing down his importance.

On March 15, or just three days after his arrival, Wyse presented a draft of a contract. Everything was going as smoothly as could be hoped for. Five days later, having made only minor modifications, Salgar and Wyse fixed their signatures to the document, and three days after that, on March 23, 1878, President Parra, who had exactly one week left in office, did the same. Confirmation by the Colombian Senate took longer, but by mid-May, the concession at last in his pocket, Wyse was on his way back to Panama, going this time by steamer down the Magdalena.

At Panama City he learned from Pedro Sosa of the little that Sosa and Réclus had accomplished, yet took no time to do anything more. Rather, he wound up his affairs in the least time possible, sold off the supplies left over from the expeditions, made Sosa a gift of the surveying instruments, and departed. He seems to have felt obliged only to see Nicaragua—to travel the route the Americans had settled on—and it was another journey in record time. He crossed from San Juan del Norte, going by steamer up the San Juan, then over the lake. The Americans had "much simplified" his task, he was to report. In fact, their Nicaragua Expedition had been their largest and most extensive. To plot their canal line they had had to chop a path nearly the length of the entire valley, or more than twice the distance across Panama, and much of the time the men had worked in swamps in water up to their shoulders. Their survey was an accomplishment Wyse especially could appreciate. He himself paused only long enough to pick up a few rock samples.

From Nicaragua he went to Washington, but by way of San Francisco, another odd side of the story, since he could so easily have returned to Colón, taken a steamer to New York, and saved himself several thousand miles. The impression is that he wanted to appraise financial interest in San Francisco, the American city that stood to gain the most from the canal. But possibly he wanted only to take the transcontinental railroad, to ride like Phileas Fogg the "uninterrupted metal ribbon." Whatever his reasons, he can be pictured flying along in a Union Pacific parlor car, observing "the varied landscape" as Fogg had, checking his watch at the Great Salt Lake, or taking some air during the stop at Green River Station.

At the Navy Department in Washington he was received by Commander Edward P. Lull and A. G. (Aniceto Garcia) Menocal, authors of both the Nicaragua and Panama surveys. Lull had had overall command; Menocal, a Cuban by birth, had been foremost of the civilian engineers assigned by Admiral Ammen "to place the results of the work beyond the reach of criticism."

The conversation was cordial and for Wyse perfectly fruitless. The Americans showed great interest in his travels, and Wyse, who spoke excellent English, made much of their pioneering efforts in the jungle. But it was their maps and plans that Wyse had come for and he was politely told that these were not available, that the department "did not feel disposed" to grant his request. He asked if he might pay his respects to Admiral Ammen, but Admiral Ammen, he was told, was not available.

So it was with the Bogotá contract only—the famous Wyse Concession—that Wyse sailed from New York; no survey of his own, not even a map of Panama other than one made by the railroad twenty-five years before. For the moment, however, the concession was enough. That its cash value could be phenomenal went without saying.

The agreement was this:

The United States of Colombia granted the Société Civile—the Türr Syndicate—the exclusive privilege, good for ninety-nine years, to construct a canal across the Isthmus of Panama. As a guarantee of their good faith, the grantees were obligated to deposit 750,000 francs in a London bank no later than 1882. It was required that surveys be made by an international commission of competent engineers, for which three years were allowed, and the grantees were permitted two additional years in which to organize a canal company, and then twelve years to build the canal.

Colombia in turn was to get 5 percent of the gross revenue from the canal for twenty-five years, 6 percent for the next twenty-five years, 7 percent for the next twenty-five years, and 8 percent for the final years of the concession. The minimum payment, however, was never to be less than $250,000, which was the same as Colombia's share in the earnings of the Panama Railroad.

Colombia conceded to the company, without charge, 500,000 hectares (1,235,500 acres) of public lands, in addition to a belt of land 200 meters (219 yards) wide on each side of the canal. The terminal ports and the canal itself were declared neutral for all time. At the end of ninety-nine years the canal would revert to Colombia.

Further conditions were stipulated, but the crucial ones were these:

The concession could be transferred (i.e., sold) to other individuals or financial syndicates, but under no circumstances could it be sold to a foreign government. It was left to the grantees to negotiate "some amicable agreement" with the Panama Railroad concerning its rights and privileges.

Once reunited in Paris, Wyse and Réclus quickly put together a plan to present to de Lesseps. It was for a sea-level canal following the line of the Panama Railroad and again they resorted to a tunnel as the essential feature. De Lesseps voiced no objections to any of it. Nor did he register any serious dissatisfaction with Wyse's so-called survey. The one dissenting voice at this stage was that of a young Hungarian engineer named Bela Gerster, who had served with Wyse on both expeditions and who pointedly refused to sign Wyse's final report. Gerster prepared his own minority report, but when he took it to a number of French newspapers none were interested in printing it.

Some loose ends had to be attended to before de Lesseps could convene his canal congress. He had to have a guarantee that the Americans would attend—their presence was essential to the prestige of the affair—and he needed a commitment from the Panama Railroad Company that there would be no problem over the "amicable agreement" required by the Wyse Concession. Actually, he wanted to buy the railroad. So back Wyse sailed once more, early in 1879, arriving at New York, where he saw the president of the Panama Railroad Company, a clever Wall Street speculator named Trenor W. Park. Standing up to greet Wyse, Park looked no larger than a twelve-year-old boy, but he had come as far as he had in the business world by making the most of every advantageous position, and at the moment he was in an extremely advantageous position, as he and Wyse both appreciated. The details of the Bogotá contract had become public knowledge by now, and if an amicable understanding could *not* be reached with Trenor Park, the major stockholder in the railroad, then obviously the contract was worthless.

It was within Park's power to decide whether Wyse or de Lesseps need go a step further with their plans.

Park was "not altogether reluctant" to sell the railroad. His price, he told Wyse, was $200 a share, or twice its market value at the moment. Park, it was understood, owned fifteen thousand shares.

In Washington next, Wyse not only succeeded in seeing Admiral Ammen, but was presented to the Secretary of State, William Evarts, and later to President Hayes, who expressed great interest in the forthcoming Paris congress. Evarts, however, seemed as suspicious as Palmerston had been about Suez. The ill-fated attempt by Napoleon III to make Maximilian emperor of Mexico had left Evarts, like many Americans, extremely uneasy about France and her aspirations in the Western Hemisphere and anything but trustful of anyone with the name Bonaparte, even so amiable a Bonaparte as Lieutenant Wyse. So it was a difficult interview.

At length Evarts agreed that the United States should participate in the congress but only Ammen and A. G. Menocal would be permitted to go as authorized delegates. They could join in the technical discussions—to "communicate such scientific, geographical, mathematical, or other information . . . as is desired or deemed important"—but they were to have no official powers or diplomatic function, no say concerning the canal policy of the United States.

Shortly afterward in Paris, sometime in the early spring of 1879, just before the opening of the congress, Charles de Lesseps met with his father in the office of Dr. Henri Bionne, one of the most respected figures in the Türr Syndicate.

At age thirty-eight, Charles was nearly bald, and with his dark brows and thick dark beard, he looked a good deal older than he was. Like his father, he was a man of great pride and natural courtesy. He was also a capable administrator and this, plus a good deal of common sense and a capacity for hard work, had won him wide admiration at Suez, where he had served as his father's principal aide.

He was intelligent, rather than brilliant, careful, considerate, but with none of his father's glamour or his need for public acclaim. Charles was a chess player.

The demands on him at Suez had been heavy. His only child, "Little Ferdinand," had died in infancy of cholera at Ismailia in 1865. Still, he idolized his father no less than ever and remained his good right arm in numerous ways. Charles, as would be said later, was above all a devoted son. More, he was a son who knew his devotion was returned in full.

Charles was strongly opposed to the Panama venture and had been from the day Lieutenant Wyse first came to La Chesnaye to present his plan. To Charles the whole scheme was a kind of madness.

The account we have of the scene in Bionne's office is Charles's own, provided years later in a private memoir.

"What do you wish to find at Panama?" he asked his father. "Money? You will not bother about money at Panama any more than you did at Suez. Glory? You've had enough glory. Why not leave that to someone else? All of us who have worked at your side are entitled to a rest. Certainly the Panama project is grandiose . . . but consider the risks those who direct it will run! You succeeded at Suez by a miracle. Should not one be satisfied with accomplishing one miracle in a lifetime?"

Then, not waiting for a reply, he added: "If you decide to proceed with this, if nothing will stop you . . . if you want me to assist you, then gladly I will take whatever comes. I shall not complain no matter what happens. All that I am I owe to you; what you have given me, you have the right to take away."

Ferdinand de Lesseps replied that he had already made up his mind. What he did not say, what perhaps he was unable to admit to himself just yet, was the extent to which his trust in Charles had influenced that decision.

orn in 1930, Sherwin Nuland has called himself "an unassimilated immigrant's son from the Bronx." He had already been accepted to the Johns Hopkins University School of Medicine when he decided to try for Yale as well. He visited New Haven and after an interview was taken by the dean of admissions to an afternoon tea served by faculty wives. "Never mind that I felt completely out of my depth. I had arrived at a place where I was sure I didn't belong, and for that reason was equally sure where I *did* belong. When I got the Yale acceptance a week later it somehow seemed right. It has seemed right for half a century." He received his M.D. from Yale in 1955 and is now clinical professor of surgery at the Yale School of Medicine. After contributing to the literature of medical history for some years, in 1988 he wrote *Doctors: The Biography of Medicine* and in 1994 *How We Die: Reflections on Life's Final Chapter,* which was given the National Book Award. Later books include *The Wisdom of the Body* (1997), *The Mysteries Within: A Surgeon Reflects on Medical Myths* (2000), and a biography, *Leonardo da Vinci* (2000). He also writes for a wide range of periodicals, including the *New Yorker* and the *New York Review of Books,* and serves on the Bioethics Committee of the Yale–New Haven Hospital.

THE MYSTERIES WITHIN, EXCERPT FROM
"THE HEART: CRACKING THE VALVE"

The first time I took part in an operation on a human heart, I was a third-year student newly assigned to the cardiac surgery service, whose chief was a man I'll call Dr. James Jackson Wiggins Brock, a soft-spoken but nevertheless extremely intense South Carolinian then in the early phases of the most productive years of what would be a distinguished career. Dr. Brock's gentle drawl belied a compulsive attention to even the minutest detail of each operative procedure. So demanding was he in his meticulousness that an operation took two or three times longer in his hands than it might when done by most other surgeons. The extra hours were spent satisfying his insistent thoroughness and almost obsessional determination to do things in the safest possible manner.

As maddening as it was to his assistants, the methodical exactitude of Brock's technique paid large dividends. In those days before open heart surgery and high-tech anesthesia, he had accumulated an enviable record of success, with extremely low rates of mortality and complications. For certain of the operations done at that time, in fact, an approach that to others seemed unnecessarily finicky and even timid was the reason that no one in the country had a higher success rate than he did.

Unlike most surgeons, who placed the medical student either far down the operating table or awkwardly positioned at the end of one of the retractors that held the wound open, Brock kept the neophyte at his right side during the entire procedure. Although one could never know what was going on in the surgeon's vigilantly focused mind or perceive the sensation in his sometimes tentative fingertips, the student enjoyed an ideal view of even the smallest detail of each operation. He might be totally enervated by the time the last stitch had been placed anywhere from five to twelve or more hours after the induction of anesthesia, but he had seen cardiac surgery from a perspective available to students in few other hospitals.

The patient was a thirty-one-year-old woman whom I'll call Lily Stewart (both for confidentiality and because I don't remember her name), suffering from a condition called mitral stenosis, in those days and now most commonly encountered years or decades after a childhood or adolescent bout of rheumatic fever. The disease causes scarring and the accumulation of thick fibrous tissue on the edges of the valve that lies between the reservoirlike left atrium (which receives oxygenated blood returning from the lungs) and the ventricle below it (which is the powerful pumping chamber that forces the blood out to the body). The flexibility of the valve is thus impaired, preventing it from opening and closing as easily as it should. Not only that, but the scarring causes adhesions between the two delicate leaflets of tissue that form the valve, further inhibiting its movements. The result is a narrowing that partially obstructs the blood flow downward from the atrium into the ventricle. Some of the blood accordingly backs up into the lungs, causing congestion and progressive shortness of breath. As the condition worsens, breathing becomes very difficult and the right side of the heart may weaken and fail in its attempt to push blood through the lungs. The disease is diagnosed by its symptoms and by the presence of a murmur with a characteristic rumble, immediately following a snapping sound caused by the contracting atrium forcing the resistant valve open by pushing a bolus of blood against it.

Mitral stenosis was one of the earliest cardiac diseases to be treated successfully by surgery, in an operation called valvulotomy—literally, opening up the valve. Some ten or a dozen attempts were made in the 1920s with only two surviving patients. The results being so poor, no further such operations were known until the mid 1940s, when several successes, first in Philadelphia and shortly thereafter in Boston and London, were achieved. Following these, the operation soon became standardized, so that by the time I was a student on the wards between 1953 and 1955, many thousands were being done in hospitals throughout the world. With slight variations, two methods were in favor. In one, the valve leaflets were separated by a specially designed knife inserted through the heart wall; in the other, the surgeon cut a small hole in the atrium, just large enough to accept his index finger, which he then lowered into the valve so that he could force it open. Either way, the idea was to free up the fibrous tissue and separate the fused leaflets, in order to allow them to move more freely.

Because Lily Stewart had been in the hospital for a week before she arrived in the operating room, I had had plenty of opportunity to spend time with her and assess her condition. The medical student evaluation of a newly admitted patient takes—or at least took in 1953—about two hours, so that the full history could be heard and a thorough physical examination completed. This alone meant that I knew my patient at least as well as did the other members of the team, and probably better than anyone except Dr. Brock himself.

Mrs. Stewart was a thin, ginger-haired woman who would have appeared pale but for the high flush over her cheekbones and the slight bluish tinge of her lips and earlobes, caused by decreased oxygenation of the blood as it made its difficult way through the crowded circuit of the lungs. Most striking was the shortness of breath, even when she was at rest and sitting up with three pillows behind her head. Removing even one of them worsened her breathing problems, and she found the loss of two unmanageable. During the admission interview, she answered my questions with very short sentences, because respirations became more difficult each time she began to speak. Obviously, her lungs were congested with backed-up blood under high pressure. The breathlessness made her fidgety; she picked at the bedclothes from time to time during our conversation and constantly held her chin high in an attempt to get more air. Speaking to her was like trying to have a conversation with someone who has just crossed the finish line of a marathon.

Mrs. Stewart had recently begun to experience a new symptom that she said was even more alarming to her than the shortness of breath with which she had long been familiar: Several times during our interview, she was seized with an alarming paroxysm of coughing, during which she spat small amounts of bright-red sputum into a Kleenex she held always ready in her hand. The tiny vessels in the lungs were under such high pressure that they were spontaneously rupturing.

Being a very young man, I was much impressed—perhaps sympathetic is a better word—with one of my patient's symptoms that was completely new to me. She had stopped having intercourse with her husband six months earlier because the combination of the emotion and the necessity for at least an element of position-change or recumbency had each time worsened the distress of her air hunger so suddenly that she was invariably thrown into an acute and terrifying episode that felt like she was drowning in the gurgly, pinkish secretions that would begin coming up from her lungs. Actually, it was her husband who told me about this—even had she wanted to, she did not have the breath to string together enough words to relate the entire story.

Over the few days following her admission, my visits to Mrs. Stewart were brief. Not only did her breathing problems preclude all but the most momentary exchanges, but she was quite obviously too exhausted with the effort of respiration for any but those contacts that were absolutely necessary. When she tried to nap she was likely to awaken suddenly after only a few minutes, gasping for the oxygen that made its way only with great difficulty into the swollen blood vessels around the air sacs in her heavy lungs. It was clear that she could not long survive in such a state. Though the risk was great, she was desperate to have the operation.

Lily Stewart was the sort of patient who in those more blunt-spoken times we used to call a cardiac cripple. Even before the rapid worsening that had brought her to this present fearful condition, she could do no housework, was unable to care for her two young children, and rarely went outdoors. Not only had her days become unlivable but there were not many of them left. Her only chance for survival was the high-risk surgery. Just before she was wheeled into the OR suite on the designated morning, she wordlessly gripped her husband's hand and kissed him for what he later told me he was sure would be the last time.

When I arrived at the OR, Mrs. Stewart was sitting up on a gurney outside of room 3. Although her eyes were closed, small, fresh tears rested on her lashes. Hurrying by, I spied Dr. Brock entering the senior surgeons' locker room. As I would later discover was his invariable habit, he had stopped at his patient's side and stood by her for a few moments, speaking gently and doing all that he could to be encouraging. Whatever were the turbulent thoughts that must have been racing through the worried mind of that uncommon man, he would never have conveyed to a patient anything but optimism and quiet reassurance. He could hardly have felt them himself on that portentous morning that we were now embarking upon with such a sense of foreboding. Uncertainty, fretfulness, impatience—those who served as his assistants bore the brunt of his complex bundle of emotional tics, but never did a single patient suspect that their surgeon was anything other than a self-assured icon of solidity.

Like the rest of us, Brock was worried, first of all, about what might happen during the induction of anesthesia. Even in the most skillful of hands, these preliminary manipulations can precipitate a sudden abnormality of rhythm or a worsening of heart failure from which a patient as sick as ours might not be rescuable. But luck was with the anesthesiologist and Mrs. Stewart. The induction was accomplished without untoward event, the breathing tube was slid into her windpipe, and her sleeping body was rotated on the table so that she lay on her right side, ready for the operation to begin. The resident, whom I'll call Fred Clarke, and I took up our positions after the intern had swabbed the chest with antiseptic solution and applied the large drapes so that only a wide swath of its left side was exposed.

With a long sweep of his arm, Fred cut through the skin and underlying skimpy layer of fat, making a gradually curving incision that began alongside the breastbone and ran backward over the chest wall, ending at a point some two inches below the tip of the shoulder blade behind. The muscles he exposed with the cut were some of those well known to bodybuilders—the latissimus dorsi, the serratus anterior, and a bit of the trapezius—but in our patient they were so thin that cutting through them with the scalpel and tying off their blood vessels was the work of only a few minutes. As each of them came into view, I was asked its name and function, questions so routinely put to medical students that I was well prepared for them.

Soon the length of the fourth rib lay exposed before us, like an arching strut protecting the vital organs that pulsed and breathed, expanded and contracted, within the rigidly encased cavity of the chest. Using a set of scraperlike tools, Fred peeled away the rib's fibrous covering, finally detaching the bone from the deep muscles that lay between it and the ribs just higher and lower, numbers three and five. Once the rib was stripped of its thin cover, it was a simple matter to divide its attachment to the cartilage in front and then cut across its narrow width far back among the vertical muscles running up and down alongside the spinal column. Fred lifted the rib out of its snug cradle and cut through the pleura, that final filmy layer lining the inside of the chest cavity.

The first thing I saw as the pleura fell away under Fred's scalpel was the spongy pinkness of the underlying lung, sliding up and down under the incision as the breathing machine forced anesthetic gas and oxygen into it and then allowed the exhaled mixture to escape. More than the usual pressure was being required to expand its turgid texture, but I did not know that at the time. To me, the salmon-coral color, the smooth gliding motion of the great lobed organ under the pleura, the certainty that I was about to see the heart—all of it was exhilarating.

A double-bladed spreading retractor was now put into place and ratcheted up in the gap where the fourth rib had been. The motion forced ribs three and five widely apart and made the long narrow opening in the chest wall big enough to easily accept the insertion of two pairs of hands, various instruments, and a few large cloth pads moistened with warm saline solution. The pads were spread out over the lung, and the entire package gently drawn backward out of the way, exposing the sturdy fibrous envelope called the pericardium, through which the powerful pulsations of the contained heart could now be seen.

Until this point, conversation had been continuous, but focused only on the job at hand. The word that had been used to describe Lily Stewart's condition was *precarious,* and her operation was not one to be approached with anything but extreme gravity. Fred, in most circumstances a cheerful fellow whose easy banter kept the members of his team distracted from the serious tasks before them, was uncharacteristically subdued that morning. Perhaps he was identifying with the young husband, a man about his own age waiting anxiously outside the OR, the future of his family and of his life hanging by tenuous threads on the events unfolding on that operating table. Or the resident may simply have been concerned with the probability that his chief would be even more demanding—or worse yet, unreasonable—than usual on that particularly nerve-wracking day, when any small mishap might be lethal to a young woman already so close to death.

The relationship between Fred Clarke and the chief was complex. Like most of our residents in those days, Fred had matured in the crucible of overseas service in World War II. At thirty-nine, Brock was only about five years older than his resident, and though far more experienced at surgery, he had enormous respect for the younger man's dependability and judgment. It was clear that he saw Fred more as a supportive and confident younger brother than a trainee. The two spoke to each other almost as equals. It was well known among the students that when feeling less than sure of himself, Brock depended on Fred's reassuring presence to steady him. But there was never any doubt about who the boss was.

So intent on our work had the entire team been that no one noticed the surgeon enter from the scrub room, water dripping from his upraised forearms and ready to be gowned. When Brock was completely outfitted in the surgeon's sterile regalia, we repositioned ourselves around the table.

I took up my place alongside and up-table of him, our bodies touching from shoulder to knee. I had been warned that he would be hesitant, uncertain, and particularly irritable when doing such a hazardous operation, but he seemed remarkably sure of himself and decisive as he took over command from Fred. Apprehensive as I was—it was my first cardiac operation and the patient was desperately ill—I felt reassured by the warmth of the chief's body next to mine. He had a few words with the anesthesiologist and Fred about the patient's status, asked me a question or two about cardiac physiology, and got right down to work.

The very first thing Brock did was to make a long up-and-down slit in the pericardium. He peeled its edges back out of the way and exposed the living, beating heart. Though it may have appeared flabby and sick to every other person in that room, the fist-sized dynamo of thrusting power which just then seemed to fill my entire field of vision was a sight so unprecedented in its glorious fulfillment that I felt as though I had been waiting to see it since the day I was born.

For here was indeed the beginning of life, the sun of the microcosm, and as far as I was concerned it was at that moment more brilliant than the sun of the *mac*rocosm. It was my own household divinity—nourishing, cherishing, quickening my whole body as I stared at it. It was the source of all action, of all energy, of all the driving force that a human being possesses. I was dumbstruck in its presence, so distracted by the ineffable beauty of the thing that I let my fingers loosen from the flat, ribbonlike retractor I had been given to hold the lung out of the way with. I was jerked back to reality by Brock's instant outburst of displeasure, although in fact the brief sample of his legendary temper was mild: "C'mon, son, wake up. This little lady needs you to pay attention to her!"

The problem, of course, was not that I had been asleep, but quite the opposite: something in me had been awakened. I stood there in a heightened state of awareness, all of it focused on the magnificence before me and none of it on my assigned task. Brock's admonition broke—or at least weakened—the spell. My rapt absorption receded just enough to disperse the drifting thoughts and return me to the company of the operating team.

In continuity with the side of the atrium is its antechamber—the auricle—a flattened appendage lying against it much as an ear does alongside the head. It is as though nature designed the auricle for the benefit of the cardiac surgeon. Because it is essentially a cul-de-sac off the atrium, it allows him to enter that reservoir unobtrusively. This is what Brock now proceeded to do.

Having placed a specially designed clamp across the auricle and inserted a series of anchoring stitches, he cut a slit into its wall just large enough to admit his right index finger. As he carried out these maneuvers, Lily Stewart's hypersensitive heart demonstrated just how easily it could become agitated, breaking into an alarming shower of irregular beats. With this, the blood pressure dropped about 20 millimeters of mercury, but only until the irregularity spontaneously abated after Brock stopped the forward motion of his finger. With a heart that is so easily upset, it behooves the surgeon to move with extra caution, and Brock's usual deliberate slowness became a circumspect crawl.

With utmost care, the surgeon began again to advance his finger into the auricle and announced that he was moving it gradually through the atrium and down toward the diseased valve. Watching that finger disappearing bit by bit into the depths of the heart, I tried to visualize the scene within, as the disembodied digit made its silent way through the streaming blood, coming ever closer to its fateful destination. The perilous journey was interrupted several times by brief runs of irregular beats. Finally, after what seemed an hour but must have been only a few minutes, Brock announced that he was positioned just above the valve and was preparing to enter it.

It was part of Brock's scrupulously organized protocol at this point in the operation to call out the numbers "1, 2, 3!" to let the operating team and the anesthesiologist know that he was set to enter the valve itself. The purpose of the signaling was to alert all warriors that the battle was about to begin in earnest and everyone had better be prepared for any untoward eventuality, be it rhythm disturbances, hemorrhage, or even cardiac arrest. He was the man whose surgical motto was "An emergency prepared for is not an emergency," and all possibilities had to be covered. For James Jackson Wiggins Brock, it was not enough to wear both belt and suspenders—I always suspected that he also pinned his trousers to his shirt.

After the sound of "3!" the room became completely silent for the briefest of moments, until the stentorian trumpeting of "ON!" and another cascade of arrhythmia proclaimed to the heavens and to us that the Brock finger was plunging into the valve. It stayed there only long enough for the chief to feel the nature of the obstruction and shout "OFF!", the declaration—along with the resumption of a normal heartbeat—of withdrawal back into the atrium. He announced that the leaflets were fused tightly together and the opening admitted only the very tip of his finger. A particularly forceful thrust would be required to free up the tissue and relieve the constriction. The need for such a maneuver certainly magnified the danger, but there was no other choice. Success would depend on Brock's ability to force the valve open without either causing an uncontrollable and therefore lethal irregularity of rhythm or cracking it so widely that retrograde flow up into the atrium would occur to cause worsening of the back pressure on the lungs. Such a serious regurgitation was even worse, if it is possible to imagine such a thing, than the stenosis itself. In other words, if Brock applied too little pressure, he would fail to sufficiently open the valve; if he applied just a bit too much, he would kill his patient.

Had Brock been a man who easily shared his anxieties for all to see, Fred would have no doubt leaned forward across the table at this point and *sotto voce* encouraged him with something like, "She's lucky you're her surgeon, Jim," or some similar proof of unquestioning confidence and solidarity. But saying something like that was tantamount to announcing to everyone in that room the unavoidable truth that was so obvious but must remain at all costs hidden—the chief's almost paralyzing fear of taking the next essential step in the operation. But the significant word here was *almost.* Whatever tremblings may have afflicted his courage as he paused there momentarily with his fingertip hovering above the straitened valve, none of us clustered around that operating table doubted that he would proceed. Though he could easily have declared the valve inoperable and retreated with a live but still critically ill patient, he would never do such a thing. As I would learn in later years, Brock was a man with an overpowering conscience, and his sense of responsibility would figuratively shout in his ear at moments like these. And of course, there across the table from him stood Fred, like a human gyroscope of stability. Not only that, but Fred's very presence was a challenge to action—and a demand, too.

The ultimate instant had now come. Not only was this my first meeting with a live human heart but it was also the first time I had ever been at an operation where a single maneuver might either cure or kill a patient, all within a period of a few seconds.

I was not optimistic. There were no effective anti-arrhythmic medications in 1954. Having just witnessed how badly this heart responded to the relatively minor stimulation of an exploring finger, I felt sure that any vigorous attempt to push the valve open would cause a problem so uncontrollable that death was certain. I was no longer spellbound by the heart's ineffable beauty. Though I continued to watch it carefully, my thoughts had again drifted off, this time out through the large swinging doors of the OR suite, to the small waiting room outside where Paul Stewart paced anxiously back and forth across the well-worn carpet.

I was yanked back by the stentorian sound of Dr. Brock trumpeting out the numbers as though their reverberation would reinforce his will: "1, 2, 3, ON!"— and he plunged his finger down into the valve orifice amid a staccato shower of violent irregularities in the heartbeat. It was like watching fireworks. The chief was standing on a stool now, and I could feel his upper arm against my shoulder. It moved slightly just then, and I sensed that he was about to withdraw his finger from the valve and back into the safety of the atrium, his job undone. The "OFF!" that now echoed through the room had a note of desperation in it. Brock looked across the operating table at his assistant and almost whined, as though he were on the verge of something near tears, "I can't do it, Fred. I just can't get my finger through the valve, dammit. It's too tight—I know I'll kill her if I keep pushing." And then plaintively, but in a way as though he was begging to be contradicted, "Now you wouldn't want me to try again and maybe kill her, would you, Fred?" and more insistently, "Would you?" But Fred would, and it was as though Brock had anticipated he would.

"Go ahead, Jim. I know you can do it. I've seen you crack tougher ones before. You have to try again." Fred spoke very gently, but his tone was firm. He was not to be denied. The words were precisely what Brock was asking for. As I watched it unfold over the few seconds it took, that scenario seemed not to be new. Perhaps it had been played out more than once before between the two men. The surgeon needed to be told that he must make another attempt. Without Fred, he might quit, and never forgive himself his failure. He had made the resident his appointed conscience, and all of us listening to their exchange somehow knew it.

Fred had given his chief no choice, and no choice was just what Brock wanted. The chief mumbled something that was lost in his cloth mask, and I could feel his body steadying itself for the next move, as though in reflection of his stiffened resolve. Never having experienced such a situation before, I had no idea what to think. I knew only what lay behind Fred's urging: Better to lose this young woman's life in a vain attempt at cure than watch her die within the next few weeks by drowning in the backed-up fluid in her lungs. But I was far too inexperienced to understand the ineradicable feeling of guilt that goes with a death on the operating table. It would be years before I knew the intense loneliness of the surgeon when responsibility reaches such a magnitude; it would be years before I knew that the certainty of having no choice makes even the most wavering of captains become courageous.

Brock leaned into the table and I saw the top of his hand move as he began to advance his finger toward the bottom of the atrium and that unyielding valve. "1, 2, 3, ON!" He literally shouted it this time, while the heart started up its terrifying outburst of uncoordinated convulsions, as though little explosions were occurring all over the ventricles. As he hunched forward to press down into the valve, I suddenly felt something give, and the tightness in Brock's shoulder instantly relaxed. The burst of release transmitted from inside the heart was so palpable that I believe I may not only have felt it but heard it, too. It was like a sudden pop, and though I had never before experienced it, I somehow knew that it was just right. There was something about the sensation of resistance overcome to tell me that Brock had expertly separated the leaflets without injuring their delicate structure. Instantaneously, the valve had become as close to normal as it was possible to make it.

With "OFF!" the surgeon pulled his finger back into the atrium and the disordered rhythm stopped as suddenly as it had started. I felt as though I had experienced a miracle. I even began to imagine that the blood-choked lung was already becoming softer under my retractor. Perhaps I wasn't imagining it—it might well have been true.

Brock pulled his finger up out of the auricle, clamped the incision in its wall, and stepped down off the stool and away from the table, a broad grin wrinkling up his surgical mask. His blue eyes twinkled like a Santa Claus who had just delivered a particularly handsome and well-deserved gift. Though not very tall, standing there after that Olympian moment he seemed a giant. Fred looked over at him with genuine admiration, like a kid who has never really doubted that his older brother would beat up the schoolyard bully. Very quietly but obviously meaning it, he said—yes, he did say it—"She's lucky you're her surgeon, Jim."

It was the resident's turn to lower his finger into the valve, which he did with a respectful imitation of his chief's precautionary numbering. Having confirmed its near normalcy, he withdrew, sewed up the small opening in the wall of the auricle, and began to close the chest, as Dr. Brock went out toward the waiting room to give good news to Paul Stewart. Not a word was said about the moments of hesitancy.

When the dressing had been applied, our reviving patient was transferred back to her gurney and wheeled to the recovery room. By that time, she was wide awake and the breathing tube was ready to be removed. When it came out, I could scarcely believe the evidence before my eyes. This young woman, previously short of breath to the point of air hunger, was inhaling and exhaling as well as the nurse who stood by her bed. She lay almost flat on one pillow, and there was not a touch of blueness on her lips. The tears of despair had dried hours earlier, but when she became fully awake and realized that she had been given a new life, tears of joy appeared in their place. A fingertip had cured her, and also converted a third-year medical student into an acolyte of cardiac surgery.

I would, of course, go on to become Jim Brock's research fellow and then his resident, as had Fred before me. But somehow, it never felt completely comfortable. I finished all the training, was awarded a cardiac fellowship at the same renowned English hospital where the first European mitral valvulotomy had been done, and spent several years doing a series of heart cases as an attending surgeon, but my own heart was never wholly in it. From the beginning, I recognized that there was an intensity and single-mindedness in the psyche of cardiac surgeons that I did not share. I could not identify with them, could not see myself focused so totally on a single organ and a particular kind of surgical tour de force that excluded all others. And, of course, I had discovered the abdomen, a soft and welcoming place with a variety of vistas and challenges that suited the pace of my personality far better than did the high-risk, tightwire adventures that took place within the ribbed solidity of the chest's unyielding encasement. Abdominal surgeons are like me—they walk often among the commonest diseases, and thrive on jousting with their multiple complexities. They do seem to require great heights of attainment, but not as uninterruptedly as their cardiac colleagues—their need is not reawakened each day.

If the chest is a fortress that must be stormed in order to reach the rich pleasures within, then the abdomen has been for me a nurturing home of many variegated rooms, where my spirit may be tested, but is just as often nourished and
expanded.

Still, I have never lost my fascination with the heart. Though it is no longer
my household divinity, it has been like a first love, always in the background of
my thoughts as she looked the very first time I saw her, but nowadays never the
chief object of my devotion, or my desire.

Stephen Sandy

native of Minnesota, Stephen Sandy graduated from Yale College in 1955. While at Yale, he heard Wallace Stevens and Robert Frost give readings, and he has a vivid memory of a 1955 visit by William Carlos Williams: "From a car that has pulled up in front of the Elizabethan Club on a spring afternoon, several, including myself, help Williams out and into the club. He sits in the tea room facing a packed little audience. Mrs. Williams, Flossie, sits in the back row, near the pipe racks. Mostly Williams takes questions. Someone asks, 'How much money, Dr. Williams, do you make, say, in a year, from your writing?' (A Williams revival in full swing means that he has fifteen books in print.) Williams considers and replies, slowly, chuckling, 'I have no idea.' Then he calls out in a surprisingly loud, brisk voice, 'Floss, how much money did we ever make in a year off writing?' She shoots back instantly and in the same tone, 'Four hundred dollars, Bill, four hundred.'" Sandy's own poems, which keep a close eye on the natural world, have been collected in *Stresses in the Peaceable Kingdom* (1967), *Roofs* (1971), *Riding to Greylock* (1983), *Man in the Open Air* (1988), *Thanksgiving over the Water* (1992), *The Thread: New and Selected Poems* (1998), *Black Box* (1999), and *Octave* (2001).

A BAMBOO BRUSHPOT

It was for my table, to put my pencils in
while I considered a fresh way to begin,
this brushpot chance had brought my way, a coarse
bamboo copy of a Chinese emperor's
minutely carved in boxwood. My bamboo showed
a mountain wall with billowing cliff that flowed
in tumult round its sides, then fell away—
revealing a tableau of men at play.
It told of one who ruled well long ago:
Old Xie An, now seated at a low
table; around him attendants in court dress;
all concentrating on a game of chess.

The minister would play, but he can hear
the sound of messengers, whose charioteer
draws up his team around the bend. The horses
neigh; the news is of vast enemy forces
invading the Northern frontier. Xie An plays;
deliberation rules while he surveys
his partner's options, and the partner makes
his move. The game continues. A new day wakes
the far side of the wall. News from the North:
for two days victory flew back and forth;
now Xie An has conquered.
                              He refrains
from looking up. At the board his hand remains
poised for a move. Aloof alike from word
of victory or defeat, he has not stirred.

This botched pot's crudely carved, volume and line;
of humble pulp that won't admit the fine
detail that pleased an emperor once, and yet
that cloud-capped game's too earnest to forget.
May he continue play beside my chair
and I, to news just made, turn a deaf ear;
go to confusion's bleachers as to school,
greet squalid terror with stolidity;
and the cloudy invader with such deliberate cool
as showed an old man's skeptic mastery.

WILD DUCKS

Nine mallards amiably swim
the stream's treadmill. Sedate,
intent; bills front, they form
a V unmoving as kites

swimming the unseen wind.
Upstream they go together;
they glide as if upstream
some hand guides them there.

With button eyes not looking
they move, unmoved, in the pull
of taut, positioning strings,
the hand's extended will.

THE TACK

Strait in are other chambers within
chambers, the bottom of which no
one has yet reached.—Samuel Taylor Coleridge

Pruning pine branches, lopping bittersweet June
Out back, bitten by some creature invisible
    Or just missed, this
Was down time. I rested under the inveterate
White pine, the dark shape on my arm draped blood,
Surprising crimson scarf, how soon a welt
As broad as a Mac, rising like inky dough!
    A small invasion,

Yet fear gunned through my limbs, a pinprick panic
The blood cried *run* to; then, *what have I caught,*
    What has caught me?
The odd sensation scouted through me casually
As a cancer; like a teenager high and wilding
On a spree. Inside the house then, inside a solace
Of walls, out of the unveiled threat of heat,
    Sun like a weight.

I sat there reading at the little desk
Facing the north wall; close there, dead ahead
   On the paneled wall,
The fresh gleam of a thumbtack, boss on pine,
Shone back its steely convex eye at me.
In the tack head I saw the bow window, bow seat, the plaid
Squab in the sun, all curving in sunlight, conforming
   To its circumference:

To my left, the darker hemisphere of chamber,
Like the bull's-eye of Arnolfini's wedding portrait,
   In shadow but gleaming
With hints of dresser and door ajar around me,
This face like anybody's in a convex mirror,
But tiny, far, a pinpoint in the shadows
Pulling me in. A self, shuffled under
   By a sudden other.

I watched the bruise mushroom. Coleridge, despairing
Because he'd fallen from his friend and turned
   From Sara; ill
And opium-numb—en route to the Siberia
Of tacky Malta—found terror, then found what
He'd hoped to find: in St. Michael's cave, the same
Chambers, the columns, the same chasm he'd
   Imagined, writing

Osorio. It was thus to his liking, those lofty wells;
So the stung pruner grew chummy with his swelling,
   What's happened here?
Unfolding to *hello, there!* finding whatever
It was, was him now. Acceptance. The familiar;
This melting welcome, shy; reflexive; of
Such unaccounted-for increase to his
   Anatomy.

Then tender as a new baked loaf my old arm
Felt hardly part of me, bicep and bone
   Diminished under
The swelling's pillow. The beveled head of tack
No longer beamed a guttering eye; it was
Only a tack, flush with the wood, its wire

Needling deep, parting the tense pine fiber.
    When the fly stung

It was as if a curtain might have fallen,
Snuffing life out like a milkweed the wind sends
    Scudding to dust
And generations among the weeds; or I
As quickly disappear as a pricked balloon
One moment full of it, the next a tiny scumbag
Broken, moist on the needles under a pine
    Beside the road.

I watched how in the beady thumbtack's head
I was a millimeter shy of vanishing.
    The swelling held.
No pain. All right then. The floppy discs of memory
Kept printing feedback out, once meaningful
Segues now were synapses uncoupled:
A boyhood spanking; the homeless man in the subway
    Who talked with me;

The stray connections some deerfly had dredged up
Were nothing, though I kept falling through the net
    Of now, vertiginous.
My butt, he'd cried at ten on the rumpled bed
Though no one heard, for Father had put up
The razor strop; hurried outside. The hurt
Was his possession. Those stings of guilt fell through him
    Like a slow rain.

That November when I went down below
To a soiled stillness, the cold platform stood
    Unechoing, empty,
Surrendered to a slow clock. I sat on a bench
Bent on my thoughts, the unabashed abandon
Of the city, in the streets the poor on watch
As from the hillside of abandonment;
    Deserted village

Of the collective heart, center ungrieving
And forsaken. When I looked up a panhandler—
    His ragged shape

Looming against the gray fluorescent twilight
Of that limbo station—stood before me; stood
In his pants—or his pants hung around him like
A voting booth. And he was in there somewhere,
    Making choices.

The beggar began then, bowing slightly, palms
Pressed together. I gave him—money. He said,
    "Bless you, young man."
He touched his hands to his lips—for the buck I gave—
And blessed me. My nod elicited first one
Then another remark about my goodness. I shrugged.
Out of the dark the boisterous train came on
    Pushing before it

The black air of the tunnel against us. The rest
Of his life and the rest of mine were about to be
    Two different things.
Under his filthy anorak he wore
A filthy undershirt, each stitch picked out
In grime; and the flesh was stained, and dark. Again
He bowed, "God bless you," and the track below gleamed
    With oncoming light.

And Coleridge, deep in the cave, saw "crown upon crown,
A tower of crowns, the models of trees in stone."
    Nature had doubled
An infinite beauty in his fantasies.
But they were imageless; rested in darkness until
His torch gave form to them. Here was a forest,
"A bushy-branched oak, all forms of ornament
    With niches for images

Not there." Whatever he found, first found itself
In him; there were no images now. Stalactite
    To stalagmite, drip
By cold calcareous drip. No vaulted chambers,
"No saints or angels." One shaft descended hundreds
Of feet, until "the smoke of torches became
Intolerable." And he rose for air to the blue,
    The resolute day.

Down there in his corner with dignity, the tramp
Bore witness, accosted me from the homeless land
    Emerging from nowhere,
From polluted night, like one of Van Gogh's miners,
Like the coal miner up from a Pennsylvania hill
Shining the little lamp on his forehead straight
In my startled face. "Here now," I said and took
    A ten from my wallet

And handed it over. His last word died in the roar
Of the train arriving; I left him to wander, to con
    Or bless more travelers;
Yet watching the burnished thumbtack, tunnel mirror,
I caught his rushy odor still, the white wine
Of his urine; understood that blessings were; that I
Had been chosen, even as I was punctured by
    The awaited fly.

David R. Slavitt

avid R. Slavitt graduated magna cum laude from Yale College in 1956 and went on to study for his M.A. at Columbia University. It was Dudley Fitts who suggested that Slavitt attend Yale, "where they'd leave me alone, which was mostly what they did. I always supposed that Yale understood that they didn't have a whole lot to tell writers, so they left us largely to our own devices, which meant they didn't do us any harm. Harvard, in the fifties, would have been chancier." On the other hand, he did study with Cleanth Brooks and Robert Penn Warren, and has since turned out to be a writer of quite astonishing range. His sixteenth volume of poems, *Falling from Silence,* appears in 2001. He has written plays and song lyrics, nineteen novels under his own name, and nine others under a pseudonym, plus four books of nonfiction and twenty-two books of translations—of texts by authors ranging from Aeschylus, Seneca, and Ovid to King David and the Hebrew prophets.

AT SNOWBIRD

The scurry of prairie dogs and more earnest marmots'
munching across the alpine meadow appear
blithe. And the mule deer, ambling into the clearing,
fearless, incurious even (it has seen
hikers before), suggests that peaceable kingdom
we may not believe in but yearn for still: we pause
to take in the mountains' breathtaking otherness,
the evergreen tang in the air, the white-noise rush
of snowmelt rivulets some clever set designer
thought might go just here. (Thus, we distrust
our eyes, our ears, the skin on the back of the neck
where the midmorning sun assures us, as fond fathers
would their fortunate sons, that all is well.)
But mind is working—the prairie dogs and marmots
know, never forget, and forage faster
for the sound of that rushing water, the noise time makes,
the year's turning, the end of the food and warmth:
winter is coming. They are the ones, if they stopped
a moment to look at us, frivolous, blithe, who would gape
at our get-ups' funny hats and impressive boots.
We do not hibernate; we do not migrate
up the mountain or down as the seasons change—
as if we were still in Eden, or had just stepped out.

CAPE COD BEACH

The flashing green light at the Wychmere jetty
seems in this fog to forget from time to time
its business—announcing where we are and the danger
the rocks pose at the harbor's entrance. The years
will bring to us all such moments, but I can remember
only too clearly glaring sun on this sand
where we spread our blankets, or sailing out there on the water
blue years ago, but black and cold now, where a huge

fog bank looms twenty yards or so offshore
like some nocturnal predator with a taste
for happy times and places. Let it come

to devour at last what remains of this strip of beach,
children at play in that dazzling sun, and loss
for which it is stupid to think these waves still sigh.

THE BATTLE AGAINST HUMBABA

So far, so good, but I wait for word
that Gilgamesh or Enkidu
will send for me one day to join them

to fight the monster, Humbaba, who waits
for us all with his visage like coiling guts.
I am no hero of epic, nor even

a minor player whose name appears
once in the text and again in the index.
But Humbaba waits, and sooner or later,

I shall confront him whose shout is the roar
of the hurricane wave that overwhelms
the fishermen's huts on the beach and the houses

of merchants inland, whose coffers of gold
cannot protect them. I shall go forth
(or else he will come to me) to do battle

to suffer the agonies heroes suffer
and lie as Enkidu lay, so dead
that Gilgamesh saw the maggot fall

out of the nose and knew then to stop
his weeping and bury the body at last.
You don't believe me? Only wait

and you, too, will hear the horrid tread
in the still of the night of Humbaba's approach.
As long as you can, you'll laugh it off,

but that doesn't stop him. Lock the doors
and set the alarm—but it does no good:
Humbaba comes to fight and will win.

Larry Kramer

i received absolutely no encouragement at Yale to become a writer," says Larry Kramer. "I was rejected for Daily Themes, and when I submitted a short story instead of a research paper on Melville for my English seminar, my professor called me in. 'I hear you are very good in that production of "Home of the Brave" they're doing in the dining hall. Perhaps you should consider becoming an actor.'" After graduating from Yale College in 1957, Kramer indeed went to work in show business. During the 1960s he lived in London and wrote two films, *Here We Go Round the Mulberry Bush* and the acclaimed *Women in Love,* based on D. H. Lawrence's classic novel. As a playwright, he has written *The Normal Heart* (1985), the longest-running play at Joseph Papp's Public Theater in New York City, and *The Destiny of Me* (1992), which received an Obie and the Lucille Lortel Award for Best Play. His novel *Faggots* appeared in 1978, and his political writings, *Reports from the Holocaust: The Making of an AIDS Activist,* appeared in 1989. He cofounded Gay Men's Health Crisis in 1981 and has been a vociferous AIDS activist, founding ACT UP in 1987. He is currently at work on *The American People,* a long novel about the plague.

THE DESTINY OF ME, EXCERPT FROM ACT 1

(NED WEEKS, *middle-aged, enters a hospital room with his suitcase.*)

NED: I grew up not far from here. The trees were just being chopped down. To make room for Eden Heights. That's where we lived. That's what they named places then.

(HANNIMAN, *a nurse, pushes in a cart with medical stuff on it, including* NED's *records. She is black.*)

HANNIMAN: The eleventh floor is our floor—Infectious Diseases. We ask that you don't leave this floor, or the hospital, or the Institute's grounds, or indeed go to any other floor, where other illnesses are housed. Dr. Della Vida says it's better to have you on our side. I tell him you're never going to be on our side. You're not here to cause some sort of political ruckus? Are you?

NED: (*Unpacking some books.*) What better time and place to read *The Magic Mountain?*

HANNIMAN: Are you?

NED: I'm here for you to save my life. Is that too political?

(DR. ANTHONY DELLA VIDA *enters. He is short, dynamic, handsome, and very smooth, a consummate bureaucrat. He beams hugely and warmly embraces* NED.)

TONY: Hello, you monster!

NED: I never understand why you talk to me . . .

TONY: I'm very fond of you.

NED: . . . after all I say about you.

HANNIMAN: "Dr. Della Vida runs the biggest waste of taxpayers' money after the Defense Department." In the Washington *Post.*

TONY: No, in the Washington *Post* he compared me to Hitler.

HANNIMAN: No, that was in the *Village Voice.* And it was "you fucking son-of-a-bitch of a Hitler."

TONY: Where was it he accused me of pulling off the biggest case of scientific fraud since laetrile?

NED: *Vanity Fair.*

TONY: (*Studying* NED's *file.*) All your numbers are going down pretty consistently. You didn't listen to me when you should have.

NED: Ah, Tony, nobody wants to take that shit.

TONY: They're wrong.

NED: It doesn't work.

TONY: Nothing works for everybody.

NED: Nobody believes you.

TONY: Then why are you here?

NED: I'm more desperate. And you sold me a bill of goods.

TONY: You begged me you were ready to try anything.

NED: I asked you when you were going to strike gold with *something*. You've spent two billion dollars.

TONY: No, sir! You asked me if I had anything I would take if I were you.

NED: No, sir! You said to me, "I've got it." And I said, "The cure!" And you said, "If you quote me I'll deny it." You slippery bastard.

TONY: You're the slippery bastard!

HANNIMAN: Yep, he sure is on our side.

NED: (*Reading from a newspaper clipping.*) "Dr. Della Vida has discovered a method to suppress the growth of the virus in mice by 80–90% . . ." The *New York Times.*

TONY: For over a decade you have mercilessly condemned that newspaper's coverage of this illness. Suddenly they're your experts?

NED: (*Another clipping.*) ". . . reconstituted genes will be introduced in transfusions of the patient's own blood . . . cells given new genetic instructions, to self-destruct if they are infected." *The Lancet.* (*A third clipping.*) "Conclusion: The success of this theory in *in vitro* experiments, followed the successful inoculation of three West African sooty mangabey monkeys, leads one to hope that human experimentation can commence without further delay." The *New England Journal of Monkeys.* I'll be your monkey.

HANNIMAN: Don't say that. We have to guarantee each chimp a thirty-thousand-dollar retirement endowment. Their activists are better than your activists.

TONY: How have you been feeling? (*Starts examining* NED.)

NED: Okay physically. Emotionally shitty. We've lost.

TONY: You *are* depressed. That's too bad. You've been very useful.

HANNIMAN: Useful?

TONY: All your anger has kept us on our toes.

HANNIMAN: They have yelled at, screamed at, threatened, insulted, castigated, crucified every person on our staff. In every publication. On every network. From every street corner. Useful?

NED: Who is she? I've been infected for so long, and I still don't get sick. What's that all about? Everyone thinks I *am* sick. Everyone around me *is* sick. I keeping waiting *to* get sick. I don't know why I'm *not* sick. All my friends are dead. I think I'm guilty I'm still alive.

TONY: Not everybody dies in any disease. You know that. Your numbers could even go back up on their own. Why is my hospital surrounded by your army of activists? Am I going to be burned at the stake if I can't restore your immune system?

NED: I'm not so active these days.

TONY: You?

NED: (*Softly.*) They don't know I'm here.

HANNIMAN: Why don't I believe that?

NED: What have we achieved? I'm here begging.

(NED *suddenly reaches out and touches* TONY*'s face.* HANNIMAN*'s back is turned.*)

This new treatment—you can't even stick it into me legally. Can you?

TONY: Ned—I do think I'm on to something. You've really got to keep your mouth shut. You've got to promise me. And then you've got to keep that promise.

NED: The world can't be saved with our mouths shut.

TONY: Give me lessons later.

NED: How long can you keep me alive? I've got work to finish. Two years. Can you do that?

TONY: You know there aren't any promises. Two years, the way you look now, doesn't seem impossible.

NED: How about three? It's a very long novel. Why are you willing to do this for me?

HANNIMAN: Because if it works, you'll scream bloody murder if anyone stands in his way. Because if it doesn't work, you'll scream bloody murder for him to find something else. That's *his* reasoning. Now *I* would just as soon you weren't here. Period.

TONY: (*To* HANNIMAN.) Give him the double d.d.b.m. (*Leaves.*)

NED: What's a double d.d.b.m.?

(*From the cart,* HANNIMAN *wields an enormous needle.* ALEXANDER, *a young boy, is seen dimly on the side. He's wet from a shower, and wrapped in towels. He comes closer to see what's going on.*)

HANNIMAN: Mice and chimps were easy. You're our first one who can talk back. Drop your drawers and bend over.

ALEXANDER: What's she doing?

NED: I want my Mommy.

ALEXANDER: Mommy's not home yet.

HANNIMAN: You even wrote in *The Advocate* you'd heard I was a lesbian.

NED: You're Mrs. Dr. Della Vida?

(*She rams the hypodermic into his ass.*)

(*Screams.*) We consider that a compliment!

ALEXANDER: Why are you here? (*No answer.*) Please tell me what's happening!

HANNIMAN: (*Still injecting him.*) I think it takes great courage for you to set foot anywhere near here. My husband works twenty hours a day and usually sleeps the other four in one of these rooms. I'm pregnant and I don't know how. Or why. With the number of patients we're seeing, I'm bearing an orphan. (*Extracts the hypodermic and takes a larger one.*)

NED: That wasn't it?

(*She laughs. She administers the second needle even deeper. He screams again, louder.*)

ALEXANDER: Tell me what's going on!

NED: I'm starring in this wonderful play about euthanasia.

(HANNIMAN *finishes and leaves.*)

ALEXANDER: Where's Benjamin? Where's *anyone?* Don't you have any friends? At a time like this? Something awful's happening. Isn't it? (*No answer.*) Will you give me a hug?

NED: Get lost, Lemon.

ALEXANDER: Just remember—*I* was here. (*Leaves.*)

NED: (*Changing from his street clothes.*) What do you do when you're dying from a disease you need not be dying from? What do you do when the only system set up to save you is a pile of shit run by idiots and quacks? What do you do when your own people won't unite and fight together to save their own lives? What do you do when you've tried every tactic you can think of to fight back and none of them has worked and you are now not only completely destitute of new ideas but suddenly more frightened than you've been before that your days are finally and at last more numbered and finite and that an obit in the *New York Times* is shortly to be yours? Why, you talk yourself into believing the quack is a genius (*Massages his sore ass.*) and his latest vat of voodoo is a major scientific breakthrough. And you check yourself in. So, here I am. At the National Institutes of Quacks.

They still don't know how this virus works inside our bodies. They still don't know how this disease progresses and what really triggers this progression. They still don't know if the virus could be hiding someplace else—its major home might not even be in the blood at all. Finally, in total desperation, my kids out there prepared a whole long list of what they still don't know; we even identified the best scientists anywhere in the world to find the answers.

When we were on the outside, fighting to get in, it was easier to call everyone names. But they were smart. They invited us inside. And we saw they looked human. And that makes hate harder.

It's funny how everyone's afraid of me. And my mouth. And my temper. They should only know I can't get angry now to save my soul. Eight years of screaming at one idiot to wake up and four more years of trying to get another idiot to even say the word can do that. They knew we couldn't keep up the fight and that eventually they'd be able to kill off all the faggots and spics and niggers. When I started yelling, there were forty-one cases of a mysterious disease. Now a doctor at Harvard is predicting a billion by the new century. And it's still mysterious. And the mystery isn't why they don't know anything, it's why they don't *want* to know anything.

So what does all this say about the usefulness of . . . anything?

Yes, the war is lost.

And I'd give anything to get angry again.

ALEXANDER: (*Reappearing, still wrapped in towel.*) You are not going to die!

NED: Go away.

ALEXANDER: If you die I die!

NED: Please go away.

ALEXANDER: I kept you alive for quite some time, thank you very much!

NED: Lemon—get the fuck out of here.

ALEXANDER: I was here first! Are you rich and successful and famous? Two of them? One? Did you fall in love? (No answers.) Every single second of my entire life I've wanted for there to be somebody! I gave you great stuff to work with. How did you fuck it up? Excuse me for saying so, but I think you're a mess.

Calvin Trillin

 orn in Kansas City in 1935, Calvin Trillin graduated from Yale in 1957. A few years later, he joined the *New Yorker* as a staff writer, traveling around the country for material to convert into a remarkable series called "U.S. Journal." From 1978 through 1985, he was a columnist for the *Nation,* and since 1990 he has contributed a weekly swatch of comic verse to the magazine. In 1996 he returned as a columnist to *Time,* where in the early 1960s he had been a cub reporter. Trillin has written and presented two one-man shows off-Broadway and has been called "the Buster Keaton of performance humorists." He has published two comic novels, a collection of short stories, travel books, a collection of light verse, three books on food (gathered in 1994 into a single volume, *The Tummy Trilogy*), and many books of reportage and essays, among them *Uncivil Liberties* (1982), *With All Disrespect* (1985), *If You Can't Say Something Nice* (1988), *Enough's Enough* (1990), and *Too Soon to Tell* (1995). A memoir of his Yale roommate, *Remembering Denny,* appeared in 1993, and his book *Messages from My Father* in 1996. Most of his books are about looking around, while these latter two are about looking back. In a backwards glance at his own Yale years, Trillin writes: "Although grades were expressed numerically during my time at Yale, Daily Themes instructors used letters to mark the vignettes we were required to hand in five days a week—A, B, C, D, and W. Nobody knew for sure what W stood for, but most people thought it meant Worthless. The instructors were free with their W's. It was not uncommon for someone to hand in a theme he was particularly proud of and receive a W+— Worthless Plus. One of the lessons I took away from Daily Themes was that whatever I'm about to turn in could probably use another draft."

The man was stubborn. Take the coffee incident. This happened after I was living away from home, working as a reporter in the South. I was back in Kansas City for a visit, and my father and mother and I were sitting at the kitchen table. My mother had just made coffee. After pouring a cup for me, she asked if I wanted some milk in it.

"I don't use milk," I said.

"Well, I'll tell you one thing," my father said. "If you were blindfolded, you couldn't tell if there was milk in it or not."

As it happened, my father had never tasted coffee in his life. Was he a Mormon? No, he was not a Mormon. A health nut? No. The only nutritional theory I can remember his propounding was that you couldn't gain more weight from eating something than the food itself weighed, so devouring a one-pound box of intensely rich chocolate candy couldn't put on more than one pound. ("It stands to reason" was how he usually introduced that theory, among others.) Was he someone who had some rare allergy to coffee beans or caffeine? No, he thought of allergies as the sort of affliction that cropped up among my mother's relatives, who apparently constructed elaborate defenses against illnesses, real and imagined, and were described around our house as "nervous."

He didn't drink coffee because at some point in his childhood he had sworn that he never would. My father had sworn off any number of things. As a young man, he smoked for a few years and then swore off cigarettes. He swore off liquor before he was old enough to taste any—supposedly because of his disgust at the smell of stale beer in the taverns where he sold newspapers as a boy. As far as I can remember, he never gave any specific reason for swearing off coffee. It may be that coffee just got caught up in the boyhood oath against liquor, tossed in because it was also something grownups drank. I think he also must have sworn off swearing; if you ran him out of patience, his strongest expression was "For cryin' out loud!" I sometimes imagined my father as swearing off things just to keep in practice—the sort of person who looks at himself in the mirror after shaving one day and, for no particular reason, says to the image he sees, "You have hit your last bucket of driving-range golf balls" or "No more popcorn for you, young fella."

The act of swearing off, in other words, seemed to overwhelm whatever had triggered it. It's possible, I suppose, that over the years my father could have forgotten why he struck something off the rolls. In his case, though, forgetting what had been behind some absolute prohibition would not have been an argument for ending it. If he swore off something, it stayed sworn off. He had no need to offer explanations for the ban, because it applied to him alone. He didn't harangue people about the wickedness of demon rum; I have no reason to believe that he thought it was wicked. He had nothing against anyone else's drinking coffee, including me. He wasn't questioning my ability to tell the difference between black coffee and coffee with milk as a way of telling me that coffee wasn't worth drinking. He spoke in a perfectly agreeable tone, as if he were passing on some interesting fact about coffee that he had just read in the Kansas City *Star*.

I also spoke in a perfectly agreeable tone. I said, "Does it occur to you that, as someone who has never tasted coffee, with or without milk, you may not be a great authority on this subject?"

"I don't care what you say," my father said, using an opening phrase he often employed even if you hadn't said anything. "Blindfolded you wouldn't know if there was milk in it or not." This is stubborn.

My mother's view was that my father's stubbornness was perfectly understandable if you considered the family he came from. In my mother's conversations about relatives, just about everyone was permanently assigned one characteristic—usually a less than noble characteristic, like cheapness or slovenliness or a tendency to spoil children—that could be illustrated in one phrase. If I had inquired, while I sipped my coffee, about a relative I'll call Doris, my mother's reply would have begun, no matter what milestones had occurred in Doris's life since my previous visit to Kansas City, no matter what acts of kindness or charity Doris had performed, "You know Doris—sink full of dirty dishes." Whatever their individual characteristics, my father's relatives had been assigned the group characteristic of stubbornness. When the subject of the St. Joe people came up—my father had grown up in St. Joseph, Missouri, about fifty miles north of Kansas City, and when I was a child a lot of his relatives still lived there—my mother often summed up her feelings with one forcefully expressed word: "Mules!"

My mother accepted without question the notion that such characteristics as stubbornness run in families. In her mind, I think, it was partly a matter of what would now be called genetic predisposition. When I displayed behavior that she considered obstinate—that happened with some regularity—she would tell me that I took after my father's family, the St. Joe people. I was not troubled by this. There seemed to be only two alternatives, and what little boy wants to take after people who are nervous? When I got angry with my parents as a child, I stomped up to my room and remained there, silently smoldering, for periods that reflected impressive stubbornness—or so I thought until I read, many decades later, about a young man in Thailand who, denied a motorcycle by his parents, went to his room to sulk and was still there twenty-two years later. My mother also seemed to believe that the stubbornness of my father's family was, in effect, cultural: some tribes in New Guinea put rings in their noses; the St. Joe people practiced pigheadedness. She was perfectly willing to admit that her own mother's family had customs that encouraged nervousness. She nodded in confirmation when my father demonstrated the variety of their nervous gestures—a medley of tics and snorts that looked like something out of a Danny Kaye movie. It was she as often as my father who reminded us that some of her cousins drank a glass of warm water before retiring, to settle their stomachs.

I suppose I absorbed some of this belief in family characteristics, because when I found myself trying to figure out how my father's family became involved in the unlikely journey that took them to St. Joe in the first place, stubbornness was the first explanation I thought of. There was a lot about my father that was strictly western Missouri. He spoke with an accent that would be familiar to anyone who remembers the speeches of Harry S Truman. By his description, a golf drive that disappeared in the clouds or a towering home run that cleared the fence at Rup-pert Stadium was "hit all the way to Clay County." A woman approaching middle age was "no spring chicken." A diminutive person weighed "seventy-five pounds soaking wet, with his boots on." It was from him that I picked up the not altogether elegant Midwestern phrase "I haven't had so much fun since the hogs ate my little sister." His childhood reminiscences were of St. Joe, around the time of the Great War; the one that stuck in my mind was that he had dislocated his shoulder jumping off a barn that once belonged to Jesse James, perhaps the best-known resident that St. Joseph, Missouri, has ever had.

But my father had actually been brought to St. Joe at the age of two, in around 1909. His family—then known as Trilinsky—was from a place that was always described as "near Kiev." I've sometimes said that a child growing up in Kansas City, unfamiliar with the world of the shtetl, could get the impression that people who came from "near Kiev" had lived in the suburbs. Except that it would have had to be an extremely poor suburb—like one of those sorry, badly used farm towns which Midwestern cities sometimes envelop as they expand. I never heard the name of the place mentioned. I knew nothing of what life had been like near Kiev, or how the decision had been made to leave for a strange country several thousand miles away. It wasn't a secret. The people who knew—my grandparents' generation—simply didn't talk about it to me, maybe because I didn't ask. My father, of course, had virtually no memories of the Old Country to talk about. I asked him once if he remembered anything at all about Russia—that part of the world was referred to in my family as Russia, not the Ukraine—and he said that he had a vague memory of getting his foot stuck in the mud.

About all I knew of how my father's family got to St. Joe was that they went there directly from Galveston, Texas, where the boat from the Old Country had landed. When I was a child, I didn't realize that there was anything out of the ordinary in getting on a boat in darkest Europe, getting off in Galveston, Texas, and going straight from there to St. Joseph, Missouri. Only later did it occur to me that what I had learned in school about the great wave of immigration from Southern and Eastern Europe at the turn of the century said nothing at all about the route my family had taken from suburban Kiev to St. Joseph, Missouri—the home of the Pony Express and, of course, Jesse James. Ellis Island was mentioned. The Statue of Liberty was mentioned. The Lower East Side was mentioned. There was not a word about Galveston, Texas. How did this family—a family indistinguishable from thousands of other poor Eastern European Jewish families saying their farewells to the czar, a family that could have been expected to fetch up on, say, Delancey Street—land in Galveston?

Could it have been stubbornness? According to one of the theories I came up with, my grandfather and his brother-in-law, my Uncle Benny Daynovsky, were talking to a friend of theirs one day in the suburbs of Kiev about where you land when you go to America. I knew that my grandfather and Uncle Benny went to America first, followed a couple of years later by my grandmother and my father and his older sister. In the conversation I imagined, the only two places any of the participants had ever heard of in America were New York and Texas. The friend said that when you went to America you landed in New York. My grandfather shook his head. "No," he said. "Texas." By the time they all actually left for the New World, my grandfather knew that the place you landed when you went to America was indeed New York, but he was willing to travel a couple of thousand miles out of his way in steerage rather than admit that he'd been wrong. Mules!

Tom Wolfe

t om Wolfe has written two novels, *The Bonfire of the Vanities* (1987) and *A Man in Full* (1998), and ten other books, including *The Electric Kool-Aid Acid Test* (1968), *Radical Chic and Mau-Mauing the Flak Catchers* (1970), *The Right Stuff* (1979), *From Bauhaus to Our House* (1981), and *Hooking Up* (2000). For the rest, let Mr. Wolfe have the floor:

"I entered the Yale Graduate School in American Studies in the fall of 1951 after graduating from Washington and Lee. The greatest teacher I had at Washington and Lee—for that matter, the greatest teacher I ever had anywhere—was a recently minted Ph.D. from the Yale American Studies program named Marshall Fishwick. At W&L he offered a one-year course in American intellectual and art history, covering everyone from Cotton Mather, Jonathan Edwards, and Rembrandt Peale to Frederick Jackson Turner, Charles and Mary Beard, Ruth Benedict, William James, and Frank Lloyd Wright. Right away I was sold. I was determined to go to graduate school in American Studies at Yale. With Marshall Fishwick's prodigious help, I was one of five students who made it that year.

"For me, the two sides of the experience, the personal and the academic, contrasted sharply. Psychologically, no one should enter an academic doctoral program until he is in his late sixties. Early eighties would be better. I was twenty-one. There I'd be, in the spring, in Nature's season of the rising sap, sitting in a cubicle in the upper reaches of the stacks of Sterling Memorial Library, that Gothic highrise of the world's entombed wisdom, staring out of a cruelly narrow leper's window at a meanly cropped little rectangle of the world outside . . . a shaft of brilliant blue sky crossed, as in a Chinese painting on silk, by a few green shoots of a tree, whose limbs and trunk I couldn't even see, bursting . . . *bursting!* . . . with buds, about to *explode* with a dionysian procreativity . . . while I sat immobile in the gloom and fantasized about Maggie a Girl of the Stacks, a townie (yes, you red-ballpoint-toting thought police, we called them "townies") whose job it was to fight Shelf Failure (a Sterling Memorial term) and put the books back on the shelves in their proper places, as she padded about . . . *shoop shoop* . . . in a pair of mules, which was a 1950s term for a pair of backless bedroom slippers . . . while, as I say, I fantasized about Maggie and simultaneously pored over books from the metal Klamp-it—on shelves above my dim little desktop . . . searching for signs of Victorian color theory in Melville . . . resonances of Carlyle's use of the tropes of *chiasma* and *anaphora* in Thoreau . . .

similarities between the use of *conjunctio* (the metronomical repetition of the conjunction *and,* often in place of relative pronouns) in early Hemingway and the Bible's second Book of Samuel . . . the influence of symbolic logic on pre–World War II American historians . . . status skews in the American bureaucracy situation (the Germanic double noun in place of adjective and noun was fashionable in sociology at the time). . . . Psychologically, being a twenty-one-year-old Yale graduate student in the 1950s was like being trapped in seat F in the middle section of the 46th row in an absolutely packed fourteen-hour flight from New York to Tokyo with some tireless logorrheic like Susan Sontag in seat E gassing into your left ear about Bosnia and another one like Richard Dawkins in seat G gassing into your right ear about memes, which seem to be little people who sprinkle fairy dust on genes in order to make the theory of evolution account for cultural change as well as everything else. . . .

"Nevertheless, in terms of my future as a writer, my time at Yale was a turning point. I had majored in English at Washington and Lee, and I arrived at Yale with the typical liberal arts major's disdain for the social sciences. But sociology was one of the disciplines we had to tackle in American Studies. Our teacher, John Sirjamki, was a tall, saturnine Finn from the Midwest. He wasn't an exciting teacher like Marshall Fishwick, but he was patient with liberal artistes like me. We could call him at home anytime, except between 7:30 and 8:00 P.M., Monday through Friday, when he listened to *The Lone Ranger* on the radio. He introduced me to Max Weber, Durkheim, Tocqueville, Kurt Lewin, Talcott Parsons. By the time I had finished my dissertation in the late summer of 1956 (I didn't receive my Ph.D. until Commencement, 1957), I was convinced that (a) Weber was the most important thinker of the twentieth century (and Parsons, the most underrated) and that (b) sociology was, or should be, the monarch of the entire kingdom of knowledge, with all other subjects, including physics and biology, as its provinces.

"My dissertation was about a 1930s Communist front called the League of American Writers, whose roster by 1938 included most of the major writers in the United States. But the subject of this dissertation was only incidentally politics and literature. In my hands, writers such as E. Hemingway and J. Dos Passos came across like remote figures from Sumerian history. My approach was entirely sociological. Was the social makeup of the American writing craft, whose members traditionally have thought of themselves as independent and idiosyncratic, such that the Communist Party could rationally regard it as a manipulable mass in the Leninist sense of the term? My dissertation, like that last sentence, was supremely-to-the-point-of-terminally boring to read.

"I saw to that. At the time, the 1950s, my subject was more than a bit radio-active for a doctoral dissertation, and I was desperate to clear the last hurdle and get out into that sunny, blue-skyed, bursting-budded, sap-gorged world beyond the leper's window.

"I didn't complete my dissertation until September of 1956, too late to get a decent job teaching. Besides, after nine straight years of academe, I was campus-whipped. So I took a job as a general assignment reporter on a newspaper in Springfield, Massachusetts, up the road.

"I could scarcely believe it. From my very first day on the job Yale served me well. My first assignment was to do a story about a family of ten the town's welfare department had discovered living on the dirt floor of a cellar in the Second Ward, after the mother had wound up in the hospital from eating dirt. This I immediately recognized as a symptom of profound depression, often accompanying the disease yaws. Ulrich B. Phillips had recorded its high incidence among antebellum plantation laborers in his grand work, *Life and Labor in the Old South,* one of the historic staples of the American Studies program at that time. *The Springfield Union* thought that they had a genius on their hands—a general assignment reporter who could draw historical parallels for dirt-eating in the Second Ward.

"From that day to this the social context of the human beast—which I believe to be inseparable from his mental life—has been the setting of practically everything I have written, whether in fiction or nonfiction. The three fundamental human desires are to ward off death, to avoid irksome toil, and to procreate—and all three exist at the service of a single overarching impulse: to believe in and assert the superiority of 'my kind.' Not 'me' but 'my kind.' I won't tarry to dilate upon that point. I will only add that lately I have become a chronicler of what is right now the hottest field in all of academia: neuroscience. I have written two long pieces on the subject; on its social history and impact, I hasten to add, not its science. I happen to agree with the field's most eminent thinker, Edward O. Wilson, in his call for 'consilience,' namely, that there should be a single academic discipline within which all others would be seen as subsets. The only thing is, Wilson got it precisely backwards. The social sciences are not subsets of evolutionary biology. Evolutionary biology is a subset of sociology, both in a strictly biological sense and, above all, in a social sense. (No? Just wait. History will absolve me.) In any event, the story of evolutionary biology and the evolutionary biologists, such as Wilson and Dawkins, is one of the most hilarious chapters in the Human Comedy.

"But Wilson is a Harvard professor, and I digress. So let me turn immediately to a Yale man, Sherman McCoy, and to the social context that has made his agonized psyche what it is."

At that very moment, in the very sort of Park Avenue co-op apartment that so obsessed the Mayor . . . twelve-foot ceilings . . . two wings, one for the white Anglo-Saxon Protestants who own the place and one for the help . . . Sherman McCoy was kneeling in his front hall trying to put a leash on a dachshund. The floor was a deep green marble, and it went on and on. It led to a five-foot-wide walnut staircase that swept up in a sumptuous curve to the floor above. It was the sort of apartment the mere thought of which ignites flames of greed and covetousness under people all over New York and, for that matter, all over the world. But Sherman burned only with the urge to get out of this fabulous spread of his for thirty minutes.

So here he was, down on both knees, struggling with a dog. The dachshund, he figured, was his exit visa.

Looking at Sherman McCoy, hunched over like that and dressed the way he was, in his checked shirt, khaki pants, and leather boating moccasins, you would have never guessed what an imposing figure he usually cut. Still young . . . thirty-eight years old . . . tall . . . almost six-one . . . terrific posture . . . terrific to the point of imperious . . . as imperious as his daddy, the Lion of Dunning Sponget . . . a full head of sandy-brown hair . . . a long nose . . . a prominent chin . . . He was proud of his chin. The McCoy chin; the Lion had it, too. It was a manly chin, a big round chin such as Yale men used to have in those drawings by Gibson and Leyendecker, an aristocratic chin, if you want to know what Sherman thought. He was a Yale man himself.

But at this moment his entire appearance was supposed to say: "I'm only going out to walk the dog."

The dachshund seemed to know what was ahead. He kept ducking away from the leash. The beast's stunted legs were deceiving. If you tried to lay hands on him, he turned into a two-foot tube packed with muscle. In grappling with him, Sherman had to lunge. And when he lunged, his kneecap hit the marble floor, and the pain made him angry.

"C'mon, Marshall," he kept muttering. "Hold still, damn it."

The beast ducked again, and he hurt his knee again, and now he resented not only the beast but his wife, too. It was his wife's delusions of a career as an interior decorator that had led to this ostentatious spread of marble in the first place. The tiny black grosgrain cap on the toe of a woman's shoe—

—she was standing there.

"You're having a time, Sherman. What on earth are you doing?"

Without looking up: "I'm taking Marshall for a wa-a-a-a-alk."

Walk came out as a groan, because the dachshund attempted a fishtail maneuver and Sherman had to wrap his arm around the dog's midsection.

"Did you know it was raining?"

Still not looking up: "Yes, I know." Finally he managed to snap the leash on the animal's collar.

"You're certainly being nice to Marshall all of a sudden."

Wait a minute. Was this irony? Did she suspect something? He looked up.

But the smile on her face was obviously genuine, altogether pleasant . . . a lovely smile, in fact . . . *Still a very good-looking woman, my wife* . . . with her fine thin features, her big clear blue eyes, her rich brown hair . . . *But she's forty years old!* . . . No getting around it . . . Today *good-looking* . . . Tomorrow they'll be talking about what a *handsome* woman she is . . . Not her fault . . . *But not mine, either!*

"I have an idea," she said. "Why don't you let *me* walk Marshall? Or I'll get Eddie to do it. You go upstairs and read Campbell a story before she goes to sleep. She'd love it. You're not home this early very often. Why don't you do that?"

He stared at her. It wasn't a trick! She was sincere! And yet *zip zip zip zip zip zip zip* with a few swift strokes, a few little sentences, she had . . . *tied him in knots!—thongs of guilt and logic!* Without even trying!

The fact that Campbell might be lying in her little bed—*my only child!*—the *utter innocence of a six-year-old!*—wishing that he would read her a bedtime story . . . while he was . . . doing whatever it was he was now doing . . . *Guilt!* . . . The fact that he usually got home too late to see her at all . . . *Guilt on top of guilt!* . . . He doted on Campbell!—loved her more than anything in the world! . . . To make matters worse—*the logic of it!* The sweet wifely face he was now staring at had just made a considerate and thoughtful suggestion, a logical suggestion . . . so logical he was speechless! There weren't enough white lies in the world to get around such logic! And she was only trying to be nice!

"Go ahead," she said. "Campbell will be so pleased. I'll tend to Marshall."

The world was upside down. What was he, a Master of the Universe, doing down here on the floor, reduced to ransacking his brain for white lies to circumvent the sweet logic of his wife? The Masters of the Universe were a set of lurid, rapacious plastic dolls that his otherwise perfect daughter liked to play with. They looked like Norse gods who lifted weights, and they had names such as Dracon, Ahor, Mangelred, and Blutong. They were unusually vulgar, even for plastic toys. Yet one fine day, in a fit of euphoria, after he had picked up the telephone and taken an order for zero-coupon bonds that had brought him a $50,000 commission, *just like that,* this very phrase had bubbled up into his brain. On Wall Street he and a few others—how many?—three hundred, four hundred, five hundred?—had become precisely that . . . Masters of the Universe. There was . . . no limit whatsoever! Naturally he had never so much as whispered this phrase to a living soul. He was no fool. Yet he couldn't get it out of his head. And here was the Master of the Universe, on the floor with a dog, hog-tied by sweetness, guilt, and logic . . . Why couldn't he (being a Master of the Universe) simply *explain* it to her? Look, Judy, I still love you and I love our daughter and I love our home and I love our life, and I don't want to change any of it—it's just that I, a Master of the Universe, a young man still in the season of the rising sap, deserve *more* from time to time, when the spirit moves me—

—but he knew he could never put any such thought into words. So resentment began to bubble up into his brain . . . In a way she brought it on herself, didn't she . . . Those women whose company she now seems to prize . . . those . . . those . . . The phrase pops into his head at that very instant: *social X rays* . . . They keep themselves so thin, they look like X-ray pictures . . . You can see lamplight through their bones . . . while they're chattering about *interiors* and *landscape gardening* . . . and encasing their scrawny shanks in metallic Lycra tubular tights for their Sports Training classes . . . And it hasn't helped any, has it! . . . See how drawn her face and neck look . . . He concentrated on her face and neck . . . *drawn* . . . No doubt about it . . . Sports Training . . . turning into *one of them*—

He managed to manufacture just enough resentment to ignite the famous McCoy temper.

He could feel his face grow hot. He put his head down and said, "Juuuuuudy . . ." It was a shout stifled by teeth. He pressed the thumb and the first two fingers of his left hand together and held them in front of his clamped jaws and blazing eyes, and he said:

"Look . . . I'm all—set—to—walk—the—dog . . . So I'm—going—out—to—walk—the—dog . . . *Okay?*"

Halfway through it, he knew it was totally out of proportion to . . . to . . . but he couldn't hold back. That, after all, was the secret of the McCoy temper . . . on Wall Street . . . wherever . . . the imperious excess.

Judy's lips tightened. She shook her head.

"Please do what you want," she said tonelessly. Then she turned away and walked across the marble hall and ascended the sumptuous stairs.

Still on his knees, he looked at her, but she didn't look back. *Please do what you want.* He had run right over her. Nothing to it. But it was a hollow victory.

Another spasm of guilt—

The Master of the Universe stood up and managed to hold on to the leash and struggle into his raincoat. It was a worn but formidable rubberized British riding mac, full of flaps, straps, and buckles. He had bought it at Knoud on Madison Avenue. Once, he had considered its aged look as just the thing, after the fashion of the Boston Cracked Shoe look. Now he wondered. He yanked the dachshund along on the leash and went from the entry gallery out into the elevator vestibule and pushed the button.

Rather than continue to pay around-the-clock shifts of Irishmen from Queens and Puerto Ricans from the Bronx $200,000 a year to run the elevators, the apartment owners had decided two years ago to convert the elevators to auto-matic. Tonight that suited Sherman fine. In this outfit, with this squirming dog in tow, he didn't feel like standing in an elevator with an elevator man dressed up like an 1870 Austrian army colonel. The elevator descended—and came to a stop two floors below. *Browning*. The door opened, and the smooth-jowled bulk of Pollard Browning stepped on. Browning looked Sherman and his country outfit and the dog up and down and said, without a trace of a smile, "Hello, Sherman."

"Hello, Sherman" was on the end of a ten-foot-pole and in a mere four sylla-bles conveyed the message: "You and your clothes and your animal are letting down our new mahogany-paneled elevator."

Sherman was furious but nevertheless found himself leaning over and picking the dog up off the floor. Browning was the president of the building's co-op board. He was a New York boy who had emerged from his mother's loins as a fifty-year-old partner in Davis Polk and president of the Downtown Association. He was only forty but had looked fifty for the past twenty years. His hair was combed back smoothly over his round skull. He wore an immaculate navy suit, a white shirt, a shepherd's check necktie, and no raincoat. He faced the elevator door, then turned his head, took another look at Sherman, said nothing, and turned back.

Sherman had known him ever since they were boys at the Buckley School. Browning had been a fat, hearty, overbearing junior snob who at the age of nine knew how to get across the astonishing news that McCoy was a hick name (and a hick family), as in Hatfields and McCoys, whereas he, Browning, was a true Knickerbocker. He used to call Sherman "Sherman McCoy the Mountain Boy."

When they reached the ground floor, Browning said, "You know it's raining, don't you?"

"Yes."

Browning looked at the dachshund and shook his head. "Sherman McCoy. Friend to man's best friend."

Sherman felt his face getting hot again. He said, "That's it?"

"What's it?"

"You had from the eighth floor to here to think up something bright, and that's it?" It was supposed to sound like amiable sarcasm, but he knew his anger had slipped out around the edges.

"I don't know what you're talking about," said Browning, and he walked on ahead. The doorman smiled and nodded and held the door open for him. Browning walked out under the awning to his car. His chauffeur held the car door open for him. Not a drop of rain touched his glossy form, and he was off, smoothly, immaculately, into the swarm of red taillights heading down Park Ave-nue. No ratty riding mac encumbered the sleek fat back of Pollard Browning.

In fact, it was raining only lightly, and there was no wind, but the dachshund was having none of it. He was beginning to struggle in Sherman's arms. The power of the little bastard! He put the dog down on the runner under the awning and then stepped out into the rain with the leash. In the darkness the apartment buildings on the other side of the avenue were a serene black wall holding back the city's sky, which was a steaming purple. It glowed, as if inflamed by a fever.

Hell, it wasn't so bad out here. Sherman pulled, but the dog dug into the runner with his toenails.

"Come on, Marshall."

The doorman was standing outside the door, watching him.

"I don't think he's too happy about it, Mr. McCoy."

"I'm not, either, Eddie." And never mind the commentary, thought Sherman. "C'mon, c'mon, c'mon, Marshall."

By now Sherman was out in the rain giving the leash a pretty good pull, but the dachshund wasn't budging. So he picked him up and took him off the rubber runner and set him down on the sidewalk. The dog tried to bolt for the door. Sherman couldn't give him any more slack on the leash or else he was going to be right back where he started. So now he was leaning one way and the dog was leaning the other, with the leash taut between them. It was a tug-of-war between a man and a dog . . . on Park Avenue. Why the hell didn't the doorman get back in the building where he belonged?

Sherman gave the leash a real jerk. The dachshund skidded forward a few inches on the sidewalk. You could hear his toenails scraping. Well, maybe if he dragged him hard enough, he would give up and start walking just to keep from being dragged.

"C'mon, Marshall! We're only going around the corner!"

He gave the leash another jerk and then kept pulling for all he was worth. The dog slid forward a couple of feet. He slid! He wouldn't walk. He wouldn't give up. The beast's center of gravity seemed to be at the middle of the earth. It was like trying to drag a sled with a pile of bricks on it. Christ, if he could only get around the corner. That was all he wanted. Why was it that *the simplest things*—he gave the leash another jerk and then he kept the pressure on. He was leaning like a sailor into the wind. He was getting hot inside his rubberized riding mac. The rain was running down his face. The dachshund had his feet splayed out on the sidewalk. His shoulder muscles were bulging. He was thrashing from side to side. His neck was stretched out. Thank God, he wasn't barking, at least! He *slid.* Christ, you could hear it! You could hear his toenails scraping along the sidewalk. He wouldn't give an inch. Sherman had his head down, his shoulders hunched over, dragging this animal through the darkness and the rain on Park Avenue. He could feel the rain on the back of his neck.

He squatted down and picked up the dachshund, catching a glimpse of Eddie, the doorman, as he did. Still watching! The dog began bucking and thrashing.

Sherman stumbled. He looked down. The leash had gotten wrapped around his legs. He began gimping along the sidewalk. Finally he made it around the corner to the pay telephone. He put the dog down on the sidewalk.

Christ! Almost got away! He grabs the leash just in time. He's sweating. His head is soaked with rain. His heart is pounding. He sticks one arm through the loop in the leash. The dog keeps struggling. The leash is wrapped around Sherman's legs again. He picks up the telephone and cradles it between his shoulder and his ear and fishes around in his pocket for a quarter and drops it in the slot and dials.

Three rings, and a woman's voice: "Hello?"

But it was not Maria's voice. He figured it must be her friend Germaine, the one she sublet the apartment from. So he said: "May I speak to Maria, please?"

The woman said: "Sherman? Is that you?"

Christ! It's Judy! He's dialed his own apartment! He's aghast—paralyzed! "Sherman?"

He hangs up. Oh Jesus. What can he do? He'll bluff it out. When she asks him, he'll say he doesn't know what she's talking about. After all, he said only five or six words. How can she be sure?

But it was no use. She'd be sure, all right. Besides, he was no good at bluffing. She'd see right through him. Still, what else could he do?

He stood there in the rain, in the dark, by the telephone. The water had worked its way down inside his shirt collar. He was breathing heavily. He was trying to figure out how bad it was going to be. What would she do? What would she say? How angry would she be? This time she'd have something she could really work on. She deserved her scene if she wanted it. He had been truly stupid. How could he have done such a thing? He berated himself. He was no longer angry at Judy at all. Could he bluff it out, or had he really done it now? Had he really hurt her?

All at once Sherman was aware of a figure approaching him on the sidewalk, in the wet black shadows of the town houses and the trees. Even from fifty feet away, in the darkness, he could tell. It was that deep worry that lives in the base of the skull of every resident of Park Avenue south of Ninety-sixth Street—a black youth, tall, rangy, wearing white sneakers. Now he was forty feet away, thirty-five. Sherman stared at him. Well, let him come! I'm not budging! It's my territory! I'm not giving way for any street punks!

The black youth suddenly made a ninety-degree turn and cut straight across the street to the sidewalk on the other side. The feeble yellow of a sodium-vapor streetlight reflected for an instant on his face as he checked Sherman out.

He had crossed over! What a stroke of luck!

Not once did it dawn on Sherman McCoy that what the boy had seen was a thirty-eight-year-old white man, soaking wet, dressed in some sort of military-looking raincoat full of straps and buckles, holding a violently lurching animal in his arms, staring, bug-eyed, and talking to himself.

Sherman stood by the telephone, breathing rapidly, almost panting. What was he to do now? He felt so defeated, he might as well go back home. But if he went back immediately, it would be pretty obvious, wouldn't it? He hadn't gone out to walk the dog but to make a telephone call. Besides, whatever Judy was going to say, he wasn't ready for it. He needed to think. He needed advice. He needed to get this intractable beast out of the rain.

So he dug out another quarter and summoned up Maria's number into his brain. He concentrated on it. He nailed it down. Then he dialed it with a plodding deliberation, as if he were using this particular invention, the telephone, for the first time.

"Hello?"

"Maria?"

"Yes?"

Taking no chances: "It's me."

"Sherman?" It came out Shuhhh-mun. Sherman was reassured. That was Maria, all right. She had the variety of Southern accent in which half the vowels are pronounced like *u*'s and the other half like short *i*'s. Birds were *buds,* pens were *pins,* bombs were *bums,* and envelopes were *invilups.*

"Listen," he said, "I'll be right over. I'm at a telephone booth. I'm only a couple of blocks away."

There was a pause, which he took to mean she was irritated. Finally: "Where on earth have you been?" Where un uth have you bin?

Sherman laughed morosely. "Look, I'll be right over."

The staircase of the town house sagged and groaned as Sherman walked up. On each floor a single barc 22-watt circular fluorescent tube, known as the Landlord's Halo, radiated a feeble tubercular-blue glow upon the walls, which were Rental Unit Green. Sherman passed apartment doors with innumerable locks, one above the other in drunken columns. There were anti-pliers covers over the locks and anti-jimmy irons over the jambs and anti-push-in screens over the door panels.

In blithe moments, when King Priapus reigned, with no crises in his domain, Sherman made this climb up to Maria's with a romantic relish. How bohemian! How . . . *real* this place was! How absolutely *right* for these moments when the Master of the Universe stripped away the long-faced proprieties of Park Avenue and Wall Street and let his rogue hormones out for a romp! Maria's one room, with its closet for a kitchen and another closet for a bathroom, this so-called apartment of hers, fourth floor rear, which she sublet from her friend Germaine—well, it was perfect. Germaine was something else again. Sherman had met her twice. She was built like a fire hydrant. She had a ferocious hedge of hair on her upper lip, practically a mustache. Sherman was convinced she was a lesbian. But so what? It was all real! Squalid! New York! A rush of fire in the loins!

But tonight Priapus did not rule. Tonight the grimness of the old brownstone weighed on the Master of the Universe.

Only the dachshund was happy. He was hauling his belly up the stairs at a merry clip. It was warm and dry in here, and familiar.

When Sherman reached Maria's door, he was surprised to find himself out of breath. He was perspiring. His body was positively abloom beneath the riding mac, his checked shirt, and his T-shirt.

Before he could knock on the door, it opened about a foot, and there she was. She didn't open it any farther. She stood there, looking Sherman up and down, as if she were angry. Her eyes gleamed above those remarkable high cheekbones of hers. Her bobbed hair was like a black hood. Her lips were drawn up into an O. All at once she broke into a smile and began chuckling with little sniffs through her nose.

"Well, come on," said Sherman, "let me in! Wait'll I tell you what happened."

Now Maria pushed the door all the way open, but instead of ushering him inside, she leaned up against the doorjamb and crossed her legs and folded her arms underneath her breasts and kept staring at him and chuckling. She was wearing high-heeled pumps with a black-and-white checkerboard pattern worked into the leather. Sherman knew little about shoe designs, but it registered on him that this one was of the moment. She wore a tailored white gabardine skirt, very short, a good four inches above the knees, revealing her legs, which to Sherman's eyes were like a dancer's, and emphasizing her tiny waist. She wore a white silk blouse, open down to the top of her breasts. The light in the tiny entryway was such that it threw her entire ensemble into high relief: her dark hair, those cheekbones, the fine features of her face, the swollen curve of her lips, her creamy blouse, those creamy flan breasts, her shimmering shanks, so insouciantly crossed.

"Sherman . . ." Shuhhh-mun. "You know what? You're cute. You're just like my little brother."

The Master of the Universe was mildly annoyed, but he walked on in, passing her and saying: "Oh boy. Wait'll I tell you what happened."

Without altering her pose in the doorway, Maria looked down at the dog, who was sniffing at the carpet. "Hello, Marshall!" Muhshull. "You're a wet little piece a salami, Marshall."

"Wait'll I tell you—"

Maria started to laugh and then shut the door. "Sherman . . . you look like somebody just . . . *balled you up*"—she balled up an imaginary piece of paper—"and threw you down."

"That's what I feel like. Let me tell you what happened."

"Just like my little brother. Every day he came home from school, and his belly button was showing."

Sherman looked down. It was true. His checked shirt was pulled out of his pants, and his belly button was showing. He shoved the shirt back in, but he didn't take off the riding mac. He couldn't settle in here. He couldn't stay too long. He didn't know quite how to get that across to Maria.

"Every day my little brother got in a fight at school . . ."

Sherman stopped listening. He was tired of Maria's little brother, not so much because the thrust of it was that he, Sherman, was childish, but because she insisted on going on about it. At first glance, Maria had never struck Sherman as anybody's idea of a Southern girl. She looked Italian or Greek. But she talked like a Southern girl. The chatter just poured out. She was still talking when Sherman said:

"You know, I just called you from a telephone booth. You want to know what happened?"

Maria turned her back and walked out into the middle of the apartment, then wheeled about and struck a pose, with her head cocked to one side and her hands on her hips and one high-heeled foot slewed out in a carefree manner and her shoulders thrown back and her back slightly arched, pushing her breasts forward, and she said:

"Do you see anything new?"

What the hell was she talking about? Sherman wasn't in a mood for anything new. But he looked her over dutifully. Did she have a new hairdo? A new piece of jewelry? Christ, her husband loaded her with so much jewelry, who could keep track? No, it must be something in the room. His eyes jumped around. It had probably been built as a child's bedroom a hundred years ago. There was a little bay with three leaded casement windows and a window seat all the way around. He surveyed the furniture . . . the same old three bentwood chairs, the same old ungainly oak pedestal table, the same old mattress-and-box-spring set with a corduroy cover and three or four paisley cushions strewn on top in an attempt to make it look like a divan. The whole place shrieked: Make Do. In any event, it hadn't changed.

Sherman shook his head.

"You really don't?" Maria motioned with her head in the direction of the bed.

Sherman now noticed, over the bed, a small painting with a simple frame of blond wood. He took a couple of steps closer. It was a picture of a nude man, seen from the rear, outlined in crude black brushstrokes, the way an eight-year-old might do it, assuming an eight-year-old had a notion to paint a nude man. The man appeared to be taking a shower, or at least there was what looked like a nozzle over his head, and some slapdash black lines were coming out of the nozzle. He seemed to be taking a shower in fuel oil. The man's flesh was tan with sickly lavender-pink smears on it, as if he were a burn case. What a piece of garbage . . . It was sick . . . But it gave off the sanctified odor of serious art, and so Sherman hesitated to be candid.

"Where'd you get that?"

"You like it? You know his work?"

"Whose work?"

"Filippo Chirazzi."

"No, I don't know his work."

She was smiling. "There was a whole article about him, in the *Times.*"

Not wanting to play the Wall Street philistine, Sherman resumed his study of this masterpiece.

"Well, it has a certain . . . how can I say it? . . . directness." He fought the urge to be ironic. "Where did you get it?"

"Filippo gave it to me." Very cheery.

"That was generous."

"Arthur's *bought* four of his paintings, great big ones."

"But he didn't give it to Arthur, he gave it to you."

"I wanted one for myself. The big ones are Arthur's. Besides, Arthur wouldn't know Filippo from . . . from I don't know what, if I hadn't told him."

"Ah."

"You don't like it, do you."

"I *like* it. To tell you the truth, I'm rattled. I just did something so goddamned stupid."

Maria gave up her pose and sat down on the edge of the bed, the would-be divan, as if to say, "Okay, I'm ready to listen." She crossed her legs. Her skirt was now halfway up her thighs. Even though those legs, those exquisite shanks and flanks of hers, were beside the point right now, Sherman couldn't keep his eyes off them. Her stockings made them shiny. They glistened. Every time she moved, the highlights shimmered.

Sherman remained standing. He didn't have much time, as he was about to explain.

"I took Marshall out for a walk." Marshall was now stretched out on the rug. "And it's raining. And he starts giving me a very hard time."

When he got to the part about the telephone call itself, he became highly agitated even in the description of it. He noticed that Maria was containing her concern, if any, quite successfully, but he couldn't calm down. He plunged on into the emotional heart of the matter, the things he felt immediately after he hung up—and Maria cut him off with a shrug and a little flick in the air with the back of her hand.

"Oh, that's nothing, Sherman." That's nuthun, Shuhmun.

He stared at her.

"All you did was make a telephone call. I don't know why you just didn't say, 'Oh, I'm sorry. I was calling my friend Maria Ruskin.' That's what I woulda done. I never bother lying to Arthur. I don't tell him every little thing, but I don't lie to him."

Could he possibly have used such a brazen strategy? He ran it through his mind. "Uhmmmmmmmm." It ended up as a groan. "I don't know how I can go out at 9:30 at night and say I'm walking the dog and then call up and say, 'Oh, I'm sorry, I'm really out here calling Maria Ruskin.' "

"You know the difference between you and me, Sherman? You feel sorry for your wife, and I don't feel sorry for Arthur. Arthur's gonna be seventy-two in August. He knew I had my own friends when he married me, and he knew he didn't like them, and he had his own friends, and he knew *I* didn't like *them*. I can't stand them. All those old Yids . . . Don't look at me as if I've said something awful! That's the way Arthur talks. 'The *Yiddim.*' And the *goyim,* and I'm a *shiksa.* I never heard of all that stuff before I met Arthur. I'm the one who happens to be married to a Jew, not you, and I've had to swallow enough of this Jewish business over the past five years to be able to use a little of it if I feel like it."

"Have you told him you have your own apartment here?"

"Of course not. I told you, I don't lie to him, but I don't tell him every little thing."

"Is this a little thing?"

"It's not as big a thing as *you* think it is. It's a pain in the neck. The landlord's got himself in an uproar again."

Maria stood up and went to the table and picked up a sheet of paper and handed it to Sherman and returned to the edge of the bed. It was a letter from the law firm of Golan, Shander, Morgan, and Greenbaum to Ms. Germaine Boll concerning her status as the tenant of a rent-controlled apartment owned by Winter Real Properties, Inc. Sherman couldn't concentrate on it. He didn't want to think about it. It was getting late. Maria kept going off on tangents. It was *getting late.*

"I don't know, Maria. This is something Germaine has to respond to."

"Sherman?"

She was smiling with her lips parted. She stood up.

"Sherman, come here."

He took a couple of steps toward her, but he resisted going very close. The look on her face said she had very close in mind.

"You think you're in trouble with your wife, and all you've done is make a phone call."

"Hah. I don't think I'm in trouble, I know I'm in trouble."

"Well, if you're already in trouble, and you haven't even done anything, then you might as well do something, since it's all the same difference."

Then she touched him.

King Priapus, he who had been scared to death, now rose up from the dead.

Sprawled on the bed, Sherman caught a glimpse of the dachshund. The beast had gotten up off the rug and had walked over to the bed and was looking up at them and switching his tail.

Christ! Was there by any chance some way a dog could indicate . . . Was there anything dogs did that showed they had seen . . . Judy knew about animals. She clucked and fussed over Marshall's every mood, until it was revolting. Was there something dachshunds did after observing . . . But then his nervous system began to dissolve, and he no longer cared.

His Majesty, the most ancient king, Priapus, Master of the Universe, had no conscience.

Sherman let himself into the apartment and made a point of amplifying the usual cozy sounds.

"Attaboy, Marshall, okay, okay."

He took off his riding mac with a lot of rustling of the rubberized material and clinking of the buckles and a few *whews.*

No sign of Judy.

The dining room, the living room, and a small library led off the marble entry gallery. Each had its familiar glints and glows of carved wood, cut glass, ecru silk shades, glazed lacquer, and the rest of the breathtakingly expensive touches of his wife, the aspiring decorator. Then he noticed. The big leather wing chair that usually faced the doorway in the library was turned around. He could just see the top of Judy's head, from behind. There was a lamp beside the chair. She appeared to be reading a book.

He went to the doorway.

"Well! We're back!"

No response.

"You were right. I got soaking wet, and Marshall wasn't happy."

She didn't look around. There was just her voice, coming from out of the wing chair:

"Sherman, if you want to talk to someone named Maria, why do you call me instead?"

Sherman took a step inside the room.

"What do you mean? If I want to talk to *who*?"

The voice: "Oh, for God's sake. Please don't bother lying."

"*Ly*ing—about *what*?"

Then Judy stuck her head around one side of the wing chair. The look she gave him!

With a sinking heart Sherman walked over to the chair. Within her corona of soft brown hair his wife's face was pure agony.

"What are you *talking* about, Judy?"

She was so upset she couldn't get the words out at first. "I wish you could see the cheap look on your face."

"I don't know what you're *talking* about!"

The shrillness in his voice made her laugh.

"All right, Sherman, you're going to stand there and tell me you didn't call here and ask to speak to someone named Maria?"

"To *who*?"

"Some little hooker, if I had to guess, named Maria."

"Judy, I swear to God, I don't know what you're talking about! I've been out walking Marshall! I don't even *know* anybody named Maria! Somebody called here asking for somebody named Maria?"

"Uhhh!" It was a short, unbelieving groan. She stood up and looked at him square in the eyes. "You *stand* there! You think I don't know your voice on the phone?"

"Maybe you do, but you haven't heard it tonight. I swear to God."

"You're lying!" She gave him a hideous smile. "And you're a rotten liar. And you're a rotten person. You think you're so swell, and you're so cheap. You're lying, aren't you?"

"I'm *not* lying. I swear to God, I took Marshall for a walk, and I come back in here, and *wham*—I mean, I hardly know what to say, because I truly don't know what you're talking about. You're asking me to prove a negative proposition."

"*Negative proposition.*" Disgust dripped from the fancy phrase. "You were gone long enough. Did you go kiss her good night and tuck her in, too?"

"Judy—"

"Did you?"

Sherman rolled his head away from her blazing gaze and turned his palms upward and sighed.

"Listen, Judy, you're totally . . . totally . . . utterly wrong. I swear to God."

She stared at him. All at once there were tears in her eyes. "Oh, you swear to God. Oh, Sherman." Now she was beginning to snuffle back the tears. "I'm not gonna—I'm going upstairs. There's the telephone. Why don't you call her from here?" She was forcing the words out through her tears. "I don't care. I really don't care."

Then she walked out of the room. He could hear her shoes clicking across the marble toward the staircase.

Sherman went over to the desk and sat down in his Hepplewhite swivel chair. He slumped back. His eyes lit on the frieze that ran around the ceiling of the little room. It was carved of Indian redwood, in high relief, in the form of figures hurrying along a city sidewalk. Judy had had it done in Hong Kong for an astonishing amount . . . *of my money.* Then he leaned forward. *Goddamn her.* Desperately he tried to relight the fires of righteous indignation. His parents had been right, hadn't they? He deserved better. She was two years older than he was, and his mother had said such things *could* matter—which, the way she said it, meant it *would* matter, and had he listened? Ohhhhh no. His father, supposedly referring to Cowles Wilton, who had a short messy marriage to some obscure little Jewish girl, had said, "Isn't it just as easy to fall in love with a rich girl from a good family?" And had he listened? Ohhhhhh no. And all these years, Judy, as the daughter of a Midwestern history professor—*a Midwestern history professor!*—had acted as if she was an intellectual aristocrat—but she hadn't minded using his money and his family to get in with this new social crowd of hers and start her decorating business and smear their names and their apartment across the pages of these vulgar publications, *W* and *Architectural Digest* and the rest of them, had she? Ohhhhhhhhh no, not for a minute! And what was he left with? A forty-year-old bolting off to her Sports Training classes—

—and all at once, he sees her as he first saw her that night fourteen years ago in the Village at Hal Thorndike's apartment with the chocolate-brown walls and the huge table covered with obelisks and the crowd that went considerably beyond bohemian, if he understood bohemian—and the girl with the light brown hair and the fine, fine features and the wild short skimpy dress that revealed so much of her perfect little body. And all at once he *feels* the ineffable way they closed themselves up in the perfect cocoon, in his little apartment on Charles Street and her little apartment on West Nineteenth, immune to all that his parents and Buckley and St. Paul's and Yale had ever imposed on him—and he *remembers* how he told her—in *practically these words!*—that their love would transcend . . . *everything*—

—and now she, forty years old, starved and Sports Trained to near-perfection, goes crying off to bed.

He slumped back in the swivel chair once more. Like many a man before him, he was no match, at last, for a woman's tears. He hung his noble chin over his collarbone. He folded.

Absentmindedly he pressed a button on the desktop. The tambour door of a *faux*-Sheraton cabinet rolled back, revealing the screen of a television set. Another of his dear weeping decorator's touches. He opened the desk drawer and took out the remote-control gadget and clicked the set to life. The news. The Mayor of New York. A stage. An angry crowd of black people. Harlem. A lot of thrashing about. A riot. The Mayor takes cover. Shouts . . . chaos . . . a real rhubarb. Absolutely pointless. To Sherman it had no more meaning than a gust of wind. He couldn't concentrate on it. He clicked it off.

She was right. The Master of the Universe was cheap, and he was rotten, and he was a liar.

A. R. Gurney

born in 1930, A. R. Gurney graduated from Williams College before coming to study at the Yale School of Drama, where he earned an M.F.A. in 1958. He has written three novels and several screenplays and teleplays but is best known for his remarkable plays, the first of which, *Love in Buffalo,* was performed in New Haven in 1958. They include *The Problem* (1973), *The Middle Ages* (1977), *The Perfect Party* (1986), *The Cocktail Hour* (1988), *Love Letters* (1988), *Sylvia* (1995), and *Labor Day* (1998). Perhaps his best known play is *The Dining Room* (1982), a gently satirical comedy of manners. "I don't write about rebels or dissenters or gangsters," he once told an English interviewer. "I write about my own people, the Americans you see haunting Harrods in midsummer." Of his time at Yale, Gurney writes: "My father, his three brothers, my own brother, and my father-in-law all attended Yale, but I was dangerously rebellious and went to Williams. When I finally reached New Haven in 1955, after a stint in the navy, I tried to take advantage of the larger university's broader opportunities: I enrolled in the Drama School, but took extra courses from Cleanth Brooks and Norman Holmes Pearson, became a freshman counselor, subscribed to Bob Kiphuth's exercise program, and ate evening meals at the Law School. People seem to think the 1950s were a narrow and circumscribed era, but remembering my time at Yale, I don't think so."

FROM *THE DINING ROOM*

(*An old man and his middle-aged son come on from the Right. The old man is Harvey, his son is Dick. The light is dim in the dining room now, except Downstage, by the French windows*)

HARVEY: (*As he enters*) We'll talk in here. No one will disturb us. Nobody comes near a dining room anymore. The thought of sitting down with a number of intelligent, attractive people to enjoy good food well cooked and properly served . . . that apparently doesn't occur to people anymore. Nowadays people eat in kitchens, or in living rooms, standing around, balancing their plates like jugglers. Soon they'll be eating in bathrooms. Well, why not? Simplify the process considerably.

DICK: Sit down somewhere, Pop.

HARVEY: (*Coming well Downstage, pulling a chair down, away from the table*) I'll sit here. We can look out. There's a purple finch who comes to the feeder every evening. Brings his young.

(*Dick pulls up a chair beside him. Behind, in the dim light, three women begin to set the table, this time for an elaborate dinner. A great white tablecloth, candles, flowers, the works. The process should be reverential, quiet, and muted, not to distract from the scene, Downstage*)

HARVEY: (*Taking an envelope from his inside pocket*) Now. I want to go over my funeral with you.

DICK: Pop—

HARVEY: I want to do it. There are only a few more apples left in the barrel for me.

DICK: You've been saying that for years, Pop.

HARVEY: Well, this time it's true. So I want to go over this, please. You're my eldest son. I can't do it with anyone else. Your mother starts to cry, your brother isn't here, and your sister gets distracted. So concentrate, please, on my funeral.

DICK: All right, Pop.

HARVEY: (*Taking out a typewritten document*) First, here is my obituary. For both newspapers. I dictated it to Miss Kovak down at the office, and I've read it over twice, and it's what I want. It's thorough without being self-congratulatory. I mention my business career, my civic commitments, and, of course, my family. I even touch on my recreational life. I give my lowest score in golf and the weight of the sailfish I caught off the Keys. The papers will want to cut both items, but don't you let them.

DICK: O.K., Pop.

HARVEY: I also want them to print this picture. (*He shows it*) It was taken when I was elected to chair the Symphony drive. I think it will do. I don't look too young to die, nor so old it won't make any difference.

DICK: All right, Pop.

HARVEY: (*Fussing with other documents*) Now I want the funeral service announced at the end of the obituary, and to occur three days later. That will give people time to postpone their trips and adjust their golf games. And I want it at three-thirty in the afternoon. This gives people time to digest their lunch and doesn't obligate us to feed them dinner. Notice I've underlined the word *church*. Mr. Fayerweather might try to squeeze the service into the chapel, but don't let him. I've lived in this city all my life, and know a great many people, and I want everyone to have a seat and feel comfortable. If you see people milling around the door, go right up to them and find them a place, even if you have to use folding chairs. Are we clear on that?

DICK: Yes, Pop.

(*By now the table has been mostly set behind them. The women have gone*)

HARVEY: I've listed the following works to be played by Mrs. Manchester at the organ. This Bach, this Handel, this Schubert. All lively, you'll notice. Nothing gloomy, nothing grim. I want the service to start promptly with a good rousing hymn—"Onward, Christian Soldiers"—and then Fayerweather may make some brief—underlined *brief*—remarks about my life and works. Do you plan to get up and speak, by the way?

DICK: Me?

HARVEY: You. Do you plan to say anything?

DICK: I hadn't thought, Pop . . .

HARVEY: Don't, if you don't want to. There's nothing more uncomfortable than a reluctant or unwilling speaker. On the other hand, if you, as my eldest son, were to get on your feet and say a few words of farewell . . .

DICK: (*Quickly*) Of course I will, Pop.

HARVEY: Good. Then I'll write you in. (*He writes*) "Brief remarks by my son Richard." (*Pause. Looks up*) Any idea what you might say?

DICK: No, Pop.

HARVEY: You won't make it sentimental, will you? Brad Hoffmeister's son got up the other day and made some very sentimental remarks about Brad. I didn't like it, and I don't think Brad would have liked it.

DICK: I won't get sentimental, Pop.

HARVEY: Good. (*Pause. Shuffles documents; looks up again*) On the other hand, you won't make any wisecracks, will you?

DICK: Oh, Pop . . .

HARVEY: You have that tendency, Dick. At Marcie's wedding. And your brother's birthday. You got up and made some very flip remarks about all of us.

DICK: I'm sorry, Pop.

HARVEY: Smart-guy stuff. Too smart, in my opinion. If you plan to get into that sort of thing, perhaps you'd better not say anything at all.

DICK: I won't make any cracks, Pop. I promise.

HARVEY: Thank you. (*Looks at documents; looks up again*) Because you love us, don't you?

DICK: Yes, Pop.

HARVEY: You love us. You may live a thousand miles away, you may have run off every summer, you may be a terrible letter-writer, but you love us all, just the same. Don't you? You love me.

DICK: (*Touching him*) Oh, yes, Pop! Oh, yes! Really!

(*Pause*)

HARVEY: Fine. (*Puts his glasses on again; shuffles through documents*) Now at the graveside, just the family. I want to be buried beside my brothers and below my mother and father. Leave room for your mother to lie beside me. If she marries again, still leave room. She'll come back at the end.

DICK: All right, Pop.

HARVEY: Invite people back here after the burial. Stay close to your mother. She gets nervous at any kind of gathering, and makes bad decisions. For example, don't let her serve any of the good Beefeater's gin if people simply want to mix it with tonic water. And when they're gone, sit with her. Stay in the house. Don't leave for a few days. Please.

DICK: I promise, Pop.

(*Annie, the maid from the first scene, now quite old, adds candlesticks and a lovely flower centerpiece to the table*)

HARVEY: (*Putting documents back in the envelope*) And that's my funeral. I'm leaving you this room, you know. After your mother dies, the table and chairs to you. It's the best thing I can leave you, by far.

DICK: Thanks, Pop.

(*Annie exits into the kitchen*)

HARVEY: Now we'll rejoin your mother. (*He gets slowly to his feet*) I'll put this envelope in my safe-deposit box, on top of my will and the stock certificates. The key will be in my left bureau drawer. (*He starts out, then stops*) You didn't see the purple finch feeding its young.

DICK: (*Remaining in his chair*) Yes I did, Pop.

HARVEY: You saw it while I was talking?

DICK: That's right.

HARVEY: Good. I'm glad you saw it.

(*He goes out slowly. Dick waits a moment, lost in thought, and then replaces the chairs.*)

born in Philadelphia in 1930, Romulus Linney is a playwright and novelist whose fascination with historical figures has yielded work of a remarkable depth and richness. "My time at the Yale School of Drama was 1953–54," he recalls, "with two years off for the army, finishing in 1958. I began as an actor, became a director, and shortly after graduation, to my surprise, a writer. Yale was a good place to learn a great many things I didn't know I was learning, which later proved to be the most valuable. I had a very good time there, and remember it with gratitude and affection." *The Sorrows of Frederick,* a vivid psychological portrait of Frederick II of Prussia, opened in 1967, and his *Childe Byron,* in which the poet's ghost tells of his scandalous life, was first performed in 1977. Among his other plays of note are *Holy Ghosts* (1971), *Old Man Joseph and His Family* (1978), *The Death of King Philip* (1979), *Heather Valley* (1987), *"2"* (1990), and *True Crimes* (1996). He has won two Obie awards, and in 1999 the American Academy of Arts and Letters awarded him the Award of Merit for Drama. He has also written three novels. His monologue, *The Cure,* appears here for the first time.

Characters: A Midwife
Place: Appalachia
Time: 1800–2000

(*Lights up on a calm but vigorous woman in late middle age, with white hair, rocking quietly in a slat-backed rocking chair. There is a leather pouch at her side.*)

MIDWIFE

Black haw tea is good for women moon-bleeding. Watermelon seeds make tea for kidney stones. Dew off a straw can rub away freckles. If you break your bed, a relative's coming to visit. Dream about catching a fish, you'll get pregnant. You keep bees? If a body dies, tell them bees. Jest say it to the hive and don't fergit. Otherwise, at the funeral, they'll plain rise up and go. I'm daft?

(*She chuckles at us, smiles, and rocks.*)

Three ways in the Smoky Mountains fer a woman to live her own life. Midwifing is best, since no strong man hereabouts will abide a foot-first baby ripping out his woman's guts. Strong men run away from that. So if you know how to turn that baby in the womb, they will call you ma'am, and leave you alone. Otherwise, they'll marry you and work you to death, or leave you an old maid so your mother can work you to death. Nother way, just kill a man. Any man. Hide behind a tree and shoot the son of a bitch. Act wild, drink your likker by yourself, and play like you enjoy it. They respect that. Number three, chew yourself to salvation.

(*She reaches into the leather pouch, pulls out a root, shaped like a tiny man.*)

Gin sang. Means root of life, bottom of everythang. Grows wild in the mountains, once ever seven year, and I know where. Looks like a little man. See, his head, arms, and his legs and his little horn hanging right yonder. Relish that. I'm alone now but I married. Lots. Would again.

(*Points to her white hair.*)

Snow on the roof don't mean there ain't fire in the house. Five men. One died a decent farmer. Second, half-man, half-buzzard. We went together like cheese and chalk, but not once did I lower my eyes to him, not in field, church, porch, or bed. He died, mortified, he said, by a witch. I'd been called that for a long time, so almost everybody believed I killed him, but such is the onery fascination of men, I turned around and married again, three times. Good men too, one even bettern that. Fifteen grandchildren, and thirty-eight great-grandchildren, and an eleven-year-old great-great-grandchild I am trying to keep from running off with a scoundrel. Maybe she will, maybe she won't, since the children who loved me when they was young change their minds growing up, and look at me slant-wise now.

(*She leans forward.*)

I don't purpose to frighten young women. Men are all right, if you know where sang grows, chew it, be patient, let every soul see the root of life you are eating up looks like a man.

(*She smiles and rocks.*)

I knowed I had "second sight" when I was just a girl. The Company had come into the cove where we lived and started the mine. They opened the mountain, built the houses all alike up the one hill, commenced the company store where we had to trade. The men went off to the mines, my Daddy with them. A coal mine, it's just a big road underground. With rooms off of it. Men go into them rooms and pull out the coal, sometimes standing up and breathing all right, sometimes on their knees ten hours a day gulping black dust and dirt. Whichever, they git the coal out of the mine. And when they do, they move backwards, pulling out ribs of coal past old four by fours left to hold everthang up. They can't leave nothing. Not one piece. They have to what's call "retreat," pulling out with them ever last rib of the mine.

(*She looks off into the distance, seeing the past.*)

My Daddy walked off to his work that morning. I yelled when I seen him walking right toward her. A woman dressed in snow white rainment, a-smiling at him, who kept smiling while he walked to her, then past her and through her, then on down into the mine. When they pulled out the coal ribs that day, the mountain fell in on them. One hundred and twenty-three men died, my father with them, leaving a hundred and two widows, a hundred sixty-five fatherless chilluns, me amongst them, with second sight. Everbody had heard me that morning when I cried out: "Daddy! She's waiting fer ye! Don't ye see her? There, at the mouth of the mine! You'll die in there!" It commenced then, calling me witch.

(*She closes her eyes.*)

Sperits. Beautiful death-wimmen, always in white amongst thc black dust which never touches 'em. I seen they wasn't no wimmen at all but great beasts protecting their mountain home with the dire destruction of tunneling fools. I could see them, second sight. I still can. I can't see Daddy, though. But I remember him. Pulled my ear. Take his knuckle, like this one here, to the top of my head. Spin it around and say, buzzzz. Just another man, going into the mine, the pieces of him dug out later. The Company gave my mother a check for twenty-five dollar and said we could stay in the house, until the end of the month. I don't know the cure for that.

(*She opens her eyes, rocks.*)

For years I wasn't allowed in town. No sluts, said the church ladies. No witches, said the police. No midwives, said the doctors. Then not long ago this man come all the way from Paris, France, to see people like me and nobody else. He said for a hundred years babies been birthed all wrong. Under blinding bright light, washed in cold alcohol water in steel basins, stinging in their eyes, their hearts beating hard enough to kill a grown man. Plain terrified scared, and sometimes never given to no mother at all, until days later. He asked if he could watch me. I said, "Shore, if you stay out of my way." He did. I keep the lights low, the woman breathing deep, and the husband quiet. Afterwards, I use my Lysol, and chase them germs away. I treat the eyes and wash the baby clean and proper, but I wash it in a sweetwood basin in warm water and I quick put that baby back to its mother's flesh, soon as I mortally can. The little hearts, I almost touch, a-beating in panic, slow down, get calm, and commence to feel some better about life we must endure. Sometimes look like they smile. The Frenchman said, "You are right and the doctors here are wrong. This baby will be a happy child." The doctors throwed him out of town. But I know this. When you come into the world under blinding light, in a tile cold room, washed off by alcohol in steel basins, and such, then finally, you get to your Momma, oh, what relief, and what do you expect the rest of life to be, but crazy madness for other bodies, whiskey, drugs, and what all, to take away your screaming? It's a wonder we ain't all worse than we are.

(*She smiles, rocks, chews.*)

I live chalk-line straight with men. I love my Daddy dead in the mine. My Momma at thirty looking seventy. For a cure I chew gin sang. And that child running down that mountain yonder will always be as pleasant to me as the flowers are made.

(*Lights fade.*)

Mark Strand

ark Strand was born in 1934 on Prince Edward Island in Canada but was raised in the United States. After graduating from Antioch, he came to the Yale School of Art in 1957 to study with Josef Albers. Though he earned his B.F.A. in 1959, it turned out that Yale taught him more about poetry than painting. "While painting," he recalls, "I had the feeling that whatever I was was diminished by my work, that visual experience could not represent or take the place of other experience. Though my poetry was not good, I felt it offered the opportunity for intellectual growth. For me, writing was thinking." Though he has continued to write about painting—and published books on Edward Hopper and William Bailey—he has become a poet of rare stature, his work at once spare, elegant, and surprising. His first book appeared in 1974, and since then his notable collections include *Reasons for Moving* (1968), *The Story of Our Lives* (1973), and *Dark Harbor* (1993). In 1990, he was named the nation's Poet Laureate. The poems here are from his collection *Blizzard of One,* published in 1998 and awarded the Pulitzer Prize.

THE NEXT TIME

I

Nobody sees it happening, but the architecture of our time
Is becoming the architecture of the next time. And the dazzle

Of light upon the waters is as nothing beside the changes
Wrought therein, just as our waywardness means

Nothing against the steady pull of things over the edge.
Nobody can stop the flow, but nobody can start it either.

Time slips by; our sorrows do not turn into poems,
And what is invisible stays that way. Desire has fled,

Leaving only a trace of perfume in its wake,
And so many people we loved have gone,

And no voice comes from outer space, from the folds
Of dust and carpets of wind to tell us that this

Is the way it was meant to happen, that if only we knew
How long the ruins would last we would never complain.

II

Perfection is out of the question for people like us,
So why plug away at the same old self when the landscape

Has opened its arms and given us marvelous shrines
To flock towards? The great motels to the west are waiting,

In somebody's yard a pristine dog is hoping that we'll drive by,
And on the rubber surface of a lake people bobbing up and down

Will wave. The highway comes right to the door, so let's
Take off before the world out there burns up. Life should be more

Than the body's weight working itself from room to room.
A turn through the forest will do us good, so will a spin

Among the farms. Just think of the chickens strutting,
The cows swinging their udders, and flicking their tails at flies.

And one can imagine prisms of summer light breaking against
The silent, haze-filled sleep of the farmer and his wife.

III
It could have been another story, the one that was meant
Instead of the one that happened. Living like this,

Hoping to revise what has been false or rendered unreadable
Is not what we wanted. Believing that the intended story

Would have been like a day in the west when everything
Is tirelessly present—the mountains casting their long shadow

Over the valley where the wind sings its circular tune
And trees respond with a dry clapping of leaves—was overly

Simple no doubt, and short-sighted. For soon the leaves,
Having gone black, would fall, and the annulling snow

Would pillow the walk, and we, with shovels in hand, would meet,
Bow, and scrape the sidewalk clean. What else would there be

This late in the day for us but desire to make amends
And start again, the sun's compassion as it disappears?

SOME LAST WORDS

1
It is easier for a needle to pass through a camel
Than for a poor man to enter a woman of means.
Just go to the graveyard and ask around.

2
Eventually, you slip outside, letting the door
Bang shut on your latest thought. What was it anyway?
Just go to the graveyard and ask around.

3
"Negligence" is the perfume I love.
O Fedora. Fedora. If you want any,
Just go to the graveyard and ask around.

4
The bones of the buffalo, the rabbit at sunset,
The wind and its double, the tree, the town . . .
Just go to the graveyard and ask around.

5
If you think good things are on their way
And the world will improve, don't hold your breath.
Just go to the graveyard and ask around.

6
You over there, why do you ask if this is the valley
Of limitless blue, and if we are its prisoners?
Just go to the graveyard and ask around.

7
Life is a dream that is never recalled when the sleeper awakes.
If this is beyond you, Magnificent One,
Just go to the graveyard and ask around.

THE VIEW

For Derek Walcott

This is the place. The chairs are white. The table shines.
The person sitting there stares at the waxen glow.
The wind moves the air around, repeatedly,
As if to clear a space. "A space for me," he thinks.
He's always been drawn to the weather of leavetaking,
Arranging itself so that grief—even the most intimate—
Might be read from a distance. A long shelf of cloud
Hangs above the open sea with the sun, the sun
Of no distinction, sinking behind it—a mild version
Of the story that is told just once if true, and always too late.
The waitress brings his drink, which he holds
Against the waning light, but just for a moment.
Its red reflection tints his shirt. Slowly the sky becomes darker,
The wind relents, the view sublimes. The violet sweep of it
Seems, in this effortless nightfall, more than a reason
For being there, for seeing it, seems itself a kind
Of happiness, as if that plain fact were enough and would last.

Leslie Epstein

orn in Los Angeles in 1938, Leslie Epstein grew up in a family of screen-writers; his father Philip and his uncle Julius wrote *Casablanca, Arsenic and Old Lace, The Man Who Came to Dinner,* and many other films. He graduated summa cum laude from Yale in 1960, continued his stud-ies as a Rhodes Scholar at Oxford and later at UCLA, then returned to the Yale School of Drama, where he completed his doctorate in 1967. He has published eight books of fiction, including *P. D. Kimerakov* (1975), *Goldkorn Tales* (1985), *Pandaemonium* (1997), and *Ice Fire Water: A Leib Goldkorn Cocktail* (1999). His novel *King of the Jews* (1979) has been translated into eleven languages and is con-sidered a classic of Holocaust literature. Epstein taught at Queens College until 1978 and for many years now has been director of the Creative Writing Program at Boston University. He recalls his being asked to leave Yale, after a run-in with then mayor Richard Lee of New Haven, and the ensuing ruckus that led to his reinstatement. "Indeed," he writes, tongue-in-cheek, "historians have already be-gun to cite this injustice, together with the response it provoked, as the true birth pangs of the counterculture. Some years later, the Jewish quota was abandoned, Bobby Seale was camped on the New Haven Green, and a knock on the Elihu door was answered by—her blouse unbuttoned, a babe at her breast—a co-ed. *Après moi, le déluge.* " In *King of the Jews,* I. C. Trumpelman is the leader of a ghetto that is under the control of German forces. Before his own people Trum-pelman is a king, with his picture on ghetto postage stamps (to mail nowhere) and on ghetto currency (to buy nothing). Before the Germans, however, he is a slave who must lick his master's boots. In the following scene, Trumpelman re-turns from a meeting with the occupiers and approaches the children of the orphanage, who have only a short time to live.

Late that same afternoon Trumpelman arrived back at Tsarskoye Selo. The Obergruppenführer dropped him off in his new Double Six. The Elder could hardly walk. His clothes were ripped, his cloak gone. There was only one lens left in his frame. He did not go into the mansion, but around it, to the gardens in back. Though early in springtime, the fresh green stems of garlic were pushing out of the ground. Trumpelman sank down among them; wearily, he shut his eyes.

No telling how long he might have stayed there if Bettsack, the schoolmaster, had not walked by carrying what looked like a gigantic squash. *Smuggling!* said the Elder to himself, and keeping low, keeping hidden, he followed the young teacher to the edge of the plowed-up field. There the orphans—both the old-timers and the ones who had joined the Asylum in the last years before the move to the Balut—were waiting. They all had caps on, and coats, and were holding such things as nuts, the head of a cabbage, and a pink India-rubber ball. The sun had dropped well down in the sky, and the air was chilly now. Bettsack was a thin fellow, poorly whiskered, with threads that stuck up from his collar. He made his way to the center of the field, set down the gourd—it was as big as a washbasin, really—and began to call through his hands.

"Stations, children! Positions, if you please! You! Shifter! Leibel Shifter! Further back. Further back! Tushnet! You go back, too!"

The children began to scatter over the field. Shifter, the mad boy, the dog, kept going backward. Every minute or so he would stop, but Bettsack waved him farther on, until he was practically out of sight. "Stop!" the schoolmaster shouted. But Shifter still backpedaled, and the message to him had to be passed from orphan to orphan, from Krystal to Atlas to Tushnet, across the length of the field.

Finally they all held still. Bettsack bent down and picked up the dried squash; he just had the strength to lift it over his head. The next thing you knew the schoolmaster, a grown-up, responsible person, was rapidly spinning around. "Flicker!" he gasped to the boy who was nearest. "Citron!" he called, to the lad next farthest out. "Begin rotation!"

Trumpelman could hardly believe what he saw: both boys, and then Gutta Blit, and then all the others began to spin on the spot. It was like madness. Round and round they went, stepping all over their shadows. "West to east, Miss Atlas! Not like a clock!" Rose Atlas stopped; she reversed direction. The rest kept going, holding their little spheres. Bettsack had begun to stagger a little. The breath came visibly from his mouth.

"Now! Revolutions!"

Little Usher Flicker—between his fingers he had a pea from a pod—began to trip around the teacher, in a circle more or less. A bit farther out Citron was

doing the same. The amazing thing was that as both boys went in this circular or-
bit, they did not stop whirling about. Gutta Blit, with the pink rubber ball, was
spinning like a dervish too, and also Krystal, and so was everyone soon. Even
Leibel Shifter, way out on the edge of the field, a half kilometer off, had started to
run. However, because of the distance between him and Bettsack, he hardly
seemed to be moving. Flicker, for instance, had run three times about the center,
before Shifter, his legs thrashing, covered any noticeable ground. It would take
him forever to complete a revolution.

"Attention! Moons!" Bettsack, with red patches that showed through his
beard, with his necktie coming undone, practically shrieked this.

From behind the hill that led to the cemetery grounds fifteen, twenty, more
than twenty children came pouring. What they did, with a whoop, with a shout,
was to pick out some of the whirling orphans—Gutta, Rose Atlas, the puffing
Mann Lifshits—and then begin to race as fast as they could around them. For a
time the whole field was covered with these whizzing children, making circles inside of circles, curves within curves.

Then Trumpelman stood up in the dimming light; he walked into their midst.
Through his split, puffy lips, he demanded of the reeling Bettsack, "What is the
meaning of this? Speak!"

The schoolmaster dropped his squash. He started screaming. "It's the whole
solar system! Including the new planet of Pluto! In correct proportions! According to the system of Sir J. Frederick Herschel!" Then he threw his arms around
the Asylum Director, clinging to him the way a drunkard does to a post. Just then
Nathan Hobnover, an eight-year-old boy, came roaring over the hilltop, making
a sizzling sound: *zzzzzzz!*

"Comet," said Bettsack, and sank down about Trumpelman's ankles.

The exhausted children saw the old man in tatters; they wobbled to a halt.
Mann Lifshits, whose heavy cabbage represented Jupiter, simply dropped, as did
his eleven moons. One by one the others collapsed. They lay on their backs, with
their coats spread, their breath coming up in a mist. Only the man from Vilna,
for all his scratches and bruises, remained on his feet. Then he sat down, too.
Tushnet caught his breath before anyone else and addressed the schoolmaster.

"Sir, what will happen when the sun goes out?" He was some way off, but it
was so still you could easily hear him.

Bettsack said, "What do you mean, Tushnet? It goes *down*. It does not go *out*."

"I mean, when it burns up. Will we burn up, too?"

A high voice broke in. "It can't just go on forever. Sometime it has to run out
of fuel."

"That is only a theory, Flicker. It has not been proved."

"But what if it's true? What then? Everything will be dark. It makes me nervous." That was Rose Atlas.

"I don't think it will burn up," said Mann Lifshits, from his spot on the ground. "It'll just get colder and colder. Everything on earth will get colder, too. It will be like the ice age. Nothing but ice."

"But it scares me," Rose replied.

"Listen," said Bettsack. "This is speculation. In any case, it won't happen for thousands of years."

"See? You said it was going to happen! It's going to happen!"

"We'll all be frozen to death!"

"Please!" their instructor said. "Why do you worry? In a thousand years none of us will be alive."

"I don't care! I don't want it to go out! I hate the idea of the cold!"

"I do, too!"

"No one alive! No one! There won't even be animals on the earth. It's terrible!"

"Don't talk about it! Don't think about it!"

The children began to whimper and moan. So Bettsack spoke in a loud, firm voice. "Pay attention, if you please. The sun is not going to stop burning. It is made in a certain way. And even if it should go out after all, by then men will have invented spaceships, and they will fly off to live somewhere else. To other planets, to other worlds. There is nothing that science cannot achieve. Perhaps in the universe we shall meet other forms of life. Perhaps even people just like ourselves. Think of that! What a wonderful day that will be! How much we shall learn!"

The moaning had completely stopped. Everything was quiet. Then, so that everyone's heart leaped and pounded, there was an awful wail from Leibel Shifter. "Help! I'm so far away! Help! I'm afraid!"

Trumpelman, sitting upright, answered. "Come. All of you. Come closer."

Silently, on all fours, the boys and girls began to crawl toward the center. They drew near to Trumpelman, who, through his swollen eyes, his single lens, was staring off to the west. They looked, too.

There, on the horizon, the real sun was leaking something. Red stuff, like jam, came out of it and spread over the nearby sky. "Like a raspberry drop," said Usher Flicker. He took the Elder's hand. Citron, a new boy, had curly blond hair coming from under his cap. He laid his head across the Elder's knees. Dark Gutta Blit leaned on his shoulder.

"It's beautiful," she whispered, gazing off to where the sun, cut by the earth's edge, still pumped the sweet-looking syrup from its center. All the children—the planets, the satellites, Hobnover the comet, and at last even Shifter—pressed close to Trumpelman, and to each other. They were like his missing cape.

John Guare

orn in New York City in 1938, John Guare studied at the Yale School of Drama and took his M.F.A. in 1963. His first play—it was called *Universe* and the author was eleven—was mounted in 1949. Among his subsequent plays are *A Play of Brecht* (1969), with music by Leonard Bernstein and lyrics by Stephen Sondheim, *The House of Blue Leaves* (1971), *Landscape of the Body* (1977), *Bosoms and Neglect* (1979), *Lydie Breeze* (1982), *Six Degrees of Separation* (1990), and *Four Baboons Adoring the Sun* (1995). His plays have won many awards, including the Tony, the Olivier, and the Obie. In addition, he has written several screenplays, notably the script for Louis Malle's *Atlantic City* (1981). His writing has all the wit and logic of dreamwork, with a Balzacian appetite for the flow of social currents and a romantic's sense of the damaged soul. One memory of his time at Yale remains vivid to him: "A couple of weeks after I got to Yale in 1960, I knew Yale was really different. T. S. Eliot came to speak. I was in such thrall I had no idea what he said or read. There was T. S. Eliot right in front of me. Years later, I met a guy who was on the honor committee that escorted Eliot on stage that night. I said, 'What did Eliot do that night at Woolsey Hall?' He said, 'I have no idea either.' As a matter of fact, I've never met anyone who knew what he said. All that was left was the awed white noise accompanying the appearance of the great man."

(*A young black man*—PAUL—*enters, supported by* THE DOORMAN. PAUL *is in his early twenties, very handsome, very preppy. He has been beaten badly. Blood seeps through his white Brooks Brothers shirt.*

OUISA *follows at a loss.*

THE DOORMAN *helps* PAUL *to the sofa and stands at the door warily.*)

PAUL: I'm so sorry to bother you, but I've been hurt and I've lost everything and I didn't know where to go. Your children—I'm a friend of—

OUISA: (*To us*) And he mentioned our daughter's name.

FLAN: (*To us*) And the school where they went.

OUISA: (*To* FLAN) Harvard. You can say Harvard.

FLAN: (*To us*) We don't want to get into libel.

PAUL: I was mugged. Out there. In Central Park. By the statue of that Alaskan husky. I was standing there trying to figure out why there is a statue of a dog who saved lives in the Yukon in Central Park and I was standing there trying to puzzle it out when—

OUISA: Are you okay?

PAUL: They took my money and my briefcase. I said my thesis is in there—

FLAN: His shirt's bleeding.

OUISA: His shirt is not bleeding. *He's* bleeding.

PAUL: (*A wave of nausea*) I get this way around blood.

FLAN: Not on the rug.

PAUL: I don't mind the money. But in this age of mechanical reproduction they managed to get the only copy of my thesis.

FLAN: Eddie, get the doctor—

PAUL: No! I'll survive.

FLAN: You'll be fine.

(FLAN *helps* PAUL *out of the room.* THE DOORMAN *goes.*)

OUISA: (*To us*) We bathed him. We did First Aid.

GEOFFREY: (*Leaving*) It's been wonderful seeing you—

OUISA: (*Very cheery*) No no no! Stay!—

(*To us*) Two million dollars two million dollars—

GEOFFREY: My time is so short—before I leave America, I really should see—

FLAN: (*Calling from the hall*) Where are the bandages!?—

OUISA: The Red Cross advises: Press edges of the wound firmly together, wash area with water—

GEOFFREY: May I use your phone?

OUISA: You darling old poop—just sit back—this'll only take a mo—

(*Calling*) Flan, go into Woody's room and get him a clean shirt.

Geoffrey, have you seen the new book on Cézanne?

(*To us*) I ran down the hall to get the book on Cézanne, got the gauze from my bathroom, gave the Cézanne to Flan who wanted the gauze, gave the gauze to Geoffrey who wanted Cézanne. Two million dollars two million dollars—

(FLAN *comes back in the room.*)

FLAN: He's going to be fine.

OUISA: (*To us*) And peace was restored.

(PAUL *enters, slightly recovered, wearing a clean pink shirt. He winces as he pulls on his blazer.*)

PAUL: Your children said you were kind. All the kids were sitting around the dorm one night dishing the shit out of their parents. But your kids were silent and said, No, not our parents. Not Flan and Ouisa. Not the Kittredges. The Kittredges are kind. So after the muggers left, I looked up and saw these Fifth Avenue apartments. Mrs. Onassis lives there. I know the Babcocks live over there. The Auchinclosses live there. But you lived here. I came here.

OUISA: Can you believe what the kids said?

FLAN: (*To us*) We mentioned our kids' names.

OUISA: We can mention our kids' names. Our children are not going to sue us for using their names.

PAUL: But your kids—I love them. Talbot and Woody mean the world to me.

FLAN: He lets you call him Woody? Nobody's called him Woody in years.

PAUL: They described this apartment in detail. The Kandinsky!—that's a double. One painted on either side.

FLAN: We flip it around for variety.

PAUL: It's wonderful.

FLAN: (*To us*) Wassily Kandinsky. Born 1866 Moscow. Blue Rider Exhibition 1914. He said "It is clear that the choice of object that is one of the elements in the harmony of form must be decided only by a corresponding vibration in the human soul." Died 1944 France.

PAUL: It's the way they said it would be.

OUISA: (*To us*) Geoffrey had been silent up to now.

GEOFFREY: Did you bitch your parents?

PAUL: As a matter of fact. No. Your kids and I . . . we both liked our parents . . . loved our—look, am I getting in the way? I burst in here, hysterical. Blood. I didn't mean to—

FLAN AND OUISA: No!

OUISA: Tell us about our children.

FLAN: (*To us*) Three. Two at Harvard. Another girl at Groton.

OUISA: How is Harvard?

PAUL: Well, fine. It's just there. Everyone's in a constant state of luxurious despair and constant discovery and paralysis.

OUISA: (*To us*) We asked him where home was.

FLAN: (*To us*) Out West, he said.

PAUL: Although I've lived all over. My folks are divorced. He's remarried. He's doing a movie.

OUISA: He's in the movies?

PAUL: He's directing this one but he does act.

FLAN: What's he directing?

PAUL: *Cats.*

OUISA: Someone is directing a film of *Cats?*

FLAN: Don't be snooty.

PAUL: You've seen it? T.S. Eliot—

FLAN: Well, yes. Years ago.

OUISA: A benefit for some disease or school—

FLAN: Surely they can't make the movie of *Cats.*

OUISA: Of course they can.

PAUL: They're going to try. My father'll be here auditioning—

OUISA: Cats?

PAUL: He's going to use people.

OUISA: What a courageous stand!

PAUL: They thought of lots of ways to go. Animation.

FLAN: Animation would be nice.

PAUL: But he found a better way. As a matter of fact, he turned it down at first. He went to tell the producers—as a courtesy—all the reasons why you couldn't make a movie of *Cats* and in going through all the reasons why you couldn't make a movie of *Cats,* he suddenly saw how you could make a movie of *Cats*—

OUISA: Eureka in the bathtub. How wonderful.

FLAN: May we ask who—

OUISA: (*To us*) And it was here we pulled up—ever so slightly—pulled up closer—

FLAN: (*To us*) And he told us.

OUISA: (*To us*) He named the greatest black star in movies. Sidney—

FLAN: Don't say it. We're trying to keep this abstract. Plus libel laws.

OUISA: Sidney Poitier! There. I don't care. We have to have truth. (*To us*) He started out as a lawyer and is terrified of libel. I'm not.

(PAUL *steps forward cheerily.*)

PAUL: (*To us*) Sidney Poitier, the future Jackie Robinson of films, was born the twenty-fourth of February 1927 in Miami during a visit his parents made to Florida—legally?—to sell tomatoes they had grown on their farm in the Bahamas. He grew up on Cat Island, "so poor they didn't even own dirt" he has said. Neglected by his family, my father would sit on the shore, and, as he told me many times, "conjure up the kind of worlds that were on the other side and what I'd do in them." He arrived in New York City

from the Bahamas in the winter of 1943 at age fifteen and a half and lived
in the pay toilet of the bus station across from the old Madison Square
Garden at Fiftieth and Eighth Avenue. He moved to the roof of the Brill
Building, commonly known as Tin Pan Alley, and washed dishes at the
Turf Restaurant for $4.11 a night. He taught himself to read by reading the
newspaper. In the black newspaper, the theater page was opposite the
want ad page. Among his 42 films are *No Way Out,* 1950; *Cry, the Beloved
Country,* 1952; *Blackboard Jungle,* 1955; *The Defiant Ones,* 1958; *Raisin in
the Sun,* 1961; *Lilies of the Field,* 1963; *In the Heat of the Night,* 1967; *To Sir
With Love,* 1967; *Shoot to Kill,* 1988; and, of course, *Guess Who's Coming to
Dinner?* He won the Oscar for *Lilies of the Field* and was twice named top
male box-office star in the country. My father made no films from 1977 to
1987 but worked as director and author. Dad said to me once, "I still don't
fully understand how all that came about in the sequence it came about."

(PAUL *returns to the sofa.*)

PAUL: Dad's not in till tomorrow at the Sherry. I came down from Cambridge.
Thought I'd stay at some fleabag for adventure. Orwell. Down and Out. I
really don't know New York. I know Rome and Paris and Los Angeles a lot
better.

OUISA: We're going out to dinner. You'll come.

PAUL: Out to dinner?

FLAN: Out to dinner.

PAUL: But why go out to dinner?

OUISA: Because we have reservations and oh my god what time is it? Have we lost
the reservations and we don't have a damn thing in the house and it's
sixteenth-century Florence and there's genius on every block.

GEOFFREY: Don't mock.

(*She kisses* GEOFFREY.)

PAUL: You must have something in the fridge.

FLAN: A frozen steak from the Ice Age.

PAUL: Why spend a hundred dollars on a bowl of rice? Let me into the kitchen.
Cooking calms me. What I'd like to do is calm down, pay back your
kids—

OUISA: (*To us*) He mentioned our kids' names—

FLAN: (*To us*) Two. Two at Harvard. A daughter at Groton.

PAUL: who've been wonderful to me.

OUISA: They've never mentioned you.

FLAN: What are they supposed to say? We've become friends with the son of
Sidney Poitier, barrier breaker of the fifties and sixties?

GEOFFREY: Your father means a great deal in South Africa.

OUISA: (*To us*) Even Geoffrey was touched.

PAUL: I'm glad of that. Dad and I went to Russia once to a film festival and he was truly amazed how much his presence meant—

OUISA: Oh no! Tell us stories of movie stars tying up their children and being cruel.

PAUL: I wish.

GEOFFREY: You wish?

PAUL: If I wanted to write a book about him, I really couldn't. No one would want to read it. He's decent. I admire him.

OUISA: He's married to an actress who was in one of—she's white? Am I right?

PAUL: That is not my mother. That is his second wife. He met Joanna making *The Lost Man.* He left my mother, who had stuck by him in the lean years. I had just been born. *The Lost Man* is the only film of my father's I can't bring myself to see.

OUISA: Oh, I'm sorry. We didn't mean to—

PAUL: (*Bright*) No! We're all good friends now. His kids from that marriage. Us— the old kids. I'd love to get in that kitchen.

FLAN: (*To* OUISA) What should we do?

OUISA: (*To us*) It's Geoffrey's only night in New York.

GEOFFREY: I vote stay in.

OUISA, FLAN AND PAUL: Good!

(PAUL *goes off to the kitchen.*)

OUISA: (*To us*) We moved into the kitchen.

FLAN: (*To us*) We watched him cook.

OUISA: (*To us*) We watched him cook and chop.

FLAN: (*To us*) He sort of did wizardry—

OUISA: (*To us*) An old jar of sun-dried tomatoes—

FLAN: (*To us*) Leftovers—tuna fish—olives—onions—

(PAUL *returns with three dishes heaped with food.*)

PAUL: Here's dinner. All ready.

OUISA: Shall we move into the dining room?

PAUL: No, let's stay in here. It's nice in here.

(OUISA, FLAN *and* GEOFFREY *take plates skeptically.*)

OUISA: Have you declared your major yet?

PAUL: You're like all parents. What's your major?

FLAN: Geoffrey, Harvard has all those great titles the students give courses.

OUISA: The Holocaust and Ethics—

FLAN: Krauts and Doubts.

(*They eat. Surprise. It's delicious.*)

GEOFFREY: This is the best pasta I've ever—

PAUL: My father insisted we learn to cook.

FLAN: Isn't he from Jamaica? There's a taste of—

GEOFFREY: The islands.

PAUL: Yes. Before he made it, he ran four restaurants in Harlem. You have good buds!

GEOFFREY: See? Good buds. I've never been complimented on my buds—

PAUL: (*To* GEOFFREY) You're from—

GEOFFREY: Johannesburg.

(*Pause*)

PAUL: My dad took me to a movie shot in South Africa. The camera moved from this vile rioting in the streets to a villa where people picked at lunch on a terrace, the only riot the flowers and the birds—gorgeous plumage and petals. And I didn't understand. And Dad said to me, "You meet these young blacks who are having a terrible time. They've had a totally inadequate education and yet in '76—the year of the Soweto riots—they took on a tremendous political responsibility. It just makes you wonder at the maturity that is in them. It makes you realize that the 'crummy childhood' theory, that everything can be blamed in a Freudian fashion on the fact that you've had a bad upbringing, just doesn't hold water." Is everything okay?

(FLAN, OUISA *and* GEOFFREY *are mesmerized, and then resume eating.*)

FLAN, OUISA AND GEOFFREY: (*While eating*) Mmmmmm . . . yes.

GEOFFREY: What about being black in America?

PAUL: My problem is I've never felt American. I grew up in Switzerland. Boarding school. Villa Rosey.

OUISA: There is a boarding school in Switzerland that takes you at age eighteen months.

PAUL: That's not me. I've never felt people liked me for my connections. Movie star kid problems. None of those. May I?

FLAN: Oh, please.

(PAUL *pours a brandy.*)

PAUL: But I never knew I was black in that racist way till I was sixteen and came back here. Very protected. White servants. After the divorce we moved to Switzerland, my mother, brother and I. I don't feel American. I don't even feel black. I suppose that's very lucky for me even though Freud says there's no such thing as luck. Just what you make.

OUISA: Does Freud say that? I think we're lucky having this dinner. Isn't this the finest time? A toast to you.

GEOFFREY: To *Cats!*

FLAN: Blunt question. What's he like?

OUISA: Let's not be star fuckers.

FLAN: I'm not a star fucker.

PAUL: My father, being an actor, has no real identity. You say to him, Pop, what's new? And he says, "I got an interesting script today. I was asked to play a lumberjack up in the Yukon. Now, I've been trained as a preacher, but my church fell apart. My wife says we have to get money to get through this winter. And I sign up as part of this team where all my beliefs are challenged. But I hold firm. In spite of prejudice. Because I want to get back to you. Out of this forest, back to the church . . ." And my father is in tears and I say Pop, this is not a real event, this is some script that was sent to you. And my father says "I'm trying it out to see how it fits on me." But he has no life—he has no memory—only the scripts producers send him in the mail through his agents. That's his past.

OUISA: (*To us*) I just loved the kid so much. I wanted to reach out to him.

John Lahr

ohn Lahr, who graduated from Yale in 1963, is the only drama critic to have twice won the prestigious George Jean Nathan Award. He has been drama critic for the *New Yorker* since 1992 and is the author of fifteen books on the theater, including a biography of his father, the actor Bert Lahr, *Notes on a Cowardly Lion* (1969), a biography of the playwright Joe Orton, *Prick Up Your Ears* (1978), and *Light Fantastic: Adventures in Theater* (1996). He has also written numerous stage adaptations and movie scripts and is the author of two novels, *The Autograph Hound* (1973) and *Hot to Trot* (1974). "I remember standing on the corner of York and Elm Streets," he writes. "I was a senior, and after a summer internship on the *Miami Herald,* I was thinking about going into journalism and becoming a foreign correspondent. I ran into my professor, Robert Penn Warren, on the corner. I asked him what he thought about journalism. You know, he said, after you've mastered the form, the routine might get a little bit boring. Then, I don't know quite why because I had no ambitions then in this area, I asked him how he thought up the characters in a novel. Usually when he was shaving, he said. The light changed, and we went our ways. But that moment—both the advice and the observation—stayed with me. He was right about journalism; and later, when I'd written a novel of my own, I realized he was right about inventing a character, too. What meant so much to me about the encounter was that Professor Warren didn't discount my dream. In fact, he made the whole hard process of getting your thoughts on paper feel possible, ordinary even, just like shaving."

THE LION AND ME

On November 6th, 1998, twenty-six years after "The Wizard of Oz" was last released and on the eve of its sixtieth anniversary, a spiffy, digitally remastered print
of the film arrived in eighteen hundred movie theatres throughout the land.
With a rub rub here and a rub rub there, "The Wizard of Oz," which never
looked bad, has been made to look even better. Dorothy's ruby slippers are rubier.
Emerald City is greener. Kansas, a rumpled and grainy black-and-white world,
has been restored to a buff, sepia Midwestern blandness. And, since everything
that rises nowadays in America ends up in a licensing agreement, new Oz merchandise will shower the planet like manna from hog heaven.

The last time I watched "The Wizard of Oz" from start to finish was in 1962,
at home, with my family. My father, Bert Lahr, who played the Cowardly Lion,
was sixty-seven. I was twenty-one; my sister, Jane, was nineteen. My mother,
Mildred, who never disclosed her age, was permanently thirty-nine. By then, as a
way of getting to know the friendly absence who answered to the name of Dad, I
was writing a biography—it was published, in 1969, as "Notes on a Cowardly
Lion"—and I used any occasion with him as field work. This was the first time
we'd sat down together as a family to watch the film, but not the first time a Lahr
had been secretly under surveillance while viewing it. The family album had
infra-red photographs of Jane and me in the mid-forties—Jane in a pinafore, me
in short pants—slumped in a darkened movie house as part of a row of well-
dressed, bug-eyed kids. Jane, who was five, is scrunched in the back of her seat in
a state of high anxiety about the witch's monkey henchmen. I'm trying to be a
laid-back big brother: my face shows nothing, but my hands are firmly clutching
the armrests.

Recently, Jane told me that for weeks afterward she'd had nightmares about
lions, but what had amazed her most then was the movie's shift from black-and-
white to Technicolor, not the fact that Dad was up onscreen in a lion's suit. Once,
around that time, while waiting up till dawn for my parents to return from a costume party, I heard laughter and then a thud in the hall; I tiptoed out to discover
Dad dressed in a skirt and bonnet as Whistler's Mother, passed out on the floor.
That was shocking. Dad dressed as a lion in a show was what he did for a living,
and was no big deal. Our small, sunless Fifth Avenue apartment was full of Dad's
disguises, which he'd first used onstage and in which he now occasionally appeared on TV. The closet contained a woodsman's props (axe, jodhpurs, and
boots); a policeman's suit and baton; a New York Giants baseball outfit, with cap
and cleats. The drawers of an apothecary's cabinet, which served as a wall-length
bedroom bureau, held his toupées, starting pistol, monocle, putty noses, and
makeup. In the living room, Dad was Louis XV, complete with sceptre and peri-
wig, in a huge oil painting made from a poster for Cole Porter's "Du Barry Was a

Lady" (1939); in the bedroom, he was a grimacing tramp in Richard Avedon's heartbreaking photograph of him praying, as Estragon, in "Waiting for Godot" (1956).

Over the decades, the popular memory of these wonderful stage performances has faded; the Cowardly Lion remains the enduring posthumous monument to Dad's comic genius. While we were growing up, there was not one Oz image or memento of any kind in the apartment. (Later, at Sotheby's, Dad acquired a first edition of L. Frank Baum's "The Wonderful Wizard of Oz.") The film had not yet become a cult. Occasionally, a taxi-driver or a passerby would spot Dad in the street and call out, "Put 'em up, put 'em *uuuhp!*" Dad would smile and tip his tweed cap, but the film's popularity didn't seem to mean as much to him as it did to other people.

As we grew older and more curious, Mom had to prod Dad out of his habitual solitude to divulge tidbits of information to us. So, as we assumed our ritual positions around the TV—Mom propped up with bolsters on the bed, Jane sprawled on the floor with our Scotch terrier, Merlin, me on the chaise longue, Dad at his desk—the accumulated knowledge we brought to the movie was limited to a few hard-won facts. To wit: Dad had held out for twenty-five hundred dollars a week with a five-week guarantee, which turned into a twenty-six-week bonanza because of the technical complexities of the production numbers; in the scene where the Lion and Dorothy fall asleep in the poppy field and wake to find it snowing, the director, Victor Fleming, had asked for a laugh and Dad had come up with "Unusual weather we're havin', ain't it?"; his makeup took two hours a day to apply and was so complicated that he had to have lunch through a straw; he wore football shoulder pads under his twenty-five-pound lion suit; and his tail, which had a fishing line attached to it, was wagged back and forth by a stagehand with a fishing rod who was positioned above him on a catwalk. It was only memories of the Munchkins, a rabble of a hundred and twenty-four midgets assembled from around the world, that seemed to delight Dad and bring a shine to his eyes. "I remember one day when we were supposed to shoot a scene with the witch's monkeys," he told me. "The head of the group was a little man who called himself the Count. He was never sober. When the call came, everybody was looking for the Count. We could not start without him. And then, a little ways offstage, we heard what sounded like a whine coming from the men's room." He went on, "They found the Count. He got plastered during lunch, and fell in the latrine and couldn't get himself out."

Dad, in his blue Sulka bathrobe, with the sash tied under his belly, was watching the show from his Victorian mahogany desk, which was positioned strategically at a right angle to the TV. Here, with his back to the room, he sat in a Colonial maple chair—the throne from which, with the minutest physical adjustment, he could watch the TV, work his crossword puzzles, and listen to the radio all at the same time. Except to eat, Dad hardly ever moved from this spot. He was almost permanently rooted to the desk, which had a pea-green leatherette top and held a large Funk & Wagnall's dictionary, a magnifying glass, a commemorative bronze medal from President Eisenhower's Inauguration (which he'd attended), various scripts, and the radio. On that afternoon, long before Dorothy had gone over the rainbow and into Technicolor, Dad had donned his radio earphones and tuned in the Giants' game. "Bert!" Mom said. "Bert!" But Dad didn't answer.

This was typical. At dinner, after he finished eating, Dad would sometimes wander away from the table without so much as a fare-thee-well; at Christmas, for which he never bought presents, the memories of his unhappy childhood made the ritual exchange of gifts almost unbearable, so he'd slip back to his desk as soon as possible. Now, just as his ravishing Technicolor performance was about to begin, he'd drifted off again, retreating into that private space.

That was irrefutably him up there, disguised in a lion's suit, telling us in the semaphore of his outlandishness what he was feeling in the silence of his bedroom. It was confusing, and more disturbing than I realized then, to see Dad so powerful onscreen and so paralyzed off it. "Yeah, it's sad believe me missy / When you're born to be a sissy / Without the vim and *voive*," Dad sang, in words so perfectly fitting his own intonation and idiom that it almost seemed he was making them up. In a sense, the song *was* him; it was written to the specifications of his paradoxical nature by E. Y. (Yip) Harburg and Harold Arlen, who had already provided him with some of his best material, in "Life Begins at 8:40" (1934) and "The Show Is On" (1936).

"I got to the point where I could do him," Arlen told me. And Harburg, who once said that he could "say something in Bert's voice that I couldn't with my own," saw social pathos in Dad's clowning. "I accepted Bert and wanted him for the part because the role was one of the things 'The Wizard of Oz' stands for: the search for some basic human necessity," he said. "Call it anxiety; call it neurosis. We're in a world we don't understand. When the Cowardly Lion admits that he lacks courage, everybody's heart is out to him. He must be somebody who embodies all this pathos, sweetness, and yet puts on the comic bravura." He added, "Bert had that quality to such a wonderful degree. It was in his face. It was in his talk. It was in himself."

When the song began onscreen, Dad swivelled around in his chair to watch himself; once the song was over, he stepped forward and switched over to football.

"Dad!" we cried.

"Watch it in Jane's room," he said.

"Is it gonna kill you, Bert?"

Dad's beaky profile turned toward Mom; his face was a fist of irritation.

"Look, Mildred, I see things," he said. "Things I coulda . . . I'm older now. There's stuff I coulda done better." Mother rolled her eyes toward the ceiling. I returned us to Oz. Dad pulled the headphones up from around his neck and went back to the hand of solitaire he'd started. His performance was enough for the world; it wasn't enough for him.

Onscreen, the Lion was panic-stricken but fun; his despair was delightful. ("But I could show my prowess / Be a lion, not a mouesse / If I only had the *noive*.") The Lion had words for what was going on inside him; he asked for help and got it. At home, there were no words or even tears, just the thick fog of some ontological anxiety, which seemed to have settled permanently around Dad and was palpable, impenetrable—it lifted only occasionally, for a few brilliant moments. "I do believe in spooks. I do. I do. I do" is the Cowardly Lion's mantra as the foursome approach the Wicked Witch's aerie. In life, Dad was constantly spooked, and his fear took the form of morbid worry. It wasn't so much a state of mind as a continent over which Dad was the bewildered sovereign. Onstage, Dad gave his fear a sound—"*Gnong, gnong, gnong!*" It was a primitive, hilarious yawping, which seemed to sum up all his wide-eyed loss and confusion. Offstage, there was no defining it. The clinical words wheeled out these days for his symptoms—"manic depressive," "bipolar"—can't convey the sensual, dramatic, almost reverent power of the moroseness that Dad could bring with him into a room, or the crazy joy he could manufacture out of it onstage. It was awful and laughable at the same time. We couldn't fathom it; instead, we learned to live with it and to treat him with amused affection. He was our beloved grump. He was perpetually distracted from others, and, despite his ability to tease the last scintilla of laughter from a role, he had no idea how to brighten his own day. "I listened to the audience, and they told me where the joke was," he told me backstage at S. J. Perelman's "The Beauty Part" (1962) after he'd got a howl from a line that had no apparent comic payoff. Why couldn't he listen as closely to us?

When you kissed Dad on the top of his bald head—it smelled deliciously like the inside of a baseball glove—he didn't turn around; when you talked to him, he didn't always answer; sometimes he even forgot our names. That was the bittersweet comedy of his self-absorption. But the Lion confessed his fears, he looked people in the eye, he was easy to touch (even Dorothy, in their first fierce encounter, puts a hand on him); he joined arms with the others and skipped off down the Yellow Brick Road. At the finale, their victory was a triumph of collaboration. In private, as even our little family get-together made apparent, Dad never collaborated; he never reached out (in all the years I went off to camp or college, he wrote me only one letter, and it was dictated); he never elaborated on what weighed him down and kept us under wraps. But there was a gentleness to his bewilderment, which made both the audience and the family want to embrace him.

His laughter was a comfort to the world; in his world, which was rarely humorous, we comforted him. All the family forces were marshalled to keep Dad's
demons at bay and "to be happy," an instruction that translated into specific behavior that would generate no worries—good humor, loyalty, gratitude, obedience, and looking good.

If Dad had had a tail, he would have twisted it just as the Lion did; instead, he
had to make do with his buttons and with the cellophane from his cigarette
packs, which he perpetually rolled between his fingers. What was Dad afraid of?
We never knew exactly. Things were mentioned: work, money, Communists,
cholesterol, garlic, the "Big C." Even a fly intruding into his airspace could bring
a sudden whirlwind of worry as he tried to stalk the pest with a flyswatter. "The
son of a bitch has been hit before," he would say, lashing at the fly and missing.
Dad's global anxiety seeped into the foundation of all our lives; it was hard to see,
and, when it was finally identified, it had to be fortified against. One of the most
efficient ways to do this was to treat Dad as a metaphor—a sort of work of art,
whose extraordinary and articulate performing self was what we took to heart instead of the deflated private person who seemed always at a loss. Any lessons Dad
taught about excellence, courage, perseverance, discipline, and integrity we got
from his stage persona. His best self—the one that was fearless, resourceful, and
generous, and that told the truth—was what he saved for the public, which included us; otherwise, as every relative of a star knows, the family had to make do
with what was left over. Even at the end of our Oz viewing, Dad brushed aside
our praise, which seemed only to increase his anxiety. As he shuffled into the
kitchen to get some ice cream, he glanced over at Mom. "If I'd made a hit as a *human being*, then perhaps I'd be sailing in films now," he said.

When "The Wizard of Oz" opened in New York, on August 17, 1939, fifteen
thousand people were lined up outside the Capitol Theatre by 8 A.M. Dad's photograph was in the window of Lindy's, across the street, and the *Times* declared
his roar "one of the laughingest sounds since the talkies came in." "Believe me it
was a tonic for my inferiority complex which is so readily developed in Hollywood," Dad wrote to Mildred, who would become Mrs. Lahr in 1940. As an
animal, in closeup, and eight times as large as life, Dad, with his broad, burlesque
energy, was acceptable; there was no place for his baggy looks and his clowning,
eccentric mannerisms in talking pictures except on the periphery of romantic stories. Despite his huge success, Metro soon dropped his option. He signed for a
Broadway musical, "Du Barry Was a Lady." "Well, how many lion parts are
there," Dad said as he departed from Hollywood.

Over the years, especially after my son was born, in 1976, I'd catch glimpses of
Dad as the Lion, but, perhaps out of some residual loyalty to his bias, I could
never sit through the film. The hubbub around the movie irritated me, because

the other accomplishments of the performers were swept away in the wake of its unique and spectacular success. I think Dad knew that he was a hostage to technology: a Broadway star whose legend would go largely unrecorded while, by the luck of a new medium, performers who couldn't get work on Broadway would be preserved and perpetuated in the culture. Nowadays, the general public doesn't know about the likes of Florenz Ziegfeld, Abe Burrows, Ethel Merman, Bea Lillie, Billy Rose, Walter Winchell, Clifton Webb, and Nancy Walker, whose stories intersected with Dad's.

What lives on is the Cowardly Lion. When I watch him now, I don't see just the Lion; I see the echoes—the little touches and moves—of those long-forgotten sensational stage performances that Dad condensed into his evergreen role. His floppy consonants, slurred vowels, malapropisms, and baritone vibrato all derived from the collection of sophisticated operatic sendups he'd developed first for Harburg and Arlen's "Things" (from "Life Begins at 8:40") and "Song of the Woodman" (from "The Show Is On"), to be perfected in "If I Were King of the Forest":

Each rabbit would show respect to me,
The chipmunks genuflect to me,
Tho' my tail would lash
I would show compash
For ev'ry underling
If I, if I were king.
Just king.

The Cowardly Lion's boxing bravado ("I'll fight you both together if you want! I'll fight you with one paw tied behind my back! I'll fight you standin' on one foot! I'll fight you wit' my eyes closed!") and his woozy body language (the shoulder rolls, the elbows akimbo, the bobbing head) were grafted onto the Lion from Dad's portrayal of the punch-drunk sparring partner Gink Schiner, in his first Broadway hit, "Hold Everything" (1928). And when the Wizard awards the Cowardly Lion his medal for courage, even Dad's vaudeville act, "What's the Idea" (1922–25), came into play: he swaggered like the policeman he had impersonated while trying to both arrest and impress the hoochy-coochy dancer Nellie Bean. "Read what my medal says—'Courage,'" the Lion says. "Ain't it de truth. Ain't it de *trooth*."

In later years, one of the many canards that grew up about the film was that there was a feud between the old pros and the young Judy Garland—that they had tried to upstage her and push her off the Yellow Brick Road. "How could that be?" my godfather, Jack Haley, who played the Tin Man, told me. "When we go off to see the Wizard, we're locked arm in arm, and every shot is a long shot. How can you push someone out of the picture with a long shot?" Although

Garland wasn't pushed out, her "Over the Rainbow," which became the anthem of a generation, was almost cut from the movie three times. According to Dad, Harburg hadn't liked the original tune, which he found too symphonic and heroic. Years later, when I was working on a book about Harburg's lyrics, Arlen explained the deadlock, which Ira Gershwin had finally been called in to arbitrate. "I got sick to my stomach," Arlen told me. "I knew Ira didn't like ballads. He only liked things with a twinkle. Ira came over, listened, and said, 'That's a good melody.' I knew the heat was off. Yip tried out a few musical notions and came up with the lyric." Another of their favorite numbers, written for "Oz," was one called "The Jitter Bug," in which bugs bite the travellers, who begin to dance with the trees and flowers. It was cut for reasons of pace and of balance, and though it gave Dad a big dance number, he never expressed regret over the loss of the material. What he remembered was the hard work and the offscreen hacking around. "Smith's premium ham!" the old pros yelled at one another before takes. "Vic Fleming had never experienced guys like us," Dad told me. "Some legitimate directors can't imagine anybody thinking about something else and when he yells 'Shoot!' just going in and playing." He went on, "We'd kid around up to the last minute and go on. You could see he got mad and red-faced. Some actors try and get into the mood. They'll put themselves into the character. I never did that. I'm not that—let's say—dedicated."

Dad died on December 4, 1967, the day I finished my book about him. He had never read any part of it. I saw him again in a dream on January 25, 1977. I'd been arguing about comedy with the distinguished English actor Jonathan Pryce, and had stepped out of his dressing room to cool off, and there was Dad in the corridor. "He was wearing his blue jacket with padded shoulders," I wrote in my diary. "He smelled of cologne, and he felt soft when I hugged him. I said, 'I love you.' I can't remember if he answered. But it felt completely real, with all the details of his presence—smell, feel, look, silence—very clear. I woke up sobbing." I added, "When will we meet again?"

So far, he has not reappeared in my dreams; but, in another sense, as the reissue of "The Wizard of Oz" only underscores, he has never really gone away. He's a Christmas ornament, a pen, a watch, a beanbag toy, a bracelet charm, a snow globe, a light sculpture, a bedroom-wall decoration. (Neiman Marcus's Christmas catalogue includes Dad in "The Wizard of Oz" bedroom—"the ultimate child's bedroom"—which, at a hundred and fifty thousand dollars, is more than twice as much as he was paid for the movie.) In the space of only two days this fall, on the merchandise channel QVC, a new offering of Oz paraphernalia sold about a million and a half dollars, which seems to prove the claim on the Warner Bros. fact sheet that " 'The Wizard of Oz' has Universal Awareness." I should be outraged by all this, I suppose, since Dad's estate gets no money. I should deplore the trivialization of him as an artist and bemoan the pagan impulse to make household gods of mortal endeavor. (When Dad took up painting, in his last years, and realized that there was a market for Cowardly Lion artifacts, even he got the franchise itch, and stopped doing flowers and vegetables in order to churn out lions, which he signed and sold to friends.) But, if I'm honest with myself, these tchotchkes comfort me. They are totems of Dad's legacy of joy, and of his enduring life in the century's collective imagination.

I'm an orphan now, but I'm full of gratitude for the world that made me. I get letters from older readers who knew my parents, and who tell me in passing how proud Dad was of Jane and me. It's nice to know. I think Dad loved us, but it was in the nature of his way of loving that the knowledge is not bone deep. So the marketed trinkets work for me like Mexican *milagros*—talismans that are extensions of prayer and are tacked by the prayerful onto crosses in thanks for the miracle of survival. I'm pushing sixty now, but I find that the conversation with one's parents doesn't end with the grave. I want Dad back to finish the discussion—to answer some questions, to talk theatre, to see me now. Almost anywhere in the city these days, I can turn the corner and run into him. I stroll past a novelty store on Lexington Avenue, and there's Dad as a cookie jar. I steal a peek at the computer of a young woman in the Public Library, and, by God, there he is as a desktop image. I go to buy some wrapping paper at the stationery store, and his face stares at me from the greeting-card rack. "Hiya, Pop," I find myself saying, and continue on my way.

William Matthews

Poet William Matthews (1942–1997) was born in Cincinnati, Ohio, and graduated from Yale College in 1965. He wrote eleven books of poems, including *Ruining the Road* (1970), *Sleek for the Long Flight* (1972), *Rising and Falling* (1979), *A Happy Childhood* (1985), *Blues If You Want* (1989), and *Time and Money,* which won the National Book Critics Circle Award in 1995. A final book, *After All,* was published posthumously in 1998. What he once wrote in praise of W. H. Auden could be said of Matthews himself: "The language has used him / well and passed him through. / We get what he has collected." He was a poet who "got" a good deal. His interests ranged from Horace to Mingus, from Freud to Nabokov, baseball to haute cuisine. He was a poet of wry wit and casual sophistication. He found the lyrical in the vernacular, the memorable in the mundane.

NABOKOV'S BLUES

The wallful of quoted passages from his work,
with the requisite specimens pinned next
to their literary cameo appearances, was too good

a temptation to resist, and if the curator couldn't,
why should we? The prose dipped and shimmered
and the "flies," as I heard a buff call them, stood

at lurid attention on their pins. If you love to read
and look, you could be happy a month in that small
room. One of the Nabokov photos I'd never seen:

he's writing (left-handed! why did I never trouble
to find out?) at his stand-up desk in the hotel
apartment in Montreux. The picture's mostly

of his back and the small wedge of face that shows
brims with indifference to anything not on the page.
The window's shut. A tiny lamp trails a veil of light

over the page, too far away for us to read.
We also liked the chest of specimen drawers
labeled, as if for apprentice Freudians,

"Genitalia," wherein languished in phials
the thousands he examined for his monograph
on the Lycaenidae, the silver-studded Blues.

And there in the center of the room a carillon
of Blues rang mutely out. There must have been
three hundred of them. Amanda's Blue was there,

and the Chalk Hill Blue, the Karner Blue
(*Lycaeides melissa samuelis* Nabokov),
a Violet-Tinged Copper, the Mourning Cloak,

an Echo Azure, the White-Lined Green Hairstreak,
the Cretan Argus (known only from Mt. Ida:
in the series Nabokov did on this beauty

he noted for each specimen the altitude at which
it had been taken), and as the ads and lovers say,
"and much, much more." The stilled belle of the tower

was a *Lycaeides melissa melissa.* No doubt
it's an accident Melissa rhymes, sort of, with Lolita.
The scant hour we could lavish on the Blues

flew by, and we improvised a path through cars
and slush and boot-high berms of mud-blurred snow
to wherever we went next. I must have been mute,

or whatever I said won from silence nothing
it mourned to lose. I was back in that small
room, vast by love of each flickering detail,

each genital dusting to nothing, the turn,
like a worm's or caterpillar's, of each phrase.
I stood up to my ankles in sludge pooled

over a stopped sewer grate and thought—
wouldn't you know it—about love and art:
you can be ruined ("rurnt," as we said in south-

western Ohio) by a book or improved by
a butterfly. You can dodder in the slop,
septic with a rage not for order but for the love

the senses bear for what they do, for the detail
that's never annexed, like a reluctant crumb
to a vacuum cleaner, to a coherence.

You can be bead after bead on perception's rosary.
This is the sweet ache that hurts most, the way
desire burns bluely at its phosphorescent core:

just as you're having what you wanted most,
you want it more and more until that's more
than you, or it, or both of you, can bear.

ONIONS

How easily happiness begins by
dicing onions. A lump of sweet butter
slithers and swirls across the floor
of the sauté pan, especially if its
errant path crosses a tiny slick
of olive oil. Then a tumble of onions.

This could mean soup or risotto
or chutney (from the Sanskrit
chatni, to lick). Slowly the onions
go limp and then nacreous
and then what cookbooks call clear,
though if they were eyes you could see

clearly the cataracts in them.
It's true it can make you weep
to peel them, to unfurl and to tease
from the taut ball first the brittle,
caramel-colored, and decrepit
papery outside layer, the least

recent the reticent onion
wrapped around its growing body,
for there's nothing to an onion
but skin, and it's true you can go on
weeping as you go on in, through
the moist middle skins, the sweetest

and thickest, and you can go on
in to the core, to the bud-like,
acrid, fibrous skins densely
clustered there, stalky and incomplete, and these are the most
pungent, like the nuggets of nightmare

and rage and murmury animal
comfort that infant humans secrete.
This is the best domestic perfume.
You sit down to eat with a rumor
of onions still on your twice-washed
hands and lift to your mouth a hint

of a story about loam and usual
endurance. It's there when you clean up
and rinse the wine glasses and make
a joke, and you leave the minutest
whiff of it on the light switch,
later, when you climb the stairs.

107TH & AMSTERDAM

A phalanx of cabs surges uptown in tune
to the staggered lights and two young black
men spurt across the dark avenue (two A.M.)

ahead of them: *We're here, motherfuckers,
don't mess up.* Three of five cabs honk: *We're here
too, older and clawing for a living, don't*

fuck up. The cabs rush uptown and the lights
go green ahead like a good explanation.
Everyone knows this ballet. Nobody falls or brakes.

Tonight I talked for hours and never said
one thing so close to the truculent heart of speech
as those horn blats, that dash across Amsterdam,

not to persuade nor to be understood but
a kind of signature, a scrawl on the air:
We're here, room for all of us if we be alert.

orn in Michigan in 1939, Thomas McGuane graduated from Michigan State University in 1962 and came then to the Yale School of Drama, where he took his M.F.A. in 1965. "My most persistent memories," he writes, "are of the endless days in Sterling Library, where I read medieval bestiaries, modern novels, and fishing books. I particularly remember covertly following Robert Penn Warren around the card catalogs, trying to figure out what he was reading." McGuane's first novel, *The Sporting Club,* appeared in 1969. Eleven other books have followed, among them *The Bushwhacked Piano* (1971), *Ninety-two in the Shade* (1973), *Panama* (1977), and *Nothing but Blue Skies* (1992). He has also written screenplays and many essays on sports. A flamboyant stylist, he now lives in Montana, whose big skies mirror the spaciousness of his fiction, its burly elegance.

Years ago, a child in a tree with a small caliber rifle bushwhacked a piano through the open summer windows of a neighbor's living room. The child's name was Nicholas Payne.

Dragged from the tree by the piano's owner, his rifle smashed upon a rock and flung, he was held by the neck in the living room and obliged to view the piano point blank, to dig into its interior and see the cut strings, the splintered holes that let slender shafts of light ignite small circles of dark inside the piano.

"You have spoiled my piano."

The child would remember the great wing of the lid over his head, the darkness, the cut wires curling upon themselves, the smell of spice and the sudden idea that the piano had been sailed full of spice from the Indies free of the bullet holes that would have sent it to the bottom, resonant with uncut strings, its mahogany lid slicing the wind and sheltering a moist and fragrant cargo of spice.

What an idea.

After that, wisdom teeth, a perfect horror: one tooth slipping out as easily as an orange seed popping from between your fingers; the other less simple, requiring the incision of a flap of skin and the chiseling through a snarl of impacted roots and nerves, the tooth coming away in splinters and his very mortality flashing from the infected maw.

Then: a visit to his grandfather's farmstead. Abandoned. The windows glinted blank on a hay field gone entirely to pigweed. Wingnuts made soft black moons in the punky wood of ruined shutters. When he shielded his eyes at the front porch window and saw into the old kitchen, he perceived the pipes of myriad disconnections, jutting and pointing into space; and, in the half-light of a far corner, a white enamel water heater, a rash of rust broken out on its sides, crouched like a monster. When he kicked in the front door, it swung wide and wobbling; its lock spilled screws far too long. He started to explore but quit at the bathroom where a tub poised lightly as a dancer on cast-iron lion's feet, its faucets dry, bulbous.

Years away but, he thought, in direct sequence, a woman sat on a blue stool striking at her hair with a tortoise-shell comb. And behind, on the bed, Nicholas Payne, her seducer, sighted between the first two toes of his right foot, wishing his leg were a Garand rifle.

There were any number of such things from that epoch, but a handful seemed to make a direct footpath to lunacy: a stockbroker's speckled face, for example, his soft, fat eyes and his utterly larval voice.

He was too young to have to make such connections, rolling across an empty early-morning city, red-eyed in an eggstained bathrobe, a finger in each corner of his mouth drawing it down to a grotesque whitening slit through which he pressed his tongue. Since they found him curiously menacing, the attendants supplied a canvas coat with longish sleeves. It was insulting and unnecessary.

That was some time ago now, and he recovered at home. When he was being odd, he would sometimes, at night, go to his bedroom window, ungirdle, and urinate on the walnut trees radiant below him in the moonlight. Sometimes he boiled eggs on the electric range and forgot to eat them or went into the closet and stood in the dark among all the dusty shoes. He had an old cello, painted blue, and he often sawed upon it. One night he took the pliers to its strings and that was that.

His family said that he could not be trusted around a musical instrument.

Then, just when he was doing so well in school, he lit out on a motorcycle. And nowadays that trip would come to him in happy little versions and episodes. Anyone could see that he was going to pull something like that again. Even his mother's friend who had managed the Longines Symphonette could see he was fixing to pull something. She taught piano, and Payne took from her.

But all Payne could remember was that first cross-country trip. He was on an English Matchless motorcycle and headed for California. Nebraska seemed so empty he sometimes could scarcely tell he was in motion. Those were soil-bank days and you had to watch out for pheasants on the road. Payne felt intuitively that a single, mature rooster could disable an English racing machine. Later, he recalled two cowboys outside of Vernal, Utah, in a windstorm, chasing a five-dollar bill across a feed lot.

A girl rode with him from Lordsburg, Colorado, to Reno, Nevada, and bought him a one-pound jar of Floyd Collins Lilac Brilliantine to keep his hair in place on the bike.

And California at first sight was the sorry, beautiful Golden West silliness and uproar of simplistic yellow hills with metal wind pumps, impossible highways to the brim of the earth, coastal cities, forests and pretty girls with their tails in the wind. A movie theater in Sacramento played *Mondo Freudo.*

In Oakland, he saw two slum children sword fighting on a slag heap. In Palo Alto, a puffy fop in bursting jodhpurs shouted from the door of a luxurious stable, "*My horse is soiled!*" While one chilly evening in Union Square he listened to a wild-eyed young woman declaim that she had seen delicate grandmothers raped by Kiwanis zombies, that she had seen Rotarian blackguards bludgeoning Easter bunnies in a coal cellar, that she had seen Irving Berlin buying an Orange Julius in Queens.

In the spring of that year, San Francisco was dark with swamis. He didn't stay long. Until that fall he lived north of San Francisco in a rented house, in the town of Bolinas. The memory of that now isolated these months to a single morning when he had turned out at dawn and gone to the window. Looking across the meadow that was the southern end of the low, vegetated mesa he lived upon, he could see the silver whale shape of fog that lay in from the sea, stilled, covering Bolinas, the lagoon and the far foothills. The eucalyptus around the house was fragrant in the early wet sun and full of birds. Firing up the motorcycle, he went spinning down Overlook Road toward the ocean rim of the mesa, straight toward the wall of fog at the cliff. Shy of the edge, he swung down onto Terrace Road and dropped quite fast through the eucalyptus and cedar, really as fast as he could go, through repetitive turns, the smells by-passing his nose to go directly to the lungs, the greenery overhead sifting and scattering shadows, the dips in the road cupping sunlight, the banked turns unfolding his shadow, the whole road flattening out, gliding along the base of the Little Mesa, down the corrugated concrete ramp onto the beach where he found himself in the fog with the sun melting it into streamers and the beach dark, streaked, delicately ridged like contour plowing; and everywhere the rock underpinning nosing through the sand and Payne obliged to steer a careful fast course with the front wheel swimming a little, until he reached Duxbury reef where he once caught a big, blushing octopus the color of any number of slightly gone-off tulips, as well as gunnysacks of monkeyface eels, cabezone and cockles—provender. He set about now getting mussels, snatching them off the rocks impatiently with less philosophical dedication to living off the land than to eating mussels at intervals of twice a week steamed in sixty cents a quart, third-press mountain white, and fennel. When he finished his work, he sat on the largest boulder at the end of the reef, the base of which was encircled with drifting kelp, weed and the pieces of a splintered hatch cover. The fog retreated to an almost circular perimeter within which a violet sun shone. The sea stood in a line of distant mercury. The sanderlings raced along the edge of the sea in almost fetid salt air. And Payne, thinking of home and knowing he would *go* home, saw with some concision that, as a citizen, he was not in the least solid. In a way, it was nice to know. Once he began to see himself as societal dead weight, a kind of energetic relaxation came over him and he no longer felt he was merely looking for trouble.

The homecoming itself was awash in vague remembered detail; the steamer dock on Sugar Island looked draped in rain. He remembered that. It was wet, middling season in Michigan; he forgot which one. There were a number of them. And this: the condemned freighter *Maida* towed by tugs toward a chalky wafer of sun, toward the lead-white expanse of Detroit River, black gleaming derricks, slag—the whole, lurid panorama of cloacal American nature smarm debouching into Lake Erie where—when Payne was duck hunting—a turn of his oar against the bottom brought up a blue whirring nimbus of petroleum sludge and toxic, coagulant effluents the glad hand of national industry wants the kids to swim in. This was water that ran in veins. This was proud water that wouldn't mix. This was water whose currents drove the additives aloft in glossy pools and gay poison rainbows. This was water the walking upon of which scarcely made for a miracle.

Moping on an abandoned coal dock, Payne rehearsed his imagined home. He tried by main force to drag back the bass-filled waters he actually remembered. He dreamed up picturesque visions of long packed lawns planing to the river and the lake in a luminous haze beyond. He recollected freighters and steamers sailing by, the side-wheeled and crystal-windowed palaces of the D & C Line that had so recently gone in stately parade up the Canadian channel, the sound of their orchestras borne across the water to Grosse Ile.

But this time the *Maida* toiled before him on the septic flow, vivid with arrows of rust thrusting downward from dismal scuppers. On deck, a handful of men rather specifically rued the day. Life in the U.S.A. gizzard had changed. Only a clown could fail to notice.

So then, failing to notice would be a possibility. Consequently, he fell in love with a girl named Ann who interested herself in the arts, who was quite beautiful and wild; and who, as no other, was onto Payne and who, to an extent that did not diminish him, saw through Payne. In the beginning, theirs was one of those semichemical, tropistic encounters that seem so romantic in print or on film. Ann had a beautiful, sandy, easy and crotch-tightening voice; and, responding to it, Payne had given her the whole works, smile after moronic smile, all those clean, gleaming, square, white teeth that could only be produced by a region which also produced a large quantity of grain, cereals, and corn—and stopped her in her tracks to turn at this, this what? this *smiler,* his face corrugated with the idiocy of *desire* and the eclectic effects of transcontinental motorcycle windburn, a grin of keenness, blocky, brilliant, possibly deranged. And stared at him!

He went to her house. He croaked *be mine* from behind the rolled windows of his Hudson Hornet which in the face of her somewhat handsome establishment appeared intolerably shabby. He felt a strange tension form between his car and the house. The mint-green Hornet was no longer his joy. The stupid lurch of its paint-can pistons lacked an earlier charm. The car was now spiritually unequal to him. The wheel in his hands was far away, a Ferris wheel. The coarse fabric of the seats extended forever. All gauges: dead. The odometer stuttered its first repetition in 1953 when Payne was a child. A month ago he'd had a new carburetor installed. When he lifted the hood, it sickened him to see that bright tuber of fitted steel on the vague rusted engine surfaces. The offensive innocence of mushrooms. A thing like that takes over. A pale green spot on a loaf of bread is a fright wig inside of a week. These little contrasts unhinge those who see them. The contrast between his car and her house was doing that now. He could barely see through the windshield, but clear glass would have been unendurable. The world changed through these occlusions. Objects slid and jumped behind his windshield as he passed them. He knew exactly how a building would cross its expanse progressively then jump fifteen degrees by optical magic. Don't make me go in that house. Just at the center of the windshield a bluish white line appeared like a tendril turning round itself downward and exploded in a perfect fetal lizard nourished by the capillaries that spread through the glass.

Gradually, he worked himself from the machine, went to the door, was admitted, went through to the back where Ann Fitzgerald was painting a white trellis and, paint brush in her right hand, dripping pale paint stars in the dirt. "Yes," she said, "I will." Indicating only that she would see him again. "Stay where you are," she said. An instant later she photographed him with a large, complex-looking camera. "That will be all," she smiled.

The steamer dock, the former property of the Sugar Island Amusement Company, defunct 1911, was a long balconied pier half-slumped under water. Near the foot of the pier, abandoned in the trees, was an evocative assortment of pavilions, ticket stands and stables. There were two carved and lofty ramps that mounted, forthright, into space. And the largest building, in the same style as the pavilion, was a roller rink. This building had come to be half-enveloped in forest.

It was nighttime and the ears of Nicholas Payne were filled with the roar of his roller-skated pursuit of the girl, Ann, at speed over the warped and undulant hardwood floor. He trailed slightly because he glided down the slopes in a crouch while she skated down; and so she stayed in front and they roared in a circle shuddering in and out of the light of the eight tall windows. Payne saw the moon stilled against the glass of one unbroken pane, gasped something like *watch me now* and skated more rapidly as the wooden sound sank deeper into his ears and the mirrored pillar that marked the center of the room glittered in the corner of his eye; he closed the distance until she was no longer cloudy and indefinite in the shifting light but brightly clear in front of him with the short pleatings of skirt curling close around the soft insides of thigh. And Payne in a bravura extension beyond his own abilities shot forward on one skate, one leg high behind him like a trick skater in a Dutch painting, reached far ahead of himself, swept his hand up a thigh, and had her by the crotch. Then, for this instant's bliss, he bit the dust, hitting the floor with his nose dragging like a skeg, landing stretched out, chin resting straight forward and looking at the puffy, dreamy vacuity midway in her panties. Ann Fitzgerald, feet apart, sitting, ball-bearing wooden wheels still whirring, laughed to herself and to him and said, "You asshole."

Paul Monette

aul Monette (1945–1995) was a poet and novelist whose best work was a pair of memoirs—*Borrowed Time* (1988), a harrowing account of nursing his lover through an AIDS illness and death, and *Becoming a Man* (1992), a memoir of growing up a confused and closeted homosexual and eventually discovering his own identity and strength. The book won the National Book Award for nonfiction in 1992. He began as a poet and published four collections: *The Carpenter at the Asylum* (1975), *No Witnesses* (1981), *Love Alone: Eighteen Elegies for Rog* (1988), and *West of Yesterday, East of Summer: New and Selected Poems, 1973–1993* (1993). He wrote six novels, among them *Taking Care of Mrs. Carroll* (1978) and *Halfway Home* (1991). His *Last Watch of the Night: Essays Too Personal and Otherwise* appeared in 1994, and an animal fable, *Sanctuary,* was published posthumously in 1997. Chapters of *Becoming a Man* dwell on his undergraduate years at Yale (1963–1967) and discuss his introduction to poetry: "I took the two-semester course in the moderns, Cleanth Brooks in the fall and John Hollander in the spring. These luminous divines could hardly have been more different from one another in approach—Brooks the brilliant exemplar of New Criticism; Hollander the working poet in the flesh, mad eyes and the tongue of a fallen angel when he read. Though I was never much of a scholar in my studies, I discovered with a growing confidence a capacity to walk through the walls of a poem."

Stevie had been in the hospital for about a week and a half, diagnosed with PCP, his first full-blown infection. For some reason he wasn't responding to the standard medication, and his doctors had put him on some new exotic combination regimen—one side effect of which was to turn his piss blue. He certainly didn't act or feel sick, except for a little breathlessness. He was still miles from the brink of death. Not even showing any sign of late-stage shriveling up—let alone the ravages of end-stage, where all that's left of life is sleep shot through with delirium.

Stevie was reading the paper, in a larky mood because he'd just had a dose of Ativan. I was sitting by the window, doodling with a script that I had to finish quickly in order to keep my insurance. "I miss Puck," he announced to no one in particular, no response required.

And I stopped writing and looked out the window at the heat-blistered parking lot, the miasma of low smog bleaching the hills in the distance. "You think Puck's going to survive me?"

"Yup," he replied. Which startled me, a bristle of the old denial that none of us was going to die just yet. Even though we were all living our lives in "dog years" now, seven for every twelvemonth, I still couldn't feel my own death as a palpable thing. To have undertaken the fight as we had for better drugs and treatment, so that we had become a guerrilla tribe of amateur microbiologists, pharmacist/shamans, our own best healers—there were those of us who'd convinced ourselves in 1990 that the dying was soon going to stop.

AIDS, you see, was on the verge of becoming a "chronic manageable illness." That was our totem mantra after we buried the second wave, or was it the third? When I met Steve Kolzak on the Fourth of July in '88, he told me he had seven friends who were going to die in the next six months—and they did. It was my job to persuade him that we could fall in love anyway, embracing between the bombs. And then we would pitch our tent in the chronic, manageable clearing, years and years given back to us by the galloping strides of science. No more afflicted than a diabetic, the daily insulin keeping him one step ahead of his body.

So don't tell me I had less time than a ten-year-old dog—admittedly one who was a specimen of roaring good health, still out chasing coyotes in the canyon every night, his watchman's bark at home sufficient to curdle the blood. But if I was angry at Stevie for saying so, I kept it to myself as the hospital stay dragged on. A week of treatment for PCP became two, and he found himself reaching more and more for the oxygen. Our determination, or mine at least, to see this bout as a minor inconvenience remained unshaken. Stevie upped his Ativan and mostly retained his playful demeanor, though woe to the nurse or technician who thought a stream of happy talk would get them through the holocaust. Stevie's bark was as lethal as Puck's if you said the wrong thing.

And he didn't get better, either, because it wasn't pneumonia that was killing him. I woke up late on Friday, the fifteenth of September, to learn they'd moved him to intensive care, and I raced to the hospital to find him in a panic, fear glazing his flashing Irish eyes as he clutched the oxygen cup to his mouth. They pulled him through the crisis with steroids, but still wouldn't say what the problem was. Some nasty bug that a sewer of antibiotics hadn't completely arrested yet. But surely all it required was a little patience till one of these drugs kicked in.

His family arrived from back East, the two halves of the divorce. Yet it looked as if the emergency had passed, such is the false promise of massive steroids. I mean, he looked *fine*. He was impish and animated all through the weekend; it was we who had to be vigilant lest he get too tired. And I was so manically certain that he'd pull through, I could hardly take it in at first when one of the docs, shifty-eyed, refined the diagnosis: "He's having a toxic reaction to the chemo."

The chemo? But how could that be? They'd been treating his KS for sixteen months, till all the lesions were under control. Even the ones on his face: you had to know they were there to spot them, a scatter of faded purple under his beard. Besides, KS wasn't a sickness really, it was mostly just a nuisance. This was how deeply invested I was in denial, the 1990 edition. Since KS had never landed us in the hospital, it didn't count. And the chemo was the treatment, so how could it be life-threatening?

Easily, as it turned out. The milligram dosage of bleomycin, a biweekly drip in the doctor's office, is cumulative. After a certain point you run the risk of toxicity, your lungs seizing with fibrous tissue—all the resilience gone till you can't even whistle in the dark anymore. You choke to death the way Stevie did, gasping into the oxygen mask, a little less air with every breath.

Still, there were moments of respite, even on that last day. "I'm not dying, am I?" he asked about noon, genuinely astonished. Finally his doctor came in and broke the news: the damage to the lungs was irreversible, and the most we could hope for was two or three weeks. Stevie nodded and pulled off the mask to speak. "Listen, I'm a greedy bastard," he declared wryly. "I'll take what I can get." As I recall, the idea was to send him home in a wheelchair with an oxygen tank.

I cried when the doctor left, trying to tell him how terrible it was, though he knew it better than I. Yet he smiled and put out a hand to comfort me, reassuring me that he felt no panic. He was on so much medication for pain and anxiety that his own dying had become a movie—a sad one to be sure, but the Ativan/ Percodan cocktail was keeping the volume down. I kept saying how much I loved him, as if to store the feeling up for the empty days ahead. Was there anything I could do? Anything left unsaid?

He shook his head, that muzzy wistful smile. Then his eyebrows lifted in surprise: "I'm not going to see Puck again." No regret, just amazement. And then it was time to grab the mask once more, the narrowing tunnel of air, the morphine watch. Twelve hours later he was gone, for death was even greedier than he.

And I was a widower twice now. Nothing for it but to stumble through the week that followed, force-fed by all my anguished friends, pulling together a funeral at the Old North Church at Forest Lawn. A funeral whose orations smeared the blame like dogshit on the rotting churches of this dead Republic, the politicians who run the ovens and dance on our graves. In the limo that took us up the hill to the gravesite, Steve's mother Dolores patted my knee and declared with a ribald trace of an Irish brogue: "Thanks for not burning the flag."

We laughed. A mere oversight, I assured her. She knew that Steve and I had spent a fruitless afternoon the previous Fourth of July—our anniversary, as it happened—going from Thrifty to Target trying to find stars-and-stripes to burn at our party. No such luck: all the flags we found were plastic or polyester, the consistency of cheap shower curtains. A perfect symbol, we realized, of the country we had lost during the decade of the calamity.

We buried the urn of his ashes high on a hill just at the rim of the chaparral, at the foot of a California live oak. The long shadow of our grieving circle fell across the hillside grass where I had buried Roger four years before; the shadow fell on my own grave, as a matter of fact, which is just to the left of Roger's, as if I will one day fling an arm about him and cradle us to sleep. After the putrefaction of the flesh, a pair of skeletons tangled together like metaphysical lovers out of Donne. And my other bone-white arm reaching above my skull, clawing the dirt with piano-key fingers, trying to get to Steve's ashes, just out of reach.

But what has it all got to do with the dog, exactly? My friend Victor stayed with me for the first week of Widowhood II. When at last he went off to juggle the shards of his own dwindling immunity, and I woke to a smudged October morning, my first thought wasn't *Oh poor me,* about which I had already written the book, but rather: *Who's going to take care of Puck?* What nudged me perhaps was the beast himself, who sprawled across the middle of the sagging double bed, permitting me a modest curl of space on the far left side.

You must try to appreciate, I never used to be anything like a rapturist about dogs, Puck or any other. My friend César used to say that Puck was the only dog he knew who'd been raised without any sentimentality at all. I was such a manic creature myself during his formative years that it was all he could do to scramble out of my lurching way, and not take it personally when I'd shoo him away for no reason. This was not the same as having trained him. He rather tumbled up, like one of those squalling babies in Dickens, saved in the nick of time from a scald of boiling water by a harried Mrs. Micawber.

And yet when Roger died, and I thought I had died along with him, the only thing that got me out of bed, groggy at sunset, was that Puck still had to be fed. I could see in his limpid, heartstopping eyes that he knew Roger was not coming back; or maybe he had acquired a permanent wince seeing me sob so inconsolably, hour after hour, gallantly putting his chin on the bed with a questioning look, in case I wanted company. I remembered asking my brother in Pennsylvania if the dog could be shipped to him when I died, an event that seemed at the time as close as the walls of this room. But I didn't really like to think of Puck snuffling about in the fields of Bucks County, he whose breeding made him thrive in the desert hills of Southern California.

Half Rhodesian ridgeback, half black lab—or half Zimbabwean ridgeback, I ought to say, since one of my earliest encounters with political correctness occurred in Laurel Canyon Park. In the early eighties it was a place where we could run our dogs off lead, one eye peeled for the panel truck of Animal Control. A sixty-dollar ticket if they caught you—or in this case, if they caught Puck, who left the paying of municipal fines in my capable hands.

He was one of a litter of nine, his mother a purebred ridgeback, tawny and noble, her back bisected by the stiff brush of her ridge, which ran from just behind her shoulders and petered out at her rump. A dog bred to hunt lions, we'd heard, especially prized for being able to go long stretches without any water, loping across the veldt. As a sort of modulation of its terrifying bark, a bay of Baskerville proportions, the ridgeback had developed over time a growl as savage as that of the lions it stalked. Try to get near a ridgeback when he's feeding, you'll see what I mean. You feel like one of those helpless children at the zoo, about to lose an arm through a chain-link fence, waving a box of Cracker Jacks in the roaring face of the king.

Ah but you see, there were compensating factors on the father's side. For Nellie, fertile mother of Puck and his eight siblings, had gotten it on with a strapping black lab high up in Benedict Canyon. A lab who was considered most *déclassé*, perhaps a bit of a half-breed himself, so friendly and ebullient that his people were always in peril of being knocked over or slobbered on. Not at all the sort of genes that Nellie's owners were seeking to rarefy even further. We were told all this in a rush by Nellie's starlet mistress, herself the achingly pretty daughter of a wondrously tucked and lifted movie star of the fifties—a pair who looked like sisters if you squinted, beautiful and not much else, the perfect ticket in L.A. to a long and happy journey on the median strip of life.

This was at a Thanksgiving supper in Echo Park—not the year we found the murdered Latino in the driveway as we left, but I think the year after. In any case, Roger and I had been worrying over the issue of a watchdog for some time now, as a security system cheaper by far than the alarm circuits that wired the hills around us, shrieking falsely into the night. The starlet daughter assured us that ridgebacks were brilliant sentries, ferociously protective.

We went back and forth in the next few weeks, warned by both our families that it was just another thing to tie us down. Besides, we traveled too much, and it wasn't fair to an animal to be getting boarded all the time. None of them understood how stirred we'd been the previous spring, when a whimper brought us to the front door one stormy night. A bedraggled one-eyed Pekingese dripped on the tile, matted and scrawny and quaking in the rain. The most improbable creature, the very last dog that either of us would have chosen. But we couldn't send him back out in the whirlwind either, a bare *hors d'oeuvre* for the sleek coyotes that roamed our canyon in pairs.

We put signs on the trees up and down Kings Road, FOUND instead of the usual LOST (for cats, especially, disappeared with alarming frequency in the hills). Nobody called to claim the one-eyed runt, and it started to look as if we were stuck with him. Without consultation, Roger began to call him Pepper and comb him out. I resisted mightily: *This was not by a long shot what anyone would call a watchdog.* I felt faintly ridiculous walking Pepper with his string leash, as if I'd become an aging queen before my time. Thus I withheld my sentiments rigorously, leaving most of the care and feeding to Roger—though now and again I'd permit the orphan to perch on my lap while I typed.

And then about three weeks later we were strolling up Harold Way, Roger and Pepper and I, past the gates to Liberace's spread. We turned to a cry of delight, as a young black woman came running down the driveway. "Thass my mama dog!" she squealed, scooping the one-eyed dustmop into her arms. In truth, Pepper seemed as overjoyed as she, licking her with abandon. The young woman called uphill to the kitchen yard, summoning her mother: "Grits home!" And a moment later an equally joyous woman came trundling toward us, crisp white uniform and billowing apron worthy of Tara.

No, no, of course we wouldn't dream of taking money. This joyous reunion was all the reward we needed. And so we trudged on home, trying not to feel even more ridiculous as we hastily put away the doll-sized bowls by the kitchen door that had held Pepper/Grits's food and water. We laughed it off, or tried to anyway, gushing appropriately when the daughter appeared at our door that evening, bearing a peach pie almost too pretty to eat. "This is like Faulkner," Roger declared as we sliced the bounty. Faulkner, I replied, would not have used a Pekingese.

We never saw Pepper again—never even had the chance to ask how he'd lost that eye. But it goes to show how primed we were at the end of the year, when the starlet called nearly every day to say the litter was going fast. We thought we'd go over and have a look, but the only time the lot of us were free was Christmas morning. "Now we don't have to take one," I admonished Roger as we turned up the dirt road. A minute later we were in the kitchen, inundated by the scrambling of nine puppies. "Pick a lively one," I said, though the sheer explosion of canine anarchy didn't seem to have produced a sluggard or a runt. They squirmed out of our hands and yapped and chased. We couldn't have been said to have actually made a choice. The starlet and her human pups were waiting impatiently in the living room to open their gifts. Roger and I exchanged a shrug, and I reached for the one that was trying to crawl behind the refrigerator.

"You don't owe me anything," the starlet trilled. "Just the fifty bucks for his shots." We waved and promised to send a check, clamoring into the car with our erupting bundle. A black lab followed us barking down the drive. The father, we supposed. "He's not going to be *that* big, is he?" murmured Roger in some dismay. By the time we got home we were calling him Puck, in part because some friends of ours had just named a daughter Ariel, and we'd liked the Shakespearean spin of that, the sense that we were bringing home a changeling. The first thing Puck did when he tottered into the house was make for the Christmas tree, where he squatted and peed on a package from Gump's.

I don't remember a whole lot after that, not for the first five years, so assiduously was I trying to avoid the doggy sort of bathos. I do recall how fretful Roger was for the first six months, waiting for Puck to lift his leg instead of squatting. And the moment of triumph when he finally did, on a bush of wild anis. His main lair was beneath my butcher-block desk in the study—where he lies even as I write this, his head propped uncomfortably on the wooden crossbeam that holds the legs in place. We quickly learned that he wouldn't be budged from any of his makeshift doghouses, which came to include the undercave of every table in the house. A lion's growl of warning if you got too close.

I fed him, I walked him. As I say, I was crazed in those years like a starlet myself, frantic to have a script made, fawning as indiscriminately as a puppy over every self-styled producer who left a spoor in my path. I was so unbearably sophisticated, convinced I could reconfigure the Tracy/Hepburn magic, so glib and airy-fairy that my shit didn't stink. For a time I even began to question my life with Roger, and Puck as well, as being perhaps too bourgeois for words.

None of the scripts got made, of course. I was tossed on my ass as a loser and a failure, unable to get my calls returned, no matter how desperately I courted the assistants of assistants. I fell into a wrongheaded love affair with a hustler—literally, the fifty-bucks-a-pop variety—which reminds me, I never paid the debt to the starlet for Puck's shots, which would have been a lot better use of the money. Within a few weeks the hustler had sucked all my marrow and moved on. I careened through a year of near-breakdown, writing plays but mostly whining, and nearly driving Roger away in the process.

Yet we never stopped taking that evening walk, along the rim of the hill that led from Kings Canyon to Queens, Puck rooting ahead of us through the chaparral. I'm not quite sure how he managed to serve two masters, but was clearly far too well-bred to choose sides. We simply represented different orbits, centered of course on him. I was the one who sat at the desk while he slept at my feet all day, and Roger the one who came home at six, sending him into paroxysms of excited barking. The late-night walk was a threesome, no hierarchy of power. I'm not saying it kept Roger and me together, all on its own, but the evening stroll had about it a Zen calm—so many steps to the bower of jacarandas at Queens Road, so many steps home.

I remember the first time the dog howled, when a line of fire trucks shrilled up the canyon to try to cut off a brushfire. Puck threw back his head and gave vent to a call so ancient, so lupine really, that it seemed to have more in common with the ravening of fire and the night stalk of predators than with the drowsy life of a house pet. The howl didn't erupt very often; usually it was kicked off by a siren or a chorus of baying coyotes up-canyon quarreling with the moon. And it was clear Puck didn't like to have us watch him when he did it, especially to laugh or applaud him. He'd been seized by a primal hunger, sacred even, and needed to be alone with it. Usually it lasted no more than a minute, and then he'd be back with us, wagging and begging for biscuits.

We didn't have him fixed, either. More of an oversight than anything else, though I wonder now if it didn't have something to do with the neutering Roger and I had been through during our own years in the closet. It meant of course that Puck could be excruciatingly randy. His favorite sexual activity was to hump our knees as we lay in bed reading at night, barking insistently if we tried to ignore his throbbing need. We more or less took turns, Roger and I, propping our knees underneath the comforter so Puck could have his ride. He never actually came, not a full load, though he dribbled a lot. I can't say if all this made him more of a gay dog or not.

Except for that nightly erotic charge he never actually jumped up on people, though he could be a handful when friends came over, turning himself inside out to greet them. And for some reason—probably having to do with the turkey and ham on the buffet—he loved parties, the bigger the better, wagging about from guest to guest all evening, one eye always on the kitchen and the disposition of scraps.

A dog's life, to be sure, but not really a life destined for heroics—huddling beside a wounded hiker to keep him warm or leading smoke-blinded tenants from a conflagrated house. That was all right: heroics weren't part of the contract. I once read about a woman in England who applied for a seeing-eye dog but specified that she wanted one who'd flunked. She wasn't *very* blind, you see, and besides she wasn't very good at passing tests herself. So she wanted a sort of second-best companion to muck along with her, doing the best they could. My sentiments exactly. I wasn't planning on any heroics in my life either. Puck didn't have to save me and Roger, and we didn't have to save him.

Except he did, save us in the end. I don't see how he could have known about the insidious onset of AIDS, the dread and the fevers, the letting of blood by the bucketful for tests that told us nothing, and finally Roger's exile to UCLA Medical Center, sentence without parole. I suppose Puck must've picked up on my own panic and grief, suddenly so ignored that he probably counted himself lucky to get his supper. I had no expectations of him except that he stay out of the way. It was then that I began to let him out on his own late at night.

Nobody liked that. Several about-to-be-former friends thought it was terribly irresponsible of me, leaving the dog prey to the coked-up traffic that thundered up the hill when the clubs on the Strip closed. Not to mention those coyotes traveling in packs from trash barrel to trash barrel. They didn't understand how rigorously I'd admonish Puck that he not go far and come back straightaway, any more than they understood that they were just displacing the helplessness they felt over Roger's illness. One time Roger's brother had a near-foaming tantrum about the sofa in the living room, grimy and doubtless flea-infested from years of dog naps. "You can't expect people to visit," Sheldon sputtered. "It smells like a kennel in here."

No, it actually smelled like death, when you came right down to it. The whole house did. And frankly, the only one who could live with the stink, the battlefield stench of shallow unmarked graves, was Puck. Those who proposed re-upholstery as a general solution to keeping death away stopped in less and less, good riddance. The ones who thought we were letting the dog run wild were lucky I didn't sic him on them. Only I really understood, because I saw it happen, how Puck would temper his huge ebullience if Roger was feeling a little fragile. Always there to be petted, sometimes a paw on your knee to nudge you into it.

The world narrowed and narrowed, no end to the tunnel and thus no pin of light in the distance. Not to say there weren't precious months, then weeks, then days, that still had the feel of normalcy. I'd cook up a plate of spaghetti, and we'd sit in the dining room talking of nothing at all, just glad to have a lull in the shelling. And we both looked over one night and saw Puck sitting at attention on his haunches, the sable sheen of his coat set off by the flash of white at his heart, head lifted as if on show, utterly still. In all probability he was just waiting for leftovers. But Roger, bemused and quietly beaming with pride, studied the pose and finally said, "Puck, when did you get to be such a noble beast?"

We both laughed, because we knew we'd had nothing to do with it. But from that point on, Noble Beast became the changeling's nickname. If he took the pose beside you, it meant he wanted his chest scratched. Nothing dramatic, you understand, but somehow Puck came to represent the space left over from AIDS. With no notion of the mortal sting that shaped our human doggedness, he managed to keep the real world ambient, the normal one. Filling it edge to edge with what the thirteenth century divine, Duns Scotus, called "thisness." There gets to be almost nothing more to say about the daily choke of drugs to get down, the nurses streaming in to start the IV drips, the numbing reports to the scatter of family and those few friends who've squeaked through with you. Nothing more to say except what the dog brings in, even if it's mostly fleas.

That last morning, when the home nurse woke me at seven to say it was very bad, Roger virtually comatose, no time to wait for our noon appointment at UCLA, I leapt out of bed and got us out of there in a matter of minutes. I don't remember the dog underfoot. Only holding Roger upright as we staggered down the steps to the car, talking frantically to keep him conscious. Puck would've been perched on the top step watching us go, he'd done that often enough. But I don't really know what he *saw*, any more than I knew what Roger saw—what dim nimbus of light still lingered with one eye gone blind overnight six months before, the other saved by a thrice-daily blast of Acyclovir, but even it milked over with a cataract.

He died that night, and the weeks after are a cataract blur of their own. Somebody must've fed the dog, for I have the impression of him wandering among the houseful of family and friends, trying to find someone who'd lead him to Rog. When we brought home from the hospital the last pitiful overnight bag, the final effects as it were, and Roger's father shook out the maroon coat sweater and put it on for closeness' sake, Puck began to leap up and down, dancing about the old man in a circle, barking deliriously. Because he could still smell life in there.

Have we gotten sentimental yet—gone over the edge? I spent the first annihilating year of grief dragging myself out of bed because somebody had to let the dog out, writing so I wouldn't have to think. I can't count the times when I'd crawl under one of the tables where Puck lay sleeping, to hold him so I could cry. He grumbled at being invaded, but his growl was pretty *pro forma*. And somewhere in there I started to talk to him, asking him if he missed Rog, wondering out loud how we were ever going to get through this—daft as a Booth cartoon. He sat unblinking, the Noble Beast as listener.

I don't know when it started, his peculiar habit of barking whenever visitors would leave. He'd always barked eruptively in greeting, whenever he heard the footfall of a friend coming up the stairs outside. But this new bark was something far more urgent, angry, and troubled, a peal of warning, so that I'd have to drag him back by the collar as one bewildered friend or another made his drowned-out goodnights. "He doesn't like people to leave," I'd tell them, but I didn't understand for months what he was warning them of: that if they left they might not come back, might get lost the way Roger did. Don't leave, stay here, I'll keep you safe as I keep this man. Meaning me.

Still, he got over the grief sooner than I, testimony to his blessed unconsciousness of death. He became himself again, inexhaustible, excited anew by the dailiness of life. I'm afraid I'd aged much more than he, maybe twenty years for the twenty months of Roger's illness. Puck was just six, a warrior still in his prime. I had to do a fair bit of traveling there for a while, the self-appointed seropositive poster child. And Puck would lie waiting under my desk, caretaken by Dan the housesitter, ears perked at every sound outside in case it was me returning from the wars.

Like Argos, Odysseus' dog. Twenty years old and shunted aside because he was too frail to hunt anymore. Waiting ten years for his master's return from Troy, and the only one in the palace to recognize the king beneath the grizzle and the tattered raiment. The earliest wagging tail in literature, I believe. There was no shyness in that time of gods and heroes when it came to the sentiments of re-union, let alone what loyalty meant. So I would come home from ten days' book-touring, from what seemed a mix of overweening flattery and drive-time call-ins from rabid Baptists who painted me as the incarnation of Satan; I would return scarcely able to say who the real Monette was, indeed if there was one anymore—till Puck ran out to welcome me.

Around that time I began to feel ready to risk the heart again, I who hadn't really had a date in fifteen years. I "lingered hopefully" (to quote the advice that Stevie Smith's lion aunt read out to her niece from the lovelorn column); lingered hopefully, I say, at the edges of various parties, in smoke-filled *boîtes*, even at rallies and protests, looking to connect. Held back by my own sero status as much as anything, unsure if I wanted to find only another positive, or whether a lucky negative might rescue my brain from the constant pound of AIDS.

I was on a stationary bike at the gym, pumping hard and going nowhere (too sweaty to be lingering hopefully), when a young man or thirty or so came up and stood before me, catching my eye with a bright expectant nod. "Excuse me," he said, "but aren't you Edmund White?"

"Not exactly," I retorted. Yet it was such an eccentric pickup line that I let him pick me up with it. At least he was literate. I waxed quite eloquent about Ed's work, was quite modest about my own, and gave no further thought to the not-so-subtle omen that the young man might have no interest whatever in Monette, real or otherwise. After all, if you want to read *Moby-Dick, Jane Eyre* just won't do.

A few nights later he came over for Chinese takeout. And took an immediate dislike to Puck—nothing personal, he assured me, all dogs really—especially not wanting to sit on the dog-haired sofa in his ice-cream linen trousers. Puck re-turned the compliment in spades, grumping beneath the coffee table, growling when the young man came too close to me. I apologized for Puck's ragged man-ners, then deftly turned the subject to AIDS, my own reality check.

His green eyes lit on me. "There's no reason for anyone to die of that," he ob-served. "All you have to do is take care of yourself. People who die of it, that's just their excuse."

Too stunned or too Episcopalian to savage my first date since puberty, I left the growling to Puck. But I only barely restrained his collar when the young man left, wincing palely at the mastiff shrill of the dog's goodbye.

Stevie had it easier all around. He liked Puck's attitude from the first, recognizing a certain orneriness and perversity that neatly matched his own. If you wanted Puck to come over to you, it did no good to call unless you had a biscuit in hand. In fact I had been bribing him so long—a Meaty Bone to get him outside, another to bring him in—that he acted as if you must be crazy to order him around without reward. It had to be *his* idea to clamber up on the bed or play with a squeak toy. With the latter he wasn't into give-and-take in any case, but snatched it out of your hand and disappeared with it into his lair. Needless to say, "fetch" wasn't in his vocabulary.

I had to learn to back off and feint with Stevie, three months' uncertain courtship. He'd never really made the couple thing work before, and couldn't imagine starting now in the midst of a minefield. It required the barricades for us, going to Washington in October with ACT UP to take over the FDA. A sobbing afternoon spent lurching down the walkways of the quilt, a candle march along the reflecting pool with a hundred thousand others. Then massing at FDA headquarters in Maryland, not even dawn yet (and I don't do mornings), standing groggily with Vito Russo as we briefed the press. A standoff most of the day, squads of cops huddled as if at a doughnut stand, trying not to arrest us.

And then a small gang of six, all from L.A., found a lacuna in the security. Somebody smashed a ground-floor window, and the L.A. guerrillas poured in—Stevie bringing up the rear, impish as Peter Pan himself. When they dragged him out in handcuffs twenty minutes later, the look that passed between us was the purest sign I could've wanted of his being in love with life again. Civil disobedience as aphrodisiac. Within a day we were lovers for real, unarmed and no turning back.

But he wouldn't move in, not to my place. I thought it had to do with the freight of memory, too much Roger wherever you looked. Then I understood how determined he was not to turn the house on Kings Road into a sickroom again—a sickroom that only went one way, to the hospice stage and the last racked weeks. From his own falling numbers, and then the bone-chilling arrival of the first lesion on the roof of his mouth, he knew he'd be out of here sooner than I. (Unless of course I got hit by the bus that seronegatives were forever invoking to prove we were all a hairsbreadth away from the grave—a bus that was always as far behind schedule as we were ahead of it.)

So Stevie began the search for an apartment near me in West Hollywood. Even then we almost broke up a couple of times. He was too far sunk in the quicksand of the endless doctoring, too out of control to be loved. He savaged me one day, calling me blameless even as the arrows found the target of my heart, then fell into a three-day silence. To Victor, who served as go-between in the pained negotiation that followed, he declared: "Why am I breaking up with Paul? I don't know. I like his dog too much."

Oh, that. The fear of getting too attached to the things of life, till you sometimes feel you're better off lying in bed with the shades all down, no visitors welcome. And NO GIFTS, as the invitations all pointedly warn whenever we agree to a final birthday or one more Christmas. No more things to add to the pile that will only have to be dispersed, the yard sale more certain than heaven or hell.

Happily, Puck and I won out. Steve found a place just blocks away, a postmod apartment behind the Pacific Design Center. And twice a day I'd duck my head under the desk and propose to Puck: "You want to go over to Stevie's?" Then an explosion of barking and dancing, and a long whine of backseat driving as we headed downhill to Huntley Street. As soon as he saw the house, Puck would leap from the moving car to leave his mark on the bushes, then bark me into the downstairs garage as if I were some recalcitrant sheep.

Stevie was usually in bed, his IVs having doubled, with nothing better to do than flip the remote between one numb banality and the next. Television gave him a place to center his anger, I think, railing at the bad hair and the laugh tracks. A business where he had once commanded so much power—and now his big-screen set practically needed windshield wipers, there was so much spit aimed at it.

But his face would brighten like a kid's when Puck tore in and bounded onto the bed, burrowing in and groaning with pleasure as Stevie gave him a scratch. "Puck, you're better than people," he'd praise the beast—a real irony there, for the beast preferred people to dogs any day.

As for sentiment, Stevie carried that off with the effortless charm he once squandered on agents and actors and network VPs. We'd be driving to one of the neighborhood restaurants, pass a street dog rooting for garbage, and Steve would give an appraising look and wonder aloud: "You think he's a friend of Puck's?" No response required from me, as the answer was quickly forthcoming: "I think he is."

In fact, the question went international quite soon thereafter. With so much medicine required on a daily basis, bags of IV drugs to be kept chilled, the only way we could travel was by ship. So we cruised through the final year—Monte Carlo to Venice, Tahiti to Bora Bora, Greece and Turkey—spending the fat disability checks from Columbia.

One day ashore in the Iles des Saintes, a necklace of pirate lagoons below Guadeloupe, we motorbiked to the highest point, winding through denuded fields, for goats were the main livestock here. We sat on a wall of mortared conchs and looked out to sea. It was one of those moments you want to stop time, knowing what torments lie waiting at journey's end. From a shack behind us emerged a gaggle of children, and behind them a tiny black goat still wobbly on its kid legs. No way could it keep up with the children running downhill to the harbor. So the goat crossed the road to where we were, made for Stevie, and butted his knee, so gently it might have been a kiss. Then did it again.

"Friend of Puck's, definitely," Stevie observed with a laugh. A laugh fit for paradise, utterly careless, a holiday from dying.

So what do you carry with you once you have started to leave the world behind? Stevie was right that last Monday in the ICU: he was never going to see Puck again. Didn't even have a chance to say goodbye, except inside. For his part Puck made his own bewildered peace, still tearing into Huntley Street as we packed and gave away one man's universe of things, the beast still hoping against hope that Stevie himself would walk in any minute.

I understand that a housedog is yet another ridiculous privilege of having means in a world gone mad with suffering. I've seen the scrawny dogs that follow refugees around in war after pointless war. The dogs have disappeared from the starvation camps of Somalia, long since eaten in the dogless camps of Laos and Bangladesh. There is nothing to pet in the end. Perhaps it is worse than sentimental, the direst form of denial, to still be weeping at dog stories. But I admit it. Puck has gone gray in the face now, stiff in the legs when he stands, and I am drawn to stories about dogs who visit nursing homes and hospitals, unafraid of frailty and the nearness of death. Dogs, in a word, who don't flunk.

And I weep these incorrigible tears. Two years ago I was in a posh photo gallery in New York with a friend, and we asked to see the Wegmans. I maintained a rigorous connoisseur's posture, keeping it all high-toned, for there were those who were very suspicious of the popularity of Man Ray, the supreme model in Wegman's canine fantasias. There was a general wariness that Wegman's audience might be more interested in dogs than art. In my case doubly so, since to me at least Puck could have been Man Ray's twin. Same color, same shape, same humanness.

Now of course Man Ray was gone, and though he'd been replaced in the studio by the sleek and estimable Fay—no mean model herself—prices for a vintage Man had gone through the roof. Anyway, this curatorial assistant, very 57th Street, brought out of a drawer with white gloves three big Polaroids of Man. In one the dog was stretched on his back with his paws up; no gimmicks or costume accessories here, just a dog at rest. You could tell he was old from the shiver of gray on his snout. I found it so unbearably moving that I choked on tears and could not look at another.

After Stevie was buried, I figured Puck and I were set for twilight, seven years for every twelvemonth, a toss-up still as to who'd go first. We didn't plan on letting anyone else in. Not depressed or even defeated yet—just exhausted, hearts brimful already with seized days and a sort of Homeric loyalty, we shared a word-less language and had no expectations. Like the old man and his dog in DeSica's masterpiece *Umberto D,* who cannot save each other but can't leave either. They'd rather starve together.

Then I met Winston. It was a bare two months since Steve had died, and Victor and I had just returned from three weeks' melancholy touring in Europe, weeping in cathedrals so to speak. I recall telling Victor on the flight home that I could probably still connect with someone, but only if that someone could han-dle the steamship-load of AIDS baggage I carried with me. Somehow Winston could juggle it with his own, or perhaps the risk and intoxication of love made even the dead in our arms lighter. By Christmas we were lovers, and Puck couldn't help but give us his blessing, so showered was he by Winston with rub-ber bones and pull toys: "This dog has got nothing to play with!"

The dog was not the only one. And because there is never enough time any-more, by mid-January we were deep into the chess match of Winston's move into Kings Road. Just one small problem, really—a four-year-old boxer called Buddy. He'd grown up on a ranch, free to run and in titular charge of a barnful of horses and a tribe of cats. The first meeting of our two unfixed males wasn't promising. Buddy jumped on Puck right off, sending the two of them into a whirlwind ball of snarling and gnashing, leaving Winston and me no choice but to wade in and pull them apart. Buddy was clearly the aggressor here, but then we were on his territory.

The situation didn't improve when Buddy came to stay at Kings Road. Puck was outraged that his slumbering twilight had been invaded. He stuck to his lairs and growled with ferocious menace if Buddy came anywhere near. In fact, if we weren't absolutely vigilant we had a sudden dogfight on our hands. There was nothing for it but to separate them at opposite ends of the house, the doors all closed. It was like a French farce, with the constant flinging and slamming of doors, and enough entrances and exits to rival the court of the Louis.

You get used to compromises when everyone you know is dying. It was clear that Buddy was a pussycat at heart, his gentle spirit every bit as benign as Puck's lab side, except when they were together. And Buddy was meticulously trained as well, as rigorous as a Balanchine dancer, responding with infinite grace to all of his master's commands. Responding to food alone, Puck didn't know quite what to make of the military precision of his housemate.

Puck was fed on the front porch, Buddy in the back yard. It was no more peculiar in its way than families who can't stand one another, sitting silent at the dinner table, invisible lines drawn. If Winston and I hadn't been able to laugh about it, I'm not sure it could have gone on so long. But by April he had bitten the bullet and had Buddy fixed, though we were warned it could take six months for the pugnacity around Puck to abate. Puck's balls followed on the chopping block in June, since the vet assured me Puck would have fewer problems aging, less chance of tumors if he were fixed.

They didn't really seem any different that summer, except that Puck wouldn't hump our knees with the same rollicking passion. He humped all right, but it seemed more of an afterthought, a memory trace, over in a matter of seconds. I didn't have much leisure to notice, frankly, with my own numbers falling precipitously and three ribs broken from taking a dive off a trotting horse. The walls of AIDS were closing in, no matter how tortuous my progress through the drug underground, scoring the latest miracle. It was all I could do not to drown in my own panic, or take it out on Winston. My attitude toward the dogs was more impatient than ever, but Puck had been there before. There were times when dogs just had to be dogs—no neediness, please, and no misbehaving. The merest tick became a problem I couldn't handle.

By the end of summer I'd started to run daily fevers—99.5 at five P.M., like clockwork. My T-cells continued to tumble, under a hundred now. Winston had to fly up to Seattle over Labor Day weekend to visit his former lover, John, who'd taken a very bad turn. It was the first time I'd had the two dogs by myself. All I really wanted to do was sit at the word processor, only three or four pages to go in *Becoming a Man.* And it seemed I spent all day opening and closing doors, a solo performer in a farce.

Finally I'd had it. I called Buddy in from the bedroom, Puck from the fleabag sofa. I sat them down at opposite ends of the study, threatening them direly if they dared make a move toward each other. They both blinked at me as I lectured them: this separate-but-equal shit had got to stop. "Now lie down and be good boys," I commanded with a final flourish.

And they did. Puzzled, I am sure, by the heat of my remark.

There were still rough edges, of course. Now that they managed to be together without attacking, they began to steal toys from each other, swooping in and snatching, the growls just short of a major explosion. The problem was, Puck didn't know how to play—he was as loath to share as a bully in kindergarten or the spoiled brat who takes his baseball home so nobody else can enjoy it. The toys would pile up in his lair, guarded like meat. Buddy—such a prince—was the one who was eager to play in earnest, and yet he'd yield to Puck and forgo the tearing around the house he loved—turning the other cheek, so to speak, rather than bristling. It may have been the loss of balls that let it happen, but clearly Buddy preferred to have a friend than to be on top.

Gradually Puck learned to give a little back, permitting Buddy to do his racing about with a mauled stuffed Dumbo in his mouth, while Puck stood ground and barked. But if Buddy gets credit for teaching Puck the rudiments of play, the pedagogy went the other way when it came to making noise. When Buddy first arrived he didn't make a peep, never having been needed as a watchdog at the ranch. Thus he'd watch with a certain fascination as Puck, alert to every sound outside, especially the arrival of delivery men, ran to the front door bellowing doom. It took a fair amount of time for Buddy to get the hang of it—a softer bark in any case, here too letting Puck be the lead singer—but now they both leap up clamoring, barreling by one another as they scramble to investigate.

In fact it's Puck who's had to yield in the watchdog department. After all, Buddy's hearing is finer, his high-pointed ear like radar. Puck's has dimmed in his twelfth year, so he doesn't quite catch the slam of every car door. More often now Buddy's the one who pricks to the sound of something out there, the first to woof, so that Puck's scramble to join the fray is an act of following.

And Puck has been more than a little grateful to turn the rat chores over to Buddy. We have brown field rats, not so horrible as the gray vermin that haunt the docks and garbage dumps of the world. Sometimes one gets in because the kitchen door is open to the back yard, to give the dogs access. A couple of times Puck and I have surprised a rodent in the kitchen, and I shriek and Puck barks, and somehow the freaked-out rat scoots away.

But Buddy's a ratter. He sniffs them out and waits for them to make their move from under the stove or the washing machine. He'll wait for hours if necessary. And when the rodent makes a dash for the kitchen door, Buddy's on him—unafraid to clamp his jaws around the squirming intruder and give him a bad shake. He doesn't kill them, just scares the bejesus out of them. If I were a rat I would not be coming back soon. And since I can't stand to trap them anymore—that awful springing snap as the trip-arm breaks a leg or neck—I much prefer the Buddy method of pest control.

It would be too simple to call them brothers now, these two dogs, too anthropomorphic by half. Each has retained the marks and idiosyncracies of his breed quite distinctly. Buddy is what is called a "flashy fawn," because all four paws are white as well as his breastplate and a marvelous zigzag just behind his ears. He can't stand getting wet, doesn't even like to be in the garden after it's been watered, practically walking on tiptoe. While Puck no longer dives into the pool as he used to, swimming laps with Roger, water is still his element. On a very hot day he'll still step down in and dog-paddle in a tight circle to cool off.

Not brothers then, but comrades. Like any other dogs they sleep more than anything else, but sometimes now they do it flank to flank, almost curled about each other. When they sit on their haunches side by side in the kitchen doorway, lingering hopefully for biscuits, they are most definitely a pair. (Puck taught Buddy to beg, by the way, a serious breach in his training.) When they go outside together, Buddy knows he can go no further than the edge of the terrace, not down the steps. Puck on the other hand sprawls himself on the landing at the top of the stairs, one step down from the terrace, his lifelong perch for overseeing the neighborhood. Thus Buddy stands above Puck, though one would be hard put to say who's taking care of whom.

That they look after each other is clear. It's an act of faith among conservative zoologists that there's no homosex in the animal world. Gay is a human orientation, period. But just as I've come to understand, late in my own dog years, that being gay is a matter of identity much larger than carnality, I don't think the mating instinct is all the story. What the two dogs have is an easy sort of intimacy, the opposite of straight men. Thus they sniff each other's buttholes as casually as men shake hands. Not gay then, exactly, even though both have grown up surrounded by a tribe of us: call them different, that comes closest. As if being together has changed them so that they've become more than themselves—a continuum of eccentricities traded off and mimicked, grounded by their willingness to be tamed, loyal before all else. Not unlike Winston and me, and we're as gay as they come.

Meanwhile, twilight deepens. The dogs whoop with delight when Ande the nurse comes to call, once a week these days so I can get my IV dose of Amphotericin. They do not see her as a chill reminder of my sickness, any more than I do. We humans sustain this life as best we can, propelled by the positive brand of denial, the nearest approximation we can make to the bliss of dogs and their mortal ignorance. Thus I can watch Puck age and feel it tear at me, while he can't watch me dwindle or even see the lesions. Somehow it makes him wiser than I am, for all my overstuffed brains, book-riddled and smart to a fault.

We go along as we always have, a household of four instead of two. Every few weeks Puck and I cross Kings Road to visit Mrs. Knecht, our neighbor who lost her husband in '85 to a sudden heart attack. She endures in her eighties, a tribute to her Austrian stalwartness, her family wiped out in the camps. Assaulted by the indignities of age, Mrs. Knecht doesn't have a lot of pleasures anymore, but Puck is one. I'm terrified that he'll knock her down when he barrels into her house, that he'll take her hand off when she feeds him biscuits. But that is what she likes best about him, I think, his indomitable eagerness, his stallion force. Mrs. Knecht is our good deed, Puck's and mine, but also serving to remind all three of us that life goes on among the loyal.

Nights we stay up later than Buddy and Winston, a couple of hours at least. Buddy curls in his basket under the bedroom window, and Winston like Roger sleeps without pills, deeper than I ever get. I can't really say that Puck stays up with me as I potter around in the still of the night. He sleeps too, though always near me, and he would call it keeping me company if he had words. All he knows is, nothing is likely at this hour to bother us or require his vigilance. It will go on like this forever, as far as Puck can see. For his sake I try to see no further, relishing these hours out of time.

It has already been decided: if I go first Winston has promised to care for him, to keep what's left of the family together. If Puck goes first, perhaps a painless shot to end some arthritic misery, I promise nothing. The vets will tell you, there are suicides in the parking lot after the putting down of pets. For some it's the last straw.

But for tonight I'm glad we have endured together and, as they say in the romance genre, lived to love again. We will not be returning from Troy, either of us, but meanwhile we are one another's link to the best of the past, a matter of trust and bondedness that goes all the way back to prehistory. One of us is descended from wolves; one of us knows he's dying. Together we somehow have the strength to bear it, tonight at least, when the moon is down and no creature howls. What we dream is exactly the same, of course, that nothing will change.

At two A.M. he whimpers at the door to go out, and I let him go. Usually he's back in half an hour, but you never know what will take him further, what trail will beckon him up through the chaparral. He knows me too well. That I'll wait up all night if necessary till he comes panting home. That even if I rail at him like a crabby parent, he'll still get a biscuit before the lights go out. Because all that matters to either of us is that the other one's still here—fellow survivors of so much breakage to the heart, not a clue when the final siren will sound. But guarding the world for dear life anyway, even as it goes. Noble beast.

C hristopher Tilghman graduated from Yale in 1968. He was a French major but most remembers the semester spent harmonizing Bach chorales in a music theory course. "This is a technical business with more obscure rules than mahjong; at a glance, it would seem that once given a soprano line, the composer has very few options. Each week I would start full of ambition for Art, but by the middle of the week the rules began to take over, and by the end what I produced was technically okay but sounded awful. When all the students had presented their solutions, we would turn to Bach and see what he did. Week after week, we were left with our mouths hanging open. So glorious; so unexpected. Where the rules stymied us, they seemed to lead him to greater heights; where the strictures of the form confined us, they seemed to compress Bach's genius into a transcendent essence. For thirty years I have been trying to figure out what this means to me." Part of his answer can be found in the emotional connections and disconnections he traces in the lives his fiction illuminates. *In a Father's Place,* a collection of stories, appeared in 1990. His novel *Mason's Retreat* was published in 1996, and another collection of stories, *The Way People Run,* in 1999.

THINGS LEFT UNDONE

On the morning his son was born, Denny McCready walked out to the banks of the Chesapeake to see the dawn. As a farmer does on his endless spirals, lost in meditation to the tractor's unwavering drone, he had been picturing and re-picturing this moment for some months as his own special celebration, a complete joy making its own music in the background. Just as he had imagined, the first yellow light dappling the water was full of promise; he could breathe in the textured Bay air and smell the sharp fragrance of the honeysuckle growing along the fence lines behind him. But his heart was not suddenly filled with the majesty of it all. He looked down at his stained hands, resting without task at his side, and they reminded him of season after season, drought followed by too much rain, sickness and health. He took one last glance across the water to Hail Point, a fragile stand of loblolly pines slowly being undermined by the tides and storms, and then he turned, feeling almost as if his love had been found insufficient even as his son was still wet from his first reach lifeward.

Denny began to feel better when he settled in on the telephone, working through the list of friends and family that Susan had prepared weeks ago. On his way through the farmyard he had stopped by the milking parlor, found his father and the hired man, and received a round of congratulations, pats on the back. The baby was named Charles after Denny's father. The sun-creased scowl on the old man's face relaxed for a time into a smoother reflection of satisfaction: it was right for a man to have children, and grandchildren, just as it was right for a farmer to have a dog. The moment was over fairly quickly—it was time to move the milkers to the cows on the other aisle—but as Denny left the others to their labors, he looked back with the sensation that these familiar routines were no longer his, that his life had now slipped slightly out of his control.

A few hours later, showered and shaved, he was back at the hospital. Susan's eyes showed black rings of fatigue, but she had demanded the baby and he lay at her side.

"I don't know how you could sleep at a time like this," she said, assuming that he had. Denny's big round face seemed to eclipse the sun at her window; she could smell the farm on his clothes, a pungent sweetness in contrast to all these metallic fumes. It seemed odd, and wonderful to her, that the future of this rough and self-reliant man would now be softened by a child.

He did not want to tell her about visiting the rivershore. "Why did I have to call Jack Hammond?" he asked. "He seemed surprised and not happy to be woke up."

"He's your uncle," she said.

"My uncle? I haven't seen him since before we graduated. I had to tell him my last name."

"S-h-h." She looked down at the small bundle, a pointy old man's face rimmed with a red rash, shrouded in a light blue blanket. His eyes were now closed, and when the nurse came in and took him to be checked over by the pediatrician he was so firmly bound in his blanket that he looked stiff, like a mummy.

"Why are you being so ornery?" Susan asked when they were alone.

He wondered why, and he looked around this hospital room, pleasant by any standard he could think of, a whiteness that spoke of hope and a busy hum that sounded like rest. He looked at Susan, drifting off in this borrowed bed; she seemed as haggard and puffy as his mother had when she was dying of cancer, perhaps even in this very same room, nearly ten years earlier. He had the sudden feeling that for families as well as hospital rooms, birth and death were really the same thing.

He banished these thoughts, wondering what was next and why it was taking so long, and then the door opened, and a trio of doctors walked in. One of them had a sort of pleased look on his face, as if he had just been proven right. When Susan was again alert, the doctors told them that the boy had cystic fibrosis, that his insides and lungs were already plugged, that he might not survive the week, and if he did he would probably not live long enough to enter kindergarten. The doctors—even the smug one—said it kindly, over the period of an hour or so, but that is what they said.

For the first months of his son's life, Denny could barely bring himself to touch him. He heard air passing through those small lips and pictured his lungs as blackened ruins dripping with tar. He watched Susan happily nursing the boy, passing her hand over the smooth contours of his silky head, luxuriating with the weight in her arms. It surprised him that she seemed, at these moments, so satisfied with her baby, despite all that awaited them. On late afternoons, when Denny came home from the fields, he usually found Susan and the baby in the kitchen. Sometimes, even before he entered the house, he could hear the deep jarring, thud, thud, thud of Susan's firm hands on the baby's back, the prescribed regimen for loosening what Denny thought of as the crusts and plugs of tar. The boy never seemed to mind this; Susan had learned how to drive the blow through the small body, and not to let it hit with a slap on his skin. But even so, Susan always ended the procedure by rubbing and massaging him, which made him giggle and coo. In time it became part of a sensuality between them, a kind of game, starting her hand down for one more blow, stopping just short and then folding into a caress, her broad palms covering his entire back. When Charlie had begun to talk, he said to his mother, "Smooth me," and Denny watched, almost embarrassed, as she passed her flesh—the inside of her forearms, her cheeks—over his body.

Back when Charlie was still a newborn, when the first untroubled and unknowing smiles began to appear, Denny prayed that this could all happen quickly, before he gave too much of his love, before he surrendered too much of his hope. It took almost to the end of Charlie's life for Denny to realize that this prayer was monstrous, that he had asked for an end of his own pain in the place of a cure for his son. Susan would make him pay for this. But by then Denny had also learned that of all the pain a human can endure, not allowing oneself to feel love is the worst; that denying love to oneself can destroy, from the inside.

In the hospital, during what they had all finally decided would be his last hours or days, Denny sat beside Charlie while Susan went home to eat and perhaps to cry in the solitude of the shower. Charlie was awake, naked except for a diaper, an oxygen tube, and an IV. He was breathing somewhat easily and his eyes were at rest on his father. Denny reached over to take his hand, and then began to stroke his small chest, running his fingertips around the cushioned indent of his nipples. Charlie smiled and closed his eyes halfway. "Smooth me, Daddy," he said.

"You okay?" he asked. "Can you breathe good?"

"Smooth me, please."

Denny dropped his hand down to the flat, starved stomach, to the navel that had opened too wide for the poisons that had been concocted from his parents' mingled blood. Charlie held still for those hands, rough and work-stained as they were, as Denny traced the lines of his body. "This is what it feels like here," Denny thought, rubbing the shoulder. "This is a tickle. This is a pat." He even lightly twisted a finger until the eyes reflected irritation and discomfort. He followed the sinews of each leg and then reached the top at the elasticized leg holes of the diapers.

"Smooth me, Daddy," said Charlie, and then Denny realized what the boy was asking him to do, or was it that Denny realized that there was one gift left to bestow? What does it feel like there? What will I miss? Denny could do this for a son, not for a daughter. As the boy, in dreamy rest now, lay still on his sheet, Denny parted the tapes of the diaper and put his hand back on his stomach. He traced down to the penis, to the tiny purplish tip, to the vacant scrotum. Denny looked up to Charlie, and the eyes were full of surprise and joy. Denny knew there would be no shame between them, even as the penis became erect, a slight nub of a thing. Denny imagined what he himself liked, how he liked to be touched, and he tried to do it, running his thumb up and down the bottom and closing the tip into his palm. He kept at it, lightly, not even wondering for a second what a doctor or nurse would think, and Charlie finally seemed to fall asleep, a rest full of gratitude, a relief from struggle, a life, as far as it went, full of joy.

In high school, Susan DeLorey's large frame, her big hands and feet, had made her seem heavy. No one would have called her cute, or ever did. "Solid," they said, referring both to her body and to her character. Perhaps marrying Denny, who spent most of his time in those days in bitter combat with his father, was one of the less practical things she had done. But Denny had settled down enough, taken an uneasy but consistent place as a partner in the family dairy, and he had begun to seem acceptable to the town ladies in comparison with the valedictorians and Boy Scouts who had long ago up and left their families with no warning. And since high school, the cute girls, the short and skinny blondes, the pert and sassy ones, had busted out of their blue jeans and peroxide, while Susan's age caught up to her strong-boned features, straight posture, and thick brown hair.

Susan worked as the electric meter reader for all "non-metropolitan" areas of the county. It took her half time, on her own time, and if someone invited her in for a cup of coffee and a doughnut, it was her decision to make. They gave her a car, with a whip antenna for its citizens-band radio, which flexed coyly as she drove from farm to farm. She had inherited this deal from her father, and it came with her to the marriage like a dowry. When Denny was courting her, after they had both spent their twenties dating others, she sometimes worried that it was the job he had fallen in love with.

After Charlie was born she contemplated giving the job up, and Denny had persuaded her not to. He said that she needed more than ever to get out of the house, and that she could bring the baby along, just as they had always planned. When Charlie died she was behind by two or three months on her accounts, and two weeks after the funeral she began to work overtime. For the most part, the customers, at least the ones that tended to be home during the day, were friends and admirers of hers. She came back from those first few days of meter reading in a car loaded with hams, and sticky buns, and roasted chickens, and pickled green tomatoes.

One evening, exhausted from a two-hundred-mile day, she was leaning across to gather some of these consoling gestures when she realized that her mind had slipped back in time for a moment, and that she thought she was reaching for Charlie in his car seat. She blinked past the illusion and saw that it was a casserole in her arms, and the hideous image of this food, and the shock of reliving the entire loss in a split second, gripped her in panic and she began to scream.

Denny heard her and came running out, opening the car door to receive her kicks and punches; he staggered off dazed from a good blow to his right eye, and she came after him, trying to hurt him. The hired hand saw her standing over Denny, kicking at him, and sprinted over the width of the farmyard. They called for Dr. Taylor, and he knocked her out with a full syringe of Nembutal.

Denny was off duty for the morning milking, and he was sitting at her bedside when she woke up. Their bed was a four-poster that had been her grandmother's, and Susan had made muslin curtains with ruffles to match the canopy. She had loved to sew before Charlie was born, lacy things, feminine touches of lace here and there throughout the house, as if to mark off a boundary for the odors and substances of farm life. Denny hadn't complained, but to this day, especially to this day, he felt as if he slept in her private space. "How do you feel?" he asked.

"My head aches."

"So does mine," he said, rubbing his eye.

"I'm sorry, Denny." She cried rarely, and almost always for others, but this time, her face gripped by her large hands, her elbows clamped against her breasts, Denny could tell that she wept for herself.

"It's all over now. We can look ahead." He meant for these words to soothe, and he repeated them a few times. He didn't feel he needed to argue the point and therefore did not put a lot of emphasis behind them.

She snapped up from her clenched recline and opened her full face to him. "It's that simple for you? You think now that Charlie's gone I'll just let you back?"

Denny knew what she meant, and he knew it wasn't fair, not entirely. She had all too easily let him free of the pain. She had gathered everything that hurt into herself, every one of Charlie's laughs and mangled words. That's mine, she seemed to say; I'm going to save that one for later. She had gone to each doctor's appointment loaded with questions, and night after night she studied the packets of information from parents' organizations and disease foundations. Denny could only scan these materials, squinting to screen the truths into a blur, looking for mention of a miracle cure. It seemed to Denny that everything in her mind had been backwards. Right up to the day Charlie died, she had been helping him learn his numbers and letters, and from the vantage point of an alphabet that would remain half unlearned forever, she seemed capable of staring into the deep almost cheerfully. Denny used to hear her teaching Charlie lessons for use later in life, and he had to cover his ears with his hands. Denny knew what Susan was saying, but it wasn't as simple as she made it sound.

"Are you God now, Susan?"

"No. There's no word for what I am. I'm a mother who lost her child."

Denny almost argued that he was a father who had lost his, but he didn't think the loss was comparable, at least, not in their house. He had often wondered what kind of father he would have been if Charlie had been healthy, and whether he would have behaved all that differently. Who knew? But this he could say to the mother who had lost her child: that he was a man who lost the person who would have become his best friend.

"I'm trying," he said finally, "to make you feel better. I want you to feel better." He spoke gingerly, not assuming too much, as if he was sharing her feelings out of kindness.

She heard these tones, and came bounding back. "Why didn't you love him? That was all he asked, to be loved by his mother and father."

Denny thought back to the last months of Charlie's life, and the last night at the hospital. How could she ask that? What could she be thinking of? He had no answer. He looked back at her blankly, and then said, "I'm trying to keep you from losing everything else."

She softened at this, even put out her hand to his. "Maybe you are. But there isn't anything you can do now." She got up, still in the T-shirt and underpants that Denny had left on her the night before. He looked at the curve of her hips, and he wanted suddenly to make love, to fall back into bed again like newlyweds. He could honestly picture this as something that might make things better, because it had been some years since they had really made love. For many months after Charlie was born they had not even tried, and then occasionally they had joined, and they did not have to remind each other that there was fate in their mingled fluids, they did not need to admit to each other that when Denny was done and had withdrawn, the cold drops of his poisonous semen burned on the sheet between them. They did not need to confess that any time their flesh touched—a simple caress, a brush of the hands—their thoughts bored deep through the skin and into the code of damaged chromosomes.

Denny believed, as he watched his long-legged wife walk across the bedroom, that they could leave this behind now. He was ready, at this moment, with the sharp tremble of desire. But she closed the door of the bathroom behind her, and then turned on the shower, and when she came back out to the kitchen, she was dressed in her jeans and was holding her account book, her No. 2½ pencils, a flashlight, a can of Halt, and her thermos. "I might be late this afternoon," she said. "I've got to go all the way to Grangerfield."

Charlie died in May, and the long, buttery Chesapeake summer moved through plantings, through the flowering of the soybean plants toward the tasseling of the corn. Denny threw himself into this work, this nurturing, but he stopped the tractor now and again on the rivershore and thought back to that unlucky morning, back to a moment, now jumbled in his memory, when he had hoped that just beginning a life was enough to give it meaning. He made his turns on the tractor, and many times as he approached the riverbank he imagined what would happen if he simply kept going, down over the crumbling yellow clay and onto the pebbled beach, and then into the warm brackish ripples and out onto the sandbars, a mile or two into the Chester River before the water reached higher than his axles.

Susan was often away from the farm these days, even into the early evening, still catching up on her accounts, maybe, or hanging around with old high school friends to whom she'd never before paid the least attention. They all had babies, even big kids now, and after the difficulty of getting pregnant in the first place, and then Charlie, Denny could hardly imagine Susan wanting to spend time in someone else's happy chaos. But he had nothing better to offer, the gray silence of the house, the farm. As Susan said earlier in the summer, the real crop on this family farm was death. She said they weren't living there anymore as much as waiting to see who went next: the logical one—Denny's father; the unnecessary one—Susan; or the unexpected one—Denny himself. None of them had gained anything other than front-pew seats at the funerals. She said that Denny could not offer life to her, or she to him, the promise of it, and he knew well enough what she meant.

Evening after evening, after milking, Denny walked the length of the farmyard in the knowledge that the three men on the place, himself, his father, and the latest teenage hand, were all heading home to empty houses.

"It appears that your wife ain't spending too much time at home these days," said Denny's father on one of those evenings in August. They were standing in the roadway between their two houses, and the heat in the milking parlor had drained them both. He wasn't being hostile calling her "your wife"; he was of an older school.

"Her private affairs are her business," Denny argued.

The old man agreed. "I'm not anyone to pry. But things have to be managed, don't they?" This was an old point, his refrain from the years when Denny fought against him and against the endless repetitive details of the farm life.

"You don't manage a marriage like fences and Johnson grass, Dad. There's nothing I can do."

The old man gave him the same disappointed look that he had worn during those arguments in his teenage years, and Denny simply stared back, as he had done years ago. "There is always something," said his father, his eyes filling.

Denny nodded once more, and took those words home with him, across the broad lawn, and waited up for Susan to come back. It was seven-thirty when she pulled in. She was wearing her pale green shirt, with a new satiny scarf tied over the tops of her shoulders. She was carrying a sack of groceries, and she started to put them away, a bag of flour, a few cans of corned beef hash, frozen vegetables, without greeting him. He wondered if she thought of him anymore as she walked up and down the aisles of the Acme, what he liked; he could not imagine her putting much attention on shared meals, just on food, just on the common need to eat something.

"Sue," he said.

"Huh?"

"I'm not stupid. I'm trying to help." She seemed not to pick up on his invitation to confess. He added, "You can trust me."

She glanced over; the light was beginning to fade and neither of them had turned on a lamp. "I never said you were stupid."

"So where are we at?"

"I think we're just floating, as long as you ask what I think. I think I'm just waiting. I don't think anything that has happened all summer is real."

"I'm dairying," he stated. "That's real."

"Denny, as long as you ask—"

"I am," he interrupted, "I am asking."

"Well, I'm seeing someone. I'm seeing someone who makes me feel better."

The truth hit his gut; he could not deny that. But he could also not deny that he and Mandy Towle, in the occasional circling and looping through lives in small towns, had fallen together a few times over the years. "Why?" he asked.

She shrugged.

"Don't think I don't know why you are doing this. Another man."

Her eyes darted, but she only shook her head and told him that he could not possibly know what she was thinking.

"You're going to leave me behind, is that it?"

"Stop."

"Throw me off like a Kleenex?"

She did not respond to this right away, but continued to lean against the kitchen counter as she considered things, and she began slowly to get more and more angry, and Denny could not divine if it was because he had located her private truth, but at last she wheeled around for something to throw at him and came up with a canister of flour, which would have been almost funny, an explosion of white mist. Denny waited, readying himself to avoid the sharp edges of the tin, but after a few moments she put it down. "You asshole," she said, and went into her bedroom.

Denny slept, as he had been doing for a month or two, in the spare room. In the morning he leaned into her room and said, "I'm sorry. You can do what you like. That's all I wanted to say." But she was already gone.

Denny had a gift for machines. Before he was out of his teens, other farmers, even mechanics in town, began to seek him out to perform magic with a welder and metal lathe. He could do this, engineering answers not on paper but with his hands. The shop, from which these bits of genius came, was at the end of the barn complex closest to his house. It had been the granary, and the walls were still lined with rodent-proof tin. There was a single low window that looked down toward the creek, and in the afternoon, when the light came sideways, orange off the water, the grease-shined floor and tin walls glowed, a radiance that started at the feet and worked upwards as the sun fell. Early in Denny's marriage, his friends used to gather in the shop on winter Saturdays, drinking beer around someone's project, and the women gathered with Susan, cooking and drinking wine and Irish Mist, and after everyone staggered home and after he and Susan had made love a little on the dirty side, Denny lay back in the four-poster and thought the future was offering itself to him not in years, which no one could predict, but in seasons, certain and always new.

The winter Susan was living in town—she had moved in with her friend Beth, on Raymond Street, but spent most of her time in Chestertown—Denny closed himself into his shop. The maw of the vise stayed open, and the roller chest of Snap-On tools remained untouched. Often, at the end of milking, he went straight there, sat down in his cold Morris chair, and stared out the low window across the lawn and to the creek, to the black winter water lapping at a brittle rim of tidal ice. Occasionally, when the weather wasn't too cold, Denny slept the night in that chair, and then, painfully stiff and foul breathed, he stole over to the house for breakfast, eating quietly as if she were asleep behind the thin partition of the kitchen. Early in the fall he went into town a few times to see Mandy Towle. They'd always liked each other, and she deserved a lot better than two failed marriages, one of them to a man from Ken County who was now in jail for house-renovation schemes that preyed on the elderly. She deserved a lot better than Denny, in these circumstances, which they both understood. She sent him home the last time, back to his shop, with a sisterly hug.

His father often stopped in to check on him, and occasionally sat down to talk. They stayed on dairying, for the most part, which wasn't a subject that held a lot more cheer than the remains of Denny's family life. Just sell the goddamn place, Denny said once; sell out and move to Florida. You deserve it. When his father hid his eyes, Denny knew the old man still hoped for the best.

"Do you think she's going to come back?" Denny asked. He knew that Susan had called his father once or twice.

"I expect what she's going through has a shape of its own."

Denny and Susan talked when they ran into each other in the street, and people could look out the windows of Todman's Insurance, or Latshaw's Jewelers, or Price and Gammon Hardware, and see them meeting like old sweethearts. The town was full of these almost-forgotten couplings, kids who had maybe once or twice fucked each other in his father's haywagon, or all winter long in her father's Buick, and what remained was a county full of people who treated each other like siblings, with the accidental intimacy of brothers and sisters who had shared the same bathroom. That's how it felt to Denny, meeting Susan on the street, and she seemed to want it that way, as if by wiping out their marriage she could eliminate her pain. Time, after all, had run out on them, had perhaps been running out on them for years: quality time, as the doctor said, had given way to the dry consolations of memory. "Until death do us part" would perhaps, despite love, turn out to be not long enough.

Denny brought these thoughts back into his workshop, these repetitious looping stabs at reason, all these variations on history. He tried to make sense of it, but he was finally bored by this hibernation, and as if in prayer, his thoughts had begun to wander. He could not say exactly from where or why the idea had come to him, but as the first stirrings of warmer weather came on the March winds, he realized that he had begun to concentrate more and more on the water, on the highways it offered, down the Bay perhaps, and out to sea. His father hated the water; most farmers did. All it did was steal away land, a furrow or two between planting and harvesting in stormy summers. Kids went out on the water to drink beer. Watermen went out there to do God knew what. The Bay, that long question mark out there beyond Kent Island: Denny's father had raised him to believe the Bay was not only wet and dangerous but immoral, a slippery surface choppy with wasted money.

But the water called to Denny. It seemed to offer refreshment for his soul; it was as if he had recognized that he had been looking at only the land side of his life all these years, and had been missing what was perhaps the fuller half. He spent hours imagining boats, revarnishing and repainting the woodwork, over-hauling the engine in the cooked odors of a clean bilge. He could not imagine why, up to now, he had never been curious about them. They seemed self-contained and sufficient, at once economical in space and extravagant with amenity.

In late spring Denny got in touch with the watermen at the Centreville landing, for whom he had repaired and built all sorts of labor-saving devices, and told them he wanted a workboat. The watermen were willing to help him, an intruder on the water, as long as he didn't tell anyone; when they found a good boat in Crisfield, they brought it up for him at night.

The following day, after knock-off, he drove it into the creek and dropped anchor at the farm. His father, as Denny had expected, was standing on the creek bank ten minutes later.

"What in hell is this?" the old man yelled.

Denny paddled over in a dingy that had been thrown into the deal, and stood beside his father to admire the view. It looked like a destroyer, a dropping curve that started high and fixed at the bowsprit and then seemed to go on forever, like a view. "It's a boat," said Denny finally.

The old man was speechless; all the slack he'd given to Denny this winter, and this was what came of it, a boat? Like some goddamn rich Philadelphian? "Just tell me what in hell you mean to do with it."

"I don't know, Dad," said Denny. It was the truth. One thing Denny had learned during his winter months was to tell the truth. "Maybe I'll do some crab-bing. Maybe you and me will go out and have picnics," he shouted as his father retreated back up the lawn to his house. "Maybe you and me will take it through the Narrows and down the Bay. Maybe we'll just keep going south."

For the next six or seven Sundays, through May and into the first heat of June, Denny threw himself into his project. He had never had much regard for water-men as mechanics: they tended to make repairs under way with vise-grips, and then forget about them when they returned to port. Denny was delighted to have so much to do. His father continued to grumble for a week or two, but relented in the end to the point of putting an aluminum lawn chair under the shade of the lone mulberry tree and passing his Sundays on the bank. Occasionally they chatted with each other across the few feet of water.

One day in June, Denny had his head deep into dark thwarts of the hull, but heard the scrape of the lawn chair over the shells and pebbles of the bank. He assumed it was his father and did not come up for air for twenty minutes, and when he did finally it was Susan he saw. She was wearing a yellow shirt, which made her dark hair shine. Denny could not believe how lovely she looked, a wife on the shore awaiting a sailor returning from a long cruise. He poled his flat-bottomed dingy to her.

"I see you've got yourself a project." She was humoring him, as if the boat was childish, like electric trains.

"It feels good to be fixing something, for a change." He came down hard on the last word.

She looked over at him, and betrayed no emotions. She was wearing white pants and earrings, and Denny could smell the slight shade of her perfume.

"So who you dressing up for today?" he said.

She gave him no answer, no anger, no hurt. "Denny, a lot has happened to us, hasn't it?"

He shrugged, but it was clear to him that she had said this in preparation for something. Asking for a divorce, most likely. Get the unpleasantness over with, then drive back out to Route 50 and meet up with her accountant from Chestertown, or whatever he was, the person she dressed up for.

She continued. "None of it made much sense, did it? I mean, why did Charlie have to die?"

"Charlie's dying is the only thing that made any sense at all," Denny snapped back. "He had cystic fibrosis. Remember? What happened to him started happening from the moment he was conceived. It's a disease that began millions of years ago, some cell or something that crawled out of the water ass-backwards. Who the hell knows where it come from?" Denny realized he was shouting. "Charlie made sense, Sue. It's what happened to us in the meantime that doesn't make sense."

She raised her hands, almost as helplessly as if shielding herself from a pistol shot. "Okay. Okay," she yelled. "What happened to us. You want to whip my ass, Denny. Do it."

They looked at each other for a few minutes, across the oily shine of the boat's pistons, laid out on a rag.

"What I mean is," she began again, "that we've lived through some times I never expected, and we've done things I never imagined doing."

He shrugged, but she was right enough about that, right enough to say that everything she had done or thought since Charlie was born was contrary to logic, especially treating him as if he were to blame for it.

"I want to come home," she said. "I haven't seen any one since Christmas," she added.

"Why?"

"Because it doesn't make me feel better. I still want to die," she said. Her radiance, from a distance, had been an illusion. She looked very bad, haggard and worn out from within. Denny wondered if she had been looking this miserable all winter and whether he was just now noticing because he had turned the corner. But he did not want to feel sorry for her yet. He got up, grabbed a handful of oyster shells, and flung them in a spray far across the water. A heron, feeding in the green shade of the other side of the creek, took this as a sign that it ought to move on, and it leaned forward, chest almost on the water, and then kicked its long legs into the flapping of its wings. It skimmed slow, unlikely, doomed, until it busted out into the sunlight and headed out to the rivershore.

"Jesus," said Denny finally. "You've slapped me from one side of this county to the other; I'm so bruised by you that my piss is purple. There's some mercy in this somewhere, isn't there?"

She looked at him and nodded, and it was a look he had not seen in a long time. She could not have been offering herself as mercy, but as faith. Her eyes suggested, her head tipped toward the house, but still, he could ignore these gestures and they could vanish as if they had been nothing. Denny did not know how to tell her yes; instead, he nodded back at her, and if she expected the beginning of a caress on the way across the lawn, she did not show it. As they entered the bedroom, Denny was telling himself, as he had not done in many years, that he would soon make love to this woman in front of him.

She undressed with her back to him and turned to face him. He had forgotten the strength of her body, how broad and powerful she looked across her upper chest, how quick and nimble she looked at the tuck of her waist, how sufficient and frank she looked from the stretched points of her hipbones to the inside of her thighs. Denny had also undressed, and she gave him a little smile as they stood and looked at each other across the room. Her eyes dropped to his penis, and his to the patch of her pubic hair, and he pictured the outstretched arms of her tubes, the encyclopedia drawings with each ovary clutched at the curled extreme, and he pictured a line of eggs like pearls, some perfect, some flawed, ready to drop one by one into potential life, and then beyond. He pictured the grip of her uterus. She was looking at his penis, and he knew she also was tracing backwards to unanswered questions of that genetic disease, following on the long, circuitous route to his balls, where there were sperm cells by the billions, enough to conceive an epidemic.

They stood facing each other, naked as if new, and they understood that they needed far more than pleasure to make him erect and to open her to him. And with that understanding, pleasure did come to him, and she smiled again, this time more slyly, as he stiffened.

"Hello, Denny," she said, a joke from long ago.

He said nothing—this was as always—as they finally joined on the bed. He traced her lines, and searched for wetness and warmth, and very soon she was sliding one leg under him, and he did not ask what she knew about this minute in her month, and did not ask whether she had, in anticipation of this moment, driven over with her diaphragm in place, and did not ask whether she might want him to hunt through the bedstand for a condom. He allowed himself to be guided in. They rested for a moment, centered and tied in this way. He began to move, and long before he thought he was ready for an orgasm he was ejaculating inside her, and he pictured it not as a burst but as a showering, a mist like soft rain. Susan felt him come, and she too imagined what was happening inside her body, and it was a tumbling she thought of first, like the tumbling of an egg on its passage outward, and then—though she had not expected it—pleasure came to her also, and she pictured a wall, a brick wall slowly giving way to his continued motion and to the rhythmic encouragement of her own flesh.

Two months later, on a Sunday, Susan sat on the porch and looked across the barnyard to the water. She could see out the creek, across the wide mouth of the river to Eastern Neck, and then, on clear days such as this one, across the dark line of the Bay and toward the smudged air of Baltimore. She knew Denny would be out there somewhere on his boat, but when she glanced up, she could not see him. She had a cup of coffee resting precariously on her thigh, and was reading the *Sun* in the streams of September light; she was warmed by the sensations and was happy to read the movie reviews, though she went to the show only rarely, with her friends Beth and Delia from town, and when she did, the other two spent the whole time making silly cracks about how beautiful were the male actors and how skinny the women.

When Susan thought about love and men these days, and about the past year, and about her son, her thoughts came ordered like a liturgy. It was necessary, in terms of fairness, for her to start always with her own general confession, with a listing of the things she had done. She did not think having an affair with Jack Marston was a particularly kind or clever thing to do. But Susan, as she considered these things, also had to go forward and admit that she had at least taken up once again a hope for the future because of it. Once she had confessed, she could proceed to a thanksgiving, to say that she was grateful that Denny had given her what he could, freedom, if not understanding; and then, because Susan did not blink at herself or at Denny or at the eternal pain losing a child had caused her, she gave thanks that Jack Marston had been there, because, in retrospect, without him she might have done something even less clever, killed herself, maybe. And finally, in her supplications, she could pray for the people in her life, for Denny's health and happiness, her mother and his father, for her sisters and their children. But not for herself, yet. She did not know what she wanted next; she did not know whether this move back, which she had done a few weeks after they made love, would work. She was waiting patiently for a sign. All she knew was that she feared nothing: she would never again be afraid, just a little hesitant, just a little reluctant to invite notice or comment.

She glanced down the length of the barns, silver in the morning light, and watched her father-in-law wash his car. He did this every Sunday morning in his milking clothes, before changing and then sleeping in front of the television. He had, last winter, called her a "loose woman." She had not argued with him; if she had, she would have told him that ever since Charlie had been born it seemed everyone on the place simply wanted her gone, and that she had done precisely that. She might have tried to explain to him that she had taken with her all those bits of Charlie's life that needed a resting place somewhere far from the farm. But during her marriage, she'd never argued with Denny's father, and he had a dim talent for her ways of thinking. Susan had always thought of her father-in-law as a man-child, and a girl-child at that, with a front tooth missing from her occasional frightened smile, a sort of waif trapped in an old man's rough and blemished body.

When Susan came back out onto the porch from filling her coffee cup, she saw that the old man had finished with his car, had walked down the long lawn to the water, and was staring out into the river. With his jug ears, his hearing had always been remarkable; he could sit in the barnyard and tell, from nothing audible to her, that the baler had broken down on the point field or that the hired hand was now in fourth gear on the Kubota and was heading for home. Perhaps he had heard Denny's boat coming in. It was a restful sight, the man under the waterside mulberry tree.

He turned slightly as she approached and then looked back out to the river.

"Is he coming in?" she asked.

"Sounded like it."

She took up her place beside him. The water was dappled gold; the slight onshore breeze was clean, clean but rich, like the air that came with the fresh-shucked oysters she used to buy for frying. She could smell the fresh milk warming on his clothes. "Do you see him?"

He waved his hand outward. There were several boats in view, indistinguishable to her except, perhaps, for the sailboats way over by the Narrows.

"What's he up to, with this boat?" the old man asked. He began by spitting out the words, but ended with a genuine question.

She stopped halfway around. "He likes being out on the water. He thinks it will save him."

The old man protested, this time with the beginning of a sarcastic snarl. "Save him from what? Seems to me what will save us—"

She put her hand out onto his shoulder and he stopped abruptly. They both looked at her hand, big, strong, a mother's hand, resting on his thinning frame, the white of her flesh against the green of his chino jacket. They both recognized that she had never done this before, that except for some early handshakes and the usual bumps in the narrow parlor when she filled in at milking, they had never touched in any way. A slight breeze, flavored with cattle, rose up behind them. It seemed almost miraculous for them to be joined on this small point of land. "Denny always took things hard," he said, after she had withdrawn. "That's all I'm trying to say."

Susan thought about Denny for a second, the man high in the tractor or deep, confident with his tools, in the guts of the combine.

"I don't suspect you know that he was a soft boy. He liked to be held by his mama."

Susan had guessed this, but it made tears come to her eyes anyway.

"By the time you knew him, he was fresh enough," said the old man. He pulled out a handkerchief—a washrag they used to clean the teats before plugging them into the milkers—and held it out for her. She knew what it was, still damp with disinfectant, and she took it. "He was even softer than his sisters. One year he planted a flower garden over behind the equipment bays and he made bouquets and vases of flowers, you know, to give. It was a girlish thing to do," the man said, sounding as confused now, and as unsure, as he must have been thirty years earlier, a dairy farmer with a boy who loved flowers. "The teachers were partial to him."

Susan listened, and waited for more, wanted these images to do their job, feeling as if these tears could be the ones she had been waiting for all this time.

"If I had it to do over again . . ." he began, and then stopped. Neither of them needed him to describe how he had reacted to this child.

"What?" she asked. She brought her hand to her face and felt the oily release of mucus on her fingertips.

"Sometimes I look at him and I catch a glimpse of that soft boy. In his eyes, I expect. It's like he is asking me for something. I always figured he would get it from his own family, but that wasn't to be. I always hoped you could make it right."

"I—" she said, ready to tell him she couldn't do it alone, but he talked past her.

"I wish you could see the boy like I do," he interrupted.

He had ended on a sort of question, a plea perhaps, and now seemed to want her to respond. But she no longer had anything to say, no answers to a father so troubled by his son, no apologies to a father who loved his boy. They waited as she blew her nose, and they both turned their stares out to the water, as if worried Denny might sneak up in his boat and overhear this conversation.

She did not want her thoughts to turn toward sorrow. This had not helped her. To ward off the impulse, she thought back for a moment to herself as a schoolgirl, without blemish, living in the uncomplicated glow. She had always liked herself best in her Brownie uniform; because the older girls wore precisely the same costume, Susan didn't feel so awkwardly big and tall. Perhaps at some point, in the past year or two, she had let the girl in the brown dress out of her grasp, let her fall away as if disappearing down a sweet but deep well. She no longer felt, as she had in her younger adulthood, that she was living as two people, the girl and the woman.

"I sometimes think all of us out here just gave up a little early," she said.

"Speak for yourself," he said, but it wasn't said harshly. It was more of an absolution than a retort.

"Oh," she said. "I've got plenty to confess. I expect that goes without saying."

The old man put up his hand to stop her. He turned to go, but seemed reluctant to leave this brilliant September day and to let this conversation stop. He looked at her, and made her realize that he believed the next step was hers.

"Charles," she said. She rarely used his name.

"What?"

"I can't fix everything. You know that. It's not as if I have any magic." She did not know why she was so certain that this was what he wanted.

"I'm not asking for magic. You've come home. That's enough to keep from offending the dead," he said finally. "The boy and my wife." He began to walk away, heading up toward his house. Susan found herself waving to him as he departed, and then turned quickly to see that Denny had entered the mouth of the creek, a tall weather bow, unnaturally, stunningly white, plowing toward her out of the molten sunlight.

She waited on the creek bank, sitting in the dry autumn grasses. Denny caught the mooring ball and was making the line fast. He seemed in a good mood, his skin a golden reflection in the tea-colored water. He looked fine as a waterman, big-chested over the low sides of the boat. Suddenly, as she looked upon this graceful scene, from deep in her lungs came a wave of joy, a relief as if for the first time in years her whole body had relaxed. She could feel it in her chest and in her shoulders. Could it be, Susan wondered, that this morning, this very moment, was what she had been waiting for, that mourning would end with the same abruptness as it had begun, begun with the words, out of a sleep, as any parent fears it most, a strange doctor saying *Wake up, wake up, it's about your son Charlie.* But Charlie isn't even born yet, she had told herself as she roused; how can doctors be waking me up with bad news about Charlie?

"Hey," Denny called out as he poled close.

"Sh-h-h," she said, putting a finger to her lips. She did not know why it was necessary for him not to talk. She watched him struggle for a second or two with an answer, perhaps even an angry complaint about being cut short when all he was saying was hello. Since she had moved back they had been careful with each other, and had not probed for feelings, and had sat silent for phrases or thoughts they did not understand. Asking for explanations would have done no good. Susan wished that her life and her marriage were that simple; she could hardly remember the time when it was, when words took care of what words were supposed to and touch handled the rest.

"Can you be with me here for a minute?" she asked.

He sat down beside her on the bank. He had moved a little beyond her, and when she turned in her seat to face him she saw the old man watching them from the patch of grass in front of his house. The three of them hoping for a peace or for a change, depending on her. It was maybe not much of an audience. Out of all the people she had known in her life, her own family, her girlfriends, the boys and men, her electric company customers, out of the planet's billions, only these few, this assortment, looked to her. Was that enough to make any of this worth it?

"A real pretty day out there," said Denny, Denny the soft boy, the one who loved flowers.

She moved over closer to him, her knees parting the grass as if she were still in school, still looking up at Denny from her spot at the senior picnic. She took his hand, spread it out between hers, attempting to flatten the natural cup of his palm with her thumbs. She could feel the pulses of blood, stunning bursts of life-giving pressure.

"It may be over," she said. She held her breath, waiting to see how this would feel, once said. A *V* of geese honked overhead, a cow bellowed angrily from the holding yard, a school of small fish breached the surface in front of them in a gravelly shower. She was glad to have these other voices join in with hers.

"I'm hoping so too," he answered.

She wished, for a moment, that he had not used this word. Of course she had hoped for many things, beginning with herself, things done and things left undone. She had hoped to be a mother, but for the moment, once risked, it was better to put that hope aside. Especially with the new knowledge and choices that could be revealed in a drop of her fluid, conceiving life seemed to have much too much to do with death. She had hoped not to be still thinking in such terms, but she was. She had hoped—maybe "pretended" would be a better word—that Denny could suddenly become someone quite different, starting with what she had learned was a slight defect, a trivial speck of dust, located on the long arm of his chromosome 7. Denny could also be more communicative, less defensive, more open to suggestion, less interested in sex, more interested in love; he could not have that palm-sized birthmark on his left flank and his breath could be nicer when he awoke. Hope, in other words, seemed a little beside the point for Susan.

He said, "It didn't seem anyone did anything wrong, anyway. That's the thing. Neither of us did anything wrong."

She quieted him once more, and this time he seemed content to sit with her in the grass. She could see Denny's father disappearing into his house; she could see the inevitable lineup of cows beginning at the far gate, drawn by the pressure of time as they measured it. She felt Denny remove his hand from its splayed captivity, and she looked down to see him moving to pick up one of hers. She would know everything when he did. There was no way for either of them to lie on this one: the moment had come, almost five years reduced to a slight clasp of his hand. It could be a little too tight and then relax too abruptly; a sort of half-hearted greeting, something for a cousin, something to be gotten over. That would mean that they would live out their lives side by side, but that it would never be sweet again. His grasp could be too loose, a kind of forgetful drape, the kind of thing you do to keep your balance. If so, they would drift apart in a year or two, and perhaps he would lose the farm and start drinking. Or he could run his hand into hers, flatten it against her palm and find the fit for his fingers; he could search and then, slowly, take what she gave him, herself, and he could draw the two of them together, and this is what she expects, and it will be enough, not perhaps for every man and every woman, but for her, and for him, for now.

orn in New York City in 1948, and a distant relative of the late Canadian Prime Minister Pierre Trudeau, Garretson Beekman Trudeau graduated from Yale in 1970 and later took his M.F.A. in graphic arts there. As an undergraduate, he wrote a comic strip for the *Yale Daily News* called "Bull Tales" that poked "sophomoric fun at mixers, campus revolutionaries, Yale President Kingman Brewster—but mostly at the football huddles of 'B.D.' Yalies recognized the jock as Brian Dowling, standout Yale quarterback." That strip evolved into *Doonesbury,* which debuted the fall after Trudeau's graduation and quickly became a success. He has compared the work to "having a term paper due every Friday for thirty years." He has written many essays, teleplays, and the book and music for a musical based on the strip, but he works most effectively at the odd juncture of writing and art that is called "graphic writing"—which can trace its history back to Egyptian hieroglyphics. Trudeau is a sort of graphic Balzac, chronicling the ambitions and absurdities of his generation with political acumen and a deft satirical touch. Beginning in 1971, collections of *Doonesbury* strips were gathered as books; there are now dozens of them.

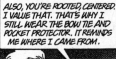

illiam Logan graduated from Yale College in 1972, and his time there coincided with a good deal of political turmoil. "At eighteen I planned a Ph.D. in game theory and political choice theory, and sophomore year took two graduate courses in service of this mad idea," he recalls. "The bombing of Cambodia and the student strike following put an end to my politics. My senior spring at Yale, two teachers, divergently brilliant, taught me how to apply my battered ingenuities, my lust for the organizations of science and math, to the DNA of language. These men were Richard Howard and David Milch, and to them I owe a long debt." Logan's passion for organization subsequently resulted in taut, rigorously speculative poems whose analytical energies, severe tone, and dark wit display a masterful touch. Five collections of his poems have appeared: *Sad-faced Men* (1982), *Difficulty* (1985), *Sullen Weedy Lakes* (1988), *Vain Empires* (1998), and *Night Battle* (1999). He is also a critic of standing and in 1988 was awarded the Citation for Excellence in Reviewing by the National Book Critics Circle. Two collections of his essays and reviews have been published: *All the Rage* (1998) and *Reputations of the Tongue* (1999), a finalist for the National Book Critics Circle award in criticism.

GARBO

Like Garbo you took to your room, a headache
coming on, but yours lasted months, years.
Ordinary life went on around you, on the sidewalk

six feet from your blinded windows. You ordered in.
Manhattan promises the cold blood of risk
when you're young; at fifty it's the half-lit world you know,

rent-controlled apartment, life overdue in installments,
each pleasure cast-iron or crumbling, a renovation.
No one believes in Freud when the antidepressants kick in—

the new therapy is an alarm clock of Elavil or Prozac.
Who hasn't felt his forties a fast-forward film?
Under a maple on campus, still appealingly young,

I slit open proofs of my studio photographs,
trying to find one way to bewilder you into love.
In minutes they faded in unforgiving sun, forgiven sin,

my hollow faces sweet and pale as pastry.
One night I huddled in my car and wept,
wept for years, and woke up cured. Seeing you

in a Manhattan restaurant, the second time
this decade, I hardly recognized who you were.
Then that smile, and I felt myself falling again.

MUSIC LESSONS

Every Good Boy Deserves Favor. Again, *ritardo.*
Each Saturday the clubfoot teacher scored
posture and its struggling notes. Was it there art learned

its cruel deceits? I sat in the car while faltering scales
fell like distant, miniature empires, struggled to rise.
Finally my teary sister would emerge, piano books

spilling from her gabardine arms. Again, *forte.*
The minor world of Chevrolet was mine,
cracked leather beneath rich odor of cigarettes.

What immature khan ever wanted more,
to hear the Abyssinian and still dream?
Sputnik's flawed arc stole night on night

through the doldrums of the Eisenhower years, the wars
over or not yet begun, a brief sleep between nightmares
under the blurred aegis of the H-bomb.

The age demanded, not a question mark,
but the whisper of ellipsis or bang of exclamation.
Our grace was to be permitted to live

where art, like the atom, embraced the eternal present,
notes pocking the surface of the infinite, the finite
where *Eleven Greedy Boyars Demand Freedom.*

SMALL TOWN

Quite early, there was something to answer for,
the two-room schoolhouse boiled in the dusty yard,
the broken backs of saltbox houses, two centuries old,

staggering beneath the overhang of the Baltimore oriole.
The clapboard facade of the Methodist church
fronted the common cemetery, scene of lichen and stitched stone,

teaching the corpus of Christian love, or Christian benefit.
Ten years beyond the burning, not a word was spoken,
though we were tiny incarnations of the Word

with our Sunday-school badges of good attendance.
Each sermon grabbled the air, swallowed like surf
in dunes a mile away. We lived in glacial rock,

there on the long aftermath of Peter's charity,
Paul's prejudicial letters, a church founded
(allegedly) by fishermen. In our deviant sect,

one more heresy moved the fractured service,
while local fishermen netted the pope's encyclicals:
fish on Friday and grace the rest of the week.

Suspended beyond the harms of a world
that buried its war dead and kept silence,
we were left to discover the zeitgeist for ourselves.

THE PAST

Between the visible and invisible lies the alteration.
The skin of my father turned hard at death,
no longer itself but the idea of itself,

who once had taken a machine to an unkempt field.
The Platonic order lounged underground, secretive
as the star-nosed mole burrowing onto the far shore.

Raise us from our prostrate, inviolate forms,
salt zephyrs peeling off the river, the river gone
in that form, that form only, mere prayer or potency.

The past lies beneath our actions like a nail bed,
guilt without justification in the breeze's coil and frieze.
The seasons waver in their stillness. Along the tide,

where spent sand crabs dug their living graves,
the hillocks of the Vineyard arched and fell,
sailors tore their catch from the billowing whale,

the barnacled cod, until the banks went dry,
abandoning the wind-scorched steeple like a rifle sight,
the graveyard tilting on its survey mark.

In the particular robin's-egg sky of the past,
the froth of honeysuckle withered at the wall
as death built its sand-castle cities around us.

Ted Tally

born in North Carolina in 1952, Ted Tally majored in drama at Yale (B.A., 1974) and then studied playwriting at the Yale School of Drama (M.F.A., 1977). His best-known play, *Terra Nova,* about Robert Scott's and Roald Amundsen's race to the South Pole, was written as his master's thesis and first staged as a student production in 1977. It was soon mounted by the Yale Repertory Theater, and a later off-Broadway production earned an Obie Award. The play has since become a mainstay of regional theaters around the country, and among its many foreign productions is a televised version by the BBC. Tally's other plays include *Hooters* (1978), *Coming Attractions* (1982), *Silver Linings* (1983), and *Little Footsteps* (1986). Also an accomplished screenwriter, he includes among his movie credits *The Silence of the Lambs* and *All the Pretty Horses.* "In the 1970s, Yale was a paradise for self-motivated theater junkies," Tally recalls. "Student productions sprang up everywhere, scores of them a year. I wrote my first several plays for such performances, and not only wrote them but got to produce, direct, design, and in some cases, act in them, too. The tickets, I remember, cost fifty cents. No dining hall or common room or courtyard ever seemed to be without its makeshift stage, its precariously constructed lighting scaffold, and its gawky young Willy Loman or Lady Bracknell or Macbeth, emoting away wildly in a nimbus of gray hair powder. You'd close one show, usually after just a weekend of performances, then immediately start rehearsing the next one. By springtime, smudgy posters festooned every gate, kiosk, and phone pole on campus: Beckett! Shaw! The Greeks! Jacques Brel, Joe Orton, Arthur Kopit! Nothing seemed impossible—nor should it be, to nineteen-year-olds. Like a wise, bemused parent, Yale understood that sometimes it could teach us best by letting us teach ourselves."

TERRA NOVA: PROLOGUE AND EXCERPT FROM ACT 1

Prologue
Darkness and silence.

Time passes. A shudder of wind. Pause. Again.

Suddenly, an image appears, huge against a cyclorama, filling the entire back of the stage. It towers over our heads. The image is a black-and-white photograph, rear-projected. It shows a vast moonlit seascape, the water filled with chunks of ice. Now a series of such photographs will flash in succession. Each will brighten for a moment, then fade:

A three-masted steamship at sea. We see it in full-length silhouette, an ominous dark shape without detail. It is Scott's ship, the Terra Nova.

The same ship, now in heavy seas. We look forward from amidships. Sailors in sou'westers are manning pumps on the port side.

(Again the strange windsong is heard, chill and stronger, rising sharply in pitch before subsiding again.)

The ship trapped in packed ice. It looms huge in the foreground. Two men stand on the ice near the bow.

The ship is now quite far away. The foreground is filled with ice and water. (The wind is a cry of rage or pain, coming closer and growing louder.)

The ship is so far away we can no longer see it. We see only an endless plain of ice.

Then a long, grey mountain range, with snow-capped peaks.

Then a tortured surface where drifts of snow have been whipped into frozen waves.

Then a vast panorama in which the only perceivable detail can be found in the sky, which is grey-streaked and threatening. There is no part of these final images which offers any human comfort or shelter whatsoever.

The last slide holds, as simultaneously the wind is full upon us. It shrieks to impossible towers of sound. It is awesome, deafening—the fabric of the air itself torn apart in the hands of giants. As the sound smashes against us, the final slide brightens and brightens until finally it shows no contrasts at all, but is just a blank square of light, as if the photograph itself had been burned away by a pure white flame.

As the slide whitens and the wind howls, a spot slowly creates a pool of light, and in this pool is revealed the figure of a man—who is Scott himself. He wears Antarctic clothing. He is kneeling on one knee, hunched over rigidly. Using a pencil, he is writing in a small notebook balanced on his knee. The effort of writing is enormously difficult for him; he seems battered by the wind. Now as the wind reaches its peak, he looks slowly up and stares out at us. His features are strained and weary. The wind continues to whipsaw impossibly louder and louder until suddenly it stops, as abruptly and cleanly as if sliced with an axe. There is a silence which seems more deafening than the wind, and Scott still kneels as before.

SCOTT (*softly*): Message to the Public. The causes of the disaster are these.

Act I
As Scott returns to his writing, a spot comes up on Amundsen, very dapper in white tie and tails.

AMUNDSEN: Ladies and gentlemen! Distinguished guests. And my fellow members of the Royal Geographical Society. I believe that concludes our lantern program at this time. I feel certain that our speaker for tonight needs little introduction from me. (*He looks at Scott, smiles*) Therefore! Let me hasten to present—England's own hero of the Antarctic—Captain Robert—Falcon—Scott!

Amundsen gestures broadly, as additional spots hit Scott. An expectant silence.

SCOTT (*writing, with difficulty*): I do not think human beings ever came through such a month as we have come through . . . And we should have succeeded—in spite of the weather—except—except for the . . . I can't make—my hands. (*To Amundsen, helplessly*) I can't move the pencil.

Amundsen is embarrassed. Slight pause. He gestures again, more grandly.

AMUNDSEN: Captain—Scott!
SCOTT: How am I to write if I can't move the pencil?
AMUNDSEN (*in a stage whisper*): Scott—what's the matter?
SCOTT: What?
AMUNDSEN: Are you ill, man? Are you indisposed?
SCOTT: No, no, I just—my hands.
AMUNDSEN: Really, this is most irregular. (*He smiles reassuringly to the audience*) The members are waiting.
SCOTT (*peering out*): They're . . .
AMUNDSEN: Waiting. We're all waiting. To hear.
SCOTT: Ah! (*Pause*) To hear?
AMUNDSEN: About the race.
SCOTT: Ah yes. Yes. (*Bitterly*) Everyone loves a race.
AMUNDSEN: Mustn't disappoint them, Scott. So many wanting to know.

SCOTT: It's just my hands, don't you see. And only—if I might rest now for a bit, because I'm so frightfully tired.

AMUNDSEN (*evenly*): Not now, old man. After.

SCOTT: After, yes. (*Pause*) Afterwards I may rest?

A spot comes up on Kathleen, upstage from Scott. She is a pretty woman in her early thirties, wearing a light, flowing summer dress. Her hair is up, set for a party.

KATHLEEN: Con? Is something the matter?

SCOTT (*still kneeling, facing out*): Kathleen! My hands—I can't feel the pencil. And yet this fellow says—says . . .

KATHLEEN: Why don't you come in now? It's getting dark.

SCOTT: No, no, Kath—listen to me, there isn't much time. I have to tell you— about the most extraordinary *place* I've been.

KATHLEEN: Oh yes.

SCOTT: The things I've seen there! Terrible and wonderful! Flames exploding in air.

KATHLEEN: Mountains of crystal . . .

SCOTT: Colors falling from the sky.

KATHLEEN: Yes.

SCOTT: Silence, like a scream into wind.

KATHLEEN: Silence like sleep.

SCOTT: Like sleep, yes.

KATHLEEN: Like a dream.

SCOTT: So many things to tell—but my hands . . .

KATHLEEN: Con? We're going to have a son.

SCOTT: A son . . .

KATHLEEN: Last night when I woke I knew. I crept out and ran down to the beach. I swam out quietly, in a calm sea, as far as my strength would take me.

SCOTT: Kath, I can't write any longer . . .

KATHLEEN: I floated with my face turned up to the moon. I thought, "my son will love the nights, and he will love the sea."

SCOTT: Tell him—tell our boy that I said . . .

KATHLEEN: Yes.

SCOTT: That I said . . . (*His voice trails off*)

AMUNDSEN (*delicately, after a pause*): The Captain has, I believe, a most unusual and—ah, a most *important*—announcement to make to us at this time. And so now, without any further ado, I give you—Robert Scott.

There is a sound of wind, softly. Scott looks about, as if aware for the first time of his surroundings, his audience. He rises with slow determination, moves downstage and faces front. He removes his mittens and pulls off his balaclava.

Amundsen exits.

Kathleen watches Scott closely.

SCOTT: My fellow members of the Society. (*Loudly and firmly*) We are all engaged, all of us here in this room tonight, in a great scientific race, in
which our national pride is at stake. No human footprints have yet appeared at the South Geographic Pole. When they do first appear—and I
assure you that day is very close—I intend that they shall be British
footprints! My new ship, the *Terra Nova,* will steam down the Thames on
the morning of May thirtieth, and her destination is Antarctica. I *am*
going back, I am going to try a second time—and this time I shall not return until I've planted the Union Jack on the bottom of the earth!

*Towards the end of the above, there is the sound of lusty singing approaching. Scott's
men—Bowers, Wilson, Oates and Evans—are singing a chantey.*

BOWERS		What shall we do with a drunken sailor?
		What shall we do with a drunken sailor?
		What shall we do with a drunken sailor?
WILSON	*singing together offstage*	Ear-ly in the mor-nin'?
OATES		Put 'em in the scuppers with a hosepipe on 'em,
EVANS		Put 'em in the scuppers with a hosepipe on 'em,
		Put 'em in the scuppers with a hosepipe on 'em,
		Ear-ly in the mor-nin'!

*By the end of the second stanza of the chantey, Bowers, Wilson, Oates and Evans
enter, hauling their sled. Bowers, Wilson and Oates are in the lead, hauling on leather
traces. Evans trails, pushing. The sled is very heavy, and awkward to move. It is piled
high with supply boxes and lashed over with tarpaulin.*

As the men enter, Kathleen turns and goes.

The Lights cover the entire stage.

Bowers spots an obstruction in their path.

BOWERS (*breathlessly*): Whoa! Bit of a crack here!

*They stop. All but Evans come forward and kneel to examine the "crack" which bars
their way. Evans sits on the back of the sled, grateful to catch his breath.*

OATES: That's not a crack. That's another bleeding crevasse.
BOWERS: There's a thin crust over it.
WILSON (*to Bowers*): Can you see bottom, Birdie?
BOWERS (*lordly*): I can see a Chinaman, on his way up.

As Scott speaks again, they kneel in silence, studying the ground. They are not certain that the ice immediately ahead of them will bear the weight of the sled.

SCOTT (*still facing front; continuing his speech*): There is another man who will attempt the race. I mean the Norwegian, Roald Amundsen. Listen to the means by which our Mr. Amundsen thinks fit to achieve the Pole. He intends to take along huge teams of dogs, whip them into hauling his men overland to the Great Barrier Glacier, then slaughter them when he has no further use for them and feed on the fresh dog meat! Well. I leave it to you to decide how sporting that is.

Oates sighs and gets up.

OATES: Help me pull us up to the edge. Come on, Birdie, put your scrawny little back to it.

They pick up the traces again.

Together—One! Two! Three!

They heave at the lines, straining mightily, but the sled will not budge. They collapse, puffing.

SCOTT: My own men have trained until they're in the peak of condition, and we intend to march it on foot.

OATES: Nothing. Stuck again.

WILSON: The runners are iced up.

They rest on the sled, catching their breath.

SCOTT: To the Pole and back—on foot!

WILSON (*wearily*): There's only one thing for it.

BOWERS: Go back two hundred miles and turn starboard, 'stead of port.

OATES: Build a bridge of ice.

BOWERS: Wait here for the spring thaw—'cept there isn't any.

WILSON: Thank you. No, I mean we'll have to unload again.

The others groan noisily.

OATES: Unload! You're off your chump. (*He chops at the ice around the base of the runners*)

SCOTT: Only we English could so believe in an ideal . . .

BOWERS: Nothing like the army, is it, Titus?

OATES: Cavalry, not army!

BOWERS: All the same to me, mate.

WILSON (*sarcastically*): Let's just *talk* it across!

SCOTT: Only we will so achieve it . . .

OATES: Well I say it's bloody stupid to unload if we can yank it!

BOWERS: And I say we just bloody well tried that, didn't we?

OATES: Then let's ask the Captain!

BOWERS: Fine!

WILSON: Yes, Robert—what do you say?

SCOTT (*still facing front*): Not with cheap tricks, or cruelty to brute beasts, but with the pride of English manhood!

WILSON (*after a slight pause*): Robert, did you hear me?

Scott turns and stares at them.

SCOTT: What?

OATES: The crevasse.

BOWERS: Do we yank or unload, Captain?

SCOTT (*after a pause*): Yes, yes, of course. (*He goes to them briskly*) Wilson, Bowers, slip your traces back along the sides. Foot the back ends of the runners and when I signal, pull like the devil. The rest of us lifting the front corners. Ready? Heave!

They all tug together; the front end of the sled is slowly lifted a few inches and yanked forward, after a tremendous effort. They once again catch their breath, Bowers half-collapsing over the side of the sled.

You see how simple it is, Bowers? We've moved it all of eight inches further along, and all it's cost you is the chance ever to have children.

BOWERS (*grimacing*): If you're referring to that ungodly popping noise, that was Mr. Oates, thank you. My last one blew a hundred miles back.

OATES: The footing is better on this side.

WILSON: I hope to God we've seen the last of that soft powder.

BOWERS: Well—let's get on with it, then. (*Passing Scott*) Ev'nin', Captain. Lovely weather for ducks!

They drag the sled rather easily now, over the stage and off. Evans, pushing, must struggle a bit to keep up.

EVANS (*puffing, as he passes Scott*): Ev'nin', sir.

SCOTT: Evans.

Bowers, Wilson and Evans exit, singing.

Oates lingers at the edge of the stage. In the distance we hear the sound of singing again, gradually trailing off.

BOWERS			Hoo-ray and up he rises!
WILSON	}	(*offstage*)	Hoo-ray and up he rises!
EVANS			Hoo-ray and up he rises!
			Ear-ly in the mor-nin'!

Scott looks at Oates curiously.

OATES: Captain Scott—may I have a word with you?

SCOTT: Certainly, Oates.

OATES: It's Evans, sir.

SCOTT: What about him?

OATES (*reluctantly*): Well he's not pulling his weight, sir.

SCOTT (*surprised*): Evans?

OATES: Yes, sir. He tires easily for a big man. I don't like it.

SCOTT: Do you mean he's shirking?

OATES: No, but he's slowing the pace, that's certain, and he favors his left hand.

SCOTT: I see. Put him on point so he can rest a bit, but don't let him see he's getting any sort of special attention. If you can, get a look at that hand. I
don't like the sound of that. (*Pause*) I won't have the pace slowed, Oates.
We've got to do five more miles this afternoon.

OATES (*grinning*): We'll do five easily enough, Captain. We'll do eight. We're all
in good spirits.

SCOTT: I can depend on you, Oates.

OATES: It's not me. All I have to do is mention the Norwegians, and they fairly fly.

SCOTT: Splendid. Well then, that's all, Oates. Carry on.

OATES: Yes, sir. I mean aye aye, sir. (*He starts to go then hesitates*) Firmer crust
here, Captain. Maybe things will start to look up, this side of the glacier.

SCOTT: I hope so, Oates. I sincerely do.

OATES: Yes, sir. (*Pause*) Well.

Oates exits.

*The wind is heard softly. The Lights fade to a spot on Scott. After a moment of uncer-
tainty he faces out front again.*

During the following, Amundsen enters upstage, unseen.

SCOTT: In—conclusion—ladies and gentlemen. No journey ever made with dogs
can approach that glory which is realized when a party of men go forth to
face hardships unaided, and by days and weeks of splendid physical exertion, succeed in solving some problem of the great unknown. Our final
victory over Norway will be all the sweeter, all the nobler, because we will
know we've taken the prize by playing the game as it *ought* to be played!

Scott concludes as if expecting a great ovation. Instead we hear only one pair of hands clapping, mockingly. Scott turns, is startled to see Amundsen, revealed upstage behind the scrim. He now wears high boots and a huge dark coat with a bristling fur collar. The Spot fades on Scott. Light glows through the cyclorama; an eerie wash of color fills the stage. Amundsen stops clapping, and, after a pause, speaks. All trace of the M.C.'s manner is now gone: he speaks in his own harsh, slightly accented voice.

AMUNDSEN: Success is a bitch. Grab her, and have her—but don't stand under her window with a mandolin.

Scott turns, his eyes wander over the audience.

SCOTT: The explanations I have to go through, the flag-waving, even at the Society! They call themselves scientists, but for three years now their stinginess has frustrated my efforts to open a whole new *continent* for science.

AMUNDSEN: For science? What can that possibly have to do with you? (*He moves down through a slash in the scrim*) A strange science, to tell you a thousand pound sled can be manhauled across sixteen hundred miles. (*Pause*) I consult a chart and a caloric table. It tells me that on the eightieth day of my journey, according to precise schedule, the seventeenth animal must be converted to protein. And that is science.

SCOTT: Of a certain kind, perhaps.

AMUNDSEN (*shrugging*): Two methods, one goal. (*Pause*) Most men squander their chances. Their lives pass as if they slept—at the end a vague sadness, then . . . (*He makes a little gesture*) But you—and me. How many in the world like us, eh? We concentrate, we wait—for what? One place, one turning. The pattern revealed. (*Pause*) Suppose we could stand on another planet, English, and see our whole lives at once?

SCOTT: How like another planet it must feel to stand at the bottom of the earth.

AMUNDSEN: And what a moment to be there first. Oh yes. How many lifetimes would we give for that? (*Pause*) You and me, we're the same, eh? But you act the fine gentleman, and I'm only a filthy barbarian. A killer of dogs.

SCOTT: I said nothing of the kind.

AMUNDSEN: A foreigner, then. It's the same thing to you.

SCOTT: You don't play the game.

AMUNDSEN: Oh yes, the English game. By which you mean that peculiar love affair between your race and Man's Best Friend. Shall I tell you a little secret? It's only the big ones I shoot. With the puppies I like to snap off the heads and drink the blood.

SCOTT: I don't find you very amusing. And you know precisely what I mean.

AMUNDSEN: Do I? Oh, yes. (*Pause*) You're angry because I swore to take the North Pole, and leave the South to you.

SCOTT: Yes, damn it. You betrayed my trust for the shabby little advantage of a few weeks head start. You lied to me in front of the whole world!

AMUNDSEN: It wasn't a lie. I meant what I said, for as long as it was convenient. (*Pause*) Oh, but I did *want* the North! More than you've ever wanted anything in your life. From the time I sat in the firelight and listened to tales of huge icecaps, where perhaps the gods still walked the earth . . . But you see—the American beat me there. Do you know what it is to see a dream strangled in newspaper cuttings? No. . . . Well, I can't see the point of being the second man in history to reach the North Pole—can you? (*Pause*) I'm going South, English.

SCOTT: You're at liberty to try. A decent sense of courtesy towards a brother explorer is more than I have any right to expect.

AMUNDSEN: Think of it as a sporting gesture, Scott! Just a bit of healthy open-air competition. Isn't that part of playing your damned game? As for the dogs, I won't apologize for common sense. A husky is fifty pounds of dinner hauling you along until you need to eat it.

SCOTT: There *are* rules. Codes, standards, among civilized men! One doesn't cease behaving properly simply because one is entering a wilderness. All the more reason to set an example. (*Pause*) You'll never understand. You're not English.

AMUNDSEN: But I do understand. Playing the game means treating your dogs like gentlemen, and your gentlemen like dogs. You're an infant, tickling yourself with a razor!

KATHLEEN (*off*): Con?

AMUNDSEN (*urgently*): Listen to me, English. Success is a bitch. You can grab her and have her if your plan is right—and that's all. Not because you made her swoon with your virtue. So learn a passion for details. That's not so romantic, but it can keep bread in your belly and your backside out of the snow. (*He turns to go*)

KATHLEEN (*off*): Con!

SCOTT: Amundsen—wait!

Kathleen appears, upstage. She carries a small wrapped gift in one hand.

AMUNDSEN: I *will* wait—in the one place I can afford to wait for a man as determined as you. In the meantime—think of the details.

SCOTT: Amundsen! (*He starts to go to Amundsen*)

Amundsen goes.

Scott stands looking after him.

KATHLEEN: Con. You said you were going upstairs to rest.

SCOTT: I—couldn't sleep. (*Pause*) I dreamt of Amundsen again.

KATHLEEN: Was he very frightening?

SCOTT: Frightening enough. I came down here. I wanted—I don't know what I wanted.

George Bradley

n o writer gets anywhere without the drive to continue, but the path along which one perseveres is very often a matter of chance," writes George Bradley. "In my case, it was my great good fortune to encounter Richard Howard at an impressionable age. Howard taught a seminar in writing poetry three out of my four years at Yale, and his instruction was worth the cost of tuition in itself. Exceptional teachers are rare in any field, but perhaps all the more so in writing." After graduating from Yale in 1975, he continued to study writing at the University of Virginia. His first book, *Terms to Be Met,* was selected by James Merrill for the Yale Younger Poets Prize in 1985. He has published two further collections, *Of the Knowledge of Good and Evil* (1991) and *The Fire Fetched Down* (1996). The poems printed here are from his forthcoming book, *Some Assembly Required.* Like Wallace Stevens, he is in the line of philosophical poets eager to test experience against ideas, and with a bracing wit. In addition he has edited *The Yale Younger Poets Anthology* (1998). For his work he has received the Witter Bynner Prize from the American Academy of Arts and Letters and the Lavan Award from the Academy of American Poets.

THE U.S.A. TODAY

Homespun *sangfroid* composed of *kaffeeklatsch*,
The calm was as persistent as crab grass,
And one witnessed hardly any gnashing of teeth,
The ritual breast-beating and rending of garments
Effectively preempted by trips to the hardware store
And close inspection of box scores in the sports pages,
By annual drives for the American Cancer Society
And endless discussion concerning inconsequential variations in the ongoing
    entertainment of weather.
So the city fathers sent out the fire engines to process,
And an ironclad normality prevailed, though if this
Be courage or stupidity, boredom or despair,
Remained hidden even from themselves,
Good citizens practicing the standard necromancies
And battening on their own ambition,
Who in sunlight ripened a rictal grin
And by night admitted into dreams
The children they had been
To stand whimpering by the side of the bed
While the gold threads were torn out of their scalps,
Their rosy complexions once more drained of blood,
The thin limbs hacked from their hairless bodies
And buried in separate boxes before dawn,
That renewed adults, awaking to the vision
Of an order still to be delivered, might hunger
For the shewbread of astonishment and pick up
The drive-thru punishment of one day's understanding.

APOLÓGIA

If our ears were not pavilions of desire,
Bright canopies, billows pitched and spread,
Painted sails upon the restless main of thought;
If they were not gardens, damp enclosures thick
With fruit and vivid bloom, not winding palaces,
Not rococo cathedrals and frivolous gazebos
And castles of caprice, eccentric merlons perched

In architectural defiance upon the wildest crag,
Then—O Acting Assistant to an Acting Editor—
We might oblige remark, hark as you would hear.

And if our speech were not another dialect,
Our own rude gutturals, our sympathetic clicks,
The odd stress and persistent superfluous schwa;
If our words weren't cultivations and gibberish
To that communal, quick, quotidian chameleon
That darts and squeaks, vigorous on its twig,
Then—O Interim Director of an Underfunded Series—
We might state your case and say your grace,
Offer up the bread that mumbles on your plate.

And further, if fierce rapidity weren't in the air,
This violent mistral, this manic will to change
That rips the sound out of our mouths and steals
Our *sfumature,* a turbulent simoom of difference
Withering pun to explanation, the surreptitious
To blank stare; if the tramontana of mutation
Were not always at our throats, why then—
O Temporary Muck-a-Muck of the Edifice on Paper—
Then we might deal plainly with plain truths,
Simply say what soothes, might seek and suffer
Little clarity, accept the sentence of the meek.

But Muck-a-Muck, our ears are shameless, self-indulged;
Our words remain our intimates and the paraphrase
Of dream, melodies that echo down enchanted corridors;
And the wind that howls above this house tonight
Sweeps our idea away like leaves torn from the trees.
Who will be left to satisfy but us and what is not?
We testify at other hearings, before a terrible tribunal
Of flimsy things: the model irony of strangers,
The enthused naïfs of day, the unresponsive innocence
Pressed to remove us and be all we have been.

MY POEM MEETS TAMERLANE

Many things happen in Chester, Connecticut,
but the invasion of Tamerlane is not one of them.
Instead, the streets are plowed and the buses run,
my Mr. Coffee radio-alarm swings into action,
and I'm just wondering if a sense of civic responsibility
isn't the instinct to mediocrity, when another account
of the cosmos gets tossed on my porch, containing
A) nothing whatsoever about my poetry, and B)
such shenanigans that I conclude the notion
of civic responsibility is a thing of the past, until
I notice an item about bloodshed in the Caucasus
(the Congo, the Murex Coast, the Transoxiana),
where vengeance remains the one idea and starvation
sinks its fangs into the blown bellies of children
as it has since Man knoweth not to the contrary
(dust is rising off the steppe, say, in A.D. 1395,
and the far cry of trumpets forecasts extinction;
as my poem is invested by Tamerlane, fear
sweeps its populace as the dawn wind sweeps water),
meaning a passable ennui is not short of perfection,
i.e., if the urge to eminence accomplishes such havoc
surely we need always all the mediocrity we can get.
Then who am I to complain of disregard
when all history comes to an unmarked grave,
when obscurity lies in ambush at each road's end,
when earth is a mother with a dead thing at her breast?
Who shall record the myriad configurations of pain?
And what is to tell but of hope gone under the ground?
Friend, Tamerlane the Great rides this and every day,
and the corpses stretch to infinity behind him.
They must rot where they fall. And I sing one life,
I find joy and the prospect of peace. Sing not
and my bones have already been scattered.

Christopher Buckley

t he son of writer William F. Buckley, Jr., Christopher Buckley comes by his wit naturally. He graduated cum laude from Yale in 1976, where he was Class Historian and editor of the *Yale Daily News Magazine*. By age twenty-five, he was managing editor of *Esquire* magazine, and five years later he published his first book, *Steaming to Bamboola: The World of a Tramp Freighter*. *Wry Martinis* (1997) is a collection of essays and articles, and Buckley has written five novels as well: *The White House Mess* (1986), *Wet Work* (1991), *Thank You for Smoking* (1994), *God Is My Broker* (1998), and *Little Green Men* (1999). He is the founding editor of *Forbes FYI* magazine. In a well-known satirical memoir called "Stoned in New Haven," Buckley recalls his undergraduate years. It was a time, after the upheavals of the 1960s, when either dope or careerism had become obsessions and the word *weenie* was coined: "A weenie was identified by a bluish skin pallor, a result of over exposure to the fluorescent lighting in the underground Cross Campus Library, thick glasses, pimples, a plastic shirt-pocket guard, a calculator worn on the belt, a shrill, whining lamentation brought on by the loudspeaker announcement that the library would close in fifteen minutes, and a right arm that automatically jerked upward during class whenever a question was asked of anyone but him."

The day I turned nineteen, I went down for my physical and had my first and only experience of Army life. I took with me a letter from Dr. Murphy, my childhood doctor, describing in uncompromising detail the asthma that had been a major part of my life, occasionally severe enough to put me in the hospital for a week. As I shuffled along the line from urinalysis to the hemorrhoid inspection I tried to look wan and generally tubercular, ready to faint if any voice were raised in my direction. One Army doctor looked at my letter with an unimpressed scowl. My hands got clammy and I wiped them on my forehead, hoping the perspiration would give my brow a nicely febrile sheen. At last I came to the end of the line, to a table at which three doctors reviewed the other doctors' evaluations and ruled on them.

"Asthma?" said one of them, looking up.

I nodded feebly and made an emphysematous sound resembling a yes, intended to make him understand the asthma had left me with a dearth of pleura, which I was conserving in order to participate in the sacrament of last rites, which in my case was obviously more or less imminent.

After the longest pause I have ever waited through, he said, "Rejected."

I waited until I was a few blocks from the examination center before breaking into a full run. (They might have been watching.) I have never since run so fast. When a mile later I hit the campus and saw my roommate and some friends across the quadrangle, I broke into a sprint. A few yards from them I jumped and in midair shouted, "I FLUNKED!" loudly enough to cause nearby heads to turn and wonder, probably, what inversion of academic values had caused this deranged jubilation.

Twelve years later, on a November day in Washington, D.C., I watched as the Vietnam Veterans Memorial was dedicated. At the edge of the crowd where I stood there was a Marine, about forty years old, ramrod-stiff and impeccable in ceremonial dress. He turned suddenly from the proceedings and, walking a few paces away, took off his glasses, put two fingers of a white-gloved hand to the bridge of his nose, and began to weep.

Watching his grief made me feel like an intruder. I felt I had no business there, so I left the grounds.

There was a lot of talk that weekend about healing. It was true the veterans finally did get the welcome home and a measure of the appreciation and recognition that they had always deserved. A group of college students in a Georgetown bar stood up and applauded when a group of vets walked in. That alone seemed a remarkable enough event for President Reagan to make prominent mention of it in a speech shortly afterward.

In a city once known for its spectacular antiwar demonstrations, there were no sour notes, only the ads on television for a movie that had just opened: Sylvester Stallone working out his post-traumatic stress disorders on a small American town—with an M-16 and everything short of close air support. Good timing, Hollywood! But when it was over—the parade, the speeches, reunions, workshops, the fifty-six-hour vigil at the National Cathedral during which the names of the 57,939 dead and missing were read aloud—there was no doubt it really had been a homecoming. Myra MacPherson wrote in *The Washington Post,* "Now there is some meager measure of reconciliation; some who used to taunt them [the homecoming soldiers] at army camps and airports—the student deferred taunting those less privileged draftees or those who felt compelled to serve their country—admit guilt and shame."

It's been ten years now since the troops came home, but until recently I had never once heard anyone admit to guilt or shame over not having gone to Vietnam—not in hundreds of conversations about the war. I find this strange; *meager,* I think, is the operative word.

The gap between those who went to war and those who stayed behind was larger in the Vietnam War than in any other war in our history. Fifty-three million Americans came of age between the signing of the Gulf of Tonkin Resolution on August 7, 1964, and April 30, 1975, the day Saigon fell to the Communists. Of those fifty-three, eleven million served in the military; and of those eleven, fewer than three went to Indochina. That leaves forty-two million Americans who did not serve. Twenty-six million of these were women, who weren't called (though the sixty-five hundred women who did serve were essential to the war effort). About sixteen million were men who were deferred, exempted, or disqualified or who evaded the draft. About 80 percent of the Vietnam generation did not participate in the dominant event of their time. About 6 percent of military-age males saw actual combat.

If the millions tend to blur, consider: How many of your friends went to Vietnam?

It wasn't until the memorial opening that I stood face-to-face with my own guilt and shame. These feelings are, I acknowledge, somewhat illogical. My medical disability is genuine—even as I write this I take periodic hits off my asthma inhaler. Into the bargain I suffer from a rather unpleasant vascular malady called Horton's cluster headache. I did not dodge the draft, starve myself, shoot off a toe, act psycho, or go to Sweden. So whence this permanent malaise? Go figure. Guilt is a pretty personal affair, and it's not my business to tell people how they should feel about not having gone to Vietnam. But now that the vets have finally come home and the healing has begun, it may be time for those of us who do have misgivings about not having fought to think, out loud, about the consequences of what we did—and didn't do.

For those who never left, there is no ceremony and no coming home; if the healing is to be complete, then all the wounds from that war will need healing.

Those of my parents' generation who missed World War II were devastated by not being part of it. When an uncle of mine talks about being just too young for that war, he uses the word *traumatic*. He once told me that for him and many of his peers Korea came "almost as a relief."

But it's hard to compare World War II and Vietnam. A lot of people I know say there's no good reason to feel guilty about having missed Vietnam. There's an echo in their arguments from *Henry IV, Part I:*

. . . but for these vile guns,
He would himself have been a soldier.

They say it was a lousy war on every score. They talk about My Lai, body counts, fraggings, Agent Orange, the Phoenix Program, the inability to distinguish enemies from friendlies; about the long list of horrors that seem peculiar to Vietnam. They feel vindicated, and some of them are startled at the question of whether they feel any guilt or shame at having sat out the war. Okay, some say, the "Baby killer!" business did get out of hand. Any movement has its excesses. But it was our movement, our resistance to the war, our not going that convinced the White House and the Pentagon and the Congress to end the war.

True, but six months after the fall of Saigon in 1975 James Fallows examined an entrenched fallacy of the antiwar movement in an article for *The Washington Monthly* called "What Did You Do in the Class War, Daddy?" The article had, in the words of the *Monthly*'s editor, Charles Peters, "tremendous impact. It was a turning point in a generation, being willing to open itself up to other than cliché-left truths about Vietnam."

Fallows described how as a Harvard student he had starved himself down to 120 pounds and affected a suicidal disposition at his Army physical. As the doctor wrote "unqualified" on his form, "I was overcome by a wave of relief, which for the first time revealed to me how great my terror had been, and by the beginning of the sense of shame which remains with me to this day."

His article was a brilliant and scathing indictment of a system that sent the sons of the working class off to fight its war while allowing the overwhelming majority of the sons of the middle and upper classes to avoid it. One of Fallows's most penetrating self-criticisms was that while those in the antiwar movement (of which he was a part) convinced themselves they were the "sand in the gears of the great war machine" by burning their draft cards and marching, the real way—the courageous way—to have ended the war would have been to *go* to war.

"As long as the little gold stars," he wrote, "kept going to homes in Chelsea and the backwoods of West Virginia, the mothers of Beverly Hills and Chevy

Chase and Great Neck and Belmont were not on the telephones to their congressmen, screaming *you killed my boy,* they were not writing to the President that his crazy, wrong, evil war had put their boys in prison and ruined their careers. It is clear by now that if the men of Harvard had wanted to do the very most they could to help shorten the war, they should have been drafted or imprisoned en masse."

Fallows's argument seems to me airtight; but there are a lot of people who persist in the fallacy, and this has contributed to the anger that many vets understandably feel. Who made the real sacrifice, anyway? Some who never went to Vietnam or into the military did suffer because of it, though the numbers are relatively minuscule: of 209,517 accused draft offenders, 3,250 were imprisoned and 3,000 became fugitives. But, as Paul Starr, author of *The Discarded Army: Vietnam Veterans After Vietnam,* wrote, "the conflict was waged without any privation at home, and the result has been an enormous disproportion of sacrifice. A few have been asked to die; virtually nothing has been asked of everyone else."

Whatever sacrifices were made at home, the ones made on the field of battle cost more, and it is hard—for me, anyway—to disagree with something James Webb, the twice-wounded, highly decorated Marine and author of *Fields of Fire,* told *Time* magazine apropos the gap between vets and nonvets: "We're going to have to lead this country side by side. We're going to have to resolve this. The easiest way is for people who didn't serve in those years to come off this pretentiousness of moral commitment and realize that the guys who went to combat are the ones who suffered the most. They are also the ones who gave the most."

The hard, psychological evidence is that what most people who didn't go to Vietnam feel is neither guilt nor regret but relief. Two years ago the Center for Policy Research submitted an exhaustive nine-hundred-page study to the Veterans Administration and Congress called *Legacies of Vietnam.* Its results, if not surprising, were interesting. It found that only a bare minority of nonveterans, 3.5 percent, feel that staying out of the military had a negative impact on their lives. Thirty-six percent feel it had a positive effect. When asked how staying out of the service had benefited them, the majority said it was by enabling them to pursue their education and career. The next-highest majority said that staying out gave them a competitive advantage over their veteran peers. A veteran, I think, would find this last datum depressing and disheartening.

The question, though, of whether nonvets ought to feel vindicated by the conduct and results of the Vietnam War is, in a sense, beside the point. War is war and combat is combat, and ever since the first jawbone was raised in anger men have felt a terrible need to prove themselves on the field of glory.

"I have heard the bullets whistle," wrote George Washington about his adventures in the French and Indian War, "and believe me, there is something

charming in the sound." A century later, watching a Federal charge be repulsed at
Fredericksburg, Robert E. Lee mused, "It is well that war is so terrible, or we
should grow too fond of it." Vietnam may have performed a great national service by demonstrating for my generation the truth of the general's remark.

The lore is full of stories of those who got out of the war. But for some, not
getting into the Army and not getting to Vietnam had nearly as traumatic or profound an impact as being left out of the Normandy landing had on those of another generation. Their stories are far rarer than the other category, but also
worth the telling.

One fellow I know is convinced his entire family has been historically cheated.
His grandfather was fourteen when World War I ended; his father was fourteen
when World War II ended; he was fourteen when the Vietnam War ended.

Robert Owen was thirteen when his brother Dwight was killed in a Vietcong
ambush in 1967. (Dwight's name is inscribed in the lobby of the State Department in Washington, along with those of other recipients of the Secretary's
Award, the State Department's highest honor.) Robert worshiped Dwight, and
the death hit him very hard.

Six years later Owen was a freshman at Stanford, watching television in his
dormitory, when the news showed the first batch of POWs setting foot on the
tarmac at Subic Bay. When Jeremiah Denton, who'd been a prisoner of the North
Vietnamese for seven years, stepped to the microphone and said, "God bless
America," Owen suddenly found tears running down his cheeks.

Not long afterward the Marines happened to be on campus recruiting. Owen
had not awakened with the idea of signing up, but when he read an ad in that
morning's student newspaper saying, DON'T BE GOOD LITTLE NAZIS: STOP THE MA-
RINE RECRUITING, he went down for an interview. The protesters outside were
trying physically to prevent anyone from getting in. Owen, who has the build of
a pentathlon competitor, shoved his way through. He signed up for the Platoon
Leader program. Then came the physical. He flunked it because of a lacrosse injury to his knee. Then began a long, consuming quest.

During the four years following graduation, he tried to get into a half dozen
California police departments. Each time, the knee kept him out. In desperation,
he offered to sign insurance waivers. No one would accept such an arrangement.

Nineteen-eighty found him in the same part of the world where Dwight had
gone in answer to his own call, on the Cambodia-Thailand border, processing
refugees from Pol Pot's reign of terror for the International Rescue Committee.
Then the word came that his father was dying, and he returned home to take care
of him. During that ordeal he tried twice to enlist, in the Marines and in the
Navy's SEAL (commando) program, but the Achilles' knee kept showing up on
the X rays. As he was going out the door the Navy doctor suggested he try some
other branch of the government. Now he works on Capitol Hill.

After telling the long story one night recently at a Chinese restaurant in Georgetown, he said he'd finally come to a realization that allowed him peace of mind. After all the attempts to put himself in positions where he'd have to prove himself, he'd finally decided that "if and when the test ever comes, I'm going to get my red badge of courage, or die trying."

In the silence that followed, the fortune cookies came and we cracked them open. His read: YOUR WISDOM HAS KEPT YOU FAR AWAY FROM MANY DANGERS.

My friend Barnaby writes from Paris a fourteen-page letter imbued with something like regret, about what not going has meant to him. (Unlike me, he was never called. If he had been, he would have gone.) He mentions a well-known novelist he knows who, when drunk, tells people he was a fighter pilot in Vietnam. (He wasn't.) But Barnaby understands the novelist's dilemma and alludes to something Hemingway once said: that if a writer goes to war for a year, he will have enough to write about for the rest of his lifetime.

He remembers a man he met once in a bar in Vermont, a construction worker who'd been stalking deer in the woods for a week with a bow. He invited the man back to his cabin for a drink, and the man told Barnaby about his year in Vietnam as a gunner on river patrol boats. This was, incidentally, three years before *The Deer Hunter* opened.

"It had started to rain heavily as we finished the beer. It was a chilly November. I offered him the couch next to the fire, but he declined, saying he had a tent, and that there was an eight-point buck he'd been closing in on for three days. He thought he could get him at dawn. We shook hands at the door and he stepped out into the cold wet night. There wasn't an ounce of fear in him, and I knew that he thought I was soft—I hadn't been to Vietnam—but he didn't hold it against me, perhaps because of the way I listened to him talk."

Barnaby dwells on the word *pledge*. "I knew [at the time] that we had pledged to support that country. While I never liked the phrase, 'My country do or die,' I get a lump in my throat when I hear the pledge of allegiance. I think the word pledge is one of the most beautiful in the world. . . . To stand by a pledge can be an ordeal, and the pledge is only as good as the man who makes it. I will never know how good my pledge is."

Both Owen and Barnaby were looking for something, obviously: for a test of manhood, a chance to prove themselves under circumstances far more grueling than the challenges civilian, peacetime life throws our way: college exams, job deadlines, love affairs, wind surfing. I think some of the stories we've all heard about getting out of the draft or about antiwar demonstrations have a kind of wistful quality to them, as if those telling them are trying to relate ersatz war experiences.

One friend who was in a lot of demonstrations confessed how disappointed he was that he'd never been gassed, "because then it would have been my war too."

Another tells a story of taking multiple doses of LSD before being inducted, which, after an understandably complicated series of events, resulted in his getting off. It's a funny, and in some ways harrowing, story. It's his war story.

There's an undercurrent of envy here. I certainly feel it, at least. I have a number of friends who served in Vietnam. One was with Special Forces, another was in Army intelligence, another with the CIA. They all saw death up close every day, and many days dealt it themselves. They're married, happy, secure, good at what they do; they don't have nightmares and they don't shoot up gas stations with M-16s. Each has a gentleness I find rare in most others, and beneath it a spiritual sinew that I ascribe to their experience in the war, an aura of *I have been weighed on the scales and have not been found wanting.*

The word *veteran* comes from the Latin for *experienced.* But it's not the same experience we gain by passing through the gradual, attenuated rites of passage of lives measured out with coffee spoons. In his extraordinary book about his experiences in Vietnam, *A Rumor of War,* Philip Caputo wrote, "We learned the old lessons about fear, cowardice, courage, suffering, cruelty, and comradeship. Most of all, we learned about death at an age when it is common to think of oneself as immortal. Everyone loses that illusion eventually, but in civilian life it is lost in installments over the years. We [in Vietnam] lost it all at once, and, in the span of months, passed from boyhood through manhood to a premature middle age."

In that passage, they learned something very hard to obtain outside the battlefield: the "communion between men [in infantry battalions] is as profound as any between lovers. Actually, it is more so. It does not demand for its sustenance the reciprocity, the pledges of affection, the endless reassurances required by the love of men and women. It is, unlike marriage, a bond that cannot be broken by a word, by boredom or divorce, or by anything other than death. Sometimes even that is not strong enough. Two friends of mine died trying to save the corpses of their men from the battlefield. Such devotion, simple and selfless, the sentiment of belonging to each other, was the one decent thing we found in a conflict otherwise notable for its monstrosities."

At the heart of Dr. Johnson's saying that "every man thinks meanly of himself for not having been a soldier" are a great many childish, mud- and blood-splattered romantic notions and dreams of glory. In the context of what Caputo is saying, maybe the best reason for agreeing with the doctor is that by not putting on uniforms, we forfeited what might have been the ultimate opportunity, in increasingly self-obsessed times, of making the ultimate commitment to something greater than ourselves: the survival of comrades.

The fragging stories blurred an important realization: if anything is clear about the ethos of the American soldiers in Vietnam, it is that they weren't fighting for democracy, or against communism, but for each other.

Dr. Arthur Egendorf, a clinical psychologist now in private practice who served with Army intelligence in Vietnam and who was a principal author of the congressional study *Legacies of Vietnam,* says that for nonveterans of Vietnam, the effects of not going are "mostly negligible, not the sort of thing to talk about as mental illness. Maybe some feel actual guilt, but mostly what we see is a kind of vague malaise." Guilt—severe guilt—is still having nightmares thirteen years later because, as in the case of one of Egendorf's friends, your unit was wiped out while you were on a reconnaissance patrol. The man in question blocked from conscious recollection the names of his friends who were killed in the attack: "We went to the Vietnam memorial together, and he literally could not mobilize himself to touch the wall because he was so ashamed of not being able to remember the names of those who died. Now," says Egendorf, putting all this in sobering perspective, "*that's* guilt."

But he does have "an impression" about the impact not going had on the generation that in the main didn't.

"If there is one major strand," he says, "that is played out among the nonveterans, it's this whole thing about nonengagement, noncommitment. Service got a bad name in the last war. People who didn't serve felt vindicated for keeping clean. And the main cost of all that is much more social than in any obvious sense individual. You see a declining trust in public institutions of all sorts. It's a suspicion that *I got away with something.* There's no neurotic guilt, but there is a lingering need to cover up and justify a posture of nonengagement. It means that there are a lot of lives that are less vital because of it."

Egendorf is not at all critical of those who, as he says, took a stand against the war on political or moral grounds; in fact, he admires the courage of those who undertook nonviolent protest.

On the other hand, he says that in the course of undertaking the *Legacies* survey, he began to find that a majority of Vietnam-generation males evinced attitudes he describes as "turned-off, who cares, don't count on me."

"*That's* where the main cost lies. The form of the war experience becomes 'I got off scot-free, ha ha ha.' And that is *not* a posture on which you can build a creative, constructive, determined, self-respecting life. Those kinds of virtues come out of a sense of having given oneself, having served, standing for something. Caring enough, putting your neck out.

"So when you have deliberately not done those things—and the zeitgeist was to justify pulling out, cover your duff—then you have people fooling themselves about how to make it in the world. They bullshit themselves into thinking the great virtue is staying aloof, being noncommittal. But that's precisely what *doesn't* work. What works is to commit yourself to what you care about."

Egendorf has two last observations on all this. The first is that this guilt—or malaise—is a waste of time. It doesn't do anyone any good. "At first," he says, "it seems like a badge of worthiness. *At least I'm suffering.* It can lead to a kind of belated hero worship [of vets]. But that's useless, really, and ultimately self-destructive. What we need to muster for vets is dignity and respect. We're all partners in a prearranged marriage. There's no illusion of romance, but we do need to have respect for each other. And if we're going to have that, we're going to need forgiveness—for ourselves."

The other is that "people called the shots as best they could at the time. It's not an excuse, but a question of recognizing that the dumb thing we all do is blame ourselves for not having known what it took some crucial experience to teach us. Guilt becomes a kind of booby prize. What we need much more than that is a fresh look at what now calls for commitment."

Whether it's guilt or malaise, what I do know for certain is that if someday I have a son and he asks me what I did in the Vietnam War, I'll have to tell him that my war experience, unlike that of his grandfather, consisted of a hemorrhoid check.

Most people I know who avoided the war by one means or another do not feel the way I do, and I'm in no position to fault their reasons or their justifications.

But I do know some others who are still trying to come to terms with all this. And sometimes it comes to the surface, a sense of incompleteness . . .

"I didn't suffer with them. I didn't watch my buddies getting wiped out next to me. And though I'm relieved, at the same time I feel as though part of my reflex action is not complete."

. . . of an unpaid debt . . .

"I haven't served my country. I've never faced life or death. I'm an incomplete person. I walk by the memorial and look at the names and think, 'There but for the grace of God . . .'"

. . . of how easy it was . . .

"The dean once told me, 'You know, the one thing your generation has done is made martyrdom painless.'"

. . . of having missed history's bus . . .

"It's guilt at not having participated. At not having done anything. I blew up neither physics labs in Ann Arbor nor Vietcong installations. I just vacillated in the middle. It's still confusing to me. Only in the last few years have I tried to straighten it out in terms of my country. And now I know I should have gone, if only to bear witness."

Rosanna Warren

t he daughter of poet and novelist Robert Penn Warren and novelist Eleanor Clark, Rosanna Warren graduated summa cum laude from Yale in 1976. Her poems—intensely imagined and vividly written—have been gathered in *Snow Day* (1981), *Each Leaf Shines Separate* (1984), and *Stained Glass* (1993). She has also written a children's book and a verse translation of Euripides' *Suppliant Women*. She is a professor at Boston University and a chancellor of the Academy of American Poets. "Poetry at Yale, during my undergraduate years," she recalls, "was for me an oblique affair. I was passionately concerned to avoid taking classes with my parents' friends (most of the English department faculty, sad to say). I was also concerned with writing poems, under cover of painting paintings. The artists who guided my eyes and hands—William Bailey, Bernard Chaet, Gretna Campbell—at the same time, unwittingly (or was it wittingly?) taught me to make shapes in words. And by great good luck, shyly and unofficially, I met Richard Howard, Mark Strand, and John Hollander, and found unofficial ways to learn from their generosity."

MOMENT

When you turned to me—you in bed, still sleepwarm, against the pillows,
I across the room, skirt zipped, stockings on—
and you asked, so quietly,

"Was that a truthful answer?"

and outside our narrow third-story window
the Norway maple was poking odd thumbs into the sky
and a skim milk early morning light leaked down the street,
down front porch steps, around grimed collars of snowbanks,
and the oval Victorian mirror of my dresser
reflected all that, with odd angles of rooflines, gutters, chimneys jutting into its
        peripheral vision,

your question cut
like a knife so sharpened it
slices clean and the surprised flesh doesn't know for a moment how to bleed,

and I answered, after a pause
in which the strangeness felt like a form of love,

"No."

5 P.M.

Down Fairview, you could pluck the spine of reflected streetlight
from asphalt.

The afternoon's flesh lies loosely, likely to slip.
Rose of Sharon with its maimed hands, privet, dead morning glory,
        rhododendron

have delivered their secrets
to January rain, to the drench of early dark,

to the long-fingered interrogations of a season that prayed for snow
and was disappointed. Therefore it dissolves

tree knots, aluminum siding, cement embankments, beveled porch columns
into streaming sheets, gutter whorls, cataracts

down alley stairs; therefore it loosens roots
of azaleas defunct in ornamental gray pressed-stone garlanded pots

and floods the sarcophagi; therefore the ex-Presbyterian fieldstone church
on the corner of Fairview and South

announces "The Boston School of Modern Languages"
in an eddy of street torrents and regurgitating storm drains

and foists its mute megaphone clamped to a chimney pot
against the gargled sky.

PORTRAIT: MARRIAGE

Through the dark feathering of spruce boughs and crosshatch
     of naked lower branches, through
splatters of beechlight and beyond the shuddered patch
of sky trapped in the pond's net of depth and shade,
     you flicker into view
     a moment, then subside

into mingled inks and umbers, like the paper birch
     reflected: shaft of brilliance probing
the pond's amnesia: whole: fractured at a touch:
that's how I've seen you over the years,
     light robing and disrobing
     an image upon shaken waters;

that's how I've held you, as one embraces and loses
     the muscled slide of water in mid-
stroke, cold, hauling forward to new darkness as
it passes. Now, almost invisible at the pond's edge,
     you rake years of mud,
     leaf-mire, twiggy sludge,

and pitch it into the barrow where I hear the clank
     of tines on the metal lip, the lurch
as you trundle it back to mulch the iris bank.
Time, lord knows, has many bodies, and we learn
     slowly enough: dredge
     of mortal muck, burn

of sunlight on birchbark and, more shiftily, on
     the reflected birch. Here, you're back: flash
of ripped white T-shirt, a holler. Yes, I'll come down
and keep you company. I want to feel
     you for a moment—slapdash,
       sweaty, whole—

as the woods hang back from us. Let's make this scar
     in chiaroscuro, in the leaflit air,
let's leave traces in the fibrous soil where we are
standing for now, since now is a proposition
     molded over and over
       in water, loam, and stone.

Wendy Wasserstein

orn in Brooklyn in 1950, Wendy Wasserstein graduated from the Yale
School of Drama in 1976, where her classmates included playwrights
Christopher Durang and Albert Innaurato and actress Meryl Streep.
Wasserstein had already had a play produced off-Broadway, but her
first critical success came with *Uncommon Women* (1977) and *Isn't It Romantic*
(1981). *The Heidi Chronicles* (1988) won the Pulitzer Prize, the Tony Award for
best play, the Drama Desk Award, the New York Drama Critics' Circle prize, and
several others. *The Sisters Rosensweig* (1992) won the Outer Critics Circle Award.
She has written many other plays, screenplays, as well as a collection of comic essays, *Bachelor Girls* (1990). Baby-boomer, overeducated, anxiously feminist
women are her subject, and as she says, "serious issues and serious people can be
quite funny."

Scene 1

1965. A high-school dance, with folding chairs, streamers, and a table with a punch bowl. Two sixteen-year-old girls enter, SUSAN, *wearing a skirt and a cardigan sweater, and* HEIDI *in a traditional A-line dress. The girls find a corner and look out at the dance floor as they sing and sway to the music. "The Shoop Shoop Song" is playing. "Does he love me? I wanna know. How can I tell if he loves me so."*

SUSAN:

> Is it in his eyes?

HEIDI:

> Oh, nooooooo, you'll be deceived.

SUSAN:

> Is it in his eyes?

HEIDI:

> Oh, no, he'll make believe.

SUSAN: Heidi! Heidi! Look at the guy over at the radiator.

HEIDI: Which one?

SUSAN: In the blue jeans, tweed jacket, and the Weejuns.

HEIDI: They're all wearing that.

SUSAN: The one in the vest, blue jeans, tweed jacket, and Weejuns.

HEIDI: Cute.

SUSAN: Looks kinda like Bobby Kennedy.

HEIDI: Kinda. Yup, he's definitely cute.

SUSAN: Look! He can twist and smoke at the same time. I love that! SUSAN *unbuttons her sweater and pulls a necklace out of her purse.*

HEIDI: Susie, what are you doing?

SUSAN: Heidi, men rely on first impressions. Oh, God, he's incredible! Heidi, move!

HEIDI: What, Susie?

SUSAN: Just move! The worst thing you can do is cluster. 'Cause then it looks like you just wanna hang around with your girlfriend. But don't look desperate. Men don't dance with desperate women. Oh my God! There's one coming. Will you start moving! Trust me.

HEIDI *begins to move. She doesn't notice a boy,* CHRIS BOXER, *coming over to her.*

CHRIS: Hi.

HEIDI: Hi.

CHRIS: Hi. I'm Chris Boxer, Student Council president here.

HEIDI: I'm Heidi Holland, editor of the newspaper somewhere else.

CHRIS: Great. I knew I could talk to you. Do you want to dance? *Begins to twist.*

HEIDI: I'm sorry. I can't leave my girlfriend. *Moves back to* SUSAN.

SUSAN: I don't believe this.

HEIDI: This is my girlfriend, Susan Johnston. We came to the dance together.

CHRIS: Oh, I thought you were alone.

SUSAN: She is. We just met.

CHRIS: Well, very nice to meet you both. *Begins to walk away.*

SUSAN: Chris, don't go.

HEIDI: Please don't go. We can all dance together. We can form a line and hully-gully, baby.

CHRIS, *uncomfortable, looks around:* Well, that's the headmaster. I guess I have to go and, uh, ask him how it's going. Keep the faith. *He snaps his fingers.*

HEIDI: We will.

CHRIS *begins to walk away again.*

SUSAN *calls after him:* Nice meeting you. *Begins whispering to* HEIDI. I can't believe you did that. Heidi, we're at a dance! You know, girl meets boy. They hold hands walking in the sand. Then they go to the Chapel of Love. Get it?

HEIDI: Got it.

"Satisfaction" begins to play.

VOICE: The next dance is gonna be a Ladies' Choice.

SUSAN, *thrilled:* All right. Let's get organized here. Heidi, stand in front of me. I can't ask Twist and Smoke to dance with my skirt this long. What should I say to him? SUSAN *rolls up her skirt.*

HEIDI: Ask him how he coordinates the twisting with the smoking.

SUSAN: You know, as your best friend, I must tell you frankly that you're going to get really messed up unless you learn to take men seriously.

HEIDI: Susan, there is absolutely no difference between you and me and him. Except that he can twist and smoke at the same time and we can get out of gym with an excuse called "I have my monthly."

SUSAN: Shit! It's still too long. *Continues to roll the waist of her skirt until it is mid-thigh.* Can you get home all right by yourself?

HEIDI: He'll never even suspect I even know you.

SUSAN: Wish me luck!

HEIDI *kisses her on the cheek:* Luck!

SUSAN *jumps back in horror:* Heidi! Don't!

HEIDI: Keep the faith! *Snaps her fingers as* CHRIS BOXER *did.*

SUSAN: Shhhhh! Don't make me laugh or my skirt will roll down.

HEIDI: I'll call you tomorrow.

SUSAN *exits as she waves good-bye to* HEIDI. HEIDI *sits on a chair, takes out a book, reads it for a moment, then puts it on her lap as she stares out. "Play with Fire" is played.* PETER, *a young man in a St. Mark's school blazer, approaches. He looks at her. She smiles and looks down.*

PETER: You must be very bright.

HEIDI: Excuse me?

PETER: You look so bored you must be very bright.

HEIDI: I'm sorry?

PETER: Don't be sorry. I appreciate bored people. Bored, depressed, anxious. These are the qualities I look for in a woman. Your lady friend is dancing with the gentleman who looks like Bobby Kennedy. I find men who smoke and twist at the same time so dreary.

HEIDI: Not worth the coordination, really.

PETER: Do you have any?

HEIDI: I can sit and read at the same time.

PETER: What book is that?

HEIDI: *Death Be Not Proud.*

PETER: Of course.

HEIDI: A favorite of mine at dances.

PETER: I was drawn to you from the moment I saw you shielding that unfortunate wench rolling up her garments in the tempest.

HEIDI: I'm sorry.

PETER: Please. Don't apologize for being the most attractive woman on this cruise.

HEIDI: Cruise?

PETER: She docks tonight in Portsmouth. And then farewell to the *Queen Mary.* Forever to harbor in Long Beach, California. *C'est triste, n'est pas?*

HEIDI: *Ce n'est pas bon.*

PETER, *excitedly:* Our tragic paths were meant to cross. I leave tomorrow for the sanatorium in Zurich. *Coughs.*

HEIDI: How odd! I'm going to the sanatorium in Milan. *Coughs. He offers her his handkerchief. She refuses.*

PETER: My parents are heartbroken. They thought I was entering Williams College in the fall.

HEIDI: My parents put down a deposit at Vassar.

PETER: We've only this night together. I'm Peter, a small noise from Winnetka. I tried to pick out your name . . . Amanda, Lady Clara, Estelle . . .

HEIDI: It's . . .

PETER: No, don't tell me. I want to remember you as you are. Beside me in the moonlight, the stars above us . . .

HEIDI: The sea below us.

PETER: Glenn Miller and the orchestra. It's all so peaceful.

HEIDI: Mmmmmm. Quite peaceful.

"The Shoop Shoop Song" is heard again.

PETER: The twist-and-smokers are heaving themselves on their lady friends. This must be the final song. Would you do me the honor of one dance?

HEIDI: Certainly.

PETER: Ahhh! "The Shoop Shoop Song." Baroque but fragile.

HEIDI: Melodic but atonal.

PETER: Will you marry me?

HEIDI: I covet my independence.

PETER: Perhaps when you leave the sanatorium, you'll think otherwise. I want to know you all my life. If we can't marry, let's be great friends.

HEIDI: I will keep your punch cup, as a memento, beside my pillow.

PETER: Well, shall we hully-gully, baby?

HEIDI: Really, I . . .

PETER: Don't worry. I'll teach you.

He begins to do a form of shimmy line dance. Holding Heidi's hand, he instructs her. The dance is somewhat interpretive and becomes a minuet. They sing as they dance together.

PETER:

    How 'bout the way he acts?

HEIDI:

    Oh, noooo, that's not the way.

PETER:

    And you're not listenin' to all I say.
    If you wanna know if he loves you so . . .

Takes Heidi's waist and dips her.

PETER:

    It's in his kiss.

HEIDI & PETER:

        Oh, yeah! It's in his kiss!

They continue to dance as the lights fade.

Scene 2

1968. A dance. There are "Eugene McCarthy for President" signs. "Take a Piece of My Heart," by Janis Joplin and Big Brother and the Holding Company, can be heard. A hippie in a Sergeant Pepper jacket smokes a joint. When HEIDI *enters, he offers her a drag.* HEIDI, *wearing a floral shawl, refuses and stands by the food table.* SCOOP ROSENBAUM, *intense but charismatic, in blue jeans and work shirt, goes over to her. He takes a beer from a bucket on stage.*

SCOOP: Are you guarding the chips?

HEIDI: No.

SCOOP: Then you're being very difficult.

HEIDI: Please, help yourself.

SCOOP: Where are you going?

HEIDI: I'm trying to listen to the music.

SCOOP: Janis Joplin and Big Brother and the Holding Company. A— singer. C+ band. Far less innovative than the Kinks. You know, you really have one hell of an inferiority complex.

HEIDI: I do?

SCOOP: Sure. I have no right to say you're difficult. Don't you believe in human dignity? I mean, you're obviously a liberal, or you wouldn't be here.

HEIDI: I came with a friend.

SCOOP: You came to Manchester, New Hampshire, in a blizzard to ring doorbells for Gene McCarthy because of a friend? Why the fuck didn't you go skiing instead?

HEIDI: I don't ski.

SCOOP *offers* HEIDI *a potato chip:* B— texture. C+ crunch. You go to one of those Seven Sister schools?

HEIDI: How did you know?

SCOOP: You're all concerned citizens.

HEIDI: I told you, I came because of a friend.

SCOOP: That's bullshit. Be real. You're neat and clean for Eugene. You think if you go door to door and ring bells, this sucker will become president, and we'll all be good people, and wars in places you've never heard of before will end, and everyone will have enough to eat and send their daughters to Vassar. Like I said, neat and clean for Eugene.

HEIDI: Would you excuse me?

SCOOP *smiles and extends his hand to her:* It's been lovely chatting with me.

HEIDI: A pleasure.

SCOOP: What's your name?

HEIDI: Susan.

SCOOP: Susan what?

HEIDI: Susan Johnston. See ya.

SCOOP: Hey, Susan Johnston, wouldn't you like to know who I am?

HEIDI: Uh . . .

SCOOP: C'mon. Nice girl like you isn't going to look a man in the eye and tell him, "I have absolutely no interest in you. You've been incredibly obnoxious and your looks are B–."

HEIDI: Why do you grade everything?

SCOOP: I used to be a very good student.

HEIDI: Used to?

SCOOP: I dropped out of Princeton. The Woodrow Wilson School of International Bullshit.

HEIDI: So what do you do now?

SCOOP: This and that. Here and there.

HEIDI: You work for McCarthy? Well, you *are* at a McCarthy dance.

SCOOP: I came with a friend. Susan, don't you know this is just the tip of the iceberg? McCarthy is irrelevant. He's a C+ Adlai Stevenson. The changes in this country could be enormous. Beyond anything your sister mind can imagine.

HEIDI: Are you a real-life radical?

SCOOP: You mean, do I make bombs in my parents' West Hartford basement? Susan, how could I be a radical? I played lacrosse at Exeter and I'm a Jew whose first name is Scoop. You're not very good at nuance. And you're too eager to categorize. I'm a journalist. I'm just here to have a look around.

HEIDI: Do you work for a paper?

SCOOP: Did they teach you at Vassar to ask so many inane questions in order to keep a conversation going?

HEIDI: Well, like I said, I have to go meet my friend.

SCOOP: Me too. I have to meet Paul Newman.

HEIDI: Please tell him Susan says "Hi."

SCOOP: You don't believe I have to meet Paul Newman.

HEIDI: I'm sure you do.

SCOOP: I'm picking him up at the airport and taking him and Mr. McCarthy to a press conference. Paul's a great guy. Why don't you come drinking with us? We can rap over a few brews.

HEIDI: I'm sorry. I can't.

SCOOP: Why not?

HEIDI: I just can't.

SCOOP: Susan, let me get this straight. You would rather drive back to Poughkeepsie with five virgins in a Volkswagen discussing Norman Mailer and birth control on dangerous frozen roads than go drinking with Eugene McCarthy, Paul Newman, and Scoop Rosenbaum? You're cute, Susan. Very cute.

HEIDI: And you are really irritating!

SCOOP: That's the first honest thing you've said all night! Lady, you better learn to stand up for yourself. I'll let you in on a scoop from Scoop.

HEIDI: Did they teach you construction like that at Princeton?

SCOOP: I dig you, Susan. I dig you a lot.

HEIDI: Can we say "like" instead of "dig"? I mean, while I am standing up for myself . . .

SCOOP: I like you, Susan. You're prissy, but I like you a lot.

HEIDI: Well, I don't know if I like you.

SCOOP: Why should you like me? I'm arrogant and difficult. But I'm very smart. So you'll put up with me. What?

HEIDI: What what?

SCOOP: You're thinking something.

HEIDI: Actually, I was wondering what mothers teach their sons that they never bother to tell their daughters.

SCOOP: What do you mean?

HEIDI: I mean, why the fuck are you so confident?

SCOOP: Ten points for Susan!

HEIDI: Have we moved on to points, from letter grades?

SCOOP: There's hope for you. You're going to be quite the little politico.

HEIDI: I'm planning to be an art historian.

SCOOP: Please don't say that. That's really suburban.

HEIDI: I'm interested in the individual expression of the human soul. Content over form.

SCOOP: But I thought the point of contemporary art is that the form becomes the content. Look at Albers' "Homage to a Square." Three superimposed squares, and we're talking perception, integration, isolation. Just three squares, and they reflect the gross inadequacies of our society. Therefore, your argument is inconclusive.

HEIDI: Don't give me a Marxist interpretation of Albers.

SCOOP: You really are one fuck of a liberal! Next thing you'll tell me is how much Herbert Marcuse means to you. What?

HEIDI: Nothing.

SCOOP: I don't fuckin' believe it! You've never read Marcuse!

HEIDI: Isn't Paul Newman waiting for you, Scoop?

SCOOP: Isn't your friend waiting for you, *Heidi? Jumps up.* Basket, Rosenbaum. Thirty points. The score is 30 to 10.

HEIDI: How did you know my name?

SCOOP: I told you I'm a journalist. Do you really think anything—*takes out the paper to show her*—gets by the *Liberated Earth News?*

HEIDI: That's your paper?

SCOOP: Editor in chief. Circulation 362 and growing. Okay. Truth. I know your name is Heidi because it says so right here—*looks in the paper and then up at her breast*—on your name tag. Heidi. H-E-I-D-I.

HEIDI: Oh!

SCOOP: Ohh!

HEIDI: Oh, well . . . *Begins to pull the tag off.*

SCOOP: You don't have to look at the floor.

HEIDI: I'm not.

SCOOP: I've got nothing on you so far. Why are you so afraid to speak up?

HEIDI: I'm not afraid to speak up.

SCOOP: Heidi, you don't understand. You're the one this is all going to affect. You're the one whose life this will all change significantly. Has to. You're a very serious person. In fact, you're the unfortunate contradiction in terms—a serious good person. And I envy you that.

HEIDI: Thank you. I guess.

SCOOP: Yup. You'll be one of those true believers who didn't understand it was all just a phase. The Trotskyite during Lenin's New Economic Policy. The worshiper of fallen images in Christian Judea.

HEIDI: And you?

SCOOP: Me? I told you. I'm just here to have a look around.

HEIDI: What if you get left behind?

SCOOP: You mean if, after all the politics, you girls decide to go "hog wild," demanding equal pay, equal rights, equal orgasms?

HEIDI: All people deserve to fulfill their potential.

SCOOP: Absolutely.

HEIDI: I mean, why should some well-educated woman waste her life making you and your children tuna-fish sandwiches?

SCOOP: She shouldn't. And, for that matter, neither should a badly educated woman. Heidella, I'm on your side.

HEIDI: Don't call me Heidella. It's diminutive.

SCOOP: You mean "demeaning," and it's not. It's endearing.

HEIDI: You're deliberately eluding my train of thought.

SCOOP: No. I'm subtly asking you to go to bed with me . . . before I go meet Paul Newman.

Pause.

HEIDI: Oh.

SCOOP: You have every right to say no. I can't guarantee absolute equality of experience.

HEIDI: I can take care of myself, thanks.

SCOOP: You've already got the lingo down, kiddo. Pretty soon you'll be burning bras.

HEIDI: Maybe I'll go "hog wild."

SCOOP: I hope so. Are you a virgin?

HEIDI: Excuse me?

SCOOP: If you choose to accept this mission, I'll find out one way or the other.

HEIDI,   *embarrassed:* That's okay.

SCOOP: Why do you cover your mouth when you talk about sex?

HEIDI: Hygiene.

SCOOP   *takes her hand away from her mouth:* I told you. You're a serious good person. And I'm honored. Maybe you'll think fondly of all this in some Proustian haze when you're thirty-five and picking your daughter up from Ethical Culture School to escort her to cello class before dinner with Dad, the noted psychiatrist and Miró poster collector.

HEIDI: No. I'll be busy torching lingerie.

SCOOP: Maybe I'll remember it one day when I'm thirty-five and watching my son's performance as Johnny Appleseed. Maybe I'll look at my wife, who puts up with me, and flash on when I was editor of a crackpot liberal newspaper and thought I could fall in love with Heidi Holland, the canvassing art historian, that first snowy night in Manchester, New Hampshire, 1968.

HEIDI: Are you guarding the chips?

SCOOP: No. I trust them.

He kisses her passionately as "White Rabbit" begins playing. SCOOP *then looks at his watch and gathers his coat. He begins to leave the room and turns back to* HEIDI. *She looks at her watch and follows him. He clenches his fist in success.*

Karl Kirchwey

arl Kirchwey was born in 1956 and graduated from Yale in 1979. He is the author of three collections of poems: *A Wandering Island* (1990), *Those I Guard* (1993), and *The Engrafted Word* (1998). He has won the Rome Prize in Literature and was the influential director of the 92nd Street Y Unterberg Poetry Center in New York City from 1987 to 2000. In September 2000, he became director of creative writing and senior lecturer in the arts at Bryn Mawr College. His poems are elegantly knotted and cunningly argued. "On Tuesday afternoons each week, in the autumn of my senior year (this is now more than twenty years ago)," writes Kirchwey, "I sat in a Georgian conference room in Silliman College around a polished wood table. The room's only furnishing was a large disheveled pile of mimeographed poems in the middle of the table. The poet drew from this pile, seemingly at random, in the course of our two hours together. And he talked—with a depth and range of knowledge, and with a vehemence of opinion, I had never heard before. It was as if all other disciplines, all other fields of knowledge, were skills necessary to the understanding of poetry. I had made my own gestures toward mastering the skills I thought necessary for a vocation I did not yet know. I had studied music. I had studied a different modern language every year. Now, as I listened, it was poetry that comprehended the world. It comprehended me and everyone else at that table. But only if we could be educated out of our pieties, our commonplace ways of seeing and feeling. Suddenly the vocation of poet became real to me and even the wretched academic and personal stumblings of my preceding three years made a kind of sense. Poetry was something to which one could devote one's life."

DEER ISLE

What was I reading on the spavined bed?
You sang to the dark pines and the granite shore,
patient, measure by measure, getting it right:
And though worms destroy this body,
yet in my flesh shall I see God.
Later we sat together and drank Moosehead
and watched a crossbill parse the cones of spruce—
a heap of gold flakes, a dark period—
and there was a sufficiency in all of it.
Then dusk came, and the bitter gray water
brimmed in silence over the broken stones.
The cottage is gone from where it stood once;
the lines are gone that swam before my eyes,
the senses' proof: but you signed the air hugely.

I-91

Bowling down the Interstate
in my plush jewel, my '91 Merc,
listening to a jive station
in the odometer's glow
as Hartford swam into view,

I saw the red skirts of a hawk
flash like an exclamation
and stoop by the freckled rib
of the steel barrier,
unspooling, in one dead drop,

toward what it had seen there
on the pallid median:
the pungent rag of a skunk,
a mad raccoon on its side,
or the bloated corpse of a doe.

Numbers scrolled backward and stopped,
or seemed to, anyway.
That cheek, famished by the air

of snowless February,
those wings, mantled on the void—

what were the crystal cube,
the lights threaded in their loop,
or song in ecstasy's counterfeit,
next to that helix, splayed
by the will's sudden compression,

driven and consummate?

FIVE ISLANDS

(for Joseph Donovan)

In front of the Church of Our Lady of the Rocks,
    the Five Islands Banana Company truck is delivering again.
Why bananas for a church? All is not what it looks
    to be. Sparrows are busy around the Corinthian

columns which, in a few weeks, will be complicated
    with ivy, their flutes infested and percolating
with song, the world's body pierced and penetrated
    by those houseless birds and their secret fluttering

among the crooked runners of my vainglory.
    In the wisdom of God, the world through wisdom did not
know God. But why bananas for a church? Again I see
    a galvanized roof blazing in sunlight;

a board across two stones is loaded with manioc,
    mottled grapefruit and a crown of bananas
like a fist upthrust in greeting, out of the woodsmoke,
    the wet scent and the difference of that place,

the aroma of life for them maybe leading to life,
    those whose names I saw in gold on a church wall
in Castries once: Victor Regis, Michael Octave,
    Sandra Saint-Ange, Ruth Theobalds, Marcellus Raphael;

or the boat that slept, past the lifting wave, on its side,
    glimpsed through the blue smoke of an idling motor
in Passion Week, which was called *Help Me God*.
    (The truck is delivering to a hospital around the corner.)

DURING THE BALKANS WAR

The afternoon sun, departing, lights up
    the woods opposite in one recondite knoll
as if to say—Have you considered the ardor deep
    in this particular color sequence, at all?

Blown up by the guns of learning, four walls of a schoolhouse
    stagger back, lost in the gold of a glade
(the globe's round O, the stained and variegated Mercators),
    the easy shells pitched in from a bend in the road

where the rising earth-tones, spattered sugar maple
    and burning sumac have anticipated
the human taste for cruelty without scruple:
    their cattle shot, their eiderdowns gutted,

and the brain of Pajazit Deliaj placed on a mattress
    to witness his murdered wife Hava's body.
Once a child read a history book in this place
    and raised her eyes to the infant century,

her mind lit up by so much gold past the windows,
    past the smell of damp wool, of plaster-and-lath
—like the haggard gold of Albanian Kosovo's
    churches, claimed by the Serbs and their Orthodox faith.

October 1998

David Hirson

orn in New York City, David Hirson graduated from Yale College in 1980. As a student he was commissioned to translate Alessandro Scarlatti's 1690 opera *Gli equivoci nel sembiante,* which was performed at Yale and later broadcast on public radio. He went on to study at Oxford and began writing for the *Times Literary Supplement* and the *London Review of Books.* His first play, *La Bête*—an astonishing display of virtuosity, set in the time of Molière and written in rhyming couplets—opened on Broadway in 1991 and received the Outer Critics Circle's John Gassner Award. Its London production earned him the 1992 Laurence Olivier Award for comedy of the year. His second play, *Wrong Mountain,* opened on Broadway in 2000. Echoing what many writers feel, Hirson writes: "I doubt I would have become any kind of writer without the encouragement of a great teacher. Alice Miskimin, a Chaucer scholar who led my section of English 25 in freshman year, managed to divine, from the lumpish incomprehensibility of my undergraduate prose, a voice (or a sensibility, at least) that she took it upon herself to cultivate. A decade later, after my first play opened on Broadway, I sent her a copy of the text with a letter of thanks, wondering if she would even remember me. She did, and her reply sparkled with a quality of mind and generosity of spirit that made me envy my eighteen-year-old self for ever having had the luck to encounter her. 'It will last,' she said of the play; for me, what has lasted from English 25 is a sense of how rigor and anarchy can happily co-exist in a work of art, and a love of language that was inspired by a teacher in whose debt I shall always remain."

Before the curtain rises, Dorine appears. She surveys the audience and is gone.

The antechamber of the dining room in the actors' cottage: a blazing white environment furnished with a gilt chair and table. Busts of Greek and Roman orators line the cornice. Enter Elomire, storming into the room, followed by Bejart.

ELOMIRE:

    I shall not tolerate another word.

BEJART:

        But Elomire . . .

ELOMIRE:

                Enough, I said . . .

BEJART:

                        I heard!

ELOMIRE:

    THAT COCKATRICE . . . !

BEJART:

                    Shhhhhhh!

ELOMIRE: (*Whispering, but viva voce.*)

                    Do it! Throw him out!!

BEJART:

    Good Lord! You whisper . . .

ELOMIRE:

                  . . . louder than I shout?

So I've been told. Well, good! It's for the better.
(*Booming.*)
LET'S HOPE WE'RE OVERHEARD DOWN TO THE LETTER . . . !

BEJART:

    You carry on as if we had a choice!

ELOMIRE:

    We do!

BEJART:

        No!

ELOMIRE:

            Bejart, listen to my voice:
Our patronage, you say, requires that we
Add one more player to our company;
The rationale for this escapes me quite . . .
(*Bejart begins to protest, but Elomire anticipates.*)
        BUT . . . knowing that the Court is always right,

I'm willing to oblige without dispute.

However, on one point I'm resolute:

A rash selection simply isn't wise,

(*Pointing to the other room.*)

And *that* bombastic ninny I despise!

Naught could induce me, save a Holy Writ,

To share the stage with that dull hypocrite!

(*Bejart extracts a document from his sleeve.*)

What's that?

BEJART:

                         A writ.

ELOMIRE:

                    You mock me.

BEJART:

                              Au contraire:

(*Elomire, gasping, snatches the document from Bejart's hand and buries his
     nose in it.*)

The Prince, it seems, *adores* Monsieur Valere;

And though you say he cannot be abided,

Apparently the matter's been decided . . . !

ELOMIRE: (*Slumping into a chair, groaning.*)

     O GOD!! I'M GOING TO DIE!!

BEJART:

                         Well, even so . . .

ELOMIRE:

     BUT I *DETEST* Valere . . . !!

BEJART:

                         We know, we *know:*

Repeatedly you've made that understood!

Withal, the fact remains, our livelihood

Depends upon a Court decree, and since

Valere's thought so amusing by the Prince,

Not only are we bound to cast him . . . WORSE!

(*Bejart points to a specific clause in the document; Elomire reads, incredulously.*)

ELOMIRE:

     "The troupe—might—even—stage his—comic verse"!?

I'm breaking out in hives! This is obscene!

What verse? That doggerel that, in between

Great gulps of *my* Bordeaux, he dared recite?—

In love with his own voice, the *parasite!*

"Self-cherishing" is much too mild a phrase

To give a sense of the coquettish ways
He forms a sentence, flirting like a girl:
The tiny cough that says,
(*With a tiny cough.*)
                                        "I've dropped a pearl,"
The eyelids all a-flutter, and the sniff
While striking poses with his handkerchief!
For all of that, he never speaks . . . he *spits!*
I almost drowned in that man's affricates!
AND HE COMPARES HIMSELF TO SCARAMOUCHE!!
O, really, he's just so grotesquely *louche*
On all accounts I'd say. Don't you agree?

BEJART: (*Hedging.*)
Well, what about his generosity
In showing admiration for your plays . . . ?

ELOMIRE:
I'd much prefer his censure to his praise!
Beware of men who laud you to the skies:
It is *themselves* they mean to lionize!
Valere finds what he thinks I'd like to hear,
Then spouts some panegyric that will steer
The conversation back to his *renown!*
(*Imitating Valere.*)
"But have you seen my own, *The Dying Clown?*"
(*Ridiculing it.*)
The Dying Clown!

BEJART:
                                        I saw it!

ELOMIRE: (*Surprised.*)
                                        Really? Where?

BEJART:
A year ago in Brussels, at a fair.

ELOMIRE:
Well, was it good?

BEJART:
                                        I don't remember now;
(*But he gradually begins to remember.*)
It was a pantomime . . . he had a . . .
(*Squinting in disbelief at the memory.*)
                                        . . . COW . . .
Dressed up as Anne of Austria!

ELOMIRE: (*Keening.*)

O PLEASE!!

(*Slumping to his knees.*)

> Look here Bejart: I'm getting on my knees
> To beg the Lord that we be spared this hell:
> "Dear God, we pray . . ."

(*To Bejart.*)

. . . get on your knees as well!

(*Bejart ignores him.*)

> "DEAR GOD, WE PRAY . . ."

(*Clutching the pocket of Bejart's coat and pulling him down to his knees.*)

. . . I *mean* it, man, get *down!*

> "DEAR GOD, WE PRAY YOU LOOK UPON THIS TOWN
> WHERE SEVEN HUMBLE ACTORS MAKE THEIR HOME
> THANKS TO PRINCE CONTI, BY WHOSE GRACE WE ROAM
> THE COUNTRYSIDE ITINERANT NO MORE . . ."

BEJART:

> Amen.

ELOMIRE:

> *Amen?* What did you say that for?

BEJART:

> I thought you'd finished.

ELOMIRE:

No.

BEJART: (*Fed up with the histrionics.*)

May we get up!?

ELOMIRE:

> "DEAR GOD . . ."

BEJART:

I'm standing . . .

ELOMIRE: (*Reaching out and restraining Bejart.*)

". . . FROM THY BRIMMING CUP

> OF MERCY LET US DRINK . . ."

BEJART: (*Trying to stand.*)

Let go!

ELOMIRE:

STAY THERE!

BEJART:

> O, stop it, Elomire! Since when is prayer
> A genuine expression of your creed . . . ?

ELOMIRE:

    When all else fails, goddammit!

BEJART:

                            Damn indeed.

ELOMIRE:

    All right, then: tell me, what do you propose
    Aside from *"pity, that's the way it goes"?*
    How very helpful, what a good solution;
    I do applaud your stunning contribution . . .

BEJART:

    We simply have no choice!

ELOMIRE:

                       Depressing beast.

BEJART:

    At least I'm honest . . .

ELOMIRE:

                    At the *very* least!
    Such honesty makes liars of us all:
    Just *kneeling* next to you makes me feel small!
    Forgive my lack of rectitude, but I,
    Immorally, must falsely hope, or die;
    Because the merest thought that this *Valere*
    Should be forever tangled in my hair
    Is so repellent, so abjectly grim,
    That, forced to choose between an hour with him
    And hanging by my thumbs in Zanzibar . . .

BEJART:

    Now don't you think you're taking this too far . . . ?

ELOMIRE:

    . . . or writhing in a scalding tub of lye . . .

BEJART:

    What would it hurt to give the man a try . . . ?

ELOMIRE:

    . . . or rotting in a ditch consumed by lice . . .

BEJART:

    In time, I'm sure we'll find he's very nice . . .

ELOMIRE:

    . . . or wracked with plague, bubonic glands protruding . . .

(*Enter Valere.*)

VALERE:

    GENTLEMEN! I hope I'm not intruding . . .

ELOMIRE: (*Through clenched teeth.*)
>
> That *voice!* Mon *Dieu!*

VALERE: (*Seeing Elomire kneeling.*)
>
> > > Good Lord! You're deep in prayer . . .

BEJART:
>
> No, no. Come in. Come in, Monsieur Valere.

ELOMIRE: (*Rolling his eyes at Bejart.*)
>
> Come *in* . . . ?

VALERE: Well Heaven Bless Us! *NOW* I see:
>
> It was a sudden burst of piety
> That took you from the table, am I right?

(*Bejart opens his mouth to speak.*)
>
> I'm so relieved! I thought, perhaps, your flight
> Was caused by something *I* had said or done . . .

(*Elomire opens his mouth to speak.*)
>
> No, don't explain. GOD BLESS US EVERY ONE!
> I, too, am *very* pious, *most* devout:
> I cross myself . . . twelve times (or thereabout)
> *Before* I take my morning tea each day!
> At lunch I'm up to forty; and I'd say
> By nightfall it's . . . a staggering amount;
> But what a foolish waste of time to count!

(*Sniffs and extends handkerchief.*)
>
> DEVOTION COMES TO NOTHING IF WE COME
> TO SUMMARIZE DEVOTION IN A SUM.

(*A slight cough, eyelids flutter, and a self-loving bow.*)
>
> A tiny play on words . . . doth please you not?
> I swear I made it up right on the spot!
> I don't know *how* I do it, I just . . . do.
> These epigrams, they . . . come to me as dew
> Collects upon a budding daffodil . . .
> A curse? A blessing? Call it what you will,
> It's mine to bear this "genius of the word"—
> DID I SAY "GENIUS"?: I think it's absurd
> When people call you that, don't you agree?
> To us it comes like breath: so naturally.
> It seems like sorcery to those below!
> I cite that telling phrase from Cicero:
> "DE BONUM EST" . . . "DIS BONUM EST" . . . O, shit . . .
> Well, anyway, you get the gist of it.
> I *do* love Latin. Does it show? It's *true!*

I'm something of a scholar in it, too.
I've read them all (yes, even *I'm* impressed)
From Cicero to . . .
(*Nervous gulp.*)

                 . . . you know . . . all the rest . . .
Whom I could quote in full without abatement:
But I digress . . .

ELOMIRE: (*Under his breath.*)

           O, what an understatement.

VALERE:

That meal! You must have gone to great expense!
How cruel of me to keep you in suspense!
DID I enjoy it? *WAS* the meal a hit?
(*A long pause.*)

He turns them slowly, slowly on the spit.
(*Thinking he has tortured them, he expounds jubilantly.*)

Be at your ease, my friends! I thought the meal
Was excellent . . . if not . . . you know . . . "ideal."
The vinaigrette: a touch acidic, no?
And I prefer less runny *haricots*;
(*Singing this line.*)

More butter in the velouté next time;
And who, for heaven's sake, told you that lime
Could substitute for lemon in soufflé . . . ?
These tiny points aside, please let me pay
My compliments to all your company,
So generous in breaking bread with me
(Albeit bread that was a wee bit stale);
But I don't want to nitpick. Did I fail
To mention what a charming group they *are?*
Marquise-Therese! *She's* going to be a *star!*
No, no . . . I'm *sure* of it! I *know* these things!
So
(*Cupping his hands over imaginary breasts.*)

       "gifted," and I'm told she even sings!
As for the others, well they tend to be
A little too . . .
(*With a theatrical flourish.*)

            . . . "theatrical" for me . . .
But, *darling,* otherwise, words can't *describe*
My deep affection for your little tribe

With whom, I do amuse myself to think,
I shall be privileged to eat and drink
(As we have done this evening) every night!
That is, of course, assuming it's all right.
Am I mistaken? Stop me if I am . . .
But it seemed obvious to this old ham
That we had an immediate rapport!
Well-educated people I adore!
It's such a joy to know there's no confusion
When I, whose speech is peppered with allusion,
Refer to facts which few but scholars know:
Arcane, pedantic things like . . .

(*Nervous gulp.*)

                                    . . . Cicero . . .

And . . . other larnèd oddments of that kind
(*Indicating himself.*)

          (Which, to the truly cultivated mind,
          Are common knowledge more than erudition . . .)
          But I digress!
(*Slapping his own wrist.*)

               O, damn me to perdition!
(*To himself.*)

          "SHUT UP! SHUT UP! GIVE SOMEONE *ELSE* A CHANCE!"
(*He covers his mouth with his hands for a beat; then, unable to contain himself for
          more than a second, he plows on.*)

          I've had that said to me all over France . . .
          All over Europe, if the truth be told:
          To babble on completely uncontrolled
          Is such a dreadful, *dreadful, DREADFUL* vice!
          Me, I keep my sentences concise
          And to the point . . . (well, nine times out of ten):
          Yes, humanly, I falter now and then
          And when I do, naive enthusiasm
          Incites a sort of logorrheic spasm:
          A flood! I mean I don't come up for air!
          And even though such episodes are rare
          I babble on . . . you can't *imagine* how . . .
          (My God! I'm almost doing it right now!)
          NO, NO! I'M ONLY JOKING! NOT TO FEAR!
          In fact, I'm far *more* guilty, so I hear,
          Of smugly showing that "My lips are sealed . . ."

When *I'm* the leading expert in the field!
Of haughtily refusing to debate
When I could easily pontificate!
Instead, I turn away with icy mien
And look . . . intimidatingly serene:
As if—you know—the wisdom of the ages
Were silently inscribed upon the pages
Of some majestic tablet in my mind.
But I lay claim to nothing of the kind!
It's others who surround me with this lore;
Myself, I know I'm just a troubadour
With very few accomplishments to boast . . .
But, then, I'm more self-critical than most.
You think me *too* self-critical?! Alack,
Ten thousand *more* have launched the same attack!
(*Weighing the gem.*)
That's awfully good: ". . . have launched the same attack!"
"Ten thousand *more* have launched the same attack!"
(*With an oratorical flourish.*)
"YOU THINK ME TOO SELF-CRITICAL?! ALACK,
TEN THOUSAND *MORE* HAVE LAUNCHED THE SAME
ATTACK!
(*The gem is priceless! Thunderstruck.*)
That's *VERY* close to genius, don't you think?
If only . . .
(*Searching the room with his eyes.*)
. . . YES! You *HAVE* a quill and ink!
(*Rushes to them.*)
I *would* be very grateful . . . may I please?
No time to lose when lightning strikes the trees!
What did I say again? How did it go?
(*As he thinks, a rolling hand gesture to Elomire and Bejart.*)
(Keep talking . . . I'm still listening, you know:
This won't take me a second.) Yes, that's right!
(*Scribbling it down.*)
"Ten thousand more . . ." O, what a pure delight!
One must act quickly on one's inspirations
That they're preserved for future generations;
Behaving otherwise, it seems to me,
Ignores the grave responsibility
Imposed on us (for it's not ours to choose)

By . . . what?
(*Forms inverted commas with fingers.*)
               . . . "the lyric gift" . . . "the tragic muse" . . .
I translate rudely from the words in Greek;
But any tongue sounds coarse when used to speak
Of something so ineffable and high.
Believe me, greater scriveners than I . . .
(All right, not "greater," "different": is that fair?)
Have racked their brains and torn out all their hair
In vain pursuit of some linguistic sign
By which mankind might utter the divine.
But what?—"afflatus"? "talent"?—they're too crude,
And I'm a stickler for exactitude
Who chafes at clumsy, earthbound turns of phrase.
True eloquence rings out like godly praise:
There's no mistaking it, it just takes wing.
And, frankly, my own phrase, "THE WONDROUS *THING,*"
Seems loftiest . . . more lofty than the Greek!
O! HOW DISGRACEFUL! SLAP ME ON THE CHEEK!
WHAT HUBRIS! WHAT VULGARITY! WHAT NERVE!
NO, SLAP ME! SLAP ME! THAT'S WHAT I DESERVE!
What gall that *I,* the commonest of sods,
Presume to speak more finely than the gods!
Of *course* it may be true, that's not the *point!*
What's ugly is my choosing to anoint
Myself instead of giving you the chance.
No doubt you both must look at me askance
For such a gross, conceited indiscretion:
I pray it won't affect your good impression.
I'm so relieved to get *that* off my chest!
Now that we've put that nagging point to rest
I shall return to my initial theme,
Which is, in short, in fact, to wit, I deem
By way of introduction, SILENCE ALL:
(*A pause. Then, with fatuous self-ridicule.*)
I HAVEN'T GOT A CLUE! BLANK AS A WALL!
NO, *REALLY,* I'M QUITE SENILE! IT'S NO JOKE!
MY HEAD IS LIKE AN EGG WITHOUT A YOLK!
AND DON'T THINK THIS IS JUST A WAY OF STALLING . . .
MY MIND HAS *BUCKLED*—ISN'T THAT *APPALLING!?*
THERE'S NOTHING BUT A SPACE BETWEEN MY EARS!

(*Change of tone.*)

   One time I had amnesia in Algiers,
   Where everyone is *black* who isn't *white!*
   (But that's another tale . . .

(*With a wink.*)

            . . . some other night.)
   Suffice to say I lost a whole December . . .
   Or was it August? . . . Whoops, I don't remember!
   You see how absent-minded I can get!?

(*Acting both parts.*)

   "WHEN DID YOU HAVE AMNESIA?" "I FORGET!"

(*He laughs, thrilled.*)

   Is that not comic genius? I must use it!
   I'd better write it down before I lose it!
   What did I say . . . again . . . about forgetting . . . ?
   O CHRIST! I've just FORGOTTEN! How UPSETTING!

(*Shaking his fist at the sky.*)

   COME BACK! COME BACK, YOU TANTALIZING GEM!
   YOU TEASE! YOU BITCH! YOU FICKLE APOTHEGM!
   I GAVE YOU LIFE, AND NOW YOU FLY FROM ME!!

(*Apologetically.*)

   This happens with annoying frequency.
   It leads me to exclaim and caterwaul!
   Well! Now you've *really* seen me, *warts and all.*

(*Suddenly remembering.*)

   ALGERIAN AMNESIA! . . .

(*Disappointed.*)

            . . . no, that's wrong;
   O, never mind. More gems will come along;
   They always do. Now *where* was I? . . . Ah, yes:
   You've seen me in a state of stark undress,
   My warts exposed, my manner slightly odd:
   Well, what would you prefer? Some cheap facade
   Of blemishless perfection? Not from ME!

(*With a dismissive flick of the wrist.*)

   GO ELSEWHERE, YE WHO SEEK DISHONESTY;
   MY LIFE IS TRUTH, AND TRUTH MY GREATEST PASSION!

(*Dawning, a revelation.*)

   Good heavens, both of you are looking . . . ashen!
   I've been *too* honest, haven't I? But *when?*
   WHY CAN'T I LEARN RESTRAINT LIKE OTHER MEN

INSTEAD OF SPILLING EVERYTHING AT ONCE?

(*Realizing.*)

       THE VINAIGRETTE! OF COURSE! I'M SUCH A DUNCE!

       HOW COULD I? Please accept my deep regret!

(*Putting on his best face.*)

       Look, I . . . *enjoy* . . . acidic . . . vinaigrette . . .

       It really makes me . . .

(*Exploding.*)

       . . . GAG!!! . . . O!!! THERE, YOU SEE!

       I CANNOT LIE! *DAMN* MY INTEGRITY!

       I *want* to spare your feelings, yes I do;

       But that means saying things that aren't true,

       And of my meagre talents, that's not one.

       You see, I find that dwelling in the sun

       Of honest criticism brings more joy

       Than rotting in the darkness of some coy

       And sycophantic coterie of slaves.

       God! Eloquence comes over me in waves!

       Did you hear *that* one? We *all* raised our brows . . .

       Permit me . . . just the . . . tiniest of bows,

(*He bows.*)

       I thank you very much, you're far too kind;

       As Cicero has famously opined,

       "To hear one's peers applaud," . . . no! that's not it!

       You know the one . . . the *famous* one . . .

(*Exasperated.*)

       . . . O, shit!

       THE . . . ONE ABOUT . . . THE NOBLEMEN . . . COMPETING . . .

(*After a desperate pause.*)

       Well, it's so famous it's not worth repeating.

       The point is, when a man whom I revere

       As highly as the famous ELOMIRE

(*Bows to him.*)

       Should greet my stabs at wit with such approval,

       I faint . . .

(*He slumps into a chair.*)

       . . . go fetch a cart for my removal!

       It's true. No, absolutely, I'm not acting:

       The lights grow dim, my pupils are contracting,

       My knees go wobbly and my knuckles white,

       I'm fading out. Goodnight, sweet world, goodnight . . .

(*Pause.*)

I'm totally unconscious now, I swear.
CAN ANYBODY HEAR ME? ARE YOU THERE?
Perhaps you think I'm being too dramatic;
But, really, I just droop when I'm ecstatic.

(*Snaps wide awake.*)

What *causes* that? Do either of you know?
A mystic in Gibraltar said I'm low
In some peculiar energy which lies
(For Leos, Capricorns, and Geminis)
Astride the cusp of Saturn's largest moon.
Well, *fine*. But does that tell me *why* I swoon?
Of course it doesn't! What a lot of bunk!
Believe in that stuff and you're really sunk!
Thank God our age has banished superstitions!
(Except for things like sprites and premonitions
Which I think almost certainly are true;
And voodoo dolls and fetishism, too,
Seem eminently credible to me—
And tarot cards and numerology
And cabalistic rituals and such . . .)
But that *astrology!* Now there's a *crutch*
That's used by *fools* with *half* a brain, or *none* . . .

(*Slaps his forehead, and is struck by a vision.*)

WELL, SPEAK OF VISIONS! SOFT! I'M HAVING ONE!

(*He describes the vision, eyes half-closed.*)

We're standing in a public square in Ghent
(I think it's Ghent. It looks like Ghent.

("*Let's just say it's Ghent.*")

It's *Ghent.*)

A scarlet banner reads: "A Great Event:
AUGUSTE VALERE and ELOMIRE Present
Their Brilliant Spectacle Hailed All Through France . . ."
(And then the title:) "ROMAN . . . ," no, "ROMANCE
OF . . .

(*Trying to make it out.*)

. . . SOMETHING . . . SOMETHING . . ." Then: "The Town of
Ghent."

(*Impatiently triumphant.*)

(I . . . *told* you it was Ghent.) Then there's a tent
Around which throngs the very cream of Flanders!

(*Pauses to savor it.*)

A rousing vision (though it almost panders—
By promising *such* glory—to my dream
That like two cloths sewn neatly at the seam
Our talents might, someday, this world enfold).
A fancy, merely? Or a truth foretold?
Won't someone say *which* of the two he thinks it?
No, no. Don't answer: that would only jinx it, ·
And fate's a cranky governess gone gray
(I coined that phrase in Zürich, by the way,
When I was EIGHT YEARS OLD! YES, ONLY *EIGHT!*
Precocious? *Try* PHENOMENAL! *Try* GREAT!
The envy I provoked just knew no ends.

(*Rubbing his hands together.*)

Imagine how despised I was by friends!
My tutor fell in love with me of course;
He thought my every word a *tour-de-force!*
I pitied him for doting on me so,
But, then, I *was* a . . . *strapping* lad, you know . . .
Don't look at me as if I led him on!

(*With increasing vehemence, obviously reliving some past tribunal.*)

You'd blame a *child* before you'd blame a *don!!??*
I ONLY DID WHAT I WAS TOLD TO DO!!

(*Full abreaction.*)

LIES! I NEVER JUMPED HIM! THAT'S NOT TRUE!

(*Quickly regaining himself.*)

Good heavens! Suddenly it all came back!
So sorry . . . seems I wandered off the track . . .)
Um . . . FATE! . . . that's right . . . a governess gone gray:
She guides our every movement, and I'd say
Her stewardship goes well beyond the grave;
But if all things are fated, why be brave . . . ?
Or noble? Or industrious? Or fair?

(*Schoolmasterish pause, "do I see hands?"*)

Is that all you can do? Just blankly stare?
Don't tell me this has *never* crossed your mind!
If not, you've waltzed through life completely blind!
Such questions are essential, don't you see?
A solid grounding in philosophy
Is vital to a proper education!
It never entered my imagination

That you could lack this bare necessity . . .
(*The things I just* assume! *Well, foolish me!*)
At risk of sounding pompous or uncouth,
I'd like to list some volumes from my youth
Which might flesh out the . . .

(*Expressing this as if it were the perfect metaphor, unconscious of the contradiction.*)

         . . . bald spots in your learning.

They've made *my* brain more subtle and discerning,
Those great Moroccan-bound and gold-tooled classics,
Which we—the prefects—in our flowing cassocks
Had tucked beneath our arms . . .

(*Bringing fingers to nose.*)

         . . . I smell them, still!

Indulge me for a moment, if you will.
I recommend you read—no, I insist . . .
An author whom, *remarkably,* you've missed
Since he's the cornerstone of ancient thought
(And—if he's not already—*should* be taught
To every child in every French lycée:)
His name, of course, is . . . wait, it *starts* with "A" . . .
A *very* famous name, don't help me out;
I *know* it's "A"; it's "A" without a doubt.
It starts with "A." It's "A."

(*Slight pause.*)

         Or *maybe* "D."

(*Banishing the ambiguity.*)

No, "A." It's "A." I'm sure it's "A."

(*Another ambiguity.*)

         Or "P."

It *could* be "P."

(*Slight pause.*)

         Or "M."

(*Now he's got it!*)

         IT'S "M"! IT'S *"M"!!*

(*Crestfallen.*)

O, never mind. It could be all of them.
Well, this is terrible; I'm just appalled.
My God! He wrote the famous . . . WHAT'S-IT-CALLED,
COME ON! Don't leave me hanging on a limb!
You're acting like you've never heard of him,
And *everybody* has. He's world renowned!

His writings turned philosophy around
By altering the then-prevailing view—
That what is real is really falsely true—
To what is true is really falsely real . . .
(*A perplexed squint; then, resuming.*)
Well, *either* way, it's BRILLIANT! Don't you feel?
And I'm not saying I don't see the *holes;*
Still, it's a stunning glimpse into our souls
No matter *how* you slice it, Q.E.D.
(He won a prize for it . . . deservedly.)
But who remembers prizes? It's the *FAME!*
The names of brilliant men like . . . what's-his-name . . .
Can never be forgotten: *that's* the PRIZE!
Such men live on when everybody dies!
They *laugh* at famine, pestilence and drought:
And isn't that what life is all about?
(*Deep breath, as a signal of summation.*)
In any case, we've really talked a streak!
Aren't you exhausted? Me? I'm feeling WEAK!!
We've hardly met, and yet you're like my brother
(*Playfully sparring.*)
The way we banter and play off each other.
We've chatted, chortled, changed our points of view,
We've laughed a little, cried a little, too,
We've had some hills, some valleys and plateaus,
We've traded secrets, quipped in cryptic prose,
We've dropped our guards, we've learned to give a damn!
We've proudly cried, "Yes! This is who I am!"
We've said it all, and then . . . found more to say;
In short, we've, quote, "just talked the night away."
And surely that's a sign, at least to me,
That this—our partnership—was *meant* to be!
For though we're strangers (in a narrow sense),
In several ways more striking and intense—
Our gift for words, our love of the sublime—
We've known each other since the dawn of time!
(*Weighing the gem.*)
O, *very* pretty: ". . . since the dawn of time!"
(*With an oratorical flourish.*)
"WE'VE KNOWN EACH OTHER SINCE THE DAWN OF TIME!"
(*Concluding, slapping hands together.*)

Well, good! That's all I really planned to *say,*
Except to thank you for a fine soirée
(*Treading on eggshells, as if he's saying it for the first time.*)
Spoiled only by acidic vinaigrette,
(*Hearing a bell.*)
But then I've said that . . . more than once, I'll bet!
My head is in the clouds: pay no attention!
It's off in some ethereal dimension
Where worldly thoughts not instantly deleted
Are roundly and mechanically repeated
As if to pacify the earth below.
How galling it must be for you to know
That even as we speak, within my mind
I might be off in some place more refined—
That even though I'm present by convention,
You may not really have my full attention . . .
I don't mean *you specifically,* dear friend!
Good heavens! Would I dare to condescend
To someone as illustrious as you!?
I mean, of course, the *common* people who
Would stoop to kiss my hem they so adore me:
Forgive them, Lord! They know not how they bore me
With idle chatter of their simple ways!
I'm sorry, but my eyes begin to glaze
And it's a chore to keep myself awake
When someone's telling me about a rake
Or if his soil will yield a healthy grape.
I smile and nod, but silently escape
To knowledgeable regions in my dome
More crowded than a Roman hippodrome!
I have, for instance (and it's not a fluke)
Verbatim recall of the Pentateuch!
Incredible? It's *true!* Just watch and see:
From Genesis to Deuteronomy
I now recite the Scriptures, LEARNED BY HEART!!:
"IN THE BEGINNING . . ."
(*Squinting, trying to remember more.*)
                                    . . . yes, well that's the start;
(*Moving right along.*)
It goes on just like that till Moses dies.
A superhuman task to memorize?

Not really. It's so *good,* it rather *stuck . . .*
(*To himself.*)

But I digress! SHUT UP YOU STUPID CLUCK,
AND LET *THESE* GENTLE PEOPLE TALK A MITE!
(*Dramatically extending handkerchief.*)

Look, gag me with this handkerchief, all right?
I know that sounds extreme, and I'm a stranger,
But trust me: you are in the gravest danger!
For my digressions (left unchecked) can reach
The vast proportions of a major speech;
And you have no *idea* how close I am
To just that sort of frantic dithyramb!
So why not spare yourselves a living hell
And gag me!
(*He touches the handkerchief to his mouth, snapping it away long enough to finish the line; he continues to do so, the handkerchief hovering.*)

GAG ME! TIE ME UP, AS WELL!
RESTRAIN ME! DISCIPLINE ME! HOLD ME BACK!
HUMILIATE ME! GIVE THE WHIP A CRACK!
DISGRACE ME: MAKE ME BARK AND WEAR A DRESS
AND LICK THE FILTHY FLOOR WHEN I DIGRESS!
But in the meantime, gagged I *should* remain:
It's better that way, no? It's such a sane
And healthy way to curb my domination.
I find it a *complete* abomination
(No matter how distinguished one might be)
When every word is "ME ME ME ME ME."
ME, I'm far too interested in others;
And frankly, friends, were I to have my "druthers"
I'd utter not a peep for weeks untold,
Preferring to . . . absorb the manifold
Of human speech: the "babel" of the masses.
Just stop and *listen* to the lower classes!
You'll have an education when you're done
That rivals twenty years at the Sorbonne!
For in their mindless grunts, the bourgeoisie
Express what I call "wise stupidity."
But no one listens anymore, I fear,
And when I die, so too will disappear
That subtle art, whose practice now grows faint.
And I'm not saying I'm some stained-glass saint

Who *always* listens. Always? No, indeed!
My God! I'm human! Cut me and I bleed!
It's simply that, as far as mortals go,
I'm sensitive (and some say too much so)
To any nuance in a conversation
Which *might, PERHAPS,* suggest my domination.
Thus, in mid-sentence often I just cease . . .
(Despite the countless times I've held my peace
When, in the end, I might as well have chattered
Since only *I* said anything that mattered!
I know that sounds repulsive, but it's true.)
The point is, this is something that I do
Against all logic; so don't be distraught
If, in the middle of a brilliant thought,
I stop like this . . .

(*Freezes; continues.*)

                    . . . depriving you of more;
Or if, commanding reverence from the floor
For awesome skills debating pro *or* con,
I simply stop like this . . .

(*Freezes; continues.*)

                    . . . and don't go on!
A trifle strange, *n'est-ce pas?* But, if you please,
Ask any of my many devotees:
They'll tell you that this quirk (at first appearing)
In time becomes . . .

(*Freezes; continues.*)

                    . . . incredibly endearing!

(*Guffaw of self-delight.*)

To *me* it seems *obnoxious,* heaven knows;
But most say it's a charming trait that grows
More sweet with each encounter! TELL ME WHY!
I just don't see it . . . but: then who am I?
At any rate, THE GAG! OF COURSE! Let me:
Observe with what profound simplicity
It does the job. I think you'll be surprised.
VOILÀ!

(*He stuffs the gag into his mouth, then continues, half-audibly.*)

Now isn't this more civilized!
I'm silenced and I think we're *all* relieved!

We've nipped me in the bud, and thus retrieved
The limelight for our precious Elomire.
Speak on, my friend! This player longs to hear
If in posterity you'll deign to share
Your splendid name with one AUGUSTE VALERE!
Please answer lest I talk you both to death:
(*Removes the gag.*)
I wait on your reply with bated breath.
(*Valere stuffs the gag back into his mouth, assumes a theatrical pose and: blackout.*
Lights up quickly. Silence. A moment passes. Elomire and Bejart circle the frozen
Valere, reaching out to touch him and jerking their fingers back. Finally, Elomire faces
him directly.)

BEJART:

Do you think he's ill?

ELOMIRE:

O, yes.

BEJART:

Then we should . . .

ELOMIRE:

No, Bejart! Be still!
Let's use this brief caesura while we can!
MONSIEUR VALERE: You seem to be a man
In love with words, a *true* aficionado . . .

VALERE:

I'm *that* transparent!?

ELOMIRE:

Yes . . .

VALERE:

But it's bravado!
Don't let my gift—"the silver tongue"—deceive you;
I'm *really* foolish . . .

BEJART:

Yes, we both believe you.

ELOMIRE:

Yes, we both believe you.

VALERE: (*Bowing.*)

You're gentle . . .

ELOMIRE:

Nonetheless it's very clear
That language is a thing which you hold dear . . .

VALERE:

Too mild! Too mild! It's more than dear to me!
I liken syntax to morality—
Its laws inviolate in such a way
That damned is he who dares to disobey!
Diction, like aesthetics, is more free:
It's where we show our creativity
By choosing metaphors and ways of speech—
I'd say "the shell-crushed strand"; you'd say "the beach."
Semantics is like . . . (hang on . . . let me see . . .
I've *used* aesthetics and morality . . .)
Semantics is like . . . SWIMMING! . . . (no, that's bad!
O, DAMMIT! DAMMIT! DAMN, I thought I had
A brilliant speech developing! *DOMMAGE!*)
Well . . . back to our exciting persiflage . . .
(*Deep inhale, eyes cross.*)
Where were we . . . ?

Martha Hollander

artha Hollander graduated from Yale College in 1980. "In my senior year at Yale," she writes, "I was chosen, along with three other students from other colleges, to participate in the Connecticut Poetry Circuit, a series of poetry readings at high schools and colleges around the state. It offered a privileged glimpse of writing as a profession: two or three times a week we put aside our classes, our friends, our perpetual loads of schoolwork, and went out on the road, reading in front of audiences as small as ten and as large as five hundred, in every conceivable environment. One bitter January day we gave a reading in a huge auditorium at a boarding school. The audience was a few hundred; attendance was mandatory. Afterwards we were scheduled to meet with the students and answer questions. I was expecting them to be shy, maybe embarrassed, or bored and sullen, but instead they clustered around us in the drafty student center, pestering us with questions. They wanted to know *everything* about writing. One boy said, 'You know, I'm glad to know all this because I really need to get stuff down—it's very hard being fifteen.' I was profoundly struck, not merely by his sweetness and candor, but by the great gulf that suddenly loomed between me and this boy barely five years my junior, between the anxious child-who-wrote I had recently been and the writer I had apparently become." Hollander teaches art history at Hofstra University and has published *Always History* (1985) and *The Game of Statues* (1990), which won the Walt Whitman Award from the Academy of American Poets.

MYSTERY DATE

Creeping along in a coat the color of smog,
poking fastidiously with a scuffed cane,
he crosses my path every few years.
He resembles Max, the early video warrior
who shuffled across the TV screen in mask
and prison stripes every day when I was five:
there was a prize for catching him.
Later came the game for older girls.
Shake the dice, turn over a card,
and find your date: is he a dream or a flop?
A creep, a nerd, jock, genius, or hunk?
The ten-year-olds finger their cards
and try out orgasmic sighs, waiting for
the big surprise, the perfect match, the one.
Here he is, in sixties Mad. Ave. splendor,
macho hollows brushed into his jaws,
his tanned fingers fitting expertly around
his bat, his briefcase, his big surfboard.
Thirty years later, the glossy catalogues
from the singles clubs reveal, in summer colors,
Tony and Ron and Ted, tall and fit,
smiling, T-shirted, financially secure.

He followed me here: I knew him years ago
when I squeezed him into my narrow college bed.
His voice was a heartland monotone; his face
fused itself around a quivering nose
that intruded and rebuked, pointing his way.
He followed me here, materializing one day
in my first apartment, then sending a postcard
from the tropics. Ten years afterwards,
at a conference down south, he sprang
into view like a patch of kudzu, dark
and bitter in an academic blue blazer.
Next year, on Park Avenue, he inched
toward the glittering rush of evening traffic
and stole my taxi. Last night, in the rain,
he crossed our path as we wrangled about marriage.

One day in the train station you vanished,
for apparently, you'd never existed at all.
How easily our life together could shrink
to a delusion fed by insomnia
and the fluorescent miseries of Amtrak!
I expected to shrug, go home and start all over,
and I weighed each choice: you might have never been.
You might never reappear. Or worst, emerge
(a smudge at the edge of the platform, of my eye)
as him, the creature whose name you share,
who shuffles this way, nose twitching, cane erect,
advancing steadily as the years advance.

THE MEMORY-GLASS

Nobody remembers the memory-glass,
so here, for the first time, is the recipe.
Rescue a wineglass, already antiqued
with sweat and lipstick, ashes and champagne,
and stuff it with the hours-old remains
of a four-course dinner. Then seal it over
with a film of wax dripped from a nearby candle
like fat on a heavy broth, ice on a swamp.
Leave it on the table for posterity.

Nobody remembers the memory-glass,
and no wonder: it was a bar mitzvah favorite,
a game for boys becoming men, the litmus test
of full-blown sublime disgustingness.
And here they are, as a grimy blue Polaroid
fixed them once: some sullen, some grinning, hair
in their eyes, with endless noses and legs,
sneakers as immense as the hooves of centaurs.
As softer and sadder men, they all refuse
to comment on this party pastime,
but inside each one lurks the masturbating
sulking boy, all dressed up, laboring
at his stuffed parody of a *Yahrzeit* candle,
using garbage to spell eternity.

Nobody remembers the memory-glass
precisely because, like all time-capsules,
it insists on recalling all the wrong things.
The newest one of these, I've heard, is called
The Capsule of Civilization, an assemblage
of our era's millennial vanity and panic.
There's the usual multicultural hello;
male and female, waving, as unerotic
and unheroic as drawings in sex manuals;
the solar system (with a helpful arrow);
the Sistine ceiling, Bach, the pyramids,
a microchip, the Beatles, dental floss.
Dental floss? It looks like nothing on earth,
a minty tool for measuring, sewing, murder.
Future cultures will be mystified.

Nobody remembers the memory-glass
except you. No need to seal you away
like a pharaoh; no need to fossilize you
like the faded food glistening with shellac
in the windows of old Chinese restaurants.
There are more elegant immortalities,
like the sidelong view of your face in repose,
a profile of plunges and ascents along
a moonlit mountain range. This living line
slices through the world like a key,
an EEG, the mark you make for the end of time.

David Leavitt

born in Pittsburgh in 1961, David Leavitt had published a story in the *New Yorker* while still an undergraduate at Yale. He graduated in 1983 and published his first book of stories, *Family Dancing,* a year later. Two years later his first novel, *The Lost Language of Cranes,* appeared. Since then he has published nine more books, most recently the novels *The Page Turner* (1998) and *Martin Bauman* (2000). "While at Yale," he writes, "I took courses in English and American literature with Harold Bloom, John Hollander, Margaret Ferguson, and Margaret Mahar (among many others), while simultaneously writing short stories under the tutelage of John Hersey, Gordon Lish, and Michael Malone. A rich sort of cross-fertilization resulted: I learned about the craft of fiction from Margaret Ferguson (with whom I studied Milton) and about the art of criticism from Gordon Lish. I'll never forget the gloomy February afternoon when during a Keats and Shelley seminar Maggie Mahar says, 'What Shelley is trying to convey here is the atmosphere of a gloomy February afternoon when your work's boring, your friends are boring, but most of all, you're boring.' Nor will I forget the hours spent in the rear smoking section of the underground library, writing 'Territory,' the first story in my first book: snow outside, and across the white formica table a very intense-looking girl smoking furiously as she took notes for some Lacanian interpretation of Jane Austen. That library, for all its drear, was for me the architectural equivalent of a blank page."

It was the tunnel—its imminence—that all of them were contemplating, that afternoon on the train, each in a different way; the tunnel, at nine miles the longest in the world, slicing under the gelid landscape of the St. Gotthard pass. To Irene it was an object of dread. She feared enclosure in small spaces, had heard from Maisie Withers that during the crossing the carriage heated up to a boiling pitch. "I was as black as a nigger from the soot," Maisie Withers said. "People have died." "Never again," Maisie Withers concluded, pouring lemonade in her sitting room in Hartford, and meaning never again the tunnel but also (Irene knew) never again Italy, never again Europe; for Maisie was a gullible woman, and during her tour had had her pocketbook stolen.

And it was not only Maisie Withers, Irene reflected now (watching, across the way, her son Grady, his nose flat against the glass), but also her own ancient terror of windowless rooms, of corners, that since their docking in Liverpool had brought the prospect of the tunnel looming before her, black as death itself (a being which, as she approached fifty, she was trying to muster the courage to meet eye to eye), until she found herself counting first the weeks, then the days, then the hours leading up to the inevitable reckoning: the train slipping into the dark, into the mountain. (It was half a mile deep, Grady kept reminding her, half a mile of solid rock separating earth from sky.) Irene remembered a ghost story she'd read as a girl—a man mistakenly believed to be dead wakes in his coffin. Was it too late to hire a carriage, then, to go *over* the pass, as Toby had? But no. Winter had already started up there. Oh, if she'd had her way, they'd have taken a different route; only Grady would have been disappointed, and since his brother's death she dared not disappoint Grady. He longed for the tunnel as ardently as his mother dreaded it.

"Mama, is it coming soon?"
"Yes, dear."
"But you said half an hour."
"Hush, Grady! I'm not a clock."
"But you said—"
"Read your book, Grady," Harold interrupted.
"I finished it."
"Then do your puzzle."
"I finished that, too."
"Then look out the window."
"Or just shut up," added Stephen, his eyes sliding open.
"Stephen, you're not to talk to your brother that way."
"He's a pest. Can't a fellow get some sleep?"
Stephen's eyes slid shut, and Grady turned to examine the view. Though nearly

fourteen, he was still a child. His leg shook. With his breath he fogged shapes onto the glass.

"Did I tell you it's the longest in the world? Did I tell you—"

"Yes, Grady. Now please hush."

They didn't understand. They were always telling him to hush. Well, all right, he would hush. He would never again utter a single word, and show them all.

Irene sneezed.

"Excuse me," she said to the red-nosed lady sitting next to her.

"Heavens! You needn't apologize to *me*."

"It's getting cold rather early this year," Irene ventured, relieved beyond measure to discover that her neighbor spoke English.

"Indeed it is. It gets cold earlier every year, I find. Judgment Day must be nigh!"

Irene laughed. They started chatting. She was elegantly got up, this red-nosed lady. She did needlepoint with her gloves on. From her hat extended a fanciful *aigrette* that danced and bobbed. Grady watched it, watched the moving mountains outside the window. (Some were already capped with snow.) Then the train turned, the sun came blazing into the compartment so sharply that the red-nosed lady murmured, "Goodness me," shielded her eyes, pulled the curtain shut against it.

Well, that did it for Grady. After all, hadn't they just told him to look at the view? No one cared. He had finished his book. He had finished his puzzle.

The tunnel would never arrive.

Snorting, he thrust his head behind the curtain.

"Grady, don't be rude."

He didn't answer. And really, behind the curtain it was a different world. He could feel warmth on his face. He could revel in the delicious sensation of apartness that the gold-lit curtain bestowed and that only the chatter of women interrupted. But it was rude.

"Oh, I know, I know!" (Whose voice was that? The red-nosed lady's?) "Oh yes, I know!" (Women always said that. They always knew.)

Harold had his face in a book. Stephen was a bully.

"Oh dear, yes!"

Whoever was talking, her voice was loud. His mother's voice he could not make out. His mother's voice was high but not loud, unless she shouted, which she tended to do lately. Outside the window an alpine landscape spread out: fir groves, steep-roofed wooden houses, fields of dead sunflowers to which the stuffy compartment with its scratched mahogany paneling bore no discernible relation. This first-class compartment belonged to the gaslit ambiance of stations and station hotels. It was a bubble of metropolitan, semipublic space sent out into the wide world and from the confines of which its inmates could regard the uncouth spectacle of nature as a kind of *tableau vivant*. Still, the trappings of luxury did little to mask its fundamental discomforts: seats that pained the back, fetid air, dirty carpets.

They were on their way to Italy, Irene told Mrs. Warshaw (for this was the red-nosed lady's name). They were on their way to Italy for a tour—Milan, Venice, Verona, Florence, Rome (Irene counted off on her fingers), then a villa in Naples for the winter months—because her sons ought to see the world, she felt; American boys knew so little; they had studied French but could hardly speak a word. (Mrs. Warshaw, nodding fervently, agreed it was a shame.)

"And this will be your first trip to Italy?"

"The first time I've been abroad, actually, although my brother Toby came twenty years ago. He wrote some lovely letters for the *Hartford Gazette*."

"Marvelous! And how lucky you are to have three handsome sons as escorts. I myself have only a daughter."

"Oh, but Harold's not my son! Harold's my cousin Millie's boy. He's the tutor."

"How nice." Mrs. Warshaw smiled assessingly at Harold. Yes, she thought, tutor he is, and tutor he will always be; he looked the part of the poor relation, no doubt expected to play the same role in the lady's life abroad that his mother played in her life at home: the companion to whom she could turn when she needed consolation, or someone to torture. (Mrs. Warshaw knew the ways of the world.)

As for the boys, the brothers: the older one looked different. Darker. Different fathers, perhaps?

But Irene thought: she's right. I do—*did*—have three sons.

Harold tried to hide inside his book. Only he thought: they ought to treat me with more respect. The boys ought to call me Mr. Prescott, not Cousin Hal, for they hardly know me. Also, he smarted at the dismissive tone with which Aunt Irene enunciated the word "tutor," as if he were something just one step above the level of a servant. He deserved better than that; deserved better than to be at the beck and call of boys in whom art, music, the classical inspired boredom at best, outright contempt at worst. For though Uncle George, God rest his soul, had financed his education, be that as it may, it was not Uncle George who had gotten the highest scores in the history of the classics department. It was not Uncle George whose translations of Cicero had won a prize. Harold had done all that himself.

On the other hand, goodness knew he could never have afforded Europe on his own. To his charges he owed the blessed image of his mother's backyard in St. Louis, his mother in her gardening gloves and hat, holding her shears over the roses while on the porch the old chair in which he habitually spent his summers reading, or sleeping, or cursing—my God, he wasn't in it! It was empty! To them he owed this miracle.

"And will your husband be joining you in Naples?"

"I'm afraid my husband passed away last winter."

"Ah."

Mrs. Warshaw dropped a stitch.

The overdecorated compartment in which these five people were sitting was small—four feet by six feet. Really, it had the look of a theater stall, Harold decided, with its maroon velvet seats, its window like a stage, its curtain—well, like a curtain. Above the stained headrests wrapped in slipcovers embellished with the crest of the railway hung six prints in reedy frames: three yellowed views of Rome—Trajan's Column (the glass cracked), the Pantheon, the Coliseum (over which Mrs. Warshaw's aigrette danced); and opposite, as if to echo the perpetual contempt with which the Christian world regards the pagan, three views of Florence—Santa Croce, the Duomo, the Palazzo Vecchio guarded by Michelangelo's immense nude David—none of which Harold, who reverenced the classical, could see. Instead, when he glanced up from his book, it was the interior of the Pantheon that met his gaze, the orifice at the center of the dome throwing against its coffered ceiling a coin of light.

He put down his book. (It was Ovid's *Metamorphoses,* in Latin.) Across from him, under the Pantheon, Stephen sprawled, his long legs in their loose flannel trousers spread wide but bent at the knees, because finally they were too long, those legs, for a compartment in which three people were expected to sit facing three people for hours at a time; asleep, or pretending to be asleep, so that Harold could drink in his beauty for once with impunity, while Mrs. Warshaw did her needlework, and Grady's head bobbed behind the curtain, and Aunt Irene said she knew, she knew. Stephen was motionless. Stephen was inscrutable. Still, Harold could tell that he, too, was alert to the tunnel's imminence; he could tell because every few minutes his eyes slotted open, the way the eyes of a doll do when you tilt back its head: green and gold, those eyes, like the sun-mottled grass beneath a tree.

He rarely spoke, Stephen. His body had the elongated musculature of a harp. His face was elusive in its beauty, like those white masks the Venetians wear at Carnival. Only sometimes he shifted his legs, in those flannel trousers that were a chaos of folds, a mountain landscape, valleys, passes, peaks. Most, Harold knew, if you punched them down, would flatten; but one would grow heavy and warm at his touch.

And now Harold had to put his book on his lap. He had to. He was twenty-two years old, scrawny, with a constitution his doctor described as "delicate"; yet when he closed his eyes, he and Stephen wore togas and stood together in a square filled with rational light. Or Harold was a great warrior and Stephen the beloved *eremenos* over whose gore-drenched body he scattered kisses at battle's end. Or they were training together, naked, in the gymnasium.

Shameful thoughts! He must cast them out of his mind. He must find a more worthy object for his adoration than this stupid, vulgar boy, this boy who for all his facile handsomeness would have hardly raised an eyebrow in the age of Socrates.

"Not Captain Warshaw, though! The Captain had a stomach of iron."

What were they talking about? The channel crossing, no doubt. Aunt Irene never tired of describing her travel woes. She detested boats, detested hotel beds, detested tunnels. Whereas Harold, if anyone had asked him, would have said that he looked forward to the tunnel not as an end in itself, the way Grady did, but because the tunnel meant the south, meant Italy. For though it did not literally link Switzerland with Italy, on one side the towns had German names—Göschenen, Andermatt, Hospental—while on the other they had Italian names—Airolo, Ambri, Lurengo—and this fact in itself was enough to intoxicate him.

Now Stephen stretched; the landscape of his trousers surged, earthquakes leveled the peaks, the rivers were re-routed and the crust of the earth churned up. It was as if a capricious god, unsatisfied with his handiwork, had decided to forge the world anew.

"Ah, how I envy any traveler his first visit to Italy!" Mrs. Warshaw said. "Because for you it will be new—what is for me already faded. Beginning with Airolo, the Campanile, as the train comes out the other end of the tunnel . . ."

Harold's book twitched. He knew all about the Campanile.

"Is it splendid?" Irene asked.

"Oh, no." Mrs. Warshaw shook her head decisively. "Not splendid at all. Quite plain, in fact, especially when you compare it to all those other wonderful Italian towers—in Pisa, in Bologna. I mustn't forget San Gimignano! Yes, compared to the towers of San Gimignano, the Campanile of Airolo is utterly without distinction or merit. Still, you will never forget it, because it is the first."

"Well, we shall look forward to it. Grady, be sure to look out for the tower of . . . just after the tunnel."

The curtain didn't budge.

Irene's smile said: "Sons."

"And where are you traveling, if I might be so bold?"

"To Florence. It's my habit to spend the winter there. You see, when I lost the Captain, I went abroad intending to make a six months' tour of Europe. But then six months turned into a year, and a year into five years, and now it will be eight years in January since I last walked on native soil. Oh, I think of returning to Toronto sometimes, settling in some little nook. And yet there is still so much to see! I have the travel bug, I fear. I wonder if I shall ever go home."

As if memory had momentarily transfixed her, Mrs. Warshaw gazed toward the curtained window.

"Ah, beloved Florence!" she exhaled. "How I long once again to take in the view from Bellosguardo."

"How lovely it must be," echoed Irene, though in truth she had no idea where Bellosguardo was, and feared repeating the name lest she should mispronounce it.

"Florence is full of treasures," Mrs. Warshaw continued. "For instance, you must go to the Piazza della Signoria and look at the Perseus."

Harold's book twitched again. He knew all about the Perseus.

"Of course we shall go and see them straight away," Irene said. "When do they bloom?"

When do they bloom!

It sometimes seemed to Harold that it was Aunt Irene, and not her sons, who needed the tutor. She was ignorant of everything, and yet she never seemed to care when she made an idiot of herself. In Harold's estimation, this was typical of the Pratt branch of the family. With the exception of dear departed Toby (both of them), no one in that branch of the family possessed the slightest receptivity to what Pater called (and Harold never forgot it) "the poetic passion, the desire of beauty, the love of art for its own sake." Pratts were anti-Paterian. Not for them Pater's "failure is forming habits." To them the formation of habits—healthy habits—was the essence of success. (It was a subject on which Uncle George, God rest his soul, had taken no end of pleasure in lecturing Harold.)

Still, Harold could not hate them. After all, they had made his education possible for him. At Thanksgiving and Christmas they always had a place for him at their table (albeit crammed in at a corner in a kitchen chair). "Our little scholarship boy," Aunt Irene called him. "Our little genius, Harold."

Later, after Uncle George had died, and Toby had died, and Toby the Second as well, Irene had come to him. "Harold, would you like to see Europe?" she'd asked, fixing his collar.

"More than anything, Aunt Irene."

"Because I'm planning a little tour this fall with the boys—following my brother's itinerary, you know—and I thought, wouldn't it be marvelous for them to have a tutor, a scholar like yourself, to tell them what was what. What do you think, Harold? Would your mother mind?"

"I think it's a capital idea."

"Good."

So here he was.

So far, things hadn't gone well at all.

In Paris, Harold had decided to test the boys' receptivity to art by taking them to the Louvre. But Grady only wanted to ride the Metro, and got infuriated when Harold explained that there was no need to take the Metro: the museum was

only a block from their hotel. Then they were standing in front of the *Mona Lisa,*
Harold lecturing, Grady quivering with rage at having been deprived of the
Metro, Stephen leaning, inscrutable as always, against a white wall. Harold spoke
eloquently about the painting, and as he spoke, he felt the silent pressure of their
boredom. They had their long bodies arranged in attitudes of sculptural indifference, as if to say, we have no truck with any of this. Curse our mother for pulling us out of our lives, and curse our father for dying, and our brother for dying,
and curse you. To which Harold wanted to answer: Well, do you think I like it
any more than you do? Do you think I enjoy babbling like an idiot, and being
ignored? For the truth was, the scrim of their apathy diffused his own sense of
wonder. After all, he was seeing all this for the first time, too: not a cheap reproduction, but *La Gioconda.* The real thing. How dare they not notice, not care?

Yes, Harold decided that morning, they were normal, these boys. They would
never warm to art. (And as if to prove his point, they now gravitated away from
his lecturing and toward an old man who had set up an easel and paints to copy a
minor annunciation—their curiosity piqued by some low circus element in the
proceedings: "Gosh, it looks exactly like the original!" an American man standing
nearby said to his wife.) Why Aunt Irene had insisted on bringing them to
Europe in the first place Harold still couldn't fathom; what did she think was
going to happen, anyway? Did she imagine that upon contact with the Sack of
Rome, the riches of Venice, some dormant love of beauty would awaken in them,
and they would suddenly be transformed into cultured, intellectual boys, the sort
upon whom she could rely for flashes of wit at dinner parties, crossword solutions
on rainy afternoons? Boys, in other words, like their brother Toby, or their uncle
Toby, for that matter, who had kept a portrait of Byron on his desk. Grady, on
the other hand, couldn't have cared less about Byron, while Stephen, so far as
Harold could tell, liked only to lean against white walls in his flannel trousers,
challenging the marble for beauty. Really, he was too much, Stephen: self-
absorbed, smug, arrogant. Harold adored him.

There was a rapping on the compartment door.

"Entrez," announced Mrs. Warshaw.

The conductor stepped in. Immediately Grady pulled back the curtain, splay-
ing the light. Stephen's eyes slotted open.

"Permit me to excuse myself," the conductor said in tormented French, "but
we are approaching the St. Gotthard tunnel. I shall now light the lamps and
make certain that the windows and ventilators are properly closed."

"Bien sûr."

The conductor was Italian, a handsome, sturdy fellow with a thick black mustache, blue eyes, fine lips. Dark hairs curled under his cuffs, rode down the length
of his hands to the ends of his thick fingers.

Bowing, he stepped to the front of the compartment, where he got down on his knees and fiddled with the ventilator panel. As he knelt he winked manfully at Grady.

"Oh, I don't like tunnels," Irene said. "I get claustrophobic."

"I hope you don't get seasick!" laughed Mrs. Warshaw. "But never mind. When you've been through the St. Gotthard as often as I have, you shall sleep right through, as I intend to do."

"How long is it again?"

"Nine miles!" Grady shouted. "The longest in the—" And winced. He had broken his vow.

"Nine miles! Dear Lord! And it will take half an hour?"

"More or less."

"Half an hour in the dark!"

"The gas jets will be lit. You needn't worry."

The conductor, having finished with the ventilators, stood to examine the window latches. In securing the one on the right he pressed a wool-covered leg against Harold's knees.

"Va bene," he said next, yanking at the latch for good measure. (It did not give.) Then he turned to face Harold, over whose head the oil lamp protruded; raised his arms into the air to light it, so that his shirt pulled up almost but not quite enough to reveal a glimpse of what was underneath (what *was* underneath?); parted his legs around Harold's knees. Harold had no choice but to stare into the white of that shirt, breathe in its odor of eau de cologne and cigar.

Then the lamp was lit. Glancing down, the conductor smiled.

"Merci mesdames," he concluded merrily. Then, to Harold: "Grazie, Signore." Harold muttered, "Prego," kept his eyes out the window.

The door shut firmly.

"I shall be so happy to have my first glimpse of Milan," Irene said.

Why French for the women and Italian for him?

They had been traveling forever. They had been traveling for years: Paris, the gaslit platform at the Gare de Lyon, a distant dream; then miles of dull French farmland, flat and blurred, and then the clattery dollhouse architecture of Switzerland, all that grass and those little clusters of chalets with their tilted roofs and knotty shuttered windows, like the window the bird would have flown out of on the cuckoo clock . . . if it had ever worked, if Uncle George had ever bothered to fix it. But he had not.

Really, there was nothing to do but read, so Harold read.

Orpheus: having led Eurydice up from the Underworld, he turned to make sure she hadn't tired behind him. He turned even though he had been warned in no uncertain terms not to turn; that turning was the one forbidden thing. And what happened? Exactly what Orpheus should have expected to happen. As if his eyes themselves shot out rays of plague, Eurydice shrank back into the vapors and died a second death; fell back down the dark well. This story of Orpheus and Eurydice Harold had read a hundred times, maybe even five hundred times, and still it frustrated him; still he hoped each time that Orpheus would catch on for once and not look back. Yet he always looked back. And why? Had love turned Orpheus's head? Harold doubted it. Perhaps the exigencies of story, then: for really, if the episode had ended with the happy couple emerging safely into the dewy morning light, something in every reader would have been left slavering for the expected payoff.

Of course there were other possible explanations. For instance: perhaps Orpheus had found it impossible not to give into a certain impulse to self-destruction; that inability, upon being told "Don't cross that line," to resist crossing it.

Only God has the power to turn back time.

Or perhaps Orpheus, at the last minute, had changed his mind; decided he didn't want Eurydice back after all. This was a radical interpretation, albeit one to which later events in Orpheus's life lent credence.

Harold remembered something—*Huck Finn,* he thought—you must never look over your shoulder at the moon.

Something made him put his book down. Stephen had woken up. He was rubbing his left eye with the ball of his fist. No, he did not look like his brother; did not look like any Pratt, for that matter. (Mrs. Warshaw was correct about this, though little else.) According to Harold's mother, this was because Aunt Irene, after years of not being able to conceive, had taken him in as a foundling, only wouldn't you know it? The very day the baby arrived she found out she was pregnant. "It's always like that," his mother had said. "Women who take in foundlings always get pregnant the day the foundling arrives."

Nine months later Toby was born—Toby the Second—that marvelous boy who rivaled his adopted brother for athletic skills, outstripped him in book smarts, but was handsome, too—Pratt handsome, with pale skin and small ears. Toby had been a star pupil, whereas Irene had had to plead with the headmaster to keep Stephen from being held back a grade. Not that the boys disliked each other: instead, so far as Harold could tell, they simply made a point of ignoring each other. (And how was this possible? How was it possible for anyone to ignore either of them?)

"Be kind to your Aunt Irene," his mother had told him at the station in St. Louis. "She's known too much death."

And now she sat opposite him, here on the train, and he could see from her eyes that it was true: she had known too much death.

Harold flipped ahead a few pages.

"Throughout this time Orpheus had shrunk from loving any woman, either because of his unhappy experience, or because he had pledged himself not to do so. In spite of this there were many who were fired with a desire to marry the poet, many were indignant to find themselves repulsed. However, Orpheus preferred to center his affection on boys of tender years, and to enjoy the brief spring and early flowering of their youth: he was the first to introduce this custom among the people of Thrace."

Boys of tender years, like Stephen, who, as Harold glanced up, shifted again, opened his eyes and stared at his cousin malevolently.

And the train rumbled, and Mrs. Warshaw's aigrette fluttered before the Coliseum, and the cracked glass that covered Trajan's Column rattled.

They were starting to climb at a steeper gradient. They were nearing the tunnel at last.

From the *Hartford Gazette,* November 4, 1878: Letter Six, "Crossing from the Tyrol into Ticino," by Tobias R. Pratt.

As we began the climb over the great mountain of San Gottardo our *mulattiere,* a most affable and friendly fellow within whose Germanic accent one could detect echoes of the imminent south, explained that even as we made our way through the pass, at that very moment men were laboring under our feet to dig a vast railway tunnel that upon completion will be the longest in the world. This tunnel will make Italy an easier destination for those of us who wish always to be idling in her beneficent breezes . . . and yet how far the Piazza della Signoria seemed to us that morning, as we rose higher and higher into snowy regions! It was difficult to believe that on the other side the lovely music of the Italian voice and the taste of a rich red wine awaited us; still this faith gave us the strength to persevere through what we knew would be three days of hard travel.

To pass the time, we asked our guide his opinion of the new tunnel. His response was ambivalent. Yes, he admitted, the tunnel would bring tourism (and hence money) to his corner of the world. And yet the cost! Had we heard, for instance, that already one hundred men had lost their lives underground? A hint of superstitious worry entered his voice, as if he feared lest the mountain—outraged by such invasions—should one day decide that it had had enough and with one great heave of its breast smash the tunnel and all its occupants to smithereens. . . .

And Irene thought: he never saw it. He had been dead two years already, by the time it was finished.

And Grady thought: finally.

And Mrs. Warshaw thought: I hope the Signora saved me Room 5, as she promised.

And Harold watched Stephen's trousers hungrily. Glimpses, guesses. All he had ever known were glimpses, guesses. Never, God forbid, a touch; never, never the sort of fraternal bond, unsullied by carnal need, to which epic poetry paid homage; never anything—except this ceaseless worrying of a bone from which every scrap of meat had long been chewed; this ceaseless searching for an outline amid the folds of a pair of flannel trousers.

Yes, he thought, leaning back, I should have been born in classical times. For he genuinely believed himself to be the victim of some heavenly imbroglio, the result of which was his being delivered not (as he should have been) into an Athenian boudoir (his mother someone wise and severe, like Plotina) but rather into a bassinet in a back bedroom in St. Louis where the air was wrong, the light was wrong, the milk did not nourish him. No wonder he grew up ugly, ill, ill-tempered! He belonged to a different age. And now he wanted to cry out, so that all of Switzerland could hear him: I belong to a different age!

The train slowed. Behind the curtain Grady watched the signs giving way one to the next, one to the next: GÖ-SCHE-NEN, GÖ-SCHE-NEN, GÖ-SCHE-NEN.

"By such songs as these the Thracian poet was drawing the woods and rocks to follow him, charming the creatures of the wild, when suddenly the Ciconian women caught sight of him. Looking down from the crest of a hill, these maddened creatures, with animal skins slung across their breasts, saw Orpheus as he was singing and accompanying himself on the lyre. One of them, tossing her hair till it streamed in the light breeze, cried out: 'See! Look here! Here is the man who scorns us!' and flung her spear—"

Darkness. Harold shut his book.

As soon as the train entered the tunnel the temperature began to rise. Despite the careful labors of the conductor, smoke was slipping into the compartment: not enough to be discernible at first by anything other than its dry, sharp smell; but then Harold noticed that no sooner had he wiped his spectacles clean, they were already filmed again with dust; and then a gray fog, almost a mist, occupied the compartment, obscuring his vision; he could no longer distinguish, for instance, which of the three little prints across the way from him represented the Pantheon, which Trajan's Column, which the Coliseum.

Mrs. Warshaw's head slumped. She snored.

And Grady pressed his face up against the glass, even though there was nothing to see outside the window but a bluish-black void, which he likened to the sinuous fabric of space itself.

And Irene, a handkerchief balled in her fist, wondered: Do the dead age? Would her little Toby, in heaven, remain forever the child he had been when he had died? Or would he grow, marry, have angel children?

And Toby her brother? Had *he* had angel children?

If Toby was in heaven—and not the other place. She sometimes feared he might be in the other place—every sermon she'd ever heard suggested it—in which case she would probably never get closer to him than she was right now, right here, in this infernal tunnel.

She glanced at Stephen, awake now. God forgive her for thinking it, but it should have been him, repairing the well with George. Only Stephen had been in bed with influenza, so Toby went instead.

Punishment? But if so, for what? Thoughts? Could he be punished for thoughts?

Suddenly she could hardly breathe the searing air—as if a hundred men were smoking cigars all at once.

Midway—or what Harold assumed was midway—he thought he heard the wheels scrape. So the train would stall, and then what would they do? There wouldn't be enough oxygen to get out on foot without suffocating. The tunnel was too long. Half a mile of rock separated train from sky; half a mile of rock, atop which trees grew, a woman milked her cow, a baker made bread.

The heat abashed; seemed to eat the air. Harold felt the weight of mountains on his lungs.

Think of other things, he told himself, and in his mind undid the glissando of buttons on Stephen's trousers.

Yet the smell in his nostrils—that smell of cigars—made him think of the conductor.

Light scratched the window. The train shuddered to a stop. Someone flung open a door.

They were outside. Dozens of soot-smeared passengers stumbled amid the tracks, the visible clouds of smoke, the sloping planes of alpine grass. For they were there now. Through.

The train throbbed. Conductors, stripped to their waistcoats, took buckets and mops and swabbed the filthy windows until cataracts of black water pooled outside the tracks.

People had died. Her brother in Greece, her child and her husband in the backyard.

There was no heaven, no hell. The dead did not age because the dead *were not.* (Still, she fingered the yellowed newspaper clippings in her purse; looked around for Stephen, who had disappeared.)

And meanwhile Harold had run up the hill from the train, and now stood on a low promontory, wiping ash from his spectacles with a handkerchief.

Where was Stephen? Suddenly she was terrified, convinced that something had happened to him on the train, in the tunnel. "Harold!" she called. "Harold, have you seen Stephen?"

But he chose not to hear her. He was gazing at the Campanile of Airolo, vivid in the fading light.

In Airolo, Harold looked for signs that the world was becoming Italy. And while it was true that most of the men in the station bar drank beer, one or two were drinking wine; and when he asked for wine in Italian, he was answered in Italian, and given a glass.

"Grady, do you want anything?"

Silence.

"Grady!"

He still wasn't talking to them.

Aunt Irene had gone into the washroom. She was not there to forbid him from drinking, so he drank. Around him, at tables, local workers—perhaps the same ones who had dug the tunnel—smoked and played cards. Most of them had pallid, dark blonde faces, Germanic faces; but one was reading a newspaper called *Il Corriere della Sera,* and one boy's skin seemed to have been touched, even in this northernmost outpost, by a finger of Mediterranean sun.

Italy, he thought, and gazing across the room, noticed that Stephen, darker by far than any man in the bar, had come inside. A hand in his pocket, he was leaning against a white wall, drinking beer from a tall glass.

Apart.

He is from here, Harold realized suddenly. But does he even know it?

Probably not.

The conductor strode into the bar. Harold turned, blushing, to contemplate his wine, wondering when the necessary boldness would come: to look another man straight in the eye, as men do.

Aunt Irene had at last emerged, with Mrs. Warshaw, from the washroom. "Harold, I'm worried about Stephen," she said. "The last time I saw him was when we got off the—"

"He's over there."

"Oh Stephen!" his mother cried, and to Harold's surprise she ran to him, embraced him tightly, pressed her face into his chest. "My darling, I've been worried sick about you! Where have you been?"

"Can't a man take a walk?" Stephen asked irritably.

"Yes, of course. Of course he can." Letting him go, she dabbed at her eyes. "You've grown so tall! You're almost a man! No wonder you don't like Mother hugging you any more. Oh, Stephen, you're such a wonderful son, I hope you know, I hope you'll always know, how much we treasure you."

Stephen grimaced; sipped at his beer.

"Well, we're through it," Mrs. Warshaw said. "Now tell me the truth, it wasn't so bad as all that, was it?"

"How I long for a bed!" Irene said. "Is Milan much further?"

Mrs. Warshaw smiled benevolently. "Just a few hours, dear," she said, patting her hand. "And only short tunnels from now on, I promise you."

after graduating summa cum laude from Brooklyn College in 1981, Gloria Naylor came to Yale and earned her M.A. in Afro-American Studies in 1983. She decided to leave the program after her first year. As she writes, "I was working on my second novel and found the demands of academia were taking me away from my literary endeavors. I went to John Blassingame, my program director, with these concerns and he hit upon a plan where I would complete my course work along with the other students, but instead of a standard thesis I could submit my second novel as partial fulfillment of the requirements for my graduate degree. Thus, *Linden Hills* was born at Yale, just as *The Women of Brewster Place* had been born at Brooklyn College." In addition to *The Women of Brewster Place* (1982) and *Linden Hills* (1985), Naylor has published *Mama Day* (1988), *Bailey's Café* (1992), which she adapted for the stage, and *The Men of Brewster Place* (1998). She has taught at Princeton, New York University, Brandeis, and the University of Kent.

The sunlight was still watery as Ben trudged into Brewster Place, and the street had just begun to yawn and stretch itself. He eased himself onto his garbage can, which was pushed against the sagging brick wall that turned Brewster into a dead-end street. The metallic cold of the can's lid seeped into the bottom of his thin trousers. Sucking on a piece of breakfast sausage caught in his back teeth, he began to muse. Mighty cold, these spring mornings. The old days you could build a good trash fire in one of them barrels to keep warm. Well, don't want no summons now, and can't freeze to death. Yup, can't freeze to death.

His daily soliloquy completed, he reached into his coat pocket and pulled out a crumpled brown bag that contained his morning sun. The cheap red liquid moved slowly down his throat, providing immediate justification as the blood began to warm in his body. In the hazy light a lean dark figure began to make its way slowly up the block. It hesitated in front of the stoop at 316, but looking around and seeing Ben, it hurried over.

"Yo, Ben."

"Hey, Eugene, I thought that was you. Ain't seen ya round for a coupla days."

"Yeah." The young man put his hands in his pockets, frowned into the ground, and kicked the edge of Ben's can. "The funeral's today, ya know."

"Yeah."

"You going?" He looked up into Ben's face.

"Naw, I ain't got no clothes for them things. Can't abide 'em no way—too sad—it being a baby and all."

"Yeah. I was going myself, people expect it, ya know?"

"Yeah."

"But, man, the way Ciel's friends look at me and all—like I was filth or something. Hey, I even tried to go see Ciel in the hospital, heard she was freaked out and all."

"Yeah, she took it real bad."

"Yeah, well, damn, I took it bad. It was my kid, too, ya know. But Mattie, that fat, black bitch, just standin' in the hospital hall sayin' to me—to me, now, 'Whatcha want?' Like I was a fuckin' germ or something. Man, I just turned and left. You gotta be treated with respect, ya know?"

"Yeah."

"I mean, I should be there today with my woman in the limo and all, sittin' up there, doin' it right. But how you gonna be a man with them ball-busters tellin' everybody it was my fault and I should be the one dead? Damn!"

"Yeah, a man's gotta be a man." Ben felt the need to wet his reply with another sip. "Have some?"

"Naw, I'm gonna be heading on—Ciel don't need me today. I bet that frig, Mattie, rides in the head limo, wearing the pants. Shit—let 'em." He looked up again. "Ya know?"

"Yup."

"Take it easy, Ben." He turned to go.

"You too, Eugene."

"Hey, you going?"

"Naw."

"Me neither. Later."

"Later, Eugene."

Funny, Ben thought, Eugene ain't stopped to chat like that for a long time—near on a year, yup, a good year. He took another swallow to help him bring back the year-old conversation, but it didn't work; the second and third one didn't either. But he did remember that it had been an early spring morning like this one, and Eugene had been wearing those same tight jeans. He had hesitated outside of 316 then, too. But that time he went in . . .

Lucielia had just run water into the tea kettle and was putting it on the burner when she heard the cylinder turn. He didn't have to knock on the door; his key still fit the lock. Her thin knuckles gripped the handle of the kettle, but she didn't turn around. She knew. The last eleven months of her life hung compressed in the air between the click of the lock and his "Yo, baby."

The vibrations from those words rode like parasites on the air waves and came rushing into her kitchen, smashing the compression into indistinguishable days and hours that swirled dizzily before her. It was all there: the frustration of being left alone, sick, with a month-old baby; her humiliation reflected in the case-worker's blue eyes for the unanswerable "you can find him to have it, but can't find him to take care of it" smile; the raw urges that crept, uninvited, between her thighs on countless nights; the eternal whys all meshed with the explainable hate and unexplainable love. They kept circling in such a confusing pattern before her that she couldn't seem to grab even one to answer him with. So there was nothing in Lucielia's face when she turned it toward Eugene, standing in her kitchen door holding a ridiculously pink Easter bunny, nothing but sheer relief. . . .

"So he's back." Mattie sat at Lucielia's kitchen table, playing with Serena. It was rare that Mattie ever spoke more than two sentences to anybody about anything. She didn't have to. She chose her words with the grinding precision of a diamond cutter's drill.

"You think I'm a fool, don't you?"

"I ain't said that."

"You didn't have to," Ciel snapped.

"Why you mad at me, Ciel? It's your life, honey."

"Oh, Mattie, you don't understand. He's really straightened up this time. He's got a new job on the docks that pays real good, and he was just so depressed before with the new baby and no work. You'll see. He's even gone out now to buy paint and stuff to fix up the apartment. And, and Serena needs a daddy."

"You ain't gotta convince me, Ciel."

No, she wasn't talking to Mattie, she was talking to herself. She was convincing herself it was the new job and the paint and Serena that let him back into her life. Yet, the real truth went beyond her scope of understanding. When she laid her head in the hollow of his neck there was a deep musky scent to his body that brought back the ghosts of the Tennessee soil of her childhood. It reached up and lined the inside of her nostrils so that she inhaled his presence almost every minute of her life. The feel of his sooty flesh penetrated the skin of her fingers and coursed through her blood and became one, somewhere, wherever it was, with her actual being. But how do you tell yourself, let alone this practical old woman who loves you, that he was back because of that. So you don't.

You get up and fix you both another cup of coffee, calm the fretting baby on your lap with her pacifier, and you pray silently—very silently—behind veiled eyes that the man will stay.

Ciel was trying to remember exactly when it had started to go wrong again. Her mind sought for the slender threads of a clue that she could trace back to—perhaps—something she had said or done. Her brow was set tightly in concentration as she folded towels and smoothed the wrinkles over and over, as if the answer lay concealed in the stubborn creases of the terry cloth.

The months since Eugene's return began to tick off slowly before her, and she examined each one to pinpoint when the nagging whispers of trouble had begun in her brain. The friction on the towels increased when she came to the month that she had gotten pregnant again, but it couldn't be that. Things were different now. She wasn't sick as she had been with Serena, he was still working—no it wasn't the baby. It's not the baby, it's not the baby—the rhythm of those words sped up the motion of her hands, and she had almost yanked and folded and pressed them into a reality when, bewildered, she realized that she had run out of towels.

Ciel jumped when the front door slammed shut. She waited tensely for the metallic bang of his keys on the coffee table and the blast of the stereo. Lately that was how Eugene announced his presence home. Ciel walked into the living room with the motion of a swimmer entering a cold lake.

"Eugene, you're home early, huh?"

"You see anybody else sittin' here?" He spoke without looking at her and rose to turn up the stereo.

He wants to pick a fight, she thought, confused and hurt. He knows Serena's taking her nap, and now I'm supposed to say, Eugene, the baby's asleep, please cut the music down. Then he's going to say, you mean a man can't even relax in his own home without being picked on? I'm not picking on you, but you're going to wake up the baby. Which is always supposed to lead to: You don't give a damn about me. Everybody's more important than me—that kid, your friends, everybody. I'm just chickenshit around here, huh?

All this went through Ciel's head as she watched him leave the stereo and drop defiantly back down on the couch. Without saying a word, she turned and went into the bedroom. She looked down on the peaceful face of her daughter and softly caressed her small cheek. Her heart became full as she realized, this is the only thing I have ever loved without pain. She pulled the sheet gently over the tiny shoulders and firmly closed the door, protecting her from the music. She then went into the kitchen and began washing the rice for their dinner.

Eugene, seeing that he had been left alone, turned off the stereo and came and stood in the kitchen door.

"I lost my job today," he shot at her, as if she had been the cause.

The water was turning cloudy in the rice pot, and the force of the stream from the faucet caused scummy bubbles to rise to the surface. These broke and sprayed tiny starchy particles onto the dirty surface. Each bubble that broke seemed to increase the volume of the dogged whispers she had been ignoring for the last few months. She poured the dirty water off the rice to destroy and silence them, then watched with a malicious joy as they disappeared down the drain.

"So now, how in the hell I'm gonna make it with no money, huh? And another brat comin' here, huh?"

The second change of the water was slightly clearer, but the starch-speckled bubbles were still there, and this time there was no way to pretend deafness to their message. She had stood at that sink countless times before, washing rice, and she knew the water was never going to be totally clear. She couldn't stand there forever—her fingers were getting cold, and the rest of the dinner had to be fixed, and Serena would be waking up soon and wanting attention. Feverishly she poured the water off and tried again.

"I'm fuckin' sick of never getting ahead. Babies and bills, that's all you good for."

The bubbles were almost transparent now, but when they broke they left light trails of starch on top of the water that curled around her fingers. She knew it would be useless to try again. Defeated, Ciel placed the wet pot on the burner, and the flames leaped up bright red and orange, turning the water droplets clinging on the outside into steam.

Turning to him, she silently acquiesced. "All right, Eugene, what do you want me to do?"

He wasn't going to let her off so easily. "Hey, baby, look, I don't care what you do. I just can't have all these hassles on me right now, ya know?"

"I'll get a job. I don't mind, but I've got no one to keep Serena, and you don't want Mattie watching her."

"Mattie—no way. That fat bitch'll turn the kid against me. She hates my ass, and you know it."

"No, she doesn't, Eugene." Ciel remembered throwing that at Mattie once. "You hate him, don't you?" "Naw, honey," and she had cupped both hands on Ciel's face. "Maybe I just loves you too much."

"I don't give a damn what you say—she ain't minding my kid."

"Well, look, after the baby comes, they can tie my tubes—I don't care." She swallowed hard to keep down the lie.

"And what the hell we gonna feed it when it gets here, huh—air? With two kids and you on my back, I ain't never gonna have nothin'." He came and grabbed her by the shoulders and was shouting into her face. "Nothin', do you hear me, nothin'!"

"Nothing to it, Mrs. Turner." The face over hers was as calm and antiseptic as the room she lay in. "Please, relax. I'm going to give you a local anesthetic and then perform a simple D&C, or what you'd call a scraping to clean out the uterus. Then you'll rest here for about an hour and be on your way. There won't even be much bleeding." The voice droned on in its practiced monologue, peppered with sterile kindness.

Ciel was not listening. It was important that she keep herself completely isolated from these surroundings. All the activities of the past week of her life were balled up and jammed on the right side of her brain, as if belonging to some other woman. And when she had endured this one last thing for her, she would push it up there, too, and then one day give it all to her—Ciel wanted no part of it.

The next few days Ciel found it difficult to connect herself up again with her own world. Everything seemed to have taken on new textures and colors. When she washed the dishes, the plates felt peculiar in her hands, and she was more conscious of their smoothness and the heat of the water. There was a disturbing split second between someone talking to her and the words penetrating sufficiently to elicit a response. Her neighbors left her presence with slight frowns of puzzlement, and Eugene could be heard mumbling, "Moody bitch."

She became terribly possessive of Serena. She refused to leave her alone, even with Eugene. The little girl went everywhere with Ciel, toddling along on plump uncertain legs. When someone asked to hold or play with her, Ciel sat nearby, watching every move. She found herself walking into the bedroom several times when the child napped to see if she was still breathing. Each time she chided herself for this unreasonable foolishness, but within the next few minutes some strange force still drove her back.

Spring was slowly beginning to announce itself at Brewster Place. The arthritic cold was seeping out of the worn gray bricks, and the tenants with apartment windows facing the street were awakened by six o'clock sunlight. The music no longer blasted inside of 3C, and Ciel grew strong with the peacefulness of her household. The playful laughter of her daughter, heard more often now, brought a sort of redemption with it.

"Isn't she marvelous, Mattie? You know she's even trying to make whole sentences. Come on, baby, talk for Auntie Mattie."

Serena, totally uninterested in living up to her mother's proud claims, was trying to tear a gold-toned button off the bosom of Mattie's dress.

"It's so cute. She even knows her father's name. She says, my da da is Gene."

"Better teach her your name," Mattie said, while playing with the baby's hand. "She'll be using it more."

Ciel's mouth flew open to ask her what she meant by that, but she checked herself. It was useless to argue with Mattie. You could take her words however you wanted. The burden of their truth lay with you, not her.

Eugene came through the front door and stopped short when he saw Mattie. He avoided being around her as much as possible. She was always polite to him, but he sensed a silent condemnation behind even her most innocent words. He constantly felt the need to prove himself in front of her. These frustrations often took the form of unwarranted rudeness on his part.

Serena struggled out of Mattie's lap and went toward her father and tugged on his legs to be picked up. Ignoring the child and cutting short the greetings of the two women, he said coldly, "Ciel, I wanna talk to you."

Sensing trouble, Mattie rose to go. "Ciel, why don't you let me take Serena downstairs for a while. I got some ice cream for her."

"She can stay right here," Eugene broke in. "If she needs ice cream, I can buy it for her."

Hastening to soften his abruptness, Ciel said, "That's okay, Mattie, it's almost time for her nap. I'll bring her later—after dinner."

"All right. Now you all keep good." Her voice was warm. "You too, Eugene," she called back from the front door.

The click of the lock restored his balance to him. "Why in the hell is she always up here?"

"You just had your chance—why didn't you ask her yourself? If you don't want her here, tell her to stay out," Ciel snapped back confidently, knowing he never would.

"Look, I ain't got time to argue with you about that old hag. I got big doings in

the making, and I need you to help me pack." Without waiting for a response, he
hurried into the bedroom and pulled his old leather suitcase from under the bed.

A tight, icy knot formed in the center of Ciel's stomach and began to melt
rapidly, watering the blood in her legs so that they almost refused to support her
weight. She pulled Serena back from following Eugene and sat her in the middle
of the living room floor.

"Here, honey, play with the blocks for Mommy—she has to talk to Daddy."
She piled a few plastic alphabet blocks in front of the child, and on her way out
of the room, she glanced around quickly and removed the glass ashtrays off the
coffee table and put them on a shelf over the stereo.

Then, taking a deep breath to calm her racing heart, she started toward the
bedroom.

Serena loved the light colorful cubes and would sometimes sit for an entire
half-hour, repeatedly stacking them up and kicking them over with her feet. The
hollow sound of their falling fascinated her, and she would often bang two of
them together to re-create the magical noise. She was sitting, contentedly engaged in this particular activity, when a slow dark movement along the baseboard
caught her eye.

A round black roach was making its way from behind the couch toward the
kitchen. Serena threw one of her blocks at the insect, and, feeling the vibrations
of the wall above it, the roach sped around the door into the kitchen. Finding a
totally new game to amuse herself, Serena took off behind the insect with a block
in each hand. Seeing her moving toy trying to bury itself under the linoleum by
the garbage pail she threw another block, and the frantic roach now raced along
the wall and found security in the electric wall socket under the kitchen table.

Angry at losing her plaything, she banged the block against the socket, attempting to get it to come back out. When that failed, she unsuccessfully tried to
poke her chubby finger into the thin horizontal slit. Frustrated, tiring of the game,
she sat under the table and realized she had found an entirely new place in the
house to play. The shiny chrome of the table and chair legs drew her attention,
and she experimented with the sound of the block against their smooth surfaces.

This would have entertained her until Ciel came, but the roach, thinking itself
safe, ventured outside of the socket. Serena gave a cry of delight and attempted to
catch her lost playmate, but it was too quick and darted back into the wall. She
tried once again to poke her finger into the slit. Then a bright slender object,
lying dropped and forgotten, came into her view. Picking up the fork, Serena finally managed to fit the thin flattened prongs into the electric socket.

Eugene was avoiding Ciel's eyes as he packed. "You know, baby, this is really a
good deal after me bein' out of work for so long." He moved around her still fig-

ure to open the drawer that held his T-shirts and shorts. "And hell, Maine ain't far. Once I get settled on the docks up there, I'll be able to come home all the time."

"Why can't you take us with you?" She followed each of his movements with her eyes and saw herself being buried in the case under the growing pile of clothes.

"'Cause I gotta check out what's happening before I drag you and the kid up there."

"I don't mind. We'll make do. I've learned to live on very little."

"No, it just won't work right now. I gotta see my way clear first."

"Eugene, please." She listened with growing horror to herself quietly begging.

"No, and that's it!" He flung his shoes into the suitcase.

"Well, how far is it? Where did you say you were going?" She moved toward the suitcase.

"I told ya—the docks in Newport."

"That's not in Maine. You said you were going to Maine."

"Well, I made a mistake."

"How could you know about a place so far up? Who got you the job?"

"A friend."

"Who?"

"None of your damned business!" His eyes were flashing with the anger of a caged animal. He slammed down the top of the suitcase and yanked it off the bed.

"You're lying, aren't you? You don't have a job, do you? Do you?"

"Look, Ciel, believe whatever the fuck you want to. I gotta go." He tried to push past her.

She grabbed the handle of the case. "No, you can't go."

"Why?"

Her eyes widened slowly. She realized that to answer that would require that she uncurl that week of her life, pushed safely up into her head, when she had done all those terrible things for that other woman who had wanted an abortion. She and she alone would have to take responsibility for them now. He must understand what those actions had meant to her, but somehow, he had meant even more. She sought desperately for the right words, but it all came out as—

"Because I love you."

"Well, that ain't good enough."

Ciel had let the suitcase go before he jerked it away. She looked at Eugene, and the poison of reality began to spread through her body like gangrene. It drew his scent out of her nostrils and scraped the veil from her eyes, and he stood before her just as he really was—a tall, skinny black man with arrogance and selfishness twisting his mouth into a strange shape. And, she thought, I don't feel anything now. But soon, very soon, I will start to hate you. I promise—I will hate you. And I'll never forgive myself for not having done it sooner—soon enough to have saved my baby. Oh, dear God, my baby.

Eugene thought the tears that began to crowd into her eyes were for him. But she was allowing herself this one last luxury of brief mourning for the loss of something denied to her. It troubled her that she wasn't sure exactly what that something was, or which one of them was to blame for taking it away. Ciel began to feel the overpowering need to be near someone who loved her. I'll get Serena and we'll go visit Mattie now, she thought in a daze.

Then they heard the scream from the kitchen.

The church was small and dark. The air hung about them like a stale blanket. Ciel looked straight ahead, oblivious to the seats filling up behind her. She didn't feel the damp pressure of Mattie's heavy arm or the doubt that invaded the air over Eugene's absence. The plaintive Merciful Jesuses, lightly sprinkled with sobs, were lost on her ears. Her dry eyes were locked on the tiny pearl-gray casket, flanked with oversized arrangements of red-carnationed bleeding hearts and white-lilied eternal circles. The sagging chords that came loping out of the huge organ and mixed with the droning voice of the black-robed old man behind the coffin were also unable to penetrate her.

Ciel's whole universe existed in the seven feet of space between herself and her child's narrow coffin. There was not even room for this comforting God whose melodious virtues floated around her sphere, attempting to get in. Obviously, He had deserted or damned her, it didn't matter which. All Ciel knew was that her prayers had gone unheeded—that afternoon she had lifted her daughter's body off the kitchen floor, those blank days in the hospital, and now. So she was left to do what God had chosen not to.

People had mistaken it for shock when she refused to cry. They thought it some special sort of grief when she stopped eating and even drinking water unless forced to; her hair went uncombed and her body unbathed. But Ciel was not grieving for Serena. She was simply tired of hurting. And she was forced to slowly give up the life that God had refused to take from her.

After the funeral the well-meaning came to console and offer their dog-eared faith in the form of coconut cakes, potato pies, fried chicken, and tears. Ciel sat in the bed with her back resting against the headboard; her long thin fingers, still as midnight frost on a frozen pond, lay on the covers. She acknowledged their kindnesses with nods of her head and slight lip movements, but no sound. It was as if her voice was too tired to make the journey from the diaphragm through the larynx to the mouth.

Her visitors' impotent words flew against the steel edge of her pain, bled slowly, and returned to die in the senders' throats. No one came too near. They stood around the door and the dressing table, or sat on the edges of the two worn chairs that needed upholstering, but they unconsciously pushed themselves back against the wall as if her hurt was contagious.

A neighbor woman entered in studied certainty and stood in the middle of the room. "Child, I know how you feel, but don't do this to yourself. I lost one, too. The Lord will . . ." And she choked, because the words were jammed down into her throat by the naked force of Ciel's eyes. Ciel had opened them fully now to look at the woman, but raw fires had eaten them worse than lifeless—worse than death. The woman saw in that mute appeal for silence the ragings of a personal hell flowing through Ciel's eyes. And just as she went to reach for the girl's hand, she stopped as if a muscle spasm had overtaken her body and, cowardly, shrank back. Reminiscences of old, dried-over pains were no consolation in the face of this. They had the effect of cold beads of water on a hot iron—they danced and fizzled up while the room stank from their steam.

Mattie stood in the doorway, and an involuntary shudder went through her when she saw Ciel's eyes. Dear God, she thought, she's dying, and right in front of our faces.

"Merciful Father, no!" she bellowed. There was no prayer, no bended knee or sackcloth supplication in those words, but a blasphemous fireball that shot forth and went smashing against the gates of heaven, raging and kicking, demanding to be heard.

"No! No! No!" Like a black Brahman cow, desperate to protect her young, she surged into the room, pushing the neighbor woman and the others out of her way. She approached the bed with her lips clamped shut in such force that the muscles in her jaw and the back of her neck began to ache.

She sat on the edge of the bed and enfolded the tissue-thin body in her huge ebony arms. And she rocked. Ciel's body was so hot it burned Mattie when she first touched her, but she held on and rocked. Back and forth, back and forth— she had Ciel so tightly she could feel her young breasts flatten against the buttons of her dress. The black mammoth gripped so firmly that the slightest increase of pressure would have cracked the girl's spine. But she rocked.

And somewhere from the bowels of her being came a moan from Ciel, so high at first it couldn't be heard by anyone there, but the yard dogs began an unholy howling. And Mattie rocked. And then, agonizingly slow, it broke its way through the parched lips in a spaghetti-thin column of air that could be faintly heard in the frozen room.

Ciel moaned. Mattie rocked. Propelled by the sound, Mattie rocked her out of that bed, out of that room, into a blue vastness just underneath the sun and above time. She rocked her over Aegean seas so clean they shone like crystal, so clear the fresh blood of sacrificed babies torn from their mother's arms and given to Neptune could be seen like pink froth on the water. She rocked her on and on, past Dachau, where soul-gutted Jewish mothers swept their children's entrails off laboratory floors. They flew past the spilled brains of Senegalese infants whose mothers had dashed them on the wooden sides of slave ships. And she rocked on.

She rocked her into her childhood and let her see murdered dreams. And she rocked her back, back into the womb, to the nadir of her hurt, and they found it—a slight silver splinter, embedded just below the surface of the skin. And Mattie rocked and pulled—and the splinter gave way, but its roots were deep, gigantic, ragged, and they tore up flesh with bits of fat and muscle tissue clinging to them. They left a huge hole, which was already starting to pus over, but Mattie was satisfied. It would heal.

The bile that had formed a tight knot in Ciel's stomach began to rise and gagged her just as it passed her throat. Mattie put her hand over the girl's mouth and rushed her out the now-empty room to the toilet. Ciel retched yellowish-green phlegm, and she brought up white lumps of slime that hit the seat of the toilet and rolled off, splattering onto the tiles. After a while she heaved only air, but the body did not seem to want to stop. It was exorcising the evilness of pain.

Mattie cupped her hands under the faucet and motioned for Ciel to drink and clean her mouth. When the water left Ciel's mouth, it tasted as if she had been rinsing with a mild acid. Mattie drew a tub of hot water and undressed Ciel. She let the nightgown fall off the narrow shoulders, over the pitifully thin breasts and jutting hipbones. She slowly helped her into the water, and it was like a dried brown autumn leaf hitting the surface of a puddle.

And slowly she bathed her. She took the soap, and, using only her hands, she washed Ciel's hair and the back of her neck. She raised her arms and cleaned the armpits, soaping well the downy brown hair there. She let the soap slip between the girl's breasts, and she washed each one separately, cupping it in her hands. She took each leg and even cleaned under the toenails. Making Ciel rise and kneel in the tub, she cleaned the crack in her behind, soaped her pubic hair, and gently washed the creases in her vagina—slowly, reverently, as if handling a newborn.

She took her from the tub and toweled her in the same manner she had been bathed—as if too much friction would break the skin tissue. All of this had been done without either woman saying a word. Ciel stood there, naked, and felt the cool air play against the clean surface of her skin. She had the sensation of fresh mint coursing through her pores. She closed her eyes and the fire was gone. Her tears no longer fried within her, killing her internal organs with their steam. So Ciel began to cry—there, naked, in the center of the bathroom floor.

Mattie emptied the tub and rinsed it. She led the still-naked Ciel to a chair in the bedroom. The tears were flowing so freely now Ciel couldn't see, and she allowed herself to be led as if blind. She sat on the chair and cried—head erect.

Since she made no effort to wipe them away, the tears dripped down her chin and landed on her chest and rolled down to her stomach and onto her dark pubic hair. Ignoring Ciel, Mattie took away the crumpled linen and made the bed, stretching the sheets tight and fresh. She beat the pillows into a virgin plumpness and dressed them in white cases.

And Ciel sat. And cried. The unmolested tears had rolled down her parted thighs and were beginning to wet the chair. But they were cold and good. She put out her tongue and began to drink in their saltiness, feeding on them. The first tears were gone. Her thin shoulders began to quiver, and spasms circled her body as new tears came—this time, hot and stinging. And she sobbed, the first sound she'd made since the moaning.

Mattie took the edges of the dirty sheet she'd pulled off the bed and wiped the mucus that had been running out of Ciel's nose. She then led her freshly wet, glistening body, baptized now, to the bed. She covered her with one sheet and laid a towel across the pillow—it would help for a while.

And Ciel lay down and cried. But Mattie knew the tears would end. And she would sleep. And morning would come.

Elizabeth Alexander

lizabeth Alexander was born in New York City in 1962 and raised in Washington, D.C. She graduated from Yale in 1984 and went on to take an M.A. at Boston University and a Ph.D. at the University of Pennsylvania in 1992. She has written two books of poems, *The Venus Hottentot* (1990) and *Body of Life* (1996), a verse play, *Diva Studies,* and many essays and articles on African-American literature and culture. She has taught at Haverford and Smith. "When I was an undergraduate at Yale," she writes, "there were 'poetry people,' both students and professors, and they were largely an intimidating group. I went underground as a poet but my writing received unparalleled encouragement from two teachers in particular, Richard Brodhead and the late John Hersey. Henry Louis Gates, Jr., the late Michael Cooke, Gloria Naylor, and Robert Stepto, among many other teachers and students in the vibrant community orbiting around 'Afro-Am' (as we called the department), took care of my reading and thinking selves, as well as my soul, and all that is very close to the surface of who I am as a writer today."

THE VENUS HOTTENTOT

(1825)

1. Cuvier
Science, science, science!
Everything is beautiful

blown up beneath my glass.
Colors dazzle insect wings.

A drop of water swirls
like marble. Ordinary

crumbs become stalactites
set in perfect angles

of geometry I'd thought
impossible. Few will

ever see what I see
through this microscope.

Cranial measurements
crowd my notebook pages,

and I am moving closer,
close to how these numbers

signify aspects of
national character.

Her genitalia
will float inside a labeled

pickling jar in the Musée
de l'Homme on a shelf

above Broca's brain:
"The Venus Hottentot."

Elegant facts await me.
Small things in this world are mine.

2.
There is unexpected sun today
in London, and the clouds that

most days sift into this cage
where I am working have dispersed.
I am a black cutout against
a captive blue sky, pivoting
nude so the paying audience
can view my naked buttocks.

I am called "Venus Hottentot."
I left Capetown with a promise
of revenue: half the profits
and my passage home: A boon!
Master's brother proposed the trip;
the magistrate granted me leave.
I would return to my family
a duchess, with watered-silk

dresses and money to grow food,
rouge and powders in glass pots,
silver scissors, a lorgnette,
voile and tulle instead of flax,
cerulean blue instead
of indigo. My brother would
devour sugar-studded non-
pareils, pale taffy, damask plums.

That was years ago. London's
circuses are florid and filthy,
swarming with cabbage-smelling
citizens who stare and query,
"Is it muscle? bone? or fat?"
My neighbor to the left is
The Sapient Pig, "The Only
Scholar of His Race." He plays

at cards, tells time and fortunes
by scraping his hooves. Behind
me is Prince Kar-mi, who arches
like a rubber tree and stares back
at the crowd from under the crook
of his knee. A professional
animal trainer shouts my cues.
There are singing mice here.

"The Ball of Duchess DuBarry":
In the engraving I lurch
toward the *belles dames,* mad-eyed, and
they swoon. Men in capes and pince-nez
shield them. Tassels dance at my hips.
In this newspaper lithograph
my buttocks are shown swollen
and luminous as a planet.

Monsieur Cuvier investigates
between my legs, poking, prodding,
sure of his hypothesis.
I half expect him to pull silk
scarves from inside me, paper poppies,
then a rabbit! He complains
at my scent and does not think
I comprehend, but I speak
English. I speak Dutch. I speak
a little French as well, and
languages Monsieur Cuvier
will never know have names.
Now I am bitter and now
I am sick. I eat brown bread,
drink rancid broth. I miss good sun,
miss Mother's *sadza.* My stomach

is frequently queasy from mutton
chops, pale potatoes, blood sausage.
I was certain that this would be
better than farm life. I am
the family entrepreneur!
But there are hours in every day
to conjure my imaginary
daughters, in banana skirts

and ostrich-feather fans.
Since my own genitals are public
I have made other parts private.
In my silence I possess
mouth, larynx, brain, in a single
gesture. I rub my hair

with lanolin, and pose in profile
like a painted Nubian

archer, imagining gold leaf
woven through my hair, and diamonds.
Observe the wordless Odalisque.
I have not forgotten my Xhosa
clicks. My flexible tongue
and healthy mouth bewilder
this man with his rotting teeth.
If he were to let me rise up

from this table, I'd spirit
his knives and cut out his black heart,
seal it with science fluid inside
a bell jar, place it on a low
shelf in a white man's museum
so the whole world could see
it was shriveled and hard,
geometric, deformed, unnatural.

STRAVINSKY IN L.A.

In white pleated trousers, peering through green
sunshades, looking for the way the sun is red
noise, how locusts hiss to replicate the sun.
What is the visual equivalent
of syncopation? Rows of seared palms wrinkle
in the heat waves through green glass. Sprinklers
tick, tick, tick. The Watts Towers aim to split
the sky into chroma, spires tiled with rubble
nothing less than aspiration. I've left
minarets for sun and syncopation,
sixty-seven shades of green which I have
counted, beginning: palm leaves, front and back,
luncheon pickle, bottle glass, etcetera.
One day I will comprehend the different
grades of red. On that day I will comprehend
these people, rhythms, jazz, Simon Rodia,
Watts, Los Angeles, aspiration.

born in South Korea in 1965, Chang-rae Lee immigrated with his family to the United States at the age of three and grew up in Westchester, New York. He graduated from Yale in 1987 and now directs the M.F.A. Program in Creative Writing at Hunter College. His first novel, *Native Speaker* (1995), won the PEN/Hemingway Award and the American Book Award. His second novel, *A Gesture Life,* appeared in 1999. Lee remembers taking a course with Harold Bloom at Yale. The subject was Marlowe and Shakespeare, but at one point the discussion turned to *Paradise Lost.* One student began reading a passage from Book I, "which Professor Bloom then took up in mid-stream, reciting perhaps the next 25 lines. I was in awe, not only of his famous ability to recite, which was astounding, but of the way he was almost physically overwhelmed by the verse, possessed by it. And I thought, my god, to have a life in the language like that!"

When I was a young man, I didn't seek out the pleasure of women. At least not like my comrades in arms, who in their every spare moment seemed ravenous for any part of a woman, in any form, whether in photographs or songs or re-counted stories, and, of course, whenever possible, in the flesh. Pictures were most favored, being easy. I remember a corporal who kept illicit photographs of disrobed maidens in his radio codebook, a sheaf of images he had salvaged from a bombed-out colonial mansion in Indonesia. Whenever I walked by the com-munications tent, he would call out in a most proper voice, "Lieutenant Kurohata, sir, may I receive an opinion from you, please?"

The women in his pictures were Western, I think French or Dutch, and had been caught by the camera in compromising positions—bending over to pick up a dropped book, for example, or being attended in the bath by another nude woman. Corporal Endo had perhaps a score of these, each featuring a different scene, and he shuffled through them with an unswerving awe and reverence that made me think he might be a Christian. Of course, I shouldn't have allowed him to address me so familiarly, as I was superior to him in rank, but we were from the same province and home town, and he was exuberantly innocent and youth-ful and he never called to me if others were within earshot. I know that he had never been with a woman, but in going through his photos he seemed to have become privy to the secrets of lovemaking.

I myself, at that time, had been initiated only once, but, unlike the Corporal, I found little of interest in the hand-size tableaux. They held for me none of the drama that he clearly savored in them. Instead, they smacked of the excess and privilege of a sclerotic, purulent culture—the very forces that our nation's people were struggling against, from Papua New Guinea and Indonesia to the densely forested foothills of old Burma, where we were posted, approximately a hundred and twenty-five kilometres from the outskirts of Rangoon. The women in the photo cards were full figured, and no longer really young, though several of them were attractive in an exotic manner.

The image I preferred was the one of the bath, and although Corporal Endo offered several times to give me that particular card, I didn't want the worry of keeping it among my few personal things. Should I be killed, those items, along with my ashen remains, would be tendered to my family in Japan, as was custom-ary. In most cases, the officer in charge of such transferrals checked the package to make sure that it contained only the most necessary (and honorable) effects, but one heard of embarrassing instances when grieving elders were forced to con-front awkward last notions of their dead. I feared it would be especially shaming in my circumstance. When I was a young boy, I had left the narrow existence of my birth family and our ghetto of hide tanners and renderers—most of us were ethnic Koreans, though we spoke and lived as Japanese, if ones in twilight—to live with a Japanese couple, well-to-do and childless, who treated me as if I were their son. I believed that as adoptive parents they might shoulder the burden of my vices even more heavily than if I had been born to them, blood of their blood, as there would be no excuse but their raising of me. Indeed, I wanted to prove myself in the crucible of the battlefield, and to prove to anyone who might suspect otherwise the worthiness of raising me away from the lowly quarters of my kin. Still, being twenty-three years old and having been with only one woman, a prostitute, during my first posting, in Singapore, I was periodically given to the enticements of such base things, and unable to stop myself from stepping into the radio tent whenever the Corporal addressed me.

"Have I shown you this new series, sir?" he said one sweltering afternoon, reaching into the back flap of his codebook. His eyes seemed bright, almost feral. "I traded some of mine to a fellow in munitions. He had these. He said he was tired of them, sir."

There were several photographs pasted into a small journal which depicted women and men together, patently engaging in sexual intercourse. I had never seen such pictures before. The style of the photography was documentary, almost clinical, as though the overexposed frames were meant for a textbook on human coitus. To my mind, there was nothing remotely titillating in them, save perhaps the shocking idea that people had willingly performed the acts while someone else had photographed them.

The Corporal took more than a customary delight in these pictures. He seemed to be drawn into their stark realism, as if he desired to inhabit them somehow. In the week or two after he had first shown them to me, I encountered him several times in the camp, and in each instance I found him further disheveled in appearance, wholly unwashed and reeking most awfully, even more than the camp norm, the private journal clutched in his hands. His face had erupted in a sudden rash of pimples. He was, as I have said, callow and youthful, and, at nineteen, without much developed musculature or much hair on his lip. He was the youngest boy of a fairly prominent family in our town, and he had been trained in coded field communications to take advantage of his obvious intelligence and to avoid the likely consequences of his physical immaturity if he became an infantry regular, which, long before an enemy confronted him, would mean certain injury and possibly death at the punitive hands of superiors.

I took pity on him, though I was afraid that lurking beneath his quick mind was an instability, a defect of character which I was certain would lead him to a troubling circumstance. As one of the brigade's medical personnel, I decided to write a memorandum to Captain Ono, the physician-in-charge, advising that the

Corporal be evaluated and possibly even relieved of his duties and disarmed, but, like almost everything else in wartime, the memo was lost, or ignored.

This was in the early fall of 1944, when it seemed that our forces were being routed across the entire region. Admiral Yamamoto's transport plane had been ambushed and destroyed by American fighter planes more than a year before, and the general mood, if still hopeful, was certainly not as ebullient as it had been in the high, early times of the war, when the Burma Road fell, and then Mandalay. And now, under regular threat of attack from British and American bombers— though, as if we'd been forgotten, none ever seemed to come for us—the behavior of the brigade, and most notably that of Corporal Endo, grew increasingly more extreme.

Late one evening, he came to my tent, behind the medical quarters, and asked if he could come inside and speak to me. He had washed up, and he looked much like the Corporal of old. Although I was weary and about to retire, it was clear that the Corporal was troubled. There was a trenchant, focussed look in his eyes, as if an idea had taken a profound hold over him and he was useless before it.

He didn't speak right away, and I asked him if I might help him with something.

He replied, "Please forgive me, Lieutenant. I'm rude to request a moment from you and then waste your time." He paused for a few seconds, and then went on. "You've been most generous to me, and I feel that my conduct has been inappropriate. There is no excuse. I feel ashamed of myself, so much so that I sometimes wish I were no longer living."

"There's no need for such a sentiment, Corporal Endo," I said, concerned by his words. "If your shame comes from showing some of your pictures to me, you must obviously know that it was always my choice to look at them. You did not force them on me."

"Yes, of course, Lieutenant," he answered, bowing his head at a supplicant angle. "I'm sorry, sir, for the implication. But, if you'll excuse me, it wasn't only the pictures I was talking about. Please forgive my insolence, but it is another thing that makes me feel desperate."

He paused again, folding his arms across his belly as though he were suddenly cold. Then he said, "You see, sir, it's about the new arrivals everyone has been talking about. It's known around camp that they're scheduled to be here soon, and I've received messages for the quartermaster that the supply transport will likely arrive by tomorrow."

"What about it, Corporal?"

"Well, sir, I've looked around camp yesterday and today, and I haven't been able to see where they'll be housed, once they're here. I thought that, as one of the medical officers, you might know."

"The housing of the female volunteers will no doubt be quickly determined, but not by me. I'm not in charge of their status or medical care. That will be Captain Ono's area, as he's the chief medical officer. Anyway, I don't see why this is your concern, Corporal."

The Corporal bobbed repeatedly, his face still quite serious. "Yes, sir. Should I then speak to Captain Ono?"

I didn't answer, as I was certain that I would grow annoyed if our conversation went on any longer. But I also feared that the Corporal might provoke Captain Ono. The Captain was a controlled man, almost grimly so, wound up within himself like a dense, impassable thicket. A week earlier, he had beaten a private nearly to death for accidentally brushing him as he passed on a narrow footpath near the latrines. Ono had ordered the man to kneel, and, in plain view of onlookers, beat him with the butt of his revolver, until the private was bloody and unconscious. He treated the man soon thereafter in the infirmary, saving his life with some quick surgical work to relieve the building pressure of blood on his brain. In fairness, it was an isolated act of violence. Still, I was concerned for Corporal Endo, and so I said to him, "Will you tell me what your interest in all this is? You won't find the Captain very patient, if he agrees to speak to you at all."

The young Corporal nodded gravely. "Yes, sir. I'm grateful for your advice. You see, sir, I was hoping that I could be among the first of those who might meet the volunteers when they arrive. If there is to be a greeting in the camp, for example, I would be honored to take part."

"Corporal Endo," I said sternly. "There will be no public greeting or reception of any kind. You ought to strike any such notion from your thoughts. As to meeting the female volunteers, it is the officer corps that will first inspect them. I'm new to this myself, but enlisted men, I've been informed, will be issued their tickets shortly thereafter, and it will be up to you to hold a place for yourself on the queue. I see you are most anxious to meet the volunteers, as most of the men will be when they learn of their arrival, but I suggest that you remain as circumspect as possible. I am also ordering you not to spread further news of their arrival. There will be time enough for foment in the camp. We don't need any beforehand."

"Yes, Lieutenant."

"The other piece of advice I have is that you put away all the picture cards you've collected. Don't look at them for a while. I believe you've developed an unhealthy dependence upon them. Do you think this may be true, Corporal?"

"Yes, sir," he said regretfully.

"Then take my advice. Bundle them up and put them in the bottom of your footlocker. Or perhaps destroy them. There's an atmosphere of malaise in the camp, and I believe it's partly due to a host of anticipations, both good and bad."

The Corporal nodded. "It's assumed among the men that the British and Americans will soon mount another major offensive, in the northern and eastern territories," he said.

"No doubt they will. As the commander instructed the officers last week, we must ready ourselves for death and suffering. When the female volunteers do arrive, perhaps it would be good if you make your own visitation. This is most regular. But keep in mind, Corporal Endo, the reasons we are here. As the commander, Colonel Ishii, has told us, it is our way of life that we're fighting for, and so it behooves each one of us to carry ourselves with dignity, in whatever we do. Try to remember this. I won't always be around to give you counsel."

"Yes, sir. Thank you, sir."

"Is that all?"

"Yes, sir," he answered, rising to his feet. He bowed, but didn't lift his head immediately, and said, "Sir?"

"Corporal?"

"If I may ask, sir," he said weakly, almost as a boy would who already feared he knew the answer. "Will you be visiting the volunteers as well?"

"Naturally," I replied. "You may take your leave now, Corporal."

In truth, I hadn't yet thought of the question he'd posed, and for the rest of the night I wondered what I would do. I had wanted to assure the Corporal of the commonness of our procedures, and yet the imminent arrival of these "volunteers," as they were referred to, seemed quite removed from the ordinary. Certainly, I had heard of the mobilization of such a corps, in northern China and in the Philippines and on other islands, and, like everyone else, I appreciated the logic of deploying young women to maintain the morale of officers and foot soldiers in the field. And, like everyone else, I suppose, I assumed that it would be a familiar event, just one among the many thousands of details in a wartime camp. But when the day finally came, I realized that I had been mistaken.

The convoy arrived a week later. It had been delayed by an ambush of native insurgents and had suffered significant damage and loss of supplies. There were at least a dozen men with serious injuries, three of whom were beyond help. Two trucks had been abandoned en route, and I remember the men crowding around the remaining truck, which bore sacks of rice and quantities of other foods, like pickled radishes and dried fish. At the time, we were still in contact with the supply line, and there were modest but decent rations available to us. It was clear, however, that the supplies were steadily growing sparser with each transport. The ambush had left the truck riddled with bullet holes, and one of the sergeants ordered a few of his men to pick the truck bed clean of every last grain of rice, which had drizzled out of holes in the burlap. The soldiers looked as if they were searching for grubs. It was a pathetic sight, particularly when the sergeant lined up the men after they finished and had them pour their scavengings into his cap, which he in turn presented to the presiding officer-in-charge.

I believe we had nearly forgotten what else had been expected, when a lone transport drove slowly up the road. It turned before reaching us in the central yard, and headed to the house of the commander, a small hut of palm wood and bamboo and thatch, situated at the far end of an expansive clearing. I could see that the doctor, Captain Ono, had just emerged from the commander's quarters and was standing at attention on a makeshift veranda. The driver stopped and folded down the back gate of the truck bed. He called into the dark hold and helped to the ground an older woman wearing a paper hat. She then turned to bark raspily inside. There was no answer and the woman shouted again, louder this time. The girls then climbed down from the truck, one by one, holding their hands above their eyes, shading them from the high Burmese light.

They were dressed like peasants, in baggy, crumpled white trousers and loose shirts. One might have thought they were young boys, were it not for their braided hair. The older woman and the driver pulled each girl by the arms as she descended and stood them in a row before the steps of the veranda. That there were only five of them seems remarkable to me now, given that there were nearly two hundred men in the encampment, but at the time I hadn't thought clearly about what was awaiting them in the coming days and nights. Like the rest of the men, I was simply struck by their presence, by the white shock of their oversized pants, their dirty, unshod feet, the narrowness of their hands and their throats. And soon enough the comprehension of what lay beneath the crumpled cotton shook me, as if I'd just heard an air-raid siren, and probably had the same effect on every other man standing at attention in that dusty clay field.

Captain Ono ordered the woman to march the girls up the steps. They looked frightened, and all but one ascended quickly to the veranda landing. The last one hesitated, though just momentarily, and the Captain stepped forward and struck her in the face with the back of his hand, sending her down to one knee. He did not seem particularly enraged. He then struck her again, and she fell back limply. She did not cry out. The older woman waited until Captain Ono withdrew before helping the girl up. The Captain knocked on the door. It was opened by the house servant and the Captain entered, followed by the older woman and the five young girls.

That night there was an unusually festive air in the camp. Groups of soldiers squatted outside their tents singing songs and trading stories in the temperate night air. There had been no ration of sake in the supply shipment except for a few large bottles for the officers, but the men didn't seem to mind. Strangely enough, Corporal Endo seemed to be the only one in a dark mood, and he sought me out as I took an evening walk. As I made my way along the camp's perimeter, listening to the rhythmic din of birds and insects calling out from the jungle, I thought of the sorry line of girls entering the house. They had spent the better part of the afternoon inside with the commander, shielded from the intense heat of the day. The Captain had come to the infirmary that afternoon to inform me of my new duties. He told me that, from the next day on, I and not he would be responsible for maintaining the readiness of the girls. Very soon the fighting would resume, he said with a chilling surety, and his time and skills would be required elsewhere. Since I was the paramedical officer—field-trained but not formally educated—it would be more than appropriate for me to handle their care. They were quite valuable, after all, to the well-being and morale of the camp, and vigilance would be in order.

Corporal Endo found me just short of the southeast checkpoint, beyond which our squads were regularly patrolling. To the left, one could see the faintest glimmers of light from the commander's hut, some fifty metres away, filtering through the half-cleared vegetation of the perimeter. There was no sound, just weak electric light glowing through the slats of the hut's bamboo shutters.

"Lieutenant, sir," Endo said, addressing me gloomily, "I've been thinking all afternoon about what's to come in the next days."

"You mean about the expected offensive from the enemy?"

"I suppose, yes, that, too," he said, regarding the light from the hut. "There's been much radio traffic lately. Almost all concerning where they'll strike, and when."

"Near here, and soon," I replied, echoing what Captain Ono had told me.

"Yes, sir," Endo said, "that seems to be the conclusion. But what I was thinking of mostly was the volunteers."

"You'll have your due turn," I said, annoyed that he was still preoccupied with the issue. "It will be a day or two or three, whatever is determined. In the meanwhile, you should keep yourself busy. It's an unhealthy anticipation that you are developing, Corporal."

"But if I can make myself clear, sir, it's not that way at all. I'm not thinking about when I'll see one of them. In fact, sir, I'm almost sure of *not* visiting. I won't seek their company at all."

This surprised me. "Of course, you're not required to," I said. "No one is."

"Yes, sir, I know," he said softly, following me as I made my way along the path back toward the main encampment, which led directly past the commander's hut. We walked for some time before he spoke again. "The fellows in the communications and munitions areas drew lots this morning, to make things orderly, and by sheer chance I took first place among my rank. There was much gibing and joking about it, and some of the fellows offered me cigarettes and fruit if I would trade with them. I had to leave the tent then, and they probably thought I was being a bad winner."

We had reached the point on the path which was closest to the hut. The sentry noticed us and let us pass; he was a private I had recently treated for a mild case of dysentery. Again there was hardly a sound save the sharp, high songs of the nighttime fauna.

"So why did you leave?" I asked.

"You see, sir," he continued, "I've decided not to visit those girls. I don't really know why, because it's true that every day I've been in this miserable situation I've been thinking about being with a woman, any woman. But yesterday, after I saw them arrive in the camp, I suddenly stopped wanting that. I know I must be sick, Lieutenant. I do in fact feel sick, but I didn't come to ask for any treatment or advice. I don't want my lot anymore, but I don't want any of the others to have it, either. So I thought I could ask you to hold it for me, so none of the fellows can get to it."

He then showed me a torn-edged chit, a tiny, triangular bit of rice paper with a scribble on one side. It was nothing. His fellows would certainly just jostle for their places when the time came, chits or not. But the Corporal handed the scrap to me as if it were the last ashes of an ancestor. I thought for a moment that he had deceived me about his virginity and was suffering from an untreated syphilitic infection, but I saw only the straining earnestness of his narrow, boyish face.

I unbuttoned the chest pocket of my shirt and deposited the bit of paper. I said nothing to the Corporal. He was genuinely grateful and relieved, and he bowed almost wistfully before me, making me feel as though I had indeed come to his aid, that I had helped save him from whatever fate he imagined would befall him were he to visit the ones delivered for our final solace and pleasure. And I recall understanding this last notion. For although it was true that the talk throughout the camp was still of the glorious brightness of our ultimate victory, the surer truth, as yet unspoken, was that we were now facing our demise. Famous, of course, is the resolve of the Japanese soldier, the lore of his tenacity and courage and willingness to fight in the breach of certain death, but I will say, too, that for every man who showed no fear there were three or four or five others whose mettle was as unashamedly wan and mortal as yours or mine. As the defenders of the most far-flung sector of the occupied territory, we had little question about the terrible hours ahead of us. It was a startlingly real possibility that every man in the camp would soon be dead.

I guided Corporal Endo quickly past the commander's hut, his gaze almost rigidly locked upon the shuttered windows. We had gone some thirty paces when he grabbed me roughly by the shoulder.

I looked up and saw that the door had opened. A man stood on the open porch, his hands on his hips. He seemed to be surveying the darkened compound, and the Corporal and I both stopped in our tracks, trying not to make a sound. From the silhouette it was clearly the commander, Colonel Ishii, with his thick torso and bowlegs and the distinctly squared-off shape of his head. He was naked, and he was inhaling and exhaling deeply from his belly. These days people might call the commander a health nut, and some of his ministrations were quite peculiar. He would exercise vigorously in the early morning, an intense regimen of calisthenics and stretching which would challenge a seasoned drill sergeant. Then, sweating like a plow ox, he would deliberately allow himself to be bitten by swarms of mosquitoes, letting the ravenous insects feed freely on his belly and chest and back. It was a way of bleeding himself. One would assume he'd have suffered terribly from malaria, but he seemed perfectly fit.

The commander took a step down and I thought he must have seen us. I was ready to address him to avoid seeming as if we were trying to conceal ourselves in the darkness, but then he bent down to peer beneath the floorboards of the hut, which was set up off the ground on short posts. After a moment's inspection, he straightened and began speaking down into the crawl space, his tone eerily gentle, as if he were addressing a favorite niece who was misbehaving.

"There is little reason to hide anymore. It's all done now. It's silly to think otherwise. You will come out and join your companions."

There was no answer.

"You must come out sometime," he continued. "I suppose it's more comfortable under there than out in the jungle. I can understand that. But you know there is food inside now. The cook has made some rice balls. The others are eating them as we speak."

"I want to be with my sister," a young voice replied miserably. She was speaking awkwardly, in Japanese, with some Korean words mixed in. I hadn't heard much of that language since my childhood, and I found myself suspended, anticipating the old tenor of the words. "I want to know where she is," the girl said. "I must know. I won't come out until I know."

"She's with the camp doctor," the commander said. "She's having her ear looked at. The doctor wanted to make sure she was all right."

I wondered whether the girl knew that the doctor was the same man who had struck her sister down. There was a pause, and the commander simply stood there in his blunt nakedness, the strangest picture of tolerance.

I heard the girl's weak reply. "I promised my mother we would always stay together," she said.

The commander said to her, "That should be so. You are good to try to keep such a promise. But how can you do so from down there? Your sister will be back with you tomorrow. For now, you must come out, right at this moment. Right at this moment. I won't wait any longer."

Something must have shifted in his voice, a different note that only she could hear, for she came out, scuttling forward on her hands and knees. When she reached the open air she didn't get up but stayed crumpled at his feet. She was naked, too. The clouds had scattered, and in the dim violet moonlight the sight of them, if you did not know the truth, was almost a thing of beauty, a painter's scene, conjured to address the subject of a difficult love. The commander offered his hand and the girl took it and pulled herself up, her posture bent and tentative as though she were ill. She was crying softly. He guided her to the step of the porch, and it was there that her legs lost their power and she collapsed. The commander grabbed her wrist and barked at her to get up, the sharp report of his voice sundering the air, but she didn't move. She was sobbing wearily for her sister, and I understood that she was calling her sister's name, "Kku-taeh," which, I knew, meant bottom, or last.

The Colonel made a low grunt and jerked the girl up by her wrist. It looked as if he were dragging a skinned calf. He got her inside and a peal of cries went up. He shouted for quiet with a sudden, terrible edge in his voice. Meanwhile, the sentry had heard the outburst and run around to the front, instinctively levelling his rifle on us as he came forward. As I raised my hands, the sentry yelled "Hey there!" and I realized that Corporal Endo, inexplicably, had begun to sprint back into the darkness of the jungle.

I shouted "Don't shoot!" but the sentry had already fired once in our direction. The shot flew past well above me, though I could feel it bore through the heavy air. There was little chance that it could have hit the Corporal, or anyone else. The sentry seemed shocked at his own reaction, however, and dropped his rifle. I was relieved, but the commander had already come out of the house, his robe hastily wrapped around his middle, a shiny pistol in his hands. Over the sentry's shoulder I could see the commander take aim from the veranda and fire twice. Then a questioning, half-bemused expression flitted across the sentry's face, and he fell to the ground.

The commander walked over and motioned to me with the gun to let down my hands. He had recognized me as the doctor's assistant. "Lieutenant Kurohata," he said almost kindly, not even looking down at the sentry's body. I knew the man was dead: one of the bullets had struck him in the neck and torn away a section of his carotid artery. The ground was slowly soaking up his blood. "You are a medical man, are you not?" the colonel said. Up close he was more inebriated than I had surmised, his eyes sleepy and opaque. "You can help me then, I hope, with a small confusion I was having this evening."

He paused, as if trying to remember what he was saying, and in the background I could hear the chaotic shouts of orders and footfalls coming from the main camp. I replied, "However I am able, sir."

"What? Oh, yes. You can aid me with something. I was being entertained this evening, as you may know, and it occurred to me that there was a chance of . . . a complication. You know what I'm talking about, Lieutenant?"

"Yes, sir," I said, though in fact I had no idea.

"They are young, after all, and likely fertile." He paused a moment, and said, as if in an aside, "And, of course, being virginal, that can't protect them, can it?"

"No, sir."

"Of course not," he concurred, as if I had asked him the question.

The commander's query surprised me. He was in his mid-thirties, which is not old in the world, but this late in the war he was practically ancient; I thought that he would have known—unlike Endo and myself—the many ways of women and amour, and yet he seemed to be even more ignorant of them than we were. He crossed his arms in an almost casual pose, though he kept a tight hold on the pistol, which poked out beneath one folded arm. "One grows up with all kinds of apocrypha and lore, yes? I mean us men. A young woman naturally receives guid-ance about such matters, estimable information, while it seems we are left on our own, each by each and one by one. To our own devices."

At that moment a squad of armed men came running up to us. The com-mander raised his free hand and waved them forward. The squad leader, a corpo-ral, seemed shocked to find the lifeless body of the sentry lying in awkward repose by our feet.

"Remove him," the commander said. Two of the men lifted up the corpse by his armpits and calves. Someone gathered the dropped rifle and the bloody cap. As they left, I realized that neither the commander nor I had spoken a word of explanation to the men, nor had any of them even whispered a question.

"You'll look after this," the commander said to me matter-of-factly, referring, I understood immediately, to the death report, which was filled out whenever time and circumstances allowed. The next day I would note in the necessary form that the sentry, a Private Ozaki, had been shot dead by a forward sniper who was sought out by our patrols but never found.

I bowed curtly and the commander acknowledged me with a grunt. I waited while he ascended the low porch and went inside. As I started back for my own tent, I could hear him speaking again, in a calm, unagitated tone. "Look at my girls," I heard him saying, repeating himself slowly, with a sort of wonder, like a father who has been away much too long. "Look here at my girls."

By midmorning the day was already muggy and bright. I hadn't gone in search of Corporal Endo the night before, nor did I have any interest in doing so amid the early bustle of the day. No one knew that he had inadvertently instigated the shooting, or that he had even been present. When it was announced that patrols would be increased to prevent further sniping, I hoped he would keep quiet and let the event pass. The commander, whom I saw during his morning exercise, seemed fresh and fit.

That afternoon, the commander relinquished the girls to my care. I ordered that they be housed temporarily in one of the barracks, displacing a handful of men. A receiving house was being built by a crew of native tradesmen, who were following specifications provided by Captain Ono. I was to oversee this as well, but there was little left to be done.

The comfort house, which is how it was known, was a narrow structure with five doorways, each with a rod across the top for a sheet that would be hung as a privacy screen. The whole thing was perhaps as long as a large transport truck, ten metres or so. There were five compartments, of course, one for each of the girls; these were tiny, windowless rooms, no more than the space of one and a half tatami mats. In the middle of each space was a wide plank of wood meant for lying down on. The plank was widest where the shoulders would be, and then it narrowed again for the head, so that its shape was like the lid of an extra-broad coffin. This is where the girls would receive the men. After their duties were over, they would sleep where they could in the compartment. They would take their meals with the older Japanese woman, who was already living in her own small tent, behind the comfort house. She would prepare their food and keep hold of their visitors' tickets and make sure they had enough of the things a young woman might need, to keep herself in a minimally respectable way.

I alone was responsible for their health. The girls' well-being aside, I was to make certain they could perform their duties for the men in the camp. The greatest challenge, of course, would be preventing them from contracting venereal disease. It was well known what an intractable problem this was in the first years of fighting, particularly in Manchuria, when it might happen that two out of every three men were stricken and rendered useless for battle. In those initial years there had been comfort houses set up with former prostitutes shipped in from Japan by Army-sanctioned merchants, and the infection rate was naturally high. Now that the comfort stations were run under military ordinances and the women were not professionals but, rather, those who had unwittingly enlisted or had been forcibly conscripted into the wartime women's volunteer corps, the expectation was that disease would be kept in check. Most of the volunteers were not Japanese, of course, just normal girls from Korea and China and wherever else they could be found. Now it was the men who were problematic, and there was a stiff penalty for anyone known to be infected who did not seek treatment beforehand. I had one of the sergeants announce final call for the camp in this regard, as I hoped to quarantine anyone who might infect a girl. Only two men came forward complaining of symptoms, both of whom were in the ward already.

I was to examine the girls and state their fitness for their duties. I had put on a doctor's coat and was waiting for the women to be brought to the infirmary. The intense heat of the day seemed to treble inside the room, and my stiff white coat was another layer over my regular uniform. I hadn't eaten anything yet that day, because of the sticking temperature and a crabbed feeling of an incipient illness.

The older woman, Mrs. Matsui, poked her head in the open doorway and bowed several times. She was pale and pock-faced and dressed in the tawdry, overly shiny garb of a woman who had obviously once been in the trade. She was clearly, too, a full Japanese, and the fact of this bothered me now, to have to see her cheapness against the line of modest girls who trailed her.

They were all fairly young, ranging from sixteen to twenty-one. At the head was a tallish girl with a dark mole on her cheek. The two beside her were more retiring in their appearance, their eyes averted from me; they seemed to be cling-ing to one another, though they weren't touching at all. The next girl, I realized, was the one who had hidden beneath the commander's hut. She had a firm hold of the hand of the girl behind her, who I realized must be her sister, the one she called Kku-taeh.

She was the only one who gazed directly at me. She met my eyes as someone might on any public bus or trolley car, though her regard was instantly fixing and cool. She had a wide, oval-shaped face, and there was some bruising along the side of her jaw and upper neck. She had been housed with Captain Ono while the rest of them had gone on to entertain the commander; the doctor had re-served her, implying to the commander that she was not a virgin like the others, who would offer him the ineffable effects of their maidenhood, which to a soldier is like an amulet of life and rebirth.

I told Mrs. Matsui to ready the girls for examination and she ordered them to remove their clothing. They were slow to do so and she went up to the girl with the mole and tore at her hair. The girl complied and the rest of them began to disrobe. I did not watch them. I stood at the table with a writing board and the sheets of paper for recording their medical histories and periodic examinations. There was special paperwork for everything, and it was no different for the young women of the comfort house. The girl with the mole came to me first. I nodded to the table and she lifted herself up gingerly. She was naked and in the bright afternoon light coming from the slatted window her youthful skin was practically luminous, as though she were somehow lit from inside. For a moment I was transfixed by the strangeness of it all, the sheer exposed figure of the girl and then the four others who stood covering themselves with their hands, their half-real, half-phantom nearness, which I thought must be like the allure of pornography for Corporal Endo. But then Mrs. Matsui came around the front of the girl on the exam table and without any prompting from me spread her knees apart.

"You'll probably see they're all a bit raw today," she said hoarsely, like a monger with her morning's call. "Nothing like the first time, right? But you'll believe me when I say they'll be used to it by tomorrow."

Her cloying tone and familiarity put me off, but she was right. The girl's privates were terribly swollen and bruised, and there were dried smears of crimson-tinged discharge on her thighs and underside. Mrs. Matsui had just delivered the four of them from the commander's hut, and the faint, sour odors of dried sweat and spilled rice wine and blood and sexual relations emanated from the girl. When I reached to examine her more closely, she curled her hips away and began whimpering. Mrs. Matsui held her steady, but I didn't touch her then. I inspected the others; I didn't touch them, either, and the condition was more or less the same. I was just beginning to examine the last one, Kku-taeh, when the door swung open. It was the doctor, in his fatigues, entering the room.

"What do you think you are doing?" Ono said sharply, staring at Kku-taeh.

I answered, "The required examinations, Captain. I've nearly completed them, and I'll have the records for you shortly."

"I don't need *records* from you," he said, not hiding his irritation. He pushed Mrs. Matsui aside, then took hold of the girl by the back of her neck. Her shoulders tightened at his touch. He was applying subtle pressure, enough that she was wincing slightly, though not letting herself cry out.

"I need order from you, Lieutenant. Order and adherence to our code. What appears to elude you is the application of principle. The true officer understands this. You examined them, yes. But in doing so you abandoned far more important principles. This examination room, for example, is a disgrace and besmirchment upon our practice." He nodded at the clothes in piles on the floor. "You follow your duties but your conduct is so often middling. In truth, I remain unconvinced of you. Now you'll get them out of here and ready for receiving the officer corps tonight. The comfort house is done?"

"Yes, sir."

"Then you can leave the examination room, Lieutenant."

"Captain, sir," I said, glancing at the girl beside him. She was stony-faced and grimly silent. "I have not yet completed the examinations."

The doctor was still staring at Kku-taeh, not acknowledging my statement. Already he seemed to consider us gone. I had known from the first moment I met him that he was a man of singular resolve, and even hardness, particularly when it came to the care of his patients, and I had always admired him for this. He had a wife and a young child back in Japan, whose attractive portraits he kept on his desk. Those portraits had been steady witness to numerous bloody surgical procedures, and I thought that anyone else would surely have retired them to a private cabinet. And now he had a girl unclothed on the table, and he was pushing her to lie down on her back, his drawn, unhumored face hovering above her shallow belly.

Mrs. Matsui gathered the rest of the girls, trying to quiet Kku-taeh's sister, who refused to leave the room, with a quick slap. The three other girls had to work together to drag her out. On the table, Kku-taeh remained oddly unmoved, almost dead to her and everything else. I removed my white coat, and left it folded on the desk chair. When I shut the door I did not look back into the room.

I was relieved to be outside. I stopped at the enlisted mess tent, and the steward there offered to prepare me a cup of tea. I sat on an upended crate and waited, welcoming the small kindness. In the corner of my vision Mrs. Matsui and the others were half carrying the hysterical girl toward the comfort house, which seemed, being so newly built, a lone clean island in the growing fetor of the camp. With dusk, I knew, the officers would recommence their visitations.

I also noticed what I thought to be the slight figure of Corporal Endo, crouched at the far end of the central yard, where it gave way to dense jungle. He was sitting back on his haunches, his canvas radioman's cap pinched down over his brow to shade his eyes from the fierce daylight. He must have seen me, but he did not wave or make a gesture; he appeared to be surveying the goings on, particularly the troop of girls making their way to Mrs. Matsui's tent behind the comfort house. Perhaps he had been waiting for them to come out from the medical hut, or perhaps he had just then crouched to rest. Whatever the case, he would never tell me or anyone else. Even now, more than fifty years afterward, I wonder what might have come of Endo had the following events not occurred. Would he have married? Would he have had children? Or would he have lived a solitary life, as I have, and known only the scantest taste of a woman's love? And even now what he did next remains a mystery to me, and I remain useless before the memory, inert with fascination and dread. I keep revisiting the scene, turning it over, again and again, like one of Endo's tattered picture cards.

He rose from his crouch and began to trot toward Mrs. Matsui and the girls. The distance between them was not great, perhaps sixty or seventy metres, and I was able to see the whole event, from start to end. The Corporal was not a natural runner, and he appeared to be awkwardly exercising, though hardly a soul was exerting himself any more than was necessary those days. Some small part of me probably fathomed what he intended, and yet I simply watched like a disinterested spectator, whose sudden glint of prescience is somehow self-fulfilling.

The Corporal approached and ordered the women to halt. I could barely hear what was said, though I could gather that Mrs. Matsui was objecting to what Endo seemed to want, which was an immediate private audience with one of the girls. Mrs. Matsui was pointing toward the medical hut, but he pushed her aside. The three girls who had been supporting Kku-taeh's sister backed away, and she fell weakly to her knees; it was Endo who raised her up with a stiff pull. She was not fighting him; in fact, her movement seemed to lighten, as if he were an old acquaintance and she were pleased to see him. Some men had noticed the commotion and were calling to him, asking what he was up to, what he was doing, shouting it in a hearty, knowing way. He ignored them and dragged the girl along, quickly arriving at his original position at the edge of the bush. After the two of them disappeared into the dense foliage and had not returned for several minutes, the corporals and privates working near the trucks began to jog over, and it was then that I knew something irregular had occurred. I slipped beneath the netting of the mess tent and slowly made my way across the dusty red clay of the yard, past the officers' quarters and latrines, then past the narrow comfort house, its walls rough-hewn and smelling of fresh-cut wood, to where the canopy rose up again and the shade cooled the air. My legs felt unbearably heavy. The half-dozen or so men were gathered there, in the trodden entrance of a patrol trail, the couple in their midst, Endo sitting on the ground with the girl lying beside him.

Her throat was slashed, deeply, very near the bone. She had probably died in less than a minute. There was much blood, naturally, but it was almost wholly pooled in a broad blot beneath her, the dry red earth turned a rich hue of brown. There was little blood on her person, hardly a spatter or speck anywhere save on her collar and on the tops of her shoulders. It was as though she had gently laid down for him and calmly waited for the cut. The oddity was that he was unsoiled as well, completely untouched. There was nothing even on his hands, with which he was rubbing his close-shaven head. I asked him what had happened, but he did not seem to hear me. He sat there, his knees splayed out, his cap fallen off, an errant expression on his face, like that of a man who has seen his other self.

Finally, someone asked me what they ought to do, and, as I held rank, I told the men to take Corporal Endo under arms to the officer-in-charge. I recall, now, having remained at the trail after Endo had been escorted away. I ordered the rest of the men to fetch a stretcher for the girl's body, and for a few moments I was left alone with her. In the sudden quiet of the glade I felt I should kneel down. Her eyes were open, coal-dark but still bright. She did not look fearful or sad. And, for the first time, I appreciated what she truly looked like, the delicate cast of her young girl's face.

Endo was kept under close watch that night, and after a brief interrogation by Captain Ono he confessed to the deed. The following morning, just after dawn, in front of the entire garrison, he was executed. Mrs. Matsui was present, as was Kku-taeh, who looked upon the proceedings coldly. She stood aside from the other girls. The officer-in-charge announced that Endo had been charged not with murder but with treasonous action against the corps. He should be considered as guilty as any saboteur who had stolen or despoiled the camp's armament or rations. Endo looked small and frail; he was so frightened he could hardly walk. He had to be helped to the spot where he would kneel. By custom he was then offered a blade, but he dropped it before he could pierce his belly, retching instead. The swordsman standing beside him did not hesitate and struck him cleanly. Endo's headless body pitched lightly forward, his delicate hands outstretched, as if to break his fall.

Claire Messud

laire Messud has written two novels, *When the World Was Steady* (1994) and *The Last Life* (1999). She graduated from Yale in 1987. She then went to England, where she first took an M.A. at Cambridge and then worked as a journalist in London before returning to the United States in 1995. "I started publishing stories in campus magazines my freshman year," she recalls. "But in my sophomore year, one of my stories won the Wallace Fiction Prize—a big deal for me at the time, and the first time I'd ever received a check for anything I'd written. By the time I was a senior, I'd been publishing stories for years in the magazines and had been in every creative writing class I'd applied for . . . until I applied to be in Peter Matthiessen's fiction seminar. He put me on the waiting list, and I went and pleaded with him to let me in; which, reluctantly, he did. I was so terrified of him, and so certain that I wasn't really meant to be in the class that I could hardly open my mouth all semester. Years later, I met Peter again in London, and he commented with some surprise that I didn't seem at all like the person he remembered. Only then did it occur to me that I may have seemed surly and malevolent, rather than terrified and embarrassed." What follows here is an extract from a short novel to be published in August 2001. It is the story of Maria Poniatowski, born in the Ukraine, interned in a German labor camp, a Displaced Person after the war who, with her Polish husband, Lev, moves to Canada and works as a housekeeper. They have one son, Radek (Rod), whose wife, Anita, is of German extraction.

"It's Anita, Mrs. Ellington," Maria Poniatowski shook her head for the umpteenth time, folding her paper napkin into ever smaller squares and allowing the tears to well up in her eyes. "She is not a good girl. I told Radek right from the start."

"Nobody likes their in-laws, Maria." Mrs. Ellington, her blind eyes shut behind her looming spectacles, lifted her chin and sniffed like a hound at the breeze from the apartment's open window. "Or very few do. It's a type of affection as rare as hen's teeth."

Maria waited.

"Hen have no teeth, don't you see? It's an expression. Just an expression. My point is—look at Judith's husband, the nasty American flag-waving goat." Judith was Mrs. Ellington's daughter. "I couldn't like him if he were the last man on earth. But I'm not going to let that stop me seeing Judith, or the kids. It's beside the point."

"But Mrs. Ellington," said Maria, "Anita runs him, she runs the house. She looks down on me. She thinks I'm stupid because my English is not so good."

"Nonsense. Your English is excellent."

"Not for writing and reading, Mrs. Ellington. You know that."

"She's a high school dropout, Maria."

"I know."

"She's not worthy of your boy, let alone you. You just have to keep in mind that she's not worthy."

Maria briefly contemplated the notion of worthiness. "But what am I supposed to do, Mrs. Ellington? She doesn't invite me to the house."

"Invite them to yours, then. Invite them to Markham Street."

Maria took her employer's advice. But she found that her invitations were frequently rebuffed: Anita found it was too far, or too complicated to arrange, or her own mother was too unwell, or the children were too restless or too tired. It happened more than once that Radek would promise a family visit, for a Saturday, say, only to ring in the morning to announce that he was coming on his own: Kelly had ballet class, or soccer practice; or Paul had been sick in the night. Maria chose to believe the excuses, as her pride demanded; but when she walked out to Lev's grave on Sunday after Mass, as she did, rain or shine, in all but the most bitter winter weather, she knelt by her husband's tomb and whispered vituperation against her daughter-in-law—quietly, always, so that the neighboring spirits would not be unsettled by her ranting, but purposefully, forcefully, from a seemingly bottomless well of ill-will.

"You were right, Lev, to shut your eyes to this," she told the cold stone, as she arranged her small bouquet (culled from the garden or purchased from the

Korean greengrocer, depending on the season) in the jam jar that stood in front of it. "This Anita is so wicked. I *spoke* to Kelly, and I could tell that she wanted to come: 'I miss you, grandma,' she said to me. And the little boy, Paul! He's his father all over again, he is Radek exactly, sometimes serious, sometimes laughing. He doesn't speak on the telephone very much. I don't mean anything to him. Not yet. It's not Radek's fault, you know. It's that Anita. She's getting fat now, Lev, just like I knew she would. She's not pretty, and she doesn't take care, and she'll go like her mother, round as a potato, you wait and see. She's eating all McDonald's, says she doesn't like to cook, but that can't be good for the kids, nah? I offer cooking, but she don't want it. That mother, living with them, she's a bad one, worse. You remember her, at the wedding, all fat and purple? Hmm?"

Lev kept his counsel, but Maria drew comfort from the mere fact of his proximity. At his grave, on a rise above the Humber River just before it opened into Lake Ontario, in a field of tombstones set out in shaded alleys and lit by the water and the sky, Maria felt consoled. She knew each season, and each moment of each season, in that place, the distant road sounds and nearby birdsongs, the changing tint of the foliage. She knew the names of all the dead around Lev, as if they were his colleagues or his classmates, and some of the neglected graves she swept and tidied in discreet homage to all who must know her husband.

When Radek did bring his family to Markham Street, the visits were strained and formal. Kelly and Paul perched on the plastic-covered chesterfield in their best outfits and fidgeted irritably, staring at the wall of family photos—which included pictures of themselves at every age—or at the blank television screen. Anita and Rod hovered, somehow too large for the sitting room, their very clothes seemingly tight and ill-fitting. Maria, made nervous, heard herself squawking and loathed herself. She cooked elaborate lunches—stews and casseroles, vast bowls of boiled vegetables, fruitcakes and puddings—which her guests only picked at (even Radek, a hearty man; and even his wife, whose girth was spreading, year by year, to outstrip her husband's) and never complimented. After lunch, while the adults had tea (Anita always asked for coffee, and somehow, she didn't know why, Maria never had any to hand), the children were invariably set loose in the back garden, where they trampled Maria's rows of vegetables, her tidy flower beds, and from which—she never mentioned it, except to Lev and Mrs. Ellington—they trailed clods of mud into the kitchen, small, stubborn tracks that sometimes found their way beyond the linoleum, off the plastic runners, into the fibers of the pristine cream broadloom. By three or three-thirty, Anita would be mumbling about her mother alone at home, or about the distance they had to drive, and as if in concert, the four of them would regroup and drift toward the door, waving away the foil-wrapped remainder of the cake or the leftover stew in its Tupperware bowl. In spite of all her harbored hopes for these visits, Maria could feel nothing but relief when they were over and would spend the day's remaining hours in furious cleaning of the smears and disorder her family had wrought.

In 1989, when Kelly was ten and Paul eight, Anita's mother died of a heart attack. Maria attended the funeral, out in Oakville: the service took place in a plush, somber chapel of rest where the German lay stony and immense in her open coffin. There were few mourners. Maria was dismayed to see the desolation in her grandchildren's faces, their skin pale as the dirty snow outside—it was late November—and their eyes red and swollen with crying. She wondered whether Kelly and Paul would manifest such sorrow if she herself were to die. When her own turn came to pay her respects to the dead, she leaned over the corpse and longed to touch it, but satisfied herself with sniffing, for the ugly smells of death or of embalming fluid. She couldn't smell a thing. Even now, the old woman was, she thought, wearing far too much makeup, and her paisley dress was bunched unbecomingly at the armpits. For once, however, her fingernails were clean. Maria noticed that the coffin, brass-handled, was lined with white satin: no expense had been spared. Would they extend themselves thus for her own funeral? She wasn't at all sure.

The following spring, as if to assert their freedom, Radek and Anita bought a summer cottage in Muskoka and a motorboat. To Maria's surprise, they invited her to spend a fortnight with them there in June.

"I don't know, Mrs. Ellington," she said to her now frail employer, who, almost the age of the century, was practically a nonagenarian. "What do you think? Maybe they don't really want me to say yes? Maybe they're hoping I'll say no, because that Anita, you know, when we're together, it's difficult. Two weeks is a long time, nah?"

"Don't be ridiculous, Maria," replied Mrs. Ellington above the din of a Gilbert and Sullivan operetta, in time to which she persisted in tapping her foot despite the gravity of the discussion. "All these years you've said they don't pay you enough attention, and now they offer and you think of saying no? Muskoka's beautiful. You'll have a lovely time. And if you don't like it, you can always catch the first bus home."

Maria thought of the Greyhound from Sudbury, all those years before, with Lev by her side and Radek on her lap, headed toward Toronto, which was not yet then "home," which was pure possibility. "I suppose you're right," she said. "I know how to take the bus, at least."

In mid-June, then, in the back seat of Radek's silver LeSabre, with the tatted back of Anita's frosted head between her and the road in front, and with Paul, almost nine, nestled amiably against her thigh while Kelly bobbed beside him to the muted throb of her Walkman, Maria retraced the route toward her first Canadian residence. Nothing along the way looked especially familiar. More than forty years had passed, after all. But Maria found her stomach bolting and her heart enlarging nevertheless: there had to be some meaning in this return.

In fact, Radek and Anita's cottage was many miles from Tagomack, on Lake of Bays. The flora—the pine trees and maples, the moss on the lakeshore boulders—was as Maria remembered, as were the swarms of black flies and the crystalline water, but she could not find Tagomack in the cozy comforts of the modern cottage, with its pale blue aluminum siding and in-ground septic tank. Rod and Anita had furnished the place in a single, mammoth sweep through Ikea, so that all the rooms were in light wood and bright colors and smelled faintly of the chemicals with which the upholstery had been treated, a synthetic, new-car smell.

Maria was installed in the smallest of the three bedrooms, a cubby beside the kitchen with a view, behind the rickrack curtains, onto the hood of the Buick and toward the dirt road beyond. Her bed was narrow, and too firm for Maria's taste, and the chest of drawers, of white particleboard with plastic handles, seemed to her too flimsy to use. She put her suitcase under the bed, with all her clothes still in it, and resolved to iron each item anew as she removed it for wearing (only to discover—she ought to have known—that Anita had no iron).

Maria began to realize that, just as she did not quite know how to arrange her wardrobe in her little room, she did not know how to fit herself into the rhythms of her son and his family. They had their own habits and ways of speaking—little Kelly was, Maria thought, intolerably insolent and offhand with her father, a breach of etiquette that Anita appeared tacitly to condone—and their own, unquestioning order for the unfolding of meals, a harum-scarum free-for-all that never seemed to involve a proper *course* and only rarely required cutlery. They had their patterns for squabbling, for planning, for moving about singly or as a group, in all of which she hovered on the periphery, an afterthought. She had never had to adapt in quite this manner before, although adaptation had been, in her youth, not merely her forte but her survival. She was accustomed to accommodation into the lives of families only as a housekeeper—for the Ellingtons or the McDonalds or the Pollocks—and so, in the cottage, reverted to these known paths. She found tasks for herself without asking: she washed the windows inside and out while Rod, Anita, and the kids went swimming; she crept into the kitchen before dawn and emptied all the cupboards to scrub the shelves clean and then carefully rewashed every cup and dish and pot, all of which seemed to her filmed with stickiness and grease. She spent an afternoon weeding what had once been a flower bed along the side of the cottage, where a few stubborn nasturtiums and sweet peas still pushed; and she trimmed the wild lilac bush with a kitchen knife because Rod had no shears.

All this Anita suffered with silent, ominous disapproval, her chin trembling
with barely perceptible rage when, in her furry purple housecoat, she shuffled
into the kitchen to find it undone or when, wrapped in a mammoth, leopard-
spotted towel, she picked her way back up from the dock to discover her mother-
in-law, damp rag in hand, sudsing the picture window onto the lake from the
perch of the brand new Ikea stepladder. But when Maria, mop, bucket, and rags
in hand, decided to tackle the boathouse ("So many spiders, yeah? Filthy!" she
exclaimed with her girlish giggle, and her nose wrinkled in a simian grin), Anita
could keep quiet no longer.

"We can *afford* a cleaning lady, you know," she said, with a smile that, intended to mask her irritation, only sharpened her disdain. "We didn't invite you
up here to spend all day, every day, creeping around behind us with a scrubbing
brush!"

Maria's face opened, then closed. She put down her bucket, her mop.

"Don't be like that, Mom," said Rod in a wheedling tone. "All Anita means is
that we want you to have a holiday. You know, to take a rest. You shouldn't be
working. That's all."

Maria's hands hung at her sides. She lifted her chin as if to speak, but said
nothing.

"Besides, Mom, you know that boathouses are meant to be dirty—they're like
garages, except on water. Heck, you want the spiders to have *somewhere* to live,
don't you?"

"Yuck," Paul chimed in. "I don't. I want Grandma to kill them all."

"Well," said Anita, "I believe in live and let live, and your grandmother can
kill all the spiders she wants to at her house, but *here*—"

"I'm going to put the mop away," Maria murmured. When she had done, she
retreated to her little room and lay on her bed with her shoes on (although she
rested her heels over its foot so as not to soil the spread with her soles), staring at
the ceiling. She was too angry even to think, and although she heard Paul's
tremolo asking his mother whether Grandma wouldn't like to come swimming
and heard Anita answer, in the voice made more resonant by her recent swollen
size, that maybe Grandma was too tired just now ("tired? too tired?" Maria's inner
voice spat contemptuously), she did not move a muscle. She watched a fly buzz
around the walls. She heard the clatter of the family gathering their gear—fins
and a mask for Paul, glossy magazines and a romance novel for Anita, the super-
market sort with gilded covers (Maria knew it, saw it in her mind's eye), Kelly's
ubiquitous yellow Walkman—and the tramp of their feet on the steps, and the
rippling thud as the last, probably Rod, slammed the front door. She lay there
still, in the quiet, aware of the caterpillar ridges of the chenille bedspread beneath
her arms and legs, aware of the play of sunlight in the pines outside the window,
aware of the fly's grinding buzz as it stopped and started; paralyzed by her fury,

Maria lay in wait. She could catch the bus; she would not catch the bus. She had nine more days to endure.

Shortly after noon, Paul and Kelly came together to her door. They knocked gently before opening but did not wait for her to answer. They stood at the foot of the bed, their tangled hair wet, their T-shirts damp with the imprint of their bathings suits, their skin fresh and freckled from their morning in the water.

"Will you get up now, Grandma?" Paul whispered, as if afraid to break the churchly silence. "We're going to have lunch."

Maria peered at her grandchildren without raising her head from the pillow.

"Dad's gone into town to get sandwiches," offered Kelly. "Submarine sandwiches. And doughnuts from Tim Horton's. Please get up, Grandma."

Paul lunged forward and pressed his warm nose into her neck. "Please don't be sick, Grandma, *please?*"

"Sick?" said Maria, struggling all of a sudden to sit up. "Who's sick?"

"Mom said you were sick."

"Grandma's not sick, Paulie." Maria wondered what her daughter-in-law intended, in lying to the children. "Grandma's never sick. Strong as a horse."

Kelly giggled.

"What?"

"Say it again, Grandma," said Kelly, still smirking. Maria noticed the buds of the girl's breasts, two small points against her shirt. "You accent's so funny."

"You're making fun of Grandma now?" Maria laughed to hide her hurt. "Maybe that makes Grandma sick!"

"Never!" cried Paul, who had retreated far enough to allow her to stand but hovered still, waiting to throw his arms around her waist. "You're strong as a horse, Grandma! You just said!"

In this way, the crisis passed. In the afternoon, after the meal, eaten by Rod standing, at which Maria yearned for Mrs. Ellington's crustless white bread and her cut-glass bowl of Bick's yum-yum pickles, and watched aghast as Anita, with grotesque daintiness, downed an entire mixed-meats sub and three glazed crullers, along with a bottle of Carlsberg for which she did not bother with a glass—after this, the family gathered their belongings to go for a ride in the motorboat. Rod donned a blue baseball cap with his company's logo embroidered on it; Anita layered her fair skin with greasy suntan cream; and the children bickered over whether to bring cookies or doughnuts, Coca-Cola or 7-Up, in the iced cooler. Even Maria put on her cotton sunhat with the floppy brim, which carried about it the whiff of mothballs from the Markham Street trunk in which it was habitually stored.

It wasn't, as Maria told Mrs. Ellington later, that she didn't *enjoy* the boat ride: the pulse of the engine and the buffeting wavelets, the puffy white leatherette banquette on which she sat between her grandchildren, drinking in the breeze. She enjoyed, too, the dense trees along the shore, thick like the earth's pelt, and the glimpse of chalets and cabins among their branches. She enjoyed being hot and cold at once, hot from the sun and cold from the wind, and she enjoyed the flat, foam-tipped swathe of wake the boat left behind. She took pleasure in the water's solemn clarity, its visible depths, and the sheen of the light upon it from a distance. She liked, too, the flicker and snap of the small Canadian flag at the stern, behind her head, and the sight of other craft—two canoes and a kayak, a little sailboat, and three or four other boats, smaller than Rod's, with outboard motors that churned the glassy lake and emitted, with their roaring, close diesel fumes. She enjoyed all of this; she just didn't see the point of it. She was not a person to act without motivation, and her purpose on the water wasn't clear to her. When, in the middle of the lake, Rod turned off the engine and began to fiddle with his fishing rod and a new-looking coffee can in which Paul had gathered worms for his father, Maria realized that only she was surprised: Paul and Kelly peeled their T-shirts and slipped over the boat's side into the water to swim in circles behind the boat, while Rod settled himself up at the bow, beyond the spattered windscreen, and cast his line. Anita, with a sigh, huddled in the modest shade of the captain's seat with a Carlsberg propped between her thighs and pulled her paperback out of her beach bag.

"Not going to swim?" she asked her mother-in-law, one eye closed against the glare.

Maria, never a strong swimmer—never, in truth, a swimmer at all: when she went on holiday to Cuba, she waded in the Caribbean but never relinquished her footing; because where, in her Ukrainian childhood, in the German camp, in the cold months at Tagomack, and the busyness of real life that so swiftly succeeded them . . . where would Maria have ever learned to swim?—did not want to reveal as much to Anita. She could hear Anita's whining voice deriding her to Radek: "She can't read or write, and she can't even *swim*? What can the old bat do, besides clean houses?"

"It's too cold, for me," she said simply, and folded her hands in her lap.

"Only the Caribbean will do, eh? You've been spoiled!"

"No, no. Just too cold today."

But short of swimming, there was little to entertain Maria for the hour or more that they drifted at the heart of the lake. Rod, his back turned to his family, sat immobile and apparently content, his rod angled slightly upward and its line, not quite taut, arcing outward to the water. Anita waved at flies and turned the pulpy pages of her novel, looking up from time to time to sight her children's sleek wet heads, and then swigging, almost aggressively, as if in defiance, from her beer bottle. Paul and Kelly frolicked like porpoises, in the tireless way of children,

occasionally resting at the ladder on the side of the boat and then splashing off
again, turning somersaults or tackling one another underwater.

Maria could not have explained to Mrs. Ellington the helplessness she felt in
that hour, the hideous superfluity. It wasn't the morning's rage; it was instead an
agony, a physical agitation, a more profound sense of not-belonging than she had
ever before, in all her life, experienced. She was to this scene like the flag on the
back of the boat or like the occasional burst of an engine in the distance: a tiny,
rootless fact, an irrelevance. She followed the line of trees at the horizon and the
pale cumulus stretch above, felt the gentle chuck-sucking of the water at the
boat's underside, and for the first time she could recall, she asked herself, "How
did I get here? What am I doing here? Why is this so?"

She watched Anita reading and could not tell whether Anita was truly oblivious to her gaze or concentrating all the harder on her novel to avoid it. She
watched the children, waited—it seemed so long a wait!—for them to notice her,
smiled, and waved. She did not know that when she smiled her silver teeth
caught the sun and glittered, visible to them far off in the water.

She grew cold, in spite of the light, but she did not move around in the boat.
She imagined falling over the side, if she were to move, her flowered skirt billowing up around her neck, her sandals weighing her down, dragging her further
into the lake's somber depths. She imagined gasping for air and swallowing the
lake instead, icy gulps of the greening, blueing, ever deeper water as it closed
coldly over her skull. Would they save her? Would they try? Anita might go so far
as to put down her novel, to move her beer bottle from between her legs; she
might shade her eyes with a fleshy, pale hand and watch the gurgling eddy into
which Maria had vanished. But she would not speak or come rushing. And how
would Radek know, with his back turned; and even if he knew, what would it
mean to him? Only the children—and in truth, only Paul. But for all his frantic
diving, his spindly arms would be too weak, his flailing ineffectual. At best, he
might salvage a hank of hair or the gold chain snapped from about her neck.

All this, Maria lived through in the placid hour. She felt the pit of mourning
in her stomach: only she would mourn herself. She and Mrs. Ellington, who
needed her. Even Jack McDonald and his wife—although they would attend the
funeral, to be sure—would be only passingly sad. She was old to them, after all, of
the generation whose turn it was to die, one way or another, sooner or later. The
buffer against their own mortality. Only for Mrs. Ellington was she still the
vibrant, unlined Maria Poniatowski, of the dark cloud of hair and the easy laugh,
with the handsome young husband and bonny little boy, the young woman
whose early trials (of those Mrs. Ellington knew at least a little, knew enough),
whose losses could still be subsumed in the real joy of new life. Nobody else alive
could see her now as she had once been, the way a lover sees, with the intimate

knowledge of the intervening years between there and here, a knowledge that in its rhythmed quotidian insistence fairly obliterated those years, rendered them invisible. Were Olga to see Maria now, for example, Maria knew that she would see foremost the lost years, the ravaging. Not so with Mrs. Ellington. It did not matter, or not so much, that Mrs. Ellington was all but blind; she could still see Maria clearly, as Maria wanted to be seen.

What she felt was a sensation of the lights going out—of the people who could know her, or who cared to know her, disappearing—until, rather than not seeing, Maria was above all *unseen*. And if she were unseen, unknown, as she felt on the boat in the middle of Lake of Bays, how then could she be sure that she *was* at all, that she breathed and signified still, that she carried inside her all the irreconcilable experiences, the long, woven filament of life that stretched back through the years and across the continents? In their different ways, Maria realized, both she and Mrs. Ellington were becoming invisible. And perhaps, then, she decided, although not without a grim sense of resignation, they were doomed to each other, perhaps that was the truth: bound, in spite of themselves, to illuminate one another and to help each other to cast some semblance of a shadow.

Craig Arnold

raig Arnold was born in 1967 and graduated from Yale in 1989. He remembers the tone of the place then as "one of guarded disdain, impatient of variety, and unforgiving of enthusiasm in any form. I had to be shown where to look—the fluid allegories of Spenser, the prophetic fury of Blake, the jaunty improvisations of Frank O'Hara." Twelve years after leaving, he thinks back with a different sense of things, and probably speaks for many of the writers in this book: "I'm indebted to Yale for teaching me how to contain myself—even appreciative, as one is to a parent to whom one no longer speaks. But it is with unmixed affection and gratitude that I remember the faces, the gestures, the catches of voice, of the teachers who drew me aside, gently or roughly, and pointed me to the window out." Arnold has since published widely and taught at the University of Texas at Austin and the University of Utah. His collection *Shells*—filled with fluid, furious, jaunty poems—was chosen by W. S. Merwin as the 1999 volume in the Yale Series of Younger Poets.

OH MUSE

Men make an occupation
           breaking themselves against you
bottles cracking across a ship's prow
christening new each time
           names
painted over names
           not one of which will stick

And still they beg to be seduced
           and you oblige them
pack them up in your interminable train
and teach them all your tricks
           to be alone
and need their solitude
           and not to talk
to lose tickets and tokens
           to contemplate
the air around them colorless as tears
to lie without shame
           to make love standing up
to write letters and burn them
           last of all
to be abandoned
        dreaming blonde and barbaric angels
to picture a stillborn sense
           of standing apart
in a raw wind
        shredding a castle's battlement
to empty gaps between impermeable stones

We watch you dance in the sunny ruins
the dance you drafted
           cupped in your hips
your public belly
           self-possessed
All for the best that you are left
alone at last
        to lie back
feel the ripples your hand trailed

from a pleasure boat in a made lake
build
    blow in waves over the bank
lapse and level again to calm
Asleep now in a shipless wake
incapable of breaking
                what will we open to?

TO BE IN MY OWN BODY AS

To be in my own body as
in yours
    To sway in bone and muscle
mobile and meaning nothing
                  To need
neither to fumble nor hold on
but simply, lightly to belong
where one is put
        Thought is a fever
mind a delirium
           a fume
winding up in its own prattle
nerve to nerve
      and when it breaks
the hex of snowflake for a second
captured in crystal melts
              unique
the blush blooming out of a cheek
diffuses
    faintly how the heart
clenches a fist
        the jellyfish
fills and deliquesces
           the yellow star
flares up in a fierceness
              falls
into itself
       collapses
          Oh
God but the bodies of the world
bud
    blossom beyond edge
shyly put out petal
          swell
with the seed's pulse
           loosen their pods
wistfully
      wilt on the stem and drop
once only to blow open

once open
        only to shut
and caught up in its opening
the joy
      having so sweetly wept
in the world's body that is a flower
not to imagine anything
                              but

Rachel Wetzsteon

New Yorker, Rachel Wetzsteon graduated from Yale College in 1989. Her memories of Yale include "the long, moonlit walks I took from Pierson College up to Science Hill, brooding on poetry and planning my first tentative poems; and, more than anything else, my encounters with Marie Borroff and John Hollander, whose boundless energy and passionate erudition helped persuade me that my own desire to be a poet was not a frivolous fancy that would vanish when I graduated but something that would stay with me my whole life." So far it has. She has published two books of poems, *The Other Stars* (1994) and *Home and Away* (1998). She currently teaches at Barnard.

COMMANDS FOR THE END OF SUMMER

i.
Deepen,
leaves, not with what
has made us sorry but
with what was profound about that
sorrow.

ii.
Make me
spontaneous,
gathering winds, but don't
blow so giddily I teeter
too much.

iii.
Songs I
listened to all
summer long, accept my
thanks: to regress is not to move
backward.

iv.
Splash of
patchouli on
my wrist, remind me that
in this cauldron there is a world
elsewhere.

v.
Smile! Those
days of humid
agony have earned you
the right to a hundred purple
sunsets.

vi.
Come, fall,
I can feel you
stirring, I can hardly
wait for the things that will happen
come fall.

BLUE OCTAVO HAIKU

after Kafka

i.   In fat armchairs sat
        indolence and impatience,
        plotting my downfall.

ii.   A wicked cage flew
        across the long horizon
        searching for a bird.

iii.   I burned with love in
        empty rooms, I sternly turned
        knives within myself.

iv.   "Behold the bright gate,"
        the keeper said. "I am now
        going to shut it."

v.   Hardly was the road
        swept clean when ah! there appeared
        new piles of dry leaves.

vi.   But nothing could kill
        a faith like a guillotine,
        as heavy, as light.

vii.   Happiness? Finding
        your indestructible core;
        leaving it alone.

viii.   Into the heavens
        flew a breathless legion of
        impossible crows.

AND THIS TIME I MEAN IT

All over the city, people are crying
crocodile tears that dry up before the cause
of weeping crosses the street; interns say great things
about the men who got them their jobs,
then roll their eyes when the coast is clear. Appearing
as a way of keeping foes and bosses happy,
the habit fastens and takes hold
until it starts occurring
even among friends, so that only
with effort can the banter be decoded:
"I'll be there" means "Never will I budge,"
"No" is a subtle way of saying "Sure."

Raised in a place where the worst that can happen
happens every day, I also had a habit
of opening a gap between the mind thinking
and the mouth, expressing; only by throwing
intricate veils over what I meant
could I reach the nearest corner
without crying out for merciful armfuls
of coins, seeing-eye dogs, golden syringes dropped
from the sky. Soon, though, I wondered whether
there were two of me living in one house:
one who did the breathing
and one, all smirks and eyebrows, who cracked the jokes.
Now I suffer from other problems
but this one's gone for good. Before we met
I hovered above my feelings
like a singer above a low and difficult note,
or a dandy suspended in a balloon
over a plague-ridden village. But if my old friends
waved to me on my armored cloud,
a handshake with a new one took me
down, toward the street's precise rough music,
down toward terror and truth.

onathan Edwards (1703–1758), the most celebrated American divine, entered Yale College at the age of twelve and graduated at the top of his class; he subsequently took an M.A. in 1723, and remained at Yale as a tutor. All along he was subject to "despondencies," illnesses, and spiritual crises, further darkening his Calvinist intellectual temperament. In 1726, he left Yale to become co-pastor of his grandfather's church in Northampton, Massachusetts. He wrote more than twelve hundred sermons during his pastorate there, all of them sternly Puritanical warnings. His first book appeared in 1731, soon followed by others. His dramatic and uncompromising views of human damnation and the possibilities of redemption remain stirring. His most famous sermon, "Sinners in the Hands of an Angry God," is a superb existential study of psychic anxiety. In 1741 a religious revival known as the Great Awakening swept the colonies, and Edwards rode its tumultuous waves with difficulty, denouncing extremists. His most important work, *Treatise Concerning Religious Affections* (1746), is a profound meditation on grace and the soul. But by 1751 he was dejected by the lack of piety in the land and harried by his own parishioners. He was dismissed from his post and moved to Stockbridge as a missionary to the Indians. In early 1758, he took up the presidency of the College of New Jersey (now Princeton), but died soon after as the result of a smallpox inoculation. He is the model of early American thought.

SINNERS IN THE HANDS OF AN ANGRY GOD

A Sermon Preached at Enfield, July 8th 1741.
At a Time of great Awakenings; and attended with remarkable Impressions on many
of the Hearers.

Amos ix. 2, 3. *Though they dig into Hell, thence shall mine Hand take them; though*
they climb up to Heaven, thence will I bring them down. And though they hide
themselves in the Top of Carmel, I will search and take them out thence; and though
they be hid from my Sight in the Bottom of the Sea, thence I will command the
Serpent, and he shall bite them.

Deut. XXXII. 35.
— Their Foot shall slide in due Time.—
In this Verse is threatened the Vengeance of God on the wicked unbelieving Israelites, that were God's visible People, and lived under Means of Grace; and that,
notwithstanding all God's wonderful Works that he had wrought towards that
People, yet remained, as is expressed, *ver.* 28. void of Counsel, having no Understanding in them; and that, under all the Cultivations of Heaven, brought forth
bitter and poisonous Fruit; as in the two Verses next preceeding the Text.

The Expression that I have chosen for my Text, *Their Foot shall slide in due*
Time; seems to imply the following Things, relating to the Punishment and Destruction that these wicked Israelites were exposed to.

1. That they were *always* exposed to Destruction, as one that stands or walks in
slippery Places is always exposed to fall. This is implied in the Manner of their
Destruction's coming upon them, being represented by their Foot's sliding. The
same is express'd, Psal. 73. 18. *Surely thou didst set them in slippery Places; thou*
castedst them down into Destruction.

2. It implies that they were always exposed to *sudden* unexpected Destruction.
As he that walks in slippery Places is every Moment liable to fall; he can't foresee
one Moment whether he shall stand or fall the next; and when he does fall, he
falls at once, without Warning. Which is also expressed in that, Psal. 73. 18, 19.
Surely thou didst set them in slippery Places; thou castedst them down into Destruc-
tion. How are they brought into Desolation as in a Moment?

3. Another Thing implied is that they are liable to fall *of themselves,* without
being thrown down by the Hand of another. As he that stands or walks on slippery Ground, needs nothing but his own Weight to throw him down.

4. That the Reason why they are not fallen already, and don't fall now, is only
that God's appointed Time is not come. For it is said, that when that due Time,
or appointed Time comes, *their Foot shall slide.* Then they shall be left to fall as
they are inclined by their own Weight. God won't hold them up in these slippery

Places any longer, but will let them go; and then, at that very Instant, they shall fall into Destruction; as he that stands in such slippery declining Ground on the Edge of a Pit that he can't stand alone, when he is let go he immediately falls and is lost.

The Observation from the Words that I would now insist upon is this,

There is nothing that keeps wicked Men, at any one Moment, out of Hell, but the meer Pleasure of GOD.

By the meer Pleasure of God, I mean his sovereign Pleasure, his arbitrary Will, restrained by no Obligation, hinder'd by no manner of Difficulty, any more than if nothing else but God's meer Will had in the least Degree, or in any Respect whatsoever, any Hand in the Preservation of wicked Men one Moment.

The Truth of this Observation may appear by the following Considerations.

1. There is no Want of *Power* in God to cast wicked Men into Hell at any Moment. Mens Hands can't be strong when God rises up: The strongest have no Power to resist him, nor can any deliver out of his Hands.

He is not only able to cast wicked Men into Hell, but he can most *easily* do it. Sometimes an earthly Prince meets with a great deal of Difficulty to subdue a Rebel, that has found Means to fortify himself, and has made himself strong by the Numbers of his Followers. But it is not so with God. There is no Fortress that is any Defence from the Power of God. Tho' Hand join in Hand, and vast Multitudes of God's Enemies combine and associate themselves, they are easily broken in Pieces: They are as great Heaps of light Chaff before the Whirlwind; or large Quantities of dry Stubble before devouring Flames. We find it easy to tread on and crush a Worm that we see crawling on the Earth; so 'tis easy for us to cut or singe a slender Thread that any Thing hangs by; thus easy is it for God when he pleases to cast his Enemies down to Hell. What are we, that we should think to stand before him, at whose Rebuke the Earth trembles, and before whom the Rocks are thrown down?

2. They *deserve* to be cast into Hell; so that divine Justice never stands in the Way, it makes no Objection against God's using his Power at any Moment to destroy them. Yea, on the contrary, Justice calls aloud for an infinite Punishment of their Sins. Divine Justice says of the Tree that brings forth such Grapes of Sodom, *Cut it down, why cumbreth it the Ground,* Luk. 13. 7. The Sword of divine Justice is every Moment brandished over their Heads, and 'tis nothing but the Hand of arbitrary Mercy, and God's meer Will, that holds it back.

3. They are *already* under a Sentence of Condemnation to Hell. They don't only justly deserve to be cast down thither; but the Sentence of the Law of God, that eternal and immutable Rule of Righteousness that God has fixed between him and Mankind, is gone out against them, and stands against them; so that they are bound over already to Hell. Joh. 3. 18. *He that believeth not is condemned*

already. So that every unconverted Man properly belongs to Hell; that is his Place; from thence he is. Joh. 8. 23. *Ye are from beneath.* And thither he is bound; 'tis the Place that Justice, and God's Word, and the Sentence of his unchangeable Law assigns to him.

4. They are now the Objects of that very *same* Anger & Wrath of God that is expressed in the Torments of Hell: and the Reason why they don't go down to Hell at each Moment, is not because God, in whose Power they are, is not then very angry with them; as angry as he is with many of those miserable Creatures that he is now tormenting in Hell, and do there feel and bear the fierceness of his Wrath. Yea God is a great deal more angry with great Numbers that are now on Earth, yea doubtless with many that are now in this Congregation, that it may be are at Ease and Quiet, than he is with many of those that are now in the Flames of Hell.

So that it is not because God is unmindful of their Wickedness, and don't resent it, that he don't let loose his Hand and cut them off. God is not altogether such an one as themselves, tho' they may imagine him to be so. The Wrath of God burns against them, their Damnation don't slumber, the Pit is prepared, the Fire is made ready, the Furnace is now hot, ready to receive them, the Flames do now rage and glow. The glittering Sword is whet, and held over them, and the Pit hath opened her Mouth under them.

5. The *Devil* stands ready to fall upon them and seize them as his own, at what Moment God shall permit him. They belong to him; he has their Souls in his Possession, and under his Dominion. The Scripture represents them as his *Goods,* Luk. 11. 21. The Devils watch them; they are ever by them, at their right Hand; they stand waiting for them, like greedy hungry Lions that see their Prey, and expect to have it, but are for the present kept back; if God should withdraw his Hand, by which they are restrained, they would in one Moment fly upon their poor Souls. The old Serpent is gaping for them; Hell opens its Mouth wide to receive them; and if God should permit it, they would be hastily swallowed up and lost.

6. There are in the Souls of wicked Men those hellish *Principles* reigning, that would presently kindle and flame out into Hell Fire, if it were not for God's Restraints. There is laid in the very Nature of carnal Men a Foundation for the Torments of Hell: There are those corrupt Principles, in reigning Power in them, and in full Possession of them, that are Seeds of Hell Fire. These Principles are active and powerful, and exceeding violent in their Nature, and if it were not for the restraining Hand of God upon them, they would soon break out, they would flame out after the same Manner as the same Corruptions, the same Enmity does in the Hearts of damned Souls, and would beget the same Torments in 'em as they do in them. The Souls of the Wicked are in Scripture compared to the troubled Sea,

Isai. 57. 20. For the present God restrains their Wickedness by his mighty Power, as he does the raging Waves of the troubled Sea, saying, *Hitherto shalt thou come, and no further;* but if God should withdraw that restraining Power, it would soon carry all afore it. Sin is the Ruin and Misery of the Soul; it is destructive in it's Nature; and if God should leave it without Restraint, there would need nothing else to make the Soul perfectly miserable. The Corruption of the Heart of Man is a Thing that is immoderate and boundless in its Fury; and while wicked Men live here, it is like Fire pent up by God's Restraints, when as if it were let loose it would set on Fire the Course of Nature; and as the Heart is now a Sink of Sin, so, if Sin was not restrain'd, it would immediately turn the Soul into a fiery Oven, or a Furnace of Fire and Brimstone.

7. It is no Security to wicked Men for one Moment, that there are no *visible Means* of *Death* at Hand. 'Tis no Security to a natural Man, that he is now in Health, and that he don't see which Way he should now immediately go out of the World by any Accident, and that there is no visible Danger in any Respect in his Circumstances. The manifold and continual Experience of the World in all Ages, shews that this is no Evidence that a Man is not on the very Brink of Eternity, and that the next Step won't be into another World. The unseen, unthought of Ways and Means of Persons going suddenly out of the World are innumerable and inconceivable. Unconverted Men walk over the Pit of Hell on a rotten Covering, and there are innumerable Places in this Covering so weak that they won't bear their Weight, and these Places are not seen. The Arrows of Death fly unseen at Noon-Day; the sharpest Sight can't discern them. God has so many different unsearchable Ways of taking wicked Men out of the World and sending 'em to Hell, that there is nothing to make it appear that God had need to be at the Expence of a Miracle, or go out of the ordinary Course of his Providence, to destroy any wicked Man, at any Moment. All the Means that there are of Sinners going out of the World, are so in God's Hands, and so universally absolutely subject to his Power and Determination, that it don't depend at all less on the meer Will of God, whether Sinners shall at any Moment go to Hell, than if Means were never made use of, or at all concerned in the Case.

8. Natural Men's *Prudence* and *Care* to preserve their own *Lives,* or the Care of others to preserve them, don't secure 'em a Moment. This divine Providence and universal Experience does also bear Testimony to. There is this clear Evidence that Men's own Wisdom is no Security to them from Death; That if it were otherwise we should see some Difference between the wise and politick Men of the World, and others, with Regard to their Liableness to early and unexpected Death; but how is it in Fact? Eccles. 2. 16. *How dieth the wise Man? as the Fool.*

9. All wicked Men's *Pains* and *Contrivance* they use to escape *Hell,* while they continue to reject Christ, and so remain wicked Men, don't secure 'em from Hell

one Moment. Almost every natural Man that hears of Hell, flatters himself that he shall escape it; he depends upon himself for his own Security; he flatters himself in what he has done, in what he is now doing, or what he intends to do; every one lays out Matters in his own Mind how he shall avoid Damnation, and flatters himself that he contrives well for himself, and that his Schemes won't fail. They hear indeed that there are but few saved, and that the bigger Part of Men that have died heretofore are gone to Hell; but each one imagines that he lays out Matters better for his own escape than others have done: He don't intend to come to that Place of Torment; he says within himself, that he intends to take Care that shall be effectual, and to order Matters so for himself as not to fail.

But the foolish Children of Men do miserably delude themselves in their own Schemes, and in their Confidence in their own Strength and Wisdom; they trust to nothing but a Shadow. The bigger Part of those that heretofore have lived under the same Means of Grace, and are now dead, are undoubtedly gone to Hell: and it was not because they were not as wise as those that are now alive: it was not because they did not lay out Matters as well for themselves to secure their own escape. If it were so, that we could come to speak with them, and could inquire of them, one by one, whether they expected when alive, and when they used to hear about Hell, ever to be the Subjects of that Misery, we doubtless should hear one and another reply, 'No, I never intended to come here; I had laid out Matters otherwise in my Mind; I thought I should contrive well for my self; I thought my Scheme good; I intended to take effectual Care; but it came upon me unexpected; I did not look for it at that Time, and in that Manner; it came as a Thief; Death outwitted me; God's Wrath was too quick for me; O my cursed Foolishness! I was flattering my self, and pleasing my self with vain Dreams of what I would do hereafter, and when I was saying Peace and Safety, then sudden Destruction came upon me.'

10. God has laid himself under *no Obligation* by any Promise to keep any natural Man out of Hell one Moment. God certainly has made no Promises either of eternal Life, or of any Deliverance or Preservation from eternal Death, but what are contained in the Covenant of Grace, the Promises that are given in Christ, in whom all the Promises are Yea and Amen. But surely they have no Interest in the Promises of the Covenant of Grace that are not the Children of the Covenant, and that don't believe in any of the Promises of the Covenant, and have no Interest in the *Mediator* of the Covenant.

So that whatever some have imagined and pretended about Promises made to natural Men's earnest seeking and knocking, 'tis plain and manifest that whatever Pains a natural Man takes in Religion, whatever Prayers he makes, till he believes in Christ, God is under no manner of Obligation to keep him a *Moment* from eternal Destruction.

So that thus it is, that natural Men are held in the Hand of God over the Pit of

Hell; they have deserved the fiery Pit, and are already sentenced to it; and God is dreadfully provoked, his Anger is as great towards them as to those that are actually suffering the Executions of the fierceness of his Wrath in Hell, and they have done nothing in the least to appease or abate that Anger, neither is God in the least bound by any Promise to hold 'em up one moment; the Devil is waiting for them, Hell is gaping for them, the Flames gather and flash about them, and would fain lay hold on them, and swallow them up; the Fire pent up in their own Hearts is struggling to break out; and they have no Interest in any Mediator, there are no Means within Reach that can be any Security to them. In short, they have no Refuge, nothing to take hold of, all that preserves them every Moment is the meer arbitrary Will, and uncovenanted unobliged Forbearance of an incensed God.

Application.
The Use may be of *Awakening* to unconverted Persons in this Congregation. This that you have heard is the Case of every one of you that are out of Christ. That World of Misery, that Lake of burning Brimstone is extended abroad under you. *There* is the dreadful Pit of the glowing Flames of the Wrath of God; there is Hell's wide gaping Mouth open; and you have nothing to stand upon, nor any Thing to take hold of; there is nothing between you and Hell but the Air; 'tis only the Power and meer Pleasure of God that holds you up.

You probably are not sensible of this; you find you are kept out of Hell, but don't see the Hand of God in it, but look at other Things, as the good State of your bodily Constitution, your Care of your own Life, and the Means you use for your own Preservation. But indeed these Things are nothing; if God should withdraw his Hand, they would avail no more to keep you from falling, than the thin Air to hold up a Person that is suspended in it.

Your Wickedness makes you as it were heavy as Lead, and to tend downwards with great Weight and Pressure towards Hell; and if God should let you go, you would immediately sink and swiftly descend & plunge into the bottomless Gulf, and your healthy Constitution, and your own Care and Prudence, and best Contrivance, and all your Righteousness, would have no more Influence to uphold you and keep you out of Hell, than a Spider's Web would have to stop a falling Rock. Were it not that so is the sovereign Pleasure of God, the Earth would not bear you one Moment; for you are a Burden to it; the Creation groans with you; the Creature is made Subject to the Bondage of your Corruption, not willingly; the Sun don't willingly shine upon you to give you Light to serve Sin and Satan; the Earth don't willingly yield her Increase to satisfy your Lusts; nor is it willingly a Stage for your Wickedness to be acted upon; the Air don't willingly serve you for Breath to maintain the Flame of Life in your Vitals, while you spend your Life in the Service of God's Enemies. God's Creatures are Good, and were made for Men to serve God with, and don't willingly subserve to any other Purpose, and groan when they are abused to Purposes so directly contrary to their Nature and End. And the World would spue you out, were it not for the sovereign Hand of him who hath subjected it in Hope. There are the black Clouds of God's Wrath now hanging directly over your Heads, full of the dreadful Storm, and big with Thunder; and were it not for the restraining Hand of God it would immediately burst forth upon you. The sovereign Pleasure of God for the present stays his rough Wind; otherwise it would come with Fury, and your Destruction would come like a Whirlwind, and you would be like the Chaff of the Summer threshing Floor.

The Wrath of God is like great Waters that are dammed for the present; they increase more and more, & rise higher and higher, till an Outlet is given, and the longer the Stream is stop'd, the more rapid and mighty is it's Course, when once it is let loose. 'Tis true, that Judgment against your evil Works has not been executed hitherto; the Floods of God's Vengeance have been with-held; but your Guilt in the mean Time is constantly increasing, and you are every Day treasuring up more Wrath; the Waters are continually rising and waxing more and more mighty; and there is nothing but the meer Pleasure of God that holds the Waters back that are unwilling to be stopped, and press hard to go forward; if God should only withdraw his Hand from the Flood-Gate, it would immediately fly open, and the fiery Floods of the Fierceness and Wrath of God would rush forth with inconceivable Fury, and would come upon you with omnipotent Power; and if your Strength were ten thousand Times greater than it is, yea ten thousand Times greater than the Strength of the stoutest, sturdiest Devil in Hell, it would be nothing to withstand or endure it.

The Bow of God's Wrath is bent, and the Arrow made ready on the String, and Justice bends the Arrow at your Heart, and strains the Bow, and it is nothing but the meer Pleasure of God, and that of an angry God, without any Promise or Obligation at all, that keeps the Arrow one Moment from being made drunk with your Blood.

Thus are all you that never passed under a great Change of Heart, by the mighty Power of the SPIRIT of GOD upon your Souls; all that were never born again, and made new Creatures, and raised from being dead in Sin, to a State of new, and before altogether unexperienced Light and Life, (however you may have reformed your Life in many Things, and may have had religious Affections, and may keep up a Form of Religion in your Families and Closets, and in the House of God, and may be strict in it,) you are thus in the Hands of an angry God; 'tis nothing but his meer Pleasure that keeps you from being this Moment swallowed up in everlasting Destruction.

However unconvinced you may now be of the Truth of what you hear, by & by you will be fully convinced of it. Those that are gone from being in the like Circumstances with you, see that it was so with them; for Destruction came suddenly upon most of them, when they expected nothing of it, and while they were saying, *Peace and Safety:* Now they see, that those Things that they depended on for Peace and Safety, were nothing but thin Air and empty Shadows.

The God that holds you over the Pit of Hell, much as one holds a Spider, or some loathsome Insect, over the Fire, abhors you, and is dreadfully provoked; his Wrath towards you burns like Fire; he looks upon you as worthy of nothing else, but to be cast into the Fire; he is of purer Eyes than to bear to have you in his Sight; you are ten thousand Times so abominable in his Eyes as the most hateful venomous Serpent is in ours. You have offended him infinitely more than ever a stubborn Rebel did his Prince: and yet 'tis nothing but his Hand that holds you from falling into the Fire every Moment: 'Tis to be ascribed to nothing else, that you did not go to Hell the last Night; that you was suffer'd to awake again in this World, after you closed your Eyes to sleep: and there is no other Reason to be given why you have not dropped into Hell since you arose in the Morning, but that God's Hand has held you up: There is no other Reason to be given why you han't gone to Hell since you have sat here in the House of God, provoking his pure Eyes by your sinful wicked Manner of attending his solemn Worship: Yea, there is nothing else that is to be given as a Reason why you don't this very Moment drop down into Hell.

O Sinner! Consider the fearful Danger you are in: 'Tis a great Furnace of Wrath, a wide and bottomless Pit, full of the Fire of Wrath, that you are held over in the Hand of that God, whose Wrath is provoked and incensed as much against you as against many of the Damned in Hell: You hang by a slender Thread, with the Flames of divine Wrath flashing about it, and ready every Moment to singe it, and burn it asunder; and you have no Interest in any Mediator, and nothing to lay hold of to save yourself, nothing to keep off the Flames of Wrath, nothing of your own, nothing that you ever have done, nothing that you can do, to induce God to spare you one Moment.

And consider here more particularly several Things concerning that Wrath that you are in such Danger of.

1. *Whose* Wrath it is: It is the Wrath of the infinite GOD. If it were only the Wrath of Man, tho' it were of the most potent Prince, it would be comparatively little to be regarded. The Wrath of Kings is very much dreaded, especially of absolute Monarchs, that have the Possessions and Lives of their Subjects wholly in their Power, to be disposed of at their meer Will. Prov. 20. 2. *The Fear of a King is as the Roaring of a Lion: whoso provoketh him to Anger, sinneth against his own Soul.* The Subject that very much enrages an arbitrary Prince, is liable to suffer the most extream Torments, that human Art can invent or human Power can inflict. But the greatest earthly Potentates, in their greatest Majesty and Strength, and when cloathed in their greatest Terrors, are but feeble despicable Worms of the Dust, in Comparison of the great and almighty Creator and King of Heaven and

Earth: It is but little that they can do, when most enraged, and when they have exerted the utmost of their Fury. All the Kings of the Earth before GOD are as Grashoppers, they are nothing and less than nothing: Both their Love and their Hatred is to be despised. The Wrath of the great King of Kings is as much more terrible than their's, as his Majesty is greater. Luke 12. 4, 5. *And I say unto you my Friends, be not afraid of them that kill the Body, and after that have no more than they can do: But I will forewarn you whom ye shall fear; fear him, which after he hath killed, hath Power to cast into Hell; yea I say unto you, fear him.*

2. 'Tis the *Fierceness* of his Wrath that you are exposed to. We often read of the *Fury* of God; as in Isai. 59. 18. *According to their Deeds, accordingly he will repay Fury to his Adversaries.* So Isai. 66. 15. *For behold, the Lord will come with Fire, and with Chariots like a Whirlwind, to render his Anger with Fury, and his Rebukes with Flames of Fire.* And so in many other Places. So we read of God's *Fierceness.* Rev. 19. 15. There we read of *the Winepress of the Fierceness and Wrath of Almighty God.* The Words are exceeding terrible: if it had only been said, *the Wrath of God,* the Words would have implied that which is infinitely dreadful: But 'tis not only said so, but *the Fierceness and Wrath of God:* the Fury of God! the Fierceness of Jehovah! Oh how dreadful must that be! Who can utter or conceive what such Expressions carry in them! But it is not only said so, but *the Fierceness and Wrath of ALMIGHTY GOD.* As tho' there would be a very great Manifestation of his almighty Power, in what the fierceness of his Wrath should inflict, as tho' Omnipotence should be as it were enraged, and excited, as Men are wont to exert their Strength in the fierceness of their Wrath. Oh! then what will be the Consequence! What will become of the poor Worm that shall suffer it! Whose Hands can be strong? and whose Heart endure? To what a dreadful, inexpressible, inconceivable Depth of Misery must the poor Creature be sunk, who shall be the Subject of this!

Consider this, you that are here present, that yet remain in an unregenerate State. That God will execute the fierceness of his Anger, implies that he will inflict Wrath without any Pity: when God beholds the ineffable Extremity of your Case, and sees your Torment to be so vastly disproportion'd to your Strength, and sees how your poor Soul is crushed and sinks down, as it were into an infinite Gloom, he will have no Compassion upon you, he will not forbear the Executions of his Wrath, or in the least lighten his Hand; there shall be no Moderation or Mercy, nor will God then at all stay his rough Wind; he will have no Regard to your Welfare, nor be at all careful lest you should suffer too much, in any other Sense than only that you shall not suffer beyond what strict Justice requires: nothing shall be with-held, because it's so hard for you to bear. Ezek. 8. 18. *Therefore will I also deal in Fury; mine Eye shall not spare, neither will I have Pity; and tho' they cry in mine Ears with a loud Voice, yet I will not hear them.* Now God stands ready to pity you; this is a Day of Mercy; you may cry now with some Encouragement of obtaining Mercy; but when once the Day of Mercy is past, your most lamentable and dolorous Cries and Shrieks will be in vain; you will be wholly lost and thrown away of God as to any Regard to your Welfare; God will have no other Use to put you to but only to suffer Misery; you shall be continued in Being to no other End; for you will be a Vessel of Wrath fitted to Destruction; and there will be no other Use of this Vessel but only to be filled full of Wrath: God will be so far from pitying you when you cry to him, that 'tis said he will only *Laugh and Mock,* Prov. 1. 25, 26, &c.

How awful are those Words, Isai. 63. 3. which are the Words of the great God, *I will tread them in mine Anger, and will trample them in my Fury, and their Blood shall be sprinkled upon my Garments, and I will stain all my Raiment.* 'Tis perhaps impossible to conceive of Words that carry in them greater Manifestations of these three Things, *viz.* Contempt, and Hatred, and fierceness of Indignation. If you cry to God to pity you, he will be so far from pitying you in your doleful Case, or shewing you the least Regard or Favour, that instead of that he'll only tread you under Foot: And tho' he will know that you can't bear the Weight of Omnipotence treading upon you, yet he won't regard that, but he will crush you under his Feet without Mercy; he'll crush out your Blood, and make it fly, and it shall be sprinkled on his Garments, so as to stain all his Raiment. He will not only hate you, but he will have you in the utmost Contempt; no Place shall be thought fit for you, but under his Feet, to be trodden down as the Mire of the Streets.

3. The Misery you are exposed to is that which God will inflict to that End, that he might *shew* what that *Wrath* of JEHOVAH is. God hath had it on his Heart to shew to Angels and Men, both how excellent his Love is, and also how terrible his Wrath is. Sometimes earthly Kings have a Mind to shew how terrible *their* Wrath is, by the extream Punishments they would execute on those that provoke 'em. *Nebuchadnezzar,* that mighty and haughty Monarch of the *Chaldean* Empire, was willing to shew *his* Wrath, when enraged with *Shadrach, Meshech,* and *Abednego;* and accordingly gave Order that the burning fiery Furnace should be het seven Times hotter than it was before; doubtless it was raised to the utmost Degree of Fierceness that humane Art could raise it: But the great GOD is also willing to shew *his Wrath,* and magnify his awful Majesty and mighty Power in the extream Sufferings of his Enemies. Rom. 9. 22. *What if God willing to shew HIS Wrath, and to make his Power known, endured with much Long-suffering the Vessels of Wrath fitted to Destruction?* And seeing this is his Design, and what he has determined, to shew how terrible the unmixed, unrestrained Wrath, the Fury and Fierceness of JEHOVAH is, he will do it to Effect. There will be something accomplished and brought to pass, that will be dreadful with a Witness. When the great and angry God hath risen up and executed his awful Vengeance on the poor Sinner; and the Wretch is actually suffering the infinite Weight and Power of his

Indignation, then will God call upon the whole Universe to behold that awful Majesty, and mighty Power that is to be seen in it. Isai. 33. 12, 13, 14. *And the People shall be as the burning of Lime, as Thorns cut up shall they be burnt in the Fire. Hear ye that are far off what I have done; and ye that are near acknowledge my Might. The Sinners in Zion are afraid, fearfulness hath surprized the Hypocrites &c.*

Thus it will be with you that are in an unconverted State, if you continue in it; the infinite Might, and Majesty and Terribleness of the OMNIPOTENT GOD shall be magnified upon you, in the ineffable Strength of your Torments: You shall be tormented in the Presence of the holy Angels, and in the Presence of the Lamb; and when you shall be in this State of Suffering, the glorious Inhabitants of Heaven shall go forth and look on the awful Spectacle, that they may see what the Wrath and Fierceness of the Almighty is, and when they have seen it, they will fall down and adore that great Power and Majesty. Isai. 66. 23, 24. *And it shall come to pass, that from one new Moon to another, and from one Sabbath to another, shall all Flesh come to Worship before me, saith the Lord; and they shall go forth and look upon the Carcasses of the Men that have transgressed against me; for their Worm shall not die, neither shall their Fire be quenched, and they shall be an abhorring unto all Flesh.*

4. 'Tis *everlasting* Wrath. It would be dreadful to suffer this Fierceness and Wrath of Almighty God one Moment; but you must suffer it to all Eternity: there will be no End to this exquisite horrible Misery: When you look forward, you shall see a long Forever, a boundless Duration before you, which will swallow up your Thoughts, and amaze your Soul; and you will absolutely despair of ever having any Deliverance, any End, any Mitigation, any Rest at all; you will know certainly that you must wear out long Ages, Millions of Millions of Ages, in wrestling and conflicting with this almighty merciless Vengeance; and then when you have so done, when so many Ages have actually been spent by you in this Manner, you will know that all is but a Point to what remains. So that your Punishment will indeed be infinite. Oh who can express what the State of a Soul in such Circumstances is! All that we can possibly say about it, gives but a very feeble faint Representation of it; 'tis inexpressible and inconceivable: for *who knows the Power of God's Anger?*

How dreadful is the State of those that are daily and hourly in Danger of this great Wrath, and infinite Misery! But this is the dismal Case of every Soul in this Congregation, that has not been born again, however moral and strict, sober and religious they may otherwise be. Oh that you would consider it, whether you be Young or Old. There is Reason to think, that there are many in this Congregation now hearing this Discourse, that will actually be the Subjects of this very Misery to all Eternity. We know not who they are, or in what Seats they sit, or what Thoughts they now have: it may be they are now at Ease, and hear all these Things without much Disturbance, and are now flattering themselves that they are not the Persons, promising themselves that they shall escape. If we knew that there was one Person, and but one, in the whole Congregation that was to be the Subject of this Misery, what an awful Thing would it be to think of! If we knew who it was, what an awful Sight would it be to see such a Person! How might all the rest of the Congregation lift up a lamentable and bitter Cry over him! But alass! instead of one, how many is it likely will remember this Discourse in Hell? And it would be a Wonder if some that are now present, should not be in Hell in a very short Time, before this Year is out. And it would be no Wonder if some Person that now sits here in some Seat of this Meeting-House in Health, and quiet & secure, should be there before to morrow Morning. Those of you that finally continue in a natural Condition, that shall keep out of Hell longest, will be there in a little Time! your Damnation don't slumber; it will come swiftly, and in all probability very suddenly upon many of you. You have Reason to wonder, that you are not already in Hell. 'Tis doubtless the Case of some that heretofore you have seen and known, that never deserved Hell more than you, and that heretofore appeared as likely to have been now alive as you: Their Case is past all Hope; they are crying in extream Misery and perfect Despair; but here you are in the Land of the Living, and in the House of God, and have an Opportunity to obtain Salvation. What would not those poor damned, hopeless Souls give for one Day's such Opportunity as you now enjoy!

And now you have an extraordinary Opportunity, a Day wherein CHRIST has flung the Door of Mercy wide open, and stands in the Door calling and crying with a loud Voice to poor Sinners; a Day wherein many are flocking to him, and pressing into the Kingdom of God; many are daily coming from the East, West, North and South; many that were very lately in the same miserable Condition that you are in, are in now an happy State, with their Hearts filled with Love to Him that has loved them and washed them from their Sins in his own Blood, and rejoycing in Hope of the Glory of God. How awful is it to be left behind at such a Day! To see so many others feasting, while you are pining and perishing! To see so many rejoycing and singing for Joy of Heart, while you have Cause to mourn for Sorrow of Heart, and howl for Vexation of Spirit! How can you rest one Moment in such a Condition? Are not your Souls as precious as the Souls of the People at* *Suffield,* where they are flocking from Day to Day to Christ?

Are there not many here that have lived *long* in the World, that are not to this Day born again, and so are Aliens from the Common-wealth of Israel, and have done nothing ever since they have lived, but treasure up Wrath against the Day of Wrath? Oh Sirs, your Case in an especial Manner is extreamly dangerous; your Guilt and Hardness of Heart is extreamly great. Don't you see how generally Persons of your Years are pass'd over and left, in the present remarkable & wonderful

---

*The next neighbour Town.

Dispensation of God's Mercy? You had need to consider your selves, and wake throughly out of Sleep; you cannot bear the Fierceness and Wrath of the infinite GOD.

And you that are *young Men,* and *young Women,* will you neglect this precious Season that you now enjoy, when so many others of your Age are renouncing all youthful Vanities, and flocking to CHRIST? You especially have now an extraordinary Opportunity; but if you neglect it, it will soon be with you as it is with those Persons that spent away all the precious Days of Youth in Sin, and are now come to such a dreadful pass in blindness and hardness.

And you *Children* that are unconverted, don't you know that you are going down to Hell, to bear the dreadful Wrath of that God that is now angry with you every Day, and every Night? Will you be content to be the Children of the Devil, when so many other Children in the Land are converted, and are become the holy and happy Children of the King of Kings?

And let every one that is yet out of Christ, and hanging over the Pit of Hell, whether they be old Men and Women, or middle Aged, or young People, or little Children, now hearken to the loud Calls of God's Word and Providence. This acceptable Year of the LORD, that is a Day of such great Favour to some, will doubtless be a Day of as remarkable Vengeance to others. Men's Hearts harden, and their Guilt increases apace at such a Day as this, if they neglect their Souls: and never was there so great Danger of such Persons being given up to hardness of Heart, and blindness of Mind. God seems now to be hastily gathering in his Elect in all Parts of the Land; and probably the bigger Part of adult Persons that ever shall be saved, will be brought in now in a little Time, and that it will be as it was on that great out-pouring of the SPIRIT upon the *Jews* in the Apostles Days, the Election will obtain, and the rest will be blinded. If this should be the Case with you, you will eternally curse this Day, and will curse the Day that ever you was born, to see such a Season of the pouring out of God's Spirit; and will wish that you had died and gone to Hell before you had seen it. Now undoubtedly it is, as it was in the Days of *John the Baptist,* the Ax is in an extraordinary Manner laid at the Root of the Trees, that every Tree that brings not forth good Fruit, may be hewen down, and cast into the Fire.

Therefore let every one that is out of CHRIST, now awake and fly from the Wrath to come. The Wrath of almighty GOD is now undoubtedly hanging over great Part of this Congregation: Let every one fly out of *Sodom: Haste and escape for your Lives, look not behind you, escape to the Mountain, least you be consumed.*

FINIS.

j oel Barlow (1754–1812), born on a farm in Redding, Connecticut, first took an interest in poetry at Yale, where he graduated in 1778. (His college years were interrupted by service in the Revolutionary War.) His first published poem, in fact, was a satire about the bad food served in Yale Commons. He went on to write verse orations delivered at Yale commencements. He then self-consciously set out to write the defining American epic poem. In 1787 he published *The Vision of Columbus* in nine books—a poem whose enthusiasts ranged from George Washington to Louis XVI. He then lived abroad for seventeen years and, with such friends as Thomas Paine and Mary Wollstonecraft, wrote influentially about the political crises of the age. After stays in Germany (where he became a successful businessman), Algeria (where he was the American minister), and Paris (where he and his wife were patrons of the arts), he returned to America. Thomas Jefferson and James Madison urged him to write a history of the United States. Instead, he greatly revised his earlier epic and in 1807 published *The Columbiad*. His friend President Madison recalled Barlow to politics and asked him in 1811 to negotiate a treaty with Napoleon. Barlow tracked the emperor to Russia, where he was fleeing back to France in ignominious defeat. Barlow caught pneumonia in the turmoil and died in Poland. Among his well-known poems are "The Hasty-Pudding" (1793), *The Prospect of Peace* (1778), and "Advice to a Raven in Russia" (published posthumously).

FROM *THE COLUMBIAD*

Now grateful truce suspends the burning war,
And groans and shouts promiscuous load the air;
When the tired Britons, where the smokes decay,
Quit their strong station and resign the day.
Slow files along the immeasurable train,
Thousands on thousands redden all the plain,
Furl their torn bandrols, all their plunder yield
And pile their muskets on the battle field.
Their wide auxiliar nations swell the crowd,
And the coopt navies from the neighboring flood
Repeat surrendering signals and obey
The landmen's fate on this concluding day.
  Cornwallis first, their late all conquering lord,
Bears to the victor chief his conquer'd sword,
Presents the burnisht hilt and yields with pain
The gift of kings, here brandisht long in vain.
Then bow their hundred banners, trailing far
Their wearied wings from all the skirts of war.
Battalion'd infantry and squadron'd horse
Dash the silk tassel and the golden torse;
Flags from the forts and ensigns from the fleet
Roll in the dust and at Columbia's feet
Prostrate the pride of thrones; they firm the base
Of freedom's temple, while her arms they grace.
Here Albion's crimson Cross the soil o'erspreads,
Her Lion crouches and her Thistle fades;
Indignant Erin rues her trampled Lyre,
Brunswick's pale Steed forgets his foamy fire,
Proud Hessia's Castle lies in dust o'erthrown,
And venal Anspach quits her broken Crown.
  Long trains of wheel'd artillery shade the shore,
Quench their blue matches and forget to roar;
Along the incumber'd plain, thick planted rise
High stacks of muskets glittering to the skies,
Numerous and vast. As when the toiling swains
Heap their whole harvest on the stubbly plains,
Gerb after gerb the bearded shock expands,
Shocks, ranged in rows, hill high the burden'd lands;
The joyous master numbers all the piles

And o'er his well earn'd crop complacent smiles:
Such growing heaps this iron harvest yield,
So tread the victors this their final field.

    Triumphant Washington with brow serene,
Regards unmoved the exhilarating scene,
Weighs in his balanced thought the silent grief
That sinks the bosom of the fallen chief,
With all the joy that laurel crowns bestow,
A world reconquer'd and a vanquisht foe.
Thus thro extremes of life, in every state,
Shines the clear soul, beyond all fortune great,
While smaller minds, the dupes of fickle chance,
Slight woes o'erwhelm and sudden joys entrance.
So the full sun, thro all the changing sky,
Nor blasts nor overpowers the naked eye;
Tho transient splendors, borrow'd from his light,
Glance on the mirror and destroy the sight.
                                            Book VII, lines 713–768

    Too much of Europe, here transplanted o'er,
Nursed feudal feelings on your tented shore,
Brought sable serfs from Afric, call'd it gain,
And urged your sires to forge the fatal chain.
But now, the tents o'erturn'd, the war dogs fled,
Now fearless Freedom rears at last her head
Matcht with celestial Peace,—my friends, beware
To shade the splendors of so bright a pair;
Complete their triumph, fix their firm abode,
Purge all privations from your liberal code,
Restore their souls to men, give earth repose
And save your sons from slavery, wars and woes.

    Based on its rock of right your empire lies,
On walls of wisdom let the fabric rise;
Preserve your principles, their force unfold,
Let nations prove them and let kings behold.
EQUALITY, your first firm-grounded stand;
Then FREE ELECTION; then your FEDERAL BAND;
This holy Triad should for ever shine
The great compendium of all rights divine,
Creed of all schools, whence youths by millions draw
Their themes of right, their decalogues of law;

Till men shall wonder (in these codes inured)
How wars were made, how tyrants were endured.
   Then shall your works of art superior rise,
Your fruits perfume a larger length of skies,
Canals careering climb your sunbright hills,
Vein the green slopes and strow their nurturing rills,
Thro tunnel'd heights and sundering ridges glide,
Rob the rich west of half Kenhawa's tide,
Mix your wide climates, all their stores confound
And plant new ports in every midland mound.
Your lawless Missisippi, now who slimes
And drowns and desolates his waste of climes,
Ribb'd with your dikes, his torrent shall restrain
And ask your leave to travel to the main;
Won from his wave while rising cantons smile,
Rear their glad nations and reward their toil.
                              Book VIII, lines 384–420

   But now had Hesper from the Hero's sight
Veil'd the vast world with sudden shades of night.
Earth, sea and heaven, where'er he turns his eye,
Arch out immense, like one surrounding sky
Lampt with reverberant fires. The starry train
Paint their fresh forms beneath the placid main;
Fair Cynthia here her face reflected laves,
Bright Venus gilds again her natal waves,
The Bear redoubling foams with fiery joles,
And two dire Dragons twine two arctic poles.
Lights o'er the land, from cities lost in shade,
New constellations, new galaxies spread,
And each high pharos double flames provides,
One from its fires, one fainter from the tides.
                              Book IX, lines 1–14

   From Mohawk's mouth, far westing with the sun,
Thro all the midlands recent channels run,
Tap the redundant lakes, the broad hills brave,
And Hudson marry with Missouri's wave.
From dim Superior, whose uncounted sails
Shade his full seas and bosom all his gales,
New paths unfolding seek Mackensie's tide,
And towns and empires rise along their side;

Slave's crystal highways all his north adorn,
Like coruscations from the boreal morn.
Proud Missisippi, tamed and taught his road,
Flings forth irriguous from his generous flood
Ten thousand watery glades; that, round him curl'd,
Vein the broad bosom of the western world.

Book X, lines 213–226

ohn Trumbull (1750–1831), considered a prodigy from the start, was admitted to Yale College at age seven, though he delayed entry until the age of thirteen. He began his career as a poet in 1769 while serving as a schoolmaster. One of his best known poems, "The Progress of Dulness," appeared in 1773, and he began work on *M'Fingal* the next year while studying law with John Adams. *M'Fingal* (1782) was an immensely popular poem, celebrating the glories of the American Revolution. Trumbull was treasurer of Yale, served as Connecticut state's attorney, was elected to Connecticut's General Assembly, and was eventually appointed a judge. He was the informal leader of the Connecticut Wits, an influential neo-Augustan group of poets and writers.

FROM *M'FINGAL*

from The Town-Meeting, A.M.
When Yankies, skill'd in martial rule,
First put the British troops to school;
Instructed them in warlike trade,
And new manoeuvres of parade,
The true war-dance of Yankee reels,
And *manual exercise* of heels;
Made them give up, like saints complete,
The arm of flesh, and trust the feet,
And work, like Christians undissembling,
Salvation out, by fear and trembling;
Taught Percy fashionable races,
And modern modes of Chevy-Chases:
From Boston, in his best array,
Great 'Squire M'FINGAL took his way,
And graced with ensigns of renown,
Steer'd homeward to his native town.

His high descent our heralds trace
From Ossian's famed Fingalian race:
For though their name some part may lack,
Old Fingal spelt it with a MAC;
Which great M'Pherson, with submission,
We hope will add the next edition.

His fathers flourish'd in the Highlands
Of Scotia's fog-benighted islands;
Whence gain'd our 'Squire two gifts by right,
Rebellion, and the Second-sight.
Of these, the first, in ancient days,
Had gain'd the noblest palm of praise,
'Gainst kings stood forth and many a crown'd head
With terror of its might confounded;
Till rose a king with potent charm
His foes by meekness to disarm,
Whom every Scot and Jacobite
Strait fell in love with at first sight;
Whose gracious speech with aid of pensions,
Hush'd down all murmurs of dissensions,
And with the sound of potent metal
Brought all their buzzing swarms to settle;

Who rain'd his ministerial manna,
Till loud Sedition sung hosanna;
The grave Lords-Bishops and the Kirk
United in the public work;
Rebellion, from the northern regions,
With Bute and Mansfield swore allegiance;
All hands combin'd to raze, as nuisance,
Of church and state the Constitutions,
Pull down the empire, on whose ruins
They meant to edify their new ones;
Enslave th' Amer'can wildernesses,
And rend the provinces in pieces.
With these our 'Squire, among the valiant'st,
Employ'd his time, and tools and talents,
And found this new rebellion pleasing
As his old king-destroying treason.
    Nor less avail'd his optic sleight,
And Scottish gift of second-sight.
No ancient sybil, famed in rhyme,
Saw deeper in the womb of time;
No block in old Dodona's grove
Could ever more orac'lar prove.
Nor only saw he all that could be,
But much that never was, nor would be;
Whereby all prophets far outwent he,
Though former days produced a plenty:
For any man with half an eye
What stands before him can espy;
But optics sharp it needs, I ween,
To see what is not to be seen.
As in the days of ancient fame,
Prophets and poets were the same,
And all the praise that poets gain
Is for the tales they forge and feign:
So gain'd our 'Squire his fame by seeing
Such things, as never would have being;
Whence he for oracles was grown
The very tripod of his town.
Gazettes no sooner rose a lie in,
But strait he fell to prophesying;
Made dreadful slaughter in his course,

O'erthrew provincials, foot and horse,
Brought armies o'er, by sudden pressings,
Of Hanoverians, Swiss and Hessians,
Feasted with blood his Scottish clan,
And hang'd all rebels to a man,
Divided their estates and pelf,
And took a goodly share himself.
All this with spirit energetic,
He did by second-sight prophetic.

Timothy Dwight

imothy Dwight (1752–1817) had read the Bible at four, mastered Latin grammar at six, and entered Yale at thirteen. He graduated in 1769 and enlisted in the army as a chaplain during the War of Independence, serving with George Washington at Valley Forge. Afterward, he returned to pastoral duties and was famous as a preacher—in the spirit of his grandfather Jonathan Edwards. He was also an innovative educator and in 1795 succeeded Ezra Stiles as president of Yale. Aside from his theological writings, he was a poet of note. His satiric *Triumph of Infidelity* (1788) and his plangent *Greenfield Hill* (1794) are works of considerable intelligence and charm.

COLUMBIA

Columbia, Columbia, to glory arise,
The queen of the world, and child of the skies!
Thy genius commands thee; with rapture behold,
While ages on ages thy splendors unfold.
Thy reign is the last, and the noblest of time,
Most fruitful thy soil, most inviting thy clime;
Let the crimes of the east ne'er encrimson thy name.
Be freedom, and science, and virtue, thy fame.

To conquest, and slaughter, let Europe aspire;
Whelm nations in blood, and wrap cities in fire;
Thy heroes the rights of mankind shall defend,
And triumph pursue them, and glory attend.
A world is thy realm: for a world be thy laws,
Enlarg'd as thine empire, and just as thy cause;
On Freedom's broad basis, that empire shall rise,
Extend with the main, and dissolve with the skies.

Fair Science her gates to thy sons shall unbar,
And the east see thy morn hide the beams of her star.
New bards and new sages, unrival'd shall soar
To fame, unextinguish'd, when time is no more;
To fame, the last refuge of virtue design'd,
Shall fly from all nations the best of mankind;
Here, grateful to heaven, with transport shall bring
Their incense, more fragrant than odours of spring.

Nor less shall thy fair ones to glory ascend,
And Genius and Beauty in harmony blend;
The graces of form shall awake pure desire,
And the charms of the soul ever cherish the fire;
Their sweetness unmingled, their manners refin'd
And virtue's bright image, instamp'd on the mind,
With peace, and soft rapture, shall teach life to glow,
And light up a smile in the aspect of woe.

Thy fleets to all regions thy pow'r shall display,
The nations admire, and the ocean obey;
Each shore to thy glory its tribute unfold,
And the east and the south yield their spices and gold
As the day-spring unbounded, thy splendor shall flow,

And earth's little kingdoms before thee shall bow,
While the ensigns of union, in triumph unfurl'd,
Hush the tumult of war, and give peace to the world.

Thus, as down a lone valley, with cedars o'erspread,
From war's dread confusion I pensively stray'd—
The gloom from the face of fair heav'n retir'd;
The winds ceas'd to murmur; the thunders expir'd;
Perfumes, as of Eden, flow'd sweetly along,
And a voice, as of angels, enchantingly sung;
"Columbia, Columbia, to glory arise,
The queen of the world, and the child of the skies."

Noah Webster

oah Webster (1758–1843), born in West Hartford, Connecticut, graduated from Yale in 1778 and then studied law. When his law practice failed, he opened an elementary school, where he noticed how instructional books were all based on English usages. He thought that the ideals of the American Revolution could best be forwarded by giving children books that would reflect a distinctly American language and culture. To that end, his *American Spelling Book* appeared in 1783, followed by the *American Grammar* in 1784, and the *American Reader* in 1785. His motives were patriotic but also practical, since he realized that language is a living organism that is constantly changing. Webster's masterpiece, on which he worked for twenty-five years, was his two-volume dictionary, published in 1828. In its own way, the book is a considerable American epic, the tale of a people as told through its speech. Not only did it change spellings to reflect American usage, but it introduced and codified native words for plants, animals, and landscapes, and foreign words—like *noodle, boss, pumpkin,* and *cookie*—domesticated by immigrants. At the time of his death, Webster was living in New Haven, at work on a revised edition of the dictionary.

FROM *DISSERTATIONS ON THE ENGLISH LANGUAGE*

A regular study of language has, in all civilized countries, formed a part of a liberal education. The Greeks, Romans, Italians and French successively improved their native tongues, taught them in Academies at home, and rendered them entertaining and useful to the foreign student.

The English tongue, though later in its progress towards perfection, has attained to a considerable degree of purity, strength and elegance, and been employed, by an active and scientific nation, to record almost all the events and discoveries of ancient and modern times.

This language is the inheritance which the Americans have received from their British parents. To cultivate and adorn it, is a task reserved for men who shall understand the connection between language and logic, and form an adequate idea of the influence which a uniformity of speech may have on national attachments.

It will be readily admitted that the pleasures of reading and conversing, the advantage of accuracy in business, the necessity of clearness and precision in communicating ideas, require us to be able to speak and write our own tongue with ease and correctness. But there are more important reasons, why the language of this country should be reduced to such fixed principles, as may give its pronunciation and construction all the certainty and uniformity which any living tongue is capable of receiving.

The United States were settled by emigrants from different parts of Europe. But their descendants mostly speak the same tongue; and the intercourse among the learned of the different States, which the revolution has begun, and an American Court will perpetuate, must gradually destroy the differences of dialect which our ancestors brought from their native countries. This approximation of dialects will be certain; but without the operation of other causes than an intercourse at Court, it will be slow and partial. The body of the people, governed by habit, will still retain their respective peculiarities of speaking; and for want of schools and proper books, fall into many inaccuracies, which, incorporating with the language of the state where they live, may imperceptibly corrupt the national language. Nothing but the establishment of schools and some uniformity in the use of books, can annihilate differences in speaking and preserve the purity of the American tongue. A sameness of pronunciation is of considerable consequence in a political view; for provincial accents are disagreeable to strangers and sometimes have an unhappy effect upon the social affections. All men have local attachments, which lead them to believe their own practice to be the least exceptionable. Pride and prejudice incline men to treat the practice of their neighbors with some degree of contempt. Thus small differences in pronunciation at first excite ridicule—a habit of laughing at the singularities of strangers is followed by disrespect—and without respect friendship is a name, and social intercourse a mere ceremony.

These remarks hold equally true, with respect to individuals, to small societies and to large communities. Small causes, such as a nickname, or a vulgar tone in speaking, have actually created a dissocial spirit between the inhabitants of the different states, which is often discoverable in private business and public deliberations. Our political harmony is therefore concerned in a uniformity of language.

As an independent nation, our honor requires us to have a system of our own, in language as well as government. Great Britain, whose children we are, and whose language we speak, should no longer be *our* standard; for the state of her writers is already corrupted, and her language on the decline. But if it were not so, she is at too great a distance to be our model, and to instruct us in the principles of our own tongue.

It must be considered further, that the English is the common root or stock from which our national language will be derived. All others will gradually waste away—and within a century and a half, North America will be peopled with a hundred millions of men, *all speaking the same language.* Place this idea in comparison with the present and possible future bounds of the language in Europe— consider the Eastern Continent as inhabited by nations, whose knowledge and intercourse are embarrassed by differences of language; then anticipate the period when the people of one quarter of the world, will be able to associate and converse together like children of the same family. Compare this prospect, which is not visionary, with the state of the English language in Europe, almost confined to an Island and to a few millions of people; then let reason and reputation decide, how far America should be dependent on a transatlantic nation, for her standard and improvements in language.

Let me add, that whatever predilection the Americans may have for their native European tongues, and particularly the British descendants for the English, yet several circumstances render a future separation of the American tongue from the English, necessary and unavoidable. The vicinity of the European nations, with the uninterrupted communication in peace, and the changes of dominion in war, are gradually assimilating their respective languages. The English with others is suffering continual alterations. America, placed at a distance from those nations, will feel, in a much less degree, the influence of the assimilating causes; at the same time, numerous local causes, such as a new country, new associations of people, new combinations of ideas in arts and science, and some intercourse with tribes wholly unknown in Europe, will introduce new words into the American tongue. These causes will produce, in a course of time, a language in North America, as different from the future language of England, as the modern Dutch, Danish and Swedish are from the German, or from one another: Like remote branches of a tree springing from the same stock; or rays of light, shot from the same center, and diverging from each other, in proportion to their distance from the point of separation.

Whether the inhabitants of America can be brought to a perfect uniformity in the pronunciation of words, it is not easy to predict; but it is certain that no attempt of the kind has been made, and an experiment, begun and pursued on the right principles, is the only way to decide the question. Schools in Great Britain have gone far towards demolishing local dialects—commerce has also had its influence—and in America these causes, operating more generally, must have a proportional effect.

In many parts of America, people at present attempt to copy the English phrases and pronunciation—an attempt that is favored by their habits, their prepossessions and the intercourse between the two countries. This attempt has, within the period of a few years, produced a multitude of changes in these particulars, especially among the leading classes of people. These changes make a difference between the language of the higher and common ranks; and indeed between the *same* ranks in *different* states; as the rage for copying the English, does not prevail equally in every part of North America.

But besides the reasons already assigned to prove this imitation absurd, there is a difficulty attending it, which will defeat the end proposed by its advocates; which is, that the English themselves have no standard of pronunciation, nor can they ever have one on the plan they propose. The Authors, who have attempted to give us a standard, make the practice of the court and stage in London the sole criterion of propriety in speaking. An attempt to establish a standard on this foundation is both *unjust* and *idle.* It is unjust, because it is abridging the nation of its rights: The *general practice* of a nation is the rule of propriety, and this practice should at least be consulted in so important a matter, as that of making laws for speaking. While all men are upon a footing and no singularities are accounted vulgar or ridiculous, every man enjoys perfect liberty. But when a particular set of men, in exalted stations, undertake to say, "we are the standards of propriety and elegance, and if all men do not conform to our practice, they shall be accounted vulgar and ignorant," they take a very great liberty with the rules of the language and the rights of civility.

But an attempt to fix a standard on the practice of any particular class of people is highly absurd: As a friend of mine once observed, it is like fixing a lighthouse on a floating island. It is an attempt to *fix* that which is in itself *variable;* at least it must be variable so long as it is supposed that a local practice has no standard but a *local practice;* that is, no standard but *itself.* While this doctrine is believed, it will be impossible for a nation to follow as fast as the standard changes—for if the gentlemen at court constitute a standard, they are above it themselves, and their practice must shift with their passions and their whims.

But this is not all. If the practice of a few men in the capital is to be the standard, a knowledge of this must be communicated to the whole nation. Who shall do this? An able compiler perhaps attempts to give this practice in a dictionary; but it is probable that the pronunciation, even at court, or on the stage, is not uniform. The compiler therefore must follow his particular friends and patrons; in which case he is sure to be opposed and the authority of his standard called in question; or he must give two pronunciations as the standard, which leaves the student in the same uncertainty as it found him. Both these events have actually taken place in England, with respect to the most approved standards; and of course no one is universally followed.

Besides, if language must vary, like fashions, at the caprice of a court, we must have our standard dictionaries republished, with the fashionable pronunciation, at least once in five years; otherwise a gentleman in the country will become intolerably vulgar, by not being in a situation to adopt the fashion of the day. The *new* editions of them will supersede the *old,* and we shall have our pronunciation to re-learn, with the polite alterations, which are generally corruptions.

Such are the consequences of attempting to make a *local* practice the *standard* of language in a *nation.* The attempt must keep the language in perpetual fluctuation, and the learner in uncertainty.

If a standard therefore cannot be fixed on local and variable custom, on what shall it be fixed? If the most eminent speakers are not to direct our practice, where shall we look for a guide? The answer is extremely easy; the *rules of the language itself,* and the *general practice of the nation,* constitute propriety in speaking. If we examine the structure of any language, we shall find a certain principle of analogy running through the whole. We shall find in English that familiar combinations of letters have usually the same pronunciation; and that words, having the same terminating syllable, generally have the accent at the same distance from that termination. These principles of analogy were not the result of design— they must have been the effect of accident, or that tendency which all men feel towards uniformity. But the principles, when established, are productive of great convenience, and become an authority superior to the arbitrary decisions of any man or class of men. There is one exception only to this remark: When a deviation from analogy has become the universal practice of a nation, it then takes place of all rules and becomes the standard of propriety.

The two points therefore, which I conceive to be the basis of a standard in speaking, are these; *universal undisputed practice,* and the *principle of analogy. Universal practice* is generally, perhaps always, a rule of propriety; and in disputed points, where people differ in opinion and practice, *analogy* should always decide the controversy.

These are authorities to which all men will submit—they are superior to the opinions and caprices of the great, and to the negligence and ignorance of the multitude. The authority of individuals is always liable to be called in question—

but the unanimous consent of a nation, and a fixed principle interwoven with the very construction of a language, coeval and coextensive with it, are like the common laws of a land, or the immutable rules of morality, the propriety of which every man, however refractory, is forced to acknowledge, and to which most men will readily submit. Fashion is usually the child of caprice and the being of a day; principles of propriety are founded in the very nature of things, and remain unmoved and unchanged, amidst all the fluctuations of human affairs and the revolutions of time.

It must be confessed that languages are changing, from age to age, in proportion to improvements in science. Words, as Horace observes, are like leaves of trees; the old ones are dropping off and new ones growing. These changes are the necessary consequence of changes in customs, the introduction of new arts, and new ideas in the sciences. Still the body of a language and its general rules remain for ages the same, and the new words usually conform to these rules; otherwise they stand as exceptions, which are not to overthrow the principle of analogy already established.

But when a language has arrived at a certain stage of improvement, it must be stationary or become retrograde; for improvements in science either cease, or become slow and too inconsiderable to affect materially the tone of a language. This stage of improvement is the period when a nation abounds with writers of the first class, both for abilities and taste. This period in England commenced with the age of Queen Elizabeth and ended with the reign of George II. It would have been fortunate for the language, had the style of writing and the pronunciation of words been fixed, as they stood in the reign of Queen Ann and her successor. Few improvements have been made since that time; but innumerable corruptions in pronunciation have been introduced by Garrick, and in style, by Johnson, Gibbon and their imitators.

Such however is the taste of the age; simplicity of style is neglected for ornament, and sense is sacrificed to sound.

Although style, or the choice of words and manner of arranging them, may be necessarily liable to change, yet it does not follow that pronunciation and orthography cannot be rendered in a great measure permanent. An orthography, in which there would be a perfect correspondence between the spelling and pronunciation, would go very far towards effecting this desirable object. The Greek language suffered little or no change in these particulars, for about a thousand years; and the Roman was in a great degree fixed for several centuries.

Rapid changes of language proceed from violent causes; but these causes cannot be supposed to exist in North America. It is contrary to all rational calculation, that the United States will ever be conquered by any one nation, speaking a different language from that of the country. Removed from the danger of corruption by conquest, our language can change only with the slow operation of the causes beforementioned and the progress of arts and sciences, unless the folly of imitating our parent country should continue to govern us, and lead us into endless innovation. This folly however will lose its influence gradually, as our particular habits of respect for that country shall wear away, and our *amor patrie* acquire strength and inspire us with a suitable respect for our own national character.

We have therefore the fairest opportunity of establishing a national language, and of giving it uniformity and perspicuity, in North America, that ever presented itself to mankind. Now is the time to begin the plan. The minds of the Americans are roused by the events of a revolution; the necessity of organizing the political body and of forming constitutions of government that shall secure freedom and property, has called all the faculties of the mind into exertion; and the danger of losing the benefits of independence, has disposed every man to embrace any scheme that shall tend, in its future operation, to reconcile the people of America to each other, and weaken the prejudices which oppose a cordial union.

born in Litchfield, Connecticut, John Pierpont (1785–1866) graduated from Yale College in 1804. He first taught, later studied, and practiced law, then ran dry goods franchises—without success in any attempt. But he had begun to publish poems in 1812, and his proceeds from *Airs of Palestine* (1816) enabled him to enroll in the Harvard Divinity School. He served as a pastor in Boston, in Troy, New York, and in West Medford, Massachusetts, and eventually served as a chaplain during the Civil War. At the time of his death, he was a clerk in the Treasury Department in Washington, D.C. *The Anti-Slavery Poems of John Pierpont* (1843) so enflamed Pierpont's Boston congregation that he was forced to resign.

THE FUGITIVE SLAVE'S APOSTROPHE TO THE NORTH STAR

Star of the North! though night winds drift
    The fleecy drapery of the sky
Between thy lamp and me, I lift,
    Yea, lift with hope, my sleepless eye
To the blue heights wherein thou dwellest,
And of a land of freedom tellest.

Star of the North! while blazing day
    Pours round me its full tide of light,
And hides thy pale but faithful ray,
    I, too, lie hid, and long for night:
For night;—I dare not walk at noon,
Nor dare I trust the faithless moon,—

Nor faithless man, whose burning lust
    For gold hath riveted my chain;
Nor other leader can I trust,
    But thee, of even the starry train;
For, all the host around thee burning,
Like faithless man, keep turning, turning.

I may not follow where they go:
    Star of the North, I look to thee
While on I press; for well I know
    Thy light and truth shall set me free;—
Thy light, that no poor slave deceiveth;
Thy truth, that all my soul believeth.

They of the East beheld the star
    That over Bethlehem's manger glowed;
With joy they hailed it from afar,
    And followed where it marked the road,
Till, where its rays directly fell,
They found the Hope of Israel.

Wise were the men who followed thus
    The star that sets man free from sin!
Star of the North! thou art to us,—
    Who 're slaves because we wear a skin
Dark as is night's protecting wing,—
Thou art to us a holy thing.

And we are wise to follow thee!
    I trust thy steady light alone:
Star of the North! thou seem'st to me
    To burn before the Almighty's throne,
To guide me, through these forests dim
And vast, to liberty and HIM.

Thy beam is on the glassy breast
    Of the still spring, upon whose brink
I lay my weary limbs to rest,
    And bow my parching lips to drink.
Guide of the friendless negro's way,
I bless thee for this quiet ray!

In the dark top of southern pines
    I nestled, when the driver's horn
Called to the field, in lengthening lines,
    My fellows at the break of morn.
And there I lay, till thy sweet face
Looked in upon "my hiding-place."

The tangled cane-brake,—where I crept
    For shelter from the heat of noon,
And where, while others toiled, I slept
    Till wakened by the rising moon,—
As its stalks felt the night wind free,
Gave me to catch a glimpse of thee.

Star of the North! in bright array
    The constellations round thee sweep,
Each holding on its nightly way,
    Rising, or sinking in the deep,
And, as it hangs in mid heaven flaming,
The homage of some nation claiming.

This nation to the Eagle cowers;
    Fit ensign! she's a bird of spoil;—
Like worships like! for each devours
    The earnings of another's toil.
I've felt her talons and her beak,
And now the gentler Lion seek.

The Lion, at the Virgin's feet
    Crouches, and lays his mighty paw

Into her lap!—an emblem meet
   Of England's Queen and English law:—
Queen, that hath made her Islands free!
Law, that holds out its shield to me!

Star of the North! upon that shield
   Thou shinest!—O, for ever shine!
The negro, from the cotton-field,
   Shall then beneath its orb recline,
And feed the Lion couched before it,
Nor heed the Eagle screaming o'er it!

ames Fenimore Cooper (1789–1851) would have graduated from Yale with the class of 1806, but he was dismissed for misconduct a year earlier. Yale was an often violent place in those days, and brawls were common. But Cooper, after a scrap with a classmate, put a homemade bomb in his antagonist's door and lit it—to scare him. (Cooper's older brother had been expelled from Princeton for trying to burn down Nassau Hall.) The Yale authorities were not amused. Though Cooper had made lifelong friendship among his classmates—with the future inventor Samuel F. B. Morse, for example, and with William Jay, son of the Chief Justice of the United States—and had been extremely fond of some of his teachers, especially Benjamin Silliman, he did not apply for readmission but instead joined the navy. "I can safely say," he wrote thirty years after his expulsion, "that the lowest, the most degraded, and the most vulgar wickedness, both as to tone and deed, and the most disordered imaginations, that it has ever been my evil fortune to witness, or to associate with, was met with at school, among the sons of those pious forefathers, who fancied they were not only saints themselves, but that they also were to be the progenitors of long lines of saints." With a substantial bequest at his father's death in 1809, he resigned from the navy and moved to Cooperstown, New York. Having run through his inheritance in a few years, he turned to a literary career to support himself and his family. His first novel, *Precaution* (1820), earned him attention; his second, *The Spy* (1821), gained a huge success. *The Pioneers* (1823), *The Pilot* (1824), *The Last of the Mohicans* (1826), *The Prairie* (1827), and *The Red Rover* (1827) quickly followed. His fame preceded him abroad, and during a stay in Paris and London he befriended the great and noble, while writing novels, romances, and political commentary. He returned to America in 1833 and spent the rest of his life in Cooperstown, continuing his Leatherstocking Tales, centered on his hero, Natty Bumppo, with *The Pathfinder* (1840) and *The Deerslayer* (1841).

THE PIONEERS, OR THE SOURCES OF THE SUSQUEHANNA; A DESCRIPTIVE TALE, VOLUME 2, CHAPTER 3

> *"Men, boys, and girls,*
> *Desert th' unpeopled village; and wild crowds*
> *Spread o'er the plain, by the sweet frenzy driven."*
> *Somerville*

From this time to the close of April, the weather continued to be a succession of great and rapid changes. One day, the soft airs of spring would seem to be stealing along the valley, and, in unison with an invigorating sun, attempting, covertly, to rouse the dormant powers of the vegetable world; while on the next, the surly blasts from the north would sweep across the lake, and erase every impression left by their gentle adversaries. The snow, however, finally disappeared, and the green wheat fields were seen in every direction, spotted with the dark and charred stumps that had, the preceding season, supported some of the proudest trees of the forest. Ploughs were in motion, wherever those useful implements could be used, and the smokes of the sugar-camps were no longer seen issuing from the summits of the woods of maple. The lake had lost all the characteristic beauty of a field of ice, but still a dark and gloomy covering concealed its waters, for the absence of currents left them yet hid under a porous crust, which, saturated with the fluid, barely retained enough of its strength to preserve the contiguity of its parts. Large flocks of wild geese were seen passing over the country, which hovered, for a time, around the hidden sheet of water, apparently searching for an opening, where they might find a resting-place; and then, on finding themselves excluded by the chill covering, would soar away to the north, filling the air with their discordant screams, as if venting their complaints at the tardy operations of nature.

For a week, the dark covering of the Otsego was left to the undisturbed possession of two eagles, who alighted on the centre of its field, and sat proudly eyeing the extent of their undisputed territory. During the presence of these monarchs of the air, the flocks of migrating birds avoided crossing the plain of ice, by turning into the hills, apparently seeking the protection of the forests, while the white and bald heads of the tenants of the lake were turned upward, with a look of majestic contempt, as if penetrating to the very heavens with the acuteness of their vision. But the time had come, when even these kings of birds were to be dispossessed. An opening had been gradually increasing, at the lower extremity of the lake, and around the dark spot where the current of the river had prevented the formation of ice, during even the coldest weather; and the fresh southerly winds, that now breathed freely up the valley, obtained an impression on the

waters. Mimic waves began to curl over the margin of the frozen field, which ex-
hibited an outline of crystallizations, that slowly receded towards the north. At
each step the power of the winds and the waves increased, until, after a struggle
of a few hours, the turbulent little billows succeeded in setting the whole field in
an undulating motion, when it was driven beyond the reach of the eye, with a
rapidity that was as magical as the change produced in the scene by this expulsion
of the lingering remnant of winter. Just as the last sheet of agitated ice was disappearing in the distance, the eagles rose over the border of crystals, and soared
with a wide sweep far above the clouds, while the waves tossed their little caps of
snow into the air, as if rioting in their release from a thraldom of five months'
duration.

The following morning Elizabeth was awakened by the exhilarating sounds of
the martins, who were quarrelling and chattering around the little boxes that
were suspended above her windows, and the cries of Richard, who was calling, in
tones as animating as the signs of the season itself—

"Awake! awake! my lady fair! the gulls are hovering over the lake already, and
the heavens are alive with the pigeons. You may look an hour before you can find
a hole, through which to get a peep at the sun. Awake! awake! lazy ones! Benjamin is overhauling the ammunition, and we only wait for our breakfasts, and
away for the mountains and pigeon shooting."

There was no resisting this animated appeal, and in a few minutes Miss Temple and her friend descended to the parlour. The doors of the hall were thrown
open, and the mild, balmy air of a clear spring morning was ventilating the apartment, where the vigilance of the ex-steward had been so long maintaining an
artificial heat with such unremitted diligence. The gentlemen were impatiently
waiting for their morning's repast, each being equipt in the garb of a sportsman.
Mr. Jones made many visits to the southern door, and would cry—

"See, cousin Bess! see, 'duke, the pigeon-roosts of the south have broken up!
They are growing more thick every instant. Here is a flock that the eye cannot see
the end of. There is food enough in it to keep the army of Xerxes for a month,
and feathers enough to make beds for the whole country. Xerxes, Mr. Edwards,
was a Grecian king, who—no, he was a Turk, or a Persian, who wanted to conquer Greece, just the same as these rascals will overrun our wheat-fields, when
they come back in the fall. Away! away! Bess; I long to pepper them from the
mountain."

In this wish both Marmaduke and young Edwards seemed equally to participate, for the sight was most exhilarating to a sportsman; and the ladies soon dismissed the party, after a hasty breakfast.

If the heavens were alive with pigeons, the whole village seemed equally in
motion, with men, women, and children. Every species of fire-arms, from the
French ducking-gun, with its barrel of near six feet in length, to the common

horseman's pistol, was to be seen in the hands of the men and boys; while bows and arrows, some made of the simple stick of a walnut sapling, and others in a rude imitation of the ancient cross-bows, were carried by many of the latter.

The houses and the signs of life apparent in the village, drove the alarmed birds from the direct line of their flight, towards the mountains, along the sides and near the bases of which they were glancing in dense masses, that were equally wonderful by the rapidity of their motion, as by their incredible numbers.

We have already said, that across the inclined plane which fell from the steep ascent of the mountain to the banks of the Susquehanna, ran the highway, on either side of which a clearing of many acres had been made at a very early day. Over those clearings, and up the eastern mountain, and along the dangerous path that was cut into its side, the different individuals posted themselves, as suited their inclinations; and in a few moments the attack commenced.

Among the sportsmen was to be seen the tall, gaunt form of Leather-stocking, who was walking over the field, with his rifle hanging on his arm, his dogs following close at his heels, now scenting the dead or wounded birds, that were beginning to tumble from the flocks, and then crouching under the legs of their master, as if they participated in his feelings at this wasteful and unsportsmanlike execution.

The reports of the fire-arms became rapid, whole volleys rising from the plain, as flocks of more than ordinary numbers darted over the opening, covering the field with darkness, like an interposing cloud; and then the light smoke of a single piece would issue from among the leafless bushes on the mountain, as death was hurled on the retreat of the affrighted birds, who were rising from a volley, for many feet into the air, in a vain effort to escape the attacks of man. Arrows, and missiles of every kind, were seen in the midst of the flocks; and so numerous were the birds, and so low did they take their flight, that even long poles, in the hands of those on the sides of the mountain, were used to strike them to the earth.

During all this time, Mr. Jones, who disdained the humble and ordinary means of destruction used by his companions, was busily occupied, aided by Benjamin, in making arrangements for an assault of a more than ordinarily fatal character. Among the relics of the old military excursions, that occasionally are discovered throughout the different districts of the western part of New-York, there had been found in Templeton, at its settlement, a small swivel, which would carry a ball of a pound weight. It was thought to have been deserted by a war-party of the whites, in one of their inroads into the Indian settlements, when, perhaps their convenience or their necessities induced them to leave such an incumbrance behind them in the woods. This miniature cannon had been released from the rust, and being mounted on little wheels, was now in a state for actual service. For several years, it was the sole organ for extraordinary rejoicings that was used in those mountains. On the mornings of the Fourths of July, it would be heard, with its echoes ringing among the hills, and telling forth its sounds, for thirteen times, with all the dignity of a two-and-thirty pounder; and even Captain Hollister, who was the highest authority in that part of the country on all such occasions, affirmed that, considering its dimensions, it was no despicable gun for a salute. It was somewhat the worse for the service it had performed, it is true, there being but a trifling difference in size between the touch-hole and the muzzle. Still, the grand conceptions of Richard had suggested the importance of such an instrument, in hurling death at his nimble enemies. The swivel was dragged by a horse into a part of the open space, that the Sheriff thought most eligible for planting a battery of the kind, and Mr. Pump proceeded to load it. Several handfuls of duck-shot were placed on top of the powder, and the Major-domo soon announced that his piece was ready for service.

The sight of such an implement collected all the idle spectators to the spot, who, being mostly boys, filled the air with their cries of exultation and delight. The gun was pointed on high, and Richard, holding a coal of fire in a pair of tongs, patiently took his seat on a stump, awaiting the appearance of a flock that was worthy of his notice.

So prodigious was the number of the birds, that the scattering fire of the guns, with the hurling of missiles, and the cries of the boys, had no other effect than to break off small flocks from the immense masses that continued to dart along the valley, as if the whole creation of the feathered tribe were pouring through that one pass. None pretended to collect the game, which lay scattered over the fields in such profusion as to cover the very ground with the fluttering victims.

Leather-stocking was a silent, but uneasy spectator of all these proceedings, but was able to keep his sentiments to himself until he saw the introduction of the swivel into the sports.

"This comes of settling a country!" he said—"here have I known the pigeons to fly for forty long years, and, till you made your clearings, there was nobody to skear or to hurt them. I loved to see them come into the woods, for they were company to a body; hurting nothing; being, as it was, as harmless as a garter-snake. But now it gives me sore thoughts when I hear the frighty things whizzing through the air, for I know it's only a motion to bring out all the brats in the village at them. Well! the Lord won't see the waste of his creaters for nothing, and right will be done to the pigeons, as well as others, by-and-by. There's Mr. Oliver, as bad as the rest of them, firing into the flocks as if he was shooting down nothing but the Mingo warriors."

Among the sportsmen was Billy Kirby, who, armed with an old musket, was loading, and without even looking into the air, was firing and shouting as his victims fell even on his own person. He heard the speech of Natty, and took upon himself to reply—

"What's that, old Leather-stocking!" he cried, "grumbling at the loss of a few pigeons! If you had to sow your wheat twice, and three times, as I have done, you wouldn't be so massyfully feeling'd to'ards the divils.—Hurrah, boys! scatter the feathers. This is better than shooting at a turkey's head and neck, old fellow."

"It's better for you, maybe, Billy Kirby," replied the indignant old hunter, "and all them as don't know how to put a ball down a rifle-barrel, or how to bring it up ag'n with a true aim; but it's wicked to be shooting into flocks in this wasty manner; and none do it, who know how to knock over a single bird. If a body has a craving for pigeon's flesh, why! it's made the same as all other creater's, for man's eating, but not to kill twenty and eat one. When I want such a thing I go into the woods till I find one to my liking, and then I shoot him off the branches without touching a feather of another, though there might be a hundred on the same tree. But you couldn't do such a thing, Billy Kirby—you couldn't do it if you tried."

"What's that you say, you old, dried cornstalk! you sapless stub!" cried the wood-chopper. "You've grown mighty boasting, sin' you killed the turkey; but if you're for a single shot, here goes at that bird which comes on by himself."

The fire from the distant part of the field had driven a single pigeon below the flock to which it had belonged, and frightened with the constant reports of the muskets, it was approaching the spot where the disputants stood, darting first from one side, and then to the other, cutting the air with the swiftness of lightning, and making a noise with its wings, not unlike the rushing of a bullet. Unfortunately for the wood-chopper, notwithstanding his vaunt, he did not see his bird until it was too late for him to fire as it approached, and he pulled his trigger at the unlucky moment when it was darting immediately over his head. The bird continued its course with incredible velocity.

Natty lowered the rifle from his arm, when the challenge was made, and, waiting a moment, until the terrified victim had got in a line with his eyes, and had dropped near the bank of the lake, he raised it again with uncommon rapidity, and fired. It might have been chance, or it might have been skill, that produced the result; it was probably a union of both; but the pigeon whirled over in the air, and fell into the lake, with a broken wing. At the sound of his rifle, both his dogs started from his feet, and in a few minutes the "slut" brought out the bird, still alive.

The wonderful exploit of Leather-stocking was noised through the field with great rapidity, and the sportsmen gathered in to learn the truth of the report.

"What," said young Edwards, "have you really killed a pigeon on the wing, Natty, with a single ball?"

"Haven't I killed loons before now, lad, that dive at the flash?" returned the hunter. "It's much better to kill only such as you want, without wasting your powder and lead, than to be firing into God's creaters in such a wicked manner. But I come out for a bird, and you know the reason why I like small game, Mr.

Oliver, and now I have got one I will go home, for I don't relish to see these wasty ways that you are all practysing, as if the least thing wasn't made for use, and not to destroy."

"Thou sayest well, Leather-stocking," cried Marmaduke, "and I begin to think it time to put an end to this work of destruction."

"Put an ind, Judge, to your clearings. An't the woods his work as well as the pigeons? Use, but don't waste. Wasn't the woods made for the beasts and birds to harbour in? and when man wanted their flesh, their skins, or their feathers, there's the place to seek them. But I'll go to the hut with my own game, for I wouldn't touch one of the harmless things that kiver the ground here, looking up with their eyes on me, as if they only wanted tongues to say their thoughts."

With this sentiment in his mouth, Leather-stocking threw his rifle over his arm, and followed by his dogs, stepping across the clearing with great caution, taking care not to tread on one of the wounded birds that lay in his path. He soon entered the bushes on the margin of the lake, and was hid from view.

Whatever impression the morality of Natty made on the Judge, it was utterly lost on Richard. He availed himself of the gathering of the sportsmen, to lay a plan for one "fell swoop" of destruction. The musket-men were drawn up in battle array, in a line extending on each side of his artillery, with orders to await the signal of firing from himself.

"Stand by, my lads," said Benjamin, who acted as an aid-de-camp on this momentous occasion, "stand by, my hearties, and when Squire Dickens heaves out the signal for to begin firing, d'ye see, you may open upon them in a broadside. Take care and fire low, boys, and you'll be sure to hull the flock."

"Fire low!" shouted Kirby—"hear the old fool! If we fire low, we may hit the stumps, but not ruffle a pigeon."

"How should you know, you lubber?" cried Benjamin, with a very unbecoming heat for an officer on the eve of battle—"how should you know, you grampus? Haven't I sailed aboard of the Boadishy for five years? and wasn't it a standing order to fire low, and to hull your enemy? Keep silence at your guns, boys, and mind the order that is passed."

The loud laughs of the musket-men were silenced by the authoritative voice of Richard, who called to them for attention and obedience to his signals.

Some millions of pigeons were supposed to have already passed, that morning, over the valley of Templeton; but nothing like the flock that was now approaching had been seen before. It extended from mountain to mountain in one solid blue mass, and the eye looked in vain over the southern hills to find its termination. The front of this living column was distinctly marked by a line but very slightly indented, so regular and even was the flight. Even Marmaduke forgot the morality of Leather-stocking as it approached, and, in common with the rest, brought his musket to his shoulder.

"Fire!" cried the Sheriff, clapping his coal to the priming of the cannon. As half of Benjamin's charge escaped through the touch-hole, the whole volley of the musketry preceded the report of the swivel. On receiving this united discharge of small arms, the front of the flock darted upward, while, at the same instant, myriads of those in their rear rushed with amazing rapidity into their places, so that when the column of white smoke gushed from the mouth of the little cannon, an accumulated mass of objects was gliding over its point of direction.—The roar of the gun echoed along the mountains, and died away to the north, like distant thunder, while the whole flock of alarmed birds seemed, for a moment, thrown into one disorderly and agitated mass. The air was filled with their irregular flights, layer rising over layer, far above the tops of the highest pines, none daring to advance beyond the dangerous pass; when, suddenly, some of the leaders of the feathered tribe shot across the valley, taking their flight directly over the village, and the hundreds of thousands in their rear followed their example, deserting the eastern side of the plain to their persecutors and their fallen.

"Victory!" shouted Richard, "victory! we have driven the enemy from the field."

"Not so, Dickon," said Marmaduke; "the field is covered with them; and, like the Leather-stocking, I see nothing but eyes, in every direction, as the innocent sufferers turn their heads, in terror, to examine my movements. Full one half of those that have fallen are yet alive: and I think it is time to end the sport; if sport it be."

"Sport!" cried the Sheriff; "it is princely sport! There are some thousands of the blue-coated boys on the ground, so that every old woman in the village may have a pot-pie for the asking."

"Well, we have happily frightened the birds from this side the valley," said Marmaduke, "and our carnage must of necessity end, for the present. Boys, I will give you sixpence a hundred for the pigeons' heads only: so go to work, and bring them into the village, where I will pay you."

This expedient produced the desired effect, for every urchin on the ground went industriously to work to wring the necks of the wounded birds. Judge Temple retired towards his dwelling with that kind of feeling, that many a man has experienced before him, who discovers, after the excitement of the moment has passed, that he has purchased pleasure at the price of misery to others. Horses were loaded with the dead; and, after the first burst of sporting, the shooting of pigeons became a business, for the remainder of the season, more in proportion to the people. Richard, however, boasted for many a year, of his shot with the "cricket;" and Benjamin gravely asserted, that he thought they killed nearly as many pigeons on that day, as there were Frenchmen destroyed on the memorable occasion of Rodney's victory.

Nathaniel Parker Willis

born into a family of Maine newspaper publishers, Nathaniel Parker Willis (1806–1867) published his first book of poems, *Sketches,* in 1827, the year he graduated from Yale. Setting out as a journalist, he continued to publish collections of verse, with *Fugitive Poetry* (1829) and *Poems Delivered Before the Society of United Brothers* (1831). His work for the *New-York Mirror* took him as a foreign correspondent to Europe and the Middle East. He settled in London and befriended Walter Savage Landor and Charles and Mary Lamb, but in an air of scandal he returned to America in 1836 and began writing popular plays. He also gathered several collections of his journalistic articles and travel writings. He continued to publish books of poems as well, including *Melanie* (1835), *Poems of Passion* (1843), *Poems: Sacred, Passionate, and Humorous* (1844), and *Poems of Early and After Years* (1848). He employed Edgar Allan Poe on the *Mirror* and chronicled fashionable New York. In James Russell Lowell's *A Fable of Critics* he was characterized as "the topmost bright bubble on the wave of the Town." From his prolific pen issued books of light fiction, travel, and memoirs. During the Civil War he stayed in Washington as a correspondent and was a friend of Mary Todd Lincoln. At his funeral, his pallbearers included Henry Wadsworth Longfellow, Oliver Wendell Holmes, Richard Henry Dana, and James Russell Lowell.

THE CONFESSIONAL

"When thou hast met with careless hearts and cold,
Hearts that young love may touch, but never hold,
Not changeless, as the loved and left of old—
    Remember me—remember me—
    I passionately pray of thee!"
Lady E. S. Wortley

I thought of thee—I thought of thee,
    On ocean—many a weary night—
When heaved the long and sullen sea,
    With only waves and stars in sight.
We stole along by isles of balm,
    We furl'd before the coming gale,
We slept amid the breathless calm,
    We flew beneath the straining sail—
But thou wert lost for years to me,
And, day and night, I thought of thee!

I thought of thee—I thought of thee,
    In France—amid the gay saloon,
Where eyes as dark as eyes may be
    Are many as the leaves in June—
Where life is love, and ev'n the air
    Is pregnant with impassion'd thought,
And song and dance and music are
    With one warm meaning only fraught—
My half-snar'd heart broke lightly free,
And, with a blush, I thought of thee!

I thought of thee—I thought of thee,
    In Florence,—where the fiery hearts
Of Italy are breathed away
    In wonders of the deathless arts;
Where strays the Contadina down
    Val d'Arno with a song of old;
Where clime and woman seldom frown,
    And life runs over sands of gold;
I stray'd to lone Fiesolé
On many an eve, and thought of thee.

I thought of thee—I thought of thee,
   In Rome,—when on the Palatine
Night left the Caesar's palace free
   To Time's forgetful foot and mine;
Or, on the Coliseum's wall,
   When moonlight touch'd the ivied stone,
Reclining, with a thought of all
   That o'er this scene has come and gone—
The shades of Rome would start and flee
Unconsciously—I thought of thee.

I thought of thee—I thought of thee,
   In Vallombrosa's holy shade,
Where nobles born the friars be,
   By life's rude changes humbler made.
Here Milton fram'd his Paradise;
   I slept within his very cell;
And, as I clos'd my weary eyes,
   I thought the cowl would fit me well—
The cloisters breath'd, it seem'd to me,
Of heart's-ease—but I thought of thee.

I thought of thee—I thought of thee,
   In Venice,—on a night in June;
When, through the city of the sea,
   Like dust of silver slept the moon.
Slow turn'd his oar the gondolier,
   And, as the black barks glided by,
The water to my leaning ear
   Bore back the lover's passing sigh—
It was no place alone to be—
I thought of thee—I thought of thee.

I thought of thee—I thought of thee,
   In the Ionian Isles—when straying
With wise Ulysses by the sea—
   Old Homer's songs around me playing;
Or, watching the bewitched caique,
   That o'er the star-lit waters flew,
I listen'd to the helmsman Greek,
   Who sung the song that Sappho knew—

The poet's spell, the bark, the sea,
All vanished—as I thought of thee.

I thought of thee—I thought of thee,
    In Greece—when rose the Parthenon
Majestic o'er the Egean sea,
    And heroes with it, one by one;
When, in the grove of Academe,
    Where Lais and Leontium stray'd
Discussing Plato's mystic theme,
    I lay at noontide in the shade—
The Egean wind, the whispering tree,
Had voices—and I thought of thee.

I thought of thee—I thought of thee,
    In Asia—on the Dardanelles;
Where, swiftly as the waters flee,
    Each wave some sweet old story tells;
And, seated by the marble tank
    Which sleeps by Ilium's ruins old,
(The fount where peerless Helen drank,
    And Venus lav'd her locks of gold,)
I thrill'd such classic haunts to see,
Yet even here—I thought of thee.

I thought of thee—I thought of thee,
    Where glide the Bosphor's lovely waters,
All palace-lined, from sea to sea;
    And ever on its shores the daughters
Of the delicious East are seen,
    Printing the brink with slipper'd feet,
And oh, those snowy folds between,
    What eyes of heaven your glances meet!
Peris of light no fairer be—
Yet—in Stamboul—I thought of thee.

I've thought of thee—I've thought of thee,
    Through change that teaches to forget;
Thy face looks up from every sea,
    In every star thine eyes are set,
Though roving beneath Orient skies,
    Whose golden beauty breathes of rest,

I envy every bird that flies
    Into the far and clouded West:
I think of thee—I think of thee!
Oh, dearest! hast thou thought of me?

UNSEEN SPIRITS

The shadows lay along Broadway,
    'Twas near the twilight-tide—
And slowly there a lady fair
    Was walking in her pride.
Alone walk'd she; but, viewlessly,
    Walk'd spirits at her side.

Peace charm'd the street beneath her feet,
    And Honor charm'd the air;
And all astir look'd kind on her,
    And call'd her good as fair—
For all God ever gave to her
    She kept with chary care.

She kept with care her beauties rare
    From lovers warm and true—
For her heart was cold to all but gold,
    And the rich came not to woo—
But honor'd well are charms to sell
    If priests the selling do.

Now walking there was one more fair—
    A slight girl, lily-pale;
And she had unseen company
    To make the spirit quail—
'Twixt Want and Scorn she walk'd forlorn,
    And nothing could avail.

No mercy now can clear her brow
    For this world's peace to pray;
For, as love's wild prayer dissolved in air,
    Her woman's heart gave way!—
But the sin forgiven by Christ in heaven
    By man is cursed alway!

CITY LYRICS

Argument.—The poet starts from the Bowling Green to take his sweetheart up to Thompson's for an ice, or (if she is inclined for more) ices. He confines his muse to matters which any every-day man and young woman may see in taking the same promenade for the same innocent refreshment.

Come out, love—the night is enchanting!
    The moon hangs just over Broadway;
The stars are all lighted and panting—
    (Hot weather up there, I dare say!)
'Tis seldom that "coolness" entices,
    And love is no better for chilling—
But come up to Thompson's for ices,
    And cool your warm heart for a shilling!

What perfume comes balmily o'er us?
    Mint juleps from City Hotel!
A loafer is smoking before us—
    (A nasty cigar, by the smell!)
Oh Woman! thou secret past knowing!
    Like lilachs that grow by the wall,
You breathe every air that is going,
    Yet gather but sweetness from all!

On, on! by St. Paul's, and the Astor!
    Religion seems very ill-plann'd!
For one day we list to the pastor,
    For six days we list to the band!
The sermon may dwell on the future,
    The organ your pulses may calm—
When—pest!—that remember'd cachucha
    Upsets both the sermon and psalm!

Oh, pity the love that must utter
    While goes a swift omnibus by!
(Though sweet is *I scream** when the flutter
    Of fans shows thermometers high)—
But if what I bawl, or I mutter,
    Falls into your ear but to die,

    **Query.*—Should this be *Ice cream,* or *I scream?—Printer's Devil.*

Oh, the dew that falls into the gutter
　　Is not more unhappy than I!

TO CHARLES ROUX, OF SWITZERLAND

Written in His Album When He Was the Author's
Teacher in Modern Languages
Yale College, 1827

I would not leave that land, if I were thou—
That glorious land of mountain and of flood,
　　Whereon is graven GOD.
As if its hills were chosen for Earth's brow,
And its loud torrents gave the words he spoke,
　　Leaping from rock to rock.

I would not leave it—for its children gave
Their blood like water, for a word, "be FREE!"
　　Their last breath, "LIBERTY!"
Till Switzerland was made a mighty grave—
A land where heroes like a harvest fell—
　　The land of WILLIAM TELL.

orn in Ithaca, New York, the son of a merchant, Francis Miles Finch (1827–1907) graduated from Yale in 1849. He was class poet and edited the *Yale Literary Magazine.* Finch practiced law, and in 1880 he was named an associate judge to the New York Court of Appeals, serving until 1895. "My whole life as a lawyer," he once wrote, "has been a battle against literary longings. I have kept the most earnest part of my nature in chains. I fear I have done it so long as to make full liberty dangerous to me." His collected poems were posthumously published in 1909, and the most famous of them is "The Blue and the Gray," first published in the *Atlantic Monthly* in 1867, earning him a wide celebrity.

THE BLUE AND THE GRAY

"The women of Columbus, Mississippi, animated by nobler sentiments than are many of their sisters, have shown themselves impartial in their offerings made to the memory of the dead. They strewed flowers alike on the graves of the Confederate and of the National soldiers."

—*New York Tribune*

By the flow of the inland river,
　　Whence the fleets of iron have fled,
Where the blades of the grave-grass quiver,
　　Asleep are the ranks of the dead;—
　　　　Under the sod and the dew,
　　　　　　Waiting the judgment day;—
　　　　Under the one, the Blue;
　　　　　　Under the other, the Gray.

These in the robings of glory,
　　Those in the gloom of defeat,
All with the battle-blood gory,
　　In the dusk of eternity meet;—
　　　　Under the sod and the dew,
　　　　　　Waiting the judgment day;—
　　　　Under the laurel, the Blue;
　　　　　　Under the willow, the Gray.

From the silence of sorrowful hours
　　The desolate mourners go,
Lovingly laden with flowers
　　Alike for the friend and the foe;—
　　　　Under the sod and the dew,
　　　　　　Waiting the judgment day;—
　　　　Under the rose, the Blue;
　　　　　　Under the lilies, the Gray.

So with an equal splendor
　　The morning sun-rays fall,
With a touch, impartially tender,
　　On the blossoms blooming for all;
　　　　Under the sod and the dew,
　　　　　　Waiting the judgment day;—

Broidered with gold, the Blue;
　　Mellowed with gold, the Gray.

So, when the Summer calleth,
　On forest and field of grain
With an equal murmur falleth
　The cooling drip of the rain;—
　　Under the sod and the dew,
　　　Waiting the judgment day;—
　　Wet with the rain, the Blue;
　　　Wet with the rain, the Gray.

Sadly, but not with upbraiding,
　The generous deed was done;
In the storm of the years that are fading,
　No braver battle was won;—
　　Under the sod and the dew,
　　　Waiting the judgment day;—
　　Under the blossoms, the Blue,
　　　Under the garlands, the Gray.

No more shall the war-cry sever,
　Or the winding rivers be red;
They banish our anger forever
　When they laurel the graves of our dead!
　　Under the sod and the dew,
　　　Waiting the judgment day;—
　　Love and tears for the Blue,
　　　Tears and love for the Gray.

C larence Day (1874–1935) graduated from Yale in 1896 and went to work with his father, a governor of the New York Stock Exchange. By 1903 ill health had forced him to retire from business, and he turned to writing. He illustrated his own poems and contributed essays to the *Saturday Evening Post* and *Harper's*. His first book, the satirical *The Simian World* (1920), was praised by Oliver Wendell Holmes, and from then on Day's books appeared regularly: *The Crow's Nest* (1921), *Thoughts Without Words* (1928), *God and My Father* (1932), *In the Green Mountain Country* (1934). His most popular book, *Life with Father,* beloved by generations of readers, appeared just before his death in 1935. The play made from it by Howard Lindsay and Russell Crouse had one of the longest Broadway runs in history; the film version with William Powell and Irene Dunne was a hit, and so was a television series that aired in the 1950s. *Life with Mother* was published posthumously in 1937. The joyful humor of Day's work belied that fact that he could barely hold a pen because of the pain that tortured him constantly. His later years were spent entirely in his bedroom, but his imagination was free and vital, and he left an indelible portrait of American life.

Father had been away, reorganizing some old upstate railroad. He returned in an executive mood and proceeded to shake up our home. In spite of my failure as a singer, he was still bound to have us taught music. We boys were summoned before him and informed that we must at once learn to play on something. We might not appreciate it now, he said, but we should later on. "You, Clarence, will learn the violin. George, you the piano. Julian—well, Julian is too young yet. But you older boys must have lessons."

I was appalled at this order. At the age of ten it seemed a disaster to lose any more of my freedom. The days were already too short for our games after school; and now here was a chunk to come out of playtime three days every week. A chunk every day, we found afterward, because we had to practice.

George sat at the piano in the parlor, and faithfully learned to pound out his exercises. He had all the luck. He was not an inspired player, but at least he had some ear for music. He also had the advantage of playing on a good robust instrument, which he didn't have to be careful not to drop, and was in no danger of breaking. Furthermore, he did not have to tune it. A piano had some good points.

But I had to go through a blacker and more gruesome experience. It was bad enough to have to come in from the street and the sunlight and go down into our dark little basement where I took my lessons. But that was only the opening chill of the struggle that followed.

The whole thing was uncanny. The violin itself was a queer, fragile, cigar-boxy thing, that had to be handled most gingerly. Nothing sturdy about it. Why, a fellow was liable to crack it putting it into its case. And then my teacher, he was queer too. He had a queer pickled smell.

I dare say he wasn't queer at all really, but he seemed so to me, because he was different from the people I generally met. He was probably worth a dozen of some of them, but I didn't know it. He was one of the violins in the Philharmonic, and an excellent player; a grave, middle-aged little man—who was obliged to give lessons.

He wore a black, wrinkled frock coat, and a discolored gold watch-chain. He had small, black-rimmed glasses; not tortoise-shell, but thin rims of metal. His violin was dark, rich, and polished, and would do anything for him.

Mine was balky and awkward, brand new, and of a light, common color.

The violin is intended for persons with a passion for music. I wasn't that kind of person. I liked to hear a band play a tune that we could march up and down to, but try as I would, I could seldom whistle such a tune afterward. My teacher didn't know this. He greeted me as a possible genius.

He taught me how to hold the contraption, tucked under my chin. I learned how to move my fingers here and there on its handle or stem. I learned how to draw the bow across the strings, and thus produce sounds. . . .

Does a mother recall the first cry of her baby, I wonder? I still remember the strange cry at birth of that new violin.

My teacher, Herr M., looked as though he had suddenly taken a large glass of vinegar. He sucked in his breath. His lips were drawn back from his teeth, and his eyes tightly shut. Of course, he hadn't expected my notes to be sweet at the start; but still, there was something unearthly about that first cry. He snatched the violin from me, examined it, readjusted its pegs, and comforted it gently, by drawing his own bow across it. It was only a new and not especially fine violin, but the sounds it made for him were more natural—they were classifiable sounds. They were not richly musical, but at least they had been heard before on this earth.

He handed the instrument back to me with careful directions. I tucked it up under my chin again and grasped the end tight. I held my bow exactly as ordered. I looked up at him, waiting.

"Now," he said, nervously.

I slowly raised the bow, drew it downward. . . .

This time there were *two* dreadful cries in our little front basement. One came from my new violin and one from the heart of Herr M.

Herr M. presently came to, and smiled bravely at me, and said if I wanted to rest a moment he would permit it. He seemed to think I might wish to lie down awhile and recover. I didn't feel any need of lying down. All I wanted was to get through the lesson. But Herr M. was shaken. He was by no means ready to let me proceed. He looked around desperately, saw the music book, and said he would now show me that. We sat down side by side on the window-seat, with the book in his lap, while he pointed out the notes to me with his finger, and told me their names.

After a bit, when he felt better, he took up his own violin, and instructed me to watch him and note how he handled the strings. And then at last, he nerved himself to let me take my violin up again. "Softly, my child, softly," he begged me, and stood facing the wall. . . .

We got through the afternoon somehow, but it was a ghastly experience. Part of the time he was maddened by the mistakes I kept making, and part of the time he was plain wretched. He covered his eyes. He seemed ill. He looked often at his watch, even shook it as though it had stopped; but he stayed the full hour.

That was Wednesday. What struggles he had with himself before Friday, when my second lesson was due, I can only dimly imagine, and of course I never even gave them a thought at the time. He came back to recommence teaching me, but he had changed—he had hardened. Instead of being cross, he was stern; and instead of sad, bitter. He wasn't unkind to me, but we were no longer companions.

He talked to himself, under his breath; and sometimes he took bits of paper, and did little sums on them, gloomily, and then tore them up.

During my third lesson I saw the tears come to his eyes. He went up to Father and said he was sorry but he honestly felt sure I'd never be able to play.

Father didn't like this at all. He said he felt sure I would. He dismissed Herr M. briefly—the poor man came stumbling back down in two minutes. In that short space of time he had gallantly gone upstairs in a glow, resolved upon sacrificing his earnings for the sake of telling the truth. He returned with his earnings still running, but with the look of a lost soul about him, as though he felt that his nerves and his sanity were doomed to destruction. He was low in his mind, and he talked to himself more than ever. Sometimes he spoke harshly of America, sometimes of fate.

But he no longer struggled. He accepted this thing as his destiny. He regarded me as an unfortunate something, outside the human species, whom he must simply try to labor with as well as he could. It was a grotesque, indeed a hellish experience, but he felt he must bear it.

He wasn't the only one—he was at least not alone in his sufferings. Mother, though expecting the worst, had tried to be hopeful about it, but at the end of a week or two I heard her and Margaret talking it over. I was slaughtering a scale in the front basement, when Mother came down and stood outside the door in the kitchen hall and whispered, "Oh, Margaret!"

I watched them. Margaret was baking a cake. She screwed up her face, raised her arms, and brought them down with hands clenched.

"I don't know what we shall do, Margaret."

"The poor little feller," Margaret whispered. "He can't make the thing go."

This made me indignant. They were making me look like a lubber. I wished to feel always that I could make anything go. . . .

I now began to feel a determination to master this thing. History shows us many examples of the misplaced determinations of men—they are one of the darkest aspects of human life, they spread so much needless pain: but I knew little history. And I viewed what little I did know romantically—I should have seen in such episodes their heroism, not their futility. Any role that seemed heroic attracted me, no matter how senseless.

Not that I saw any chance for heroism in our front basement, of course. You had to have a battlefield or something. I saw only that I was appearing ridiculous. But that stung my pride. I hadn't wanted to learn anything whatever about fiddles or music, but since I was in for it, I'd do it, and show them I could. A boy will often put in enormous amounts of his time trying to prove he isn't as ridiculous as he thinks people think him.

Meanwhile Herr M. and I had discovered that I was nearsighted. On account of the violin's being an instrument that sticks out in front of one, I couldn't stand close enough to the music book to see the notes clearly. He didn't at first realize that I often made mistakes from that cause. When he and I finally comprehended that I had this defect, he had a sudden new hope that this might have been the whole trouble, and that when it was corrected I might play like a human being at last.

Neither of us ventured to take up this matter with Father. We knew that it would have been hard to convince him that my eyes were not perfect, I being a son of his and presumably made in his image; and we knew that he immediately would have felt we were trying to make trouble for him, and would have shown an amount of resentment which it was best to avoid. So Herr M. instead lent me his glasses. These did fairly well. They turned the dim grayness of the notes into a queer bright distortion, but the main thing was they did make them brighter, so that I now saw more of them. How well I remember those little glasses. Poor, dingy old things. Herr M. was nervous about lending them to me; he feared that I'd drop them. It would have been safer if they had been spectacles: but no, they were pince-nez; and I had to learn to balance them across my nose as well as I could. I couldn't wear them up near my eyes because my nose was too thin there; I had to put them about half-way down where there was enough flesh to hold them. I also had to tilt my head back, for the music-stand was a little too tall for me. Herr M. sometimes mounted me on a stool, warning me not to step off. Then when I was all set, and when he without his glasses was blind, I would smash my way into the scales again.

All during the long winter months I worked away at this job. I gave no thought, of course, to the family. But they did to me. Our house was heated by a furnace, which had big warm air pipes; these ran up through the walls with wide outlets into each room, and sound traveled easily and ringingly through their roomy, tin passages. My violin could be heard in every part of the house. No one could settle down to anything while I was practicing. If visitors came they soon left. Mother couldn't even sing to the baby. She would wait, watching the clock, until my long hour of scale-work was over, and then come downstairs and shriek at me that my time was up. She would find me sawing away with my forehead wet, and my hair wet and stringy, and even my clothes slowly getting damp from my exertions. She would feel my collar, which was done for, and say I must change it. "Oh, Mother! Please!"—for I was in a hurry now to run out and play. But she wasn't being fussy about my collar, I can see, looking back; she was using it merely as a barometer or gauge of my pores. She thought I had better dry my-self before going out in the snow.

It was a hard winter for Mother. I believe she also had fears for the baby. She sometimes pleaded with Father; but no one could ever tell Father anything. He continued to stand like a rock against stopping my lessons.

Schopenhauer, in his rules for debating, shows how to win a weak case by insidiously transferring an argument from its right field, and discussing it instead from some irrelevant but impregnable angle. Father knew nothing of Schopenhauer, and was never insidious, but, nevertheless, he had certain natural gifts for debate. In the first place his voice was powerful and stormy, and he let it out at full strength, and kept on letting it out with a vigor that stunned his opponents. As a second gift, he was convinced at all times that his opponents were wrong. Hence, even if they did win a point or two, it did them no good, for he dragged the issue to some other ground then, where he and Truth could prevail. When Mother said it surely was plain enough that I had no ear, what was his reply? Why, he said that the violin was the noblest instrument invented by man. Having silenced her with this solid premise he declared that it followed that any boy was lucky to be given the privilege of learning to play it. No boy should expect to learn it immediately. It required persistence. Everything, he had found, required persistence. The motto was, Never give up.

All his life, he declared, he had persevered in spite of discouragement, and he meant to keep on persevering, and he meant me to, too. He said that none of us realized what he had had to go through. If he had been the kind that gave up at the very first obstacle, where would he have been now—where would any of the family have been? The answer was, apparently, that we'd either have been in a very bad way, poking round for crusts in the gutter, or else nonexistent. We might have never even been born if Father had not persevered.

Placed beside this record of Father's vast trials overcome, the little difficulty of my learning to play the violin seemed a trifle. I faithfully spurred myself on again, to work at the puzzle. Even my teacher seemed impressed with these views on persistence. Though older than Father, he had certainly not made as much money, and he bowed to the experience of a practical man who was a success. If he, Herr M., had been a success he would not have had to teach boys; and sitting in this black pit in which his need of money had placed him, he saw more than ever that he must learn the ways of this world. He listened with all his heart, as to a god, when Father shook his forefinger, and told him how to climb to the heights where financial rewards were achieved. The idea he got was that perseverance was sure to lead to great wealth.

Consequently our front basement continued to be the home of lost causes.

Of course, I kept begging Herr M. to let me learn just one tune. Even though I seldom could whistle them, still I liked tunes; and I knew that, in my hours of practicing, a tune would be a comfort. That is, for myself. Here again I never gave a thought to the effect upon others.

Herr M., after many misgivings, to which I respectfully listened—though they were not spoken to me, they were muttered to himself, pessimistically—hunted through a worn old book of selections, and after much doubtful fumbling chose as simple a thing as he could find for me—for me and the neighbors.

It was spring now, and windows were open. That tune became famous.

What would the musician who had tenderly composed this air, years before, have felt if he had foreseen what an end it would have, on Madison Avenue; and how, before death, it would be execrated by that once peaceful neighborhood. I engraved it on their hearts; not in its true form but in my own eerie versions. It was the only tune I knew. Consequently I played and replayed it.

Even horrors when repeated grow old and lose part of their sting. But those I produced were, unluckily, never the same. To be sure, this tune kept its general structure the same, even in my sweating hands. There was always the place where I climbed unsteadily up to its peak, and that difficult spot where it wavered, or staggered, and stuck; and then a sudden jerk of resumption—I came out strong on that. Every afternoon when I got to that difficult spot, the neighbors dropped whatever they were doing to wait for that jerk, shrinking from the moment, and yet feverishly impatient for it to come.

But what made the tune and their anguish so different each day? I'll explain. The strings of a violin are wound at the end around pegs, and each peg must be screwed in and tightened till the string sounds just right. Herr M. left my violin properly tuned when he went. But suppose a string broke, or that somehow I jarred a peg loose. Its string then became slack and soundless. I had to re-tighten it. Not having an ear, I was highly uncertain about this.

Our neighbors never knew at what degree of tautness I'd put such a string. I didn't myself. I just screwed her up tight enough to make a strong reliable sound. Neither they nor I could tell which string would thus appear in a new role each day, nor foresee the profound transformations this would produce in that tune.

All that spring this unhappy and ill-destined melody floated out through my window, and writhed in the air for one hour daily, in sunshine or storm. All that spring our neighbors and I daily toiled to its peak, and staggered over its hump, so to speak, and fell wailing through space.

Things now began to be said to Mother which drove her to act. She explained to Father that the end had come at last. Absolutely. "This awful nightmare cannot go on," she said.

Father pooh-poohed her.

She cried. She told him what it was doing to her. He said that she was excited, and that her descriptions of the sounds I made were exaggerated and hysterical— must be. She was always too vehement, he shouted. She must learn to be calm.

"But you're downtown, *you* don't have to hear it!"

Father remained wholly skeptical.

She endeavored to shame him. She told him what awful things the neighbors were saying about him, because of the noise I was making, for which he was responsible.

He couldn't be made to look at it that way. If there really were any unpleasantness then I was responsible. He had provided me with a good teacher and a good violin—so he reasoned. In short, he had done his best, and no father could have done more. If I made hideous sounds after all that, the fault must be mine. He said that Mother should be stricter with me, if necessary, and make me try harder.

This was the last straw. I couldn't try harder. When Mother told me his verdict I said nothing, but my body rebelled. Self-discipline had its limits—and I wanted to be out: it was spring. I skimped my hours of practice when I heard the fellows playing outside. I came home late for lessons—even forgot them. Little by little they stopped.

Father was outraged. His final argument, I remember, was that my violin had cost twenty-five dollars; if I didn't learn it the money would be wasted, and he couldn't afford it. But it was put to him that my younger brother, Julian, could learn it instead, later on. Then summer came, anyhow, and we went for three months to the seashore; and in the confusion of this Father was defeated and I was set free.

In the autumn little Julian was led away one afternoon, and imprisoned in the front basement in my place. I don't remember how long they kept him down there, but it was several years. He had an ear, however, and I believe he learned to play fairly well. This would have made a happy ending for Herr M. after all; but it was some other teacher, a younger man, who was engaged to teach Julian. Father said Herr M. was a failure.

Owen Johnson (1878–1952) stayed an extra year at Lawrenceville to found and edit the *Lawrenceville Lit,* and at Yale, which he entered in 1896, he edited the *Yale Literary Magazine.* By the age of twenty-three, he had published his first novel, *Arrows of the Almighty,* a historical romance set at Yale in the 1850s. Among his other novels are *Max Fargus* (1906), and his Lawrenceville Stories, *The Prodigious Hickey* (1910) and *The Tennessee Shad* (1911). *The Varmint* (1910) introduced his readers to a character named John Humperdink Stover, the hero next of *Stover at Yale* (1911), a memorable satire on snobbery and conformity. It remains Johnson's most famous book. Many other novels followed; among them, *The Salamander* (1913), *The Wasted Generation* (1921), and *Sacrifice* (1929), all of them acute observations of social convention.

STOVER AT YALE, EXCERPT FROM CHAPTER 12

The first weeks of the competition for the crew were not exacting, and consisted mostly of eliminating processes. Stover had consequently still enough leisure to gravitate naturally into that necessity of running into debt which comes to every youth who has just won the privilege of a yearly allowance; the same being solemnly understood to cover all the secret and hidden needs of the flesh as well as those that are outwardly exposed to the admiration of the multitude.

Now, the lure of personal adornment and the charm of violent neckties and outrageous vests had come to him naturally, as such things come, shortly after the measles, under the educating influence of a hopeless passion which had passed but had left its handiwork.

About a week after the opening of the term, Stover was drifting down Chapel Street in the company of Hungerford and McCarthy, when, in the window of the most predatory haberdasher's, he suddenly was fascinated by the most beautiful thing he had ever seen adorning a window. A tinge of masculine modesty prevented his remaining in struck admiration before it, especially in the presence of McCarthy and Hungerford, whose souls could rest content in jerseys and sweaters; but half an hour later, slipping away, he returned, fascinated. Chance had been kind to him. It was still there, the most beautiful green shirt he had ever beheld—not the diluted green of ordinary pistache ice-cream, but the deep, royal hue of a glorious emerald!

He had once, in the school days when he was blossoming into a man of fashion, experienced a similar sensation before a cravat of pigeon-blood red. He peered through the window to see if any one he knew was present, and glanced up the street to assure himself that a mob was not going to collect. Then he entered nonchalantly. The clerk, who recognized him, greeted him with ingratiating unction.

"Glad to see you here, Mr. Stover. What can I do for you?"

"I thought I'd look at some shirts," he said, in what he believed a masterly haphazard manner.

"White lawn—something with a thin stripe?"

"Well, something in a color—solid color."

He waited patiently, considering solicitously twenty inconsequential styles, until the spruce clerk, casually producing the one thing, said:

"Would that appeal to you?"

"It's rather nice," he said, gazing at it. Entranced, he stared on. Then a new difficulty arose. People didn't enter a shop just to purchase one shirt, and, besides, he was known. So he selected three other shirts and added the beautiful green thing to them in an unostentatious manner, saying:

"Send around these four shirts, will you? What's the tax?"

"Very pleased to have you open an account, Mr. Stover," said the clerk. "Pay when you like."

Stover took this as a personal tribute to his public reputation. Likewise, it opened up to him startling possibilities, so he said in a bored way:

"I suppose I might just as well."

"Thank you, Mr. Stover—thank you very much! Anything more? Some rather tasty neckties here for conservative dressers. Collars? Something like this would be very becoming to you. We've just got in a very smart line of silk socks. All the latest bonton styles. Look them over—you don't need to buy anything."

When Stover finally was shown to the door, he had clandestinely and with great astuteness acquired the green shirt on the following terms:

One green shirt (imported) . . . . $ 5
Three decoy shirts   9
Four silk ties (to go with green shirt)   8
One dozen Roxburgh turndown collars (to complete same)   3
One dozen Gladstone collars (an indiscretion)   3
One half dozen silk socks (bonton style) 12
Total for one green shirt $40

By the time he had made this mental calculation he was half way up the block. Then, his extravagance overwhelming him, he virtuously determined to send back the Gladstone collars, to show the clerk that, while he was a man of fashion, he still had a will of his own.

Refreshed then by this firm conscientious resolve, he went down York Street, where he was hailed by Hungerford from an upper story, and went in to find a small group sitting in inspection of several bundles of tailoring goods which were being displayed in the center of the room by a little bow-legged Yankee with an open appealing countenance.

"I say, Dink, you ought to get in on this," said Hungerford at his entrance.

"What's the game?"

"Here's a wonderful chance. Little bright-eyes here has got a lot of goods dirt cheap and he's giving us the first chance. You see it's this way: he travels for a firm and the end of the season he gets all the samples for himself, so he can let them go dirt cheap."

"Half price," said the salesman nodding. "Half price on everything."

"I've bought a bundle," said Troutman. "It's wonderful goods."

"How much?" said Stover, considering.

"Only twenty dollars for enough to make up a suit. Twenty's right, isn't it, Skenk?"

"Twenty for this—twenty-two for that. You remember I said twenty-two."

"Let me see the stuff," said Stover, as though he had been the mainstay of custom tailors all his life.

Now the crowd was a New York one, a little better groomed than their companions, affecting the same predilections for indiscreet vests and modish styles that would make them appreciative of the supremacy of green in the haberdashery arts.

"This is rather good style," he said, with a glance at Troutman's genteel trousers. "What sort of goods do you call it?"

"Imported Scotch cheviot," said the salesman in a confidential whisper.

Stover looked again at Troutman, who tried discreetly, without being seen by the unsuspecting Yankee, to convey to him in a look the fact that it was a crime to acquire the goods at such a price.

Thus tipped off, Dink bought a roll that had in it a distinct reminiscent tinge of green, and saw it carried to the house, for fear the salesman should suddenly repent of the sacrifice.

At half past eight that night, as he and Tough McCarthy were painfully excavating a bit of Greek prose for the morrow, McNab came rushing in.

"Get out, Dopey, we're boning," said McCarthy, reaching for a tennis racket.

"Boys, the greatest bargain you ever heard," said McNab excitedly, "come in before it's too late!"

"Bargain?" said Stover, frowning, for the word was beginning to cloy.

McNab, with a show of pantomime, squinted behind the window curtains and opened the closet door.

"Look here, Dopey, you get out," said Tough, wrathfully, "you're faking."

"I'm looking for customs officers," said McNab mysteriously.

"What! I say, what's this game?"

"Boys, we've got a couple of *Cuba libre* dagos rounded up and dancing on a string."

"For the love of Mike, Dopey, be intelligible."

"It's cigars," said McNab at last.

"Don't want them!"

"But it's smuggled cigars!"

"Oh!"

"Wonderful, pure Havanas, priceless, out of a museum."

"You don't say so."

"And all for the cause of *Cuba libre*. You're for *Cuba libre,* aren't you?"

"Sure we are."

"Well, these men are patriots."

"Who found them?"

"Buck Waters. They were just going into Pierson Hall to let the sophs have all the candy. Buck sidetracked them and started them down our row. Hungerford bought twenty-five dollars' worth."

"Twenty-five? Holy cats!"

"For the cause of *Cuba libre!* Joe is very patriotic. All the boys came up handsomely."

"Are they good cigars?" said Dink who, since his purchases of the day, was not exactly moved to tears by the financial needs of an alien though struggling nation.

"My boy, immense! Wait till you smoke one!"

At this moment there came a gentle scratching at the door, and a chocolate pair appeared, with Buck Waters in the background.

"Emanuel Garcia and Henry Clay!" said McNab irreverently.

"They smuggled the cigars right through the Spanish lines," said Waters who, from constant recital, had caught the spirit of unconquerable revolution.

"How do you know?" said McCarthy suspiciously, watching the unstrapping of the cigar boxes.

"I speak French," said Waters with pride, and turning to his protégés he continued fluently, " *Vous êtes patriots, vous avez battlez, soldats n'est-ce-pas?* You see, they have had a whole family chopped up for the cause. The Cuban Junta has sent them over to raise money—very good family."

"Let's see the cigars," said Stover. "How much a box?"

Curiously enough this seemed to be a phrase of English which could be understood without difficulty.

"Fourteen dollar."

"That's for a box of a hundred," said McNab, who screwed up the far side of his face, to indicate bargaining was in order.

"Of course," said Buck Waters, "everything you give goes to the cause. Remember that."

"Try one," said McNab.

The smaller Cuban with an affable smile held up a bundle.

"Nice white teeth he's got," said Buck Waters encouragingly.

"Don't let him shove one over on you," said McCarthy warningly.

Waters and McNab were indignant.

"Oh, I say fellows, come on. They are patriots."

"If they could understand you they would go right up in the air."

"Nevertheless and notwithstanding," said McCarthy, indicating with his finger, "I'll take this one; it appeals to me."

"I'll worry this one," said Dink with equal astuteness.

They took several puffs, watched by the enthusiastic spectators.

"Well?" said McNab.

Stover looked wisely at McCarthy, flirting the cigar between his careless fingers.

"Not bad."

"Rather good bouquet," said McCarthy, who knew no more than Stover.

"Let's begin at eight dollars and stick at ten," said Dink.

At that latter price, despite the openly expressed scorn of the American allies of the struggle for Cuban independence, Stover received a box of one hundred finest Havana cigars—fit for a museum, as McNab repeated—and saw the advance guard of the liberators disappear.

"Dink, it's a shame," said McCarthy gleefully. "Finest cigars I ever smoked."

They shook hands and Stover, overcome by the look of pain he had seen in the eyes of the patriots on their final surrender at ten dollars, said, with a patriotic remorse:

"Poor devils! Think what they're fighting for! If I hadn't been so lavish to-day, I'd have given them the full price."

"I feel sort of bad about it myself."

About ten o'clock they rose by a common impulse and, seeking out the cigars with caressing fingers, indulged in another smoke.

"Dink, this is certainly living," said McCarthy, reclining in that position which his favorite magazine artist ascribed to men of the world when indulging in extravagant desires.

"Pretty high rolling, old geezer."

"I like this better than the first one."

"Of course with a well-seasoned rare old cigar you don't get all the beauty of it right at first."

"By George, if those chocolate patriots would come around again I'd give 'em the four plunks."

"I should feel like it," said Dink, who made a distinction.

The next morning being Sunday, they lolled deliciously in bed, and rose with difficulty at ten.

"Of course I don't believe in smoking before breakfast, as a general rule," said McCarthy in striped red and blue pajamas, "but I have such a fond feeling for Cuba."

"I can hardly believe it's true," said Dink, emerging from the covers like an impressionistic dawn. "Smoke up."

"How is it this morning?"

"Wonderful."

"Better and better."

"I could dream away my life on it."

"We ought to have bought more."

"Too bad."

After chapel, while pursuing their studies in comparative literature in the Sunday newspapers, they smoked again.

"Well?" said Stover anxiously.

"Well?"

"Marvellous, isn't it?"

"Exquisite."

"Only ten cents apiece!"

"It's the way to buy cigars."

"Trouble is, Dink, old highroller, it's going to be an awful wrench getting down to earth again. We'll hate anything ordinary, anything cheap."

"Yes, Tough, we are ruining our future happiness."

"And how good one of the little beauties will taste after that brutalizing Sunday dinner."

"I can hardly wait. By the way, I blew myself to a few glad rags," said Dink, bringing out his purchases, "I rather fancy them. How do they strike you?"

McCarthy emitted a languishing whistle and then his eyes fell on the cause of all the trouble.

"Keeroogalum! Where did you get the pea-soup?"

The expression did not please. However, Stover had still in the matter of his sentimental inclinations a certain bashfulness. So he said dishonestly:

"I had 'em throw it in for a lark."

"Why, the cows would leave the farm."

"Rats. Wait and see," said Dink, who seized the excuse to don the green shirt.

When Stover's blond locks were seen struggling through the collar McCarthy exploded:

"It looks like you were coming out of a tree. What the deuce has happened to you? Are you going out for class beauty? Holy cats! the socks, the socks!"

"The socks, you Reuben, should match the shirt," said Stover, completing his toilet under a diplomatic assumption of persiflage.

"Well, you are a lovely thing," said McCarthy, when the new collar and the selected necktie had transformed Stover. "Lovely! lovely! you should go out and have the girls fondle you."

At this moment Bob Story arrived, as fate would have it, with an invitation to dinner at his home.

"Sis is back with a few charmers from Farmington and they're crazy to meet you."

"Oh, I say," said Stover in sudden alarm. "I'm the limit on the fussing question."

"Yes, he is," said McCarthy maliciously. "Why, they fall down before him and beg him to step on them."

"You shut up," said Stover, with wrath in his eye.

"Why, Bob, look at him, isn't he gotten up just to charm and delight? You'll have to put a fence around him to keep them off."

"In an hour," said Story, making for the door. "Hunter and Hungerford are coming."

"Hold up."

"Delighted you're coming."

"I say—"

"There's a Miss Sparkes—just crazy about you. You're in luck. Remember the name—Miss Sparkes."

"Story—Bob, come back here!"

"Au reservoir!"

"I can't go—I won't—" But here Dink, leaning over the banister, heard a gleeful laugh float up and the sudden banging of the door.

He rushed back frantically to the room and craned out the window, to see Bob Story sliding around the corner with his fingers spread in a gesture that is never anything but insulting. He closed the window violently and returned to the center of the room.

"Damn!"

"Pooh!" said McCarthy, chuckling with delight.

"Petticoats!"

"Alas!"

"A lot of silly, yapping, gushing, fluffy, giggling, tee-heeing, tittering, languishing, vapid, useless—"

"My boy, immense! Go on!"

"Confound Bob Story, why the deuce did he rope me into this? I loathe females."

"And one just dotes on you," said McCarthy, with the expression of a Cheshire cat.

"I won't go," said Stover loudly.

"Are you going in that green symphony?"

"Why not?"

In the midst of this quarrel, Joe Hungerford entered, with a solemn face.

"You're going to this massacre at Story's?"

"Don't I look like it?" said Dink crossly.

"We'll go over together then," said Hungerford, with a sigh of relief.

"I say, help yourself to a cigar, Joe," said McCarthy, with the air of a Maecenas.

"*Cuba Libre?*" said Hungerford, approaching the box.

"And *à bas* Spain!"

Hungerford examined the cigars with a certain amount of caution which was not lost on the room-mates.

"How many of these have you smoked?" he asked, turning to them with interest.

"Oh, about three apiece."

"How do you like 'em?"

"Wonderful!" said Dink loudly.

"Wonderful!" said McCarthy.

The three lit up simultaneously.

"What did you pay for yours?" said Hungerford, with a sort of inward concentration on the flavor.

"Ten bright silver ones."

"I paid twenty-five for two. How do they taste?"

"Wonderful!"

"Troutman only paid seven-fifty for his box."

"What!"

"And Hunter only five."

"Five dollars?" said McCarthy, with a foreboding.

"But what I can't understand is this—"

"What?"

"Dopey McNab got a box at two-fifty."

A sudden silence fell on the room, while, reflectively, each puffed forth quick, questioning volumes of smoke.

"How do they smoke?" said Hungerford again.

"Wonderful!" said McCarthy, hoping against hope.

"They're not!" said Dink firmly.

He rose, went to the window, and cast forth the malodorous thing. Hungerford followed suit. McCarthy, proud as the Old Guard, sat smoking on; only one leg was drawn up under the other in a tense, convulsive way.

"They were wonderful last night," he said obstinately.

"They certainly were."

"And they were wonderful this morning."

"Not quite so wonderful."

"I like 'em still."

"And Dopey McNab bought a hundred at two-fifty."

This was too much for McCarthy. He surrendered.

Dopey McNab, at this favorable conjunction, sidled into the room with his box under his arm and the face of a boy soprano on duty.

"I say, fellows, I've got a little proposition to make."

A sort of dull, rolling murmur went around the room which he did not notice.

"I find I've been cracking my bank account—the fact is, I'm strapped as a mule and have got to raise enough to pay my wash bill."

"Wash bill, Dopey?" said McCarthy softly.

"We must wash," said Dopey firmly. "To resume. As I detest, abhor, and likewise shrink from borrowing from friends—"

"Repeat that," said Joe Hungerford.

"I will not. But for all of which reasons, I have a little bargain to propose. Here is a box of the finest cigars ever struck the place."

"A full box?"

"Only three cigars out."

"Three!" said Hungerford with a significant look at Stover.

"I could sell them on the campus for twenty, easy."

"But you love your friends," said Stover, moving a little, so as to shut off the retreat.

"Who will give me seven-fifty for it?" said McNab, with the air of one filling a beggar with ecstasy.

"Seven-fifty. You'll let it go at seven-fifty, Dopey?" said McCarthy faintly, paralyzed at such duplicity.

"I will."

"Dopey," said Dink, with a signal to the others, "what is the exact figure of that wash bill of yours?"

"Two dollars and sixty-two cents."

"Will you take two dollars and sixty-two cents for it?"

"You're fooling."

"I am very, very serious."

McNab struck a pose, while over his face was seen the conflict of duty and avarice.

"Take it," he said at last, in a glow of virtue.

"I didn't say I wanted it."

"You didn't!"

"I only wanted to know what you'd really take."

"What's this mean?" said McNab indignantly.

"Dopey, would you sacrifice it at just a little less?" said Hungerford.

But here McNab, suddenly smelling danger in the air, made a spring backwards. Hungerford, who was on guard, caught him.

"Put him in the chair and tie him," said Stover, savagely.

Which was done.

"I say, look here, what are you going to do with me?" said McNab, fiercely.

"You're going to sit there and smoke a couple of those museum cigars, for our delectation and amusement."

"Assassins!"

"Two cigars."

"Never! I'll starve to death first!"

"All right. Keep on sitting there."

"But this is a crime! Police!"

"There are other crimes, Dopey."

"Hold up," said McNab, frantically, as he perceived the cigar being prepared. "I've got to dine over at the Story's at one o'clock."

"So have we," said Hungerford, "but McCarthy will watch you for us."

"I will," said McCarthy, licking his chops.

"I've got to be there," said McNab, wriggling in a frenzy.

"Smoke right up, then. You can smoke them in twenty minutes."

"Police!"

"I say, Dink," said Hungerford, as McNab's head whipped from side to side like a recalcitrant child's. "Perhaps we'd better get in all the crowd who fell for the cigars—round 'em up."

"I'll smoke it," said McNab instantly.

"I thought you would."

They sat around, unfeelingly, grinning, while McNab, strapped in like a papoose, rebelliously, with much sputtering and coughing, smoked the cigar that Dink fed him like a trained nurse.

"Fellows, I've got to get to that dinner."

"We know that, Dopey—but there's one thing you won't do there—tell the story of the *Cuba libre* cigar."

"Say, let me off and I'll put you on to a great stunt."

"We can't be bought."

"I'll tell you, I'll trust you! We're going to have a cop-killing over in Freshman row. We've got a whole depot of Roman candles. Let me off this second cigar and I'll work you in."

"We'll be there!"

"You bandits, I'll get even with you."

"You probably will, Dopey, but you'll never rob us of this memory."

"Curse you, feed it to me quickly."

The cigar consumed to the last rebellious puff, McNab was released in a terrific humor, and departed hastily to dress, after remarking in a deadly manner:

"I'll get you yet—you brutal kidnappers."

"I think it's a rather low trick of Bob Story's," said Stover, considering surreptitiously in the mirror the effect of his new color scheme.

"Ditto here," said Hungerford.

orn in Minnesota, novelist Sinclair Lewis (1885–1951) was the first American to win the Nobel Prize for literature. He graduated from Yale in 1908. As a college student, he was friendless, awkward, and ugly; his classmates called him "God-Forbid." Though he started publishing poems in the *Yale Lit,* and studied with William Lyon Phelps, Chauncey Brewster Tinker, and Henry Seidel Canby, he gave up being "accepted" as a Yale man—and turned his bitterness into art. He went to work as a news reporter, and by 1920 he had written five novels. Then, in that same year, he published his coruscating exposé of small-town life, *Main Street,* which secured his fame. *Babbitt* followed in 1922, and its satire contributed a new word to the language. *Arrowsmith* appeared in 1925, and when it was awarded the Pulitzer Prize denied the two earlier novels because of their controversial nature, Lewis rejected the prize, thereby achieving even more notoriety. *Elmer Gantry* (1927) and *Dodsworth* (1929) were two further successes, and the Nobel Prize followed in 1930. His career declined afterward, though he continued to publish novels. Among his later books are *Ann Vickers* (1933), *It Can't Happen Here* (1945), *The Prodigal Parents* (1938), *Cass Timberlane* (1945), and *Kingsblood Royal* (1947).

I

The towers of Zenith aspired above the morning mist; austere towers of steel and cement and limestone, sturdy as cliffs and delicate as silver rods. They were neither citadels nor churches, but frankly and beautifully office-buildings.

The mist took pity on the fretted structures of earlier generations: the Post Office with its shingle-tortured mansard, the red brick minarets of hulking old houses, factories with stingy and sooted windows, wooden tenements colored like mud. The city was full of such grotesqueries, but the clean towers were thrusting them from the business center, and on the farther hills were shining new houses, homes—they seemed—for laughter and tranquillity.

Over a concrete bridge fled a limousine of long sleek hood and noiseless engine. These people in evening clothes were returning from an all-night rehearsal of a Little Theater play, an artistic adventure considerably illuminated by champagne. Below the bridge curved a railroad, a maze of green and crimson lights. The New York Flyer boomed past, and twenty lines of polished steel leaped into the glare.

In one of the skyscrapers the wires of the Associated Press were closing down. The telegraph operators wearily raised their celluloid eye-shades after a night of talking with Paris and Peking. Through the building crawled the scrubwomen, yawning, their old shoes slapping. The dawn mist spun away. Cues of men with lunch-boxes clumped toward the immensity of new factories, sheets of glass and hollow tile, glittering shops where five thousand men worked beneath one roof, pouring out the honest wares that would be sold up the Euphrates and across the veldt. The whistles rolled out in greeting a chorus cheerful as the April dawn; the song of labor in a city built—it seemed—for giants.

II

There was nothing of the giant in the aspect of the man who was beginning to awaken on the sleeping-porch of a Dutch Colonial house in that residential district of Zenith known as Floral Heights.

His name was George F. Babbitt. He was forty-six years old now, in April, 1920, and he made nothing in particular, neither butter nor shoes nor poetry, but he was nimble in the calling of selling houses for more than people could afford to pay.

His large head was pink, his brown hair thin and dry. His face was babyish in slumber, despite his wrinkles and the red spectacle-dents on the slopes of his nose. He was not fat but he was exceedingly well fed; his cheeks were pads, and the unroughened hand which lay helpless upon the khaki-colored blanket was slightly puffy. He seemed prosperous, extremely married and unromantic; and altogether unromantic appeared this sleeping-porch, which looked on one sizable elm, two respectable grass-plots, a cement driveway, and a corrugated iron garage. Yet Babbitt was again dreaming of the fairy child, a dream more romantic than scarlet pagodas by a silver sea.

For years the fairy child had come to him. Where others saw but Georgie Babbitt, she discerned gallant youth. She waited for him, in the darkness beyond mysterious groves. When at last he could slip away from the crowded house he darted to her. His wife, his clamoring friends, sought to follow, but he escaped, the girl fleet beside him, and they crouched together on a shadowy hillside. She was so slim, so white, so eager! She cried that he was gay and valiant, that she would wait for him, that they would sail—

Rumble and bang of the milk-truck.

Babbitt moaned, turned over, struggled back toward his dream. He could see only her face now, beyond misty waters. The furnace-man slammed the basement door. A dog barked in the next yard. As Babbitt sank blissfully into a dim warm tide, the paper-carrier went by whistling, and the rolled-up *Advocate* thumped the front door. Babbitt roused, his stomach constricted with alarm. As he relaxed, he was pierced by the familiar and irritating rattle of some one cranking a Ford: snap-ah-ah, snap-ah-ah, snap-ah-ah. Himself a pious motorist, Babbitt cranked with the unseen driver, with him waited through taut hours for the roar of the starting engine, with him agonized as the roar ceased and again began the infernal patient snap-ah-ah—a round, flat sound, a shivering cold-morning sound, a sound infuriating and inescapable. Not till the rising voice of the motor told him that the Ford was moving was he released from the panting tension. He glanced once at his favorite tree, elm twigs against the gold patina of sky, and fumbled for sleep as for a drug. He who had been a boy very credulous of life was no longer greatly interested in the possible and improbable adventures of each new day.

He escaped from reality till the alarm-clock rang, at seven-twenty.

III

It was the best of nationally advertised and quantitatively produced alarm-clocks, with all modern attachments, including cathedral chime, intermittent alarm, and a phosphorescent dial. Babbitt was proud of being awakened by such a rich device. Socially it was almost as creditable as buying expensive cord tires.

He sulkily admitted now that there was no more escape, but he lay and detested the grind of the real-estate business, and disliked his family, and disliked himself for disliking them. The evening before, he had played poker at Vergil Gunch's till midnight, and after such holidays he was irritable before breakfast. It may have been the tremendous home-brewed beer of the prohibition-era and the cigars to which that beer enticed him; it may have been resentment of return from this fine, bold man-world to a restricted region of wives and stenographers, and of suggestions not to smoke so much.

From the bedroom beside the sleeping-porch, his wife's detestably cheerful "Time to get up, Georgie boy," and the itchy sound, the brisk and scratchy sound, of combing hairs out of a stiff brush.

He grunted; he dragged his thick legs, in faded baby-blue pajamas, from under the khaki blanket; he sat on the edge of the cot, running his fingers through his wild hair, while his plump feet mechanically felt for his slippers. He looked regretfully at the blanket—forever a suggestion to him of freedom and heroism. He had bought it for a camping trip which had never come off. It symbolized gorgeous loafing, gorgeous cursing, virile flannel shirts.

He creaked to his feet, groaning at the waves of pain which passed behind his eyeballs. Though he waited for their scorching recurrence, he looked blurrily out at the yard. It delighted him, as always; it was the neat yard of a successful business man of Zenith, that is, it was perfection, and made him also perfect. He regarded the corrugated iron garage. For the three-hundred-and-sixty-fifth time in a year he reflected, "No class to that tin shack. Have to build me a frame garage. But by golly it's the only thing on the place that isn't up-to-date!" While he stared he thought of a community garage for his acreage development, Glen Oriole. He stopped puffing and jiggling. His arms were akimbo. His petulant, sleep-swollen face was set in harder lines. He suddenly seemed capable, an official, a man to contrive, to direct, to get things done.

On the vigor of his idea he was carried down the hard, clean, unused-looking hall into the bathroom.

Though the house was not large it had, like all houses on Floral Heights, an altogether royal bathroom of porcelain and glazed tile and metal sleek as silver. The towel-rack was a rod of clear glass set in nickel. The tub was long enough for a Prussian Guard, and above the set bowl was a sensational exhibit of tooth-brush holder, shaving-brush holder, soap-dish, sponge-dish, and medicine-cabinet, so glittering and so ingenious that they resembled an electrical instrument-board. But the Babbitt whose god was Modern Appliances was not pleased. The air of the bathroom was thick with the smell of a heathen toothpaste. "Verona been at it again! 'Stead of sticking to Lilidol, like I've re-peat-ed-ly asked her, she's gone and gotten some confounded stinkum stuff that makes you sick!"

The bath-mat was wrinkled and the floor was wet. (His daughter Verona eccentrically took baths in the morning, now and then.) He slipped on the mat, and slid against the tub. He said "Damn!" Furiously he snatched up his tube of shaving-cream, furiously he lathered, with a belligerent slapping of the unctuous brush, furiously he raked his plump cheeks with a safety-razor. It pulled. The blade was dull. He said, "Damn—oh—oh—damn it!"

He hunted through the medicine-cabinet for a packet of new razor-blades (reflecting, as invariably, "Be cheaper to buy one of these dinguses and strop your own blades,") and when he discovered the packet, behind the round box of bicarbonate of soda, he thought ill of his wife for putting it there and very well of himself for not saying "Damn." But he did say it, immediately afterward, when with wet and soap-slippery fingers he tried to remove the horrible little envelope and crisp clinging oiled paper from the new blade.

Then there was the problem, oft-pondered, never solved, of what to do with the old blade, which might imperil the fingers of his young. As usual, he tossed it on top of the medicine-cabinet, with a mental note that some day he must remove the fifty or sixty other blades that were also temporarily, piled up there. He finished his shaving in a growing testiness increased by his spinning headache and by the emptiness in his stomach. When he was done, his round face smooth and streamy and his eyes stinging from soapy water, he reached for a towel. The family towels were wet, wet and clammy and vile, all of them wet, he found, as he blindly snatched them—his own face-towel, his wife's, Verona's, Ted's, Tinka's, and the lone bath-towel with the huge welt of initial. Then George F. Babbitt did a dismaying thing. He wiped his face on the guest-towel! It was a pansy-embroidered trifle which always hung there to indicate that the Babbitts were in the best Floral Heights society. No one had ever used it. No guest had ever dared to. Guests secretively took a corner of the nearest regular towel.

He was raging, "By golly, here they go and use up all the towels, every doggone one of 'em, and they use 'em and get 'em all wet and sopping, and never put out a dry one for me—of course, I'm the goat!—and then I want one and— I'm the only person in the doggone house that's got the slightest doggone bit of consideration for other people and thoughtfulness and consider there may be others that may want to use the doggone bathroom after me and consider—"

He was pitching the chill abominations into the bath-tub, pleased by the vindictiveness of that desolate flapping sound; and in the midst his wife serenely trotted in, observed serenely, "Why Georgie dear, what are you doing? Are you going to wash out the towels? Why, you needn't wash out the towels. Oh, Georgie, you didn't go and use the guest-towel, did you?"

It is not recorded that he was able to answer.

For the first time in weeks he was sufficiently roused by his wife to look at her.

IV

Myra Babbitt—Mrs. George F. Babbitt—was definitely mature. She had creases from the corners of her mouth to the bottom of her chin, and her plump neck bagged. But the thing that marked her as having passed the line was that she no longer had reticences before her husband, and no longer worried about not having reticences. She was in a petticoat now, and corsets which bulged, and unaware of being seen in bulgy corsets. She had become so dully habituated to married life that in her full matronliness she was as sexless as an anemic nun. She was a good woman, a kind woman, a diligent woman, but no one, save perhaps Tinka her ten-year-old, was at all interested in her or entirely aware that she was alive.

After a rather thorough discussion of all the domestic and social aspects of towels she apologized to Babbitt for his having an alcoholic headache; and he recovered enough to endure the search for a B.V.D. undershirt which had, he pointed out, malevolently been concealed among his clean pajamas.

He was fairly amiable in the conference on the brown suit.

"What do you think, Myra?" He pawed at the clothes hunched on a chair in their bedroom, while she moved about mysteriously adjusting and patting her petticoat and, to his jaundiced eye, never seeming to get on with her dressing. "How about it? Shall I wear the brown suit another day?"

"Well, it looks awfully nice on you."

"I know, but gosh, it needs pressing."

"That's so. Perhaps it does."

"It certainly could stand being pressed, all right."

"Yes, perhaps it wouldn't hurt it to be pressed."

"But gee, the coat doesn't need pressing. No sense in having the whole darn suit pressed, when the coat doesn't need it."

"That's so."

"But the pants certainly need it, all right. Look at them—look at those wrinkles—the pants certainly do need pressing."

"That's so. Oh, Georgie, why couldn't you wear the brown coat with the blue trousers we were wondering what we'd do with them?"

"Good Lord! Did you ever in all my life know me to wear the coat of one suit and the pants of another? What do you think I am? A busted bookkeeper?"

"Well, why don't you put on the dark gray suit to-day, and stop in at the tailor and leave the brown trousers?"

"Well, they certainly need— Now where the devil is that gray suit? Oh, yes, here we are."

He was able to get through the other crises of dressing with comparative resoluteness and calm.

His first adornment was the sleeveless dimity B.V.D. undershirt, in which he resembled a small boy humorlessly wearing a cheesecloth tabard at a civic pageant. He never put on B.V.D.'s without thanking the God of Progress that he didn't wear tight, long, old-fashioned undergarments, like his father-in-law and partner, Henry Thompson. His second embellishment was combing and slicking back his hair. It gave him a tremendous forehead, arching up two inches beyond the former hair-line. But most wonder-working of all was the donning of his spectacles.

There is character in spectacles—the pretentious tortoise-shell, the meek pince-nez of the school teacher, the twisted silver-framed glasses of the old villager. Babbitt's spectacles had huge, circular, frameless lenses of the very best glass; the ear-pieces were thin bars of gold. In them he was the modern business man; one who gave orders to clerks and drove a car and played occasional golf and was scholarly in regard to Salesmanship. His head suddenly appeared not babyish but weighty, and you noted his heavy, blunt nose, his straight mouth and thick, long upper lip, his chin overfleshy but strong; with respect you beheld him put on the rest of his uniform as a Solid Citizen.

The gray suit was well cut, well made, and completely undistinguished. It was a standard suit. White piping on the V of the vest added a flavor of law and learning. His shoes were black laced boots, good boots, honest boots, standard boots, extraordinarily uninteresting boots. The only frivolity was in his purple knitted scarf. With considerable comment on the matter to Mrs. Babbitt (who, acrobatically fastening the back of her blouse to her skirt with a safety-pin, did not hear a word he said), he chose between the purple scarf and a tapestry effect with stringless brown harps among blown palms, and into it he thrust a snake-head pin with opal eyes.

A sensational event was changing from the brown suit to the gray the contents of his pockets. He was earnest about these objects. They were of eternal importance, like baseball or the Republican Party. They included a fountain pen and a silver pencil (always lacking a supply of new leads) which belonged in the right-hand upper vest pocket. Without them he would have felt naked. On his watch-chain were a gold penknife, silver cigar-cutter, seven keys (the use of two of which he had forgotten), and incidentally a good watch. Depending from the chain was a large, yellowish elk's-tooth—proclamation of his membership in the Brotherly and Protective Order of Elks. Most significant of all was his loose-leaf pocket note-book, that modern and efficient note-book which contained the addresses of people whom he had forgotten, prudent memoranda of postal money-orders which had reached their destinations months ago, stamps which had lost their mucilage, clippings of verses by T. Cholmondeley Frink and of the newspaper editorials from which Babbitt got his opinions and his polysyllables, notes to be sure and do things which he did not intend to do, and one curious inscription—D.S.S.D.M.Y.P.D.F.

But he had no cigarette-case. No one had ever happened to give him one, so he hadn't the habit, and people who carried cigarette-cases he regarded as effeminate.

Last, he stuck in his lapel the Boosters' Club button. With the conciseness of great art the button displayed two words: "Boosters—Pep!" It made Babbitt feel loyal and important. It associated him with Good Fellows, with men who were nice and human, and important in business circles. It was his V.C., his Legion of Honor ribbon, his Phi Beta Kappa key.

With the subtleties of dressing ran other complex worries. "I feel kind of punk this morning," he said. "I think I had too much dinner last evening. You oughtn't to serve those heavy banana fritters."

"But you asked me to have some."

"I know, but— I tell you, when a fellow gets past forty he has to look after his digestion. There's a lot of fellows that don't take proper care of themselves. I tell you at forty a man's a fool or his doctor—I mean, his own doctor. Folks don't give enough attention to this matter of dieting. Now I think— Course a man ought to have a good meal after the day's work, but it would be a good thing for both of us if we took lighter lunches."

"But Georgie, here at home I always do have a light lunch."

"Mean to imply I make a hog of myself, eating down-town? Yes, sure! You'd have a swell time if you had to eat the truck that new steward hands out to us at the Athletic Club! But I certainly do feel out of sorts, this morning. Funny, got a pain down here on the left side—but no, that wouldn't be appendicitis, would it? Last night, when I was driving over to Verg Gunch's, I felt a pain in my stomach, too. Right here it was—kind of a sharp shooting pain. I— Where'd that dime go to? Why don't you serve more prunes at breakfast? Of course I eat an apple every evening—an apple a day keeps the doctor away—but still, you ought to have more prunes, and not all these fancy doodads."

"The last time I had prunes you didn't eat them."

"Well, I didn't feel like eating 'em, I suppose. Matter of fact, I think I did eat some of 'em. Anyway— I tell you it's mighty important to— I was saying to Verg Gunch, just last evening, most people don't take sufficient care of their diges—"

"Shall we have the Gunches for our dinner, next week?"

"Why sure; you bet."

"Now see here, George: I want you to put on your nice dinner-jacket that evening."

"Rats! The rest of 'em won't want to dress."

"Of course they will. You remember when you didn't dress for the Littlefields' supper-party, and all the rest did, and how embarrassed you were."

"Embarrassed, hell! I wasn't embarrassed. Everybody knows I can put on as expensive a Tux. as anybody else, and I should worry if I don't happen to have it on sometimes. All a darn nuisance, anyway. All right for a woman, that stays around the house all the time, but when a fellow's worked like the dickens all day, he doesn't want to go and hustle his head off getting into the soup-and-fish for a lot of folks that he's seen in just reg'lar ordinary clothes that same day."

"You know you enjoy being seen in one. The other evening you admitted you were glad I'd insisted on your dressing. You said you felt a lot better for it. And oh, Georgie, I do wish you wouldn't say 'Tux.' It's 'dinner-jacket.'"

"Rats, what's the odds?"

"Well, it's what all the nice folks say. Suppose Lucile McKelvey heard you calling it a 'Tux.'"

"Well, that's all right now! Lucile McKelvey can't pull anything on me! Her folks are common as mud, even if her husband and her dad are millionaires! I suppose you're trying to rub in *your* exalted social position! Well, let me tell you that your revered paternal ancestor, Henry T., doesn't even call it a 'Tux.'! He calls it a 'bobtail jacket for a ringtail monkey,' and you couldn't get him into one unless you chloroformed him!"

"Now don't be horrid, George."

"Well, I don't want to be horrid, but Lord! you're getting as fussy as Verona. Ever since she got out of college she's been too rambunctious to live with—doesn't know what she wants—well, I know what she wants!—all she wants is to marry a millionaire, and live in Europe, and hold some preacher's hand, and simultaneously at the same time stay right here in Zenith and be some blooming kind of a socialist agitator or boss charity-worker or some damn thing! Lord, and Ted is just as bad! He wants to go to college, and he doesn't want to go to college. Only one of the three that knows her own mind is Tinka. Simply can't understand how I ever came to have a pair of shillyshallying children like Rone and Ted. I may not be any Rockefeller or James J. Shakespeare, but I certainly do know my own mind, and I do keep right on plugging along in the office and— Do you know the latest? Far as I can figure out, Ted's new bee is he'd like to be a movie actor and— And here I've told him a hundred times, if he'll go to college and law-school and make good, I'll set him up in business and— Verona just exactly as bad. Doesn't know what she wants. Well, well, come on! Aren't you ready yet? The girl rang the bell three minutes ago."

V

Before he followed his wife, Babbitt stood at the western-most window of their room. This residential settlement, Floral Heights, was on a rise; and though the center of the city was three miles away—Zenith had between three and four hundred thousand inhabitants now—he could see the top of the Second National Tower, an Indiana limestone building of thirty-five stories.

Its shining walls rose against April sky to a simple cornice like a streak of white fire. Integrity was in the tower, and decision. It bore its strength lightly as a tall soldier. As Babbitt stared, the nervousness was soothed from his face, his slack chin lifted in reverence. All he articulated was "That's one lovely sight!" but he was inspired by the rhythm of the city; his love of it renewed. He beheld the tower as a temple-spire of the religion of business, a faith passionate, exalted, surpassing common men; and as he clumped down to breakfast he whistled the ballad "Oh, by gee, by gosh, by jingo" as though it were a hymn melancholy and noble.

rchibald MacLeish (1892–1982), poet and playwright, grew up on the shores of Lake Michigan. At Yale, he was a golden boy: he was Phi Beta Kappa and made the crucial tackle to win the game against Harvard in his senior year; he was a member of Skull and Bones and chairman of the *Yale Lit.* He graduated with the class of 1915. His first volume of poems, *Tower of Ivory,* appeared two years later, just as he left for the war in France to serve with the Yale Mobile Hospital Unit. On his return, he graduated at the top of his class at Harvard Law School. He started to practice, but eager to pursue a literary career, he quit on the day he was offered a partnership in 1923. He headed for Paris, where Ernest Hemingway became a close friend, and wrote a series of books culminating in *The Hamlet of A. MacLeish* in 1928, the year he returned to the United States. His long poem *Conquistador* (1933) won the first of his three Pulitzer Prizes. He next worked for *Fortune* magazine and wrote plays for stage and radio, believing in poetry as "public speech" and in the writer's social obligations. *Land of the Free* (1938) was as much treatise as poetry. In 1939, President Franklin Roosevelt appointed him Librarian of Congress; two years later he headed the Office of Facts and Figures, and for the rest of the war he was assistant director of the Office of War Information. For a time after the war he worked with UNESCO before returning to private life. In 1949 he became the Boylston Professor of Rhetoric and Oratory at Harvard, a position he held until 1962. His *Collected Poems, 1917–52,* was acclaimed, and in 1958 his play *J. B.* was a Broadway success. His lyrics have lasted longer than his epic or political poems. Their grace, and the light they shine into modern history's darkness, ensure that several of his poems will remain classics.

ARS POETICA

A poem should be palpable and mute
As a globed fruit,

Dumb
As old medallions to the thumb,

Silent as the sleeve-worn stone
Of casement ledges where the moss has grown—

A poem should be wordless
As the flight of birds.

*

A poem should be motionless in time
As the moon climbs,

Leaving, as the moon releases
Twig by twig the night-entangled trees,

Leaving, as the moon behind the winter leaves,
Memory by memory the mind—

A poem should be motionless in time
As the moon climbs.

*

A poem should be equal to:
Not true.

For all the history of grief
An empty doorway and a maple leaf.

For love
The leaning grasses and two lights above the sea—

A poem should not mean
But be.

YOU, ANDREW MARVELL

And here face down beneath the sun
And here upon earth's noonward height
To feel the always coming on
The always rising of the night:

To feel creep up the curving east
The earthy chill of dusk and slow
Upon those under lands the vast
And ever climbing shadow grow

And strange at Ecbatan the trees
Take leaf by leaf the evening strange
The flooding dark about their knees
The mountains over Persia change

And now at Kermanshah the gate
Dark empty and the withered grass
And through the twilight now the late
Few travelers in the westward pass

And Baghdad darken and the bridge
Across the silent river gone
And through Arabia the edge
Of evening widen and steal on

And deepen on Palmyra's street
The wheel rut in the ruined stone
And Lebanon fade out and Crete
High through the clouds and overblown

And over Sicily the air
Still flashing with the landward gulls
And loom and slowly disappear
The sails above the shadowy hulls

And Spain go under and the shore
Of Africa the gilded sand
And evening vanish and no more
The low pale light across that land

Nor now the long light on the sea:

And here face downward in the sun
To feel how swift how secretly
The shadow of the night comes on . . .

LANDSCAPE AS A NUDE

She lies on her left side her flank golden:
Her hair is burned black with the strong sun.
The scent of her hair is of rain in the dust on her shoulders:
She has brown breasts and the mouth of no other country.

Ah she is beautiful here in the sun where she lies:
She is not like the soft girls naked in vineyards
Nor the soft naked girls of the English islands
Where the rain comes in with the surf on an east wind:

Hers is the west wind and the sunlight: the west
Wind is the long clean wind of the continents—
The wind turning with earth, the wind descending
Steadily out of the evening and following on.

The wind here where she lies is west: the trees
Oak ironwood cottonwood hickory: standing in
Great groves they roll on the wind as the sea would.
The grasses of Iowa Illinois Indiana

Run with the plunge of the wind as a wave tumbling.

Under her knees there is no green lawn of the Florentines:
Under her dusty knees is the corn stubble:
Her belly is flecked with the flickering light of the corn.

She lies on her left side her flank golden:
Her hair is burned black with the strong sun.
The scent of her hair is of dust and of smoke on her shoulders:
She has brown breasts and the mouth of no other country.

Philip Barry

t he master of drawing-room comedy, Philip Barry (1896–1949) wrote twenty-one plays for Broadway in fewer than thirty years. In most of them, he chronicled the foibles and fates of the well-heeled. He enrolled in Yale in 1914, and in 1918 left to do war-work in London; he returned to New Haven in 1919 and graduated. Even as a student, he kept a file of index cards with such headings as "Comedy Dialogue," "Detached Scenes," "Words and Phrases," and "Notes on Plays Seen," and after some apprentice work, his first Broadway play, *You and I,* opened in 1923; it was a hit, toured the country, and was made into a film. Among the plays that followed were *White Wings* (1926), *Holiday* (1927), *Hotel Universe* (1930; it drew on the life of his friend and Yale classmate Gerald Murphy, who had a villa near Barry's in Cannes), *The Animal Kingdom* (1932), *Here Come the Clowns* (1938), and *The Philadelphia Story* (1939), which was his greatest triumph and a treasury of silvery wit and moral depth. He had several mild successes in the 1940s, and wrote a novel; at the time of his death Barry left a play he had been working on for many years, *Second Threshold,* which was completed by his friend Robert E. Sherwood and opened on Broadway in 1951. On his gravestone are carved lines from *Hotel Universe:* "All things are turned into a roundness. Wherever there is an end, from it springs a beginning."

The sitting room of the Lords' house in the country near Philadelphia is a large, comfortably furnished room of a somewhat faded elegance containing a number of very good Victorian pieces. The entrance from the hall is at Right 2 upstage, down two broad, shallow steps. The entrance into what the family still call "the parlor" is through double doors downstage Right 1. At Left are two glass doors leading to the porch. A writing desk stands between them. There is a large marble fireplace in the back wall with chairs Right and Left of it; a stool in front of it. A grand piano in the corner at up Left. Chairs and a table are at down Left Center, and at down Right Center, a coffee table, an easy chair and a sofa. There is a large and fine portrait over the fireplace and other paintings here and there. A wall cabinet Right of fireplace contains a quantity of bric-a-brac and there is more of it, together with a number of signed photographs in silver frames, upon the tables and piano. A bookcase above doors Right 1. There are also several cardboard boxes strewn about, indicating an approaching wedding.

It is late on a Friday morning in June, an overcast day. DINAH, *who is all of fifteen years old, is stretched out on the sofa reading a set of printers' galley proofs.* TRACY, *a strikingly lovely girl of twenty-four, sits in the chair at Left, a leather writing set upon her knees, scribbling notes. She wears slacks and a blouse.* MARGARET LORD, *their mother, a young and smart forty-seven, comes in from the hall with three more boxes in her arms. She places them upon the table near* TRACY.

MARGARET [*Entering Right 1 with three boxes. Going to back of table Left*]: I'm so terribly afraid that some of the cards for these last-minute presents must have got mixed. Look at them, Tracy—perhaps you can tell. [*Puts boxes upper end of table.*]

TRACY: In a minute, Mother. I'm up to my neck in these blank thank-you notes.

DINAH [*Rises*]: This stinks! [*Goes in Center with papers.*]

MARGARET [*Back of table*]: Don't say "stinks," darling. If absolutely necessary, "smells"—but only if absolutely necessary. What is it? [*Crosses to desk—picks up three-page typed list.*]

DINAH [*Going up to piano*]: I found it in Sandy's room. It's something that's going to be in a magazine. It certainly stinks all right.

MARGARET [*At desk*]: Keep out of your brother's things, dear—and his house. [*Crossing down Left, reading:*] Ninety-four for the ceremony, five hundred and six for the reception—I don't know where we'll put them all, if it should rain. [*Looks out Left 1.*]

DINAH [*Crossing down back of table Left*]: It won't rain.

MARGARET [*Crossing below table to chair Left Center; sits*]: Uncle Willie wanted to insure against it with Lloyd's but I wouldn't let him. If I was God and someone bet I wouldn't let it rain, I'd show him fast enough. This second page is solid Cadwalader. Twenty-six.

DINAH [*Back of table*]: That's a lot of Cadwalader.

MARGARET: One, my child, is a lot of Cadwalader.

TRACY: How do you spell omelet?

MARGARET: O-m-m-e-l-e-t.

TRACY: I thought there was another "l."

[DINAH *moves up to and leans on piano, reading proof sheets.*]

MARGARET: The omelet dish from the—? [*Rises.*]

TRACY: You said it was an omelet dish.

MARGARET: It might be for fish.

TRACY: Fish dish? That sounds idiotic. [*Tears up card—starts new letter.*]

MARGARET: I should simply say "Thank you so much for your lovely silver dish."

TRACY [*Taking up card from another box*]: Here's the tag, "Old Dutch Muffin Ear, Circa 1810"—What the—[*Dropping card*] I am simply enchanted with your old Dutch Muffin Ear—with which my husband and I will certainly hear any muffin coming a mile away.

DINAH [*Crossing down back of table*]: Lookit, Tracy: don't you think you've done enough notes for one day? [*Starts to handle things on table.*]

TRACY [*Waving her off*]: Don't disturb me. [*Picking up cards, reads:*] From Cousin Horace Macomber, one pair of game shears, looking like hell. [*Picks up shears.*]

DINAH: He's so awful. What did he send the other time?

TRACY [*Writing "game shears" on the card*]: No one to speak of sent anything the other time.

MARGARET [*In armchair*]: It's such a pity your brother Junius can't be here for your wedding. London's so far away.

DINAH [*Back of table*]: I miss old Junius: you did a good job when you had him, Mother.

MARGARET: The first is always the best. They deteriorate as you go on.

[*A look between* DINAH *and* TRACY]

TRACY [*Writes note*]: There was no occasion to send anything the other time.

DINAH [*Reading the proof sheets—crossing to Center*]: This is certainly pretty rooty-tooty all right.

TRACY [*Still writing at table*]: It would scarcely be considered a wedding at all, the other time. When you run off to Maryland on a sudden impulse—as Dexter and I did—

DINAH [*Crossing back behind table Left*]: Ten months is quite long to be married, though. You can have a baby in nine, can't you?

TRACY: I guess, if you put your mind to it.

DINAH: Why didn't you?

TRACY [*Looks up from her writing*]: Mother, don't you think it's time for her nap?

DINAH: I imagine you and George'll have slews of 'em. [*Slouches to Center.*]

TRACY: I hope so, all like you, dear, with the same wild grace.

[DINAH *stops Center and looks at her.* TRACY *rises; picks up box of envelopes and places it on desk.*]

DINAH [*Center*]: Lookit: "the other time"—he's back from wherever he's been.

[TRACY *goes in to back of table Left.*]

MARGARET [*After a glance at* TRACY]: What do you mean?

DINAH: Dexter, of course. I saw his car in front of his house: [*Crossing Right*] the roadster. It must be him.

MARGARET: When? When did you?

DINAH [*At sofa*]: This morning, early, when I was out exercising The Hoofer. [*Sits on sofa Right; puts sheets on coffee table.*]

MARGARET: Why didn't you tell us?

TRACY [*Back of table, near* MARGARET's *chair*]: I'm not worried, Mother. The only trouble Mr. C. K. Dexter Haven ever gave me was when he married me.— *You* might say the same for one Seth Lord. If you'd just face it squarely as I did—[*Sits on end of table.*]

MARGARET: That will do! I will allow none of you to criticize your father.

TRACY: What are we expected to do when he treats you—

MARGARET: Did you hear me, Tracy?

TRACY [*Rising*]: All right, I give up.

MARGARET [*Softly, and taking* TRACY's *hand*]: —And in view of this second attempt of yours, it might pay you to remind yourself that neither of us has proved to be a very great success as a wife.

TRACY [*Crossing to behind table*]: We just picked the wrong first husbands, that's all.

MARGARET: That's an extremely vulgar remark.

TRACY: Oh, who cares about either of them any more—[*Crosses back of* MARGARET, *who is in chair Left Center. Crouches to embrace her.*] Golly Moses, I'm going to be happy now.

MARGARET: Darling.

TRACY: Isn't George an angel?

MARGARET: George is an angel.

TRACY: Is he handsome, or is he not?

MARGARET: George is handsome.

TRACY [*Straightens up and picks up boxes from table, also writing-case*]: Suds. I'm a lucky girl. [*Crosses Right upper.*]

DINAH: I like Dexter.

TRACY [*Continuing on her way up Right*]: Really? Why don't you ask him to lunch, or something? [*Goes out Right 2.*]

DINAH [*Looking after her for a moment—rises and crosses to Center*]: She's awfully mean about him, isn't she?

MARGARET: He was rather mean to her, my dear.

DINAH [*Over Left Center at* MARGARET's *chair*]: Did he really sock her?

MARGARET [*Still comparing lists and letters*]: Don't say "sock," darling. "Strike" is quite an ugly enough word.

DINAH: But did he really?

MARGARET: I'm afraid I don't know the details.

DINAH [*By* MARGARET *at chair Left Center*]: Cruelty and drunkenness, it said.

MARGARET: Dinah!

DINAH: It was right in the papers.

MARGARET: You read too much. You'll spoil your eyes.

DINAH [*Crossing Right to sofa*]: I think it's an awful thing to say about a man. I don't think they like things like that said about them.

MARGARET: I'm sure they don't.

DINAH [*At sofa picks up three proof sheets*]: Father's going to be hopping when he reads all this about himself in that magazine, *Destiny,* when it comes out.

MARGARET: All what? *About whom?* [*Turns to face* DINAH.]

DINAH: Father—that they're going to publish.

MARGARET: Dinah, what *are* you talking about?

DINAH [*Crossing Center with paper*]: It's what they call proof sheets for some article they're going to call "Broadway and Finance," and Father's in it, and so they just sent it on to Sandy—sort of—you know, on approval. [*Crosses Left Center.*]

MARGARET: But the article! What does the article say? [*Takes paper from her.*]

DINAH: Oh, it's partly about Father backing three shows for that dancer—what's her name—Tina Mara—and his early history—and about the stables—and why he's living in New York, instead of with us, any more, and—

MARGARET: Great heaven—what on earth can we do?

DINAH: Couldn't Father sue them for liable?

MARGARET: But it's true—it's all—[*Realizing her error, she glances at* DINAH, *then rises and crosses to Right at coffee table.*] That is, I mean to say—[*Reading sheets*]

DINAH: I don't think the part about Tina Mara is, the way they put it. It's simply full of innundo. [*Sits in armchair Left Center.*]

MARGARET [*Turning*]: Of what?

DINAH: Of innundo. [*Rests elbow on table Left.*] Oh, I do wish something would happen here. Nothing ever possibly in the least ever happens. [*Rises, crossing Right*] Next year can I go to the Conservatory in New York? They teach you to sing and dance and act and everything at once. Can I, Mother?

MARGARET [*Front of sofa, down Right*]: Save your dramatics, Dinah. Oh, why didn't Sandy *tell* me!

DINAH: Mother, why won't Tracy *ask* her own *father* to her *wedding?*

MARGARET [*Crossing over Left to the table—picks up list and three letters which she had left there*]: Your sister has very definite opinions about certain things.

DINAH [*Crosses to Left Center to* MARGARET]: She's sort of—you know—hard, isn't she?

MARGARET: Not hard—none of my children is that, I hope. Tracy sets exceptionally high standards for herself, that's all, and although she lives up to them, other people aren't always quite able to. If your Uncle Willie Tracy comes in, tell him to wait. I want to see him. [*Starts for window Left 1.*]

DINAH [*Follows her to Left*]: Tell me one thing: don't you think it's stinking not at least to *want* Father?

MARGARET [*Turning to her*]: Yes, darling, between ourselves I think it's good and stinking. [*Goes out Left 1.*]

DINAH: And I bet if Dexter knew what she—[DINAH *waits a moment, then goes to the telephone on desk and dials four numbers.*] Hello. May I please speak to Mr. Dexter Haven—what?—Dexter! It's you! [*Then affectedly*] A very great pleasure to have you back. Dinah, you goat, Dinah Lord. What?—You bet!—Lookit, Dexter, Tracy says why don't you come right over for lunch? What? But she told me to ask you.—Listen, though, maybe it would be better if you'd—Hello!—Hello! [*Taps the telephone several times to get operator. Hangs up as* TRACY *enters Right 1 with a large roll of parchment.*]

TRACY [*Entering, crossing to Left*]: Who was that?

DINAH: Wrong number.

[TRACY *moves over Left to back of table.* DINAH *moves to her.*]

TRACY [*Spreads roll of paper out on table*]: Listen, darling, give me a hand with this cockeyed seating arrangement, will you? At least hold it down.— George doesn't want the Grants at the bridal table. [SANDY LORD, *twenty-six, comes in from Right 2.*] He says they're fast. He—

SANDY [*Entering and going down Center*]: Hello, kids.

TRACY [*Rushes up Center to embrace him*]: Sandy!

SANDY: Where's Mother?

[DINAH *crosses Left Center back of armchair.*]

TRACY: She's around. How's New York?—How's Sue?—How's the baby?

SANDY: Blooming. They sent their love, sorry they can't make the wedding. Is there a party tonight, of course?

TRACY: Aunt Geneva's throwing a monster.

SANDY: Boy, am I going to get plastered. [*Crossing to armchair* L. *to* DINAH] Hello, little fellah. [*Makes a boxing pass at her.*]

DINAH: Hello, yourself.

SANDY [*Giving her a flat box*]: This is for you, Mug; get the three race horses into the paddock. It's tough. Work it out.

DINAH: Oh, thanks. [*Remains at Left Center armchair.*]

SANDY [*Turning to* TRACY]: Sue's and my wedding present comes by registered mail, Tracy—and a pretty penny it set me back.

TRACY: You're a bonny boy, Sandy. I love you.

SANDY: Mutual—

[TRACY *goes to Left armchair; looks at toy with* DINAH.]

MARGARET [*Re-enters Left 1. She carries three envelopes and the three proof sheets. As she enters*]: I was wondering about you.

SANDY [*Crosses Left below table—kisses her*]: Give us a kiss.—You look fine.— Imagine this, a *grand*mother. How's everything? [*Goes to front of table.*]

MARGARET [*Left of Left table*]: Absolute chaos.

SANDY [*Front of table Left*]: Just how you like it, eh? Just when you function best!

MARGARET: How's my precious grandchild?

SANDY: Couldn't be better; Sue, too. Ten more days in the hospital, and back home they'll be.

MARGARET [*Crossing Right below him to sofa with papers*]: I broke into your house and did up the nursery.

SANDY [*Crossing Center*]: Good girl. Where's George, Tracy?

TRACY [*Sitting on arm of chair Right*]: He's staying in the Gatehouse. He still had business things to clear up and I thought he'd be quieter there.

SANDY [*Crosses below table to Right Center*]: Did he see his picture in *Dime?* Was he sore at the "Former Coal Miner" caption?

MARGARET [*At sofa*]: What about this absurd article about your father and—er— Tina Mara in *Destiny?* Can't it be stopped?

[DINAH *goes in Center.*]

TRACY [*Rises, crossing Right*]: About Father and—let me see! [*Takes article from* MARGARET.]

SANDY: Where'd you get hold of that? [*Tries to take it from her.*]

MARGARET [*Sits sofa*]: Get ready for lunch, Dinah.

DINAH [*Going up Right, sits on step—works at puzzle*]: In a minute. I'm busy.

TRACY [*Reading sheets*]: Oh! The absolute devils—Who publishes *Destiny?* [*Sits on armchair Right.*]

SANDY [*Center*]: Sidney Kidd.—Also *Dime,* also *Spy,* the picture sheet. I worked on *Dime* for two summers, you know that.

TRACY: Stopped? It's got to be! I'll go to him myself.

SANDY [*Center*]: A fat lot of good that would do. You're too much alike. God save us from the strong. [*Crossing to behind armchair Right Center*] I saw Kidd the day before yesterday. It took about three hours, but I finally got through to him.

TRACY: What happened?

SANDY: I think I fixed things.

TRACY: How?

SANDY: That would be telling.

MARGARET: Just so long as your father never hears of it.

SANDY: I had a copy of the piece made, and sent it around to his flat, with a little note saying, "How do you like it?"

TRACY: You are a fellah.

MARGARET: Sandy!

SANDY: Why not? Let him worry a little.

[THOMAS *enters Right 2; comes down steps.*]

TRACY: Let him worry a lot!

SANDY [*Crosses up to him*]: Yes, Thomas?

THOMAS [*At door*]: Mr. Connor and the lady say they will be down directly, sir.

SANDY: Thanks, that's fine. Tell May or Elsie to look after Miss Imbrie, will you?

THOMAS: Very good, sir. [*Goes out Right 2.*]

MARGARET: What's all this?

TRACY: "Mr. Connor and—?"

SANDY [*Takes paper from* TRACY; *crossing Left Center, sits on arm of chair*]: Mike Connor—Macaulay Connor, his name is.—And—er—Elizabeth Imbrie. I'm putting them up for over the wedding. They're quite nice. You'll like them.

TRACY: You asked people to stay in this house without even asking us?

MARGARET: I think it's very queer indeed.

TRACY: I think it's queerer than that—*I* think it's paranoic! [*Rises and crosses Left Center to him.*]

SANDY: Keep your shirt on.—I just sort of drifted into them and we sort of got to talking about what riots weddings are as a rule, and they'd never been to a Philadelphia one, and—

TRACY: You're lying, Sandy.—I can always tell.

SANDY: Now look here, Tracy—

TRACY: Look where? "Elizabeth Imbrie"—I know that name! She's a—wait— damn your eyes, Sandy, she's a photographer!

SANDY: For a fact?

TRACY: For a couple of facts—and a famous one!

SANDY: Well, it might be nice to have some good shots of the wedding.

TRACY: What are they doing here?

SANDY: Just now I suppose they're brushing up and going to the bathroom. [*Rising, Right Center*] They're very interesting people. She's practically an artist, and he's written a couple of books—and—and I thought you liked interesting people.

DINAH [*Rising*]: *I* do.

[SANDY *crosses to Right armchair.* DINAH *is up on step up Right.*]

TRACY: I know—now I know! They're from *Destiny*—*Destiny* sent them!

MARGARET: *Destiny?*

SANDY [*Sitting in armchair Right*]: You're just a mass of intuition, Tracy.

TRACY: Well, they can go right back again. [*Goes to him.*]

SANDY: No, they can't. Not till they get their story.

TRACY: Story? What story?

SANDY: The Philadelphia story.

MARGARET: And what on earth's that?

SANDY: Well, it seems Kidd has had Connor and Imbrie and a couple of others down here for two months doing the town: I mean writing it up. It's to come out in three parts in the Autumn. "Industrial Philadelphia," "Historical Philadelphia"—and then the third—

TRACY: I'm going to be sick.

SANDY: Yes, dear, "Fashionable Philadelphia."

TRACY: I *am* sick. [*Turns to Center.*]

MARGARET: But why us? Surely there are other families who—

TRACY [*Crossing a bit to Left Center*]: Yes—why not the Drexels or Biddles or the qu'est-ce que c'est Cassats?

SANDY [*Seated*]: We go even further back: It's those Quakers.—And of course there's your former marriage and your looks and your general prowess in golf and fox-hunting, with a little big game on the side, and your impending second marriage into the coal fields—

TRACY [*Center*]: Never mind that!

SANDY: I don't, but they do. It's news, darling, news.

MARGARET: Is there no such thing as privacy any more?

TRACY: Only in bed, Mother, and not always there.

SANDY: Anyhow I thought I was licked—and what else could I do?

TRACY: A trade, eh? So we're to let them publish the inside story of my wedding in order to keep Father's wretched little affair quiet!

MARGARET: It's utterly and completely disgusting.

SANDY: It was my suggestion, not Kidd's. I may have been put in the way of making it. I don't know. It's hard to tell with the future President of the United States.

TRACY: What's the writer's name again?

SANDY: Connor, Macaulay Connor. I don't think he likes the assignment any more than we do—the gal either. They were handling the Industrial end.

TRACY [*Crossing to desk to phone—dials four numbers*]: My heart's breaking for them.

MARGARET [*Rises*]: I don't know what the world is coming to. It's an absolute invasion; two strange people tramping through the house, prying and investigating—

TRACY [*At the telephone*]: Maybe we're going through a revolution without know-ing it. [*In telephone*] Hello, is Mr. Briggs there?—This is Tracy Lord, Mr. Briggs.—Look, I wonder if you happen to have on hand any books by Macaulay Connor? [SANDY *rises.*] You have!—Could you surely send them out this afternoon?—Thanks, Mr. Briggs, you're sweet. [*Hangs up.* SANDY *goes in Left Center*]—If they've got to have a story, I'll give them a story—I'll give them one they can't get through the mails!

SANDY [*Left Center*]: Oh—oh—I was afraid of this—

TRACY: Who the hell do they think they are, barging in on peaceful people—watching every little mannerism—jotting down notes on how we sit, and stand, and talk, and eat and move—

DINAH [*Crossing down back of sofa*]: Will they do that?

TRACY [*Center*]: —And all in the horrible snide corkscrew English!—Well, if we have to submit to it to save Father's face—which incidentally doesn't de-serve it—I'm for giving them a picture of home life that will stand their hair on end.

MARGARET [*Right*]: You will do nothing of the sort, Tracy. [*Sits on sofa.*]

SANDY [*Left, embracing* TRACY]: She thinks she'll be the outrageous Miss Lord. The fact is, she'll probably be Sweetness and Light to the neck.

TRACY: Oh, will I? [*Turns out of his arm, to back of armchair Right.*]

SANDY: You don't know yet what being under the microscope does to people. I felt it a little coming out in the car. It's a funny feeling.

MARGARET: It's odd how self-conscious we've all become over the worldly posses-sions that once made us so confident.

SANDY [*Center*]: I know; you catch yourself explaining away your dough, the way you would a black eye: you've just run into it in the dark or something.

MARGARET: We shall be ourselves with them; very much ourselves.

DINAH [*Back of sofa*]: But Mother, you want us to create a good impression, don't you?

MARGARET [*To* SANDY]: They don't know that *we* know what they're here for, I hope?

[TRACY *sits on the arm upper end of sofa.*]

SANDY: No; that was understood.

DINAH: [*Crossing down lower end of sofa*]: I should think it would look awfully funny to them, Father's not being here for his own daughter's wedding.

TRACY: Would you now?

SANDY: That's all right; I fixed that, too. [*Goes in Right Center back of armchair.*]

TRACY: How do you mean you did?

SANDY: I told Sue to send a telegram before dinner, "Confined to bed with a cold, unable to attend nuptials, oceans of love, Father."

MARGARET: Not just in those words!

SANDY: Not exactly.—It'll come on the telephone and Thomas will take it and you won't have your glasses and he'll read it aloud to you.

MARGARET: Tracy, will you promise to behave like a lady, if only for my sake?

TRACY: I'll do my best, Mrs. Lord. I don't know how good that is.

MARGARET: Go put a dress on.

TRACY: Yes, Mother.

MARGARET [*Rises*]: There are too many legs around here.

TRACY [*Rises*]: Suds! I'll be pure Victorian, all frills and ruffles, conversationally chaste as an egg. [UNCLE WILLIE TRACY, *sixty-two, comes in from the Right 1 door.*] Hello, Uncle Willie. Where did you come from? [*Gets back of table Left for roll of paper.*]

UNCLE WILLIE [*Down Right*]: Your Great-aunt Geneva has requested my absence from the house until dinnertime. Can you give me lunch, Margaret?

MARGARET: But of course! With pleasure—

DINAH: Hello, Uncle Willie—[*She goes up—leaves toy on bookcase and stops behind armchair Right Center.*]

SANDY: How are you, Uncle Willie?

WILLIE: Alexander and Dinah, good morning. [*Crossing Center*] My esteemed wife, the old warhorse, is certainly spreading herself for your party. *I* seriously question the propriety of [TRACY *goes down Center.*] any such display in such times. But she—Why aren't you being married in church, Tracy?

TRACY [*At Left Center chair*]: I like the parlor here so much better. Didn't you think it looked pretty as you came through?

UNCLE WILLIE: That is not the point. The point is that I've sunk thousands in that church, and I'd like to get some use of it.—Give me a glass of sherry, Margaret. [*Goes in Center.*]

[DINAH *goes down* L.C. TRACY *goes to* SANDY, *back of Right Center armchair.*]

MARGARET: Not until lunchtime, my dear.

UNCLE WILLIE: These women.

MARGARET [*At Left Center*]: You're really a wicked old man, aren't you?

UNCLE WILLIE [*Points to the porch Left*]: What's that out there?

[DINAH *turns to look. He vigorously pinches her behind.*]

DINAH: Ouch!

[SANDY, *standing at upper end of sofa, is chatting with* TRACY.]

UNCLE WILLIE: Never play with fire, child. [*Looks at the* OTHERS *over Right.*] What's a-lack here? What's a-stirrin'? What's amiss?

SANDY: Uncle Willie, do you know anything about the laws of libel?

UNCLE WILLIE [*Sitting in Right armchair*]: Certainly I know about the laws of libel. Why shouldn't I? I know all about them. In 1916, I, Willie Q. Tracy, successfully defended the *Post,* and George Lorimer personally, against one of the cleverest, one of the subtlest—why? What do you want to say?

SANDY [*Sits on sofa*]: It isn't what *I* want to say—

TRACY [*Breaking in—sits at his feet on floor Center*]: Is it enough if they can simply prove that it is true?

[DINAH *goes back of him; sits on arm of sofa.*]

UNCLE WILLIE [*Turns to* TRACY]: Certainly not! Take me; if I was totally bald and wore a toupee, if I had flat feet, with these damnable metal arches, false teeth, and a case of double—

DINAH: Poor Uncle Willie.

UNCLE WILLIE: I said "*If* I had." [DINAH, *behind him, leans over and gives a derisive laugh through "haw."*]—And if such—[WILLIE *gives her a dirty look*]—facts were presented in the public prints in such a manner as to hold me up to public ridicule, I could collect substantial damages—and would, if it took me all winter.

TRACY [*Rising*]: Suppose the other way around; suppose they printed things that weren't true.

UNCLE WILLIE [*Rising and crossing Center.* TRACY *sits on arm of chair Right Center*]: Suppose they did? Suppose it was erroneously stated, that during my travels as a young man I was married in a native ceremony to a dusky maiden in British Guinea, I doubt if I could collect a cent. [*Looks off up Right 2—clears throat—crossing up.*] Who are these two strange people coming down the hall?

[*The* FAMILY *rises, frozen in their tracks a second.*]

MARGARET [*Rises*]: Oh, good gracious!

[DINAH *goes up to doorway Right 2.*]

TRACY: Come on—out. [*Goes Center, grabs* WILLIE *and leads him to down Right*]: What was she like, Uncle Willie?

[SANDY *gets in corner up Right near mantel.*]

WILLIE: Who?

TRACY [*Crossing Right*]: British Guinea?

WILLIE [*Crossing Right*]: So very unlike your Aunt Geneva, my dear.

[*And they exit Right 1.*]

MARGARET [*Crossing up for* DINAH—*takes hold of her—moves down Right with her*]: Dinah—

DINAH: But, Mother, oughtn't we—?

MARGARET: Sandy can entertain them until we—until we collect ourselves. [*Puts* DINAH *out Right 1.*]

SANDY [*Crossing to* MARGARET *at door Right 1*]: What'll I say?

MARGARET: I wish I could tell you—in a few very well-chosen words.

[*She goes out.*]

[SANDY *is alone for a moment; leans against bookcase, Right.* MIKE CONNOR, *thirty, and* LIZ IMBRIE, *twenty-eight, come in from the hall.* LIZ *has a small and important camera hanging from a leather strap around her neck.*]

LIZ [*Enters from Right 2, crossing Left Center*]: —In here?

MIKE [*Entering down Center—gazes about room—notices crystal chandelier*]: He said the sitting room. I suppose that's contrasted to the living room, the ballroom—the drawing room—the morning room the—[*He sees* SANDY.] Oh, hello again. Here you are.

[LIZ *goes over Left to Left of table and sits.*]

SANDY: Here I am. [*Goes Center.*]

MIKE [*Up Center toward mantel*]: It's quite a place.

SANDY [*Crossing up to* MIKE]: It is, isn't it?—I couldn't help overhearing you as you came in. Do you mind if I say something?

MIKE: Not at all. What?

SANDY: Your approach to your job seems definitely antagonistic. I don't think it's fair. I think you ought to give us a break.

MIKE: It's not a job I asked for. [*Goes down Left Center.*]

SANDY [*Up Right Center*]: I know it's not. But in spite of it, and in spite of certain of our regrettable inherited characteristics, we just might be fairly decent. Why not wait and see?

MIKE [*Sits Right of table Left*]: You have quite a style yourself. [SANDY *picks up stool at fireplace, crossing down Center.*] —You're on the *Saturday Evening Post*, did you say?

SANDY: I work for it.

MIKE: Which end?

SANDY: Editorial. [*Sits on stool he brought down.*]

MIKE: I have to tell you, in all honesty, that I'm opposed to everything you represent.

SANDY: *Destiny* is hardly a radical sheet: what is it you're doing—boring from within?

MIKE: — And I'm not a Communist, not by a long shot.

LIZ: Just a small pin feather in the Left Wing. [MIKE *looks at her.*] —Sorry.

SANDY: Jeffersonian Democrat?

MIKE [*Looks at him*]: That's more like it.

SANDY: Have you ever seen his house at Monticello? *It's* quite a place too.

LIZ: Home Team One; Visitors Nothing—[*Rises.*] Is this house very old, Mr. Lord? [*Goes up Left.*]

SANDY: No, there are a very few old ones on the Main Line—The Gatehouse is, of course. Father's grandfather built that for a summer place when they all lived on Rittenhouse Square. Father and Mother did this about 1910—the spring before my brother Junius was born. He's the oldest. You won't meet him, he's in the diplomatic service in London.

MIKE [*To* LIZ]: Wouldn't you know? [*Putting out cigarette on table tray*]

SANDY: *I* worked for Sidney Kidd once. What do you make of him?

MIKE [*After a short pause*]: A brilliant editor, and a very wonderful man. [*Gets cards from his pocket.*]

LIZ: Also, our bread and butter.

SANDY: Sorry to have been rude.

MIKE [*Looking through cards*]: I suppose you're all of you opposed to the Administration?

SANDY: The present one? No—as a matter of fact we're Loyalists.

MIKE [*Has a sheaf of typewritten cards and looks at them*]: Surprise, surprise.—The Research Department didn't give us much data.—Your sister's fiancé—George Kittredge—aged thirty-two.—Since last year General Manager Quaker State Coal, in charge of operation.—Is that right?

SANDY: That's right.—And brilliant at it.

MIKE: So I've heard tell. I seem to have read about him first back in '35 or '36.— Up from the bottom, wasn't he?

[LIZ *sits on arm of Left Center chair.*]

SANDY: Just exactly—and of the mines.

MIKE: Reorganized the entire works?

SANDY: He did.

MIKE: National hero, new model: makes drooping family incomes to revive again. Anthracite, sweet anthracite.—How did your sister happen to meet him?

SANDY: She and I went up a month ago to look things over.

MIKE: I see. And was it instant?

SANDY: Immediate.

MIKE: Good for her.—He must be quite a guy.—Which side of this—er—fine, aboriginal family does she resemble most, would you say?

SANDY [*Looks at him; rises*]: The histories of both are in the library; I'll get them out for you. I'll also see if I can round up some of the Living Members. [*Goes up to door Right 2.*]

LIZ: They don't know about *us,* do they? [*Goes above table.*]

SANDY [*In the doorway stops and turns*]: —Pleasanter not, don't you think?

LIZ: Much.

SANDY: That's what *I* thought—also what Kidd thought. [*Moves a step up.*]

MIKE [*Rising and going near Center*]: Look here, Lord—

SANDY [*Stops*]: Yes—?

MIKE [*Crossing up Center*]: Why don't you throw us out?

SANDY: I hope you'll never know. [*A smile and goes out Right 2.*]

LIZ: Maybe Der Kidder has been up to his little tricks. [*Goes up Left.*]

MIKE [*At mantel*]: If only I could get away from his damned paper—

LIZ: It's Sidney himself you can't get away from, dear. [*Up at piano*]

MIKE: I tried to resign again on the phone this morning.

LIZ [*Touring up Left at piano*]: —Knickknacks—gimcracks—signed photographs! Wouldn't you know you'd have to be rich as the Lords to live in a dump like this? [*Goes to Center. Sees the portrait over the mantel.*] Save me—it's Gilbert Stuart.

MIKE: A what?

LIZ: Catch me, Mike!

MIKE: Faint to the left, will you? [*Crosses down Right to sofa. He returns to the typewritten cards*] "First husband, C. K.—" Can you imagine what a guy named "C. K. Dexter Haven" must be like?

LIZ: "Macaulay Connor" is not such a homespun tag, my pet. [*Goes up Right.*]

MIKE [*Sits on sofa*]: I've been called Mike since I can remember.

LIZ: Well, maybe Dexter is "Ducky" to his friends. [*Goes over Right by steps.*]

MIKE: I wouldn't doubt it.—But I wonder what the "C. K." is for—

LIZ [*Turns upstage—looks at cabinet*]: Maybe it's Pennsylvania Dutch for "William Penn."

MIKE: "C. K. Dexter Haven." God!

LIZ [*Crossing down to upper corner of sofa*]: I knew a plain Joe Smith once. He was only a clerk in a hardware store, but he was an absolute louse.

MIKE: —Also he plays polo. Also designs and races sailboats. "Class" boats, I think they call them. Very upper class, of course.

LIZ: Don't despair. He's out, and Kittredge, man of the people, is in. [*Goes up to mantel.*]

MIKE: From all reports, quite a comer too. Political timber.—Poor fellow, I wonder how he fell for it.

LIZ: I imagine she's a young lady who knows what she wants when she wants it. [*Goes up by piano.*]

MIKE: The young, rich, rapacious American female—there's no other country where she exists.

LIZ [*Comes in Center*]: I'll admit the idea of *her* scares even me.—Would I change places with her, for all her wealth and beauty? Boy! Just ask me. [*Goes up to piano.*]

MIKE: I know how I'm going to begin. [*Leans back on the sofa, closes his eyes, and declaims:* LIZ *goes in Center slowly*] "—So much for Historical Philadelphia, so much for Industrial. Now, Gentle Reader, consider an entire section of American Society which, closely following the English tradition, lives on the land, but in a new sense. It is not the land that provides the living, it is—"

LIZ [*Back of sofa; pats his arm, then crosses Right*]: You're ahead of yourself. Wait
till you do your documentation.

MIKE: I'm tired. [*Reclines on sofa, head on upstage end*] Kidd is a slavedriver. I
wish I was home in bed. Also I'm hungry. Tell four footmen to call me in
time for lunch.

[LIZ *is taking pictures of room off Right I.*]

DINAH [*Re-enters Left from porch window, the woman of the world. Crossing Center
on her toes—hand extended*]: Oh—how do you do?—Friends of Alexander's, are you not?

MIKE [*Rises*]: How do you do?—Why, yes, we—

DINAH [*Crossing Right*]: I am Dinah Lord. My real name is Diana, but my sister
changed it.

LIZ: I'm Elizabeth Imbrie—and this is Macaulay Connor. It's awfully nice of—

DINAH [*Goes Right to them—extends an arched hand to each*]: *Enchantée de vous
voir.* [*Shakes hands with* MIKE.] *Enchanté de faire votre connaissance.* [*Shakes
hands with* LIZ.]—I spoke French before I spoke English. My early childhood was spent in Paris, where my father worked in a bank—the House of
Morgan.

LIZ: Really?

DINAH: *C'est vrai—absolument!* [*Runs up to piano—jumping over stool Center as she
goes.*] Can you play the piano? I can. And sing at the same time. Listen—
[*Plays and sings*] "Pepper Sauce Woman; Pepper Sauce Woman—"

[*This dialog goes through the song, topping it.*]

LIZ [*Speaks lowly to* MIKE *Down Right*]: What is this?

MIKE: An idiot, probably. They happen in the best of families, especially in the
best.

DINAH: —"Oh, what a shame; she has lost her name. Don't know who to blame,
walkin' along to Shango Batcheloor." [DINAH *stops singing and continues in
a dreamy voice:*] The Bahamas—how well I remember them.—Those perfumed nights—the flowers—the native wines. I was there, once, on a little
trip with Leopold Stokowski.

TRACY [*Enters Left I; stops up at piano. She has changed into a rather demure dress,
high in neck and ample in skirt*]: You were there with your governess, after
the whooping cough.

[DINAH *gestures airily.* LIZ *goes front of sofa.* MIKE *gets to downstage end.*]

DINAH [*Crossing to* TRACY *and below her to chair Left of table Left*]: —My sister
Tracy. Greetings, Sister.

TRACY: Mother wants to see you at once. At once!

DINAH: You've got on my hair ribbon.

TRACY: Your face is still dirty. [DINAH *exits Left I.* TRACY, *cool, collected and charming, all sweetness and light—crossing down to upper corner of sofa*] It's awfully

nice having you here. [*Shakes hands with* LIZ *and* MIKE.] I do hope you'll stay for my wedding.

LIZ: We'd like to very much.

MIKE: In fact, that was our idea.

TRACY: I'm so pleased that it occurred to you. [*Waves them to sit—*ALL *do so together. She in armchair Right Center.* LIZ *and* MIKE *in sofa, together*] The house is in rather a mess, of course. We all have to huddle here, and overflow onto the porch.—I hope your rooms are comfortable.

[MIKE *takes out pack of cigarettes.*]

LIZ: Oh, very, thanks.

TRACY: Anything you want, ask Mary or Elsie [*Passes cigarette box.*] They're magic. What a cunning little camera.

[MIKE *has struck match—sees* TRACY *still holds lighter toward him as she talks to* LIZ— *he slowly bends forward to accept light for cigarette—then blows his match out—she graciously smiles at him.*]

LIZ [*Lights cigarette from* TRACY's *lighter*]: It's a Contax. I'm afraid I'm rather a nuisance with it.

TRACY: But you couldn't be: I hope you'll take loads. Dear Papá and Mamá aren't allowing any reporters in—that is, except for little Mr. Grace, who does the social news. [*To* MIKE] Can you imagine a grown-up man having to sink so low?

MIKE: It does seem pretty bad.

TRACY: People have always been so kind about letting us live our simple and uneventful little life here unmolested. Of course, after my divorce last year— but I expect that always happens, and is more or less deserved. Dear Papá was quite angry, though, and swore he'd never let another reporter inside the gate. He thought some of their methods were a trifle underhanded.— You're a writer, aren't you, Mr. Connor?

MIKE [*Looks at her*]: In a manner of speaking.

TRACY: Sandy told me. I've sent for your books. "Macaulay Connor"—What's the "Macaulay" for?

MIKE: My father taught English History. I'm "Mike" to my friends.

TRACY: —Of whom you have many, I'm sure. English history has always fascinated me. Cromwell—Bloody Mary, John the Bastard—Where did he teach? I mean your father—

MIKE: In the high school in South Bend, Indiana.

TRACY: "South Bend"! It sounds like dancing, doesn't it? You must have had a most happy childhood there.

MIKE: It was terrific.

TRACY: I'm so glad.

MIKE: I don't mean it that way.

TRACY: I'm so sorry. Why?

MIKE: Largely due to the lack of the wherewithal, I guess.

TRACY: But that doesn't always cause unhappiness, does it?—not if you're the right kind of man. George Kittredge, my fiancé, never had anything either, but he—Are either of you married?

MIKE: No.

LIZ: I—er—that is, no.

TRACY: You mean *you* were, but now you're divorced?

LIZ: Well, the fact is—

TRACY: Suds—you can't mean you're ashamed of it!

LIZ: Of course I'm not ashamed of it.

MIKE [*Is staring at her*]: Wha-at?

LIZ: It was ages ago, when I was a mere kid, in Duluth. [*Flicks ashes in ashtray.*]

MIKE: Good Lord, Liz—you never told me you were—

LIZ: You never asked.

MIKE: I know, but—

LIZ: Joe Smith, Hardware.

MIKE: Liz, you're the damndest girl. [*Rises.*]

LIZ: *I* think I'm sweet. [*Smiles at* TRACY.]

[MIKE *goes to lower end corner of sofa.*]

TRACY: Duluth—that must be a lovely spot. It's west of here, isn't it?

LIZ: Sort of.—But occasionally we get the breezes.

TRACY: Is this your first visit in Philadelphia?

LIZ: Just about.

TRACY: It's a quaint old place, don't you think? I suppose it's affected somewhat by being the only really big city that's near New York.

LIZ: I think that's a very good point to make about it.

TRACY: —Though I suppose you consider us somewhat provincial?

LIZ: Not at all, I assure you.

TRACY: Odd customs, and such. Where the scrapples eat biddle on Sunday. Of course it *is* very old—Philadelphia, I mean, the scrapple is fresh weekly. How old are *you,* Mr. Connor?

MIKE [*Starts for seat—ashes to tray*]: I was thirty last month. [*Sits on sofa again.*]

TRACY: Two books isn't much for a man of thirty. I don't mean to criticize. You probably have other interests outside your work.

MIKE: None.—Unless—[*Looks at* LIZ *and smiles.*]

TRACY: How sweet! Are you living together?

MIKE [*Through the laugh*]: Why—er—no, we're not—

LIZ: That's an odd question, I must say!

TRACY: Why?

LIZ: Well—it just is.

TRACY: I don't see why. I think it's very interesting. [*Leans forward seriously, elbow on knee and chin on hand*] Miss Imbrie—don't you agree that all this marrying and giving in marriage is the damndest gyp that's ever been put over on an unsuspecting public?

MIKE [*To* LIZ]: Can she be human!

TRACY: Please, Mr. Connor!—I asked Miss Imbrie a question.

LIZ: No. As a matter of fact, I don't.

TRACY: Good. Nor do I. That's why I'm putting my chin out for the second time tomorrow. [GEORGE, *off Left, calls "Tracy." She rises.*] Here's the lucky man now. I'll bring him right in and put him on view—a one-man exhibition. [*As she moves over Left and goes off Left*] In here, George!—In here, my dear!

LIZ [*To* MIKE—*rises*]: My God—who's doing the interviewing here?

[*Puts out cigarette on table.*]

MIKE [*Rises. Back of sofa to Center*]: She's a lot more than I counted on.

LIZ: Do you suppose she caught on somehow?

MIKE: No. She's just a hellion. [*Has got to Center.*]

LIZ: I'm beginning to feel the size of a pinhead. [*Goes Right Center.*]

MIKE: Don't let her throw you.

LIZ: Do you want to take over?

MIKE: I want to go home.

[TRACY *re-enters with* GEORGE KITTREDGE, *aged thirty-two; brings him to Center.*]

TRACY [*As she crosses*]: Miss Imbrie—Mr. Connor—Mr. Kittredge, my beau.— Friends of Sandy's, George.

GEORGE [*Center*]: Any friend of Sandy's—[*Shakes hands with them.*]

LIZ [*Right Center*]: How do you do?

MIKE [*Center*]: How are you?

GEORGE: Fine as silk, thanks.

LIZ: You certainly look it.

GEORGE: Thanks, I've shaken quite a lot of coal dust from my feet in the last day or two.

TRACY [*Left Center*]: Isn't he beautiful? Isn't it wonderful what a little soap and water will do?

MIKE: Didn't I read a piece about you in *The Nation* a while ago?

GEORGE: Quite a while ago: I've been resting on my laurels since that—and a couple of others.

MIKE: Quite a neat piece of work—anticipating the Guffey Coal Act the way you did.—Or do I remember straight?

GEORGE: Anyone should have foreseen that—I was just lucky.

LIZ: A becoming modesty.

GEORGE: That's nothing to what's yet to be done with Labor relations.

TRACY: You ought to see him with the men—they simply adore him.

GEORGE: Oh—come on, Tracy!

TRACY [*Backing a few steps to Left*]: Oh, but they do! Never in my life will I forget that first night I saw you, all those wonderful faces, and the torchlights, and the way his voice boomed—

GEORGE: You see, I'm really a spellbinder.—That's the way I got her.

TRACY [*Crossing up to* GEORGE]: Except it was me who got you!—I'm going to put these two at the bridal table, in place of the Grants.

GEORGE: That's a good idea.

TRACY [*Crossing to Left, back of table*]: George, it won't rain, will it?—Promise me it won't rain. [*Looking out window*]

GEORGE [*Follows her*]: Tracy, I'll see to that personally.

TRACY: I almost believe you could.

MIKE: I guess this must be love.

GEORGE: Your guess is correct, Mr. Connor.

TRACY: I'm just his faithful Old Dog Tray.

GEORGE: Give me your paw?

TRACY [*She does*]: You've got it.

[GEORGE *takes her hand and kisses it.*]

[MARGARET *enters Right 1, followed by* DINAH. DINAH *remains in doorway.* MARGARET *goes directly to between* LIZ *and* MIKE *in front of sofa, Right.*]

MARGARET [*Shakes hands with* BOTH]: How do you do? We're so happy to have you. Forgive me for not coming in sooner, but things are in such a state. I'd no idea that a simple country wedding could involve so much. [*Crosses to* TRACY *and* TRACY *comes to her. They meet Center and beam.*] My little girl—[SANDY *enters Right 2 and crosses down to table Left near* TRACY. GEORGE *works to Left of table Left.*]—I do hope you'll be comfortable. Those rooms are inclined to be hot in this weather.—Aren't you pretty, my dear! Look at the way she wears her hair, Tracy. Isn't it pretty?

TRACY: Mighty fine.

MARGARET: I do wish my husband might be here to greet you, but we expect him presently. He's been detained in New York on business for that lovely Tina Mara. You know her work?

LIZ: Only vaguely!

MARGARET: So talented—and such a lovely person! But like so many artists—no business head, none whatever. [*Gives* TRACY *a knowing smile.* TRACY *and* SANDY *smile.* SANDY *then smirks.* EDWARD *enters from Right 2. He carries tray with sherry decanter and eight glasses.* THOMAS *follows to serve. They go up Center.*] Good morning, George!

GEORGE: Good morning, Mrs. Lord!

MARGARET: And this is my youngest daughter, Diana—

[DINAH *curtseys.*]

MIKE [*Is working his way behind sofa to down Right*]: I think we've met.

[THOMAS *gives* MARGARET *drink and napkin.*]

MARGARET: Thank you, Thomas.

[DINAH *then works her way across back of sofa to armchair Left Center—stops to get glass of sherry for* SANDY.]

SANDY [*Sitting in armchair Left Center*] Now let's all relax, and throw ourselves into things. Hi, George!

[MARGARET *sits in armchair Right Center.* TRACY *sits stool Center.* GEORGE *works slowly to behind her.*]

GEORGE: Hello, Sandy—Welcome home!

[THOMAS *serves* LIZ. DINAH *serves* SANDY *with sherry.*]

MARGARET: After lunch Sandy must show you some of the sights—the model dairy, and the stables, and the chicken farm—and perhaps there'll be time to run you out to some other places on the Main Line—Devins, Saint Davids, Bryn Mawr, where my daughter Tracy went to college—

[THOMAS *serves* MIKE, *then* THOMAS *goes up for* WILLIE*'s wine.*]

DINAH: 'Til she got bounced out on her—

MARGARET: Dinah!

UNCLE WILLIE [*Entering Right*]: It's a pretty kettle of fish when a man has to wait two mortal hours—

TRACY [*Rising*]: Papá!—Dear Papá—

UNCLE WILLIE: What's that?

TRACY [*As she rushes over Right to embrace him*]: Didn't the car meet you?

UNCLE WILLIE [*Amazed, but hardly audible*]: The car?

TRACY [*Crossing down Right*]: You Angel—to drop everything and get here in time for lunch—Isn't he, Mamá?

MARGARET: In—indeed he is.

UNCLE WILLIE: I'm not one to jump to conclusions, but—

TRACY: These are our friends, Mr. Connor and Miss Imbrie, Father.—They're here for the wedding.

MIKE: How are you, Mr. Lord?

LIZ: How do you do, Mr. Lord?

UNCLE WILLIE: Dashed fine. How are you?

[*Shakes hands with* MIKE.]

SANDY [*Over Left*]: Hi, Pops!

UNCLE WILLIE [*Crossing in Center*]: —Alexander.

DINAH [*Crossing in Center*]: Welcome back, Daddy!

UNCLE WILLIE: Dinah—Kittredge—[*He turns to* MARGARET *and bows.*] Margaret, my sweet.

[THOMAS *comes down to his Left with a sherry.* UNCLE WILLIE *takes sherry and tosses it off; glass back to* THOMAS, *who, taking stool from Center, goes up to fireplace.*]

TRACY: Mother, don't you think you ought to explain the new arrangement to Father before lunch?

MARGARET [*Taking* WILLIE *by the arm*]: Why—yes—I think I'd best. [*Having* WILLIE *by arm, takes him over Left as* DEXTER *enters. They meet Left 1.*] See here—here is the list now—Seth.

[TRACY *goes up Center.*]

SANDY [*As he sees* DEXTER *enter*]: Holy cats!

MARGARET [*As she sees him enter she turns quickly to look at* TRACY, *then speaks*]: Dexter Haven!

DEXTER [*Down at Left 1 entrance*]: Hello, friends and enemies. I came the short way, across the fields.

MARGARET: Well, this *is* a surprise.

GEORGE [*Up Center*]: I should think it is.

DEXTER: Hello, you sweet thing. [*Taking* MARGARET *by the shoulders and kissing her cheek*]

[MIKE *and* LIZ *cross.*]

MARGARET: Now you go right home at once!

UNCLE WILLIE: Remove yourself, young man!

DEXTER: But I've been invited. [*Going to* WILLIE *and shaking hands*] How are you, sir?

UNCLE WILLIE: No better, no worse. Get along.

DEXTER: Hello, Sandy.

SANDY [*Shaking hands with* DEXTER]: How are you, boy?

DEXTER: Never better. In fact, it's immoral how good I feel.

DINAH [*Works down Center*]: What—what brings you here, Mr. Haven?

DEXTER [*Crossing to her Center*]: Dinah, my angel! [*Kisses her cheek.*] Why, she's turned into a raving beauty! [*Crossing to* TRACY *as* DINAH *goes up Center*] Awfully sweet and thoughtful of you to ask me to lunch, Tray.

TRACY: Not at all.—Extra place, Thomas.

[GEORGE *crosses down Center.*]

THOMAS: Yes, Miss Tracy. [*He and* EDWARD *go out Right 2.*]

TRACY [*Right Center*]: Miss Imbrie—Mr. Connor—my former husband, whose name for the moment escapes me.

DEXTER [*Center*]: How do you do?

MIKE [*Right*]: How do you do? } [*Together*]

LIZ [*Right Center*]: How do you do?

DEXTER: —Of course I intended to come anyway, but it did make it pleasanter.— Hello, Kittredge.

[*Turns Center.*]

GEORGE: How are you, Haven?

DEXTER [*Peers at him*]: What's the matter? You don't look as well as when I last
saw you. [*He pats his arm sympathetically.*] Poor fellow—I know just how
you feel. [*He turns to* TRACY; *gazes at her fondly*] Redhead—isn't *she* in the
pink, though!—*You* don't look old enough to marry anyone, even for the
first time—you never did! She needs trouble to mature her, Kittredge.
Give her lots of it.

GEORGE: I'm afraid she can't count on me for that.

DEXTER: No? Too bad.—Sometimes, for your own sake, I think you should have
stuck to me longer, Red.

TRACY: I thought it was for life. [*Crossing to* GEORGE—*Left of him—takes his arm*]
but the nice Judge gave me a full pardon.

DEXTER: That's the kind of talk I like to hear; no bitterness, no recrimination—
just a good quick left to the jaw.

GEORGE: Very funny.

THOMAS [*Appears in the door Right 2*]: Luncheon is served, Madam.

MARGARET: Thank you, Thomas.

UNCLE WILLIE [*Crossing to Center*]: I don't suppose a man ever had a better or
finer family. [*Turns and takes* MARGARET'*s arm.*] I wake in the night and
say to myself—"Seth, you lucky dog. What have you done to deserve it?"
[*Goes up and exits Right 2, taking* MARGARET *along.*]

MARGARET [*As they go*]: And what *have* you?

[*Exits.*]

TRACY [*Crossing to Right*]: Do you mind if I go in with Mr. Connor, Miss
Imbrie?

LIZ: Why, not in the least.

SANDY [*Crossing and goes up Right back of couch, takes* LIZ'*s arm.* BOTH *exit*]:
Sandy's your boy.

TRACY [*Taking* MIKE'*s arm and up Center*]:—Because I think he's such an interesting man.

GEORGE: Come on, Dinah, I draw you, I guess.

DINAH [*Taking* DEXTER'*s arm also*]: Dexter—

DEXTER [*As they go*]: Isn't snatching one of my girls enough, you cad?

GEORGE [*At the same cue and time as they go up Right*]: You're a very bright fellow,
Haven, I'll hire you.

[*He exits.*]

TRACY [*To* MIKE—*going up*]: That's very insulting—but consistently interesting.
We must talk more.

MIKE [*Going up*]: No wonder you want to get away from all this.

[*They are* ALL *up near door Right 2 when* SETH *comes into room from Left 1.*]

SETH [*Stopping* MIKE, DEXTER, DINAH, TRACY. OTHERS *have gone*]: I don't know how welcome I am, but after Sandy's note, I thought the least I could do was to—

[DINAH *starts down but is stopped by* TRACY.]

TRACY [*As she restrains* DINAH]: *Uncle Willie!* [*She turns to* OTHERS.] Please go in, everyone. I want a word with Uncle Willie.

[*They go in—*DEXTER *turning back with a faint smile at* TRACY. *She crosses down Left, facing* SETH.]

SETH: Well, daughter?

TRACY: Well?

SETH:: Still Justice, with her shining sword—eh? Who's on the spot?

TRACY: We are; thanks to you—Uncle Willie.

CURTAIN

S tephen Vincent Benét (1898–1943) was born into a literary family. (His older sister Laura was a poet of some note, and his older brother William Rose Benét [1886–1950], who graduated from Yale in 1907, was a notable editor and poet whose verse autobiography, *The Dust Which Is God,* won the 1941 Pulitzer Prize.) Young Stephen entered Yale at the age of seventeen and quickly became a literary star on campus, running the *Yale Lit* and having his first book of poems, *Five Men and Pompey,* appear in 1915, while an undergraduate. His *Young Adventure: A Book of Poems* was then published in the Yale Series of Younger Poets in 1918. He left Yale to join the army in 1918, but because of his poor eyesight was rejected for service. He returned to Yale and graduated the following year, and he stayed on to take his M.A. in 1920, the year his *Heavens and Earth* was published. His early novels rapidly appeared—*The Beginning of Wisdom* (1921), *Young People's Pride* (1922), *Jean Huguenot* (1923), and *Spanish Bayonet* (1926)—along with poems and ballads celebrating America's folklore. It was cheaper to live in Paris, and it was there he wrote *John Brown's Body,* published in 1928. It won him the Pulitzer Prize and quickly established itself as the most popular American poem since *The Song of Hiawatha.* In 1933 he was appointed editor of the Yale Series of Younger Poets, a position he held until his death. Stories, poems, and screenplays (notably *Seven Brides for Seven Brothers*) burst from his pen, and when World War II broke out Benét—despite his poor health—wrote radio scripts and a history of the United States for distribution throughout the world. The work exhausted him, and he died in 1943. *Western Star,* begun in 1937 and the first of a projected nine-book poem about the European settlement of North America, was published posthumously in 1943 and was awarded his second Pulitzer Prize.

AMERICAN NAMES

I have fallen in love with American names,
The sharp names that never get fat,
The snakeskin-titles of mining-claims,
The plumed war-bonnet of Medicine Hat,
Tucson and Deadwood and Lost Mule Flat.

Seine and Piave are silver spoons,
But the spoonbowl-metal is thin and worn,
There are English counties like hunting-tunes
Played on the keys of a postboy's horn,
But I will remember where I was born.

I will remember Carquinez Straits,
Little French Lick and Lundy's Lane,
The Yankee ships and the Yankee dates
And the bullet-towns of Calamity Jane.
I will remember Skunktown Plain.

I will fall in love with a Salem tree
And a rawhide quirt from Santa Cruz,
I will get me a bottle of Boston sea
And a blue-gum nigger to sing me blues.
I am tired of loving a foreign muse.

Rue des Martyrs and Bleeding-Heart-Yard,
Senlis, Pisa, and Blindman's Oast,
It is a magic ghost you guard
But I am sick for a newer ghost,
Harrisburg, Spartanburg, Painted Post.

Henry and John were never so
And Henry and John were always right?
Granted, but when it was time to go
And the tea and the laurels had stood all night,
Did they never watch for Nantucket Light?

I shall not rest quiet in Montparnasse.
I shall not lie easy at Winchelsea.
You may bury my body in Sussex grass,
You may bury my tongue at Champmédy.
I shall not be there. I shall rise and pass.
Bury my heart at Wounded Knee.

THE DEVIL AND DANIEL WEBSTER

It's a story they tell in the border country, where Massachusetts joins Vermont and New Hampshire.

Yes, Dan'l Webster's dead—or, at least, they buried him. But every time there's a thunderstorm around Marshfield, they say you can hear his rolling voice in the hollows of the sky. And they say that if you go to his grave and speak loud and clear, "Dan'l Webster—Dan'l Webster!" the ground'll begin to shiver and the trees begin to shake. And after a while you'll hear a deep voice saying, "Neighbor, how stands the Union?" Then you better answer the Union stands as she stood, rock-bottomed and copper-sheathed, one and indivisible, or he's liable to rear right out of the ground. At least, that's what I was told when I was a youngster.

You see, for a while, he was the biggest man in the country. He never got to be President, but he was the biggest man. There were thousands that trusted in him right next to God Almighty, and they told stories about him that were like the stories of patriarchs and such. They said, when he stood up to speak, stars and stripes came right out in the sky, and once he spoke against a river and made it sink into the ground. They said, when he walked the woods with his fishing rod, Killall, the trout would jump out of the streams right into his pockets, for they knew it was no use putting up a fight against him; and, when he argued a case, he could turn on the harps of the blessed and the shaking of the earth underground. That was the kind of man he was, and his big farm up at Marshfield was suitable to him. The chickens he raised were all white meat down through the drumsticks, the cows were tended like children, and the big ram he called Goliath had horns with a curl like a morning-glory vine and could butt through an iron door. But Dan'l wasn't one of your gentlemen farmers; he knew all the ways of the land, and he'd be up by candlelight to see that the chores got done. A man with a mouth like a mastiff, a brow like a mountain and eyes like burning anthracite— that was Dan'l Webster in his prime. And the biggest case he argued never got written down in the books, for he argued it against the devil, nip and tuck and no holds barred. And this is the way I used to hear it told.

There was a man named Jabez Stone, lived at Cross Corners, New Hampshire. He wasn't a bad man to start with, but he was an unlucky man. If he planted corn, he got borers; if he planted potatoes, he got blight. He had good-enough land, but it didn't prosper him; he had a decent wife and children, but the more children he had, the less there was to feed them. If stones cropped up in his neighbor's field, boulders boiled up in his; if he had a horse with the spavins, he'd trade it for one with the staggers and give something extra. There's some folks bound to be like that, apparently. But one day Jabez Stone got sick of the whole business.

He'd been plowing that morning and he'd just broke the plowshare on a rock that he could have sworn hadn't been there yesterday. And, as he stood looking at the plowshare, the off horse began to cough—that ropy kind of cough that means sickness and horse doctors. There were two children down with the measles, his wife was ailing, and he had a whitlow on his thumb. It was about the last straw for Jabez Stone. "I vow," he said, and he looked around him kind of desperate— "I vow it's enough to make a man want to sell his soul to the devil! And I would, too, for two cents!"

Then he felt a kind of queerness come over him at having said what he'd said; though, naturally, being a New Hampshireman, he wouldn't take it back. But, all the same, when it got to be evening and, as far as he could see, no notice had been taken, he felt relieved in his mind, for he was a religious man. But notice is always taken, sooner or later, just like the Good Book says. And, sure enough, next day, about suppertime, a soft-spoken, dark-dressed stranger drove up in a handsome buggy and asked for Jabez Stone.

Well, Jabez told his family it was a lawyer, come to see him about a legacy. But he knew who it was. He didn't like the looks of the stranger, nor the way he smiled with his teeth. They were white teeth, and plentiful—some say they were filed to a point, but I wouldn't vouch for that. And he didn't like it when the dog took one look at the stranger and ran away howling, with his tail between his legs. But having passed his word, more or less, he stuck to it, and they went out behind the barn and made their bargain. Jabez Stone had to prick his finger to sign, and the stranger lent him a silver pin. The wound healed clean, but it left a little white scar.

After that, all of a sudden, things began to pick up and prosper for Jabez Stone. His cows got fat and his horses sleek, his crops were the envy of the neighborhood, and lightning might strike all over the valley, but it wouldn't strike his barn. Pretty soon, he was one of the prosperous people of the county; they asked him to stand for selectman, and he stood for it; there began to be talk of running him for state senate. All in all, you might say the Stone family was as happy and contented as cats in a dairy. And so they were, except for Jabez Stone.

He'd been contented enough, the first few years. It's a great thing when bad luck turns; it drives most other things out of your head. True, every now and then, especially in rainy weather, the little white scar on his finger would give him a twinge. And once a year, punctual as clockwork, the stranger with the handsome buggy would come driving by. But the sixth year, the stranger lighted, and, after that, his peace was over for Jabez Stone.

The stranger came up through the lower field, switching his boots with a cane—they were handsome black boots, but Jabez Stone never liked the look of them, particularly the toes. And, after he'd passed the time of day, he said, "Well, Mr. Stone, you're a hummer! It's a very pretty property you've got here, Mr. Stone."

"Well, some might favor it and others might not," said Jabez Stone, for he was a New Hampshireman.

"Oh, no need to decry your industry!" said the stranger, very easy, showing his teeth in a smile. "After all, we know what's been done, and it's been according to contract and specifications. So when—ahem—the mortgage falls due next year, you shouldn't have any regrets."

"Speaking of that mortgage, mister," said Jabez Stone, and he looked around for help to the earth and the sky, "I'm beginning to have one or two doubts about it."

"Doubts?" said the stranger, not quite so pleasantly.

"Why, yes," said Jabez Stone. "This being the U.S.A. and me always having been a religious man." He cleared his throat and got bolder. "Yes, sir," he said, "I'm beginning to have considerable doubts as to that mortgage holding in court."

"There's courts and courts," said the stranger, clicking his teeth. "Still, we might as well have a look at the original document." And he hauled out a big black pocketbook, full of papers. "Sherwin, Slater, Stevens, Stone," he muttered. "I, Jabez Stone, for a term of seven years—Oh, it's quite in order, I think."

But Jabez Stone wasn't listening, for he saw something else flutter out of the black pocketbook. It was something that looked like a moth, but it wasn't a moth. And as Jabez Stone stared at it, it seemed to speak to him in a small sort of piping voice, terrible small and thin, but terrible human. "Neighbor Stone!" it squeaked. "Neighbor Stone! Help me! For God's sake, help me!"

But before Jabez Stone could stir hand or foot, the stranger whipped out a big bandanna handkerchief, caught the creature in it, just like a butterfly, and started tying up the ends of the bandanna.

"Sorry for the interruption," he said. "As I was saying—"

But Jabez Stone was shaking all over like a scared horse.

"That's Miser Stevens' voice!" he said, in a croak. "And you've got him in your handkerchief!"

The stranger looked a little embarrassed.

"Yes, I really should have transferred him to the collecting box," he said with a simper, "but there were some rather unusual specimens there and I didn't want them crowded. Well, well, these little contretemps will occur."

"I don't know what you mean by contertan," said Jabez Stone, "but that was Miser Stevens' voice! And he ain't dead! You can't tell me he is! He was just as spry and mean as a woodchuck, Tuesday!"

"In the midst of life—" said the stranger, kind of pious. "Listen!" Then a bell began to toll in the valley and Jabez Stone listened, with the sweat running down his face. For he knew it was tolled for Miser Stevens and that he was dead.

"These long-standing accounts," said the stranger with a sigh; "one really hates to close them. But business is business."

He still had the bandanna in his hand, and Jabez Stone felt sick as he saw the cloth struggle and flutter.

"Are they all as small as that?" he asked hoarsely.

"Small?" said the stranger. "Oh, I see what you mean. Why, they vary." He measured Jabez Stone with his eyes, and his teeth showed. "Don't worry, Mr. Stone," he said. "You'll go with a very good grade. I wouldn't trust you outside the collecting box. Now, a man like Dan'l Webster, of course—well, we'd have to build a special box for him, and even at that, I imagine the wingspread would astonish you. But, in your case, as I was saying—"

"Put that handkerchief away!" said Jabez Stone, and he began to beg and to pray. But the best he could get at the end was a three years' extension, with conditions.

But till you make a bargain like that, you've got no idea of how fast four years can run. By the last months of those years, Jabez Stone's known all over the state and there's talk of running him for governor—and it's dust and ashes in his mouth. For every day, when he gets up, he thinks, "There's one more night gone," and every night when he lies down, he thinks of the black pocketbook and the soul of Miser Stevens, and it makes him sick at heart. Till, finally, he can't bear it any longer, and, in the last days of the last year, he hitches up his horse and drives off to seek Dan'l Webster. For Dan'l was born in New Hampshire, only a few miles from Cross Corners, and it's well known that he has a particular soft spot for old neighbors.

It was early in the morning when he got to Marshfield, but Dan'l was up already, talking Latin to the farm hands and wrestling with the ram, Goliath, and trying out a new trotter and working up speeches to make against John C. Calhoun. But when he heard a New Hampshireman had come to see him, he dropped everything else he was doing, for that was Dan'l's way. He gave Jabez Stone a breakfast that five men couldn't eat, went into the living history of every man and woman in Cross Corners, and finally asked him how he could serve him.

Jabez Stone allowed that it was a kind of mortgage case.

"Well, I haven't pleaded a mortgage case in a long time, and I don't generally plead now, except before the Supreme Court," said Dan'l, "but if I can, I'll help you."

"Then I've got hope for the first time in ten years," said Jabez Stone, and told him the details.

Dan'l walked up and down as he listened, hands behind his back, now and then asking a question, now and then plunging his eyes at the floor, as if they'd bore through it like gimlets. When Jabez Stone had finished, Dan'l puffed out his cheeks and blew. Then he turned to Jabez Stone and a smile broke over his face like the sunrise over Monadnock.

"You've certainly given yourself the devil's own row to hoe, Neighbor Stone," he said, "but I'll take your case."

"You'll take it?" said Jabez Stone, hardly daring to believe.

"Yes," said Dan'l Webster. "I've got about seventy-five other things to do and the Missouri Compromise to straighten out, but I'll take your case. For if two New Hampshiremen aren't a match for the devil, we might as well give the country back to the Indians." Then he shook Jabez Stone by the hand and said, "Did you come down here in a hurry?"

"Well, I admit I made time," said Jabez Stone.

"You'll go back faster," said Dan'l Webster, and he told 'em to hitch up Constitution and Constellation to the carriage. They were matched grays with one white forefoot, and they stepped like greased lightning.

Well, I won't describe how excited and pleased the whole Stone family was to have the great Dan'l Webster for a guest, when they finally got there. Jabez Stone had lost his hat on the way, blown off when they overtook a wind, but he didn't take much account of that. But after supper he sent the family off to bed, for he had most particular business with Mr. Webster. Mrs. Stone wanted them to sit in the front parlor, but Dan'l Webster knew front parlors and said he preferred the kitchen. So it was there they sat, waiting for the stranger, with a jug on the table between them and a bright fire on the hearth—the stranger being scheduled to show up on the stroke of midnight, according to specifications.

Well, most men wouldn't have asked for better company than Dan'l Webster and a jug. But with every tick of the clock Jabez Stone got sadder and sadder. His eyes roved round, and though he sampled the jug you could see he couldn't taste it. Finally, on the stroke of 11:30 he reached over and grabbed Dan'l Webster by the arm.

"Mr. Webster, Mr. Webster!" he said, and his voice was shaking with fear and a desperate courage. "For God's sake, Mr. Webster, harness your horses and get away from this place while you can!"

"You've brought me a long way, neighbor, to tell me you don't like my company," said Dan'l Webster, quite peaceable, pulling at the jug.

"Miserable wretch that I am!" groaned Jabez Stone. "I've brought you a devilish way, and now I see my folly. Let him take me if he wills. I don't hanker after it, I must say, but I can stand it. But you're the Union's stay and New Hampshire's pride! He mustn't get you, Mr. Webster! He mustn't get you!"

Dan'l Webster looked at the distracted man, all gray and shaking in the firelight, and laid a hand on his shoulder.

"I'm obliged to you, Neighbor Stone," he said gently. "It's kindly thought of. But there's a jug on the table and a case in hand. And I never left a jug or a case half finished in my life."

And just at that moment there was a sharp rap on the door.

"Ah," said Dan'l Webster, very coolly, "I thought your clock was a trifle slow, Neighbor Stone." He stepped to the door and opened it. "Come in!" he said.

The stranger came in—very dark and tall he looked in the firelight. He was carrying a box under his arm—a black, japanned box with little air holes in the lid. At the sight of the box, Jabez Stone gave a low cry and shrank into a corner of the room.

"Mr. Webster, I presume," said the stranger, very polite, but with his eyes glowing like a fox's deep in the woods.

"Attorney of record for Jabez Stone," said Dan'l Webster, but his eyes were glowing too. "Might I ask your name?"

"I've gone by a good many," said the stranger carelessly. "Perhaps Scratch will do for the evening. I'm often called that in these regions."

Then he sat down at the table and poured himself a drink from the jug. The liquor was cold in the jug, but it came steaming into the glass.

"And now," said the stranger, smiling and showing his teeth, "I shall call upon you, as a law-abiding citizen, to assist me in taking possession of my property."

Well, with that the argument began—and it went hot and heavy. At first, Jabez Stone had a flicker of hope, but when he saw Dan'l Webster being forced back at point after point, he just scrunched in his corner, with his eyes on that japanned box. For there wasn't any doubt as to the deed or the signature—that was the worst of it. Dan'l Webster twisted and turned and thumped his fist on the table, but he couldn't get away from that. He offered to compromise the case; the stranger wouldn't hear of it. He pointed out the property had increased in value, and state senators ought to be worth more; the stranger stuck to the letter of the law. He was a great lawyer, Dan'l Webster, but we know who's the King of Lawyers, as the Good Book tells us, and it seemed as if, for the first time, Dan'l Webster had met his match.

Finally, the stranger yawned a little. "Your spirited efforts on behalf of your client do you credit, Mr. Webster," he said, "but if you have no more arguments to adduce, I'm rather pressed for time"—and Jabez Stone shuddered.

Dan'l Webster's brow looked dark as a thundercloud.

"Pressed or not, you shall not have this man!" he thundered. "Mr. Stone is an American citizen, and no American citizen may be forced into the service of a foreign prince. We fought England for that in '12 and we'll fight all hell for it again!"

"Foreign?" said the stranger. "And who calls me a foreigner?"

"Well, I never yet heard of the dev—of your claiming American citizenship," said Dan'l Webster with surprise.

"And who with better right?" said the stranger, with one of his terrible smiles. "When the first wrong was done to the first Indian, I was there. When the first slaver put out for the Congo, I stood on her deck. Am I not in your books and stories and beliefs, from the first settlements on? Am I not spoken of, still, in every church in New England? 'Tis true the North claims me for a Southerner and the South for a Northerner, but I am neither. I am merely an honest American like yourself—and of the best descent—for, to tell the truth, Mr. Webster, though I don't like to boast of it, my name is older in this country than yours."

"Aha!" said Dan'l Webster, with the veins standing out in his forehead. "Then I stand on the Constitution! I demand a trial for my client!"

"The case is hardly one for an ordinary court," said the stranger, his eyes flickering. "And, indeed, the lateness of the hour—"

"Let it be any court you choose, so it is an American judge and an American jury!" said Dan'l Webster in his pride. "Let it be the quick or the dead; I'll abide the issue!"

"You have said it," said the stranger, and pointed his finger at the door. And with that, and all of a sudden, there was a rushing of wind outside and a noise of footsteps. They came, clear and distinct, through the night. And yet, they were not like the footsteps of living men.

"In God's name, who comes by so late?" cried Jabez Stone, in an ague of fear.

"The jury Mr. Webster demands," said the stranger, sipping at his boiling glass. "You must pardon the rough appearance of one or two; they will have come a long way."

And with that the fire burned blue and the door blew open and twelve men entered, one by one.

If Jabez Stone had been sick with terror before, he was blind with terror now. For there was Walter Butler, the loyalist, who spread fire and horror through the Mohawk Valley in the times of the Revolution; and there was Simon Girty, the renegade, who saw white men burned at the stake and whooped with the Indians to see them burn. His eyes were green, like a catamount's, and the stains on his hunting shirt did not come from the blood of the deer. King Philip was there, wild and proud as he had been in life, with the great gash in his head that gave him his death wound, and cruel Governor Dale, who broke men on the wheel. There was Morton of Merry Mount, who so vexed the Plymouth Colony, with his flushed, loose, handsome face and his hate of the godly. There was Teach, the bloody pirate, with his black beard curling on his breast. The Reverend John Smeet, with his strangler's hands and his Geneva gown, walked as daintily as he had to the gallows. The red print of the rope was still around his neck, but he carried a perfumed handkerchief in one hand. One and all, they came into the room with the fires of hell still upon them, and the stranger named their names and their deeds as they came, till the tale of twelve was told. Yet the stranger had told the truth—they had all played a part in America.

"Are you satisfied with the jury, Mr. Webster?" said the stranger mockingly, when they had taken their places.

The sweat stood upon Dan'l Webster's brow, but his voice was clear.

"Quite satisfied," he said. "Though I miss General Arnold from the company."

"Benedict Arnold is engaged upon other business," said the stranger, with a glower. "Ah, you asked for a justice, I believe."

He pointed his finger once more, and a tall man, soberly clad in Puritan garb, with the burning gaze of the fanatic, stalked into the room and took his judge's place.

"Justice Hathorne is a jurist of experience," said the stranger. "He presided at certain witch trials once held in Salem. There were others who repented of the business later, but not he."

"Repent of such notable wonders and undertakings?" said the stern old justice. "Nay, hang them—hang them all!" And he muttered to himself in a way that struck ice into the soul of Jabez Stone.

Then the trial began, and, as you might expect, it didn't look anyways good for the defense. And Jabez Stone didn't make much of a witness in his own behalf. He took one look at Simon Girty and screeched, and they had to put him back in his corner in a kind of swoon.

It didn't halt the trial, though; the trial went on, as trials do. Dan'l Webster had faced some hard juries and hanging judges in his time, but this was the hardest he'd ever faced, and he knew it. They sat there with a kind of glitter in their eyes, and the stranger's smooth voice went on and on. Every time he'd raise an objection, it'd be "Objection sustained," but whenever Dan'l objected, it'd be "Objection denied." Well, you couldn't expect fair play from a fellow like this Mr. Scratch.

It got to Dan'l in the end, and he began to heat, like iron in the forge. When he got up to speak he was going to flay that stranger with every trick known to the law, and the judge and jury too. He didn't care if it was contempt of court or what would happen to him for it. He didn't care any more what happened to Jabez Stone. He just got madder and madder, thinking of what he'd say. And yet, curiously enough, the more he thought about it, the less he was able to arrange his speech in his mind.

Till, finally, it was time for him to get up on his feet, and he did so, all ready to bust out with lightnings and denunciations. But before he started he looked over the judge and jury for a moment, such being his custom. And he noticed the glitter in their eyes was twice as strong as before, and they all leaned forward. Like hounds just before they get the fox, they looked, and the blue mist of evil in the room thickened as he watched them. Then he saw what he'd been about to do, and he wiped his forehead, as a man might who's just escaped falling into a pit in the dark.

For it was him they'd come for, not only Jabez Stone. He read it in the glitter of their eyes and in the way the stranger hid his mouth with one hand. And if he fought them with their own weapons, he'd fall into their power; he knew that, though he couldn't have told you how. It was his own anger and horror that burned in their eyes; and he'd have to wipe that out or the case was lost. He stood there for a moment, his black eyes burning like anthracite. And then he began to speak.

He started off in a low voice, though you could hear every word. They say he could call on the harps of the blessed when he chose. And this was just as simple and easy as a man could talk. But he didn't start out by condemning or reviling. He was talking about the things that make a country a country, and a man a man.

And he began with the simple things that everybody's known and felt—the freshness of a fine morning when you're young, and the taste of food when you're hungry, and the new day that's every day when you're a child. He took them up and he turned them in his hands. They were good things for any man. But without freedom, they sickened. And when he talked of those enslaved, and the sorrows of slavery, his voice got like a big bell. He talked of the early days of America and the men who had made those days. It wasn't a spread-eagle speech, but he made you see it. He admitted all the wrong that had ever been done. But he showed how, out of the wrong and the right, the suffering and the starvations, something new had come. And everybody had played a part in it, even the traitors.

Then he turned to Jabez Stone and showed him as he was—an ordinary man who'd had hard luck and wanted to change it. And, because he'd wanted to change it, now he was going to be punished for all eternity. And yet there was good in Jabez Stone, and he showed that good. He was hard and mean, in some ways, but he was a man. There was sadness in being a man, but it was a proud thing too. And he showed what the pride of it was till you couldn't help feeling it. Yes, even in hell, if a man was a man, you'd know it. And he wasn't pleading for any one person any more, though his voice rang like an organ. He was telling the story and the failures and the endless journey of mankind. They got tricked and trapped and bamboozled, but it was a great journey. And no demon that was ever foaled could know the inwardness of it—it took a man to do that.

The fire began to die on the hearth and the wind before morning to blow. The light was getting gray in the room when Dan'l Webster finished. And his words came back at the end to New Hampshire ground, and the one spot of land that each man loves and clings to. He painted a picture of that, and to each one of that jury he spoke of things long forgotten. For his voice could search the heart, and that was his gift and his strength. And to one, his voice was like the forest and its secrecy, and to another like the sea and the storms of the sea; and one heard the cry of his lost nation in it, and another saw a little harmless scene he hadn't remembered for years. But each saw something. And when Dan'l Webster finished he didn't know whether or not he'd saved Jabez Stone. But he knew he'd done a miracle. For the glitter was gone from the eyes of judge and jury, and, for the moment, they were men again, and knew they were men.

"The defense rests," said Dan'l Webster, and stood there like a mountain. His ears were still ringing with his speech, and he didn't hear anything else till he heard Judge Hathorne say, "The jury will retire to consider its verdict."

Walter Butler rose in his place and his face had a dark, gay pride on it.

"The jury has considered its verdict," he said, and looked the stranger full in the eye. "We find for the defendant, Jabez Stone."

With that, the smile left the stranger's face, but Walter Butler did not flinch.

"Perhaps 'tis not strictly in accordance with the evidence," he said, "but even the damned may salute the eloquence of Mr. Webster."

With that, the long crow of a rooster split the gray morning sky and judge and jury were gone from the room like a puff of smoke and as if they had never been there. The stranger turned to Dan'l Webster, smiling wryly.

"Major Butler was always a bold man," he said. "I had not thought him quite so bold. Nevertheless, my congratulations, as between two gentlemen."

"I'll have that paper first, if you please," said Dan'l Webster, and he took it and tore it into four pieces. It was queerly warm to the touch. "And now," he said, "I'll have you!" and his hand came down like a bear trap on the stranger's arm. For he knew that once you bested anybody like Mr. Scratch in fair fight, his power on you was gone. And he could see that Mr. Scratch knew it too.

The stranger twisted and wriggled, but he couldn't get out of that grip. "Come, come, Mr. Webster," he said, smiling palely. "This sort of thing is ridic—ouch!—is ridiculous. If you're worried about the costs of the case, naturally, I'd be glad to pay—"

"And so you shall!" said Dan'l Webster, shaking him till his teeth rattled. "For you'll sit right down at that table and draw up a document, promising never to bother Jabez Stone nor his heirs or assigns nor any other New Hampshireman till doomsday! For any hades we want to raise in this state, we can raise ourselves, without assistance from strangers."

"Ouch!" said the stranger. "Ouch! Well, they never did run very big to the barrel, but—ouch!—I agree!"

So he sat down and drew up the document. But Dan'l Webster kept his hand on his coat collar all the time.

"And, now, may I go?" said the stranger, quite humble, when Dan'l'd seen the document was in proper and legal form.

"Go?" said Dan'l, giving him another shake. "I'm still trying to figure out what I'll do with you. For you've settled the costs of the case, but you haven't settled with me. I think I'll take you back to Marshfield," he said, kind of reflective. "I've got a ram there named Goliath that can butt through an iron door. I'd kind of like to turn you loose in his field and see what he'd do."

Well, with that the stranger began to beg and to plead. And he begged and he pled so humble that finally Dan'l, who was naturally kindhearted, agreed to let him go. The stranger seemed terrible grateful for that and said, just to show they were friends, he'd tell Dan'l's fortune before leaving. So Dan'l agreed to that, though he didn't take much stock in fortune-tellers ordinarily. But, naturally, the stranger was a little different.

Well, he pried and he peered at the lines in Dan'l's hands. And he told him one thing and another that was quite remarkable. But they were all in the past.

"Yes, all that's true, and it happened," said Dan'l Webster. "But what's to come in the future?"

The stranger grinned, kind of happily, and shook his head.

"The future's not as you think it," he said. "It's dark. You have a great ambition, Mr. Webster."

"I have," said Dan'l firmly, for everybody knew he wanted to be President.

"It seems almost within your grasp," said the stranger, "but you will not attain it. Lesser men will be made President and you will be passed over."

"And, if I am, I'll still be Daniel Webster," said Dan'l. "Say on."

"You have two strong sons," said the stranger, shaking his head. "You look to found a line. But each will die in war and neither reach greatness."

"Live or die, they are still my sons," said Dan'l Webster. "Say on."

"You have made great speeches," said the stranger. "You will make more."

"Ah," said Dan'l Webster.

"But the last great speech you make will turn many of your own against you," said the stranger. "They will call you Ichabod; they will call you by other names. Even in New England, some will say you have turned your coat and sold your country, and their voices will be loud against you till you die."

"So it is an honest speech, it does not matter what men say," said Dan'l Webster. Then he looked at the stranger and their glances locked.

"One question," he said. "I have fought for the Union all my life. Will I see that fight won against those who would tear it apart?"

"Not while you live," said the stranger, grimly, "but it will be won. And after you are dead, there are thousands who will fight for your cause, because of words that you spoke."

"Why, then, you long-barreled, slab-sided, lantern-jawed, fortune-telling note shaver!" said Dan'l Webster, with a great roar of laughter, "be off with you to your own place before I put my mark on you! For, by the thirteen original colonies, I'd go to the Pit itself to save the Union!"

And with that he drew back his foot for a kick that would have stunned a horse. It was only the tip of his shoe that caught the stranger, but he went flying out of the door with his collecting box under his arm.

"And now," said Dan'l Webster, seeing Jabez Stone beginning to rouse from his swoon, "let's see what's left in the jug, for it's dry work talking all night. I hope there's pie for breakfast, Neighbor Stone."

But they say that whenever the devil comes near Marshfield, even now, he gives it a wide berth. And he hasn't been seen in the state of New Hampshire from that day to this. I'm not talking about Massachusetts or Vermont.

Cole Porter (1891–1964), America's most sophisticated songwriter, was born in Peru, Indiana, and graduated from Yale in 1913. While at Yale, his visits to Manhattan earned him the sobriquet "pet of society"—while back in New Haven he wrote 300 songs (including Yale's two fight songs) and produced several musical comedies. Looking back later, he once described his undergraduate self as "a cross between Eddie Cantor and the Duke of Windsor." He was a member of the Glee Club (along with Averell Harriman, Dean Acheson, Gerald Murphy, and "Black Jack" Bouvier) and the Whiffen-poofs, and through the Yale Dramat he became a lifelong friend of Monty Woolley. His first Broadway show, the unpopular *See America First,* opened in 1916. He moved to France a year later to live the rich expatriate life, and his songs began turning up in London shows. He once estimated that he wrote a song a day throughout his life. By 1928 his music was everywhere, and in the 1930s he had a string of successes: *The New Yorkers* (1930), *The Gay Divorcée* (1932), *Nymph Errant* (1933), *Anything Goes* (1934), and *Red, Hot, and Blue* (1936). In 1937, a riding accident left him crippled for life. But his work for the stage and screen, whether mordant or vibrant, remained popular. His sardonic takes on love and loneliness barely disguised the disappointed romantic beneath. *DuBarry Was a Lady* (1939), *Mexican Hayride* (1943), *Kiss Me, Kate* (1948), *Out of This World* (1950), *Can-Can* (1953), *Silk Stockings* (1955), and *High Society* (1956) carried his fame to unprecedented heights, where it remains to this day.

BULL DOG

Verse
Way down, way down in New Haven town,
Lives Mister Yale,
Old Eli Yale.
No one ever cares to come around,
Just because of his pet "Bow-wow."
Poor old Harvard tries it once a year,
Always goes back,
Tied up in black,
For when old Yale sicks that big bull dog on,
He raises an awful row.

Refrain
Bull dog! Bull dog! Bow, wow, wow,
Eli Yale!
Bull dog! Bull dog! Bow, wow, wow,
Our team can never fail.
When the sons of Eli break through the line,
That is the sign we hail.
Bull dog! Bull dog! Bow, wow, wow,
Eli Yale!   [1911]

ANTOINETTE BIRBY

Verse 1
Miss Antoinette Birby lived way out in Derby,
A maid divinely fair.
She found it no heaven retiring at seven;
Her heart was filled with care.
'Twas truly a pity that a maiden so pretty
Should milk the cows all day,
So she took a notion to get into motion
And packed her trunk right away.
As the train pulled out of the station,
She gave forth this explanation:

Refrain 1
I'm off for New Haven, so long, goodbye,
I'm off for New Haven, I don't know why.
This leaving the family really makes me very sad,
For they are by far the best pa and ma I ever had.
But I've got to sling hash at the Taft Hotel,
As a waitress I never shall fail.
For I have a cravin' for dear old New Haven
And Yale, Yale, Yale.

Verse 2
Arrived in the city, this maiden so pretty
Did walk down Chapel Street,
And then a young fellow to whom she said "Hello"
Our heroine did meet.
Now he was a villain, but Nettie was willin',
She loved him right away.
Her scruples forsook her,
The villain he took her into a swell café.
As she took down her first few swallows,
She was heard to murmur rather incoherently as follows:

Refrain 2
I'm strong for New Haven, believe me, kid,
For this is the town where there ain't no lid.
The life in New Haven makes Derby seem so very tame,
I've learned sev'ral things that I never knew before I came.
I'm going to learn all that there is to know,
At least if I keep out of jail,
As a fountain of knowledge believe me some college
Is Yale, Yale, Yale.

Verse 3
Next morn at eleven, instead of at seven,
She woke up in dismay.
Her bean it was addled, her brain had skedaddled,
For she had passed away.
The warden he brought her a pail of ice water,
Her thirst was so intense;
Her spirit was stricken, her conscience was pricken,
Her head it felt immense

As she left the police station,
She gave out this information:

Refrain 3
I'm going back to Derby, so long, goodbye,
I'm going back to Derby, you all know why.
When I came to New Haven I was so very good and sweet and true,
But I've done sev'ral things that a girlie shouldn't oughta do.
So it's back to the milking for Antoinette,
A sadder but wiser female.
No maiden that's pretty should come to the city
And Yale, Yale, Yale.   [1913]

WE ARE PROM GIRLS

We are Prom girls.
Pretty little pink-cheeked Prom girls.
Gautier would swear that we're evil-eyed,
Browning would declare that we were ostrich-thighed.
We add pep to
Any tune that we one-step to.
You won't bore us
If you'll but adore us,
Pretty little Prom girls, we—
Pretty little Prom girls, we.   [1913]

A MEMBER OF THE YALE ELIZABETHAN CLUB

Verse
I'm a member very noted
Of a club that's often quoted
As the most exclusive club in college.
My medulla oblongata
Has an awful lot of data
On the sources of our springs of knowledge.
I delight in being chatty
With New Haven's literati
On the subject of a brand-new binding.

All the critics sing my praises
In illuminated phrases;
As a literary light I'm blinding.

Chorus
As a literary light, as a literary light,
He's blinding!
Did you get that metaphor?
I confess I could do better for—

Refrain
I'm a member of the Yale Elizabethan Club
In a very hypocritical way.
By belonging to the Yale Elizabethan Club
I've a terrible political sway.
I convert New Haven
To the bard of Avon,
And a highbrow must I be;
For I give support
To the latest college sporto,
Tea by the quart
And editions by the quarto.
Good gadzooks! But I love those books.
With a fol, with a fol,
With a hey, with a hey,
With a toureloure tourelourelay,
With a tralalalala,
With a tralalalala,
And a noney, noney, noney noney, ney,
For a member of the Yale Elizabethan Club am I!

[1913]

I WANT TO ROW ON THE CREW

Verse
Now when Willie was still an obtuse Montessori-an,
Having heard of Yale victories early Victorian,
He was mad to show oarsmanship ichthyosaurian,
On the Yale University Crew.

What a "Bright College Years" thing to do!
Though his mother regarded his scheme as chimerical,
And referred to his prospects in accents satirical,
Little Willie would chant in apostrophes lyrical
To the Yale University Crew.
Swing, swing, together!
In a voice that might rival Apollo's,
He expressed his intentions as follows:

Refrain
I want to row on the crew, Mama.
That's the thing I want to do, Mama.
To be known throughout Yale when I walk about it,
Get a boil on my tail and then talk about it.
I want to be a big bloke, Mama,
And learn that new Argentine stroke, Mama.
You'll see your slim son putting crimps in the crimson,
When I row on the (Brek-ek-co-ax-co-ax
Brek-ek-co-ax-co-ax Parabalou)
When I row on the Varsity Crew.   [1913]

I'VE A SHOOTING BOX IN SCOTLAND

Verse 1
Nowadays it's rather nobby
To regard one's private hobby
As the object of one's tenderest affections;
Some excel at Alpine climbing,
Others have a turn for rhyming,
While a lot of people go in for collections.

Such as prints by Hiroshigi,
Edelweiss from off the Rigi,
Jacobean soup tureens,
Early types of limousines,
Pipes constructed from a dry cob,
Baseball hits by Mister Ty Cobb,*
Locks of Missus Browning's hair,

*Original version: Priceless sets of Pepys and Evelyn, Footballs kicked by Tommy Shevlin.

Photographs of Ina Claire,
First editions still uncut,
Daily pranks of Jeff and Mutt,
Della Robbia singing boys,
Signatures of Alfred Noyes,
Fancy bantams,
Grecian vases,
Tropic beetles,
Irish laces,
But my favorite pastime
Is collecting country places.

Refrain 1
I've a shooting box in Scotland,
I've a château in Touraine,
I've a silly little chalet
In the Interlaken Valley,
I've a hacienda in Spain,
I've a private fjord in Norway,
I've a villa close to Rome,
And in traveling
It's really quite a comfort to know
That you're never far from home!

Verse 2
Now it's really very funny
What an awful lot of money
On exorbitant hotels a chap can squander;
But I never have to do so,
Like resourceful Mister Crusoe,
I can find a home however far I wander.

Refrain 2
I've a bungalow at Simla,
I've an island east of Maine,
If you care for hotter places,
I've an African oasis
On an uninhabited plain;
I've a houseboat on the Yangtse,
I've an igloo up at Nome,
Yes, in traveling

It's really quite a comfort to know
That you're never far from home!

Verse 3
Having lots of idle leisure
I pursue a life of pleasure,
Like a rolling stone in constant agitation
For tho' stay-at-homes may cavil,
I admit I'd rather travel,
Than collect a crop of mossy vegetation!

Refrain 3
I've a shanty in the Rockies,
I've a castle on the Rhine,
I've a Siamese pagoda,
I've a cottage in Fashoda,
Near the equatorial line!
On my sable farm in Russia
O'er the barren steppes we'll roam,
And in traveling,
It's really quite a comfort to know
That you're never far from home.

                                    [1916]

JUST ONE OF THOSE THINGS

Verse
Love can make you happy,
Love can make you blue,
Love can make your bitter life sweet,
And your sweet life bitter too.

Refrain
If ever I love again
I'll cling to the mem'ry of
The first time I fell in love,
Just one of those things.
If only I'd thought again
I wouldn't have looked! But instead

I lost both my heart and my head,
Just one of those things.
I can't tell you why it started
Or how it evolved,
But when with the dawn we parted
Life seemed to be solved.
I wouldn't have b'lieved it then,
If some gypsy had said to me,
"Your dream will turn out to be
Just one of those things."

ANYTHING GOES

Verse
Times have changed
And we've often rewound the clock
Since the Puritans got a shock
When they landed on Plymouth Rock
If today
Any shock they should try to stem,
'Stead of landing on Plymouth Rock,
Plymouth Rock would land on them.

Refrain 1
In olden days, a glimpse of stocking
Was looked on as something shocking,
But now, God knows,
Anything goes.
Good authors too who once knew better words
Now only use four-letter words
Writing prose,
Anything goes.
If driving fast cars you like,
If low bars you like,
If old hymns you like,
If bare limbs you like,
If Mae West you like,
Or me undressed you like,
Why, nobody will oppose.

When ev'ry night, the set that's smart is in-
Truding in nudist parties in
Studios,
Anything goes.

Refrain 2
When Missus Ned McLean (God bless her)
Can get Russian reds to "yes" her,
Then I suppose
Anything goes.
When Rockefeller still can hoard en-
Ough money to let Max Gordon
Produce his shows,
Anything goes.
The world has gone mad today
And good's bad today,
And black's white today,
And day's night today,
And that gent today
You gave a cent today
Once had several châteaux.
When folks who still can ride in jitneys
Find out Vanderbilts and Whitneys
Lack baby clo'es,
Anything goes.

Refrain 3
If Sam Goldwyn can with great conviction
Instruct Anna Sten in diction,
Then Anna shows
Anything goes.
When you hear that Lady Mendl standing up
Now turns a handspring landing up-
On her toes,
Anything goes.
Just think of those shocks you've got
And those knocks you've got
And those blues you've got
From that news you've got
And those pains you've got
(If any brains you've got)

From those little radios.
So Missus R., with all her trimmin's,
Can broadcast a bed from Simmons
'Cause Franklin knows
Anything goes.

I GET A KICK OUT OF YOU

Verse
My story is much too sad to be told,
But practically ev'rything leaves me totally cold.
The only exception I know is the case
Where I'm out on a quiet spree
Fighting vainly the old ennui
And I suddenly turn and see
Your fabulous face.

Refrain
I get no kick from champagne.
Mere alcohol doesn't thrill me at all,
So tell me why should it be true
That I get a kick out of you?
Some get a kick from cocaine.
I'm sure that if I took even one sniff
That would bore me terrific'ly too
Yet I get a kick out of you.
I get a kick ev'ry time I see
You're standing there before me.
I get a kick though it's clear to me
You obviously don't adore me.
I get no kick in a plane.
Flying too high with some guy in the sky
Is my idea of nothing to do,
Yet I get a kick out of you.

Thornton Wilder

t hornton Wilder (1897–1975), one of this country's greatest playwrights and novelists, grew up in Wisconsin, Hong Kong, and California. When he graduated from Yale in 1920, already a writer and with an intellectual poise and curiosity that lasted his lifetime, his professor, the redoubtable William Lyon Phelps, called him "a star of the first magnitude." In 1918 he had written his first play to be professionally staged, *The Trumpet Shall Sound.* After Yale, he studied archaeology in Rome and taught French at Lawrenceville. His first novel, the astonishingly sophisticated *The Cabala,* appeared in 1926, and a year later *The Bridge of San Luis Rey* was acclaimed and won the Pulitzer Prize. *The Woman of Andros* (1930) and *Heaven's My Destination* (1935) solidified his reputation. Then he wrote his most successful and enduring work, *Our Town* (1938), also awarded the Pulitzer Prize. It has since become around the world the most produced American play in history. *The Merchant of Yonkers* followed in 1939, and *The Skin of Our Teeth* in 1942—which won him his third Pulitzer. Wilder interrupted his career to work in military intelligence during World War II. He returned to fiction with *The Ides of March* (1948), *The Eighth Day* (1967), and *Theophilus North* (1973). Wilder's home, from which he was often absent and on the road, was in Hamden, Connecticut, near Yale, where he maintained a loose connection over decades, and he was a familiar presence on the campus. *Pullman Car Hiawatha* was published in 1931 and within a year had been performed forty-one times on stages in sixteen states. Wilder had written the play in France, and it reflects his fascination with European avant-garde expressionist theater of the day. It clearly foreshadows the great plays he wrote a little later in his career. In a letter to his family, Wilder himself called the play one of his "Cosmic ones!!"

PULLMAN CAR HIAWATHA

Characters

	THE STAGE MANAGER
Compartment Three:	AN INSANE WOMAN, Mrs. Churchill
	A MALE ATTENDANT, Mr. Morgan
	THE FEMALE ATTENDANT, A trained nurse
Compartment Two:	PHILIP
Compartment One:	HARRIET, Philip's young wife
Lower One:	A MAIDEN LADY
Lower Three:	A MIDDLE-AGED DOCTOR
Lower Five:	A STOUT, AMIABLE WOMAN OF FIFTY
Lower Seven:	AN ENGINEER, Bill, going to California
Lower Nine:	AN ENGINEER, Fred
	THE PORTER, Harrison
	GROVER'S CORNERS, OHIO
	THE FIELD
	THE TRAMP
	PARKERSBURG, OHIO
	THE WORKMAN, Mr. Krüger, a ghost
	THE WORKER, a watchman
	A MECHANIC
The Hours:	TEN O'CLOCK, ELEVEN O'CLOCK,
	TWELVE O'CLOCK
The Planets:	SATURN, VENUS, JUPITER, EARTH
The Archangels:	GABRIEL, MICHAEL

Setting

A Pullman car making its way from New York to Chicago, December 1930.

At the back of the stage is a balcony or bridge or runway leading out of sight in both directions. Two flights of stairs descend from it to the stage. There is no further scenery.

At the rise of the curtain The Stage Manager is making lines with a piece of chalk on the floor of the stage by the footlights.

THE STAGE MANAGER: This is the plan of a Pullman car. Its name is Hiawatha and on December twenty-first it is on its way from New York to Chicago.
   Here at your left are three compartments. Here is the aisle and five lowers. The berths are all full, uppers and lowers, but for the purposes of this play we are limiting our interest to the people in the lower berths on the further side only.
   The berths are already made-up. It is half past nine. Most of the pas-

sengers are in bed behind the green curtains. They are dropping their shoes on the floor, or wrestling with their trousers, or wondering whether they dare hide their valuables in the pillow slips during the night.

All right! Come on, everybody!

(*The actors enter carrying chairs. Each improvises his berth by placing two chairs "facing one another" in his chalk-marked space. They then sit in one chair, profile to the audience, and rest their feet on the other. This must do for lying in bed.*

The passengers in the compartments do the same.)

LOWER ONE: Porter, be sure and wake me up at quarter of six.

THE PORTER: Yes, ma'am.

LOWER ONE: I know I shan't sleep a wink, but I want to be told when it's quarter of six.

THE PORTER: Yes, ma'am.

LOWER SEVEN (*Putting his head through the curtains*): Hsst! Porter! Hsst! How the hell do you turn on this other light?

THE PORTER (*Fussing with it*): I'm afraid it's outta order, suh. You'll have to use the other end.

THE STAGE MANAGER (*Falsetto, substituting for some woman in an upper berth*): May I ask if someone in this car will be kind enough to lend me some aspirin?

THE PORTER (*Rushing about*): Yes, ma'am.

LOWER NINE (*One of the engineers, descending the aisle and falling into Lower Five*): Sorry, lady, sorry. Made a mistake.

LOWER FIVE (*Grumbling*): Never in all my born days!

LOWER ONE (*In a shrill whisper*): Porter! Porter!

THE PORTER: Yes, ma'am.

LOWER ONE: My hot water bag's leaking. I guess you'll have to take it away. I'll have to do without it tonight. How awful!

LOWER FIVE (*Sharply to the passenger above her*): Young man, you mind your own business, or I'll report you to the conductor.

THE STAGE MANAGER (*Substituting for Upper Five*): Sorry, ma'am, I didn't mean to upset you. My suspenders fell down and I was trying to catch them.

LOWER FIVE: Well, here they are. Now go to sleep. Everybody seems to be rushing into my berth tonight. (*She puts her head out*) Porter! Porter! Be a good soul and bring me a glass of water, will you? I'm parched.

LOWER NINE: Bill!

(*No answer.*)

Bill!

LOWER SEVEN: Yea? Wha'd'ya want?

LOWER NINE: Slip me one of those magazines, willya?

LOWER SEVEN: Which one d'ya want?

LOWER NINE: Either one. *Detective Stories*. Either one.

LOWER SEVEN: Aw, Fred. I'm just in the middle of one of 'em in *Detective Stories*.

LOWER NINE: That's all right. I'll take the *Western*.—Thanks.

THE STAGE MANAGER (*To the actors*): All right!—Sh! Sh! Sh! (*To the audience*) Now I want you to hear them thinking.

(*There is a pause and then they all begin a murmuring-swishing noise, very soft. In turn each one of them can be heard above the others.*)

LOWER FIVE (*The Woman of Fifty*): Let's see: I've got the doll for the baby. And the slip-on for Marietta. And the fountain pen for Herbert. And the subscription to *Time* for George . . .

LOWER SEVEN (*Bill*): God! Lillian, if you don't turn out to be what I think you are, I don't know what I'll do.—I guess it's bad politics to let a woman know that you're going all the way to California to see her. I'll think up a song-and-dance about a business trip or something. Was I ever as hot and bothered about anyone like this before? Well, there was Martha. But that was different. I'd better try and read or I'll go cuckoo. "How did you know it was ten o'clock when the visitor left the house?" asked the detective. "Because at ten o'clock," answered the girl, "I always turn out the lights in the conservatory and in the back hall. As I was coming down the stairs I heard the master talking to someone at the front door. I heard him say, 'Well, good night . . .'"—Gee, I don't feel like reading; I'll just think about Lillian. That yellow hair. Them eyes! . . .

LOWER THREE (*The Doctor reads aloud to himself the most hair-raising material from a medical journal, every now and then punctuating his reading with an interrogative "So?"*)

LOWER ONE (*The Maiden Lady*): I know I'll be awake all night. I might just as well make up my mind to it now. I can't imagine what got hold of that hot water bag to leak on the train of all places. Well now, I'll lie on my right side and breathe deeply and think of beautiful things, and perhaps I can doze off a bit.

(*And lastly:*)

LOWER NINE (*Fred*): That was the craziest thing I ever did. It's set me back three whole years. I could have saved up thirty thousand dollars by now, if I'd only stayed over here. What business had I got to fool with contracts with the goddam Soviets. Hell, I thought it would be interesting. Interesting, what the hell! It's set me back three whole years. I don't even know if the company'll take me back. I'm green, that's all. I just don't grow up.

(*The Stage Manager strides toward them with lifted hand, crying, "Hush," and their whispering ceases.*)

THE STAGE MANAGER: That'll do!—Just one minute. Porter!
THE PORTER (*Appearing at the left*): Yessuh.
THE STAGE MANAGER: It's your turn to think.

(*The Porter is very embarrassed.*)

Don't you want to? You have a right to.
THE PORTER (*Torn between the desire to release his thoughts and his shyness*): Ah . . . ah . . . I'm only thinkin' about my home in Chicago and . . . and my life insurance.
THE STAGE MANAGER: That's right.
THE PORTER: . . . Well, thank you . . . Thank you.

(*The Porter slips away, blushing violently, in an agony of self-consciousness and pleasure.*)

THE STAGE MANAGER (*To the audience*): He's a good fellow, Harrison is. Just shy. (*To the actors again*) Now the compartments, please.

(*The berths fall into shadow.*
Philip is standing at the door connecting his compartment with his wife's.)

PHILIP: Are you all right, angel?
HARRIET: Yes. I don't know what was the matter with me during dinner.
PHILIP: Shall I close the door?
HARRIET: Do see whether you can't put a chair against it that will hold it half open without banging.
PHILIP: There.—Good night, angel. If you can't sleep, call me and we'll sit up and play Russian Bank.
HARRIET: You're thinking of that awful time when we sat up every night for a week . . . But at least I know I shall sleep tonight. The noise of the wheels has become sort of nice and homely. What state are we in?
PHILIP: We're tearing through Ohio. We'll be in Indiana soon.
HARRIET: I know those little towns full of horse blocks.
PHILIP: Well, we'll reach Chicago very early. I'll call you. Sleep tight.
HARRIET: Sleep tight, darling.

(*Philip returns to his own compartment. In Compartment Three, the male attendant tips his chair back against the wall and smokes a cigar. The trained nurse knits a stocking. The insane woman leans her forehead against the windowpane, that is, stares into the audience.*)

THE INSANE WOMAN (*Her words have a dragging, complaining sound, but lack any conviction*): Don't take me there. Don't take me there.

THE FEMALE ATTENDANT: Wouldn't you like to lie down, dearie?

THE INSANE WOMAN: I want to get off the train. I want to go back to New York.

THE FEMALE ATTENDANT: Wouldn't you like me to brush your hair again? It's such a nice feeling.

THE INSANE WOMAN (*Going to the door*): I want to get off the train. I want to open the door.

THE FEMALE ATTENDANT (*Taking one of her hands*): Such a noise! You'll wake up all the nice people. Come and I'll tell you a story about the place we're going to.

THE INSANE WOMAN: I don't want to go to that place.

THE FEMALE ATTENDANT: Oh, it's lovely! There are lawns and gardens everywhere. I never saw such a lovely place. Just lovely.

THE INSANE WOMAN (*Lies down on the bed*): Are there roses?

THE FEMALE ATTENDANT: Roses! Red, yellow, white . . . just everywhere.

THE MALE ATTENDANT (*After a pause*): That musta been Cleveland.

THE FEMALE ATTENDANT: I had a case in Cleveland once. Diabetes.

THE MALE ATTENDANT (*After another pause*): I wisht I had a radio here. Radios are good for *them*. I had a patient once that had to have the radio going every minute.

THE FEMALE ATTENDANT: Radios are lovely. My married niece has one. It's always going. It's wonderful.

THE INSANE WOMAN (*Half rising*): I'm not beautiful. I'm not beautiful as she was.

THE FEMALE ATTENDANT: Oh, I think you're beautiful! Beautiful.—Mr. Morgan, don't you think Mrs. Churchill is beautiful?

THE MALE ATTENDANT: Oh, fine lookin'! Regular movie star, Mrs. Churchill.

(*The Insane Woman looks inquiringly at them and subsides.*
    Harriet groans slightly. Smothers a cough. She gropes about with her hand and finds the bell.
    The Porter knocks at her door.)

HARRIET (*Whispering*): Come in. First, please close the door into my husband's room. Softly. Softly.

THE PORTER (*A plaintive porter*): Yes, ma'am.

HARRIET: Porter, I'm not well. I'm sick. I must see a doctor.

THE PORTER: Why ma'am, they ain't no doctor . . .

HARRIET: Yes, when I was coming out from dinner I saw a man in one of the seats on *that* side, reading medical papers. Go and wake him up.

THE PORTER (*Flabbergasted*): Ma'am, I cain't wake anybody up.

HARRIET: Yes, you can. Porter. Porter. Now don't argue with me. I'm very sick. It's my heart. Wake him up. Tell him it's my heart.

THE PORTER: Yes, ma'am.

(*He goes into the aisle and starts pulling the shoulder of the man in Lower Three.*)

LOWER THREE: Hello. Hello. What is it? Are we there?

(*The Porter mumbles to him.*)

I'll be right there.—Porter, is it a young woman or an old one?

THE PORTER: I dunno, suh. I guess she's kinda old, suh, but not so very old.

LOWER THREE: Tell her I'll be there in a minute and to lie quietly.

(*The Porter enters Harriet's compartment. She has turned her head away.*)

THE PORTER: He'll be here in a minute, ma'am. He says you lie quiet.

(*Lower Three stumbles along the aisle muttering: "Damn these shoes!"*)

SOMEONE'S VOICE: Can't we have a little quiet in this car, please?

LOWER NINE (*Fred*): Oh, shut up!

(*The Doctor passes The Porter and enters Harriet's compartment. He leans over her, concealing her by his stooping figure.*)

LOWER THREE: She's dead, Porter. Is there anyone on the train traveling with her?

THE PORTER: Yessuh. Dat's her husband in dere.

LOWER THREE: Idiot! Why didn't you call him? I'll go in and speak to him.

(*The Stage Manager comes forward.*)

THE STAGE MANAGER: All right. So much for the inside of the car. That'll be enough of that for the present. Now for its position geographically, meteorologically, astronomically, theologically considered.

Pullman Car Hiawatha, ten minutes of ten. December twenty-first, 1930. All ready.

(*Some figures begin to appear on the balcony.*)

No, no. It's not time for The Planets yet. Nor The Hours. (*They retire*)

(*The Stage Manager claps his hands. A grinning boy in overalls enters from the left behind the berths.*)

GROVER'S CORNERS, OHIO (*In a foolish voice as though he were reciting a piece at a Sunday school entertainment*): I represent Grover's Corners, Ohio. Eight hundred twenty-one souls. "There's so much good in the worst of us and so much bad in the best of us, that it ill behooves any of us to criticize the rest of us." Robert Louis Stevenson. Thankya.

(*He grins and goes out right.*
   Enter from the same direction somebody in shirt sleeves. This is a field.)

THE FIELD: I represent a field you are passing between Grover's Corners, Ohio, and Parkersburg, Ohio. In this field there are fifty-one gophers, two hundred and six field mice, six snakes and millions of bugs, insects, ants and spiders. All in their winter sleep. "What is so rare as a day in June? Then, if ever, come perfect days." *The Vision of Sir Launfal*, William Cullen—I mean James Russell Lowell. Thank you.

(*Exit.*
   Enter a tramp.)

THE TRAMP: I just want to tell you that I'm a tramp that's been traveling under this car, Hiawatha, so I have a right to be in this play. I'm going from Rochester, New York, to Joliet, Illinois. It takes a lotta people to make a world. "On the road to Mandalay, where the flying fishes play and the sun comes up like thunder, over China, 'cross the bay." Frank W. Service. It's bitter cold. Thank you.

(*Exit.*
   Enter a gentle old farmer's wife with three stringy young people.)

PARKERSBURG, OHIO: I represent Parkersburg, Ohio. Twenty-six hundred and four souls. I have seen all the dreadful havoc that alcohol has done and I hope no one here will ever touch a drop of the curse of this beautiful country.

(*She beats a measure and they all sing unsteadily:*)

"Throw out the lifeline! Throw out the lifeline! Someone is sinking today-ay . . ."

(*The Stage Manager waves them away tactfully.*
   Enter a workman.)

THE WORKMAN: Ich bin der Arbeiter der hier sein Leben verlor. Bei der Sprengung für diese Brücke über die Sie in dem Moment fahren—(*The engine whistles for a trestle crossing*)—erschlug mich ein Felsbrock. Ich spiele jetzt als Geist in diesem Stück mit. "Vor sieben und achtzig Jahren haben unsere Väter auf diesem Kontinent eine neue Nation hervorgebracht . . ."

THE STAGE MANAGER (*Helpfully, to the audience*): I'm sorry; that's in German. He says that he's the ghost of a workman who was killed while they were building the trestle over which the car Hiawatha is now passing—(*The engine whistles again*)—and he wants to appear in this play. A chunk of rock hit him while they were dynamiting.—His motto you know: "Three score and seven years ago our fathers brought forth upon this continent a new nation dedicated . . ." and so on. Thank you, Mr. Krüger.

(*Exit the ghost.*
  Enter another worker.)

THE WORKER: I'm a watchman in a tower near Parkersburg, Ohio. I just want to tell you that I'm not asleep and that the signals are all right for this train. I hope you all have a fine trip. "If you can keep your head when all about you are losing theirs and blaming it on you . . ." Rudyard Kipling. Thank you.

(*He exits.*
  The Stage Manager comes forward.)

THE STAGE MANAGER: All right. That'll be enough of that. Now the weather.

(*Enter a mechanic.*)

A MECHANIC: It is eleven degrees above zero. The wind is north-northwest, velocity: fifty-seven. There is a field of low barometric pressure moving eastward from Saskatchewan to the eastern coast. Tomorrow it will be cold with some snow in the middle western states and northern New York. (*He exits*)

THE STAGE MANAGER: All right. Now for The Hours. (*Helpfully to the audience*) The minutes are gossips; the hours are philosophers; the years are theologians. The hours are philosophers with the exception of Twelve O'clock who is also a theologian.—Ready Ten O'clock!

(*The Hours are beautiful girls dressed like Elihu Vedder's Pleiades. Each carries a great gold Roman numeral. They pass slowly across the balcony at the back, moving from right to left.*)

What are you doing, Ten O'clock? Aristotle?

TEN O'CLOCK: No, Plato, Mr. Washburn.

THE STAGE MANAGER: Good.—"Are you not rather convinced that he who thus . . ."

TEN O'CLOCK: "Are you not rather convinced that he who thus sees Beauty as only it can be seen will be specially favored? And since he is in contact not with images but with realities . . ." (*She continues the passage in a murmur as Eleven O'clock appears*)

ELEVEN O'CLOCK: "What else can I, Epictetus, do, a lame old man, but sing hymns to God? If then I were a nightingale, I would do the nightingale's part. If I were a swan, I would do a swan's. But now I am a rational creature . . ." (*Her voice also subsides to a murmur. Twelve O'clock appears*)

THE STAGE MANAGER: Good.—Twelve O'clock, what have you?

TWELVE O'CLOCK: Saint Augustine and his mother.

THE STAGE MANAGER: So.—"And we began to say: If to any the tumult of the flesh were hushed . . ."

TWELVE O'CLOCK: "And we began to say: If to any the tumult of the flesh were hushed; hushed the images of earth; of waters and of air . . ."

THE STAGE MANAGER: Faster.—"Hushed also the poles of Heaven."

TWELVE O'CLOCK: "Yea, were the very soul to be hushed to herself."

THE STAGE MANAGER: A little louder, Miss Foster.

TWELVE O'CLOCK (*A little louder*): "Hushed all dreams and imaginary revelations . . ."

THE STAGE MANAGER (*Waving them back*): All right. All right. Now The Planets. December twenty-first, 1930, please.

(*The Hours unwind and return to their dressing rooms at the right.*
The Planets appear on the balcony. Some of them take their place halfway on the steps. These have no words, but each has a sound. One has a pulsating, zinging sound. Another has a thrum. One whistles ascending and descending scales. Saturn does a slow, obstinate humming sound on two repeated low notes:)

Louder, Saturn.—Venus, higher. Good. Now, Jupiter.—Now the Earth.

(*The Stage Manager turns to the beds on the train.*)

Come, everybody. This is the Earth's sound.

(*The towns, workmen, etc., appear at the edge of the stage. The passengers begin their "thinking" murmur.*)

Come, Grover's Corners. Parkersburg. You're in this. Watchman. Tramp. This is the Earth's sound.

(*He conducts it as the director of an orchestra would. Each of the towns and workmen does his motto.*
The Insane Woman breaks into passionate weeping. She rises and stretches out her arms to The Stage Manager.)

THE INSANE WOMAN: Use me. Give me something to do.

(*He goes to her quickly, whispers something in her ear, and leads her back to her guardians. She is unconsoled.*)

THE STAGE MANAGER: Now shh—shh—shh! Enter The Archangels.

(*To the audience*) We have now reached the theological position of Pullman Car Hiawatha.

(*The towns and workmen have disappeared. The Planets, offstage, continue a faint music. Two young men in blue serge suits enter along the balcony and descend the stairs at the right. As they pass each bed the passenger talks in his sleep.*

Gabriel points out Bill to Michael who smiles with raised eyebrows. They pause before Lower Five, and Michael makes the sound of assent that can only be rendered "Hn-Hn."

The remarks that the characters make in their sleep are not all intelligible, being lost in the sound of sigh or groan or whisper by which they are conveyed. But we seem to hear:)

LOWER NINE (*Loud*): Some people are slower than others, that's all.

LOWER SEVEN (*Bill*): It's no fun, y'know. I'll try.

LOWER FIVE (*The lady of the Christmas presents, rapidly*): You know best, of
   course. I'm ready whenever you are. One year's like another.

LOWER ONE: I can teach sewing. I can sew.

(*They approach Harriet's compartment.*
   The Insane Woman sits up and speaks to them.)

THE INSANE WOMAN: Me?

(*The Archangels shake their heads.*)

What possible use can there by in my simply waiting?—Well, I'm grateful for anything. I'm grateful for being so much better than I was. The old story, the terrible story, doesn't haunt me as it used to. A great load seems to have been taken off my mind.—But no one understands me any more. At last I understand myself perfectly, but no one else understands a thing I say.—So I must wait?

(*The Archangels nod, smiling.*)

(*Resignedly, and with a smile that implies their complicity*) Well, you know best. I'll do whatever is best; but everyone is so childish, so absurd. They have no logic. These people are all so mad . . . These people are like children; they have never suffered.

(*She returns to her bed and sleeps. The Archangels stand beside Harriet. The Doctor has drawn Philip into the next compartment and is talking to him in earnest whispers.*

Harriet's face has been toward the wall; she turns it slightly and speaks toward the ceiling.)

HARRIET: I wouldn't be happy there. Let me stay dead down here. I belong here.
     I shall be perfectly happy to roam about my house and be near Philip.—
     You know I wouldn't be happy there.

(*Gabriel leans over and whispers into her ear. After a short pause she bursts into fierce tears.*)

I'm ashamed to come with you. I haven't done anything. I haven't done anything with my life. Worse than that: I was angry and sullen. I never realized anything. I don't dare go a step in such a place.

(*They whisper to her again.*)

But it's not possible to forgive such things. I don't want to be forgiven so easily. I want to be punished for it all. I won't stir until I've been punished a long, long time. I want to be freed of all that—by punishment. I want to be all new.

(*They whisper to her. She puts her feet slowly on the ground.*)

But no one else could be punished for me. I'm willing to face it all myself. I don't ask anyone to be punished for me.

(*They whisper to her again. She sits long and brokenly looking at her shoes, thinking it over.*)

It wasn't fair. I'd have been willing to suffer for it myself—if I could have endured such a mountain.

(*She smiles.*)

Oh, I'm ashamed! I'm just a stupid and you know it. I'm just another American.—But then what wonderful things must be beginning now. You really want me? You really want me?

(*They start leading her down the aisle of the car.*)

Let's take the whole train. There are some lovely faces on this train. Can't we all come? You'll never find anyone better than Philip. Please, please, let's all go.

(*They reach the steps. The Archangels interlock their arms as a support for her as she leans heavily on them, taking the steps slowly. Her words are half singing and half babbling.*)

But look at how tremendously high and far it is. I've a weak heart. I'm not supposed to climb stairs. "I do not ask to see the distant scene: One step enough for me." It's like Switzerland. My tongue keeps saying things. I can't control it.—Do let me stop a minute: I want to say good-bye.

(*She turns in their arms.*)

Just a minute, I want to cry on your shoulder.

(*She leans her forehead against Gabriel's shoulder and laughs long and softly.*)

Good-bye, Philip.—I begged him not to marry me, but he would. He believed in me just as you do.—Good-bye, 1312 Ridgewood Avenue, Oaksbury, Illinois. I hope I remember all its steps and doors and wallpapers forever. Good-bye, Emerson Grammar School on the corner of Forbush Avenue and Wherry Street. Good-bye, Miss Walker and Miss Cramer who taught me English and Miss Matthewson who taught me biology. Good-bye, First Congregational Church on the corner of Meyerson Avenue and Sixth Street and Dr. McReady and Mrs. McReady and Julia. Good-bye, Papa and Mama . . .

(*She turns.*)

Now I'm tired of saying good-bye.—I never used to talk like this. I was so homely I never used to have the courage to talk. Until Philip came. I see now. I see now. I understand everything now.

(*The Stage Manager comes forward.*)

THE STAGE MANAGER (*To the actors*): All right. All right.—Now we'll have the whole world together, please. The whole solar system, please.

(*The complete cast begins to appear at the edges of the stage. He claps his hands.*)

The whole solar system, please. Where's The Tramp?—Where's The Moon?

(*He gives two raps on the floor, like the conductor of an orchestra attracting the attention of his forces, and slowly lifts his hand. The human beings murmur their thoughts; The Hours discourse; The Planets chant or hum. Harriet's voice finally rises above them all, saying:*)

HARRIET: "I was not ever thus, nor asked that Thou
    Shouldst lead me on, and spite of fears,
    Pride ruled my will: Remember not past years."

(*The Stage Manager waves them away.*)

THE STAGE MANAGER: Very good. Now clear the stage, please. Now we're at Englewood Station, South Chicago. See the university's towers over there! The best of them all.

LOWER ONE (*The Maiden Lady*): Porter, you promised to wake me up at quarter of six.

THE PORTER: Sorry, ma'am, but it's been an awful night on this car. A lady's been
 terrible sick.

LOWER ONE: Oh! Is she better?

THE PORTER: No'm. She ain't one jot better.

LOWER FIVE: Young man, take your foot out of my face.

THE STAGE MANAGER (*Again substituting for Upper Five*): Sorry, lady, I slipped—

LOWER FIVE (*Grumbling not unamiably*): I declare, this trip's been one long series
 of insults.

THE STAGE MANAGER: Just one minute, ma'am, and I'll be down and out of your
 way.

LOWER FIVE: Haven't you got anybody to darn your socks for you? You ought to
 be ashamed to go about that way.

THE STAGE MANAGER: Sorry, lady.

LOWER FIVE: You're too stuck up to get married. That's the trouble with you.

LOWER NINE: Bill! Bill!

LOWER SEVEN: Yea? Wha'd'ya want?

LOWER NINE: Bill, how much d'ya give the porter on a train like this? I've been
 outta the country so long . . .

LOWER SEVEN: Hell, Fred, I don't know myself.

THE PORTER: CHICAGO, CHICAGO. All out. This train don't go no further.

(*The passengers jostle their way out and an army of old women with mops and pails
enter and prepare to clean up the car.*)

END OF PLAY